KONSTANTIN SAKAEV

COMPLETE
SLAV I

Responsible editor
Konstantin Sakaev

Cover designer
Milos Sibinovic

Typesetting
Piotr Pielach ‹www.i-press.pl›

First edition 2012 by Chess Evolution

Complete Slav I
Copyright © 2012 Chess Evolution

ISBN 978-83-934656-3-7

All sales or enquiries should be directed to Chess Evolution
ul. Smutna 5a, 32-005 Niepolomice, Poland

e-mail: chessevolutionshop@yahoo.com
website: www.chess-evolution.com

Printed in Poland by Drukarnia Pionier, 31-983 Krakow, ul.Igolomska 12

Table of contents

Key to symbols

=	Equality or equal chances
±	White has a slight advantage
∓	Black has a slight advantage
±	White is better
∓	Black is better
+-	White has a decisive advantage
-+	Black has a decisive advantage
∞	unclear
∞	with compensation
⇆	with counterplay
↑	with initiative
→	with an attack
Δ	with the idea
□	only move

N	novelty
!	a good move
!!	an excellent move
?	a weak move
??	a blunder
!?	an interesing move
?!	a dubious move
+	check
#	mate

Preface

The Slav Defence is currently the most popular closed opening, appearing in the opening repertoire of the overwhelming majority of top class grandmasters. A competitive chess player playing 1.d4 faces the opening in almost every tournament, and for Black it can be used in just about every second game. Over a number of years I have played various different lines of the opening with both colours and analysed it both individually and in cooperation with many well-known grandmasters. Now I have decided to give the opportunity to anyone who feels like it to enter a grandmaster's laboratory and see my professional approach to various opening lines.

Measures have been taken lest the work should swell to enormous size. Textual annotations to variations and evaluations are not given throughout the book but only in cases where I thought it to be important and not too obvious. As for the rest, a conventional abridged evaluation system has been used. All noteworthy lines have been analysed in detail. Also many novelties have been introduced with enclosed analyses. At the same time many weak and inessential moves, although in some cases with a considerable praxis, have been evaluated briefly.

I will be glad if my work turns out to be a good aid in learning the Slav Defence — an exceptionally interesting opening, rich in both strategic and tactical ideas.

This book is rated for skilled chess players.

The theoretical material is given as of July 2012.

Konstantin Sakaev

■ GAME 1

1.d4 d5 2.c4 c6 3.cxd5 cxd5

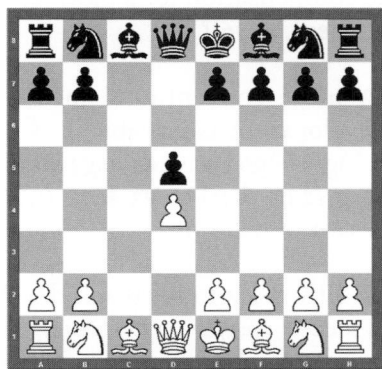

4.♗f4

This order of moves is most accurate as White may want to play ♘g1–e2

There is no point in beginning development with 4.♘f3, since c3 and f4 are the best squares for the queen's knight and queen's bishop respectively, however the king's knight can sometimes go to e2.;

4.♘c3 makes sense for White if he wants move the knight to f3 before e2-e3.Otherwise an interesting possibility is allowed: 4...♘c6 (4...♘f6 5.♗f4 ♘c6 — 4.♗f4 ♘f6 5.♘c3 ♘c6) 5.♗f4

a) 5.e4 creates no serious danger for Black

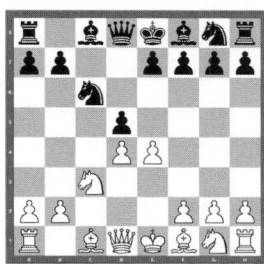

5...dxe4

a1) White is a bit better after 5... e6 6.e5 (6.exd5 exd5 7.♘f3 ♘f6 8.♗d3±) 6...♘ge7 7.♘f3 ♘f5 8.a3±;
a2) But not bad is 5...♘f6 6.e5 (6.exd5 ♘xd5 7.♘f3 leads to a reliable Panov Attack variation of the Caro-Kann Defence.) 6...♘e4=, with about equal chances.;

6.d5 ♘e5 7.♕a4+

(7.♗f4 ♘g6 8.♗g3

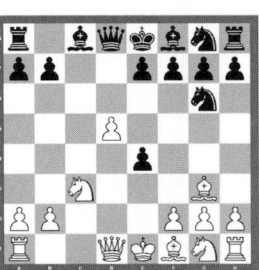

8...♘f6!N

(8...f5 9.h4 f4 (*9...h5 10.♘h3±* Dvoretzky — De Jong, Netherlands 2010) 10.♗h2 e5 11.dxe6 ♗xe6 12.h5 (*12.♕a4+ ♗d7 13.♕xe4+ ♗e7 14.0-0-0 ♘f6 15.♕xb7 ♕c8 16.♕xc8+ ♖xc8 17.f3 ♗c5±*) 12...♘e5 Aronian — Smeets, Nice 2010 13.♕a4+ ♘d7 14.0-0-0 ♘gf6 15.♘ge2±)

9.h4 e5 10.dxe6 ♗xe6 11.♗b5+ ♘d7 12.h5 ♘e7 13.♘ge2 a6 14.♘d4 axb5 15.♘dxb5 ♘f5 16.♘c7+ ♔e7 17.♘3d5+ ♗xd5 18.♘xd5+ ♔e8 19.♘c7+ ♔e7=)

7...♗d7 (*7...♘d7 8.♗f4 ♘gf6 9.0-0-0↑*) 8.♕xe4 ♘g6 9.♘f3 ♘f6 10.♕d4 e6 11.dxe6 ♗xe6 12.♗b5+ ♗d7 13.0-0 ♗e7 14.♗xd7+ ♕xd7 15.♗g5 (*15. ♕xd7+ ♘xd7 16.♖d1 ♘f6=*) 15...♕xd4 16.♘xd4 0-0 17.♘f5 ♘d5 18.♗xe7 ♘dxe7 19.♘d6 ♖ad8 = — White's position is more active but Black should achieve a draw without any problems.

b) 5.♘f3 ♘f6 6.♗f4 — 4.♗f4 ♘f6 5.♘c3 ♘c6 6.♘f3.;

5...e5!? (In practice Black usually plays *5...♘f6* which transposes below) 6.dxe5

(6.♗xe5 ♘xe5 7.dxe5 d4 8.♘e4 ♕a5+ 9.♘d2 ♘e7 10.♘gf3 ♘c6 11.g3 (*11.a3 ♗e6=*) 11...♘xe5 12.♗g2 ♘xf3+ 13.♗xf3 g6 14.0-0 ♗g7 15.♘b3 ♕b6=)

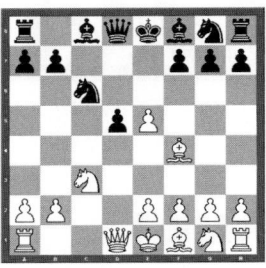

6...d4 7.♘e4 ♕a5+ 8.♘d2 Black can play in different ways, in both cases the compensation for a pawn seems sufficient. 8...f6!?

(A more conventional means of development is possible: 8...♘ge7 9.♘gf3 ♘g6 (*9...♘d5 10.g3 h6 11.h4 ♗e7 12.a3 ♗f5*) 10.g3 ♗e7 11.♗g2 0-0 12.0-0 ♖d8)

9.a3 (It's risky to let Black develop his pieces: *9.exf6 ♘xf6 10.♘gf3 ♗e7 11.e3 dxe3 12.♗xe3 ♗e6* — Strong piece activity fully compensates for the loss of a pawn.) 9...fxe5 10.b4 ♕b6 11.♗g3 ♘f6 12.♘c4 ♕d8 13.e3 e4 14.b5 ♘a5 15.exd4

(*15.♕xd4 ♕xd4 16.exd4 ♘b3 (16... ♘xc4 17.♗xc4 ♗d7) 17.♖d1 ♗e6*)

15...♗e6 — White is a little behind in development. The position is unclear.

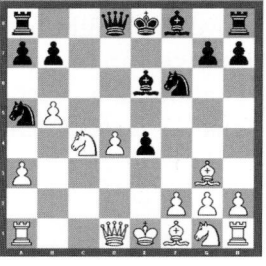

4...♘f6

4...♘c6 5.e3 (5.♘f3 ♘f6 6.♘c3 — 4...♘f6 5.♘c3 ♘c6 6.♘f3) 5...♘f6 (5...♗f5 6.♕b3±) 6.♘c3 — 4...♘f6 5.♘c3 ♘c6 6.e3

5.♘c3 ♘c6 6.♘f3 a6

Another good choice is 6...♗f5 which transposes to other variations 7.e3 — 6.e3 ♗f5 7.♘f3

a) 7.♕b3 ♘a5 8.♕a4+ ♗d7 9.♕c2 e6 10.e3 — 6.e3 ♗g4 7.♕b3 ♘a5 8.♕a4+ ♗d7 9.♕c2 e6 10.♘f3;

b) Only 7.♖c1 is of independent significance, but after 7...e6 8.♕b3 ♗d6! 9.♗xd6 (9.♕xb7 0–0 10.♕xc6 ♗xf4 11.e3 ♗d6 12.♕a6 ♖b8 13.♗b5 ♘e4∓/↑) 9...♕xd6 10.e3 0–0 11.♗e2 ♖ab8 12.0–0 ♖fc8 13.♘h4 ♗g4= the game is equal.;

7.♖c1

7.e3 ♗g4=;

7.♘e5

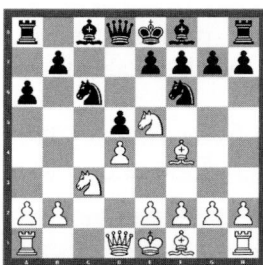

7...♕b6

a) 7...♗f5?! 8.♘xc6 bxc6 9.e3 e6 10.♗e2 ♗d6 (10...♗e7 11.0–0 0–0 12.♖c1±) 11.♗xd6 ♕xd6 12.0–0 0–0 13.♘a4±;

b) 7...e6 8.e3 ♘xe5 9.♗xe5 (9.dxe5 ♘d7 10.♗d3 g6 11.♗g3 ♗g7 12.f4 0–0 13.0–0 b5= Jobava — D. Mastrovasilis, Brasov 2011) 9...♗d7 (9...♗d6 10.♗d3 ♗xe5 11.dxe5 ♘d7 12.f4 ♕b6 13.♕d2 ♘c5 Makarov — Burmakin, St. Petersburg 2009 14.♗e2±) 10.♗d3 ♗e7 11.0–0 0–0±/= White has an advantage but it's microscopic Gustafsson — Meyer, Germany 1998;

8.♘xc6 bxc6 9.♕d2

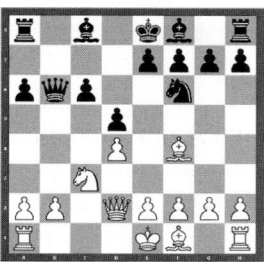

9...e6

(9...♘h5!? 10.♗e3 ♘f6 (10...e6 11.g3±) 11.♖c1 ♘g4 12.♗f4 (12.♗g5 e5 13.e3 ♖b8∞) 12...e5 13.♗xe5 ♘xe5 14.dxe5 ♖b8 15.e4 ♕xb2 16.♕xb2 ♖xb2 17.exd5 cxd5 18.♘xd5 ♗b7 19.♗c4 ♗xd5 20.♗xd5 ♗b4+ 21.♔f1 0–0=)

10.e3 ♕b7 (10...♘h5 11.♗g5 h6 12.♗h4 g5 13.♗e2 gxh4 14.♗xh5 ♖b8 15.b3±; 10...♗d7 11.♘a4 ♕b7 12.a3 ♘h5 13.♗e2 ♘xf4 14.exf4±) 11.♖c1 c5 12.♗e2 ♗d7 13.0–0 ♖c8 (13...♗c6 14.♖c2 ♗e7 15.dxc5 0–0 16.♖fc1 ♖fd8 17.♗f3 ♘d7 18.b4± Macieja — Caruana, Spoleto 2011) 14.♗e5 ♗e7

15.dxc5 ♖xc5 16.♗xf6 (*16.♕d3 a5 17.♖c2 0-0 18.♖fc1 ♖fc8=*) 16...gxf6 17.♗f3 f5 = Short — Dominguez, Habana 2010

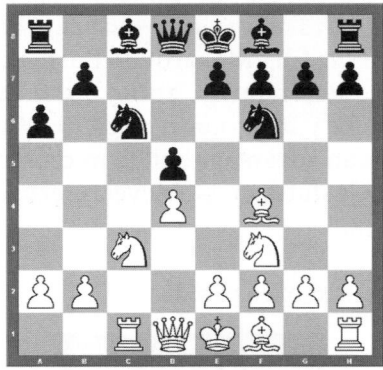

7...♘h5!

The simplest route to equalisation. The problems cannot be solved by 7...♘e4 8.♘e5

(White also has a slightly more pleasant game after 8.e3 ♘xc3 9.bxc3 ♗f5 10.♗d3 ♗xd3 11.♕xd3 e6 12.0-0 ♗e7 13.c4 dxc4 14.♖xc4 (*14.♕xc4 0-0 15.e4 ♖c8 16.d5 b5 17.♕b3 ♘a5 18.♖xc8 ♕xc8 19.♕d3 ♕c4 20.♖d1 exd5 21.♕xd5 h6 =* Ponomariov — Malakhov, Montcada 2009) 14...0-0 15.♖fc1 ♖c8 16.♘e5 ♘xe5 17.♗xe5 ♖xc4 Turov — Akopian, Kallithea 2008 18.♖xc4!± — White maintains pressure.due to his possession of the c-file)

8...♘xc3 9.♖xc3 ♗d7 10.♕b3 ♘xe5 (*10...f6 11.♘xc6 ♗xc6 12.e3 e6 13.♗d3±*) 11.♗xe5 ♗c6 12.e3 e6 13.♗e2 ♗d6 14.♗xd6 ♕xd6

15.0-0 0-0 16.♖fc1± Sargissian — M.Pavlovic, Reykjavik 2006;

7...♗f5 demands very accurate further play from Black: 8.e3 (*8.♘e5 ♖c8=*) 8...♖c8 (*8...e6 9.♕b3±*) 9.♘e5

(*9.♗e2 e6 10.0-0 ♘d7! (10...♗d6 11.♗xd6 ♕xd6 12.♘a4 0-0 13.♘c5 ♖c7 14.♕b3± Kramnik — Bareev, Moscow 2005) 11.♕b3 (11.♘d2 ♗e7 12.a3 0-0= Kasimdzhanov — Grischuk, Elista 2008) 11...♘a5 (11...♕b6 12.♕xb6 ♘xb6 13.♘h4 ♗g6±/=) 12.♕a4 ♘c6 13.♕b3 ♘a5=*)

9...e6

(*9...♘xe5 10.dxe5 (10.♗xe5 ♘d7 11.♗f4 e6=) 10...♘e4 11.♘xe4 ♖xc1 12.♕xc1 dxe4 (Risky is 12...♗xe4 13.e6! ♕a5+ (13...fxe6 14.f3 ♗f5 15.♗e5±) 14.♔e2 fxe6 15.f3 ♗f5 16.g4 ♗g6 17.♕c8+ ♔f7 18.♕xb7±) 13.♗e2 ♕a5+ 14.♕d2 ♕xd2+ 15.♔xd2 e6 16.h4 h5 (16...h6 17.g4±) 17.♗g5± — White has a more pleasant game though Black should be able to resist.*)

10.♕b3 ♘xe5 11.♗xe5 ♕d7 12.♗e2 ♘e4! 13.f3 ♘d6 14.0-0 ♘c4

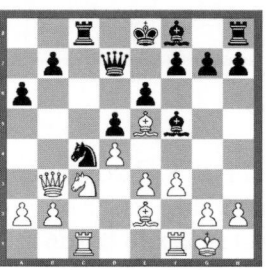

15.♖fd1!N (15.e4 ♘d2∓; 15.♗xc4 dxc4 16.♕b6 f6∓ Margvelashvili — Borovikov, Konya 2010) 15... b5 (15...♘xe5 16.dxe5 ♗c5 17.♘a4 ♗a7 18.♘b6 ♗xb6 19.♕xb6 0-0±/= 20.♖xc8 ♕xc8 21.♖d4 f6 22.exf6 ♖xf6=) 16.e4 dxe4 17.fxe4 ♗g6 18.♗xc4 ♖xc4 (18...bxc4 19.♕b6 f6 20.♗g3 ♕c6 21.♕xc6+ ♖xc6 22.d5 ♖b6±) 19.♘a4 (19.♘xb5 axb5 20.♖xc4 bxc4 21.♕b8+ ♕d8 22.♕b5+ ♕d7=) 19...♖xa4 20.♖c7 ♕d8 21.♖dc1 ♗c5 (21...♗e7 22.♖c8 0-0 23.♖xd8 ♖xd8 24.♖c7±) 22.dxc5 0-0 23.♗d6 ♖e8 (? An unclear position arises after 23...♖xe4!? — It's not easy for White to advance the c-pawn.) 24.e5 ♕g5 25.♖f1 ♖f4 = — The rook on c7 is disconnected from its base, so White cannot avoid perpetual check.

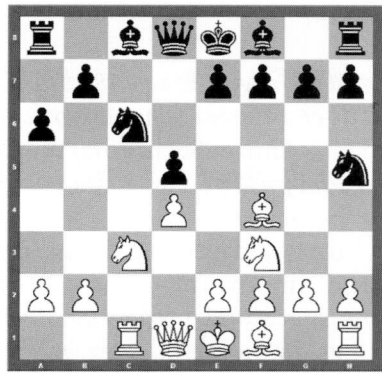

8.♗d2
8.♗e5 f6 9.♗g3 e5∓

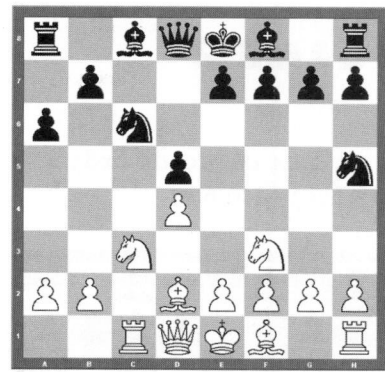

8...♘f6!
8...e6 9.e3±

9.e3 ♗g4 10.h3 ♗xf3 11.♕xf3 e6 12.♗d3
12.♕g3 ♘h5 13.♕f3 ♘f6

12... ♗d6 13.0-0
13.g4?! 13...♖c8 14.g5 ♘d7 15.♕g2 ♘b6∓ Aronian — Gelfand, Nice (blindfold) 2008

13...0-0 14.♕e2
Khairullin — I.Popov, Dagomys 2010

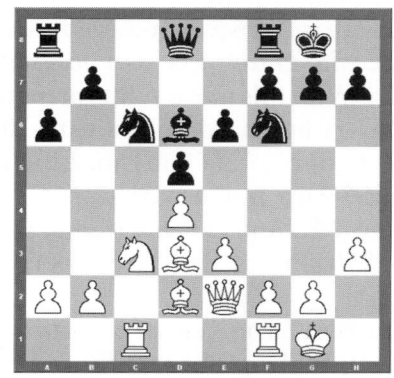

14...♖c8=

■ GAME 2

1.d4 d5 2.c4 c6 3.cxd5 cxd5 4.♗f4
♘f6 5.♘c3 ♘c6 6.e3

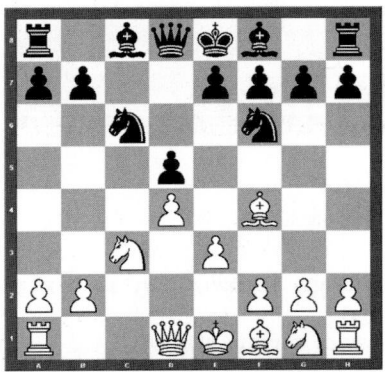

6...a6

Played to limit the scope of White's light-squared bishop on the queenside which can only be improved by a pawn advance. In reply White must generate pressure along the c-file combined with play in the centre on the dark squares.

Passive is 6...e6 7.♗d3 ♗e7 (7...♗d6 8.♗xd6 ♕xd6 9.f4 0–0 10.♘f3±) 8.h3! With this move White prepares ♘g1–f3 by guarding against ♘f6-h5. 8...0–0 9.♘f3 ♘b4 10.♗b1 (10. ♗e2!? ♘e4 11.0–0 ♗d7 12.a3 ♘xc3 13.bxc3 ♘c6 14.c4 ♘a5 15.cxd5 exd5 16.♗d3±) 10...♗d7 11.0–0 ♖c8 12.a3

(12.♕e2 ♕b6 13.a3 (13.♘e5±) 13... ♖xc3 14.bxc3 ♗b5 15.♕b2 ♗xf1 16.♔xf1± Volkov — Grachev, Taganrog 2011)

12...♘c6 13.♗d3± — White has a small but stable advantage.;

6...♗g4 An unpopular move which has undeservedly received little attention. However it's better than its reputation and is in fact quite good.

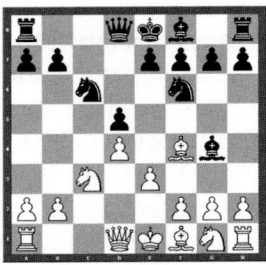

7.f3

a) 7.♗e2 ♗xe2 8.♘gxe2 e6 9.0–0 ♗e7 10.♘c1 0–0 11.♘d3 ♖c8 12.♖c1=;

b) 7.♕b3 ♘a5 8.♕a4+ (8.♕c2 ♖c8 9.♗d3 e6 10.♘ge2 ♗h5 11.0–0 ♗g6= Landa — Shirov, Sochi 2012) 8...♗d7 — 6...♗f5 7.♕b3 ♘a5 8.♕a4 ♗d7.;

7...♗d7 8.♗d3 e6 9.g4! The only e and important move. White gains space and prevents ♘f6-h5. (9.♗g5 h6 10.♗h4 ♗e7 11.♘ge2 ♘e4 12.♗xe7 ♘xc3 13.♘xc3 ♘xe7 14.f4 ♘c8±/= — White has only a symbolically more pleasant position, Morozevich — Svetushkin, PortoCarras2011) 9...♗e7 (9...♗b4 Macieja — Shirov, Warsaw 2010 10.♘ge2 0–0 11.a3±) 10.♘ge2 0–0 N White needs a lot of time to develop a kingside intitiative so Black should not be afraid. (*10...a6 11.♘g3 h6 12.h4 ♕b6 13.♕d2± Vaisser — Khalifman, New York 1994*) 11.♖c1 ♖c8 12.h4 ♘e8 13.g5∞ — The position is very complicated and chances are equal.

7.♗d3!

7.♘f3 This helps Black to solve the problem of his white-squared bishop and is therefore harmless. 7...♗g4 8.♗e2 e6 9.0-0 ♗d6 10.♗xd6 ♕xd6 = with equality.;

7.♖c1 Here Black obtains a good game as well : Most interesting is 7...♗g4 (*7...♗f5 — 6...♗f5 7.♖c1 a6*) 8.f3

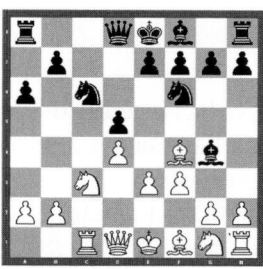

8...♗h5!? (More reliable than *8...♗d7 9.g4 e6 10.h4 ♗e7 11.♗d3 0-0 12.♗b1∞*, with unclear play, Morozevich — Sakaev, Moscow 2007) 9.g4 ♗g6 10.h4 h6 11.♗d3 (*11.♕b3 ♘a5 12.♕a4+ ♘c6=*) 11...♗xd3 12.♕xd3 e6 13.♘ge2 ♗e7 14.♔f2 h5 15.g5 ♘d7 16.♗g3 g6= Sedlak — Rublevsky, Serbia 2011

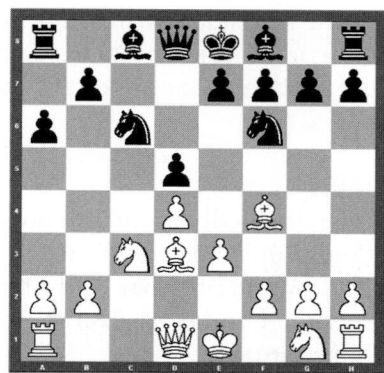

7...♗g4 8.♘ge2 e6 9.♖c1 ♗e7

9...♗xe2 10.♕xe2 ♗d6 11.♗xd6 (*11.♗g5 h6 12.♗h4 ♗e7 13.0-0 0-0 14.♘a4 ♘d7 15.♗g3± Kryakvin — Potkin, Olginka 2011*) 11...♕xd6 12.0-0 0-0 13.♘a4 ♖ac8 14.♘c5 ♖c7 15.♖c3±;

9...♗d6 10.f3 ♗h5 11.♘a4 ♗g6 12.0-0 0-0 13.♘c5 ♗xf4 14.♘xf4 ♕b6 15.♖f2± — White's pressure is very unpleasant, Landa — Hracek, Germany 2012

10.0-0 ♗h5

10...0-0 11.♘a4 ♘d7 12.f3 ♗h5 13.♕b3 ♖a7 (*13...♘a5 14.♕c2±*) 14.♗g3±

11.♘a4 ♘d7 12.♕b3 ♘a5 13.♕c3 ♘c6 14.♗g3

14.a3±

14...♖c8

14...♘b4 15.♗c7 ♘xa2 16.♕a5 ♕c8 (*16...♘xc1 17.♗xd8 ♘xe2+ 18.♗xe2 ♗xe2 19.♗xe7 ♗xf1 20.♗a3 ♗b5 21.b3±* — The penetration of the queen to e7 via b4 is inevitable, after which the kingside pawns will begin to fall.) 17.♘b6 ♘xb6 18.♕xa2 ♗xe2 19.♗xe2 ♘c4 20.♗xc4 dxc4 21.♖xc4 ♕d7 22.♗f4±

15.♘f4!N
15.a3 Undoubtedly useful but not an essential prophylaxis. After 15...♗g6 16.♘f4± White only has a minimal advantage, Landa — Svetushkin, Mulhouse 2011

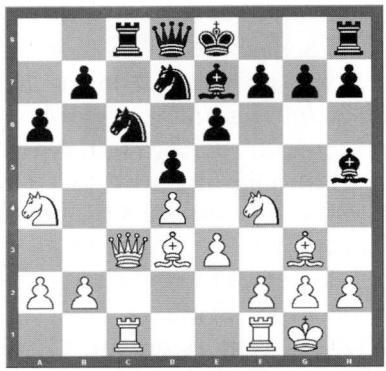

15...♗g6 16.♘xg6 hxg6 17.♖c2!±/±
White's queenside pressure is very unpleasant.

■ GAME 3

1.d4 d5 2.c4 c6 3.cxd5 cxd5 4.♗f4 ♘f6 5.♘c3 ♘c6 6.e3 ♗f5 N

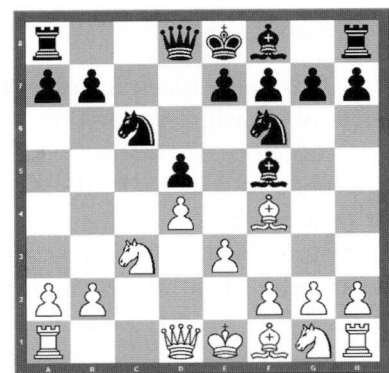

7.♖c1
This move has recently become popular. Black has not yet demonstrated a correct response.
7.♗b5 e6 8.♕a4 (8.♘f3 — 7.♘f3 e6 8.♗b5) 8...♕b6 9.♘f3 ♗e7 10.♘e5 0-0 11.♗xc6 ♖fc8 12.0-0 bxc6 13.♖fc1 Morozevich — Grischuk, Moscow 2007

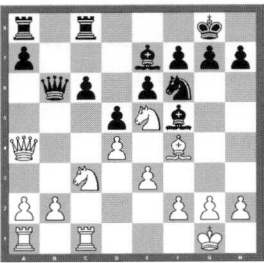

13...♕xb2!N was very strong 14.♘xc6 ♗a3!± threatening ♗f5-c2!; 7.♕b3!?

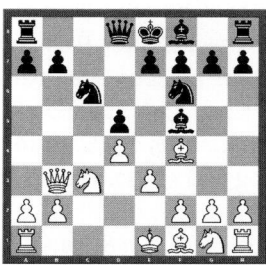

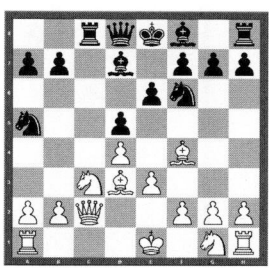

7...♘a5 8.♕a4+ ♗d7 9.♕c2

(9.♗b5 leads to simplification and equalisation 9...e6 10.♘f3 a6 11.♗xd7+ ♘xd7 12.0-0 b5 13.♕d1 (13.♕c2 ♗e7=) 13...♗e7 14.♖c1 ♖c8 15.♕d3 0-0 16.a4 b4 17.♘e2 ♕b6 18.b3=)

9...e6 (9...♖c8 10.♗d3 e6 11.♘f3 — 9...e6 10.♗d3 ♖c8 11.♘f3) 10.♗d3 (10.♘f3 ♘h5! 11.♗e5 f6 12.♗g3 g6=) 10...♖c8

(10...♘c6!? 11.a3 ♘h5 12.♗e5 ♖c8 13.♘f3 (13.h3 ♘xe5 14.dxe5 g6 15.♘f3 ♗e7=) 13...f6 14.♗g3

(14.♗xh7?! 14...fxe5 15.♕g6+ ♔e7 16.♕xh5 ♗e8 17.♕g5+ (17. ♕h3 ♔d7 18.dxe5 ♔c7∓) 17...♔d7 18.♕xd8+ ♔xd8∓ Khenkin — Savic, Budva 2009)

14...f5 15.♗h4 ♘f6 16.♘e5 ♗e7 17.f3± — White's position is slightly more pleasant.)

11.♘f3 b5 (11...♘c4 12.0-0 ♗e7 13.♘e5 0-0 14.♕e2± Kazhgaleyev — Van Kampen, Wijk aan Zee 2011; 11...♗b4 12.0-0 ♘c4 13.♗xc4 ♖xc4 14.♘e5 ♖c8 15.♕b3± Kramnik — Aronian, Shanghai 2010) 12.a3 (12. ♕e2 b4 13.♘d1 ♘c4∞) 12...♘c4 13.0-0 ♗e7 14.h3±/∞ In this complicated position, with plenty of possibilites on each move, White's chances are just a little better, I. Sokolov — Giri, Boxtel 2011

7...♖c8!
A rare move but the only one to fully equalise.
7...e6 8.♕b3 ♕b6

(8...♗b4 9.a3! (9.♗b5 0-0 10.♗xc6 ♗xc3+ 11.♖xc3 bxc6 12.♕a3 ♘e4 13.♖c1 g5! 14.♗g3 ♕b6= Ponomariov — Smeets, Nice (blindfold) 2010) 9...♗xc3+ 10.♖xc3 ♕e7

(10...♕d7 11.f3 0-0 (11...♘h5 12.♗g5 h6 13.♗h4 g5 14.♗f2±) 12.♗b5 ♖fc8 13.♘e2 a6 14.♗xc6 ♖xc6 15.♖xc6 ♕xc6 16.♔d2!±)

11.♗b5 ♖c8

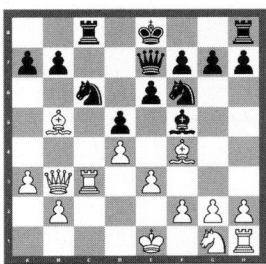

12.♗g5!N (12.♘f3 Miladinovic — Lekic, Bar 2010 12...♘e4! 13.♖c1 g5! 14.♗g3 0-0 15.0-0-0 f6∓) 12...0-0 (12...h6 13.♗xf6 ♕xf6 14.♘f3 0-0 15.0-0±) 13.♘e2 h6 (13...e5 14.♗xc6 bxc6 15.0-0-0±) 14.♗xf6 ♕xf6 15.0-0±)

9.♕xb6 axb6

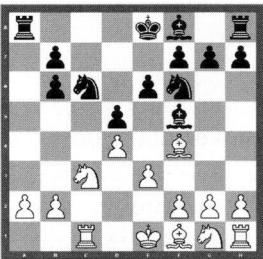

10.a3!N

a) 10.♗b5 ♗e7 (10...♗b4 11.a3 ♗xc3+ 12.♖xc3 ♔e7 13.♘e2±) 11.f3 (11.♘f3! ♘d7 12.a3±) 11...0-0 12.a3 (12.g4 ♗g6 13.a3 ♖fc8 14.♘ge2 ♘a5 15.♔f2 ♗b3 16.♖ce1 ♘e8=) 12...♖fc8 (12...♘h5 13.♗e5±) 13.♘ge2 ♘a5 14.♘a4 ♖xc1+ 15.♘xc1 Kramnik — Aronian, Wijk aan Zee 2011 15...♖c8 16.♘e2 ♘c4 17.g4 ♗c2 18.♗xc4 ♗xa4 19.♗d3 ♗c6 20.♘c3 ♘e8=;

b) 10.♘f3 ♗b4 (10...♗e7 11.♘h4!±) 11.a3 ♗xc3+ 12.♖xc3 ♖c8 13.♘d2 (13.♘h4 ♗b1! 14.♗b5 ♔e7 15.0-0 ♗a2 16.♖a1 ♘a7 17.♖xc8 ♖xc8 18.♗a4 ♘h5=) 13...♘h5 14.♗g5 f6 15.♗h4 g5 16.♗g3 ♘xg3 17.hxg3 0-0=;

10...♗e7 (10...♖c8 11.♘a4 ♘d7 12.♗b5 ♗e7 13.h4) 11.♘f3 h6 12.h4 White preserves his dark-squared bishop and gains space. 12...0-0 13.♘d2± The endgame is unpleasant for Black.;

7...a6 8.♘f3 e6 9.♕b3 ♗d6 10.♕xb7 ♘a5 11.♕xa8 ♕xa8 12.♗xd6 ♘c4

(12...♔d7 13.♗c5 ♖b8

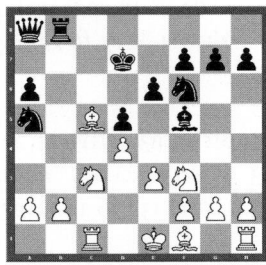

14.b3!N± The black pieces are very constricted. White possesses the only open file and has an edge.(14. ♗e2 ♖xb2 15.♘e5+ ♔e8 16.♗d1 ♕b7∞ Solak — K.Berg, Cappelle la Grande 2012; 14.♘e5+ ♔e8 15.b4 ♘b7∞ Kramnik — Gelfand, Monaco (blindfold) 2011))

13.♗xc4 dxc4 14.0-0 ♘d5 (14... ♘e4 15.♗a3 f6 16.♘a4±) 15.♖fe1 f6 16.♗a3 ♗d3 17.♘a4 ♔f7 18.♘d2± The pawn on c4 will be lost and

White will gain an obvious advantage.

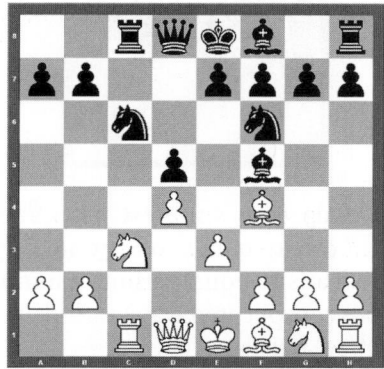

8.♘f3

8.♕b3 ♘a5 9.♕a4+ ♗d7 10.♗b5 a6 11.♗xd7+ ♘xd7=;

8.♗b5 e6 (8...a6 9.♗xc6+ ♖xc6 10.♘f3 ♘e4 11.♘e5 ♖c8 12.♕a4+ ♗d7 13.♕b3 f6 (13...♘xc3 14.♖xc3 ♖xc3 15.bxc3 ♗c8 16.0-0±) 14.♘xd7 ♕xd7 15.f3 ♘xc3 16.♖xc3±) 9.♘f3 ♘d7=

8...e6 9.♕b3

9.♘h4 ♗g4 10.♕b3 ♗b4=

9...♗b4 10.♘e5 ♕a5 11.f3

11.♘d3 ♘e4 12.♘xb4 ♘xb4 13.a3 ♘d3+ 14.♗xd3 ♘xc3 15.♕xb7 (15. ♖xc3 ♗xd3 16.♔d2=) 15...♘e4+ 16.♖c3 ♖xc3 17.♗b5+ ♖c6+ (17...♔f8 18.0-0 g5 19.♗e5 f6 20.bxc3 fxe5 21.f3=) 18.b4 0-0 19.bxa5 (19.♗xc6 ♕xa3 20.0-0 ♘d2 21.♗d6 h6 22.♕e7 ♖c8 23.b5 ♕a2 24.♖e1 ♘e4 25.♗g3=) 19...♖c1+ 20.♔e2 ♖c2+ 21.♔e1 ♖c1+=

11...♘h5

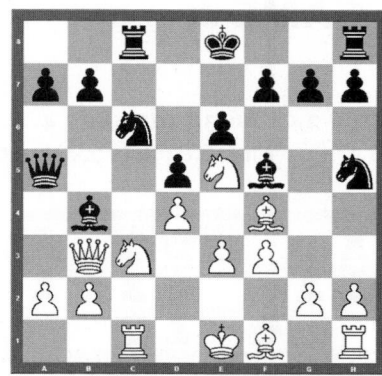

12.a3

12.♗g5 Risky. Black gets many opportunities for active play. One of them is 12...♘xe5 13.dxe5 h6 14.♗h4 d4! 15.exd4 ♘f4 16.a3 ♗xc3+ 17.bxc3 ♗d3 with sufficient compensation for the pawn.

12...♗xc3+ 13.♕xc3 ♕xc3+ 14.♖xc3 ♘xf4 15.exf4 ♔e7 16.♘xc6+ ♖xc6 17.♖xc6 bxc6 18.b4 ♗c2

18...♖a8 White has a slightly more pleasant game after 19.♗a6!±;

But quite good is 18...a6!?= followed by ♖h8-a8 then a6-a5.

19.♔d2 ♗a4 20.♗d3 ♖a8 21.♖c1 a5 22.♖c5 axb4 23.axb4 ♗b5 24.♗xb5 cxb5=

The rook endgame is drawish.

◼ GAME 4

**1.d4 d5 2.c4 c6 3.cxd5 cxd5 4.♗f4
♘f6 5.♘c3 ♘c6 6.e3 ♗f5 7.♘f3 e6**

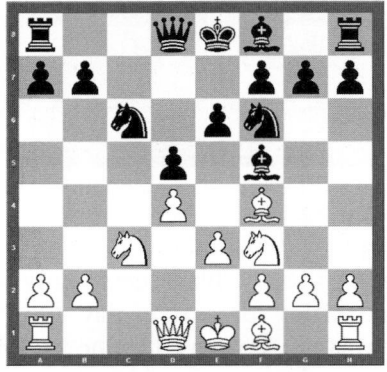

8.♕b3

8.♗b5 ♘d7 (8...♗e7 9.♘e5 ♕b6
10.♕b3 ♖c8 11.0–0 0–0 12.♗xc6 bxc6
13.♕xb6 axb6 14.♘a4 ♗d8 15.♖fc1±)
9.♕a4 (9.♖c1 ♗e7 10.♕a4?! 10...
♕b6∓; 9.0–0 ♗e7 10.♖c1 ♖c8=) 9...
♖c8 (9...♕b6 10.♘h4±) 10.0–0

(10.♗xc6 ♖xc6 11.♕xa7 ♕c8 (11...
♗d3!?) 12.♕a5 ♖a6 13.♕c7 ♕xc7
14.♗xc7 ♗b4∓)

10...a6 11.♗xc6 ♖xc6 12.♖fc1 ♗e7
13.♘e2

(13.♘d1 b5 14.♕b3 ♕c8 15.♖xc6
(15.e4 ♗xe4 16.♖xc6 ♕xc6 17.♖c1
♕a8∓) 15...♕xc6∓)

13...♕b6 14.♖xc6 bxc6 15.♖c1

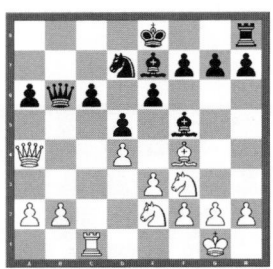

15...♗d3 The simplest. (15...♕xb2
16.♕xa6 0–0 17.♖xc6 g5 18.♗c7=
also leads to equality but in a much
more complicated way.) 16.♕d1 ♗g6
17.♕a4 ♗d3=;

8.♘e5 ♘xe5 9.♗xe5 ♘d7=;

8.♗d3 ♗xd3 9.♕xd3 ♗e7 10.0–0
0–0=

8...♗b4

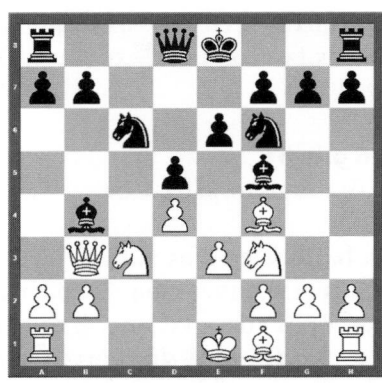

9.♗b5 0–0

9...♕a5 10.0–0 0–0 11.♖fc1! (11.♗xc6
yields nothing. 11...bxc6 12.♗c7
♕xc7 13.♕xb4 ♖ab8 14.♕a3 ♘d7=)
11...♖fc8 12.♘h4 ♗g6 13.♘xg6 hxg6
14.h3±;

9...♕e7 10.♘e5 — 9.♘e5 ♕e7
10.♗b5;

9...♗xc3+ 10.♕xc3 0–0 11.0–0 —
9...0–0 10.0–0 ♗xc3 11.♕xc3(11.
♗xc6 — 9...0–0 10.♗xc6 ♗xc3+
11.♕xc3)

10.0–0

10.♗xc6 ♗xc3+ 11.♕xc3 ♖c8 12.♘e5
♘g4 13.♘xg4 ♗xg4 14.♕b4

(14.♕a3 ♖xc6 15.♕xa7 ♖c2 16.0–
0 ♗e2 17.♖fb1 (17.♖fc1 ♖xb2 =
Abasov — Arzumanian, Kharkov
2009) 17...♕e7 18.♕a3 (18.a4 ♕b4∓;
18.♕b6 ♖fc8 19.a4 ♖8c6 20.♕b3
h5∓ — White must be careful as
the black queen and pawns can initiate a kingside attack.) 18...♕xa3
19.bxa3 b5=)

14...♖xc6 15.♕xb7 ♕a5+! Allows
a draw to be obtained from a position of strength. (Not so convincing is 15...♕c8 16.♕xc8 ♖fxc8
17.0–0 a5= Despite the extra pawn
White's chances of success are minimal. Kramnik — Anand, Bonn
(match–01) 2008) 16.b4 ♕a4 17.0–0

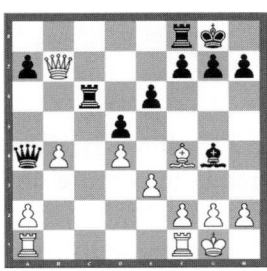

17...♗e2!N The bishop moves to the
queenside to help the major pieces
fight the white pawns.

(17...♖b6 18.♕e7 (18.♕c7±) 18...♖e8
19.♕g5 ♗f5 20.a3 ♖c6 21.h4± Ap-
pel — Nyback, Germany 2008)

18.♖fe1 ♗b5 19.h3 f6 20.♕e7 ♖f7
21.♕d8+ ♖f8 22.♕a5 ♕xa5 23.bxa5
g5 24.♗g3 ♗c4 25.♖eb1 ♖a6=

10...♗xc3

10...♕a5 — 9...♕a5 10.0–0 0–0

11.♕xc3

11.♗xc6 ♗xb2 12.♗xb7 ♗xa1
13.♖xa1 ♕b6 14.♗xa8 ♖xa8=

11...♘e4

Less concrete but nearly equal is 11...
♖c8 12.♕a3 Maintaining the tension
on the c-file also yields nothing:

a) 12.♖ac1 a6 13.♗xc6 ♖xc6 14.♕b4
♕c8 15.♖xc6 ♕xc6 16.♘e5 ♕c8
17.h3 ♘d7 18.♘xd7 ♕xd7 19.♖c1
♖c8=;

b) 12.♖fc1 ♘h5!? (12...♘e4 13.♕a3 —
12.♕a3 ♘e4 13.♖fc1) 13.♕a3 ♘xf4
14.exf4 ♕b6 15.♗xc6 ♖xc6 16.♖xc6
♕xc6 17.♕xa7 ♖c8 — Black's compensation for his pawn is sufficient
for equality, Stojanovic — Kir.Geor-
giev, Niksic (rapid)2008;

12...♘e4

a) 12...♕b6 13.♕c5 ♕a5

a1) 13...♕xc5 14.dxc5 ♘e4 (14...a6 15.♗xc6 bxc6 16.♖ac1±) 15.♖ac1±;

a2) 13...♕d8 14.♗xc6 ♖xc6 15.♕xa7 ♕c8 16.♕a3 ♘e4±;

14.♗xc6 ♕xc5 15.dxc5 bxc6 16.♖fc1±;

b) 12...a6 13.♗xc6 (13.♗e2 ♘e4 14.h3 f6=) 13...♖xc6 14.♖ac1 ♖xc1 (14...♕c8 15.b3 (15.♖xc6 ♕xc6 16.♘e5 ♕c8 (16...♕c2!?) 17.b3 ♘h5 18.♖c1 ♕d8 — Exchanging his knight for the bishop solves Black's problems despite White's control of the c-file.) 15...♘e4 16.♖xc6 ♕xc6 17.♖c1 ♕b5± — White's advantage is so small that its realisation is unlikely.) 15.♖xc1 ♕d7 16.h3 (16.♕c5 ♘e4 17.♕c7 ♕b5=) 16...♖c8 17.♖c5 ♕e8 18.♕c3 ♖xc5 19.dxc5 ♘e4 20.♕a5 f6 21.♘d4 ♗g6=;

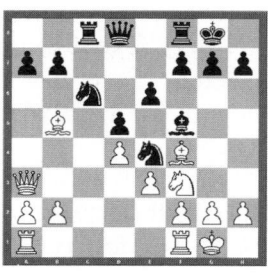

13.♖fc1 (13.♖ac1 g5 14.♗xc6 bxc6 15.♗g3 f6 — 11...♘e4 12.♕a3 g5 13.♗xc6 bxc6 14.♗g3 f6 15.♖ac1 ♖c8.) 13...g5 14.♗g3 f6 15.♗xc6 bxc6 16.♕xa7 h5 17.h3 (17.h4 g4 18.♘h2 ♘xg3 19.fxg3 ♕d6∓ 20.♘f1?! 20...♖a8 21.♕c5 ♕xc5 22.♖xc5 ♖fb8–+ Rusev — Ni Hua, Villarrobledo (rapid) 2009) 17...♘xg3 (17...g4

18.♘h4 ♘xg3 19.fxg3 ♗e4∞) 18.fxg3 ♕d6 19.♔f2 ♖a8 20.♕c5 ♕xc5 21.dxc5 ♖fb8 22.b3 e5 23.♘d2 ♖a3=

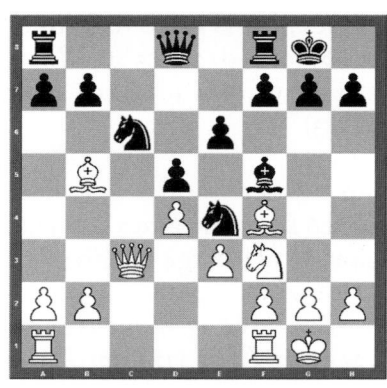

12.♕a3

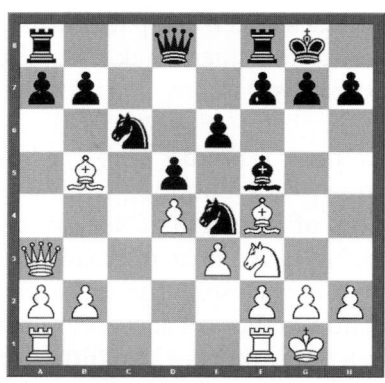

12...g5!?
12...♖c8 — 11...♖c8 12.♕a3 ♘e4

13.♗xc6

On 13.♗g3 follows 13...♕b6 = and Black is ready to capture on c6 with the queen.

13...bxc6 14.♗g3 f6

The most flexible. The white knight is deprived of the e5 square and Black retains the option to fight on either flank.

14...h5 15.h4 ♘xg3 16.fxg3 ♕c7 17.♔h2 gxh4 18.♘xh4 ♗e4 19.♖f6 ♔g7 20.♖af1 ♖ae8±

15.♖ac1
15.♖fc1 ♕b6=

15...♖c8 16.♖fd1
16.♕xa7 ♖a8∓

16...h5 17.♘d2 ♘xd2 18.♖xd2 c5 19.h4
19.dxc5 h4 20.e4 ♗g6∓ — White is forced to sacrifice the bishop.

19...gxh4 20.♗xh4 c4=
with a near equal game.

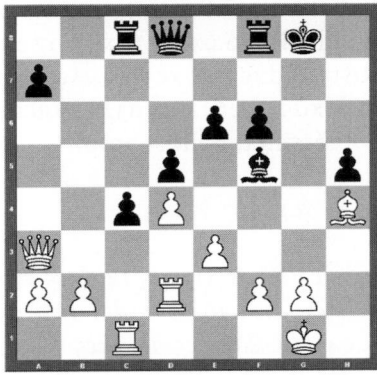

■ GAME 5

1.d4 d5 2.c4 c6 3.cxd5 cxd5 4.♗f4 ♘f6 5.♘c3 ♘c6 6.e3 ♗f5 7.♘f3 e6 8.♕b3 ♗b4

8...♕b6 White has the more pleasant endgame arising after 9.♕xb6 axb6 10.a3 ♗e7 11.♗e2 0–0 12.0–0 ♖fc8 13.♖fc1± Ivanchuk — Nakamura, Medias 2011

9.♘e5

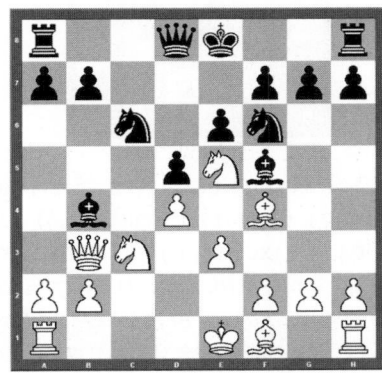

9...♗xc3+!
Only this immediate exchange allows Black to reach equality.
9...♕b6 10.♘xc6 (

10.♗e2 ♖c8! (10...♘e4 11.♘xc6 bxc6 — 10.♘xc6 bxc6 11.♗e2 ♘e4; 10...♘xe5 11.♗xe5 0–0 12.♗xf6 gxf6 13.0–0 ♗xc3 14.bxc3 ♖fc8 15.♖fc1 ♖c6 16.c4 dxc4 17.♖xc4± Macieja — Shirov, Trzcianka 2012) 11.0–0

a) 11.♘xc6 ♖xc6 12.f3 0–0=;

b) 11.f3 0-0 (11...♘xe5!? 12.♗xe5 ♘d7∞) 12.♘xc6 ♖xc6=;

c) 11.♖c1 ♘e4 12.f3 (12.g4 ♗g6 (12...♘xe5 13.♗xe5 ♗g6 14.f3 (14.♗xg7 ♖g8 15.♗h6 (15.♗e5 f6 16.♗f4 ♔e7∓) 15...♔e7∓) 14...♘xc3 15.bxc3 f6=)) 12...♘xc3 13.bxc3 ♘xe5 14.♗xe5 f6=;

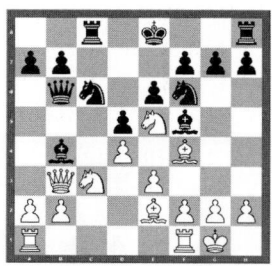

11...♗xc3 12.bxc3 (12.♕xc3 g5! 13.♗g3 ♘e4 14.♕a3 ♕b4=) 12...♘e4 13.♘xc6 (13.c4 ♘xe5 14.♗xe5 f6 15.♗f4 g5 16.♗g3 dxc4 17.♗xc4 ♕xb3 18.axb3 a6 19.f3 ♘xg3 20.hxg3 ♔e7 21.e4 ♗g6 22.♔f2=) 13...♘xc6 14.♗b5 ♘d2 15.♕a4 ♘xf1 16.♖xf1 0-0 17.♗xc6 bxc6=)

10...bxc6 11.♗e2

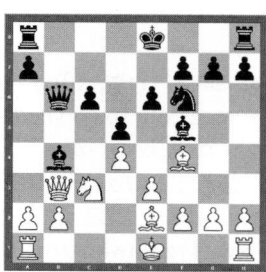

11...0-0

(11...♘e4 12.f3 ♘xc3 13.bxc3 ♗e7 14.0-0! (14.c4 ♕xb3 15.axb3 ♗b4+ 16.♔f2 a5 = — The bishop on b4 cements the queenside, Landa — Sakaev, Plovdiv 2010) 14...0-0 (14... h6 Neither can the exchange of the dark-squared bishops solve the problems: 15.c4 ♗g5 16.♗xg5 hxg5 17.cxd5±) 15.c4± — White wants to seize space with the move c4-c5. The pressure is unpleasant.

15...c5?! No chances are given by this attempt at active counterplay by Black. 16.cxd5 ♕xb3 17.axb3 exd5 18.dxc5 ♗xc5 19.♖a5 ♗b6 20.♖xd5 ♗e6 21.♖d3± Tkachiev — Fressinet, Belfort 2010)

12.0-0 ♗xc3 13.♕xc3

(13.bxc3 ♖fc8! (13...c5 14.dxc5 ♕xc5 15.♖fc1 ♘e4 16.c4 ♘d2? 17.♕b5±) 14.c4 (14.♖fc1 c5 15.dxc5 ♖xc5=) 14...c5 15.♖fd1 ♕xb3 16.axb3 ♗c2 17.♖dc1 ♗xb3 18.cxd5 ♘xd5=)

13...g5 14.♗g3 ♘e4 15.♕a3 a5 16.♖fc1 (Also noteworthy is 16.♖ac1!? with the idea of capturing with the f-pawn if ♘xg3.) 16...♘xg3 17.hxg3 a4 18.♗d3 ♗xd3 19.♕xd3 ♖fb8 20.♖c2 ♕b5 21.♕d1 h6 22.♖ac1 ♖b6 23.f4±

N.Nguen — Bu Xiangzhi, Mashhad 2011;

9...♕e7 10.♗b5 ♖c8 11.♘xc6 bxc6 12.♗a6 ♖d8 13.0-0± Morovic — Ragger, Khanty Mansyisk 2010

10.bxc3

10.♕xc3 ♘xe5 11.♗xe5 0-0 12.♕b4 ♖c8 13.♗e2 ♖c2 (13...♘e4!? 14.h4 f6 15.♗h2 ♖c2 16.f3 a5∞) 14.♗d1 ♖c4 15.♕a3

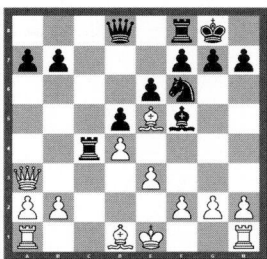

15...a6!

(15...♕b6 16.♗d6 (16.0-0 ♖fc8 17.♗b3 ♖4c6 18.♗a4 ♖c4 19.♗b3 = Martinovic — Erdos, Sibenik 2011) 16...♖fc8 17.♗c5± — Black is forced to sacrifice the exchange.)

16.0-0 ♖c6=

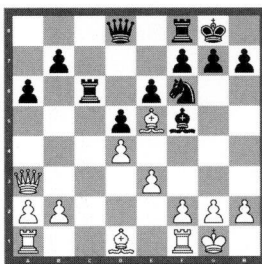

Due to his control of the c-file Black obtains equality.

10...♘xe5!

10...0-0 11.♘xc6 bxc6 12.♕a3 a5 13.♗e2± Potkin — Rublevsky, Dagomys 2010

11.♗xe5 0-0 12.♗e2

12.♕xb7 ♖c8 13.♗a6 (13.♖c1 — 12.♖c1 ♖c8 13.♕xb7) 13...♖xc3 14.0-0 ♘e4=;

12.♖c1 ♖c8 13.♕xb7 (13.♗e2 — 12.♗e2 ♖c8 13.♖c1) 13...♘e4 14.f3 ♕h4+ 15.g3 ♕h6 16.♗f4 g5 17.♗c7 g4 18.♗f4 ♘g5 19.e4 (19.fxg4 ♗e4 20.h4 ♗xh1 21.♗xg5 ♕g6∓) 19...dxe4 20.fxe4 e5 21.dxe5 ♖b8 22.♕a6 ♕xa6 23.♗xa6 ♗xe4 24.♖f1 ♘f3+ 25.♔f2 ♖fe8=

12...♖c8!N

12...♕a5 13.♗xf6 gxf6 14.0-0± T.Mueller — Roth, Untergrombach 1999

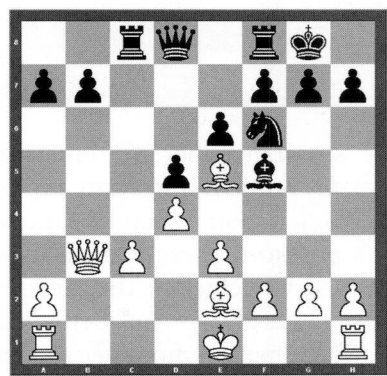

13.♖c1 ♕e7!

13...♕a5 14.♗d6 ♖fd8 15.♗b4 ♕c7 16.0-0±;

13...♘e4 14.f3 ♘d6 15.0-0 ♘c4 16.♗xc4 ♖xc4 17.♕xb7 ♕c8 18.♕xa7

♖xc3 19.♗c7 ♖xe3 20.♗f4 ♖c3 21.a4±
— The remote a-pawn can be blockaded but Black's game is still unpleasant.

14. ♗xf6 gxf6
Unnecessarily sharp for Black is 14...
♕xf6 15.♕xb7 ♖b8 16.♕a6 ♖b2 17.0–
0 ♖fb8 with compensation which
should be sufficient for equality.

**15.0–0 ♖c7 16.c4 dxc4 17.♖xc4 ♗e4
18.f3 ♗d5 19.♖xc7 ♕xc7 20.♕b2
♖c8 21.e4 ♗c6=**

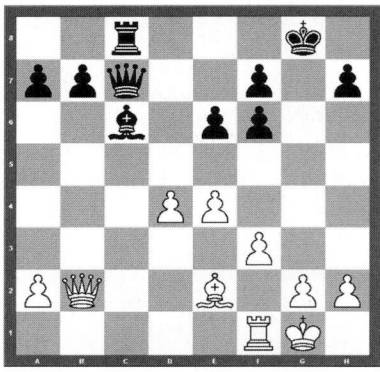

The small number of remaining
pieces prevents White from exploit-
ing Black's somewhat weakened
king's position. There is equality on
the board. Conclusion: The exchange
variation was always considered to be
a drawish opening, however modern
theory has shaken this opinion. No
wonder that many grandmasters in-
cluding Vladimir Kramnik play this
opening with White to win. At the
same time Black can solve all opening problems with accurate play.

PART 2

Winawer counter-gambit

■ GAME 6

1.d4 d5 2.c4 c6 3.♘c3 e5

A sharp blow freeing his pieces. However the immediate moves in the main branches of this variation are to be made by the queen which is a serious drawback.

4.cxd5

On the one hand the removal of pawn tension on the c-file gives the c6 square to the black knight, on the other hand it will soon be evident that it leaves the black d4 pawn without support.

4.e3 is unprincipled. Black can switch to a French Defence with reversed colours a tempo down by means of 4...e4 Of course an extra tempo will be useful for White but Black still has a good enough game.

A reliable continuation is the move 4...exd4 — Black has an easy game and free development.

4.dxe5 d4 5.♘e4 ♕a5+

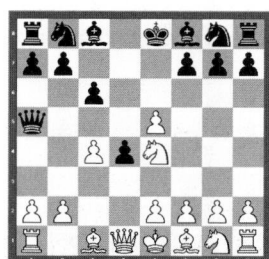

6.♗d2

(6.♘d2 ♘d7

a) 6...♕xe5 7.♘gf3 ♕d6 8.♘b3 c5 9.e3±;

b) 6...♘h6 7.♘gf3 ♘f5 8.g3 ♘d7 (8...♘e3 9.fxe3 dxe3 10.a3! ♗f5 11.♗g2± Beliavsky — Gelfand, Linares 1992) 9.♗g2 ♘xe5 10.0-0±;

7.♘gf3

(7.e6 fxe6 (7...♘e5!? 8.exf7+ ♔xf7∞ Timman — Hector, Malme 2007) 8.g3 e5 9.♗g2 ♘gf6 10.♘gf3 ♗e7 11.0-0 ♕c7 = Karpov — Bareev, Linares 1992)

7...♘xe5 8.♘xe5 ♕xe5 9.♘f3 ♕a5+

(9...♗b4+ 10.♗d2 ♕e7! (10...
♕c5 11.a3 ♗xd2+ 12.♕xd2 ♗e6
13.♕xd4 ♕xd4 14.♘xd4 ♗xc4
15.♘f5± Janssen — Smeets,
Hilversum 2007) 11.♘xd4
♘f6=/⩲)

10.♗d2 ♕b6 11.♕b3 ♗e6= Roeder
— Engqvist, Vienna 1990)

6...♕xe5 7.♘g3 ♘f6

(7...c5 8.♘f3 ♕c7 9.e3 dxe3

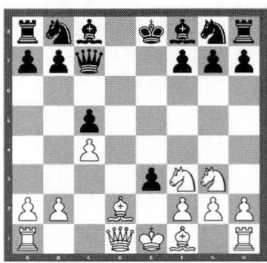

10.♕e2! (Placing the dark-squared
bishop on the long diagonal is
much more effective. White has
just a microscopic advantage after
10.♗xe3 ♘f6 11.♗d3 ♗e7 12.0–0
0–0 13.♘f5 ♗xf5 14.♗xf5 g6 15.♗h3
♘c6 16.♕c2± — then White plans
♖ad1, g2-g3 and ♗h3-g2.) 10...♘f6
11.♕xe3+ ♗e7 12.♗c3 0–0 13.♗d3
♘c6 14.0–0± — White's piece
pressure is very serious since Black
cannot move his light-squared
bishop to an active position: 14...
♗g4? 15.♗xf6 ♗xf6 16.♕e4+-)

8.♘f3 ♕d6

(8...♕c5 is extravagant. 9.a3! (Also
good enough is 9.b4 ♕d6 (Bad

is 9...♕xc4 10.e4 d3 11.♖c1 ♕a6
12.a4↑ — White develops a strong
initiative.) 10.♕c2 — The move
b2-b4 turns out to be useful, since
Black cannot secure the d4 pawn
by c6-c5.) 9...♕b6 (9...♕xc4 10.e3
♕d5 11.♘xd4±/↑ White has a simple plan: the queen moves to c2,
the bishop to c3, whereas the black
queen will not stay long in the centre as eventually it will be attacked
by the white pieces.) 10.e3!N (10.
♕c2± Grabliauskas — Leonid Mi-
lov, Berlin 1995)

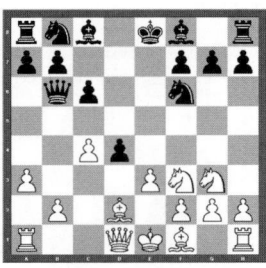

10...dxe3 11.♗xe3 c5 12.♗d3±/↑
— White's initiative is very strong
and the b2 pawn is (+) poisoned.+
— Black is already behind in development.)
9.♕c2

(If White wants a more simple
game, he can choose 9.a3!?, depriving Black of a future check on b4.

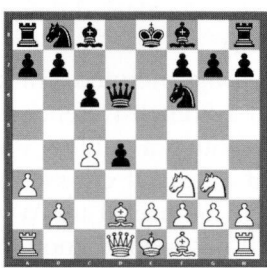

9... ♗e7 (9...c5 has also been played
10.e3 ♘c6 11.exd4 cxd4 (11...♘xd4
12.♘xd4 ♕xd4 13. ♗c3±) 12. ♗d3
♗e7 13.0-0 a5 Huebner — Kiik,
Finland 2010. Here a strong move
was 14.b4!±, since impossible is
14...axb4 15.axb4 ♖xa1 16.♕xa1
♘xb4 due to 17.♗f5! 17...0-0 18.c5!
♕xc5 19.♖c1+-) 10.e3 dxe3 11. ♗xe3
0-0 12.♕xd6 ♗xd6 13.0-0-0 ♗c7
14. ♗d3± Although Black's camp
has no weaknesses the endgame
looks advantageous for White.)
9... ♗e7

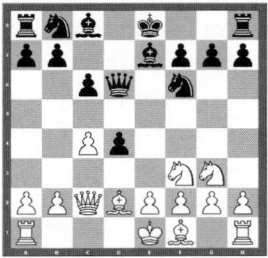

10.0-0-0

a) 10.♘f5 ♗xf5 11.♕xf5 0-0 12.g3

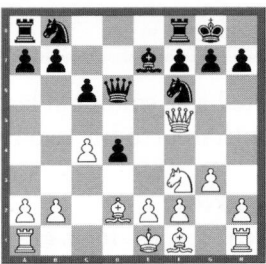

12...g6!N The right moment to drive
the queen from its active position.
(12...♘a6 Less accurate is 13.♗g2
g6 Huebner — Fontaine, Palermo
2007 (13...♘c5 14.0-0 ♘ce4 15.♗f4
♕b4 16.♗e5±) 14.♕f4!± — In the

endgame Black will have to defend the d4 pawn with the move
c6-c5, and the knight on a6 will be
out of the picture.) 13.♕c2 (13.♕f4
♕xf4 14. ♗xf4 ♗b4+!=) 13...c5 (13...
♘a6 14. ♗g2 ♘b4 15.♕d1 d3 16.0-
0±) 14. ♗g2 ♘c6 15.0-0 ♖fe8 = —
Somewhat weakened white squares
are compensated by active pieces
and the possibility of carrying out
a black-squared strategy.;

b) 10.e3 White gains little from
a plan with short castling: 10...dxe3
11. ♗xe3 0-0 (11...♘g4 12. ♗d4 ♗f6
13.0-0-0±) 12. ♗e2 ♕c7 (12...♘g4
13. ♗d2±; 12...♘a6 13.a3 ♖e8 14.0-0
♘g4 15. ♗d4 ♘c5 Hutchinson —
Coates, England 2004 16.h3 ♘f6
17.b4 ♘e6 18. ♗e5 ♕d8 19.♖ad1 ♗d7
20.♘f5±) 13.0-0 ♖e8 14.♖ad1 c5!
15.♖fe1 ♘c6 It's hard for White to
build up pressure along the central
files and he can't get the advantage
of two bishops. On 16.♘f5 follows
16... ♗f8=;

10...0-0 11.e3

(11. ♗c3 ♕f4+ 12.e3 dxe3 13.fxe3

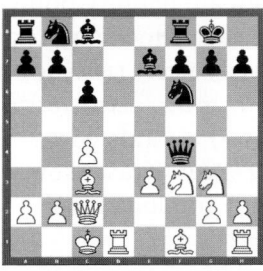

13...♕h6!N The queen is best positioned here. It attacks the white

pieces and defends the kingside. Now the move ♘f6-g4 is threatened. (In practice the following has occurred *13...♕xe3+ 14.♔b1↑* — The black queen will be attacked with tempi.) *14.♗d2 ♗d6! 15.e4 ♗f4 =* — Black has a good game.)

11...dxe3

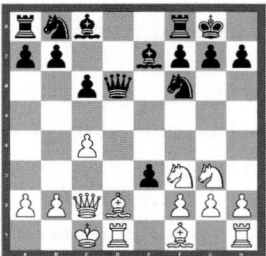

12.♗xe3

(Strategically risky for White is 12.fxe3 — If White fails to develop the initiative, the weakness on the e-file will show: 12...♕c7 13.♗c3 g6!?

a) 13...♗g4?! 14.♗d3 ♘bd7 15.♗f5↑ Kasparov — Pr.Nikolic, Mamila 1992;

b) From a reliability point of view, Black can choose 13...c5 14.♘f5 ♘c6 15.a3 ♗xf5 (*15...♘g4 16.♘xg7 ♘xe3 17.♕d2 ♘xd1 18.♕h6 ♗d6 19.♘h5→*) 16.♕xf5 g6 17.♕f4 ♕xf4 18.exf4 ♘e4= Krasenkow — Morozevich, Pamplona 1999;

14.e4 There are signs of active counterplay. *14...♘g4! 15.♕e2 ♗c5!±* — The black pieces move to

active positions and White can't uitilise the long diagonal.)

12...♕c7 13.♘f5 ♗xf5

(If Black parts with the active bishop, then White's position is also a bit better: 13...♘a6 14.♘xe7+ ♕xe7 15.h3 (*15.a3 ♗g4 16.♗e2 ♘c5=*) 15...♘b4 16.♕b3 ♗f5 17.a3 ♘a6 18.♘h4 ♗e6 19.♕c2 (*19.g4!?*) 19...♘c5 20.♗e2±)

14.♕xf5 ♘a6 15.♗d3 (*15.♘d4* yields nothing *15...g6 16.♕f3 ♘c5 17.g4=* Gustafsson — Tischbierek, Bonn 2011. Against flank play Black has sufficient counterplay along the central files.) 15...g6 16.♕f4 ♕xf4 17.♗xf4±

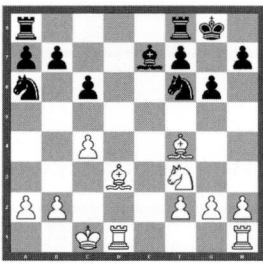

— White has a small but lasting advantage thanks to his two bishops.

4...cxd5 5.dxe5

5.♘f3 e4 6.♘e5 f6 7.♕a4+ ♘d7 8.♘xd7 (*8.♘g4 ♔f7 9.♕b3 ♘b6 10.♘e3 ♗e6∓*) 8...♗xd7 9.♕b3 ♗c6 10.♗f4 Gustafsson — Wiesnewski, Pinneberg 1996 10...♗d6 11.♗xd6 ♕xd6 12.e3 f5=;

5.e4 dxe4 6.♗b5+ (*6.d5 ♘f6 7.♗g5 ♘bd7∓*) 6...♗d7 7.dxe5 ♗b4 (*7...♘c6*

8.♗f4 ♘ge7 9.♘ge2 ♘g6 Krasenkow
— Shabalov, Moscow 1991 *10.0-0↑* —
White gains an advantage in development.) *8.♗xd7+ (8.e6 fxe6 9.♕h5+
g6 10.♕e5 ♕f6 11.♗f4 a6 12.♗c4 ♘c6
13.♕xf6 ♘xf6∓* Beliavsky — Lautier,
Belgrade 1991; *8.♗d2 ♗xc3 9.♗xd7+
♘xd7 10.♗xc3 ♘c5 11.♘h3 ♘d3+
12.♔f1 ♕d5∓* — Black has some initiative, Matthiesen — Hector, Denmark
2010.) *8...♕xd7 (8...♘xd7 9.♘ge2
♘xe5 10.0-0 ♘e7 11.♘xe4 ♘7c6± /=)
9.♗d2 ♘c6 10.♘xe4 ♗xd2+ 11.♕xd2
♕xd2+ 12.♔xd2 ♘xe5=*

5...d4 6.♘e4 ♕a5+ 7.♘d2!

*7.♗d2 ♕xe5 8.♘g3 ♘f6! 9.♘f3
♕d5=*

7...♘c6

*7...♘h6 8.♘gf3 ♘f5 9.g3 ♘c6 (9...
♘e3 10.fxe3 dxe3 11.♕b3! exd2+ (11...
♗c5 12.♘g5 0-0 13.♗g2±) 12.♗xd2±)
10.♗g2 ♘e3 11.fxe3 dxe3 12.0-0 exd2
13.♗xd2 ♕b6+ 14.♔h1 ♗e7 15.♗g5
(15.♗c3 0-0±) 15...0-0 16.♗xe7 ♘xe7
17.♕d4±* Yevseev — Sergienko, Sochi
2004

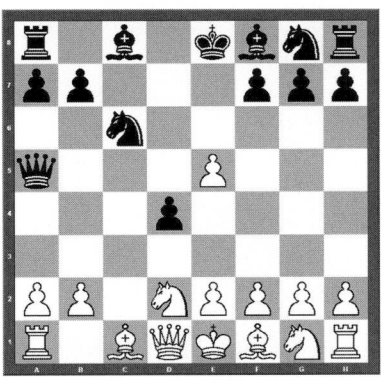

8.♘gf3 ♗g4 9.g3

9.♕b3? 9...♖d8! 10.♕xb7 ♘ge7

9...♗xf3

*9...d3 10.exd3 0-0-0 11.♗g2 ♘xe5
12.♕c2+ ♔b8 13.0-0±*

10.exf3 ♕xe5+ 11.♕e2 ♕xe2+

11...0-0-0 12.♕xe5 ♘xe5 13.♘c4±

12.♗xe2 0-0-0

12...♖d8 13.♗d3±

13.♗c4 ♖d7

*13...♗b4 14.a3 (14.♗xf7 ♘h6
15.♗e6+ ♔b8) 14...♗xd2+ 15.♗xd2
♘e5 16.♗e2 d3 17.♖c1+ ♘c6 (17...♔d7
18.f4+-* Fridman — Hector, Germany
2010) *18.♗f1±*

14.0-0 ♘f6 15.♖d1±

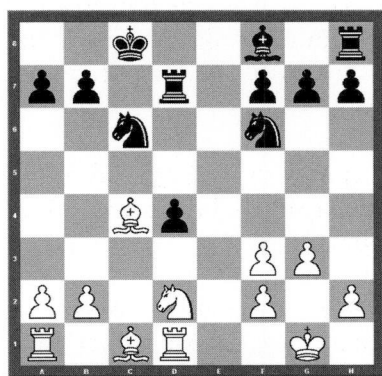

The d4 pawn is not a passed pawn
but a weakness taking into account
White's bishop pair. Black is faced
with an unpleasant defence. Conclusion: In spite of widespread opinion
the move 3...e5 is not sharp at all.
The pawn will be won back and in
most cases White stands a little bet-

ter on account of his two bishops.
I think the most promising line is
4.cxd5 cxd5 5. dxe5 d4 6. ♘e4 ♕a5+
7.♘d2 — here White presses without
any risk. The following seems to be
a good try too 4.dxe5 d4 5.♘e4 ♕a5+
6.♗d2 ♕xe5 7.♘g3 ♘f6 8.♘f3 ♕d6
9.♕c2 or 9.a3!?

PART 3 — Alekhine variation, side line

■ GAME 7

1.d4 d5 2.c4 c6 3.♘c3 dxc4
Once considered inferior this has now become popular.

4.e3
To a slow 4.a4 Black has the chance to fight for the initiative at once with 4...e5! freeing all his pieces. 5.dxe5

a) 5.e3 exd4 6.exd4 ♗e6∓ — It will take a lot of time to win back the c4 pawn.;

b) 5.♘f3 exd4 6.♘xd4

6...♘d7!?N (6...♗c5 To obtain a good game the following will suffice 7.e3 ♘f6 (An unclear endgame results from 7...♗xd4 8.♕xd4 (*8.exd4 ♗e6∓*) 8...♕xd4 9.exd4 ♗e6 10.♘e4 ♘a6 11.♘d6+ ♔d7∞) 8.♗xc4 0-0=) 7.e4 ♘e5 8.♗f4 ♘d3+ (8...♗d6 9.♕d2 ♘e7 10.0-0-0 ♘7g6∞)

9.♗xd3 ♕xd4 10.♗e2 ♕xd1+ 11.♖xd1 ♗e6 12.♗e3 Pressing Black with the f-pawn — perhaps the only possible plan for White. The endgame is double-edged and White must play it like a middlegame. 12...♘h6!? Enabling the most harmonious development of the kingside. (*12...♘f6 13.f4 ♗b4 14.f5∞; 12...a6 13.f4 b5 14.f5 ♗d7 15.0-0∞*) 13.h3 ♗b4 14.g4 f6 15.f4 ♘f7∞ — The play is double-edged but White risks more since he is already a pawn down (the thrust f4-f5 winning the pawn back is a positional concession);

5...♕xd1+ 6.♔xd1 ♗e6 7.e4 ♘a6 8.f4

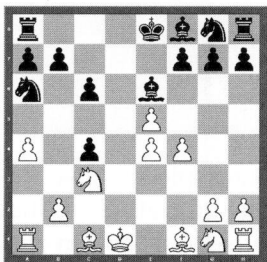

8...0-0-0+ (Apart from castling long, interesting is *8...♖d8+!?N* vacating the c8 square for the retreat of the bishop. *9.♔e2 ♘c5 10.♗e3 ♘d3∞* — Black's chances are as good as White's.) 9.♔e2 g6 10.♗e3

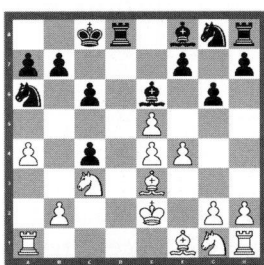

10...♘b4!N (10...♗c5 11.♘f3 f6 12.h3 fxe5 13.♘xe5 ♘f6 14.♔f3± Dub — Drozdov, Tel Aviv 2002; 10...♘c5 11.♘f3∞) 11.♘f3

(11.♗xa7 ♘d3 12.♔e3 ♗h6 13.g3 f6 14.exf6 g5 15.♗xd3 ♖xd3+ 16.♔f2 ♘xf6 17.♘ge2 gxf4 (17...♗g4!?) 18.♘xf4 ♗xf4 19.gxf4 ♖f8 20.f5 ♘xe4+ 21.♘xe4 ♖xf5+ 22.♔g1 ♖f4 23.♖e1 ♖df3∓

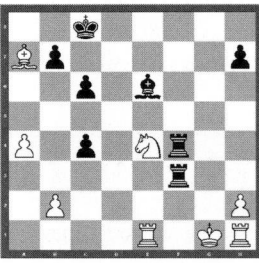

The Black pieces have developed a strong initiative — the bishop will move to d5 and in spite of the extra piece White must be concerned about his salvation.)

11...♘c2

(11...♘d3 12.♘g5 ♘xb2 (12...♗g4+ 13.♔d2±) 13.♘xe6 fxe6 14.g3±)

12.♖d1 ♘xe3 13.♖xd8+ ♔xd8 14.♔xe3 ♗c5+ 15.♔d2 ♘h6 (15... f6!?) 16.h3 (16.♘g5 ♔e7 17.♘xe6 fxe6 18.♗xc4 ♖f8 19.♖f1 g5 20.fxg5 ♖xf1 21.♗xf1 ♘f7∓ The g5 and e5 pawns are lost and thanks to his better pawn structure Black is even a little better.) 16...a6∞ — The pawn mass emerging on the queenside is no less dangerous than White's activity.

4.♘f3 b5 (4...♘f6 — 3.♘f3 ♘f6 4.♘c3 dxc4; 4...e6 — 3.♘c3 e6 4.♘f3 dxc4) 5.a4 Otherwise Black keeps the extra pawn for insufficient compensation. 5...b4 6.♘e4 ♘f6 7.♘xf6+ (On 7.♘g3 Black has many possibilities but most of all I like

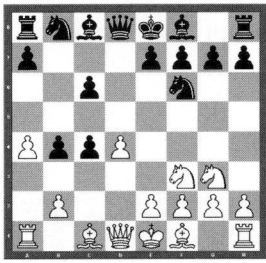

7...♕d5! preventi ng e2-e4 and preparing to defend the c4 pawn with ♗c8-a6. Also an attack on the g3 knight with the pawn thrust h7-h5-h4 is possible. If h2-h4 the white knight becomes vulnerable after ♗f8-d6.) 7...exf6 8.e3 (8.e4 ♕e7∓ — White is forced to sacrifice a pawn with insufficent compensation to equalise)

8...♕d5!N (8...♗e6 9.♗d2 ♘d7 10.♖c1 c3 11.bxc3 b3 12.♖b1 ♖b8 13.c4 b2∞) 9.♗d2 a5 — Black has the better game. The bishop is ready to defend the pawn from a6.

4...b5

4...♗e6 5.♘f3 — 3.♘f3 dxc4 4.e3 ♗e6 5.♘c3

5.a4 b4 6.♘e4 ♕d5

6...♘f6 7.♘xf6+ exf6 8.♗xc4 ♗d6 9.♘f3 0-0 10.0-0±

7.♘g3

7.f3 e6 (7...e5 8.dxe5 ♘d7 9.♘d6+ ♗xd6 10.exd6∞; 7...♘d7 8.♕c2 ♗a6 9.♘d2 b3 10.♕c3 e5 11.♗xc4 exd4 12.exd4 ♗xc4 13.♕xc4 ♕xc4 14.♘xc4 ♘b6=) 8.♘e2 ♗a6 9.♘f4 ♕a5 10.♘d2 c3 11.bxc3 bxc3 12.♘b3 ♕c7=;

7.♘d2 c3 8.bxc3 bxc3 9.♘c4 (9.♘b1 ♕a5∓ Ponomariov — Vallejo Pons, Beijing 2011) 9...♘f6 10.♕c2 ♗a6!? (10...c5=) 11.♕xc3 e5∞ Goudriaan — Khenkin, Hilversum 2011

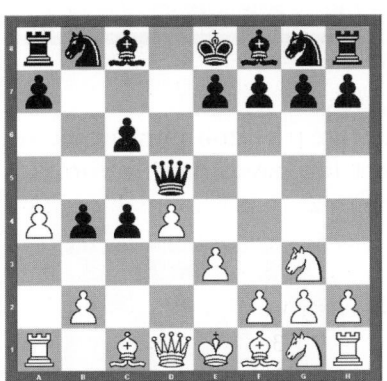

7...♘f6 8.♗e2

8.♘f3 ♗a6 (8...h5!?∞) 9.♗e2 e6 (9...h5!?∞) 10.0-0 (10.♘e5 ♕xg2 (10...c3!?∞) 11.♗f3 ♕h3 12.♘xc6 ♘bd7∓/∞) 10...♗d6 11.♗d2 h5 (11...

c5∞) 12.♘e5 (12.h4 ♘bd7∓; 12.♖e1 h4 13.e4 ♕a5∓) 12...h4 13.♗f3

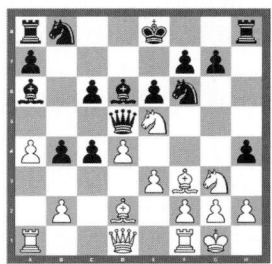

13...♕a5!N (13...hxg3 14.♗xd5 gxh2+ 15.♔h1 cxd5∞ Tkachiev — Piket, Cannes 2000) 14.♘xc6 ♘xc6 15.♗xc6+ ♔e7 16.♘e4 (16.♗xa8 hxg3-+) 16...♘xe4 17.♗xe4 c3∓

8...♗a6

8...e6 9.e4 ♕a5 (9...♘xe4 10.♗f3 f5 11.♕e2↑) 10.♗xc4 ♗a6 11.♗xa6 ♕xa6 12.♗g5 ♘bd7 13.♕e2 ♕xe2+ 14.♔xe2 c5 15.♘f3 h5 16.h4± Lysyi — S.Ernst, Plovdiv 2012;

8...e5 is quite reliable. 9.♘f3 exd4 10.exd4 ♗d6 11.♕c2

(11.♘f1 c3 12.bxc3 (12.♘e3 cxb2 13.♗xb2 ♕a5∓) 12...♘e4 13.cxb4

(13.c4

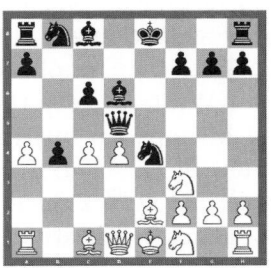

13...♕e6!N (13...♕a5 14.♗d3 ♘c3
15.♕c2± Riazantsev — Felgaer,
Moscow 2011) 14.♘e3 ♘c3 15.♕c2
♘xe2 16.♕xe2 0-0 17.0-0 ♘d7∓)

13...♗xb4+ 14.♗d2 ♘xd2 15.N1xd2
0-0=)

11...♗a6 12.♘f5 0-0

(12...b3 leads to a double-edged,
nearly equal endgame 13.♘xg7+
♔f8 14.♕f5 ♗b4+ 15.♔f1 ♘g8
16.♕xd5 (16.♘e5 ♔xg7 17.♗f3 ♕e6
18.♕g5+ ♔f8 19.♕d8+ ♔g7=) 16...
cxd5 17.♘h5∞)

13.♘e3 (13.♗f4 doesn't work in view
of the intermediate 13...b3! 14.♗xd6
♖e8 15.♕b1 ♕a5+ 16.♔f1 ♖xe2) 13...
♕e6!N

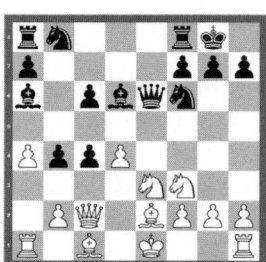

(13...♕e4 14.♕xe4 ♘xe4 15.♘xc4±
Kurnosov — Tikkanen, Helsingor
2011) 14.♗xc4 (14.♘xc4 It would be
useful for White to keep the light-
squared bishops on but impossible in view of 14...♘bd7 15.♗e3 b3!
16.♕xb3 ♖ab8 17.♕c2 ♗b4+ 18.♔f1
♖fe8 — Black's initiative is very
dangerous.) 14...♗xc4 15.♕xc4 ♘d5
16.0-0 ♘d7= — The game is equal.

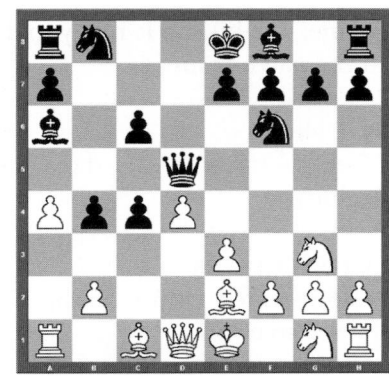

9.e4

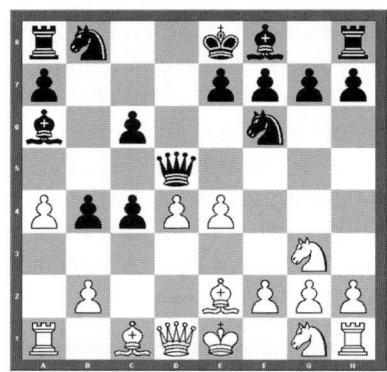

9...♕a5!

9...♘xe4 It's too dangerous to accept the pawn sacrifice: 10.♗f3 f5
11.♘1e2

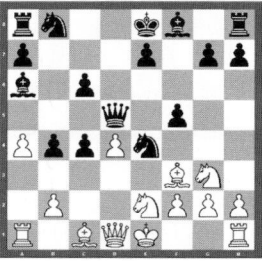

On 11...♕f7 White need not to hurry
to regain the pawn. Strongest is

a) 11...c3 12.bxc3±;

b) 11...g6 12.♘f4 ♕f7 13.0-0 ♘g5 *(13...♗h6 14.♖e1 c3 15.♘xe4 fxe4 16.♖xe4 cxb2 17.♗xb2 ♗xf4 18.d5 ♖f8 19.dxc6 ♕f5 20.♕e1 ♕c5 21.♖xb4±/→)* 14.d5 ♘xf3+ *(14...♗g7? 15.dxc6 ♘xf3+ 16.♕xf3 0-0 17.c7 ♘d7 18.♕c6± Gustafsson — Balogh, Porto Carras 2011)* 15.♕xf3 ♗b7 16.♘e6 cxd5 17.♖e1 ♘a6 18.♗f4↑

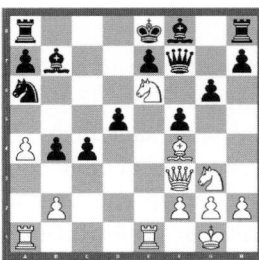

— the position has plenty of opportunities but at the same time the White has a most dangerous initiative fully compensating the material loss.;

12.0-0!, with the idea of ♘e2-f4, ♖f1-e1 after which the rook is active.

(12.♘xe4 fxe4 13.♗xe4 e6 14.♘g1!∞

(14.♗f4 ♘d7! (14...♗e7 15.♗xb8 ♖xb8 16.♗xc6+ ♔f8 17.0-0±) 15.♗xc6 ♖c8 16.d5 e5 17.♗e3 ♗d6 18.♘g3 0-0 19.0-0 (19.♘e4 ♕g6 20.♘xd6 (20.♗xd7 ♕xe4 21.♗xc8 ♖xc8 22.♕f3 ♕g6 23.♕g3 ♕c2!±) 20...♕xd6 21.0-0 ♘c5∓) 19...♘f6 20.♖e1 (20.♘f5 ♖fd8∓) 20...c3 21.bxc3 bxc3∓))

12...♘xg3 *(12...e6 13.♘f4 ♘d7 14.♖e1 0-0-0 15.♘xe4 fxe4 16.♗g4↑; 12...♘d7 13.♘xe4 fxe4 14.♗xe4 ♕f6 15.♘g3↑)* 13.hxg3↑

10.♘f3 ♘bd7

10...e6 allows the additional possibility 11.♘e5!?

11.0-0 e6 12.♗f4

12.♗g5 h6!? *(12...c3 13.bxc3 ♗xe2 14.♕xe2 bxc3= Erdos — Golod, Cappelle la Grande 2007)* 13.♗xf6 gxf6 14.♘d2 ♘b6 15.♕c1 0-0-0 16.♗xc4 ♘xc4 17.♘xc4 ♕c7 18.♖d1 h5∞ — In the following double-edged play on both flanks Black's chances are good due to his two bishops, Fridman — Starostits, Riga 2004

12...♖c8 13.♕c2 ♘b6 14.♘d2 ♗e7 15.♘xc4 ♘xc4 16.♗xc4 0-0 17.♖fd1 ♖fd8 18.♗xa6 ♕xa6 19.♖ac1 h6=

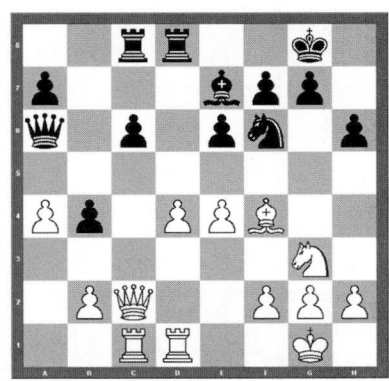

Due to the badly placed knight on g3, Black can achieve c6-c5 and equalise the game.

■ GAME 8

1.d4 d5 2.c4 c6 3.♘c3 dxc4

Once considered inferior this has now become popular.

4.e4

4...b5

4...e5 5.dxe5 (5.♘f3 exd4 6.♕xd4 ♕xd4 7.♘xd4 b5 8.a4 — 4...b5 5.a4 e5 6.♘f3 exd4 7.♕xd4 ♕xd4 8.♘xd4) 5...♕xd1+ 6.♔xd1 b5 7.♗e3 (7.a4 b4 8.♘b1 ♘d7 9.♘f3±) 7...♘d7 8.f4 ♗c5 9.♔e2± Karpov — Salov, Wijk aan Zee 1993

5.a4 b4

5...e5

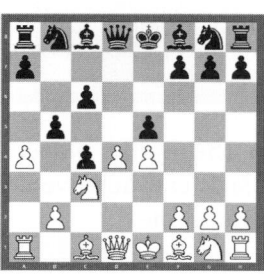

6.axb5! (6.♘f3 exd4 7.♕xd4 ♕xd4 8.♘xd4 b4 9.♘d1 ♗a6 10.♗f4 ♘f6 11.f3 ♗c5 12.♘f5 0–0 13.♖c1± Kasparov — Huebner, Belfort 1988) 6...exd4 7.♗xc4 ♘f6 (7...dxc3 8.♗xf7+ ♔e7 9.♕b3±/→; 7...♗c5 8.♘a4±; 7...♗b4 8.♖a4 a5 9.bxa6 c5 10.♖xb4 cxb4 11.♕h5 ♕d7 12.♘b5 ♗xa6 13.♕c5±/→; 7...♗e6 8.♗xe6 fxe6 9.♘ce2 e5 10.♘f3±) 8.e5 dxc3 9.♕xd8+ ♔xd8 10.exf6±/↑

6.♘b1!?

Very interesting and the only variation posing a serious danger for Black involves a pawn sacrifice:

6.♘ce2 ♗a6 7.♘f3 e6 8.♘g3 (An attempt to develop the bishop first is either risky or unambitious. 8.♗f4 ♘f6 9.♘g3 h5 10.h4 c5 11.♖c1 c3 12.bxc3 bxc3= — White cannot eliminate the c3 pawn comfortably.; The game is also about equal after 8.♗e3 ♘f6 9.♘g3 c3 10.bxc3 ♗xf1 11.♔xf1 bxc3 12.♕b3 ♘bd7= — Black will achieve c6-c5.) 8...c5! A modern treatment of the variation solving all problems. (8...♘f6 allows an unpleasant pin, at the same time White vacates the c1 square for the rook. 9.♗g5 ♕a5 10.♗e2± Gelfand — Huzman, Israel 2000)

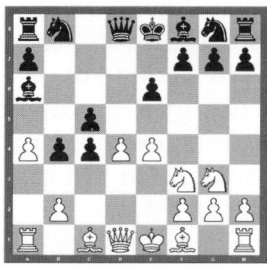

9.d5 (9.♗e3 cxd4 10.♘xd4 ♘d7 11.♘b5 ♗xb5 12.axb5 ♗c5∓ Dubov — Balogh, Aix les Bains 2011) 9...exd5 (9...♗e7? 10.♗f4 exd5 11.♕xd5 ♕xd5 12.exd5± Anand — Vallejo Pons, Bilbao 2011) 10.exd5 ♘f6 11.♗g5 (11. ♕e2+ ♕e7 12.♕xe7+ ♗xe7∓) 11... ♕xd5 12.♕xd5 ♘xd5 13.0-0-0 h6 14.♖e1+ ♗e7 15.♗xe7 ♘xe7 16.♘e4= — There is no question of a White edge; he has to maintain equality with piece activity.;

6.♘a2 ♘f6

(6...e5?! 7.♘f3 exd4 8.♗xc4 ♗a6 9.♕b3! ♗xc4 10.♕xc4 ♘d7 (10... c5 11.♘xb4!± Belov — Va.Popov, Moscow 2006) 11.♕xd4!N (11.♗g5 O.Budnikov — Romashko, Donetsk 2011 11...f6 12.♗d2 c5∞)

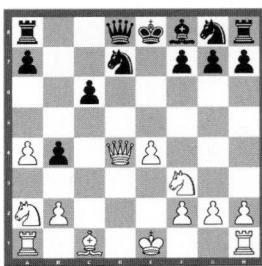

11...♘gf6 12.0-0 a5 13.♗g5±)

7.e5 (7.f3? 7...e5!±) 7...♘d5 8.♗xc4 e6

(A solid move is 8...♗f5, to which the best reply looks like 9.♘f3. The pin threat no longer exists, so there is no point in ♘e2.

a) 9.♘e2 e6 10.♘g3 (10.0-0 ♘d7 11.♗d2 a5 12.♘g3 ♗g6 13.♘c1 ♗e7 14.♘b3 0-0=) 10...♗g6 11.h4 h6 (11...h5 12.♗g5 ♗e7 13.♗xe7 ♕xe7= Kalinin — Drabke, Mulhouse 2002) 12.h5 ♗h7 13.♕g4!± (13.0-0 ♕h4 14.a5 ♗e7∞ Wojtaszek — Bartel, Warsaw 2012),

b) 9.♗g5?! The idea is to prevent e7-e6. However it has a serious drawback, as the bishop is permanently left on the kingside. 9...h6 10.♗h4 A.Kuzmin — Rausis, Dubai 1999 10...♘d7∓ — Black can at anytime play g7-g5 forcing the bishop to the unpromising g3 square.

9...e6 10.0-0 (10.♗g5 ♗e7 11.♗xe7 ♕xe7 12.♘c1 0-0=) 10...♗e7 11.♗d2 a5 12.♘c1 0-0 13.♘b3 ♘d7 14.♕e2 ♘5b6 15.♗d3 ♗xd3 16.♕xd3±

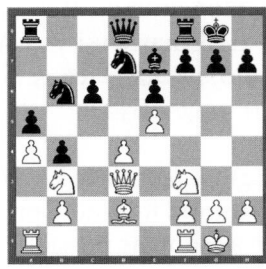

— White retains a slight edge, Bluvshtein — Feuerstack, Groningen 2010)

9.♘f3

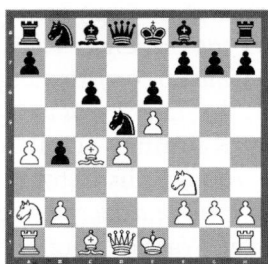

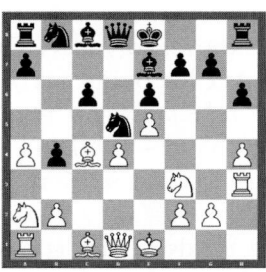

9...a5! This move appears to be slightly more accurate than 9...♗e7, though it often transposes. In any case Black has to secure the b4 pawn, at the same time he has the concrete idea of exchanging bishops via a6 and playing c6-c5 with the bishop on f8. It is important that White doesn't have time to transfer the knight to b3 and play ♖a1–c1 detering c5-c4. Instead of ♘c1–b3 White is forced to waste a tempo on ♕d1–e2.

a) 9...♗a6 10.♗xa6 ♘xa6 11.0–0 c5 12.♕d3 ♕b6 13.♗d2 ♖c8 (13...♗e7 14.♕b5+± Tomashevsky — Yilmaz, Bursa 2010) 14.♖fc1 ♖c6 15.♖c4 ♗e7 16.♘c1 0–0 17.♘b3±;

b) 9...♗e7 10.♗d2! The knight on a2 must be moved to a more promising position as soon as possible.

(The idea of developing the rook via h3 in this position is hardly good: 10.h4 h6 Taking the g5 square, which could be used as a launch pad for minor pieces. 11.♖h3

11...♗a6! (The following careless move leads to defeat: 11...0–0? in view of 12.♗xh6!; 11...♗b7 12.♗d2 a5 13.♘c1 ♘d7 14.♘b3 ♕b6 15.♖g3 g6 Kasimdzhanov — Arutinian, Yerevan 1999 16.♔f1 ♗a6 17.♗xa6 ♕xa6+ 18.♔g1±) 12.♗xa6 (12.b3 c5∓) 12...♘xa6 13.♗d2 c5 14.♕e2 ♕b6 15.♘c1 ♖c8∞ — The game is unclear.)

10...a5 11.♘c1

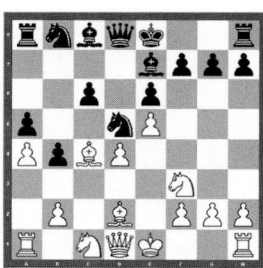

11...♗a6

(11...♘d7 12.♘b3 ♗b7 (12...h6 13.0–0 ♕b6 14.♕e2 ♗a6 15.♖fc1 0–0 16.♗xa6 ♕xa6 17.♕xa6 ♖xa6 18.♔f1± Kasparov — Svidler, Moscow 2004) 13.0–0

b1) Risky though interesting is 13.h4!? h6 14.♕e2 (14.♖h3 Van

Wely — Piket, Vlissingen 2001
14...♘5b6! 15.♗e2 c5 16.dxc5 ♘xc5
17.♘xc5 ♗xc5 18.♖c1 ♖c8∞) 14...
♕b6 L.Portisch — Hochstrasser,
Zuerich 2009 15.♖h3!±;

b2) 13.♕e2 0-0 14.♗d3 c5 15.♕e4
Avrukh — Bu Xiangzhi, Biel 2007
15...g6∞;

13...0-0

(13...h6 14.♖e1! (14.♕c2 ♕b6
(14...0-0 15.♕e4 ♗a6 16.♗xa6
♖xa6 17.♘fc1±; 14...♖c8 15.♕e4 c5
16.♖ac1± Kasparov — I.Sokolov,
Sarajevo 1999) 15.♕e4 ♗a6
16.♖fc1± Soon the knight will
move via e1 to d3 and Black cannot play c6-c5.) 14...0-0 15.♖e4↑
— the rook is transferred to g4,
after which the black king is in
danger.)

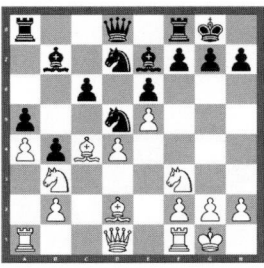

14.♗d3! (If 14.♕e2 c5 15.♖fc1 cxd4
16.♘fxd4 ♕b6 Black is nearly
equal) 14...♖c8 15.♖c1±).

12.♗xa6 It's better to lure a black
piece to a6 than to develop one's
queen prematurely.

(12.♕e2 ♗xc4 13.♕xc4 ♘b6
14.♕c2 ♕d5 15.0-0 ♘8d7 16.♘d3
c5 17.♘f4 ♕b7 (17...♕c6!∞) 18.♘h5
g6 (18...0-0 19.♗g5 ♘d5∞) 19.♘f6+
♗xf6 (19...♘xf6 20.exf6 ♗xf6
21.dxc5 ♖c8∞) 20.exf6 0-0 21.dxc5
♖fc8 22.♗e3± Volkov — Raznikov,
Oslo 2011)

12...♘xa6 (12...♖xa6 13.♘d3 ♘d7
14.♖c1±) 13.♘b3 c5 14.♖c1!±

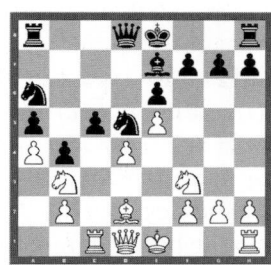

10.0-0

a) 10.♗e3 ♗e7 11.♘c1 ♗b7 12.♘b3
♘d7 13.0-0 0-0 14.♖c1?! (14.♕e2
♘xe3 15.♕xe3 ♕b6=) 14...♘xe3
15.fxe3 ♘b6 16.♗d3 (16.♘bd2 ♖c8∓;
16.♘c5 ♗xc5 17.dxc5 ♘xc4 18.♖xc4
♗a6 19.♖d4 ♕e7 20.♖f2 ♕xc5∓)
16...♘xa4 17.♕c2 g6 18.♖a1 ♘xb2!
19.♕xb2 a4 20.♘bd2 c5∓ Mamedyarov — Balogh, Ningbo 2011;

b) 10.♘g5 ♗e7 11.♕h5 (11.♘e4 0-0!
(11...♗a6 12.♗xa6 ♘xa6 13.♕g4±
Aleksandrov — Felgaer, Lugo 2007)
12.0-0 ♘d7 13.♖e1 c5∓) 11...g6
12.♕h6 ♘b6 13.♗e2 ♕xd4 14.♕g7
♖f8∞;

c) 10.♗g5 hardly makes sense. The move h6 to keep the knight out is planned. 10...♕b6 11.0-0 (*11.♘c1 ♗a6 12.♕e2 h6 13.♗e3 ♗xc4 14.♕xc4 ♘d7 15.♘b3 ♗e7 16.♖c1 0-0 17.0-0 ♖fc8 18.♕e2 c5= Computer „Deep Fritz" — Kramnik, Bonn 2006*) 11...♗a6 12.♕e2 c5 13.♘c1 ♗xc4 14.♕xc4 ♕a6 15.♕xa6 ♖xa6 16.dxc5 h6 17.♗d2 ♘d7 18.♘d3 (*18. c6 ♖xc6 19.♘b3 ♖a6 20.♖fc1 g5!*) 18...♘xc5 19.♘xc5 ♗xc5 20.♖fc1 ♖c6 21.♘d4 ♖c7 22.♘b5 ♖c6=;

d) 10.♗d2 ♗a6 11.♗xa6 (*11.♕e2 ♗xc4 (11...♕b6 12.♘c1 c5 13.♘b3 ♗xc4 14.♕xc4 ♘d7 15.0-0 cxd4∞) 12.♕xc4 ♘b6 13.♕c2 ♕d5 14.♘c1 ♘8d7 15.♘d3 c5 16.♘f4 ♕b7=* — Black has the better game, Korobov — Grigoryan, Moscow 2011) 11...♘xa6 12.♘c1 c5 13.♕e2 ♗e7! 14.♘b3 0-0 15.0-0 cxd4= — 10.0-0 ♗a6 11.♗xa6 ♘xa6 12.♗d2 c5 13.♕e2 ♗e7 14.♘c1 0-0 15.♘b3 cxd4=;

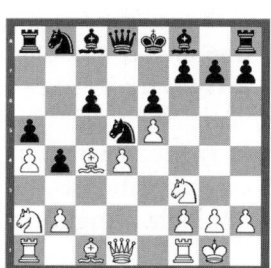

10...♗a6 11.♗xa6 ♘xa6 12.♗d2 (*12.♕e2 ♗e7 13.♗d2 0-0 14.♘c1 c5 15.♘b3 cxd4 16.♖fc1 ♘c3!=* Delchev — Khenkin, France 2008) 12...c5 13.♕e2

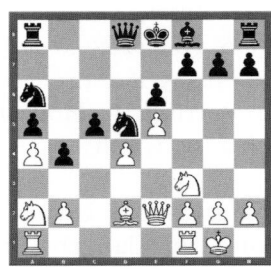

13...♗e7!

(13...♕b6 14.♘c1 cxd4

(14...♖c8?! 15.♕b5+ ♕xb5 16.axb5 ♘ac7 17.dxc5 (*17.♖xa5 c4 18.♘e2 c3!⇆*) 17...♗xc5 18.♖xa5± Ponomariov — Eljanov, Kiev 2011)

15.♘b3 d3 16.♕xd3 ♘c5 17.♘xc5 ♗xc5 18.♖ac1±)

14.♘c1 0-0 15.♘b3 cxd4 16.♘fxd4 ♘c5 17.♘c6 ♕c7 18.♘bd4 ♖fc8 19.♖fc1 ♗f8 20.♕b5 ♕b6= — Both sides chances are nearly equal.

6...♗a6

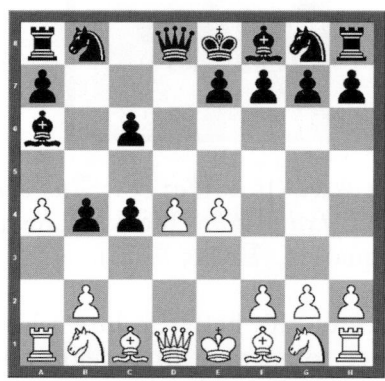

7.♕c2!

7.♗e3 ♘f6 8.f3 c5 (*8...e5 9.♘e2∞* Anand — Lautier, Monaco 1996) 9.dxc5

(*9.d5?! 9...♘bd7 (9...♕d7 10.♘d2 e6 11.dxe6 ♕xe6 12.♖c1 ♘d5 13.♕e2 ♘xe3 14.♕xe3 c3∓; 9...e6 10.dxe6 ♕xd1+ 11.♔xd1 fxe6 12.♘d2 c3 13.bxc3 ♗xf1 14.♘xf1 ♘c6∓) 10.♘d2 ♘e5 11.♘h3 e6 12.dxe6 fxe6 13.♘f2 ♕b6 14.♕c2 c3∓*)

9...♕xd1+ (*9...♘bd7 10.♘d2 e6 11.♗xc4 ♗xc5=*) 10.♔xd1 e6 11.♘d2 ♘fd7 12.♗xc4 ♗xc5 13.♔e2 ♗xc4+ 14.♘xc4 ♔e7=;

7.♘f3 ♘f6! (*7...e6 8.♗g5 ♕a5 9.♕c1 h6 10.♗e3 c3 11.bxc3 ♗xf1 12.♔xf1 ♘f6 13.e5 ♘d5 14.c4 ♕a6 15.♔g1 ♘xe3 16.fxe3 c5∞* Kozul — Vitiugov, Budva 2009) 8.e5 ♘d5 9.e6 f6 10.♗e2 ♕c8 11.0-0 ♕xe6∓ — White doesn't have full compensation.

7...♕xd4

Hardly good is 7...e5 In a number of lines the weakened white squares are evident: 8.♘f3 b3 (*8...exd4 9.♗xc4 ♗xc4 10.♕xc4 c5 11.♘e5 ♕c7 12.♕d5 ♘f6 13.♕xa8 ♕xe5 14.♘d2±*) 9.♕c3 ♕b6

(*9...♘f6*

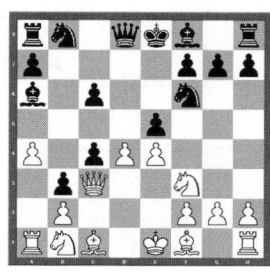

10.♘bd2!N (*10.♗xc4 exd4 11.♕xb3 ♗xc4 12.♕xc4 c5= Sargissian — Balogh, Ningbo 2011*) 10...exd4 11.♘xd4 ♗c5 12.♘f5 0-0 13.♗xc4±)

10.♗d2!N (*10.a5 ♕b7 11.♗d2 exd4 12.♕xd4 c5 13.♕d5 ♘c6 14.♗xc4 ♘f6 15.♕d3 ♘b4 16.♗xb4 ♕xb4+ 17.♘bd2 ♗xc4 18.♕xc4 ♕xc4 19.♘xc4 ♘xe4 20.0-0 ♗e7 Le Quang Liem — Felgaer, Caleta 2012 21.♖a3!±*)

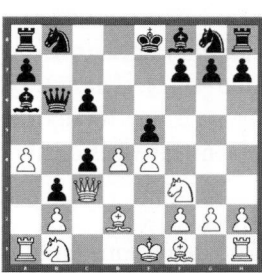

10...exd4 11.♘xd4 ♘f6 12.♗xc4±

8.♘f3 ♕b6

Wherever the black queen retreats it will lose another tempo later. If it remains on the d-file then rook to d1, therefore b6 seems more logical as the attack ♗c1-e3 is not harmful because the bishop stands passively on e3. However one must take into account

8...♛d7 9.♗xc4 e6 10.0-0 ♞f6

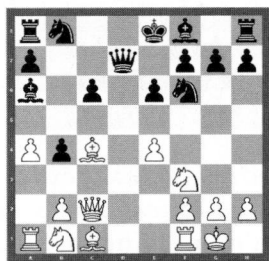

11.♖d1!N It's us eful to clarify where Black will retreat his queen. If it goes to c7 then exchanging on a6 is to White's advantage, if to b7 then it's better to wait for Black to exchange. (11.♗g5 ♗e7 12.♞bd2 h6 13.♗xf6 ♗xf6 14.♖fd1 0-0 15.e5 ♗e7 16.♞e4 Aronian — Vallejo Pons, Sao Paulo 2011 16...♛c7! 17.♗xa6 ♞xa6 18.♛c4 ♞b8! 19.♖ac1 ♖d8 20.♖xd8+ ♛xd8 21.h3 a5⩱) 11...♛b7 (11...♛c7 12.♗xa6 ♞xa6 13.♗f4!±) 12.♗g5 ♗e7 13.♗xa6 (13.♞bd2 0-0 14.♖ac1∞) 13...♞xa6 14.e5 ♞d5 15.♗xe7 ♞xe7 16.♞bd2↑ — White's initiative is dangerous

9.♞bd2!?N

9.♗e3 The development of the bishop, even with tempo, yields nothing since it belongs on g5 where it puts pressure on the knight on f6 and the bishop on e7: 9...♛c7 10.♞bd2 e6 11.♗xc4 ♗xc4 12.♞xc4 ♞f6 13.0-0 ♗e7 — White has sufficient compensation for a pawn but nothing more. Pashikian — Grigoryan,

9...c3

9...b3 10.♛c3 e6 11.♗xc4 ♗xc4 12.♛xc4±

10.♞c4∞

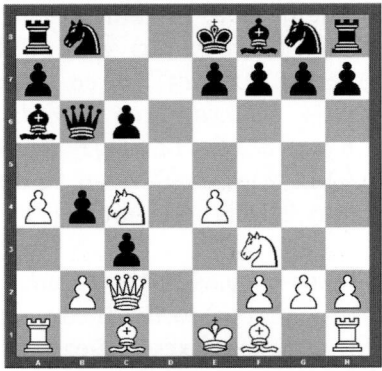

White has good compensation for the sacrificed material. Conclusion: The main line containing danger for Black in the variation 3...dxc4, appears to be 4.e4 b5 5.a4 b4 6. ♞b1! ♗a6 7.♛c2 ♛xd4 8.♞f3. In my opinion this is the most important area for the development of theory.

■ GAME 9

1.d4 d5 2.c4 c6 3.♘c3 e6 4.e3 f5

4...♘d7 is sometimes played so that if 5.♘f3 then 5...f5 transposing to a Stonewall, or 5...♘f6 turning the game into a Meran. If White on the other hand wants to play a Meran, it makes sense to play 5.♗d3, and on 5...♘f6 6.♘f3. But if White wants to play the Anti-Meran it is worth playing 5.♕c2 and on 5...♘f6 6.♘f3.;

One more potential trick to exclude some of White's possibilities is 4...♗d6 5.♗d3

(5.♘f3 On 5...f5 6.c5

(6.♘e5 leads to equality 6...♘f6 7.♗e2 0–0 8.0–0 ♘bd7 (Also quite good is 8...b6 with ♗b7 to follow.) 9.f4 ♘e4 10.♘xe4 fxe4 11.♗d2 ♘xe5 12.fxe5 (*12.dxe5 ♗e7 13.♔h1 ♗d7 14.♖c1 b5 15.cxb5 cxb5=* Tkachiev — Bareev, France 2001) 12...♖xf1+ 13.♗xf1 ♗e7 14.b4 ♗d7 15.♕b3 a6=)

6...♗c7 7.b4 I like the idea 7...♘d7!? (If the knight is developed to its usual square *7...♘f6* then later after ♘bd7 it is more difficult to play e6-e5 since the f-pawn hangs.) 8.♗d3

♘h6, and soon Black will play the freeing move e6-e5.)

5...f5 6.♘ge2 ♘f6 — 4...f5 5.♗d3 ♘f6 6.♘ge2 ♗d6.

5.g4!?

Without completing development the pawn break seems risky but interesting. Since Black is not developed either such a move is quite possible.

A good variation of the Stonewall arises if White develops normally: 5.♘f3 ♘f6 (The original plan with ♘h6 is interesting too: *5...♘d7!? 6.♗d3 ♘h6* — The bishop moves to d6 and the f6 square is left for the queen to control the e5 square better. In conjunction with the knight on h6 the plan g7-g5-g4 is possible, driving the white knight from the centre.) 6.♗d3 (*6.♘e5 ♘bd7=*) 6...♗d6 7.0–0 0–0 8.♕c2 ♘e4 9.♘e2 b6 (*9...♘d7!? 10.b3 g5!? 11.♗b2 ♕f6∞*) 10.b3 ♗b7 11.♗b2 ♕e7= — The game is equal.;

5.f4 By locking the structure White secures an bullet-proof position, but such a variation doesn't fight for an advantage.

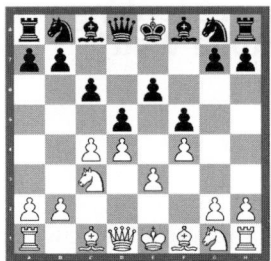

5...♘f6 6.♘f3 ♗d6

(Near equal is 6...♗e7 7.♗e2 0–0 8.0–0

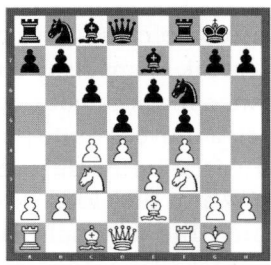

8...♘e4! The most accurate move order forcing White to decide about the c3 knight before b2-b3 and ♗c1–b2.

a) 8...b6 9.b3

a1) 9.♗d2 ♗b7 10.♕b3 c5 (10...♘e4 11.♘xe4 dxe4 12.♘e5 c5 13.♗c3±) 11.♖ad1 ♘c6 12.♘g5 ♘a5 13.♕a4 cxd4 14.♘xe6 ♕c8 15.♘xd4 ♘xc4 16.♕c2= Epishin — Malakhov, Elista 2001;

a2) 9.♕c2 ♗b7 10.cxd5 cxd5 11.♗d2 ♘c6= Karpov — Ivanchuk, Tilburg 1993;

9...♘e4 10.♘xe4! dxe4 11.♘e5 ♕c7 (11...♗b7 12.♕c2 ♘d7 13.♘xd7

♕xd7 14.c5 ♕c8 15.♗b2 ♗a6 16.♗xa6 ♕xa6 17.cxb6 ♕xb6 18.♖fc1±) 12.♗b2 ♘d7 13.d5!± Dziuba — Bareev, Warsaw (rapid) 2002 (13.♘xd7 ♗xd7=);

b) 8...♗d7 The plan of transferring the bishop to h5 is slow and unreliable: 9.♗d2 ♗e8 10.♕b3 ♕c8 11.♖ac1 ♗h5 12.cxd5 exd5 13.♗d3±;

9.♕c2 ♘d7 10.b3 b6! (10...♘xc3 11.♕xc3 ♘f6 12.♘e5 ♗d7 13.a4 ♘e4 14.♕d3 ♘f6 15.♗a3 ♖e8 16.♗h5 g6 17.♗f3± Karpov — Spassky, Leningrad 1974) 11.♗b2 ♗b7=).

7.♗e2 (7.♗d3 0–0 8.0–0 b6 9.b3 ♗b7 10.♗b2 ♘e4 11.♖c1 ♘d7 12.♕e2 Ivanchuk — Nogueiras, Lucerne 1993 12...♕e7=) 7...0–0 8.0–0 b6 9.♗d2 ♗b7 (9...♘e4 10.♗e1 ♘xc3 11.♗xc3 a5 12.♖c1 ♗a6 13.b3 ♘d7± Epishin — Haba, Brno 1994) 10.♗e1 (10.cxd5 cxd5 11.♖c1 a6 12.♘e5 ♘bd7= 13.g4? 13...fxg4 14.♘xg4 ♘xg4 15.♗xg4 ♕e7∓ Ganin — Borovikov, Alushta 1999) 10...♘bd7

(10...♘e4 11.b4 ♘xc3 12.♗xc3 ♘d7 13.♖b1 ♘f6 14.♕c2 ♗a6= (14...dxc4 15.♗xc4 ♘d5 16.♗d2 ♕e7 17.a3 ♖ac8 18.♕b3± Epishin — Tregubov, St.Petersburg 2004))

11.♘e5 ♘e4 12.b4 ♘xc3 13.♗xc3 ♘f6 14.♕b3 ♘e4= Epishin — Kosyrev, Kazan 2005.

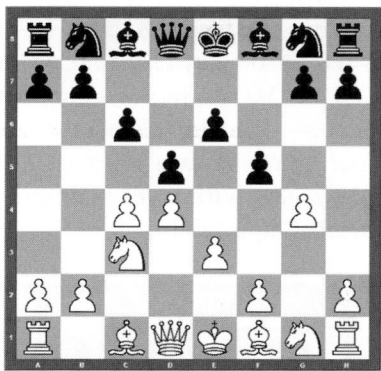

5...♘f6

5...fxg4?! contributes to White's development and is therefore dubious 6.♕xg4 ♘f6

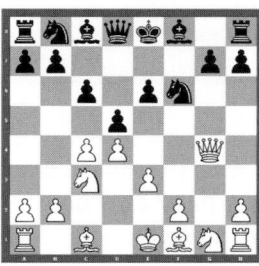

7.♕g2 (Also interesting is *7.♕g5!? c5 8.♗d2,* with the idea of 0-0-0) 7...c5 8.♘f3 ♘c6 9.♗d2!↑ — White prepares to castle long and put pressure along the d and g files, Seirawan — Yermolinsky, Key West 1994;

But very sensible and interesting is the unpopular 5...♘h6!? 6.h3 (*6.g5 ♕xg5 7.e4* Volkov — Landa, Perm 1997 *7...♕e7!±; 6.cxd5 exd5 7.g5 ♕xg5 8.e4 ♕e7 9.e5 ♘f7∓*) 6...♗d6

(*6...♗e7 7.♘f3 0-0 8.♖g1 ♘d7 9.♗d3 ♔h8 (9...dxc4 10.♗xc4 ♘b6*

11.♗d3 ♘d5 12.♗d2±) 10.g5 ♘f7 11.g6 hxg6 12.♖xg6 ♘f6±)

7.♗d3 0-0

(*7...e5 8.cxd5 0-0 9.dxe5 (9.♕c2?! Ipatov — Volkov, Moscow 2010 9... cxd5 10.♘xd5 ♘c6∓/↑) 9...♗xe5 10.♗c4 ♕f6 11.dxc6+ ♔h8 12.g5!±)*

8.♘f3 c5!? (*8...dxc4 9.♗xc4 b5 10.♗d3±; 8...♘a6 9.a3 dxc4 10.♗xc4 ♘c7 11.e4!±) 9.cxd5 (9.g5 ♘f7 10.♖g1 ♘c6 11.g6 hxg6 12.♖xg6∞) 9...exd5 10.g5 ♘f7 11.♘xd5 ♘xg5∞*

6.gxf5 exf5

6...♗b4 7.♗d2 0-0 8.♘ge2 (*8.♘h3 exf5 9.♕b3 ♗xc3 10.♗xc3±) 8...exf5*

(*8...e5?! 9.cxd5*

(*9.♕b3 ♘a6! (9...♗xc3 10.♗xc3 ♘e4 11.cxd5 cxd5 12.♗g2 ♗xf5 13.♕xb7+- M.Gurevich — Krasenkow, Erfurt 2004) 10.cxd5 ♘xd5 11.♘xd5 ♗xd2+ 12.♔xd2 cxd5 13.♗g2 ♔h8)*

9...exd4 (9...cxd5 10.dxe5 ♘g4 11.♗g2±) 10.♘xd4 cxd5 11.♕b3±)

9.♕b3 (*9.♘f4 ♗d6 10.♕f3 ♕c7=) 9... ♘a6 10.cxd5 (10.♘f4 ♗xc3 11.♗xc3 ♘c7) 10...cxd5*

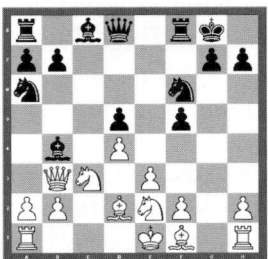

11.0-0-0 I prefer an immediate evacuation of the king despite the fact that Black doesn't have to exchange the b4 bishop for the knight. The knight on a6 counts as a positional plus for White as Black must waste two tempi transferring it to e6.

(11.♘f4 also leads to very complicated, double-edged play with minimal advantage for White 11...♗xc3 (11...♔h8 12.♗g2±) 12.♗xc3 (12.bxc3 ♘c7 13.c4 ♖e8 14.♗g2 dxc4 15.♕xc4+ ♘e6 16.0-0 ♘e4∞) 12...♘c7±/∞)

11...♗d6 12.♘b5 ♗b8 13.♔b1 ♗d7 14.f3± — The position is complicated but advantageous for White.

7.♕b3

On 7.cxd5 solves the problems?? 7...♘xd5! and Black blockades the central white squares with pieces.;

Simple development is possible 7.♘f3, although with this move White does not put pressure on the key square d5. Then logical is 7...♗e6, the most principled, fighting for the white squares. (However Black has time to complete kingside development, so 7...♗e7 is also possible, followed by castling.) 8.♕b3 (8.♘g5 ♗g8=) 8...♕b6 9.c5 ♕c7 10.♘e2 ♘e4 (10...b6 11.♘f4 ♗c8∞; 10...♘h5 Moiseenko — Kharlov, Moscow 2002 11.♘f4! ♘xf4 12.exf4 ♗e7 13.♖g1±) 11.♘f4 ♗g8∞ with a very complicated, almost equal fight.

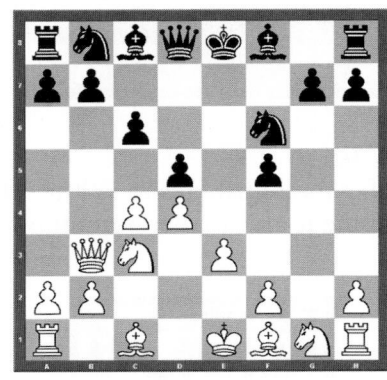

7...dxc4

7...♘a6 with the idea of transferring the knight to c7 and holding the d5 square with pieces.

8.♗xc4 ♗d6! 9.♘f3

The idea of losing two tempi just to stop Black castling appears to be dubious: 9.♗f7+?! 9...♔e7 (9...♔f8!?) 10.♗c4 b5 11.♗d3

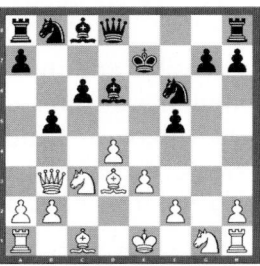

11...♘a6!N (11...♗e6 12.♕c2 b4 Stohl — Goloshchapov, Hungary 2001

13.♘ce2±) 12.a3 ♖e8∓ — Black wants to play ♔e7-f8, after which he will be ready to open up the centre.

9...♕e7 10.♘g5

Too slow is 10.a4 ♘bd7 11.a5 b5 (*11...♘e4!?; 11...♖b8!?*) 12.axb6 ♘xb6 13.♖a5 ♘fd5! 14.♗xd5 cxd5 15.♘xd5 ♘xd5 16.♕xd5 ♗b7 17.♕b5+ ♕d7

(*17...♔f8 18.♕xf5+ ♔g8 19.♖g1 ♖f8 (19...♗b4+ 20.♗d2 ♗xa5 21.♗xa5 ♖f8 22.♕e5±) 20.♖xg7+ ♔xg7 21.♕g4+ ♔f7 22.♕h5+ ♔e6 23.♕g4+ ♔f7=*)

18.♕xd7+ ♔xd7 19.♔e2 ♖hc8=

10...♘bd7!N

10...b5 11.♗f7+ ♔f8 12.♗e6↑ Khenkin — Rombaldoni, Bratto 2007;

10...♘d5 Pira — Tregubov, Auberville 2000 11.h4! h6 12.♗xd5 hxg5 13.hxg5 ♖xh1+ 14.♗xh1 ♕xg5 15.♔e2±

11.♗f7+ ♔f8 12.♗e6 ♘b6 13.♗d2 g6 (*13...h6 14.♗xc8 ♖xc8 15.♘e6+ ♔e8 16.♖g1 g5∞*) 14.♗xc8 ♖xc8 15.0-0-0 h6 16.♘e6+ ♔f7 17.♘c5+ ♔g7 18.♘e6+ ♔f7=;

11.♖g1 g6 12.e4 fxe4 13.♗e3 ♘b6 14.♗f7+ ♔f8 15.♘gxe4 ♕xf7=

11...♖f8 12.♘xd6+ ♕xd6 13.♕a3 ♕xa3 14.bxa3 ♘b6 15.♗b3 ♘bd5=

White has the bishop pair but Black controls the white squares. The chances are equal.

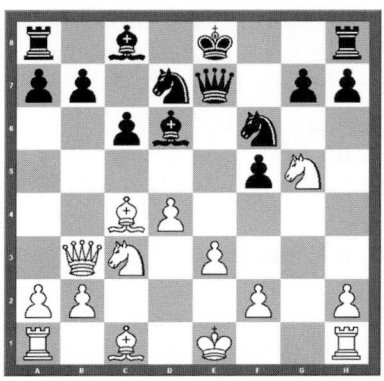

11.♘f7

■ GAME 10

1.d4 d5 2.c4 c6 3.♘c3 e6 4.e3 f5

4...♘d7 is sometimes played so that if 5.♘f3 then 5...f5 transposing to a Stonewall, or 5...♘f6 turning the game into a Meran. If White on the other hand wants to play a Meran, it makes sense to play 5.♗d3, and on 5... ♘f6 6. ♘f3. But if White wants to play the Anti-Meran it is worth playing 5. ♕c2 and on 5...♘f6 6.♘f3.;

One more potential trick to exclude some of White's possibilities is 4... ♗d6 5. ♗d3

(On 5.♘f3 f5 6.c5

(6.♘e5 leads to equality 6...♘f6 7.♗e2 0–0 8.0–0 ♘bd7 (8...b6, with subsequent ♗b7. Quite good is also) 9.f4 ♘e4 10.♘xe4 fxe4 11.♗d2 ♘xe5 12.fxe5 (*12. dxe5 ♗e7 13.♔h1 ♗d7 14.♖c1 b5 15.cxb5 cxb5=* Tkachiev — Bareev, France 2001) 12...♖xf1+ 13. ♗xf1 ♗e7 14.b4 ♗d7 15.♕b3 a6=)

6... ♗c7 7.b4 I like the idea 7...♘d7!? (If the knight is developed to its usual square 7...♘f6 then later after ♘bd7 it is more difficult to play e6-e5 since the f-pawn hangs.) 8.♗d3 ♘h6, and soon Black will play the freeing move e6-e5.)

5...f5 6.♘ge2 ♘f6 — 4...f5 5.♗d3 ♘f6 6.♘ge2 ♗d6.

5. ♗d3

A popular development scheme. White's idea is to move the king's knight to e2 and play f2-f3. With such a flexible structure many plans arise, the main one being e3-e4.

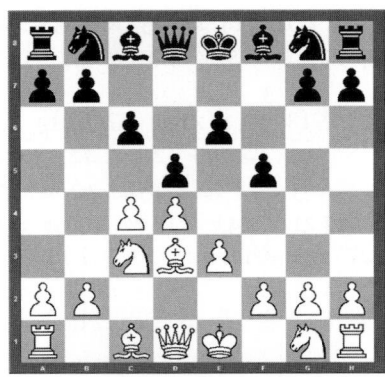

5...♘f6 6.♘ge2

6.♕c2 White gains nothing from trying to simplify: 6...♗d6 7.cxd5 cxd5 8.♘b5 ♗b4+ (8...♘c6 9.♘xd6+ ♕xd6 10. ♗d2±) 9. ♗d2 ♗xd2+! (9... ♘c6 10.♘c7+ ♕xc7 11. ♗xb4 ♗d7 12.♘f3 ♖c8 13.♕b3 ♘e4 14.♖c1± Aronian — Morozevich, Moscow 2009) 10.♕xd2 ♘e4 11.♗xe4 fxe4 12.♘e2 0–0=

6... ♗d6 7.f3

7.♕c2 0–0 8.f3 — 7.f3 0–0 8.♕c2

7...0–0 8.♕c2

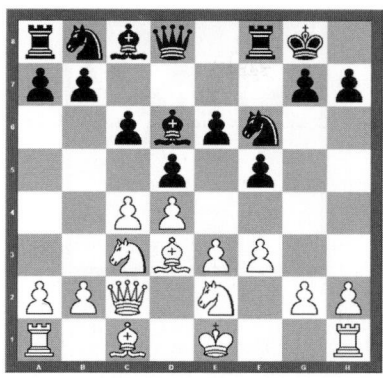

8...♘a6!

8...a6 allows White to fix the structure on the queenside: 9.c5! 9...♗c7

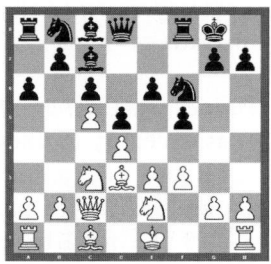

10.♗d2

a) 10.♘a4 ♘bd7 11.♗d2 ♘e4!

(11...g6 12.0-0-0 e5 13.dxe5 ♘xe5 14.♗c3 (*14.♘d4 ♘xd3+ 15.♕xd3 ♕e7 16.♔b1 ♗e6∞* Yakovich — Girya, St.Petersburg 2011) 14...♖e8 15.♗d4±)

12.fxe4 fxe4 13.♗xe4 ♕h4+ 14.g3 ♕xe4 15.♕xe4 dxe4 16.♘ec3 ♖e8!±;

b) 10.0-0 ♘bd7 11.♗d2 — 10.♗d2 ♘bd7 11.0-0;

10...♘bd7

(10...♕e7 11.0-0-0 (*11.0-0±*) 11...e5 12.dxe5 ♗xe5 13.♘a4 ♗e6 14.♘d4± Bukavshin — J.Geller, Moscow 2011)

11.0-0! (*11.0-0-0 b6 12.cxb6 ♘xb6∞*) 11...b6 12.b4±;

8...dxc4 9.♗xc4 b5 10.♗b3±;

In practice the most popular is 8...♔h8, a useful but insufficiently concrete move with such a tense position in the centre.

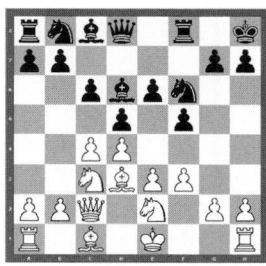

9.0-0

a) 9.cxd5 ♘xd5!

(9...cxd5 10.♘b5 ♗b4+ (*10...♘c6 11.♘xd6 ♘b4 12.♕b3 ♘xd3+ 13.♕xd3 ♕xd6±*) 11.♗d2 ♘c6 12.♗xb4 ♘xb4 13.♕d2 ♘xd3+ 14.♕xd3 ♕a5+ 15.♘bc3± Bukavshin — Ponfilenok, Kazan 2009)

10.a3 ♕h4+ (*10...♘xc3 11.♘xc3 e5=*) 11.g3 ♕h3 12.♘f4 ♘xf4 13.exf4 b6=;

b) 9.♗d2 dxc4 (9...♘a6 10.a3 dxc4 11.♗xc4 b5 12.♗d3 b4 13.♘a4±) 10.♗xc4 ♕e7 11.0-0 — 9.0-0 dxc4 10.♗xc4 ♕e7 11.♗d2;

9...dxc4 (9...a6 10.c5 ♗c7 11.♗d2 ♘bd7 12.b4 b6 13.♘a4± Kramnik — Tregubov, France 2002) 10.♗xc4 ♕e7 (10...b5 11.♗d3±) 11.♗d2 (11. e4 fxe4 12.♘xe4 ♘xe4 13.♕xe4 e5 14.dxe5 ♕xe5 15.♕xe5 ♗xe5=; 11.♘g3 ♘bd7 12.♘ce2 c5 13.♗d2 ♘b6 14.♗b3 ♗d7 15.♖ac1 ♖ac8 16.♕b1 cxd4 17.exd4 ♘fd5∓ Sargissian — Valhondo, Giblartar 2012) 11...♘bd7 12.♗b3

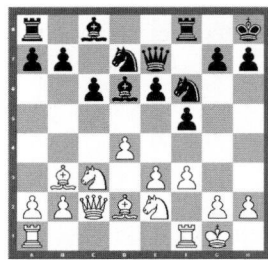

12...b5

a) 12...e5 13.♕xf5 ♘c5 14.♕c2 ♘xb3 15.axb3±;

b) 12...a5!? 13.a3 (13.♘f4 ♘b6 14.♘d3 ♘fd5 15.e4 ♘b4 16.♘xb4 ♕h4 17.f4 axb4 18.♘a4 ♘xa4 19.♗xa4±) 13... e5 14.♕xf5 (14.♖ad1∞) 14...♘c5 15.♕c2 ♘xb3 16.♕xb3 ♗e6 17.♕c2±;

13.♘f4 (13.e4 e5 14.♗e3 a5∞) 13... ♘b6

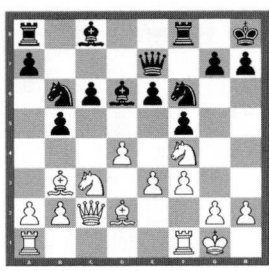

14.a4!

(14.♘ce2 e5! (14...a5 15.a3 a4 16.♗a2 ♘c4 17.♗xc4 bxc4 18.♕xc4 ♗a6 19.♕c2 ♗xf4 20.exf4 ♗xe2 21.♗b4±; 14...c5 15.dxc5 ♗xc5 Melkumyan — Zhigalko, Konya 2011 16.♘d4 ♘fd5 17.♖ac1 ♗xd4 18.♗xd5 exd5 19.exd4±) 15.dxe5 ♕xe5 16.♖ad1 c5=)

14...b4 (14...e5 15.♘d3!±; 14...♗d7 15.♘d3±) 15.♘ce2 e5 16.dxe5 ♕xe5 17.♘g3 c5 18.a5 c4 19.♗xc4 (19. axb6 cxb3 20.♕xb3 a5∓) 19...♘xc4 20.♕xc4 ♖d8 21.♖fd1 ♖b8 22.b3±

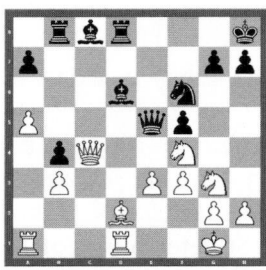

— Black has an active position but without full compensation for the pawn.

9.a3 dxc4 10.♗xc4 b5 11.♗a2

After 11.♗b3, hardly makes sense as the white bishop can potentially be subjected to c5-c4 11...♔h8 12.e4?! bad is,in view of 12...e5 13.exf5 exd4 14.♘xd4 ♘c5 15.♗a2 ♖e8+ 16.♔f1 ♗e5 17.♘xc6 ♕d6 18.♘xe5 ♕xe5∓;

If White retreats 11.♗d3 then this only confirms that the popular prophylaxis 8...♔h8 may beunnecessary, and that more concrete 8...♘a6 is more logical. 11...♕a5 (*11...b4!? 12.♘a4 ♕c7*) 12.♕b1 (*12.♖a2 b4 13.axb4 ♕b6 14.♘a4 ♕b8 15.♗xa6 ♗xa6 16.♘c5 ♕xb4+ 17.♗d2 ♕c4 18.♕xc4 ♗xc4=* Kraemer — Krasenkow, Germany 2007) 12...♕b6! The most active square for the queen to put pressure on d4 later. The c7 square also remains free for transferring the knight from a6.

(12...♕c7 13.b4 ♘b8!

(13...♗xh2 14.e4! (*14.f4 ♘g4∞* Polak — Navara, Hustopece (rapid) 2009) 14...♗g3+ 15.♔f1+-)

14.e4 fxe4 15.♘xe4 ♘xe4 16.♗xe4 h6=)

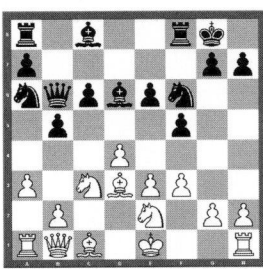

13.♗d2 (*13.e4 e5! 14.♗e3 exd4 15.♗xd4 ♗c5 16.♗xf6 ♖xf6 17.exf5 ♗e7* — Black has a good initiative

for the pawn.) 13...♘c7 (Also very interesting is *13...♗d7!? 14.b4* otherwise Black plays c6-c5 *14...♘c7 15.e4 e5 16.exf5 exd4 17.♘e4 ♘xe4 18.fxe4 ♘a6 19.a4 c5 20.axb5 ♘xb4 21.♗xb4 cxb4∞* with an unclear game.) 14.a4 ♘fd5= and Black has a good game.

11...♔h8

11...b4 12.♘a4 ♖b8 13.0-0 ♕c7 14.g3 c5 15.♗d2 bxa3 16.bxa3±

12.0-0 ♕e7

12...b4 13.♘a4 ♖b8 (*13...♕c7 14.g3 ♖b8 15.♗d2 ♕e7 16.♗c4 bxa3 17.bxa3 c5* Al.David — Feller, Paris 2010 *18.♖fb1!±*) 14.♗d2 ♕e7! Black prepares e6-e5 not c6-c5, since the weakness on e6 is more significant than c6. 15.♘f4 bxa3 16.bxa3 e5 17.dxe5 ♗xe5 18.♗c3 ♗d6 19.♖fe1 ♘c7± — White stands just a little better.

13.b4

13.♘g3 b4 14.♘ce2 c5=

13...♘c7 14.♗d2

14.e4 fxe4 15.♗g5 exf3 16.♖xf3 e5 17.♘e4 ♗g4 18.♖e3 ♕d7 19.♗xf6 gxf6 20.♘xd6 ♕xd6 21.dxe5 fxe5=

14...a5

Pushin — Volkov, Moscow 2011

15.bxa5 ♗xa3∞

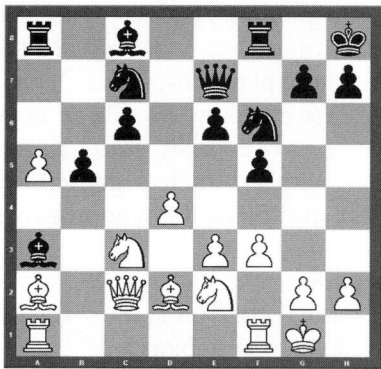

In this complicated position the chances are about equal. Conclusion: Instead of the main line Slav 4...♘f6, the transformation to positions more reminiscent of the Stonewall Dutch is quite possible. However White can decide whether he wants go in for a complex struggle usually developing the bishop to d3 and the knight to e2, or go into a closed structure retaining a microscopically small advantage.

PART 5

■ GAME 11

1.d4 d5 2.c4 c6 3.♘c3 e6 4.♘f3 dxc4
The Noteboom variation is a very demanding opening for both sides. In the main line a strong white centre and a pair of bishops are balanced by a queenside pawn mass which although not very mobile, presents a serious potential threat. The following moves lead to an unpromising line of the Catalan opening.

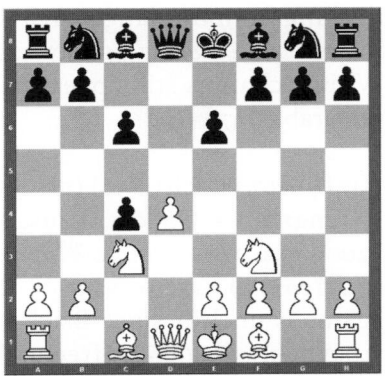

5.g3
Played after the knight has moved to c3 which in some variations will be attacked by b5-b4 with tempo.
Risky is 5.e4 b5 6.a4 ♗b4 — It's very hard to prove that White's initiative is worth a pawn.;

After 5.♗g5 Black has a large range of options.

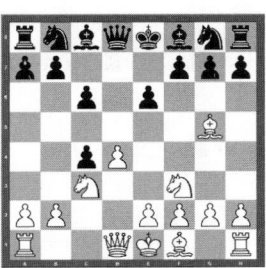

The most solid is 5...♗e7 (5...♘f6 leads to the Botvinnik Variation. Double-edged moves such as 5.. .♕c7, 5...♕a5 and 5...f6 are of little theoretical interest since 5...♗e7 equalises fully.) 6.♗xe7 ♘xe7 7.a4 (*7.e3 b5∓*) 7...♘d5 8.a5 c5 (Another route to equality is *8...b5 9.axb6 ♘xb6 10.e3 ♘8d7 11.♘d2 0-0 12.♘xc4 c5 13.♘a5 cxd4 14.♕xd4 ♘f6=* David — Galkin, Saint Vincent 2000) 9.e4 ♘b4 (*9...♘xc3 10.bxc3 0-0 11.♗xc4 ♕c7=*) 10.dxc5 ♕xd1+ 11.♖xd1 ♘8a6 12.♗xc4 ♘xc5= Kipper — Nyback, Germany 2010;

5.a4 usually transposes but gives Black additional options. 5...♗b4

a) 5...♘f6 — 3.♘f3 ♘f6 4.♘c3 dxc4 5.a4 e6;

b) 5...c5 6.e3 (*6.d5!?*) 6...♘f6 — 3.♘f3 ♘f6 4.♘c3 dxc4 5.a4 e6 6.e3 c5;

6.e3 b5 — 5.e3 b5 6.a4 ♗b4

5...b5 6.♗g2 ♗b7

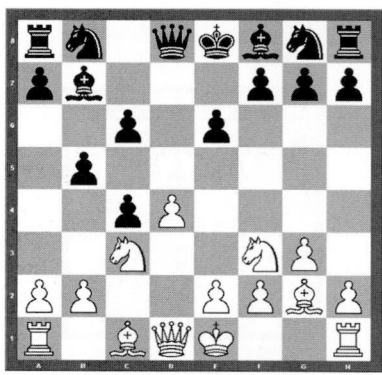

7.♘e5

7.0–0 ♘d7 8.e4 ♘gf6 9.e5 ♘d5 10.♘g5 h6!

a) 10...♘xc3 11.bxc3 ♗e7 12.♕h5 ♗xg5 13.♗xg5 ♕c7 14.f4↑ Ivanishevich — Blagojevic, Niksic 2008;

b) 10...♗e7 11.♕h5 g6 12.♕h6 ♗f8 13.♕h3 ♗e7

(13...♕b6 14.♘ce4! (*14.♘xe6 fxe6 15.♕xe6+ ♗e7∓* Swiercz — Shirov, Warsaw (rapid) 2010) 14... h6 15.♘xe6 fxe6 16.♕xe6+ ♔d8 17.♖d1±/↑)

14.♘ce4⯬;

11.♘xe6 fxe6 12.♕h5+

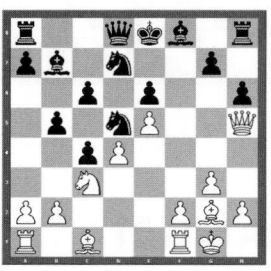

12...g6!N

(Only 12...♔e7 has been played 13.♘e4 (*13.♗g5+ hxg5 14.♕xh8 ♘7b6 15.♘e4 ♔d7∓* Shinkevich — Korobov, St.Petersburg 2010) 13...♕e8 14.♗g5+ hxg5 (*14...♘5f6 15.exf6+ gxf6 16.♗xf6+ ♘xf6 17.♘xf6 ♕xh5 18.♘xh5 ♔d6±*) 15.♕xh8 ♔d8 16.♘xg5 ♕e7 (Bad is *16...♘c7* in view of *17.f4!* with the threat f4-f5.; The idea of evacuating the king from the danger area is of interest *16...♔c8!? 17.a4 ♘c7∞*, but White's chances still appear to be preferable.) 17.♕h4!?

(*17.f4 ♔c7 18.♗h3 ♖e8!* (*18...c5* Bu Xiangzhi — Galkin, Lausanne 2000 *19.♘xe6+ ♔b6 20.♕h5 cxd4 21.♕g6±*) *19.♘xe6+ ♔b8∞* — The game is unclear since Black will inevitably play c6-c5 freeing his minor pieces.)

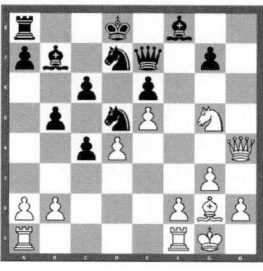

17...♔c8 18.♗h3 ♘c7 19.f4↑ —
White has the initiative.)

13.♕xg6+ ♔e7 White has a possibility of perpetual check:

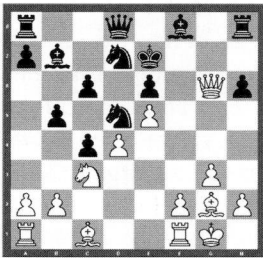

14.♗e4! (14.♗h3 ♕e8 15.♕xe6+
♔d8 16.♕f5 ♘xc3 17.bxc3 ♘b6∓ —
Black's chances look better.) 14...b4

(To 14...♕b6 15.♕g4! can be found,
with the idea of a perpetual on
the squares h4-h5. The attempt to
play for a win is dubious: (15.♗g5+
hxg5 16.♘xd5+ cxd5 17.♕xg5+
♘f6 18.♕xf6+ ♔d7∓) 15...♔d8
16.♕xe6± Leading to a complicated game but with advantage for
White.)

15.♘xd5+ cxd5 16.♗g5+ hxg5
17.♕xg5+ ♔f7 18.♕g6+ ♔e7=, with
a draw.

7...a6
7...f6?! 8.♘f3 ♘d7 9.0-0 ♘e7 10.e4
♘g6 11.e5!↑ (11.h4 ♗b4∞ Maze —
Bauer, Nice 2011);
7...♕c8 8.0-0 ♘d7 9.b3 b4 10.♘e4
♘xe5 11.dxe5 c3 12.♕d3↑ Nakamura
— Ivanchuk, Wjik aan Zee 2012

8.0-0
If 8.a4 f6! is strong, since after 9.♘f3
b4 the white knight cannot move to
a4. 10.♘e4 c5 11.♘fd2 ♗d5 12.dxc5
f5 13.♘d6+ ♗xd6 14.e4 fxe4 15.cxd6
♘f6∓

8...♘f6 9.a4
Usually this position arises from
a Catalan move order.

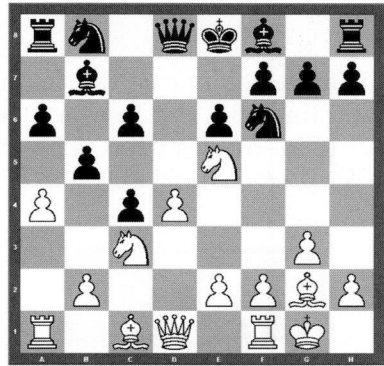

9...♘d5
9...♕c8 is not so reliable 10.e4 ♘bd7

(Also possible is 10...♗e7 11.g4 (11.
f4 ♘bd7∞) 11...♘fd7 12.♘f3 0-0∞,
with a complicated fight, Grischuk
— Aronian, Monaco (blindfold)
2011)

11.♘xd7 (11.f4 ♗e7∞) 11...♕xd7 12.e5
♘d5 13.♘e4⩲ — White has good
compensation for the pawn, Postny
— Nyback, Germany 2011.

10.e4 ♘xc3 11.bxc3 ♘d7 12.♗f4
12.f4 ♗e7 13.♘g4

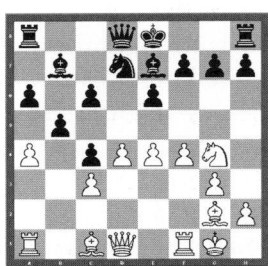

13...h5! It's better to leave the king in the centre and decide on its haven later.

(If Black boldly castles, it seems the game will end in a perpetual : 13...0–0 14.e5 ♘b6 15.f5! exf5 16.♘e3! g6 17.♘xf5! gxf5 18.♖xf5

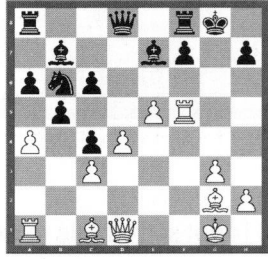

18...♗c8!□ The only move.

a) 18...♘d5 19.♗h6 ♔h8 20.♗xf8 ♗xf8 21.♖xf7+–;

b) 18...♔h8 19.♗e4 f6 (19...♘d5 20.♕f3 f6 21.♖h5 ♖f7 22.e6 ♖g7 23.♗h6+–) 20.♖h5 f5 (20...♖f7 21.e6 ♖g7 22.♗h6+–) 21.♖xh7+ ♔xh7 22.♕h5+ ♔g8 23.♕g6+ ♔h8 24.♗h6 ♗f6 25.♖f1+–;

c) 18...f6 19.♗h6±/→ Miton — Krapivin, Moscow 2004;

19.♗e4 (19.♖h5 ♘d5 20.♕c2 f5 21.exf6 ♘xf6 22.♖g5+ ♔h8 23.axb5 ♗d6 24.bxc6 ♖a7∓/∞) 19...♗xf5 (19...f6 20.♖h5 ♖f7 21.♗xh7+ ♖xh7 22.♖xh7 ♔xh7 23.♕h5+ ♔g8 24.♕g6+ ♔h8=) 20.♗xf5 ♗g5 21.♕h5 h6 22.h4 ♗xc1 23.♖xc1 ♔g7 (23...♕e7 24.♕xh6 f6 25.♖f1 ♖f7 26.♗g6 ♘d5 27.♗xf7+ ♔xf7 28.♕h7+ ♔e6 29.♕f5+ ♔f7 30.♕h7+=) 24.♕g4+ ♔h8 25.♕h5 ♔g7=)

14.♘e3 ♕c7 (It's possible to remind White immediately that he has a King too and that it's a little exposed: *14...h4!? 15.g4 h3 16.♗f3 ♕c7 17.e5 g6∓*) 15.e5 g6 16.♗a3 ♗xa3

(16...♘b6 17.♗xe7 ♕xe7 18.♕c2 ♘d5?! (18...h4∓) 19.♗xd5 cxd5 20.axb5 axb5 21.♕b2± Najer — Volkov, Taganrog 2011)

17.♖xa3 h4∓

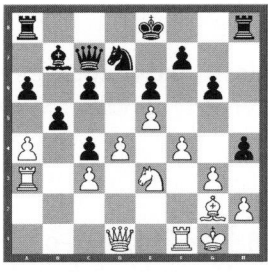

— Black is ready to play c6-c5 at any time. Additionally the king can be left in the centre or can be evacuated to the kingside or queenside.

12...♘xe5!?N

12...♗e7 13.♕g4 g6 14.♗h6!

(14.♘xd7 14...h5!N (14...♕xd7 15.♗h6 f6= Korchnoi — Wang Yue, Amsterdam 2008) 15.♕e2 ♕xd7∓)

14...♘xe5 15.dxe5 ♕c7 16.♕f4 ♖g8 17.h4⩲ Zhao Xue — Mongontuul, Shenzhen 2011

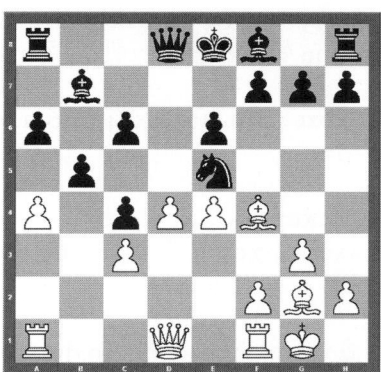

13.♗xe5 f6 14.♗f4 ♗e7 15.♕h5+ g6 16.♕h6 ♔f7=

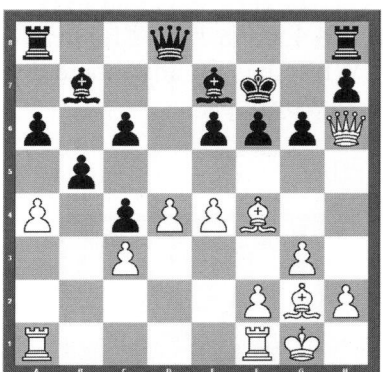

White has some compensation but it's only enough for equality.

■ GAME 12

1.d4 d5 2.c4 c6 3.♘c3 e6 4.♘f3 dxc4

The Noteboom variation is a very demanding opening for both sides. In the main line a strong white centre and a pair of bishops are balanced by a queenside pawn mass which although not very mobile, presents a serious potential threat.

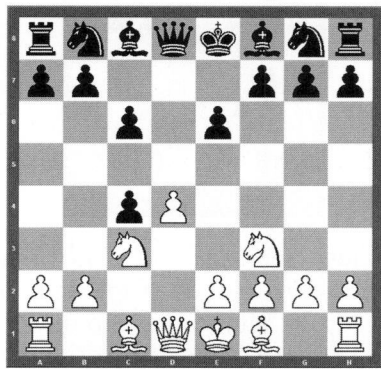

5.e3 b5 6.a4 ♗b4

6...b4 7.♘e4 ♕d5 (7...♗a6 leads to White's advantage leads After 8.♘e5 ♕d5 is answered by 9.♘g5) 8.♘ed2 c3 9.bxc3 bxc3 10.♘b1 ♗b4 11.♕c2± — White has a small but stable advantage.

6...♕b6 7.♗d2 (Not so convincing is 7.axb5 cxb5 8.b3 ♗b4 9.♕c2±) 7...♕b7!?N An inter esting move which hasn't been tested in practice. The idea is that after the exchange on b5 and b2-b3 Black would have the move b5-b4 after which ♘c3-a4 doesn't gain a tempo. In any case the queen stands awkwardly on b7 and White develops the initiative with further accurate play.

a) 7...♗b4 8.♘e4 ♗e7 (8...♘a6 9.♗xb4 ♘xb4 10.b3 ♕a5 11.♘fd2 f5 12.♘d6+ ♔e7 13.♘xc8+ ♖xc8 14.bxc4 c5 15.♗e2 cxd4 16.0–0 d3 17.axb5 dxe2 18.♕xe2 ♕b6 19.♖fb1 ♕c5 20.♖a4+–) 9.b3 a5 10.axb5 cxb5 11.bxc4 b4 12.♘e5± Mikkelsen — A.Rasmussen, Helsingor 2009;

b) 7...♘f6 8.axb5 cxb5 9.b3±;

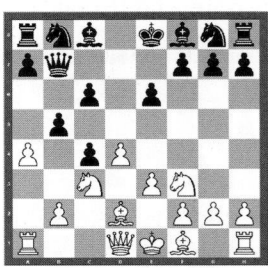

8.♘e5! (8.♘e4 ♘d7 9.b3 cxb3 10.♕xb3 b4 11.♗d3 ♘gf6 12.♖c1⩲) 8...♘d7 9.♕f3 ♘xe5 10.dxe5 a6 11.♗e2 ♘e7 12.0–0 ♘d5 13.♘e4 ♗e7 14.♘d6+ ♗xd6 15.exd6↑

7.♗d2

7.♘e5 poses no threat. Black can transpose to the main line where the knight has advanced: 7...♘f6 8.♗d2 ♗b7 9.axb5 ♗xc3 10.♗xc3 cxb5 11.b3 a5 12.bxc4 b4 13.♗b2 0–0 with a good game.

7...a5

7...♗xc3 8.♗xc3 ♘f6 9.axb5 cxb5 10.b3±;

Dubious is 7...♗b7 8.axb5

(8.b3 a5 9.axb5
a) 9.♘e4 f5 10.♘c5

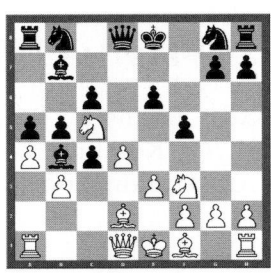

10...♗xc5!N (10...c3 11.♘xb7 ♕e7 12.♘c5 e5∞ Morozevich — Miton, Sochi 2007) 11.dxc5 ♘d7 12.axb5 cxb5 13.bxc4 b4 14.c6 ♗xc6 15.♘d4 ♕c7 16.♘xe6 ♕e5 17.♘d4 ♘e7∓;

b) 9.bxc4 bxc4 10.♗xc4 ♘f6 11.0–0 0–0=;

9...♗xc3 10.♗xc3 cxb5 — 7...a5 8.axb5 ♗xc3 9.♗xc3 cxb5 10.b3 ♗b7)

8...♗xc3 9.♗xc3 cxb5 10.d5! (10.b3 a5 — 7...a5 8.axb5 ♗xc3 9.♗xc3 cxb5 10.b3 ♗b7) 10...♘f6 (10...f6 11.dxe6 ♕xd1+ 12.♖xd1 ♘e7 13.♘d4 a6 14.♗e2±) 11.dxe6 ♕xd1+ 12.♖xd1 ♗xf3 13.exf7+ ♔xf7 14.gxf3 ♘c6 15.♖d6 ♘e7 16.♗h3 ♖hd8 17.♖a6± — White has an advantage due to the two bishops.

7...♕b6

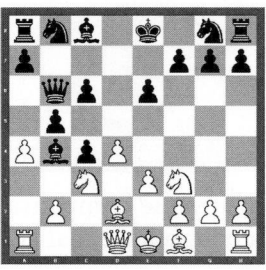

8.♘e4! (8.axb5 cxb5 9.♘e5 ♘h6!? 10.b3 ♘d7∞) 8...♘a6 (8...♗e7 9.b3 f5 10.♘g3 c3 11.♗xc3 ♘f6 12.♗e2±) 9.♗xb4

(9.♗e2 Not so convincing is 9... f5 10.♘eg5 (Also quite good is 10.♘c3. The move f7-f5 has significantly weakened Black's position.) 10...♘f6 11.0–0 h6 12.♘h3 ♗xd2 13.♕xd2 g5 14.♘e5↑ — White has a long-lasting initiative.)

9...♘xb4 10.b3 cxb3 11.♕xb3 ♕a5 12.♘fd2± — White will soon win back the pawn and retain the advantage.;

7...♕e7 8.axb5 ♗xc3 9.♗xc3 cxb5 10.d5 ♘f6 11.d6 ♕b7 12.b3

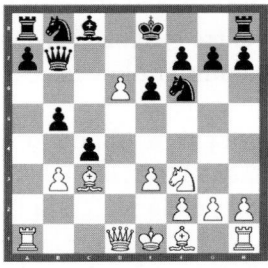

12...cxb3

a) 12...♘bd7 13.bxc4 b4 14.♗xf6 gxf6 15.♖a5 ♖b8 Ovod — Skripchenko, Sochi 2006 16.c5+-;

b) 12...0–0 13.♗xf6 gxf6 14.bxc4 bxc4 15.♗xc4 ♕b4+ 16.♘d2 ♕xd6 17.♕g4+ ♔h8 18.♕f3 ♘c6 19.♕xf6+ ♔g8 20.♖b1±;

c) 12...♘e4 13.♗xg7 ♖g8 14.♗e5 ♘d7 15.♗g3 (15.♗f4 a5 16.bxc4 b4∞) 15...♘dc5

(15...a5 16.bxc4 bxc4 (16...b4 17.♘d4±) 17.♖b1 ♕d5 18.♕c2 ♘xd6 19.♖d1 ♕f5 20.♕c1 ♘e4 21.♗xc4±)

16.♘d4 a6 17.♕h5 cxb3 (17...♘xb3 18.♘xb3 cxb3 19.♕xh7 ♖f8 20.♗e2±) 18.♕xh7 ♖f8 19.♗e2↑ — White's initiative is very dangerous.

13.♕xb3 a6 14.♕b2 ♘bd7 15.♗e2±

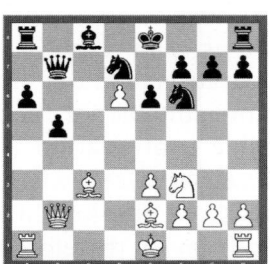

— Black's pieces are very passive and he faces a difficult defence.

8.axb5 ♗xc3 9.♗xc3 cxb5 10.b3 ♗b7 11.bxc4

11.d5? 11...♘f6 12.bxc4 b4 13.♗xf6 ♕xf6 14.♕a4+ ♘d7 15.♘d4 ♕e7! 16.♕b5 ♖b8 17.♖xa5 (17.dxe6 fxe6 18.♖xa5 ♗e4∓; 17.♕xa5 0–0! 18.♖b1 exd5 19.♕xb4 ♕e4) 17...♗xd5 18.♕a4 ♗e4 19.f3 0–0 (19...e5 20.fxe4 exd4 21.exd4 0–0 22.♗d3 ♕h4+ 23.g3 ♕f6 24.♔e2 ♕xd4 25.♖d5 ♘b6 26.♖xd4 ♘xa4∓) 20.fxe4 ♕h4+ 21.♔d1 ♘f6 22.♗d3 ♘g4 23.♘c6 (23.g3 ♕h6-+ Goldsztejn — Tregubov, Mulhouse 2011) 23...♘f2+ 24.♔d2 ♖bd8 25.♘xd8 ♕xd8 26.♔e2 ♘xh1∓ — The knight cannot be caught and the kingside pawns will soon be attacked by the black queen.

11...b4 12.♗b2 ♘f6 13.♗d3

13.c5 The attempt to blockade the queenside does not pose a threat to Black 13...0-0 14.♗b5 since Black takes control of the important d5 square.

(14.♘e5 ♕c7 15.f3 (15.♗b5 ♗xg2! 16.♖g1 ♗d5 17.f3 ♘bd7∓) 15...♘bd7 16.♘c4 ♗c6∓)

14...♗c6 15.♗a4 ♕c7 (15...♗xa4 Less accurate is 16.♕xa4 ♕d5 since d5 is more suitable for the knight. A possible continuation is 17.0-0 ♘c6 18.♖fd1 ♖fc8 19.♘d2 ♘e4 20.♘f1 f5± — The knight will be expelled from e4, therefore White's position is slightly better, Antonsen — Krasenkow, Helsingor 2011.) 16.0-0 ♗xa4 17.♕xa4 ♘c6= Korobov — Tregubov, Warsaw (blitz) 2010. In response to a later knight transfer to c4, Black can either place his knight on d5 and play f7-f5 or try e6-e5.

13...♘bd7

13...0-0 transposes with 14.0-0 ♘bd7

14.0-0 0-0

White has a strong centre coupled with the two bishops. Black has a pair of connected passed pawns on the wing. Both sides have considerable assets.

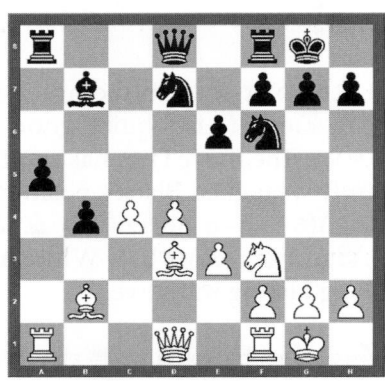

15.♘d2!

Only with this knight control over the e4 square can White can pose problems for Black.

A straightforward attempt to occupy the centre 15.♕c2 ♕c7 16.e4 runs into the counter blow 16...e5! 17.♖fe1

(17.c5 exd4 18.♗xd4 h6 19.♖fe1 (19. ♖fc1 ♗c6∓) 19...♖fe8 — 17.♖fe1 ♖fe8 18.c5 exd4 19.♗xd4 h6)

17...♖fe8 18.c5 exd4 19.♗xd4

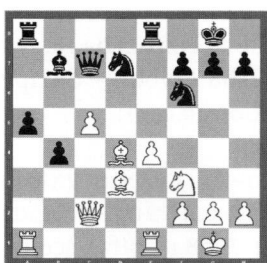

19...h6! An important preventive move. White's initiative has come to a dead-end and the connected passed pawns are evident. 20.h3 ♗c6 21.e5 (21.♘h4 ♘e5∓ Aseev — Popov, St.Petersburg 1998) 21...♘d5 22.e6 ♖xe6 23.♖xe6 fxe6 24.♗h7+ ♔h8 25.♗xg7+ ♔xg7 26.♕g6+ ♔h8 27.♕xh6 ♘f8 28.♗f5+ ♘h7 29.♗xh7 Neverov — Kramnik, Moscow 1991 29...♕g7! 30.♕xg7+ ♔xg7 31.♗c2 ♘c3−+;

15.♖e1 allows Black to organise a blockade of the white squares against this and the most convincing seems

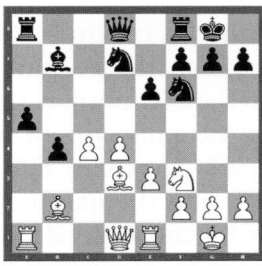

15...♗e4!

a) 15...♕c7?! 16.e4 e5 17.c5 exd4 18.♖c1±/↑;

b) 15...♘e4 16.♕c2

b1) 16.♗xe4?! 16...♗xe4 17.♘d2 ♗b7 18.e4 (18.c5 ♗c6∓) 18...e5 19.d5 f6∓;

b2) 16.♘d2!? ♘xd2 17.♕xd2 ♕c7 18.f3 f5∞;

16...f5 17.c5 ♕c7

(17...♗c6 18.♗c4 ♖e8 (18...♕e8 19.♗b3 ♘df6 20.♘e5 a4 21.♗c4 ♘d5 22.f3 ♘ef6 23.♕d3±) 19.♗b3 ♕c7 20.♖ed1 (20.♘h4 ♔h8 21.f3 ♘ef6 22.e4 fxe4 23.fxe4 ♕a7∞) 20...♔h8 (20...♗d5!?) 21.♘e1± Van Wely — Alekseev, Foros 2008)

18.♗b5 (18.♗c4 ♗d5=) 18...♗c6 19.♗a4 ♗xa4 20.♕xa4 ♖fc8=;

c) 15...♖e8 16.c5 ♗c6 17.♗c2 (17.e4 a4 18.♗c2 a3 19.♗c1 ♕c7∓ Tyomkin — Malakhov, Tallinn 1997) 17...♘e4 (17...♕c7 18.♘d2±) 18.♗a4

(18.♖e2 ♕c7 19.♘d2 1/2–1/2, Ionov — Popov, St.Petersburg 1998 (19. ♘e1 ♘ef6 20.♘d3 ♘g4 21.f4 f5∓) 19...♘xd2 20.♖xd2 ♘f6=)

18...♕c7

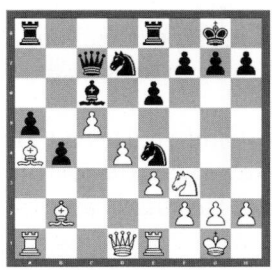

19.♕c2

c1) 19.♘d2 ♗xa4 20.♖xa4 ♘dxc5 21.dxc5 ♖ad8 (21...♖ed8 22.♗d4 ♘c3 23.♗xc3 bxc3 24.♖d4 e5 25.♖d6=) 22.♖e2 (22.♗d4 ♘xd2 23.♕xd2 e5∓ Piket — Ivanchuk, Monaco 1999) 22...♘c3 23.♗xc3 bxc3=;

c2) 19.♗xc6 ♕xc6 20.♕a4 ♕xa4 21.♖xa4 ♘dxc5! 22.dxc5 ♘xc5 23.♖aa1 a4 24.♖eb1 f6!± By placing pawns on f6 and e5 Black restricts the bishop. White is trying to draw.;

19...♖ec8 20.♖ec1 ♗xa4 (20...♕b7 21.♘e1 ♘ef6 22.f3± Svetushkin — Tzermiadianos, Olympus Riviera 2006) 21.♖xa4 f5 22.♘e1 ♘b8 23.♘d3 ♘c6 24.f3 ♘f6= — The game is near equal.;

16.♗xe4 (16.♗f1 ♗c6∓) 16...♘xe4 17.♕c2

(17.c5 ♕c7 18.♕c2 ♕c6 (18...f5 — 17.♕c2 f5 18.c5 ♕c7) 19.♖a4 ♘b6 20.♖aa1 ♘d7=)

17...f5 18.c5 ♕c7 19.♖ec1

a) 19.♖a2 ♕c6 (19...♕b7 20.♕b3 ♖fe8=) 20.♖ea1 ♕b5 21.♕a4 ♖fb8=;

b) 19.c6 ♘b6 20.♘e5 a4 21.f3 ♘d6 22.e4 fxe4 23.fxe4 ♖a5∓ Brynell — Khenkin, Helsingor 2011;

19...♕c6 20.♕a4 ♖fc8=

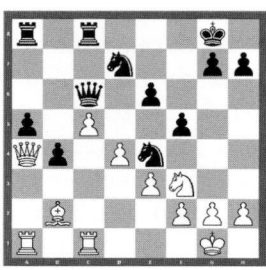

(20...♕d5 21.♘e1 f4 Brynell — Gdanski, Sweden 2011 22.exf4∞)

15...e5

15...♖e8 16.♗c2 ♘b6? J.Geller — Krapivin, Moscow 2005 17.c5 ♘bd5 18.♖e1±/↑;

15...♕c7 deserves serious attention 16.♗c2

a) 16.f4 a4 17.♖b1 ♖fd8 18.♕e2 ♘f8 19.e4 ♘6d7∞ Grachev — Malakhov, Sochi 2004;

b) 16.f3 e5 17.♗c2 — 15...e5 16.♗c2 ♕c7 17.f3

(Too slow is 17.♔h1 . The only benefit from the prophylaxis in the foreseeable future is that after a pawn exchange on d4 in some variations c4-c5 can fail due to ♘d7xc5, and the queen captures on c5 with check. 17...♖fe8 18.♕c2 (18.♗c2 exd4 19.exd4 ♘b6 20.♖c1 a4 21.d5 b3 22.♗b1 ♘bd7∓ Vitiugov — Yakovich, Aix les Bains 2011) 18...h6 19.♖fd1 e4 (19...exd4 20.exd4 ♕f4 21.♘f1± Jakovenko — Grigoryan, Aix les Bains 2011) 20.♘xe4 ♗xe4 21.♗xe4 ♘xe4 22.fxe4 ♕b7 23.e5 a4 24.c5 ♕c6∞ — The connected pawns on the queenside provide Black with sufficient counterplay.)

16...♗c6!? Not hurrying with e6-e5 and aiming to induce e3-e4 locking-in the bishop on c2. (16...e5 — 15...e5 16.♗c2 ♕c7) 17.e4 (17.f4

♕b7∞; 17.♖e1!?; 05Also interesting
is *17.f3!?,*with ♖f1–f2 to follow. Also
one must not disregard the idea
of a massive pawn advance on the
kingside (especially in the event of
Black's prophylaxis h7-h6), which
can be started with g2-g4!?)

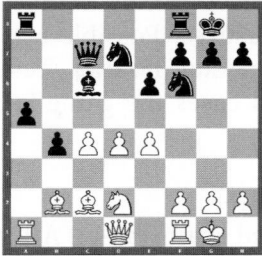

17...e5

(17...a4 18.♗xa4 (*18.d5 b3 19.♗xb3±*)
18...♘xe4 19.♘xe4 ♗xe4 20.♖e1±
Nechepurenko — Frolyanov, Sochi
2010)

18.d5 ♗b7

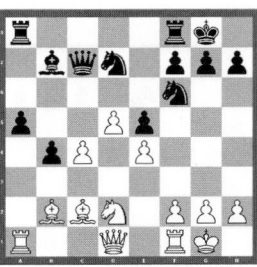

19.f4! (*19.♖e1∞; 19.♕e2∞*) 19...exf4
20.♗a4! (*20.♕f3 ♘e5 21.♕xf4
♘fd7∞*) 20...♖fc8 (*20...♖ac8
21.♗b5↑*) 21.♗d4!↑ — White has an
advantage although the black wing
pawns still pose a potential threat.

(21.♕f3 ♘c5 (*21...♘e5 22.♗xe5
♕xe5 23.♖xf4±*) 22.♗c2 (*22.♗xf6
gxf6 23.♕xf4 ♕xf4 24.♖xf4 ♔g7∞*)
22...a4 23.e5 ♘xd5 24.cxd5 a3
25.♗d4 ♕d8 26.♗xc5 ♖xc5 27.♗b3
♗xd5 28.♕xf4 ♕b6 29.♔h1 ♗xb3
30.♘xb3 ♖c7= leads to a dynami-
cally balanced position.)

15...♗c6 16.♗c2 ♕c7 — 15...♕c7
16.♗c2 ♗c6

16.♗c2
Useful prophylaxis. The bishop
leaves the d-file on which it can be
attacked and evades a potential e5-
e4 jab. Simultaneously White prevents a5-a4, and in some variations
the bishop can put pressure on the
Black's position from a4.
16.d5 ♕c7 17.♗c2± — 16.♗c2 ♕c7
17.d5

16...♕c7

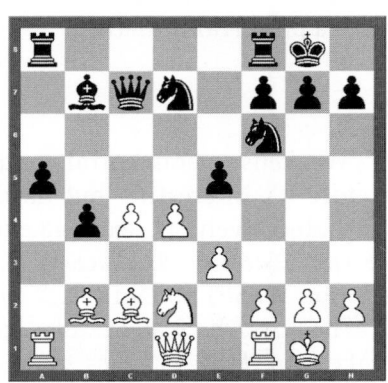

17.d5!

A straightforward idea but still dangerous for Black. After shutting-out the b7 bishop, White intends to open-up lines for his bishops with f2-f4 and start a kingside attack combined with play in the centre.

17.♗a4 ♖fd8 (*17...♘b6 18.♗b5∞*) 18.d5 and now correct is 18...♘c5 forcing the bishop to retreat back to c2.

(On 18...♘b6 strong is

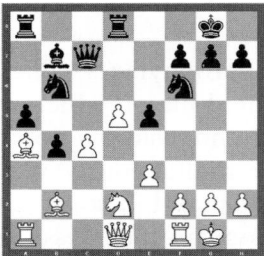

19.♗b3! (*19.♖c1 ♘xa4 20.♕xa4 ♘d7!± Sakaev — Timofeev, Moscow 2004*) 19...♘fd7 20.f4 ♖e8 21.fxe5 ♘xe5 22.♗d4 a4 23.♖xa4 ♘xa4 24.♗xa4 ♖ed8 25.♗c2↑ with a powerful initiative.)

19.♗c2∞;

17.f4 Weakens several central squares therefore it's interesting but hardly strong objectively. 17...exd4 18.exd4 ♖fe8 (*18...♗a6!?∞; 18...♖ac8∞*) 19.d5 ♖ac8 (*19...♗a6!?*) 20.♖c1 (*20.♗a4±*) 20...♕b6+ 21.♔h1 ♗a6 22.♗f5 ♖cd8 23.♘f3 (*23.♖f3!?*) 23...♘c5 24.♗d4 ♗c8 A.Zhigalko — S.Zhigalko, Minsk 2006 25.♗c2! ♗g4 26.h3 ♗xf3 27.♕xf3±/↑;

A different idea in principle lies behind 17.f3!? which has not been played yet at Grandmaster level. White takes control of the e4 square and restricts the black bishop. Subsequently he intends to maximise the strength of his centre whilst preventing Black's activity. 05After thelogical 17...♖fe8 White can continue to take preventive measures. Possible are 18.♖e1, 18.♖f2, 18.♖c1, 18.♗a4 ♗c6 19.♗b3 — in all cases the game is complicated.

17...♖fe8!N
Directed against f2-f4. All other replies allow White to develop a strong initiative:

17...♕c5 18.♔h1 ♕e7 19.f4 exf4 20.exf4!N± — The black knight cannot move to the e5 square to block the long diagonal. White's initiative is very dangerous.(*20.e4∞ Timofeev — Yudin, Tomsk 2008*);

17...♗a6

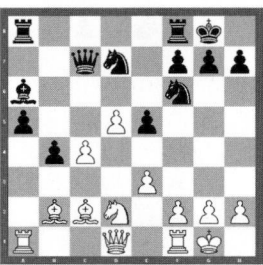

18.f4 e4

a) 18...♖ac8 19.fxe5 ♘xd5 20.e6 ♘7f6 21.cxd5 ♗xf1 (*21...♕xc2 22.♗xf6 ♗xf1 23.♕g4 ♕g6 24.♕xg6*) *fxg6 25.♗e7 ♖fe8 26.d6 ♖xe7 27.dxe7 ♗b5 28.♖xa5+-)* 22.♖c1±;

b) 18...exf4 19.♖xf4→;

19.♗a4±;

17...♖fd8 18.f4 ♖a6 *(18...h6 19.♗a4±)* 19.♗a4± Frolyanov — Galkin, St.Petersburg 2009;

17...♘b6 18.♖c1 a4

(18...g6 19.♗b1 (19.f4 ♘xc4 20.♘xc4 ♕xc4 21.e4 ♘xe4 22.♗b3 ♕b5 23.fxe5 ♘c3 24.♗xc3 bxc3 25.♖xc3 a4=) 19...♘bd7 (On *19...h5* with the idea of providing the knight with the g4 square after f2-f4, strong is a simple *20.h3!*) 20.f4 ♖a6 21.♗c2! — The white bishop is ready to jump to a4.)

19.f4 b3 20.♗xb3 axb3 21.♗xe5 ♕c5 *(21...♕d8 22.♕xb3 ♗a6 23.e4±)* 22.♕xb3 ♘bd7 23.♗d4 ♕a5 24.♕b2±

18.♔h1!
White prepares the blow f2-f4 and moves the king away from checks along the diagonal.
18.♗a4 ♖e7 19.f4 exf4 20.exf4 ♘e4 21.♘xe4 ♖xe4=;
18.♖c1 ♕d6 19.f4 exf4 20.exf4 ♖ac8∞

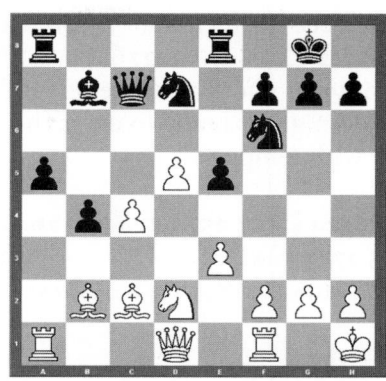

18...♘b6
18...h6 19.♗a4 ♖e7 20.f4 exf4 21.exf4↑

19.♗d3!
Black ha s weakened his control of e5, therefore White can afford to bring back the bishop to where it was previously.
19.♗b3 ♕e7 20.e4 ♘fd7 21.f4∞

19...♘bd7 20.f4 ♖e7 21.fxe5 ♘xe5 22.♗e2 ♘ed7

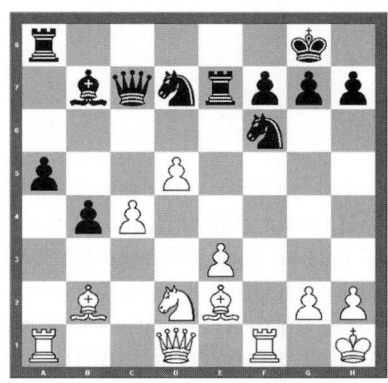

23.e4! ♘xe4

23...♖ee8 24.♖c1 ♗a6 25.c5 ♗xe2
26.♕xe2 ♘xd5 27.♗xg7 ♘f4 28.♕g4
♘g6 29.c6 ♘de5 30.♗xe5± — The
white knight is ready to enter the attack with tempo.

**24.♘xe4 ♖xe4 25.♗f3 ♖ee8 26.♖c1
♘e5 27.c5 ♘xf3**

27...♖ad8 28.d6 ♗xf3 29.♗xe5+-

28.♕xf3!

28.♖xf3 ♖ad8 29.♖g3 f6 30.d6 ♕c6
31.♗xf6 ♖d7= — Black is ready to
remove the queen to d5 or e4 and
then occupy the excellent blockading square c6 with his bishop.

**28...f6 29.♖fd1 ♖ad8 30.c6 ♗a8
31.h3±/↑**

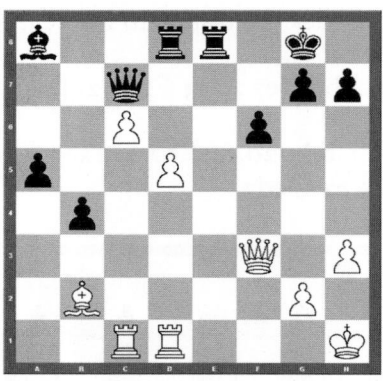

Whit e's initiative is dangerous and
Black faces a difficult defence. Conclusion: The evaluation of the Noteboom Variation is as controversial
as it was many years ago. I think the
main line analysed beginning with
15.♘d2! is the most dangerous for
Black. Additionally many variations
are often of a non-forcing nature
and energetic play by White as well
as cool-headed play by Black are required throughout the game.

PART 6 — Marshall gambit

■ GAME 13

1.d4 d5 2.c4 c6 3.♘c3 e6

Primarily played to deter the set-up with ♘f3 and ♗g5 but it allows the very dangerous variation called the Slav Gambit.

4.e4

Already on the 4th move the game sharpens dramatically and the price of a mistake is now higher than in most other opening variations. Accurate play based on deep knowledge is required from both sides and the White player needs courage and a feeling for the initiative.

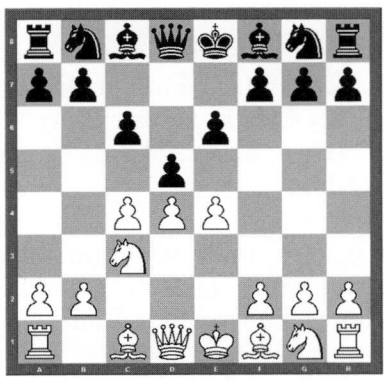

4...dxe4

On 4...♗b4, I think the most dangerous for Black is 5.♗d2!

a) Of interest is 5.♕b3!? ♗xc3+ (After 5...♗a5 White can still sacrifice a pawn: 6.♗d2! dxe4 7.0-0-0⩲, with compensation, Jobava — Drazic, Milan 2011) 6.♕xc3 dxe4 The position has not been analysed and is rich in possibilities. Ideally one would like toplay 7.f3!? (Of interest is 7.♘e2, with the idea of ♘e2-g3.; and also 7.♗f4, with the idea 0-0-0.) 7...♘f6 8.♗g5 0-0 (8...exf3 9.♘xf3 ♘e4 10.♗xd8 ♘xc3 11.♗c7 ♘e4 12.♗d3 ♘f6 13.♗d6⩲) 9.0-0-0 exf3 10.♘xf3 ♘e4 11.♕e3 ♘xg5 12.♘xg5⩲, with compensation for the pawn.;

b) In practice White usually steers the game into positional channels choosing 5.e5, or 5.cxd5 exd5 6.e5.;

5...dxc4

a) 5...♗xc3 6.♗xc3 dxe4 (6...♘f6 7.e5 ♘e4 8.♖c1! with the idea of capturing with the rook on c3 in the event of an exchange and preventing Black from playing c6-c5. 8...0-0 9.♘f3 ♘xc3 10.♖xc3 dxc4 11.♗xc4±) 7.♕g4 ♘f6 8.♕xg7 ♖g8 9.♕h6 ♘bd7 10.g3 b6 11.♘h3 ♗b7 12.♗e2±;

b) With the move 5...♘e7 Black doesn't put pressure on the centre, therefore White gains the advantage easily: 6.♘f3 ♗xc3 *(6...0-0 7.♗d3 c5 8.cxd5 exd5 9.dxc5 dxe4 10.♗xe4 ♗xc5 11.0-0 ♘bc6 12.♕c2 f5 13.♗xc6 ♘xc6 14.♘b5± —* The pawn on f5 seriously restricts the Black's light-squared bishop and his lag in development shows.) 7.♗xc3 dxe4 8.♘g5 ♘d5 *(8...e3 9.fxe3 ♘f5 10.♕g4±)* 9.♕h5 9...g6 10.♕h6 ♘xc3 11.♕g7 ♕a5 12.♕xh8+ ♔d7 *(12... ♔e7 13.♕e5±)* 13.♕e5 ♕b4 14.♕f4 ♕xb2 15.♕c1 ♕xc1+ 16.♖xc1 ♘xa2 17.♖b1±;

c) 5...dxe4 6.♘xe4 leads to the main variation by transposition 4...dxe4 5.♘xe4 ♗b4+ 6.♗d2;

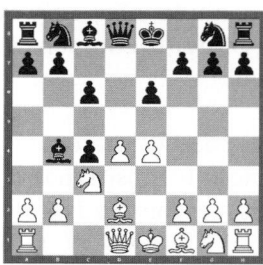

6.♗xc4 ♕xd4 7.♕e2 White gains a considerable advantage in development for the sacrificed pawn.

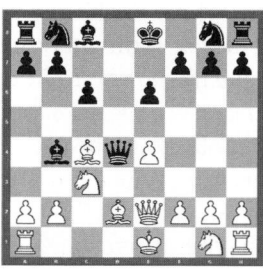

7...♘f6

a) 7...b5 8.♗d3 ♘d7 9.♘f3 ♕b6 10.0-0 ♗xc3 11.♗xc3 ♘gf6 12.a4 b4 13.a5 ♕b8 14.♗d2 *(14.♗xf6±)* 14...e5 15.♖ac1 c5 16.♗e3 ♕c7 17.♗xc5! *(17. a6 0-0 18.♘d2 ♕c6± Potkin — Vitiugov, St.Petersburg 2005)* 17...♘xc5 18.♕e3 ♘fd7 19.♗b5 0-0 20.♗xd7 ♕xd7 21.♘xe5+-;

b) 7...♕d8 8.♘f3 (Worth investigating is *8.a3!?* in order to respond to *8...♗e7* with *9.e5±* keeping the black king's knight out of the game) 8... ♘f6 9.0-0→ — 7...♘f6 8.♘f3 ♕d8 9.0-0;

c) 7...e5 8.♘f3 *(8.0-0-0 ♕c5 9.♔b1∞ Ezat — Mamedyarov, Bursa 2010)* 8...♕d6 9.a3 ♗a5 10.0-0± — White's advantage in development is very dangerous.;

8.♘f3 ♕d8 9.0-0 ♘bd7

a) 9...b5?! 10.e5 *(10.♗d3 ♗e7 11.e5↑)* 10...♗xc3 *(10...♘d5 11.♘xb5±)* 11.♗xc3 ♘d5 12.♗xd5 cxd5 13.♗b4 *(13.♕xb5+ ♗d7 14.♕d3±)* 13...♘c6 14.♗d6±;

b) 9...0-0 10.e5 ♘d5 *(10...♗xc3 11.bxc3 ♘d5 12.♗d3↑)* 11.♘xd5 ♗xd2 12.♘f6+ gxf6 13.♖ad1±;

10.e5!N *(10.a3 has also been played 10...♗e7 11.♖ac1 0-0 12.e5 ♘d5 13.♖fd1 b6∓ — White's co mpensation is hardly enough for equality, San Segundo — Shirov, Madrid 1996.)*

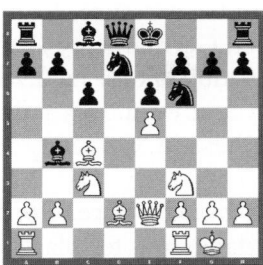

10...♘d5 11.♕e4! In this way White redeploys the queen to g4. 11...0–0

a) 11...♗e7 12.♕g4 g6 13.♗h6 b5 (*13...♕c7 14.♖fe1↑*) 14.♗e2↑;

b) 11...♘xc3 12.bxc3 ♗e7 13.♕g4 g6 14.♗h6 ♕a5 15.♖fe1 ♘b6 16.♗b3 ♕xc3 17.♘g5 ♘d5 18.♖ac1±/→ White's initiative is very strong.;

12.♗xd5 ♗xc3

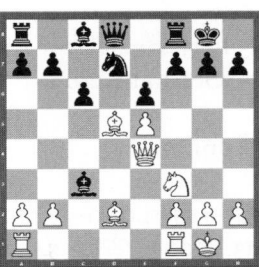

13.♘g5 A most important intermediate move! 13...g6 14.♕h4 h5 15.♗xc3 exd5 (*15...cxd5 16.♖fe1 ♘c5 17.g4↑*) 16.e6 fxe6 17.♕g3 ♕e7 18.♖fe1 ♘f6 (On *18...e5* follows *19.♘f3*, aiming to capture on e5, after which White will not only have black squared play but also the e-file.) 19.♖ad1 Black will not be able to complete the development of his pieces. 19...c5 (After.

19...♗d7 follows 20.♘e4!) 20.♘xe6 ♗xe6 21.♖xd5 ♔f7 22.♖de5 ♖ae8 23.♖xe6 ♕xe6 24.♖xe6 ♖xe6 25.♕c7+ ♖e7 26.♕xc5 ♖fe8 27.h3±

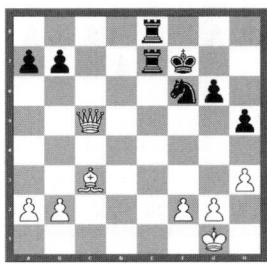

— Black has a cluster of weak squares on the kingside therefore White's advantage is indisputable.

5.♘xe4 ♗b4+ 6.♗d2
6.♘c3 Multiple mo ves by one piece in the opening are not to be recommended therefore this move does not fight for the advantage. 6...c5 7.a3 ♗a5

(A worthy option is 7...♗xc3+ 8.bxc3 ♘f6 9.♘f3 ♕a5 10.♗d2

(10.♕c2 cxd4 11.♘xd4 (*11.♗d2 d3 12.♗xd3 ♘bd7 13.0–0 ♘c5∓*) 11...0–0 12.♗e2 e5∓)

10...♘e4 11.♗d3 ♘xd2 12.♕xd2 0–0=, with equal game, Potapov — Sveshnikov, Miass 2007.)

8.♘f3 (Dubious is *8.dxc5?!* 8...♗xc3+ *9.bxc3 ♕xd1+ 10.♔xd1 ♘f6 11.f3 ♗d7 12.♗e3 ♘a6 13.♘e2 ♗a4+ 14.♔e1 ♘d7* — The endgame is more pleasant for black.; *8.♗e3 ♘f6 9.dxc5*

♗xc3+ 10.bxc3 ♕a5 11.♘f3 0-0 = — Black has an excellent game, Khismatullin — Vitiugov, Kazan 2005) 8...♘f6

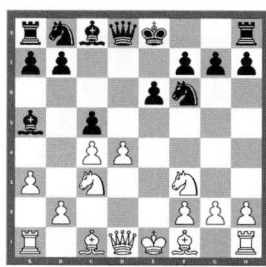

9.♗e2

(9.♗e3 ♘c6 (9...0-0 10.♕c2 cxd4 11.♗xd4 ♘c6 12.♗e3 ♗xc3+ 13.♕xc3 e5 14.♖d1 ♕e7 15.♗e2± — In this complicated position White's game looks preferable.) 10.dxc5 (10.♗e2 ♘e4 11.♖c1 cxd4 12.♘xd4 ♘xc3 13.bxc3 ♘xd4 14.♗xd4 0-0 = Mellado Trivino — Korneev, Manresa 1995) 10...♗xc3+ 11.bxc3 ♕a5 12.♕c2 ♘g4 13.♕c1 (Interesting but risky is 13.♗c1!? ♕xc5 14.a4 ♘ce5 = — Black's chances are as good as White's.) 13...0-0 (13...e5 14.h3 ♘xe3 15.♕xe3 0-0 16.♗e2 ♘d4 17.♘xd4 exd4 18.♕xd4 ♖e8 19.♕d2 ♗d7 20.0-0 ♗c6 =, with equality.) 14.♗e2 f5!? Black has reason to fight for the initiative (14...♘xe3 15.♕xe3 ♘e7 16.0-0 ♘f5 17.♕e4 ♕xc5= Zsuzsa Polgar — Lajos Portisch, Budapest 1993) 15.0-0 e5∓)

9...cxd4 (Not so convincing is 9...♘e4 10.♗d2 ♘xd2 11.♕xd2 cxd4 12.♘xd4± — Black's queenside can come under pressure, Konikowski — Meyer, Germany 1995.) 10.♘xd4 ♘e4 11.♘db5 ♕xd1+ 12.♗xd1 ♘xc3 13.♘xc3 ♗xc3+ 14.bxc3 ♗d7 = Babula — Khenkin, Germany 2003

6...♕xd4 7.♗xb4 ♕xe4+ 8.♗e2
Hardly dangerous for Black is 8.♘e2 ♘a6 9.♗f8

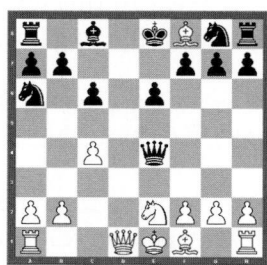

9...♘e7

(Interesting is 9...♕g6!? 10.♘f4

a) 10.♘g3 ♘e7 11.♗xe7 ♔xe7 12.♗d3 f5 13.♕e2 ♔f7 = Richter — Smeets, Germany 2012;

b) 10.♗d6!?∞;

c) 10.♕d6 f5 11.0-0-0 ♕g5+ 12.f4 ♕f6 13.♕d8+ ♔f7 14.♗a3 (14. ♖d7+ ♗xd7 15.♕xa8 ♘e7 16.♕xb7 ♖xf8 17.♕xd7 ♘c5∓/↑) 14...♕xd8 15.♖xd8 c5=;

10...♕g5 11.♕d6 ♘e7 12.h4 ♕a5+ 13.b4 ♕xb4+ 14.♕xb4 ♘xb4 15.♗xg7 ♘c2+ 16.♔d2 ♖g8 17.♘h5 ♘xa1 18.♘f6+ ♔d8 19.♘xg8 ♘xg8 20.♗xa1 ♔e7 21.g4⩲⩲ — White has good compensation for a pawn.)

10.♗xg7 ♘b4

(The other option is sharper but it also leads to equality: 10...♖g8 11.♕d4 ♕xd4 12.♗xd4 c5

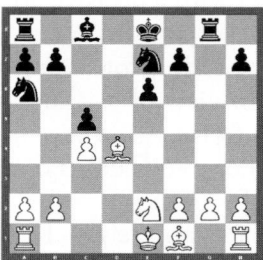

13.♗f6!? White lures the rook to g6 where it will be attacked by ♘e2-f4.

(No problems are posed by 13.♗c3 ♘b4 14.♔d2 b6 (Also interesting is *14...e5!?* Batsiashvili — Frolyanov, Yerevan 2004) 15.a3 ♘bc6 = Grigore — Kharlov, Cologne 1993)

13...♘b4 (White's idea is shown in the line *13...♖g6 14.♗c3 ♘b4 15.♘f4!±* Timofeev — Frolyanov, Taganrog 2011) 14.♔d2

(14.♖d1 N demands accurate play from Black 14...♖g6 15.♗e5 ♘ec6! (Not so strong is *15...♘bc6 16.♗c3 e5 17.f4±* The black knights are deprived of the outpost d4, since it's not worth playing f6 allowing an isolated pawn on e5.) 16.♗d6 b6 17.a3 ♘c2+ 18.♔d2 ♘2d4 19.♘xd4 (*19.♗g3 ♗b7 20.♘f4 ♖h6=*) 19...♘xd4 20.♗d3 f5 (It looks like Black also obtains

equality after *20...♖xg2 21.♗e4 ♖xf2+ 22.♔c3 ♗b7 23.♗xb7 ♖d8 24.♗e5 ♖c2+ 25.♔d3 ♖xb2 =*, but such complications are needless.) 21.♖hg1 ♗b7 22.♗g3 h5 =,with a near equal game.)

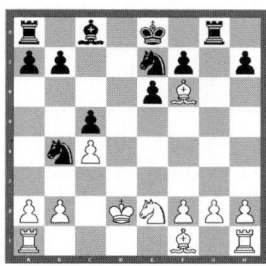

14...♖g6 15.♗c3

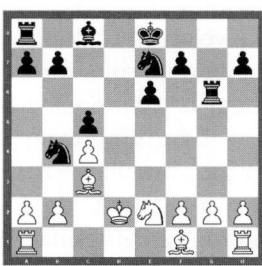

15...e5!N (*15...♗d7 16.a3 ♘bc6* Lorparizangeneh — Aghasaryan, Jermuk 2011 *17.♘f4±*) 16.♗xe5 ♗f5 17.♘f4 (*17.♘g3 0-0-0+ 18.♔c3 ♗d3 19.♖d1 ♘xa2+ 20.♔b3 ♘b4 21.♔c3 ♘a2+=*) 17...0-0-0+ 18.♔c3 ♖b6 19.g4 ♗xg4 20.♖g1 ♗f5 21.♗g7 ♘c2 22.♖c1 ♘b4 23.♖a1=)

11.♕d6

(11.♗xh8 e5 12.♕d6 (*12.♕b3 ♘c2+ 13.♔d2 ♘xa1 14.♕d3 ♕xd3+ 15.♔xd3 ♗f5+ 16.♔c3 0-0-0 17.♘g3 ♖xh8 18.♘xf5 ♘xf5 19.♗d3 ♘h4 20.g3 ♘f3 21.♖xa1 ♘c7=*) 12...♘c2+

13.♔d2 ♗f5 14.♘g3 ♕f4+ 15.♔c3 ♘d5+ 16.cxd5 ♕d4+ 17.♔b3 ♘xa1+ 18.♔a3 ♘c2+= Hera — R.Markus, Skopje 2012)

11...♘d3+ (Risky for Black is *11... ♘c2+ 12.♔d2 ♘xa1 13.♗xh8 e5 14.f3 ♕c2+ 15.♔e1± Nepomnia-chtchi — Pavasovic, Rogaska Slatina 2011)* 12.♔d2 ♘f5 13.♕xd3 ♕xd3+ 14.♔xd3 ♘xg7= The endgame looks practically equal, Aleksandrov — S. Zhigalko, Minsk 2010.

8...♘a6

8...♕xg2 is risky because Black lags in development 9.♗f3 This is the way to develop the strongest initiative (Very dangerous for Black but not so clear is *9.♕d6 ♘d7 10.0-0-0 ♕xf2∞* — By giving away another pawn White burns all his bridges and plays for mate, Bu Xiangzhi — Lu Shanglei, Xinghua 2010.) 9... ♕g5 10.♘e2 ♘d7 (*10...♘a6 11.♖g1 ♕f6 12.♗c3 e5 13.♘g3±* — White's initiative is developing of its own accord, Volkov — Grachev, Krasnodar 2002.) 11.♖g1 ♕h4 White has many tempting possibilities. Most of all I like the following way of developing the initiative:

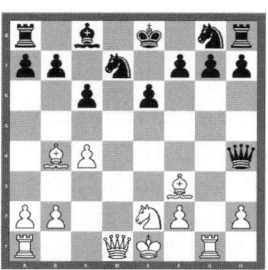

12.♖xg7! ♘e5 13.♖g3!,with the antic-ipated line: 13...♕xc4 14.♗c3 ♘xf3+ 15.♖xf3 f6 16.♕d6 e5 17.♗xe5 ♕e6 18.♕a3 ♘e7 19.♗c3 ♕e4 20.♖e3 ♕h1+ 21.♔d2 ♕d5+ 22.♖d3+- and then ♖e1 with a decisive attack.;

8...♘e7 9.♕d2 (Not so promising is *9.♘f3*, in view of *9...♘d5!*) 9...♘g6 10.♘h3 f6 (*10...♘a6 11.0-0-0 f6* — *10...f6 11.0-0-0 ♘a6*) 11.0-0-0 ♔f7

(11...♘a6 Van Wely — Krasenkow, Pamplona 1999

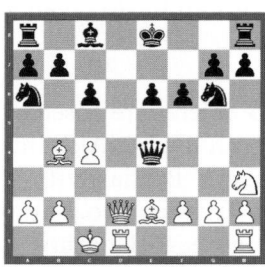

12.f3!N ♕e5 13.♗d6 ♕h5 14.f4 ♕h4 15.♖hf1+-, with decisive threats. If 15...♔f7 (If *15...♗d7 16.f5*) 16.♘g5+)

12.f3 ♕h4 13.♗c5! e5 14.♘f2 f5 15.g3 ♕f6 16.♖hf1→ — All White's pieces participate in the attack and Black is practically defenceless Khalifman — Filippov, Kazan 1995.;

8...♘d7 This rare move is very so-phisticated. White must play ener-getically: 9.♘f3 c5 10.♗c3

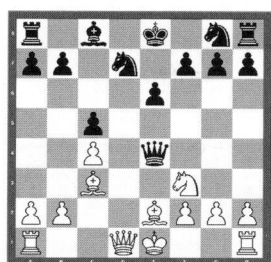

10...♘e7

(10...♘gf6 11.♕d6 ♕c6 12.♕g3 0-0
13.♖d1 (Also promising is *13.0-0-0
♘e8 14.♗d3 f6 15.♖he1 ♖f7 16.♗c2*,
with a strong initiative.) 13...♘e8
14.♗d3 f6 15.♕h4 (After *15.0-0*
follows *15...♖f7* and then *♘d7-f8*.
Without weak pawns on the kingside it's easier for Black to defend.)
15...h6 16.0-0 ♘d6

(16...♖f7 17.♗g6 ♖e7 18.♘e5 ♕c7
(In case of *18...♘xe5 19.♗xe5*
Black is nearly in zugzwang, at
the same time White intends to
bring up the rook to d3 with decisive effect, threatening to dou-
ble on the d-file and to swing
over along the 3rd rank to attack.)
19.♘g4 Black cannot defend the
threatened piece sacrifice on f6 in
various combinations.)

17.♕g3 e5 18.♘h4± — The weakening of a group of squares in Black's
camp is very serious, at the same
time he faces the opening up of the
game by f2-f4.)

11.0-0 f6

(11...0-0 12.♗d3 ♕c6 (After *12...
♕f4 13.♖e1* also follows) 13.♖e1
♘g6 Belozerov — S.Ivanov,
St.Petersburg 1994

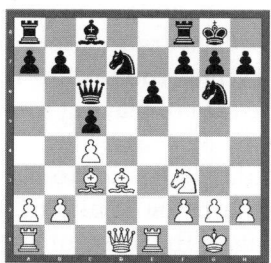

Now strong was 14.♕d2!N, depriving the black knight of the f4
square and increasing pressure
on the centre. Additionallytheth-
reatofh2-h4-h5isveryunpleasant)

12.♗d3 ♕c6 13.♕c2 ♘f8

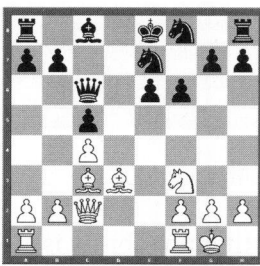

14.♖fe1!N (*14.♗e4 ♕c7 15.b4∞*
Wohlers-Armas — Roumegous,
Besancon 2006) 14...♕c7 15.♖ad1!
♗d7 16.♘g5! 16...e5 17.♕e2 (*17.f4 Not
so strong is 17...♘fg6 18.♘f3 ♘xf4
19.♘xe5 ♘xd3 20.♕xd3 ♗e6 21.♕f3
♖d8 22.♖xd8+ ♔xd8 23.♘g4 ♗xc4
24.♘xf6 gxf6 25.♗xf6 ♖f8 26.♕d1+
♔c8 27.♗xe7 ♖g8 28.♗d6±*) 17...
♘e6 (*17...h5 18.♗xe5 fxe5 19.♕xe5*

♕xe5 20.♖xe5+-) 18.♘xe6 (White's advantage is small after *18.♗xe5 fxe5 19.♘xe6 ♗xe6 20.♕xe5 ♕xe5 21.♖xe5 ♗g8 22.♗c2 g6 23.♖de1 0-0-0 24.♖xe7 ♗xc4±*) 18...♗xe6 19.f4 0-0-0 20.fxe5 f5 21.♕e3±/↑ White's ideas are to either play b2-b4, or retreat the bishop from d3, with the idea of playing rook to d6.;

Unpopular is 8...c5. However here too it's hard for White to gain an advantage. The idea of the move is that the Black's queenside is not so confined and can be developed more easily while the bishop on c5 can be attacked with tempo.

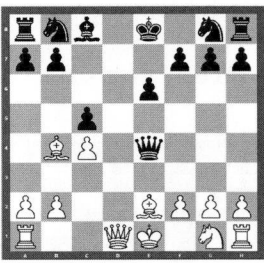

9.♗xc5 ♕xg2 10.♗f3

(The other possibility is also interesting but I like it less: *10.♕d6!? ♘d7 11.0-0-0 (11.♗f3 ♕g5 transposes to the main line) 11...♕c6* Now it's n ot worth exchanging on c6 since the black bishop can be developed on b7. Correct is

(*11...♕g5+ 12.♗e3 ♕e7 (12...♕e5 13.♕a3±) 13.♕g3±*)

12.♗a3! ♕xd6 13.♗xd6, with good compensation for a pawn, for example:

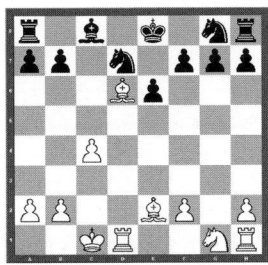

13...♘h6N

(*13...♘e7*

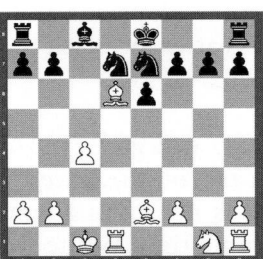

14.♗d3!N White keeps the black knight out of f5, and opens up the e-file for future use 14...♘b8 (*14... f6 rather restricts Black's game 15.f4 ♔f7 16.♘f3⩲⩱*) 15.♘e2 ♘bc6 16.♘c3 f6 17.♘b5 ♔f7 18.f4⩲⩱ — White has excellent compensation for the pawn.)

14.♗d3! f6 (*14...♘g4 15.♘h3 ♘ge5 16.♗e2 f6 17.♖hg1 g6 18.f4 ♘f7 19.♗a3 e5 20.b3⩲⩱*) 15.♗e4 (*15.f4 ♘f7 16.♗a3 b6 = — Black is ready to develop his bishop; 15.♘f3 e5 16.♗e4 ♘f8 —* the knight on f3 doesn't participate. It's restricted by the f6 and e5 pawns.) 15...e5 16.♘e2⯱.

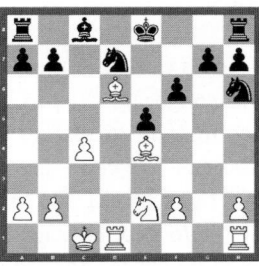

The white knight is ready to increase pressure on Black's position via c3. Another option is the blow f2-f4)

10...♕g5 11.♕d6!

a) An interesting game arises after 11.♗a3 ♘e7 12.♘e2

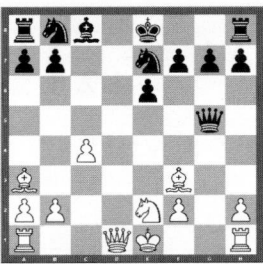

12...0-0!N

a1) 12...♘f5? 13.♖g1 ♕h4 (13...♕d8 14.♕xd8+ ♔xd8 15.0-0-0++- Jobava — Lajos Portisch, Rethymnon 2003) ;

a2) 12...♘bc6 13.♖g1 ♕f6 14.♗xc6+!N 14...♘xc6 15.♘c3 ♕e5+ 16.♔f1 a6 17.♕d3 ♕d4 18.♕e2 e5 19.♖d1 ♕h4 20.♘e4

♗h3+ 21.♔e1 ♖d8 22.♘d6+ ♖xd6 23.♖xd6±;

13.♕d6

(13.♖g1 ♕a5+ 14.♔f1 (*14.♕d2 ♕xd2+ 15.♔xd2 ♘bc6∓*) 14...♖d8 15.♕c1 ♘bc6 16.b4 ♕c7∓)

13...♖e8 14.♖g1 ♕f6 15.0-0-0 ♘bc6 16.♗e4 (*16.♗h1!?*) 16...♕xf2 17.♘c3 g6∞, but it's hard for White to demonstrate compensation for the two sacrificed pawns.;

b) 11.♗d6 yields nothing 11...♘e7 12.♘e2 (*12.♗e4 e5 13.♘f3 ♕f4 14.♕e2 ♘bc6∓*) 12...♘bc6 (*12...♘f5 13.♖g1 ♕d8 14.♗a3⯱*) 13.♖g1 ♕a5+ (*13...♕f6 14.♗xc6+ ♘xc6 15.♘c3↑*) 14.♔f1!?N

(*14.♘c3 ♘f5 15.♗e4 ♗d7 (15... ♘cd4!?) 16.♗xf5 exf5 17.♕e2+ ♗e6 18.0-0-0 0-0-0 19.♖xg7 ♕a6 = Hjartarson — Van Der Werf, Reykjavik 1996*)

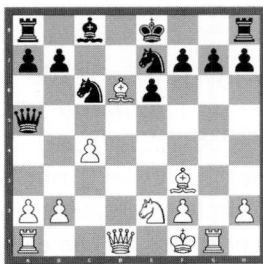

14...♘f5 15.♘g3 ♘cd4 16.♘xf5 ♘xf5 17.♕d3 (*17.♗e4 ♗d7 18.♗xf5 ♕xf5 19.♖xg7 0-0-0=*) 17...♕d8 18.c5 ♘xd6 19.cxd6 0-0 20.♖c1 a5 21.♔g2

(21.♗e4 f5 22.♖c7 ♖f7 23.♕c3 ♕f8=)
21...♖a6 22.♖gd1 ♗d7=

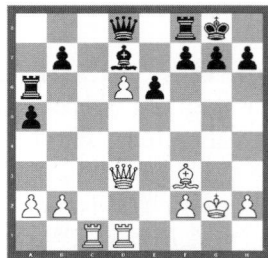

— The passed pawn on d6 is very strong but the pawn deficit and weakened white king position does not allow White to claim an advantage.

11...♘d7 12.♗a3!

(Short castling by Black should be prevented after 12.♗e3 ♕e7 13.♕d2 (There is no *13.♕g3* due to *13...♕b4+!*) 13...♘gf6 14.0–0–0 0–0∓ White has insufficient compensation for a pawn.)

12...♕a5+!N This creates some disharmony in White's camp.

a) 12...♕e5+ 13.♘e2 ♕xd6 14.♗xd6 f6 (14...♘e7 15.♘d4 a6 16.0–0–0↑) 15.♘d4 ♘e5 (15...♔f7 16.0–0–0 ♘b6 17.b3 ♘e7 Meier — Thorsteinsson, Reykjavik 2008 *18.♖he1!*, Increasing the pressure on the centre with threats of advancing the a-pawn, exchanging on e7 followed by ♘d4-f5-d6 and ♘d4-b5. White could gain a decisive advantage.) 16.♗xe5 fxe5 17.♘c6 e4 18.♗xe4 ♘f6 19.♗g2 0–0

20.♘e5 ♘d7 21.♘d3± — White's pressure in the queenside is very dangerous.

b) 12...♘e7 13.♗e4 ♘g6 (13...♕h4 14.♗c2 ♘c6 15.♘f3 ♕g4 16.♕d3 ♕f4 17.♖d1 e5 18.♖d2 f6 19.♖g1 g6 20.h3! e4 21.♕xe4+ ♕xe4+ 22.♗xe4±) 14.♘f3 ♕f4 15.♕xf4 ♘xf4 16.0–0–0 (16.♖g1 ♘f6 17.♗c2 ♘g6 18.0–0–0 ♗d7 19.♗d6 ♗c6 20.♘d4 0–0–0 21.♘xc6 bxc6 22.♖g3 ♘e8 23.♗c5 ♖xd1+ 24.♔xd1∞/= White has compensation for the pawn but it will hardly be sufficient for more than equality.) 16...♘f6 (After *16...f6* White plays *17.♖d2!*, preparing to seize the d-file with ♖hd1.) 17.♖he1 ♘xe4 18.♖xe4 ♘g6 19.♘d4 f6

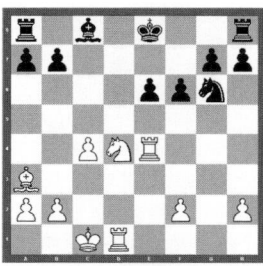

20.♘xe6

(A Sharper play which is also good for White arises after 20.♘f5!? ♔f7 21.♘d6+ ♔g8 22.♖g4! White threatens to exchange on c8 followed by penetration of the rook to d7, as well as ♖dg1 and h2-h4-h5. 22...♘e5 (22...b6 permits White to implement one of his ideas: 23.♖dg1 e5 24.♖4g3 ♗e6 25.h4+-, with the decisive threat h4-h5.; 22...e5 does not solve the problems 23.♘xc8 ♖xc8 24.♖d7 f5 25.♖g5 ♖xc4+ 26.♔d2± — Despite a two pawn deficit White dominates, while Black has no useful moves.) 23.♖g3 h5 (23...♘c6 24.♘xb7± — Thanks to his piece activity and better pawn structure, White has a large advantage.) 24.f4 h4 25.♖gg1 ♘f3 26.♖g2 e5 27.♘e8 ♗g4 28.♘xf6+ gxf6 29.♖xg4+ ♔f7 30.♖d3 ♘d4 (Black is caught in a mating net after 30...e4 31.♖d7+ ♔e6 32.♖d5 f5 33.♖g6+ ♔f7 34.♖gd6 ♖h5 35.b3 ♘xh2 36.♖d7+ ♔g8 37.♖5d6) 31.fxe5 fxe5 32.♗d6± — Black cannot keep the knight in the centre.)

20...♗xe6 21.♖xe6+ ♔f7 22.♖ed6 ♘e5 23.b3 g5 24.♗b2 ♖ae8 25.♖1d5± — White retains good winning chances.;

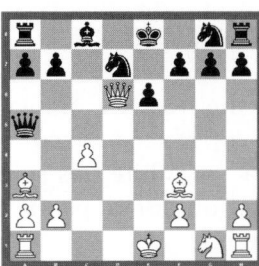

13.♔f1 ♕b6 14.♘e2

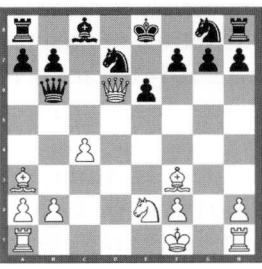

14...♕xd6

(14...f6 allows White to preserve the queens

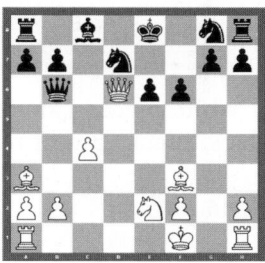

15.♕g3!

(15.♖e1 ♕xd6 16.♗xd6 ♘b6 17.b3 ♔f7 18.♘d4 ♘e7 (18...e5 19.♘b5 ♘e7 20.♗a3↑) 19.♗c5! ♖d8 20.♘b5 ♘f5 21.♗e4 e5 (21...♗d7 22.♗xf5 exf5 23.♘d6+ ♔g8 24.♖g1↑) 22.♖g1 (22.♘xa7 ♘d7 23.♘xc8 ♘xc5 24.♗xf5 ♖xa2 25.♔g2 g6 26.♗b1 ♖b2 27.♘b6 ♖dd2 28.♖hf1 ♖xb3 29.♘d5 ♖bb2 30.♖d1 ♖xd1 31.♖xd1 e4= — The bishop on b1 is greatly restricted by the black pawns so White can hardly win the position.; 22.a4 ♗e6 23.a5 ♘d7 24.♗b4↑) 22...g6 23.f4 ♗e6 24.♗xf5 ♗xf5 25.fxe5 ♘d7 26.♘d6+ ♔g8 27.♘xf5 ♘xc5 28.exf6 ♔f7 29.♘e7 ♖e8 — the f6 pawn will be lost soon, therefore Black should obtain equality.)

15...g6 16.♖e1! ♘e5 17.♘c3 ♘xf3 18.♕xf3 ♔f7 19.h4 ♗d7 20.♘e4 ♔g7 21.h5 e5 22.♖d1 ♕e6 23.♖d6 ♕f5 24.♕b3 ♗c8 (24...♗c6 25.♖xc6+-) 25.f3+-

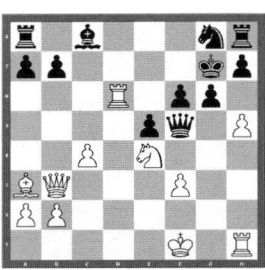

— All white pieces participate in the attack. Black cannot resist.)

15.♗xd6 f6 16.♘d4 ♘e5

(16...♔f7 17.♖e1 ♘b6 18.b3 ♘e7 (18...e5 19.♘b5 ♘e7 20.♗a3±) 19.♗c5↑ — White's initiative compensates fully for the sacrificed pawn.)

17.♗xe5 fxe5 18.♘c6! e4 19.♗xe4 ♘f6 20.♗g2 ♘d7 21.♘d4± The bishop on g2 generates strong pressure along the long diagonal and White also has a pawn advantage on the queenside, therefore it's not easy for Black to draw.

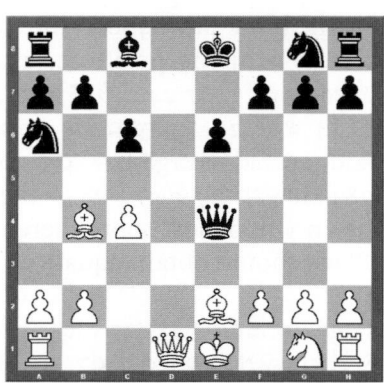

9.♗a5

This initially unobvious move creates disharmony in Black's camp.

Unpromising is 9.♗c3 Black has a reliable route to equality as well as a chance to maintain the tension 9...♘e7

(It's not easy for White demonstrate the power of his initiative after 9...f6!? 10.♘f3

(Dubious is 10.♕d6, since White's kingside development lags: 10...e5! (10...♘h6? 11.♗xf6! gxf6 12.0-0-0 ♕g6 13.♕d8+ ♔f7 14.♕xh8 ♘b4 15.♗h5 ♘xa2+ 16.♔d2 ♕xh5 17.♕xh7+ ♔e8 18.♘f3±; 10...♘e7 11.0-0-0∞) 11.♘f3

(11.♖d1 ♔f7 12.f4 (12.♕d8 ♖b8∓; 12.♘f3 ♗e6∓) 12...exf4 13.♘f3 ♘e7 14.♖d4 ♕e3 15.♗d2 ♘f5 16.♗xe3 ♘xd6∓)

11...♘h6 12.♘d2 ♕xg2 13.♗f3 ♘f7 14.♕xc6+ bxc6 15.♗xg2 ♗d7∓ — White has some compensation for a pawn but not enough.)

10...♘e7 11.0-0 0-0

(Also possible is 11...♕f4, preparing the retreat of the queen to c7. After 12.♗d3 the most reliable is 12...0-0

(12...♘c5 is interesting but still risky 13.♗c2 (13.♗b4 ♘xd3 14.♕xd3 ♔f7∞) 13...

♕xc4 14.♕d6 ♕d5 15.♕g3 0-0 16.♖ad1 ♕h5 17.♕d6 ♖e8∞ — The game is unclear.)

13.♕c2 ♕h6 — Black is ready to play e6-e5.)

12.♖e1 (After *12.♗d3* Black finds a useful square for the queen *12... ♕g4! 13.♕c2 ♘g6∓*) 12...♕f4 (*12... e5!? 13.b4∞*) 13.b4 ♕c7∞ — White's compensation should be enough for equality.)

10.♗xg7 ♖g8 11.♗f6

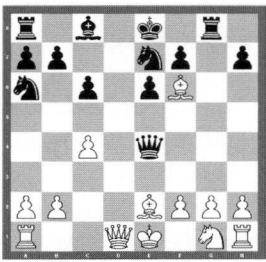

11...♕g6!N The most precise path to equality.

(Not so convincing is 11...♖g6

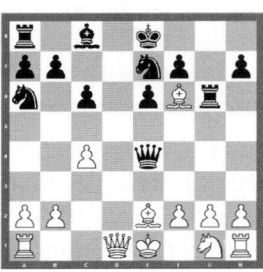

12.f3!

a) 12.♗xe7 ♔xe7 13.♕d2 e5 14.♖d1 (*14.f3 ♕d4 15.♕xd4 exd4∓*) 14...♗e6 15.f3 ♕d4 16.♕xd4 exd4 17.♔f2 ♖d8∓ Vaisser — S.Savchenko, Moscow 1992;

b) 12.♗c3 ♕xg2 13.♕d2 ♕xh1 14.0-0-0 ♘d5 15.♘f3 ♕g2 16.cxd5 exd5 17.♕d4 (*17.♖e1 ♗e6 18.♗xa6 bxa6∓*) 17...♕g4 18.♕e5+ ♗e6 19.h3 ♕g2 20.♖g1 ♕xf3 21.♖xg6 ♕h1+ 22.♔d2 hxg6 23.♕h8+ ♔d7 24.♕xa8 ♘c7 25.♕xb7 ♕h2 26.♕xa7 ♕f4+ 27.♕e3 ♕xe3+ 28.fxe3 ♗xh3∓ — White can draw with an accurate play.;

12...♕f4 13.♗xe7 ♔xe7 14.g3 ♕e3

(After 14...♕h6 strong is

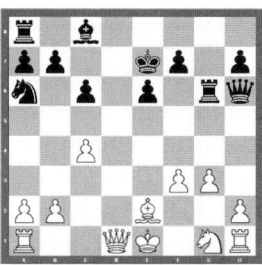

15.f4!N (*15.♕d4* Steingrimsson — Banusz, Budapest 2005 *15... c5 16.♕e4 f5 17.♕e5 ♗d7=*) 15...e5 (Wholly bad is *15...♖xg3? 16.hxg3 ♕xh1 17.♕d4 c5 18.♕e3±*, with 0-0-0 to follow Black is under attack.) 16.fxe5 ♗f5 17.♘f3 ♖d8 18.♕c1±, with an advantage.)

15.♕d3 ♕xd3 16.♗xd3 ♖g7 (Good chances for equality are given by

16...♖h6!?) 17.0‑0‑0 ♘c5 18.f4 ♗d7 19.♘f3 f6 20.♖he1 a5 Yakovich — Sherbakov, Kolontaevo 1994. Here necessary was 21.♗c2±, with b2‑b3 and a king march to c3 to follow. Then White can either increase pressure on the centre or try a2‑a3 and b3‑b4.)

12.♗h4

(12.♗c3 ♕xg2 13.♕d2 ♕xh1 14.0‑0‑0 ♘d5 15.♘f3

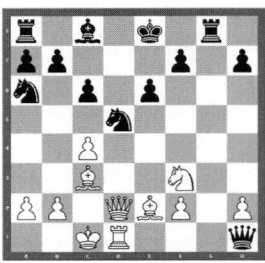

15...♕g2 (The most exact way to a draw although it seems the following is also enough for equality *15...♕xd1+ 16.♗xd1 ♘xc3 17.♕xc3 e5=*, with ♗c8‑e6 to follow.) 16.cxd5 exd5 (Risky is *16...cxd5 17.♕d4 ♗d7 18.♖g1 ♕xg1+ 19.♘xg1 ♖xg1+ 20.♔d2↑* — White's black squared play is quite dangerous.) 17.♕e3+ ♗e6 18.♗xa6 bxa6 19.♕c5 ♕xf3 20.♕xc6+ ♔e7 21.♕b7+ ♔d6 22.♕xa6+ ♔e7 23.♕b7+ ♔d6=)

12...♘b4 13.♖c1 e5 14.♘f3 ♘xa2 15.♖c2 ♗f5 16.♖d2 ♕xg2 17.♖f1 ♘b4 18.♕b3 a5

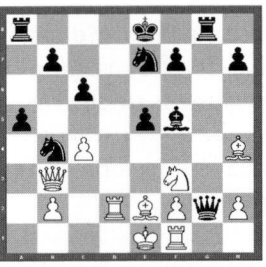

19.♕e3 ♘c2+ 20.♖xc2 ♗xc2 21.♕xe5 (21.♕b6 ♖d8 22.♕xb7 ♖d7 23.♕b8+ ♖d8 24.♕xe5 ♖d7=) 21...0‑0‑0 22.♗g3 ♖xg3 23.hxg3 ♘f5 24.♕xa5 ♘d6 25.c5 ♘e4 26.♕a8+ ♔c7 27.♕a5+ ♔c8=;

The following leads to sharp play which looks like it should end in a draw 9.♗d6 ♕xg2

a) 9...b6 10.♘f3 (*10.♕d2 leads to an unclear game 10...♗b7 11.0‑0‑0∞*) 10...♗b7 11.0‑0

(11.♘e5 leads to a draw 11...f6 12.0‑0 fxe5 13.♗h5+ g6 14.♖e1

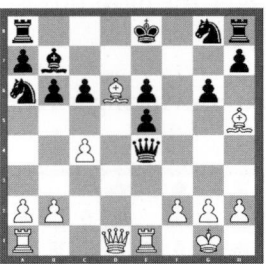

14...♕xc4! (Many opening books state that *14...♕h4 leads to a draw 15.♗g4 ♖d8 16.♖xe5 ♘c5 17.b4 ♘h6 18.bxc5 ♕xg4*, but after *19.f3 ♕h4 20.♖xe6+ ♔f7 21.g3 ♕g5 22.♕e2 ♖d7 23.f4 ♕d8 24.♖e1 ♘f5 25.g4 ♘xd6 26.cxd6 ♖f8 27.♕e5! ♕h4*

28.♖e7+ ♖xe7 29.♕xe7+ ♕xe7 30.♖xe7+ ♔f6 31.♖xb7 ♔e6 32.d7 ♔e7 33.f5 gxf5 34.d8♕+ ♔xd8 35.g5 ♖e8 36.♖xh7 ♖e4 37.h3± White has winning chances.) 15.♗xe5 ♘f6 16.♗e2 ♕d5 17.♕xd5 cxd5 18.♗xa6 ♗xa6 19.♗xf6 0-0 20.♖xe6 ♖ae8=)

11...0-0-0

a1) 11...c5 12.♘h4! 0-0-0 (12... ♕c6 13.♗f3 ♕d7 14.♗xb7 ♕xb7 15.♕g4±; 12...♕xh4 13.♕a4+ ♔d8 14.♖ad1+- Onischuk — Shulman, Minneapolis 2005) 13.♗f3 ♕xc4 14.♗xb7+ ♔xb7 15.♕f3+ ♕d5 16.♕xf7+ ♔a8 17.♕xg7 ♕xd6 18.♕xh8 ♕e7 19.♖ad1 ♖f8 20.♕e5 ♕xh4 21.♕xe6±;

a2) 11...♖d8 12.♕d2 c5 13.♖ad1 ♘f6 (13...♘e7 14.♕g5+-; 13... ♘b4 14.a3 ♘c6 15.♗d3 ♕g4 16.h3 ♕h5 17.♕f4± Cheparinov — Krasenkow, Wijk aan Zee 2008) 14.♖fe1 ♘b4 15.a3 ♕c6 16.axb4 ♘e4 17.♕f4 ♘xd6 18.♖d2 f6 19.♘h4 0-0 20.♗f3 e5 21.♗xc6 exf4 22.♖xd6 ♖xd6 23.♗xb7 cxb4 24.♗d5+ ♔h8 25.♘f5 (25.♖e7!?) 25...♖dd8 26.♘d4± White's pieces are planted firmly in the centre and therefore he has an advantage.;

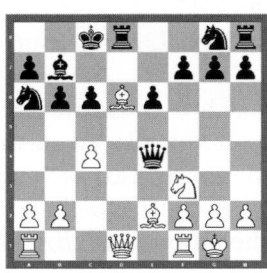

12.♘e5! ♕f5

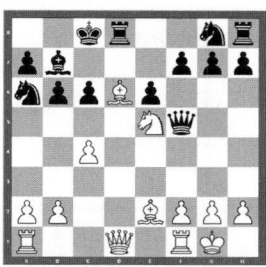

13.g4!N It turns out that the black queen is short of retreat squares. (13.♗g4 ♕f6 14.♗f3 ♘e7 15.♗xe7 ♕xe7 16.♕a4 ♕c7= Verduga — Vera, Habana 1986) 13...♕f4

(After 13...♕f6 White keeps chasing the queen: 14.f4! h6 (14...c5 15.♗f3 ♗xf3 16.♕xf3 ♖xd6 17.♖ad1+-) 15.♕d2 ♘e7 (15...♕e7 16.♖fd1 ♕e8 17.♕e3) 16.♗f3 Black has been pushed back to his last lines while White threatens to bring the rook into action with decisive effect. There is no defence against the simple ♖a1-d1, for example:

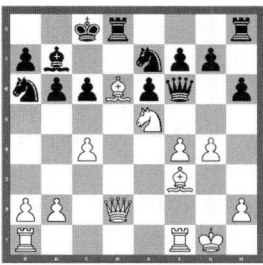

16...♘g6 (16...♘c7 17.♖ad1 ♘e8 18.♗xe7 ♖xd2 19.♗xf6 ♖xd1 20.♖xd1 ♘xf6 21.♘xf7 ♖f8 22.♘d6+ ♔c7 23.♘xb7 ♔xb7 24.g5+-) 17.♗xc6 ♗xc6 18.♘xc6 ♕h4 19.♘xd8 ♕xg4+ 20.♔h1

♖xd8 21.♖ad1+- — White has an extra exchange and the initiative so he should win.)

14.♘g6 ♕xd6 15.♕xd6 ♖xd6 16.♘xh8 ♖d7 17.♖ad1 ♖e7 18.g5±

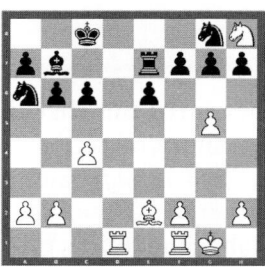

— The knight on h8 cannot be caught therefore White has a big advantage.

b) Bad is 9...♗d7, since it blocks a potential attack on the d6 bishop along the d-file. After the simple 10.♘f3 c5 11.♘e5 ♗c6 12.♘xc6 bxc6 13.0-0 it looks difficult for Black, Taimanov — Steiner, Saltsjobaden 1952;

c) 9...e5 10.♘f3 ♗g4

(10...f6 11.0-0 ♗e6 (*11...♗f5 12.♘xe5!+-*) 12.♖e1 0-0-0 13.♗d3 ♕g4 14.h3 ♕h5 15.c5 ♘c7 16.♕a4 ♘e8 17.♘d4!+-)

11.0-0 0-0-0 12.♗d3

(There is no advantage after 12.b4 ♘f6 13.c5 (*13.♖e1 ♗xf3 14.♗xf3 ♕xc4 15.♖xe5 ♘c7! 16.♖c1 ♕f4 17.♖d5 ♕xc1 18.♕xc1 ♘fxd5∓*) 13...

♘e8! 14.♗d3 (*14.♖c1 ♘xd6 15.cxd6 ♔b8= Kornev — Galkin, Sochi 2008*) 14...♕f4 (*14...♕xb4 15.♖b1 ♕a3 16.♘xe5+-*) 15.♗xe5 ♕xb4 16.♖b1 ♕a5 17.♕c2 (*17.♗xa6 ♕xa6 18.♕b3∞/=*) 17...♘xc5 18.♗f5+ (*18.♖b5 cxb5 19.♕xc5+ ♘c7 20.♖c1 ♖xd3 21.♗xc7 ♖d1+ 22.♖xd1 ♕xc7 23.♕xa7 ♗xf3 24.gxf3 ♕c2!= Vitiugov — Frolyanov, Sochi 2006*) 18...♗xf5 19.♕xf5+ ♘d7 (*19...♘e6 20.♕xf7 ♘8c7 21.♕f5⩲*) 20.♕xf7 (*20.♕h3!?∞*) 20...♖f8 21.♕b3⩲ — White has sufficient compensation for a pawn but nothing more.)

12...♕f4 13.♗xe5 ♕xe5 14.♘xe5 ♗xd1 15.♗f5+ (*15.♘xf7 ♗g4*) 15...♔c7 16.♘xf7

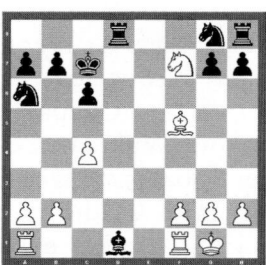

16...♘h6

c1) 16...♗h5 17.♘xd8 ♔xd8 18.g4 ♘h6 19.♖ad1+ ♔c7 20.♖d7+ ♔b6 21.♖xg7 ♘xf5 22.gxf5± Aronian — Vallejo Pons, Linares 2006;

c2) 16...♘e7 17.♘xd8! (Stronger than *17.♗xh7*, played in the well-known game Tal — Dorfman, Tbilisi 1978. If Black had gone into the line *17...♖xh7! 18.♘xd8*

♗g4 19.♘f7±, White's advantage would not have been so large.) 17...♖xd8 18.♗xh7 ♗h5 19.♖ae1 ♖d7 20.♗b1!± — The bishop has evaded all possible attacks. White has an advantage.;

17.♘xh8!

c1) 17.♘xh6?! 17...♗e2! (*17...♗h5 18.♗g4 ♗xg4 19.♘xg4 ♖d2 = Bacrot — Tregubov, Corsico 2005*) 18.♖fe1 ♖d2 19.♗g4 ♖e8∓;

c2) 17.♘xd8 ♖xd8 18.♗xh7 ♗e2;

17...♘xf5 (*17...♗e2 18.♖fe1 ♘xf5 19.♖xe2 ♖xh8 20.g4±; 17...♖xh8 18.♗xh7 ♗h5 19.♗c2 ♘b4 20.♗d1 ♗g6 21.♖e1±; 17...♗h5 18.♗xh7 ♖xh8 — 17...♖h8 18.♗xh7 ♗h5*) 18.♘f7 ♖d7 19.♘e5 ♗e2 20.♘xd7 ♗xf1 21.♘e5 ♗e2 22.f4±

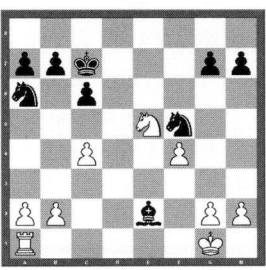

— The black knights have no outposts in the centre, therefore in this complicated endgame, with a non-standard material balance, White's chances are better.

d) 9...♘h6? Bad 10.♘f3 ♘f5 11.0-0 ♘xd6 12.♕xd6 ♕f5 13.♘e5 ♕f6 14.♘xc6+-;

10.♕d2 (*10.♗f3 ♕g5∓*) 10...♘f6 11.♗f3 ♕g6 12.0-0-0 (*12.♘e2 e5 13.0-0-0 — 12.0-0-0 e5 13.♘e2*) 12...e5 13.♗xe5

(13.♘e2 Usually transposes to the main line can also be of independent significance: 13...♗e6

a) 13...♕f5 14.♕e3 ♗e6 15.♖hg1 — 13...♗e6 14.♖hg1 ♕f5 15.♕e3;

b) 13...♗g4!?

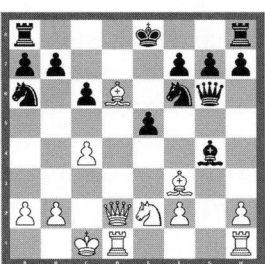

14.♖hg1

b1) If 14.♗xe5 ♗xf3 15.♖hg1 ♕f5 16.♘d4 ♕xe5 17.♘xf3 ♕c7 18.♖xg7 White can only hope for salvation by perpetual check 18...♘c5 (Also leading to a repetition is *18...♖g8 19.♖xg8+ ♘xg8 20.♕g5 ♘e7 21.♕f6 ♘g8 22.♕g5 ♘e7=*) 19.♖e1+ ♔f8 20.♘e5 ♔xg7 21.♕g5+ ♔f8 22.♘d7+ ♕xd7 23.♕xc5+ ♔g7 24.♕g5+=;

b2) 14.♗xg4 ♘xg4 15.f3 ♘f2 (*15...0-0-0 16.fxg4 ♖he8 17.♘c3*

♖e6 18.c5 ♘xc5 19.♕e3 ♖exd6 20.♕xc5 ♕g5+ 21.♔c2 ♕g6+=) 16.♗xe5 ♘xd1 17.♖xd1 ♘c5 18.b4! (*18.♘f4 ♕g5 19.♕d6 Gajewski — Kempinski, Ustron 2006 19... ♖d8 20.♕xc5 ♖xd1+ 21.♔xd1 f6 22.♗d6 ♕xc5 23.♗xc5 ♔f7∓*) 18... ♕f5 19.♗xg7 ♖g8 20.♗b2 ♘e6 21.♕d7+ ♔f8 22.♕d6+ ♔e8=;

14...0-0-0 15.♕e3 h5

(15...♖d7 16.♘c3 ♕h5 17.♘e4 ♗xf3 18.♕xa7 ♕h6+ 19.♖g5 ♖c7 (*19...♘c7 20.♘c5 ♕xg5+ 21.♔b1 ♕f5+ 22.♔a1 ♖xd6 23.♕xb7+ ♔d8 24.♖xd6+ ♘d7 25.b4±/↑ —* White's initiative is very strong. Black has to defend accurately.) 20.♕a8+ ♔d7 21.♗xc7+ ♗xd1 22.♕xh8 ♘xc7 23.♕xg7 ♕xg7 24.♖xg7 ♔e7 25.♘xf6 ♗xf6 26.♖xh7∞ — A complicated endgame with mutual chances has arisen.)

16.h3 ♖xd6 17.♖xd6 ♘b4 18.♕b3 ♕h6+ 19.♔d1 ♗xf3 20.♕xf3 ♕h7 21.♘c3 ♕c2+ 22.♔e1 e4 23.♕f5+ ♔b8 Moiseenko — Pavasovic, Dresden 2007

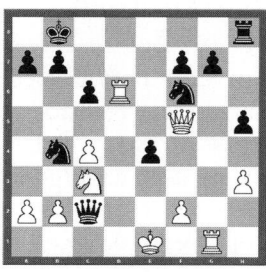

24.♕e5 ♔c8 (*24...♔a8 25.♕d4=*) 25.♕f5+=;

14.♗xe5

(14.♖hg1 ♕f5 15.♕e3 0-0-0

(15...h6 16.♘g3 ♕g5 (*16...♕f4 17.♕xf4 exf4 18.♗xf4 ♖d8 19.♗d6 ♖d7 20.b3⇄*) 17.♗xe5 ♕xe3+ 18.fxe3 ♖d8=)

16.♖g5 ♕h3 17.♘c3 e4 (*17...♕h6 18.♗xe5⇄*) 18.♕xa7 ♖xd6 19.♖xd6 ♕xf3 20.♖xc6+ bxc6 21.♕xa6+=)

14...♕f5 15.♗f4 — 12.0-0-0 e5 13.♗xe5 ♗e6 14.♘e2 ♕f5 15.♗f4)

13...♗e6! Black retains the possibility of castling long.

(13...0-0 14.♘e2 ♗g4 (*14...♕f5 15.♕e3 ♘b4 16.♘d4 ♘xa2+ 17.♔d2 ♖d8 18.♔e2 ♕g6 19.♖hg1 ♗g4 20.♗xf6 ♕xf6 21.♖xg4 c5 22.♘b5±*) 15.♗xg4 (*15.♖hg1 ♗xf3 16.♖xg6 fxg6±*) 15...♘xg4 16.♗c3 ♘c5 17.f3 ♘d3+ 18.♕xd3 ♕xd3 19.♖xd3 ♘f2 20.♖dd1±)

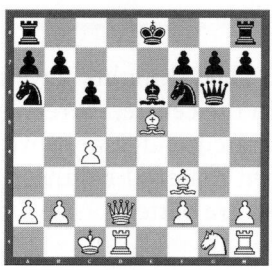

14.♘e2 ♕f5 15.♗f4 (15.♕e3? 15...
♘b4 16.♘d4 ♘xa2+ 17.♔d2 0-0-
0!+−) 15...♗xc4 (15...♕c5 16.b3 ♘d5
17.♗e5 0-0-0 18.♗d4 ♕a3+ 19.♕b2
♕xb2+ 20.♔xb2 ♘f6 21.♗xa7±
Gustafsson — Pavasovic, Rogatska
Slatina 2009)

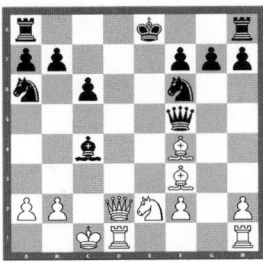

16.♖hg1

(16.♘g3 ♕c5 17.♗e3 ♕b4 (17...
♕b5 18.♘e4 ♘xe4 19.♕d7+ ♔f8
20.♗xe4⊒) 18.♘f5 ♕xd2+ 19.♖xd2

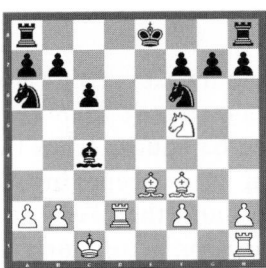

19...♔f8!N There are no queens on
the board and Black can afford to
play without connecting rooks in
return for a pair of extra pawns. After a possible (19...♗d5 20.♘xg7+↑
Gupta — Aswin,Gaziantep 2008)
20.♖g1 ♖g8 21.♗f4 ♘e8 22.♘d6
g5∓ White's piece activity will only
be enough for a draw.)

16...♗xa2 17.♕e3+ ♕e6 18.♗e5
(18.♕c3 ♕c4∓) 18...♕e7 (18...♖d8
19.♘f4⊒) 19.♗g5

a) 19.♖xg7 ♘d7 20.♖xd7 (20.♖g5 h6
21.♖f5 ♖g8 22.♘c3 0-0-0 23.♘xa2
♕e6 24.♕f4 ♖g5 25.♗g4 ♖xg4
26.♕xg4 ♘xe5 27.♖xd8+ ♔xd8∓
— Only White is in danger.) 20...
♔xd7 21.♘c3 ♘c5 22.♗g4+ ♔d8
23.♖g5 f6 24.♕xc5 ♕xc5 25.♗xf6+
♕e7 26.♗xe7+ ♔xe7 27.♘xa2 ♖ag8
28.♖e5+ ♔d6 29.♖e6+ ♔c7∓;

b) 19.♘g3 ♕c5+ (19...♘d5 20.♗xd5
♗xd5 21.♘f5 ♕c5+ 22.♕xc5 ♘xc5
23.♗xg7 ♖g8 24.♘h6 0-0-0
25.♘xg8 ♖xg8=) 20.♕xc5 ♘xc5
21.♘f5 ♖d8 (21...♗d5 22.♖ge1↑)
22.♘xg7+ (22.♘d6+ ♔f8 23.♖xg7
♔xg7 24.♘f5+ ♔g6 25.♘e7+
♔g7=) 22...♔e7 23.♘f5+ (23.♗d6+
♖xd6 24.♘f5+ ♔e6 25.♘xd6 ♗d5
26.♗xd5+ ♘xd5 27.♘c4 f5= Black's
chances are no worse thanks to his
excellent centralisation.) 23...♔e6
24.♘g7+ ♔e7=;

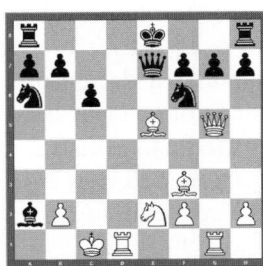

19...♘d7 20.♕xe7+ ♔xe7 21.♗d6+
♔f6 22.♘c3 ♗b3 23.♘e4+ ♔e6
24.♘g5+ ♔f6 25.♘e4+= Doric —
Pavasovic, Lasko 2011

9...b6

After 9...♗d7 10.♘f3 Black is forced to move the knight to f6 though he would like to place pawns on f6 and e5. 10...♘f6 11.0–0

a) 11.♕d6 ♕f5 12.♘e5 ♕xf2+ 13.♔xf2 ♘e4+ 14.♔f3 ♘xd6 15.♖hd1 ♔e7 16.♖d2 ♗e8 17.♖ad1 ♘f5∞ Li Chao — Shulman, Khanty-Mansyisk 2010;

b) Interesting is 11.♕d2!?N which has not occurred in practice. The best reply is

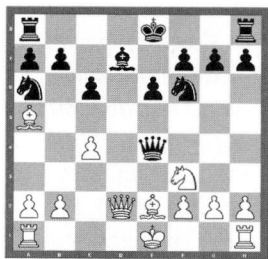

11...e5!, preventing long castling 12.0–0–0 because of 12...♗f5.

(White's idea emerges after 11...♕f5 12.0–0–0 e5 (12...♘c5 13.g4!→ — White starts a dangerous attack) 13.♖he1 (Not so clear is 13.♕d6 e4 14.♘e5 ♕e6) 13...♗e6 (13...0–0 14.g4 ♕e4 15.h3 ♗e6 16.♘g5 ♕f4 17.♕xf4 exf4 18.♘xe6 fxe6 19.♗f3±) 14.♗f1 e4 15.♘d4↑)

12.0–0 (12.♕d6 poses no problems 12...b6 13.♗c3 0–0–0 14.♘xe5 ♖he8 15.f3 ♕e3=) 12...♕f5 13.♕d6 e4 14.♘e5 ♕e6 15.c5 (White also has

compensation after 15.♖ad1 ♕xd6 16.♖xd6 ♗e6=, however there is no question of any serious advantage.) 15...♕xd6 16.cxd6 ♘c5 17.♖ac1 ♘e6 18.f3 exf3 19.♗xf3 ♘d4 20.♖ce1 ♗e6 21.♗g4 0–0 22.♗xe6 ♘xe6 23.d7

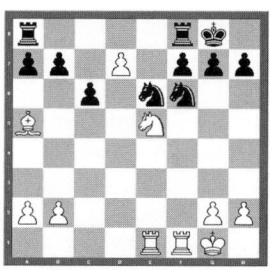

23...♖ab8= The idea of this unexpected move is to play b7-b6 with tempo and then immediately ♖b8-b7. It seems that after simplification it will be a draw.;

11...♕f5

(11...0–0 12.♖e1 ♕f4 (No better is 12...c5 13.♗d3 ♕c6 14.a3! taking the b4 square from the black knight and preparing ♗a5-c3, ♘f3-e5, and then ♖e1-e3, swinging the rook across for a kingside attack.) 13.♗f1!± White keeps the d-file open and provides e5 for the knight. White's advantage is indisputable, as his initiative is full compensation for the sacrificed pawn.)

12.♕e1! (Double-edged is 12.♗c3 ♘e4 13.♗xg7 ♖g8∞) 12...c5 (The following requires flexible play from White 12...0–0 13.♗c3 ♖fd8

14.♘e5 ♗e8 The initiative can only be developed by means of *15.f4!* *♘c5 16.♖f3!* The 3rd rank is crucial. White prepares the deployment of the rook to the kingside and enables the involvement of the bishop via d3 after a preliminary b2-b4.) 13.♖d1!N

(Less energetic is *13.♗c3 ♗c6 14.a3 ♖d8!* (Bad is *14...♘b8 15.♘e5 ♘bd7 16.♘xc6 bxc6 17.f4±* — The bishops attack squares over the whole board. Black also has a damaged pawn structure, Lysyj — Vitiugov,Serpukhov 2008) *15.♘e5 ♘b8*, with a defensible position.)

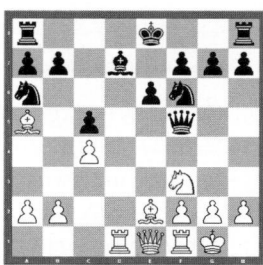

13... ♗c6 14. ♗d3 ♕h5 15.♘e5 ♘g4 16.♘xg4 ♕xg4 17.f3 Black is behind in development and the a6 knight a6 is out of the game. White has excellent prospects. For example

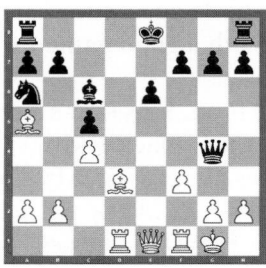

17...♕g5 (If *17...♕d4+ 18.♖f2* the black queen will be attacked.) 18.♗e4

(Interesting is *18.a3!?* *18...0–0 19.♗c2* White plans kingside play, for example: *19...♖fe8 20.♕f2 b6 21.♗c3 ♖ad8* (*21...e5 22.b4↑*) *22.f4 ♕e7 23.♖de1↑*, with a strong initiative.)

18... ♗xe4 19.♕xe4 ♕e7 20.♖d2 ♘b4 21.♖fd1 ♘c6 22.♗c3 f6 23.♖d6 ♖d8 24.♖xe6 ♖xd1+ 25.♔f2 ♖d7 26.♖xe7+ ♖xe7 27.♕d5 ♘b4 28.♗xb4 cxb4 29.c5±

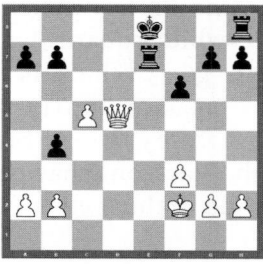

— In this resulting major piece endgame there are many intricacies. The black rooks are not coordinated and the b4 pawn will soon fall. White retains ongoing pressure and some winning chances.

9...f6 10.♘f3

(The following is not so dangerous 10.♕d8+ ♔f7

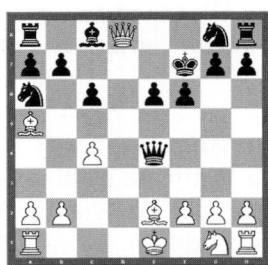

11.♘f3

a) 11.0-0-0 b6 12.♗c3 e5 13.♗d3 ♕xg2 (*13...♕f4+∞*) 14.♘e2 c5 15.♘g3 ♗e6 16.♕d6 ♘e7 17.♗e4 ♕xf2 18.♖hf1 ♕e3+ 19.♖d2 ♖ad8 20.♕xe5 ♖xd2 21.♗xd2 (*21.♗g6+ hxg6 22.♕xe3 ♖d7∓* — Black's king is safe and he has excellent play on the white squares.) 21...♕d4 22.♕h5+ g6 23.♕h4 ♘f5 24.♘xf5 ♕xc4+ 25.♗c3 ♕xf1+ 26.♔d2 ♖d8+ 27.♔e3 = — Strangely enough, Black only has perpetual check and nothing else.;

b) 11.♖d1 e5 12.♘f3 b6 13.♗c3 ♘c5 14.♗b4 ♘e7 15.♕xh8 ♗b7 16.♖d8 ♕b1+ 17.♗d1 ♕e4+ 18.♔d2 ♕f4+ 19.♔c2 ♕f5+= — Black takes the perpetual check.;

11...b6

(Also possible is 11...e5 12.♖d1 b6 13.♗c3 ♘c5 14.♗b4 ♘e7 15.♕xh8 ♗b7 16.♖d8 ♕b1+ 17.♗d1 ♕e4+ 18.♔d2 ♕f4+ 19.♔c2 ♕f5+ 20.♔c1 (*20.♔d2 ♕f4+=*) 20...♖xd8 21.♕xd8 ♘d3+ 22.♔d2 ♘xb4 23.a3 ♕f4+ 24.♔c3 ♘a2+ 25.♔b3 (*25.♔c2 ♕f5+ 26.♔b3*

♘c1+ 27.♔c3 ♘d5+ 28.♔d2 ♕f4+ 29.♔c2 ♕xc4+ 30.♔b1 ♘d3 31.♕d7+ ♔f8 32.♕d8+=*) 25...♘c1+ 26.♔c3 (*26.♔c2 ♕xc4+ 27.♔b1 c5 28.♘d2 ♕d3+ 29.♕xd3 ♘xd3 30.♗b3+ ♗d5∓*) 26... ♘a2+=, with perpetual check.)

12.♗c3 ♗b7 (*12...♘c5!?*) 13.♕d7+ ♘e7 14.♕xb7 ♘c5 15.♕c7 ♖hc8 16.♕g3 ♘f5

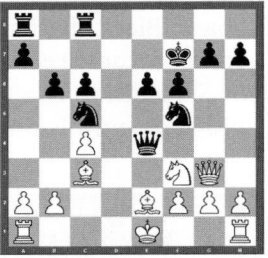

17.♕g5! (*17.♘g5+ fxg5 18.♕xg5 ♘d3+ 19.♔f1 ♖f8!∓*) 17...♔e7 (*17...h6 18.♕h5+ g6 19.♘d2 gxh5 20.♘xe4 ♘xe4 21.♗xh5+ ♔e7 22.♗b4+ c5 23.♗f3 ♘fd6 24.♗a3±*) 18.♕h5 ♘d3+ 19.♔f1 ♘f4 20.♗xf6+ ♔xf6 21.♕g5+ ♔f7 22.♖e1 ♔g8 23.♘d2 ♕e5 24.♘f3 ♕e4=, with a repetition of moves.)

10...b6 11.♘d2! (*If 11.♗c3 Black has won an important tempo for developing the kingside 11...♘e7 12.0-0 0-0∞*, with a good game.) 11...♕f4

(11...♕f5 12.♗h5+! It's important to weaken Black's kingside dark squares. 12...g6 13.♗f3 ♘e7 (*13... ♕e5+ — 11...♕f4 12.♗h5+ g6 13.♗f3 ♕e5+*) 14.♗c3 e5

(14...0-0 15.0-0 e5

(15...♖d8 16.♕e2 e5 (16...♘c5 17.♘e4±) 17.♘e4 ♕e6 18.♖ad1 ♗b7 19.♗g4 f5 (19...♘f5 20.f4!±) 20.♘g5 ♕f6 21.♗f3 h6 22.♘h3 g5 23.♗xe5 ♕e6 24.♗b8!+–)

16.♘e4)

15.0-0 0-0 (15...♕e6 16.♘e4 ♘f5 17.♘xf6+ ♕xf6 18.♗xe5 ♕xe5 19.♖e1 ♕xe1+ 20.♕xe1+ ♔f7 21.♗xc6+–) 16.♘e4 ♕e6

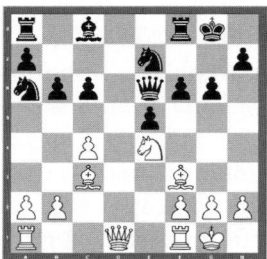

17.♖e1! White plans the destruction of the defensive pawn wedge f6-e5 which the weakening g7-g6 has enabled. 17...♘f5

(After 17...♗b7 White can use the same motif in another combination:

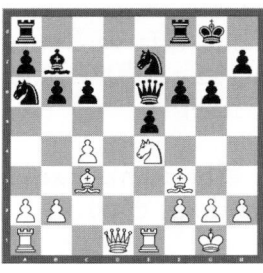

18.♘g5! ♕c8 19.♖xe5!! 19...♘f5 (19...fxe5 20.♕d6+–) 20.♕e2 ♘c5 21.♖d1 fxg5 22.b4! (Even stronger than 22.♖xc5 bxc5 23.♕e5 ♘d4 24.♖xd4 cxd4 25.♕xd4 ♔f7 26.♗g4 ♕d8 27.♕g7+ ♔e8 28.♕xb7 ♖f7 29.♕xc6+ ♔f8 30.h4 gxh4 31.♗e6± — White wins back one exchange and still has black squared play and a pair of connected pawns on the queenside.) 22...♘a4 23.♗a1+- — White's attack cannot be repelled.)

18.♘xf6+! ♖xf6 19.♖xe5 ♕d6 (White's task is easier after 19...♕d7 20.♕e2 ♗b7 21.♗g4! The main defender of the black squares is eliminated. 21...♖f7 22.♗xf5 gxf5 23.♖d1+- Riazantsev — Sjugirov, Ulan Ude 2009) 20.♕e1! To have b4 for the bishop when the knight leaves a6. (20.♕e2 ♘c7∞)

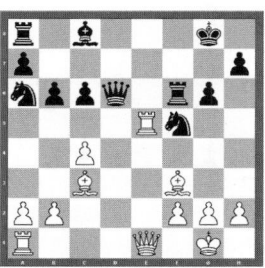

20...♖e6

(20...♘c7 21.♖d1 ♕f8 22.♗b4 c5 (22...♕f7 23.♖d8+ ♔g7 24.g4+-) 23.♗xc5 bxc5 24.♗xa8±)

21.♖d1 ♖xe5 22.♗xe5 ♕e6 23.♖d8+ ♔f7 The queen o n e6 is

in a sticky position and can only move to e7, where she can be attacked by ♖d8-h8-h7. White can exploit the situation with the problem-like

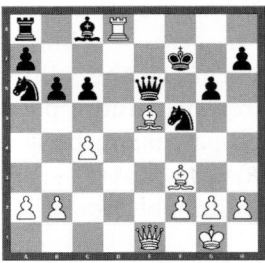

24.♗d5!! 24...cxd5 25.cxd5 ♕e7 (25...♕d7 26.♖xd7+ ♗xd7 27.♗c3 ♖e8 28.♕c1+- — There is no defence against the threats g2-g4 and ♕c1-g5.) 26.♖h8 ♕h4 27.♗c3 ♘c7 28.♕e5 ♗d7 29.g3+- Checkmate or large material losses are inevitable.)

12.♗h5+ g6 13.♗f3

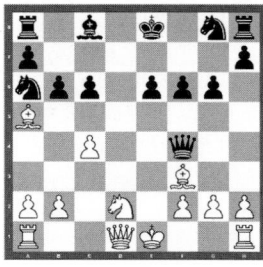

13...♕e5+

(13...♘e7 14.♗c3 0-0

(14...♘c5 15.0-0 (After 15.g3, as played in the game Volkov —

Kempinski, Dresden 2007, possible is 15...♕c7 16.♗xf6 0-0 17.♗xe7 ♕xe7 18.0-0 ♗b7 19.♕e2 ♖ad8± — White has only a minimal advantage.) 15...0-0 16.b4 ♘d7 (16...♘d3 17.♗e2 ♘e5 18.g3 ♕h6 19.♘e4±) 17.♖e1 ♕c7 18.♘e4 ♘f5 19.♕d2 e5 20.♖ad1± — It's hard for Black to complete his development.)

15.♘e4

(15.0-0 e5

(15...♕c7 16.♘e4 e5 17.♖e1 ♘f5 (17...♕d7 18.♕e2 ♕e6 19.♖ad1 ♘f5 Akobian — Shulman, 2010 20.g4 ♘h4 21.♖d6 ♕e7 22.♖xc6 ♘xf3+ 23.♕xf3 ♗e6 24.♘xf6+! ♖xf6 25.♖xe6+-) 18.♘xf6+ ♖xf6 19.♗xe5 ♕e7 20.♗xf6 ♕xf6 21.♖e8+ ♔g7 22.♕d8 ♕f7 23.♖ae1 ♗b7 24.♖1e7 ♖xd8 25.♖xf7+ ♔xf7 26.♖xd8± — The white rook is able to move from side to side. It's hard for Black to defend his pawns.)

16.♘e4 ♗f5 17.♗d2 ♕h4 18.♖e1 g5

(18...♖ad8 19.g3 ♕h3 20.♗g2 ♕g4 (20...♕h5 21.♕xh5 gxh5 22.♗h6 ♖f7 23.♖ad1+-) 21.f3 ♕h5 22.g4 ♕h4 23.gxf5 gxf5 24.♘f2±)

19.g3 ♕h6 20.h4 ♗xe4 21.♖xe4 ♘c5 22.hxg5 ♕g7)

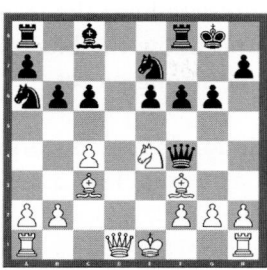

15...♘c5 16.g3 ♕f5 17.♕e2↑, with the initiative.)

14.♔f1 ♕c7 15.♗c3 e5 (15...♔f7 16.♘e4 e5 — 15...e5 16.♘e4 ♔f7) 16.♘e4 ♔f7

(16...♘c5 17.♘xc5! (17.♕d6 ♕xd6 18.♘xd6+ ♔e7 19.♗xc6 ♖b8 20.♘xc8+ ♖xc8 = Lysyi — Galkin, Sochi 2005) 17...bxc5 18.♗a5! ♕xa5 19.♗xc6+ ♔f7 20.♗xa8 ♘e7 21.♗d5+ ♔g7 22.h4± Black's compensation for the exchange is obviously insufficient.)

17.♘d6+!N

a) 17.h4 h5∞;

b) 17.b4 ♘e7 18.♕e2 ♘f5 19.h4 h5∞ Maletin — J.Geller, Moscow 2011;

c) 17.♕a4!?

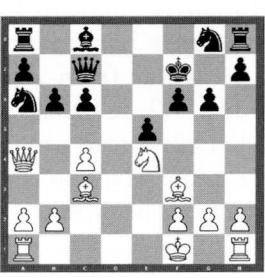

17...♖b8! With the idea b6-b5 with tempo.

(17...♘e7 18.♕a3 ♘c5 19.♘xc5 bxc5 20.♕xc5 (20.♗a5!? ♕b7 21.♖d1⩱) 20...♕b6 21.♗b4 ♕xc5 22.♗xc5 ♗f5 23.b3±)

18.♕a3 (18.♖d1 ♘e7 19.♖d6 ♘c5 20.♖xf6+ ♔g7 21.♘xc5 bxc5 22.♖f4 ♘f5 23.♖e4 ♘d4 24.h4 ♗f5 25.♖e3 h5∞; 18.g4!?∞) 18...♕e7 19.♘d6+ ♔g7 20.♗xc6 (20.♖d1 ♘h6∞) 20...♗e6 21.f4 exf4 (21...e4 22.♖e1 ♘c5 23.♘xe4 ♗xc4+ 24.♔g1 ♘xe4 25.♕xe7+ ♘xe7 26.♖xe4 ♘xc6 27.♖xc4 ♖hc8 28.♔f2±) 22.♗d2

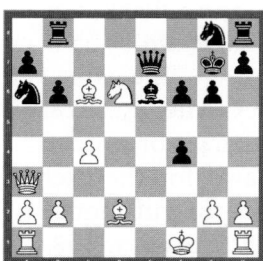

22...♘c5 23.♗xf4 ♖d8 24.♕g3 h5 25.h4 ♘h6 26.♖e1 ♖xd6 27.♗xd6 ♘f5 28.♗xe7 ♘xg3+ 29.♔g1 ♖c8 30.♗b5 ♘ce4=;

17...♔f8

(17...♔e7 A Very accurate play is required to pose problems for Black after 18.♘b5 (18.♘xc8+ ♖xc8 19.b4∞) 18...cxb5 19.♗xa8 ♕xc4+ 20.♔g1 ♗g4 21.♕e1! (21.♗f3 ♘h6=) 21...♔f7 22.h3 ♗f5

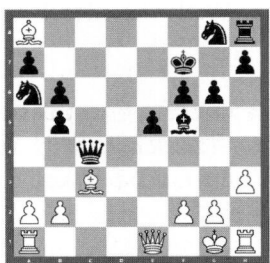

23. ♗f3!

(23.b3 ♕e6 24.g4 ♗d3 25.♖d1 (25.
♕e3 ♘e7 26.♕xd3 ♖xa8 27.♕xb5
♘c7) 25...♘e7 26.♖xd3 ♖xa8
27.♕d2 ♘c5 28.♖d6 ♕c8 29.f3
♘b7 30.♖d3 ♘c5 31.♖d6=)

23...♘e7 24.♗e2 ♕c6 25.♖c1
(After 25.a4 Black can reply 25...
bxa4! 26.♗xa6 b5 27.♗xe5 ♕xa6
28.♗g3∞ — The game is unclear.)
25...♘c5 (After 25...♖c8 White can
play 26.a4± or 26.♕f1± — Just
one pawn for the exchange isn't
enough for full equality.) 26.b4
♘d3 27.♗xd3 ♗xd3 28.♗xe5 ♗c4
29.♗g3 To connect the rooks ♔h2
is necessary. The bishop will defend the king against checks along
the diagonal. 29...h5 30.h4 ♘f5
31.♔h2 g5 32.♕d2 gxh4 33.♗f4±
— White stands better.)

18.♘b5 cxb5 19.♗xa8

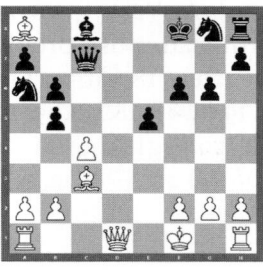

19...b4! Only to keep the f6-e5 pawn
wedge and allow the black knights
to become strong pieces.

a) Bad is 19...♕xc4+ 20.♔g1 b4, in
view of 21.♗xe5! fxe5 22.♖c1 ♕e6
23.♕d8++-;

b) After 19...bxc4 White prepares the
f2 square for his king and activates
the c3 bishop : 20.f4! exf4

b1) 20...♘c5 21.fxe5 fxe5 (21...♘d3
22.exf6±) 22.♕f3+ ♔g7 23.♖e1
♘d3 24.♕xd3±;

b2) 20...♗f5 21.fxe5 ♗d3+ 22.♔f2
♕c5+ 23.♔g3 ♘h6 24.h3±;

b3) 20...b5 21.a3 exf4 22.♕d4±;

21.♕d4 ♗e6 (21...♗f5 22.♗d5
♗d3+ 23.♔f2 ♕c5 24.♕xc5+ ♘xc5
25.♖he1±) 22.♗d5 ♗xd5 23.♕xd5
♔g7 (23...♕f7 24.♖d1±) 24.♖d1
♘c5 25.♕xc4 ♘h6 (25...♘e7 26.b4
♘f5 -25...♘h6 26.b4 ♘f5) 26.b4 ♘f5
27.♖d3 ♘e3+ 28.♖xe3 fxe3 29.bxc5
♕c6 30.♔e1! e2 31.♔f2±;

20.♗d2 ♕xc4+ 21.♔g1 ♘e7 The resulting position is very complicated
and it seems that Black can hold the
fort with correct play. At the same
time the game has an unforcing
nature. However from a practical
standpoint, White's task is easier
and he benefits from any opening
up of the game. Here are some possible directions of subsequent play:

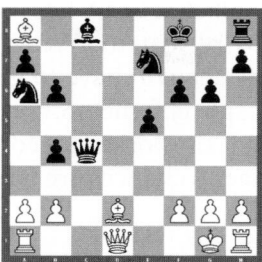

22. ♗f3

(Also interesting is 22.♖c1 ♕d4 23.♕e2 ♔g7 24.♗e3 ♕d6 25.h4 ♘c7 26.♖d1 ♘ed5 27.♗xd5 ♘xd5 28.h5 ♗e6 29.♕f3 ♖d8 30.hxg6 hxg6 31.♖xh8 ♔xh8 32.♕xf6 was threatened (If 29...g5 White has an advantage 30.h6+ ♔f7 31.♗xg5±) 30.hxg6 hxg6 31.♕g3↑ — The initiative is with White.)

22...♔g7 23.h4 The pawn wants to advance to h6, and if h7-h5 White can simply use the h2 square for his king. 23...h5 24.a3 b3 25.♖c1 ♕d4 26.♗e3 ♕xb2 27.♕d6 ♖e8 28.♖xc8 ♘xc8 29.♕d7+ ♖e7 30.♕xc8±

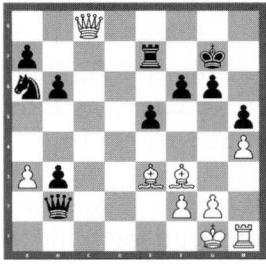

The position remains sharp but it's Black who must save himself.

The following move is not very easy 9...♕h4, with the idea of returning the queen back to base on e7. White has a lot of tempting possibilities, but most of all I like the following: 10.♗c3! (10.♘f3 ♕e7 11.0-0 ♘f6 12.♗c3 0-0∞ Bublei — Kezin, Novosibirsk 2007; 10.♕d2 ♘h6∞) 10...f6 (10...♘f6 11.♘f3 ♕h6 12.♗d3↑ — The queen is badly placed on h6, and the white bishops control the whole board.) 11.♗h5+!N White provokes a weakening of the black squares. (11.♕d6 ♘h6 12.♘f3 ♕e4 13.0-0-0 ♘f7 14.♕d2 e5 15.♗d3 ♕g4 16.h3 ♕e6∞ Thompson — Papin, Reykjavic 2012)

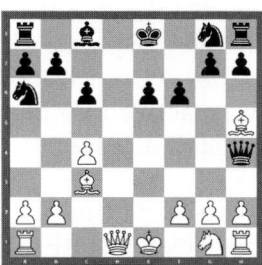

11...g6

(11...♔e7 12.♕e2 (The next is also good 12.♗e2!?) 12...g6 13.♗f3 ♔f7 14.g4 (14.g3 ♕h6 15.♗g2 e5 16.♘f3∞; 14.♗e4!?) 14...e5 15.h3↑ — White is ready to retreat the bishop to g2 and play ♘g1-f3 with tempo developing an attack.)

12.♗e2 e5 13.♘f3 ♕f4 14.0-0 ♘e7 15.♕d6 ♗g4

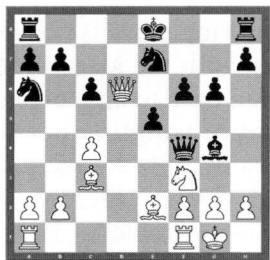

16.♘xe5

(16.♖ad1 ♗xf3 17.♗xf3 ♔f7 18.♖d4
♕xd4 (*18...♖hd8 19.♖xf4 ♖xd6
20.♗xe5 ♖e6 21.♗c3±*) 19.♗xd4
♖hd8 20.♕a3 ♖xd4 21.♖d1±)

16...♖d8 (*16...♗xe2 17.♕d7+ ♔f8
18.♖fe1 ♘c5 19.♕d6 ♕xf2+ 20.♔xf2
♘e4+ 21.♔g1 ♘xd6 22.♘d7+ ♔f7
23.♖xe2±/↑*) 17.♕xd8+ ♔xd8
18.♖ad1+ ♔c7 19.♘xg4 ♖f8 20.g3
♕f5 21.♖fe1±/↑ — White's pieces are very active and Black faces
a very difficult defence.

10.♕d6

10.♗c3 — yields nothing. Black
can use the move b7-b6 for development: 10...♗b7 (*Also good is 10...f6
11.♘f3 ♘e7 12.0-0 0-0∞, with good
play for Black*) 11.♘f3 ♘f6 (*11...♖d8
12.♗xg7 ♖xd1+ 13.♖xd1∞ Pakhomov
— S.Soloviov, Orsha 2009*) 12.♘e5
(*12.0-0 ♖d8 13.♘d2 Volkov — Sjugirov, Novokuznetsk 2008. Now good
is 13...♕f4!, with the idea of retreating
the queen to c7. White doesn't have
full compensation for the pawn.*) 12...
♖d8 13.♕c1 B.Savchenko — J.Geller,
St.Petersburg 2010. Here 13...♘c5! is
strong (*If 13...h6,keeping the white
queen out of g5, there follows 14.h4!,*

and the black queen has no good
square to retreat to. When White
plays f2-f3 she will have to go to h7.)
14.♕g5 ♖g8 15.f3 h6 16.♕c1 ♕h4+
17.g3 ♕h3∓ The position is complicated but Black's chances are preferable.

10... ♗d7

10...♘e7? 11.0-0-0 0-0 12.♕xe7
bxa5 13.♖d8+-;

10...♗b7 11.0-0-0 c5 12.♕d7+ It's
important to play two checks to deprive Black of the right to castle.
12...♔f8 13.♕d6+ ♔e8 14.♗c3 ♘b4
15.♗xb4 cxb4 16.♘f3± Kobalija —
E.Sveshnikov, Stepanakert 2004;

10...f6 11.f3 ♕f5

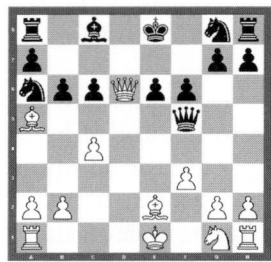

12.♗xb6!N (*12.♕xc6+ ♔f7 13.♗c3
♖b8± Williams — Domont, Grae-
chen 2009*) 12...♔f7 13.♗d3 ♕g5 (*13...
♕h5 14.g4 ♕h6 15.♗f2±*) 14.h4 ♕xg2
(*14...♕h6 15.♗f2±*) 15.♖h2 ♕xh2
16.♕xh2 axb6 17.0-0-0±;

10...bxa5 11.♖d1 f6 12.f3 ♕e3!
13.♕xc6+ ♔f7 14.♕xa8 ♘e7 15.♕e4
♕b6 It's difficult for White to castle,
that's where Black's compensation is
hidden. Yet White can gain the advantage with accurate play:

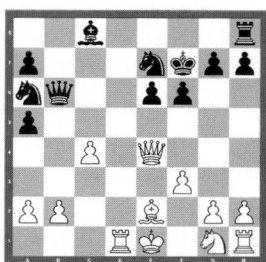

16.♕c2!N

(The following does not give an advantage 16.♕d4 ♘c5 17.♘h3 Naiditsch — Buhmann, Aix les Bains 2011 (Black also has sufficient compensation for the exchange after 17.f4 ♗b7 18.♘f3 ♘f5 19.♕f2 ♕b4+ 20.♔f1 h5) 17...e5 18.♕f2 ♗xh3 19.gxh3 ♘g6 — The black knight eyes the excellent f4 square.)

16...e5 17.♕b3! ♕xb3 18.axb3 ♘c5 19.♗d3 ♘xb3 20.♘e2 ♘c5 21.♘c3 ♗e6 22.♘e4 ♘xe4

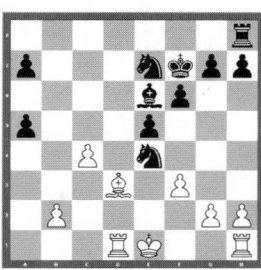

23.♗xe4! The bishop must capture. Taking with the pawn would be a positional error. 23...♖b8 24.0-0 ♗xc4 25.♖f2± — White has extinguished Black's initiative and has an extra exchange with good chances to win.

11.♗c3

11.0-0-0 0-0-0 12.♗c3 f6∓ and Black is ready to play ♘g8-h6 successfully completing development and escaping the attack, Van Wely — Gustafsson, Dortmund 2008.

11...f6
Structurally it's very beneficial for Black to align the pawns on the squares f6 and e5, but White gains extra tempi for piece play.

11...♘f6 12.♘f3 c5 13.♘e5 ♗a4! Black keeps the rook out of d1 and wants to eject the queen with ♖d8.

(13...♖d8 14.♖d1 ♕b7 15.♗f3 ♕b8 Mekhitarian — V.Sveshnikov, Reykjavik 2011

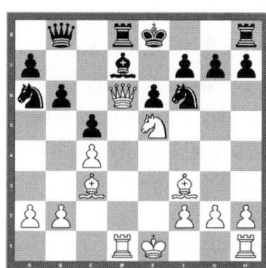

16.♕xb8!N ♘xb8 17.g4 h6 (17...♔e7 18.g5 ♘e8 19.♗h5 ♖f8 20.♗xf7 ♖xf7 21.g6+−) 18.h4 ♔e7 19.♔e2 ♗a4 20.b3 ♖xd1 21.♖xd1 ♗e8 22.b4 ♗a4 23.♖d2± — Despite the fact that it's an endgame, White can attack in a middlegame manner.)

14.f3 ♕b7

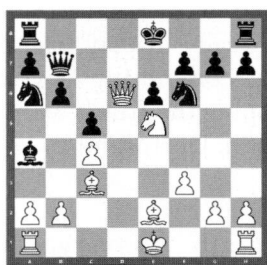

15.♕d2! (Not so strong is 15.♗d1 ♗xd1 16.♖xd1 ♖c8, and then ♕c7 or ♕e7 — White's compensation is only enough for equality.) 15...♘d7 16.♕g5 ♘xe5 17.♕xe5 0-0-0 18.0-0 f6 19.♕xe6+ ♕d7 20.♕xd7+ ♗xd7 21.a3± — White has a longlasting endgame initiative due to his two bishops.

12.♘f3

The following does not pose a serious danger for Black 12.0-0-0 0-0-0 13.♕a3 ♔b7 14.♗f3 ♕f4+ 15.♖d2 ♕c7 — White hasn't achieved anything concrete and the g1 knight isn't in the game yet.

12...♖d8!

The strongest, although in practice Black usually develops his king's knight

12...e5 13.0-0 0-0-0

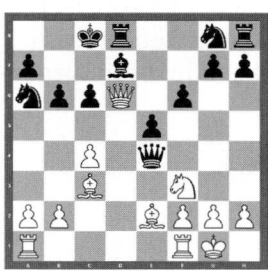

14.♖fe1!N (Not so convincing is 14.♕a3 ♔b7 15.♖fe1↑ Borovikov — Peschel, Boeblingen 2009, although here too White's initiative is very dangerous.) 14...♕g6

(14...♕f5 15.a4 (This is simpler than 15.c5 ♘xc5 16.♘xe5 ♕xf2+ 17.♔h1!+-, which is also good for White.) 15...♕e6 16.♕a3 ♘h6 17.♘d2± — White is ready for a massive attack on the queenside.)

15.a4!± — White's attack is developing of it's own accord.;

12...♘e7 13.0-0-0! ♕xe2

(13...♖d8 14.♖he1 ♘c8

a) 14...♘c5

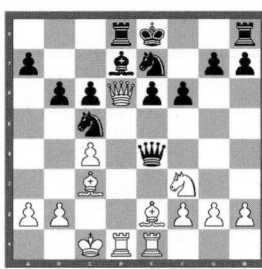

15.b4!N (15.♗f1 ♕g6 16.♗b4 ♕h6+ 17.♗d2 ♕g6 18.♗b4 ♕h6+ 1/2-1/2, Maslak — Bukavshin, Pardubice 2008) 15...♘b7 16.♕c7 c5 17.♘g5 ♕c6 (17...♕g6 18.♘e4+-) 18.♗h5+ g6 19.♕xc6 ♗xc6 20.♘xe6 ♖xd1+ 21.♗xd1+-;

b) 14...♕g6

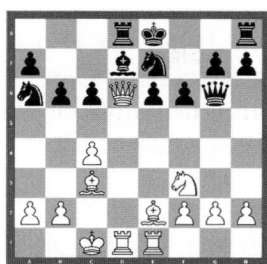

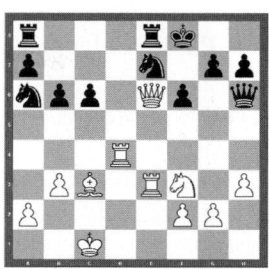

15.♗f1! (Not so clear is *15.g4 ♘c5∞*)
15...♕h6+

b1) 15...♔f7 16.♗d3 ♕h6+ (*16...
♕xg2 17.♖g1+-; 16...♕h5 17.g4
♕xg4 18.♖g1+-*) 17.♗d2 ♕h5
18.♖e5 fxe5 19.g4+-;

b2) 15...♘c5 16.♕c7 e5 17.b4 ♘e6
18.♕xa7±;

16.♖d2 ♔f7 17.g4 ♗c8 18.♕g3± —
All the White pieces can attack.;

15.♕d2 ♕g6 16.♗d3 ♕h5 (*16...♕f7
17.g4!→* — the threat g4-g5 is very
strong.) 17.♗c2 ♘c5 18.b4 ♘b7
19.♕f4 0-0 20.♕c7 ♘cd6 21.♖xd6
♘xd6 22.♕xd6 e5 23.♕c7±)

14.♕xd7+ ♔f7 15.♖he1 ♕xc4
16.♖e3 ♖he8 17.b3 ♕g4! It is important to provoke h2-h3 to deprive the
white queen of that square. However White still gains an advantage:
(*17...♕f4* leads to a immediate loss
*18.♖d4 ♕h6 19.♕xe6+ ♔f8 20.♖h4
♘c5 21.♕h3! ♕g6 22.♘d4+-* Lysyi —
Sjugirov, Moscow 2009) 18.h3 ♕f4
19.♖d4 ♕h6 20.♕xe6+ ♔f8

21.♕d6! The attack on the kingside
has failed, therefore White simply
maintains a dominating position
in the centre, and can exploit the
pinned e7 knight. 21...c5

a) 21...♖ac8 22.♖h4 ♖cd8 (*22...♕g6
23.♗xf6 gxf6 24.♖e6+-*) 23.♕a3 ♕g6
24.♖g4 ♕h6 25.♕xa6 ♘f5 26.♗d2
♘xe3 27.fxe3± — White holds the
initiative as well as a small material
advantage.;

b) 21...♘c5 22.♗b4 ♘b7 (*22...♕g6
23.♗xc5 bxc5 24.♖d1!* The most exact. White keeps control of the central files and does not give Black any
chance to exchange pieces to ease his
defence. The pinned Knight e7 is the
decisive factor, for example: *24...a5
25.♕xc5 ♕f5 26.♕d6 ♕c8 27.♘d4+-*
— White must win.) 23.♕d7 c5
(*23...♘c5 24.♗xc5 bxc5 25.♖de4
♖ad8 26.♕xa7 ♘d5 27.♕xc5+
♔g8 28.♖h4 ♕g6 29.♖xe8+ ♕xe8
30.♕c2+*) 24.♖de4 ♖ad8 25.♕xb7
♘f5 26.♗d2 ♘xe3 27.♖xe3 ♖xe3
28.fxe3!± — The white king is protected while the black queenside
pawns fall.;

c) 21...f5 22.♕xh6 gxh6 23.♖e6± Sakaev — Papin, Belgorod 2010;

22.♖d2 ♖ac8

(22...♘b4 23.♗xb4 cxb4 24.♘d4 f5 (24...♖ac8+ 25.♔d1 f5 26.♘xf5+−) 25.♕xb4±)

23.♔b2! A useful prophylaxis. The king moves out of the black rook's line of fire along the c-file and releases his rooks from the pin.

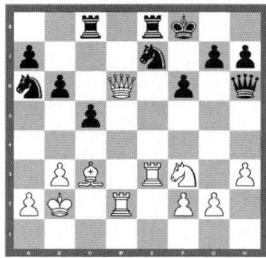

23...♘c7

a) 23...♕g6 24.g4 h6

a1) 24...♕f7 25.g5±;

a2) 24...♘c7 25.a4! The only but effective defence against ♘c7-b5. 25...♕f7 (After preparing b6-b5 with 25...a6 decisive is 26.♘h4 ♕f7 27.g5 ♘cd5 28.g6 hxg6 29.♖xd5 ♕xd5 30.♘xg6++−) 26.g5±;

25.♕d7 ♘c6 26.♘h4 ♕f7 27.♖xe8+ ♕xe8 28.♕b7 ♘c7 29.♘f5 ♘e6 30.♖d7 ♖c7 31.♖xc7 ♘xc7 32.♕xc7 ♕e2+ 33.♔c1 ♕f1+ 34.♔d2 ♕xf2+ 35.♔d3 ♕f1+ 36.♔e3 ♕xh3+ 37.♔f2 ♕xc3 38.♕xg7+ ♔e8 39.♕g8+

♔d7 40.♕d5+ ♔c7 41.♕d6+ ♔b7 42.♕d7+ ♔a6 43.♕xc6 ♕d2+ 44.♔f3 ♕xa2 45.♕e6± — The queen and the knight combine perfectly. White has excellent winning chances.;

b) 23...♖c6 24.♕d7 ♖c7 25.♕a4 ♘b8 26.g4 ♘ec6 27.g5 fxg5 28.♖xe8+ ♔xe8 29.♕c4 ♘d7 30.♕d5 ♘e7 31.♖e2 ♔f8 32.♕d2 ♘f6 33.♘xg5 ♖d7 34.♕f4 ♕g6

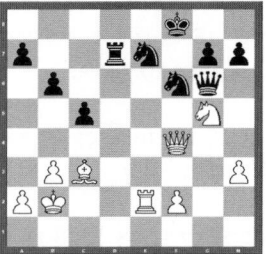

35.♔a3!! The king evades a potential check along the long diagonal. Now combinations involving a capture on f6 are very dangerous. White's threats are irresistible.;

c) 23...♘b8 24.g4 ♘bc6 (24...♖c6 25.♕g3 ♕g6 26.♘h4 ♕f7 27.g5→) 25.g5 fxg5 26.♖e6 ♕h5 27.♘e5 ♖ed8 (27...♖cd8 28.♖f6+ gxf6 29.♕xf6+ ♔g8 30.♖xd8 ♖xd8 31.♘xc6 ♕e2+ 32.♔a3 ♕a6+ 33.♘a5 ♖d4 34.♕xe7 bxa5 35.♗xd4 cxd4 36.♕xg5++−) 28.♘d7+ ♖xd7 29.♖xd7 ♖d8 30.♕c7 ♖xd2+ 31.♗xd2 ♕d1 32.♕d6 h6 33.f4 gxf4 34.♕xf4+ ♔g8 35.♗c3±;

24.a4 ♕h5 25.g4 ♕f7 (25...♕g6 26.♘h4 ♕f7 27.g5 ♘cd5 28.g6 hxg6

29.♖xd5 g5 30.♖xe7 ♖xe7 31.♘f5+-)
26.g5 ♔g8 27.gxf6 ♘f5 28.♖xe8+
♘xe8 29.♕d5 ♕xd5 30.♖xd5 ♘d4
31.♗xd4 cxd4 32.fxg7± — White
has an extra pawn and excellent
winning chances.;

On 12...0-0-0 the following is
strong 13.♘d2! ♕g6

(It's bad to accept the sacrifice of
the 2nd pawn: 13...♕xg2?! 14.♗f3
♕h3 15.♖g1 ♘c7 (15...g6 16.♖g3
♕xh2 17.♕a3 ♔b7 18.♘e4+-; 15...
♘h6 16.♕a3 ♘c5 17.0-0-0 ♔b8
18.♖xg7 ♘f5 19.♖f7 ♕xh2 20.♔b1
♕f4 21.b4 ♘b7 22.♖xf6± — White
has a strong initiative.) 16.♕a3 ♔b8
17.♖xg7 e5 (17...♕xh2 18.0-0-0 ♕f4
19.♗b4 ♗c8 20.♖g4 ♕e5 21.♗xc6↑;
17...♕h6 18.♖f7 ♕g6 19.♖f8 ♘h6
20.♖xh8 ♖xh8 21.♕e7±) 18.0-0-0
♘h6 (18...c5? 19.b4!+- — White is
better prepared for the opening
of lines. Black should lose, Volkov — Goloshchapov, Dubai 2003)
19.♗xc6 ♕e6 20.♗e4±)

14.a4!

(The following leads to a double-
edged battle 14.♕a3 ♔b7 15.♗f3
(15.0-0∞) 15...♘h6 16.♘e4 ♘f7∞)

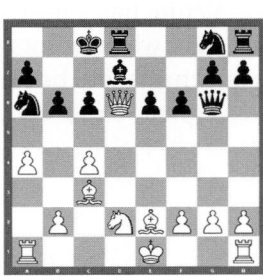

14...♗e8 15.♕xe6+ (The next
move is also interesting 15.♕a3!?
♕xg2 16.♗f3 ♕g5 17.a5 b5 18.cxb5
♘c5 19.b6∞) 15...♗d7 16.♕e4 ♖e8
17.♕xg6 hxg6 18.♔f1! (White stands
just a little bit better after 18.f3 ♗f5
19.♔f2 ♘c5 20.h3 ♘d3+ 21.♗xd3
♗xd3 22.♖he1± — One of the bishops has been exchanged.) 18...♘h6
19.a5 ♔b7 20.f3 ♘c5 21.b4 ♘e6
22.♘e4 ♘f7 23.♔f2± Due to greater
activity and the bishop pair, White
stands better.;

12...♘h6

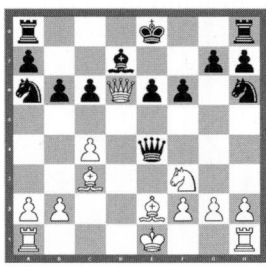

13.♖d1! ♖d8

(13...0-0-0 14.♕a3 ♔b7 15.♕e7
♘c5 16.♕xg7 ♘g4 17.♗d4

(17.♗xf6 ♖hg8 18.♕e7 ♖ge8 (18...
♘xf6 19.♕xf6±) 19.♕xd8 (19.
♕g7=) 19...♖xd8 20.♗xd8 ♗e8
21.♗e7 ♖h5 22.♗xc5 bxc5 23.♖d7+
♔b6 24.♖d2 ♘e5 25.♘xe5 ♗xe2
26.♖xe2 ♕b1+ 27.♔d2 ♕xh1
28.g3 ♕xh2 29.♘d3± — White
will inevitably capture on c5 with
the manoeuver ♖e2-e5-c5, after
which he can advance the queenside pawns. There isn't any risk but
winning chances are minimal.)

17...♖hg8 18.♕f7 ♖gf8 19.♕e7 ♖fe8 20.♗xc5! ♖xe7 21.♗xe7 ♔c8 22.♗xd8 ♔xd8 23.0-0 (The following leads to more complicated game 23.b3 ♔c7 24.♖d2 ♕b1+ 25.♗d1 ♕e4+ 26.♖e2 ♕f4 27.0-0± — White's position is preferable but Black has his trumps. He plans to play c6-c5, e6-e5 and transfer the knight along the route ♘g4-h6-f5-d4.) 23...♕xe2 24.♖d2 ♕xc4 25.♖fd1 ♕c5 26.♖xd7+ ♔c8 27.♖7d4± — The two rooks are stronger than the queen. Black faces a difficult defence)

14.♕a3 ♗c8

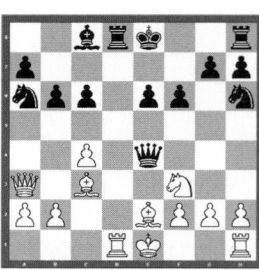

15.♘d2!N (15.♖xd8+ ♔xd8∞ Sakaev — Bukavshin, Taganrog 2011) 15...♕g6 (15...♕xg2 16.♗h5+ ♘f7 17.♗f3 ♕g6 18.♗e4 ♕g4 19.♗xc6++-) 16.♗f3

The following leads to an unclear game 16.0-0 c5 17.♕a4+ ♖d7!∞

(17...♔f7 18.♕c6 ♘f5 19.♘e4 ♖hf8 20.♕a8 ♘d4 21.♗xd4 cxd4 22.♕xa7+ ♔g8 23.♘g3 ♕c2 24.♕xb6 d3 25.♖c1 ♕a4

26.♗d1 ♕d7 (26...♕xa2 27.♖c3+-) 27.♗f3±)

16...c5

a) 16...♘f5 17.♗xc6+ ♔f7 18.0-0 ♘d4 19.♗xd4 ♖xd4 20.♕a4 (20.♘e4 ♖xe4 21.♗b5 ♕f5 22.♗xa6 ♕c5±) 20...♖hd8 (20...♕f5 21.♘f3 ♖xd1 22.♖xd1±) 21.♘e4 ♕f5 (21...♔g8 22.♖xd4 ♖xd4 23.♖d1±) 22.b4± — There are serious problems with the a6 knight.;

b) 16...♗b7 17.0-0

(17.♘e4 ♖xd1+ (17...♘f5 18.0-0 ♔f7 19.g3± — The threat c4-c5 is very unpleasant.) 18.♔xd1 ♘f7 19.♔e2 c5 20.♖d1 0-0 21.♘xf6+ gxf6 22.♗xb7±)

17...♘f5 18.♘e4 ♔f7 19.♘g3 (Also promising is 19.g3, with the idea c4-c5.) 19...♘xg3 20.hxg3 ♖he8 there is no sign of another useful move 21.b4± — The threat b4-b5 is very strong. White has an obvious advantage.;

17.♗c6+ ♔f7 (17...♗d7 18.♗e4 f5 19.♗f3 ♘b4 20.♗xb4 cxb4 21.♕xa7 e5 22.♗d5 ♗c6 23.0-0 ♖xd5 24.cxd5 0-0 25.♘c4± The position has stabilised — White has a passed pawn and Black has weak points.; If 17...♔f8 the queenside will be destroyed 18.0-0 e5 19.b4 cxb4 20.♗xb4+ ♘xb4 21.♕xb4+ ♔f7 22.♘e4 ♘f5 23.♕a3+-) 18.0-0 ♘f5

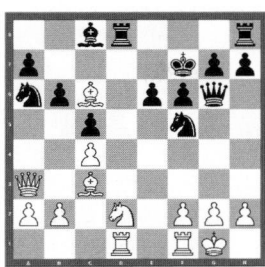

19.♘e4! The knigh t heads for g3 to protect the g2. The other options seem to lead to a draw by perpetual check:

a) 19.♕a4 ♖hf8 20.♗b5 ♔g8 21.♗xa6 ♘h4 22.g3 ♗xa6 23.♕xa6 ♖xd2 24.♗xd2 ♘f3+ 25.♔h1 ♕h5 26.♔g2 ♘h4+=;

b) 19.♗b5 ♗b7 20.g3

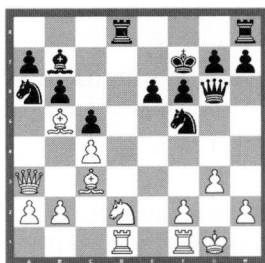

20...♘h4!

(Another tempting possibility leads to White's advantage: 20...♕h6 21.♗xa6 ♗a8 22.♕a4 ♕h3 23.f3 ♘e3

(23...♘xg3 24.♖f2 ♘h5 (24...♘f5 25.♗b5+-) 25.♗b5±)

24.♖f2 ♘xd1 25.♕xd1 ♗c6 (25...♖d3 26.♕e2 ♖hd8 27.♗b5 ♕h6 28.♘f1±) 26.♕e2 ♖d7 27.♗b5

(27.b4 ♖hd8 (27...cxb4 28.♗xb4 ♖hd8 29.c5 bxc5 30.♗c3 ♕f5 31.♗c4±) 28.bxc5 ♖d3 29.♗b4 bxc5 30.♗a5 ♖8d4 31.♗c8 h5 32.♕e1 ♕f5 33.♖e2 ♖d6 34.h3∞)

27...♗xb5 28.cxb5 ♖hd8 (28...♕f5 29.♔g2±) 29.♖f1 ♕f5 30.♘e4 ♕d5 31.f4 ♕d3 32.♕h5+ ♔g8 33.♖e1± — The game is complicated but White's chances are better.)

21.f3 (21.♗xa6 ♗f3 22.♕a4 ♕g4 23.♘xf3 ♘xf3+ 24.♔g2 ♘h4+ 25.♔g1 ♘f3+=) 21...♖d3 22.♖de1 (Bad is 22.♗xa6, in view of 22...♗xf3) 22...♖hd8 23.♗xa6 ♖xd2 24.♗xd2 ♖xd2 25.♕e3 ♖g2+ 26.♔h1 e5 27.♗xb7 ♕c2 28.f4 ♖xh2+ 29.♔g1 ♖g2+ = — Black obtains a perpetual.;

19...♖hf8 20.♘g3 ♖xd1 21.♖xd1 ♘xg3 22.hxg3 ♔g8 (An almost equal position arises after 22...♕g4 23.♕a4 ♔g8 24.♖d2 ♘b4 25.♗xb4 cxb4 26.♕xb4±) 23.♗b5 ♕c2 24.♖d2! (Just slightly more exact than 24.♖e1 ♘b4 25.♗a4 ♕f5 26.♗xb4 cxb4 27.♕xb4±, though White stands better here too.) 24...♕c1+ 25.♔h2 ♘b4

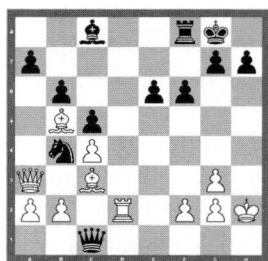

26.♕b3! (Less precise is 26.♗xb4
cxb4 27.♕xb4 a6! 28.♗a4 a5!=)
26...♗b7 (26...♕b1 27.♗xb4 cxb4
28.♕xb4 ♕e4 29.♕e7±) 27.♗xb4
cxb4 28.♕xb4±

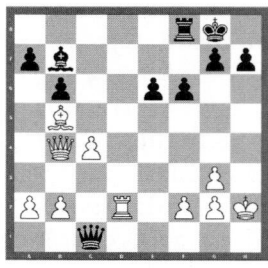

White occupies the d-file, has the
more promising bishop and chances to create a passed pawn in the
queenside. Black faces a long, unpleasant defence.

13.♘d2!?N
Although this move hasn't been
played yet, some positions arising after several moves have occurred by
transposition!
13.♕g3 ♕g6∓ Vallejo Pons — Pavasovic, Crete 2007;
13.♖d1 ♘e7 (13...c5!?) 14.♕a3 (14.
♖d4 ♕g6∓) 14...♗c8 15.♖xd8+ ♔xd8
16.♕d6+ ♗d7∓ — It's hard for White
to maintain the waning initiative.

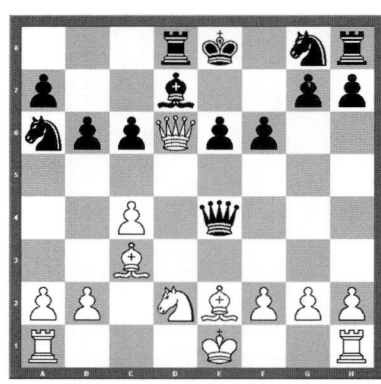

13...♕g6
Black must not accept the sacrifice of
the second pawn: 13...♕xg2 14.♗h5+
(Not so convincing is 14.0-0-0 ♕xf2
15.♖he1↑) 14...g6 15.♗f3 ♕h3 16.0-0-
0 ♘c5

(16...♔f7 17.♖he1 ♘e7 (17...e5
18.♗xc6+-) 18.♗xf6+-)

17.♖he1± — White has a powerful
attack.

14.♕a3
The following deserves examination
although it is risky, 14.h4!?, and l ate
r the pawn can expel the queen from
g6 or sometimes reach h6, destroying
the black pawn chain.;
After 14.0-0 possible is 14...c5, in addition to transposing after 14...♘e7
15.♕a3 ♗c8

14...♗c8 15.0-0
The following leads to a complicated
battle 15.♗f3 ♘e7 16.♘e4 c5 17.♕a4+
(17.♗xf6 ♗b7 18.0-0 ♗xe4 19.♗xe4
♕xe4 20.♗xe7 ♔xe7 21.♕xa6 ♖d7=

— The possession of d-file and piece activity compensates for the weakness of the e6 pawn) 17...♔f7 18.0–0 ♖hf8 (18...♘f5 19.♘g3 ♘xg3 20.hxg3 ♖d6 21.a3 ♖hd8 22.b4⯑) 19.♖ad1 ♘f5 20.♖xd8 ♖xd8 21.♖d1 ♘d4 22.♗xd4 cxd4∞

15...♘e7 16.♖ad1 c5

16...♔f7 17.♗f3 c5 18.♘e4 ♘f5 19.♘g3 ♘xg3 20.hxg3 ♖hf8 21.♗c6 ♖xd1 22.♖xd1 ♔g8 23.♗b5 ♕c2 24.♖d2! (24.♖e1 ♘b4 25.♗a4 ♕f5 26.♗xb4 cxb4 27.♕xb4±) 24...♕c1+ 25.♔h2 ♘b4 26.♕b3! ♗b7 27.♗xb4 cxb4 28.♕xb4± — Suddenly, via a different move order a position has arisen from the line 12...♘h6 13.♖d1 ♖d8 14.♕a3 ♗c8 15.♘d2 ♕g6 16.♗f3 c5 17.♗c6 ♔f7 18.0–0 ♘f5 19.♘e4 ♖hf8 20.♘g3 ♖xd1 21.♖xd1 ♘xg3 22.hxg3 ♔g8 23.♗b5 ♕c2 24.♖d2 ♕c1 25.♔h2 ♘b4 26.♕b3 ♗b7 27.♗xb4 cxb4 28.♕xb4

17.♕a4+ ♔f7

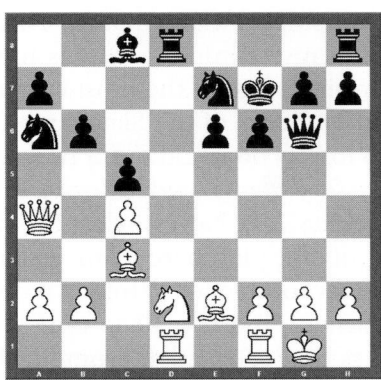

18.a3!?N

To play b2-b4 and threaten b4-b5 — one of the White's main ideas in this variation.

18.♗f3 ♘f5 19.♗e4

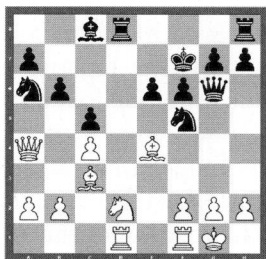

19...♕g4! The queen moves via f4 to c7 to protect the queenside.

(19...♕h5

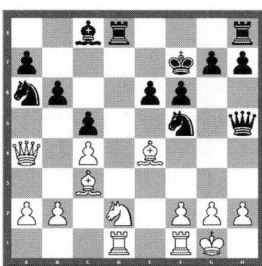

20.♖fe1!N Even though the idea 13.♘d2!?N has not occurred in practice, this position is already known, as it has arisen with a different move order.

a) 20.♗c6 ♕g4 21.g3 (21.♘f3 ♘e7 22.h3 ♕g6∞; 21.♘e4 ♕f4∞; 21.♖fe1 ♖hf8∞) 21...♖hf8∞;

b) 20.♘f3 ♖hf8 21.♗c6 ♔g8 22.♖xd8 ♖xd8 23.♖d1 ♖xd1+ 24.♕xd1 ♕f7 25.g4 ♕c7 Potapov

— Feygin, Ceske Budejovice 1995 26.gxf5! ♕xc6 27.♕d8+ ♔f7 28.♘g5+ fxg5 29.♕h8 exf5 30.♕xg7+ ♔e8 31.♕g8+ ♔e7 32.♕g7+=;

20...♖hf8 21.h3 ♕g5 22.a3↑ — White plays b2-b4 and obtains a serious initiative for the pawn.)

20.♖fe1 ♘d4 21.h3 ♕f4 22.♘f3 ♘xf3+ 23.♗xf3 ♕c7 24.a3⯬ Due to the bad position of the a6 knight White's compensation is enough for equality but there is no question of an advantage.

18...♖hf8!

18...♗b7 19.♗f3±;

18...♖d7 19.♗f3 ♘f5 20.♗c6 ♖e7 21.b4↑;

18...♘f5 19.♘f3 ♖he8 20.b4 ♗b7 21.g3 ♖xd1 22.♖xd1 ♖e7 23.♖d8 ♘d4 24.♗xd4 ♕b1+ 25.♕d1 ♕xd1+ 26.♗xd1 ♗xf3 27.♗xf3 cxd4 28.♖xd4±

19.b4 ♗b7 20.♘f3

20.♗f3 ♖xd2 21.♗xb7 ♕c2 22.♕xc2 ♖xc2⯬

20...cxb4!

A structural concession but now the c5 square is freed for the knight and the b4-b5 jab becomes ineffective.

21.axb4 ♔g8 22.h3⯱

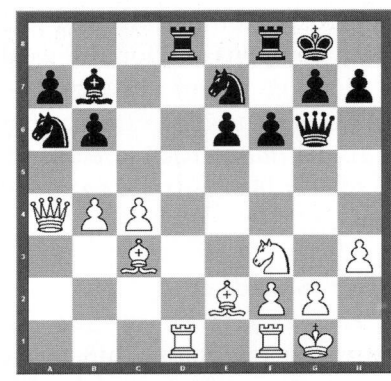

Compensation for the pawn looks sufficient but Black has counter chances. White plans to increase the piece pressure on the centre and prepare the move c4-c5. The main task for Black is to eventually transfer the a6 knight to a better position. Conclusion: In summary the most principled move after 4.e4 dxe4 5.♘xe4 ♗b4+ 6.♗d2 ♕xd4 7.♗xb4 ♕xe4+ is 8.♗e2. Here an interesting line is 8...c5, but still Black encounters problems. The more popular 8...♘a6 is objectively stronger. Regarding 9.♗d6, the only move appears to be 9...♕xg2 but it is sufficient for equality. Therefore, in my opinion, 9.♗a5 is more promising. One of the most complicated branches of the Slav gambit is 9...f6 10.♘f3 b6 11.♘d2 ♕f4 12.♗h5+ g6 13.♗f3 ♕e5+14.♔f1 ♕c7 15.♗c3 e5 16.♘e4 ♔f7. Nevertheless the nature of the play here is in general more favourable for White. Another problematic line is 9...b6 10.♕d6 ♗d7 11.♗c3 f6 12.♘f3 ♖d8!. From Black's point of view this variation looks to be the most acceptable.

PART 7

**3.♘c3 ♞f6 4.e3
Variations, that are
not entering the Meran**

■ GAME 14

1.d4 d5 2.c4 c6 3.♘c3 ♞f6 4.e3
4.♗g5 dxc4 5.a4 h6! 6.♗h4

(6.♗xf6 exf6 7.e4 ♕b6!? (7...f5
8.♗xc4 fxe4))

6...♕b6 7.♕d2 g5 8.♗g3 ♗g7 9.e4
♞h5∓;

4.♗f4 dxc4 5.a4 ♞d5∓

4...a6
4...g6 5.♘f3 — 3.♘f3 ♞f6 4.e3 g6
5.♘c3;

After 4...♗g4, correct in principle is

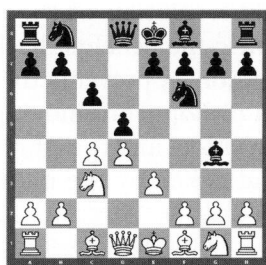

5.f3!

a) 5.♘f3 e6 — 3.♘f3 ♞f6 4.e3 ♗g4
5.♘c3;

b) 5.♕b3 ♕b6 6.h3

(6.♘ge2 dxc4

(6...♕xb3 7.axb3 ♗f5 (7...e6
8.♘g3±) 8.♘f4 e6 9.c5± — White
will push b4-b5.)

7.♕xc4 ♞a6∞)

6...♗f5 7.g4 ♕xb3 8.axb3 ♗c2 9.g5
♞fd7 10.cxd5 ♗xb3 11.♗g2

(11.e4 ♞b6 (11...cxd5 12.♘xd5 ♗xd5
13.exd5±) 12.♖a3 ♗c4 13.♗xc4
♞xc4 14.♖a1 e6 15.dxe6 fxe6∞)

11...♞b6 12.dxc6 ♞xc6 13.♘f3 e6=
Potkin — Vallejo Pons, Germany
2011;

5...♗e6

a) 5...♗c8 6.♗d3±;

b) 5...♗h5 6.♕b3±;

c) 5...♗f5 6.g4! (6.♕b3±) 6...♗c8

(6...♗e6 7.g5 ♞fd7 (7...♞h5 8.cxd5
cxd5 9.f4 g6 10.♕b3±) 8.♘ge2±)

7.g5 ♞fd7 8.f4 ♞b6 (8...e6 9.♘f3±)
9.c5 ♞6d7 10.e4 e6 11.exd5 cxd5 12.b4
♞c6 13.a3±;

6.♘ge2 dxc4 (6...♗c8 7.♘g3±) 7.♘f4
♛c8 8.e4 g6

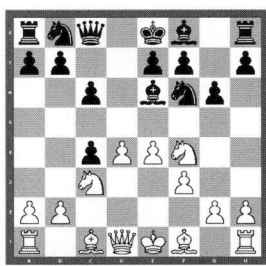

9.g4!?

a) 9.♘xe6 ♛xe6 10.♛a4 b5 11.♛a5
♘d5 (11...♗g7 12.a4±) 12.♘xd5
cxd5 13.♛xb5+ ♘d7 14.♛xd5 ♛xd5
15.exd5 ♘b6 16.b3 ♗g7 17.♗a3 (17.
bxc4 ♗xd4 18.♖b1 ♖c8 19.♗d3
♘xc4 20.♔e2±) 17...♖c8

(17...♘xd5 18.♗xc4 (18.♗c5!?) 18...
♘e3 19.♖c1 ♗xd4 20.g3±)

18.bxc4 (18.♖c1 cxb3 19.♖xc8+ ♘xc8
20.♗c5 bxa2 21.♗b5+ ♔d8 22.♔e2
♔c7 23.♖a1 ♖d8 24.♗c4 ♘d6
25.♔d3±) 18...♗xd4 19.♖c1 ♔d7
20.♗d3 ♖c7 21.♔d2 ♖hc8 22.♖he1
♗c5 23.♗xc5 ♖xc5 24.♖e4± —
Black ha s organized a good blockade but a pawn is a pawn and White
retains winning chances.;

b) 9.a4 ♗g7 10.a5±;

9...♗g7 10.h4 0–0

(10...h6 Mamedyarov — Kamsky, Sofia 2007 11.♛e2 (11.♗e3 b5
12.b3±) 11...b5 12.a4±)

11.h5 ♘a6 12.♗e3→ — Black risks
getting mated along the h-file.;

4...♗f5 5.cxd5 (5.♘f3 e6 — 3.♘f3
♘f6 4.e3 ♗f5 5.♘c3 e6; 5.♛b3 ♛b6
6.♛xb6 axb6 7.cxd5 ♘xd5 8.♘xd5
cxd5 9.♗d2 ♘c6= Epishin — Khalifman, Budapest 1996) 5...cxd5

(5...♘xd5 allows White to occupy
the centre easily: 6.♘ge2 e6 7.e4
♘xc3 8.♘xc3 ♗g6 9.♗e3 ♘d7 (9...
♗b4 10.♛b3±) 10.♗e2 White has
a small but stable advantage. An
attempt to undermine the white
centre breaks down: 10...♗b4 11.f3
0–0 12.♛b3 c5 Flear — Kasimdzhanov, France 1997 Here strongest is
13.♖d1!, preventing Black from exchanging in the centre. After 13...
♛a5 follows 14.♔f2!, with the positional threats a2-a3 and d4-d5.)

6.♛b3 ♗c8 Despite hav ing lost two
tempi, Black's play makes sense.
An early resolution of the tension
along the c-file benefits Black. Also
the pawn on e3 prevents the black-
squared bishop from moving to an
active position, and the white queen
can be attacked by the manoeuver
♘b8-c6-a5.

a) 6...♛d7 7.♘f3 ♘c6 8.♘e5 ♛c7
9.♗b5 ♗d7 (9...e6 10.♛a4 ♖c8
11.♛xa7±) 10.♘xd7 ♛xd7 11.e4 e6
12.e5 ♘e4 13.♘xe4 dxe4 14.0–0±
Black loses the e4 pawn.;

b) 6...♕b6 7.♘xd5 ♘xd5 8.♕xd5 ♕b4+ 9.♔d1 (9.♗d2 ♕xb2 10.♖c1 ♗d7 11.♘f3 e6 12.♕c4 ♘c6 13.♗e2± Tal — Fuchs, Kislovodsk 1964) 9...♗d7 10.♘f3 e6 11.♕c4± — Black has insufficient compensation for a pawn.;

7.f4 The idea behind controlling the e5 square again is to place the knight there at an opportune moment, thus preventing an exchange of knights which can facilitate Black's defence.

a) 7.♗b5+ ♘c6 (7...♗d7!?) 8.♘f3 (8.e4 ♗d7 9.♘ge2 ♘xe4=) 8...e6 9.♘e5 ♗d7=;

b) 7.♘f3 e6

(7...♘c6 leads to a transposition 8.♗d3 (8.♘e5 e6 — 7...e6 8.♘e5 ♘c6) 8...e6 — 7...e6 8.♗d3 ♘c6)

8.♗d3

(8.♘e5 gives nothing at all 8...♘c6 9.f4 ♗e7 10.♗d3 0-0 11.0-0 ♘d7! 12.♗d2 (12.♘f3 ♘b6=) 12...♘dxe5 13.fxe5 ♗d7= — One possibility is to route the black knight to c4 via a5, another is to play f7-f6 simplifying the game.)

8...♘c6 9.0-0 ♗d6 The bishop is well-placed since it prevents the white knight from invading on e5 (9...♗e7 10.♗d2 0-0 11.♖fc1± Wojtaszek — Kempinski, Warsaw 2012) 10.e4 (10.♗d2 0-0 11.♖ac1 ♗d7 12.e4 dxe4 13.♘xe4 ♘xe4 14.♗xe4 ♕b6

15.♕xb6 axb6 16.a3± — White wants to push d4-d5, then retain a better pawn structure on the queenside.) 10...dxe4 11.♘xe4 ♘xe4 (11...♘d5 12.♗g5 f6 13.♘xd6+ ♕xd6 14.♗h4 0-0 15.♗g3± Aleksandrov — Oleksienko, Chennai 2012) 12.♗xe4 0-0 13.♖d1 h6 14.d5 ♘a5 15.♕c3 f5 16.♗c2 exd5 17.♕d3 ♗e7 (17...♗e6 18.♘d4 ♗c8 19.♗d2 ♘c4 20.♗c3↑) 18.♖b1± — White wins back the pawn on d5, retaining the somewhat more active pieces.;

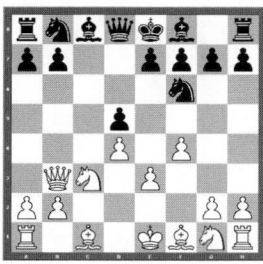

7...e6 8.♘f3 ♘c6 9.♗d3 ♗e7 10.0-0 0-0 11.♗d2 ♗d7 12.♘e5 ♖c8

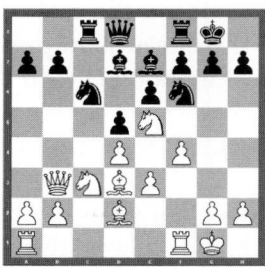

13.♖fc1! Only with this rook, so that after a later retreat of the queen to d1 the rooks will remain connected.

a) 13.♗e1 ♘a5 (*13...a6 14.♗h4 b5 15.♕d1±*) 14.♕d1 ♘c4 15.♕e2 ♘d6!=;

b) 13.♖ac1 ♘a5 14.♕d1 ♘c4 15.♗xc4 dxc4 16.b3 cxb3 17.♕xb3 ♗c6= — White has no advantage due to the bad position of the pawn on f4.;

13...♘a5 14.♕d1 ♘c4 15.♗xc4 dxc4 16.a4±

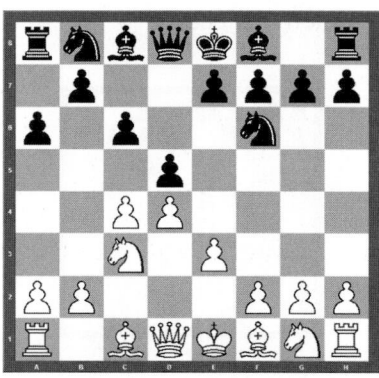

5.♕c2

The idea behind the early development of the queen is to prevent the pin of the knight on f3 with ♗c8-g4.

5.♘f3 — 3.♘f3 ♘f6 4.♘c3 a6 5.e3;

5.♗d3 does not pose any problems for Black. But if played then 5...dxc4!

a) After 5...♗g4?! promising are both 6.♕b3, and 6.♘ge2.;

b) 5...e6, then one must consider 6.c5 (*6.♘f3 dxc4 7.♗xc4 b5* with a later c6-c5, leads to a line of the Queen's Gambit Accepted advantageous for Black, where the white knight moved to c3 too early.) 6...b6 7.cxb6±;

6.♗xc4 b5 (*6...e6 7.a4 c5 8.♘f3* leads to a classical Queen's Gambit Accepted.) 7.♗e2 Otherwise Black simply plays e7-e6 and pushes c6-c5. 7...e6 8.♗f3

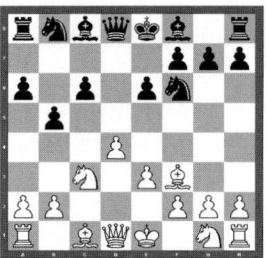

8...♗b7N

(*8...♖a7 9.a4 (9.e4 ♖d7 10.♘ge2 e5 11.♕b3 exd4 12.e5 dxc3 13.exf6 ♕xf6∓ Epishin — Dreev, Tilburg 1994) 9...b4 10.♘e4 ♘xe4 11.♗xe4 c5= Korotylev — Val.Popov, St.Petersburg 2003*)

9.♘ge2 ♘bd7 10.0-0 ♕c7= — Black pushes c6-c5 with simple play.;

After 5.♗d2 conventional play for the a7-a6 line looks most logical: 5...b5 (*5...g6 6.♘f3 ♗g7 7.♗e2 0-0 8.0-0 — 3.♘f3 ♘f6 4.e3 g6 5.♘c3 ♗g7 6.♗e2 0-0 7.0-0 a6 8.♗d2; 5...e6 6.♘f3 — 3.♘f3 ♘f6 4.e3 a6 5.♗d2 e6 6.♘c3*) 6.cxd5 (After *6.c5* good is *6...a5*, preventing the clamping of the queenside by b2-b4 and a2-a4.) 6...

cxd5 7.♘f3 e6 — 3.♘f3 ♘f6 4.♘c3 a6 5.e3 b5 6.cxd5 cxd5 7.♗d2

5...e6

5...♗g4 6.h3 ♗h5 7.♕b3 (7.♘ge2 *♗g6 8.♕b3 b5 9.cxd5 cxd5 10.♘f4 e6=*) 7...♖a7 8.cxd5 (*8.♘ge2 dxc4 9.♕xc4 b5 10.♕b3 e5 11.dxe5 ♘bd7 12.♘f4 ♘xe5 13.♘xh5 ♘xh5 14.♕c2±*) 8...cxd5 9.g4 ♗g6 10.g5

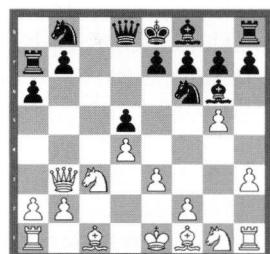

10...♘e4

a) 10...♘fd7 11.♘xd5 ♘c6 12.♘f4 e5 13.♘xg6 hxg6 14.♗d2 ♗e7 15.♘f3 e4

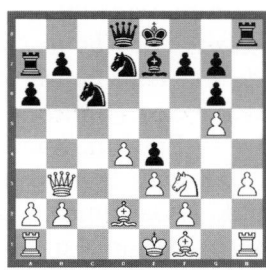

16.♘h2!N (*16.♘g1 ♗xg5 17.♘e2 ♘ce5 18.♘g1 ♘c6 19.0-0-0 ♘f6∞* Mamedyarov — Ivanchuk, Moscow 2008) 16...♗xg5 17.0-0-0± — The white knight can enter the game via g4 as well as being useful for opening up the game with the f-pawn.;

b) 10...♘g8

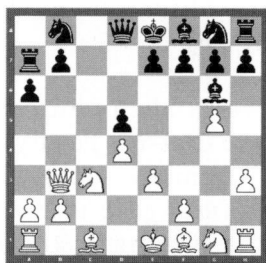

11.♕xd5!N (*11.♗g2 e6 12.e4± Bacrot — Vallejo Pons, Porto Carras 2011*) 11...♕xd5 12.♘xd5 ♗e4 13.♘c7+ ♔d7 14.f3 ♗c6 15.d5 ♔xc7 16.dxc6 ♘xc6 17.♗d2 h6 18.f4± — White has an advantage due to the two bishops.;

11.♕xd5 ♕xd5 12.♘xd5 ♘xg5 13.♗g2 (*13.♘c3 ♘c6∞*) 13...♗e4 14.♖h2 (*14.♔f1!? ♗xg2+ 15.♔xg2 ♘e4 16.f3 ♘d6 17.e4 e6 18.♘e3±*) 14...♗xg2 15.♖xg2 ♘e4 16.f3 ♘d6 (*16... ♘f6 17.♘xf6+ gxf6 18.e4 e6 19.♗e3 ♖a8 20.♘e2±* Pe.Nielsen — Stefanova, Drammen 2005) 17.♗d2 e6 18.♘f4±;

5...b5 6.b3 ♗g4

(6...g6 7.♗d3 ♗g7 8.♘f3 0-0 9.0-0 ♗e6 10.♗a3 (*10.c5±*) 10...bxc4 11.bxc4 dxc4 12.♗e2 ♘bd7 13.♘g5 ♗g4 14.♗xg4 ♘xg4 15.♘a4± Sjugirov — Gabuzyan, Plovdiv 2012)

7.♘ge2 (After 7.♗d3 follows 7...
♘bd7, with the idea of e7-e5.; 7.♗e2
♗xe2 8.♘gxe2 e6 9.0-0 ♘bd7
10.e4 dxe4 11.♘xe4 ♗e7 12.♗f4
0-0 13.♖fd1 ♘xe4 14.♕xe4 ♕b6=
Koneru — Laznicka, Caleta 2012)
7...♘bd7 8.h3

(8.♘g3 e5 (8...dxc4 9.bxc4 e5 10.♗d3
♗e7 11.0-0 0-0= Posnty — Van
Wely, Germany 2006) 9.h3 ♗e6
10.dxe5 (10.c5 g6∓) 10...♘xe5 11.f4
♘ed7 12.♗e2 (12.f5 ♗d6 13.♘ge2
b4 14.fxe6 fxe6 15.♘d1 ♘e4; 12.♗d2
Ivanisevic — Solak, Slovenia 2008
12...dxc4 13.bxc4 ♘c5∓) 12...♗d6
13.0-0 0-0 14.♖d1∞)

8...♗h5 9.♘f4 ♗g6 10.♘xg6 hxg6

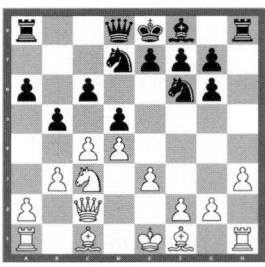

11.g3! By fianchettoing the bishop on
g2, White can castle without fearing
the advance of the black "g" pawn.

a) 11.♗d2 e5∞;

b) 11.♗e2 e6 12.0-0 ♗d6 13.e4 (After a preventive move such as 13.a3
there can follow 13...g5!?∞, developing the initiative on the kingside.)
13...b4 14.exd5 bxc3 15.dxc6 ♘b8
16.♗f3 ♕c7 17.d5 0-0 18.♗e3 exd5

19.cxd5 a5= — The white pawns have
advanced far but they are firmly
blockaded, Hracek — Dautov, Germany 2000;

c) 11.♗b2 e6 12.c5 g5∞ Shabalov —
Laznicka, Philadelphia 2010;

11...e5

(11...e6 12.♗g2 ♗e7 13.0-0 0-0
14.♖d1 (14.e4 bxc4 15.bxc4 dxc4
16.♖d1±) 14...♖c8 15.e4 b4 16.exd5
exd5 17.♘a4± S.Saric — Lukovic,
Novi Sad 2011)

12.♗g2 ♖c8 13.c5 ♗e7 14.♗b2 0-0
15.♘e2 ♕a5+ 16.♗c3 ♕c7 17.a4±
Radjabov — Movsesian, Sarajevo
2003 ;

5...g6 6.♗d3 ♗g7 7.♘f3 0-0 8.0-0
♗g4

(Solid but passive is 8...♘bd7 White
can play in various ways retaining a minimal advantage in each
case: 9.cxd5 (9.b3 b5 10.♗b2 ♗b7
11.♖ad1 ♕c7 12.e4 b4 13.♘a4 dxe4
14.♗xe4 ♘xe4 15.♕xe4∞ Tomashevsky — Epishin, Kazan 2005;
9.♖d1 ♖e8 10.b3 b5 11.♗b2 ♗b7±
Ivanchuk — Gashimov, Nice (rapid) 2010) 9...cxd5 10.♗d2 b6 11.♕b3
♗b7 12.♖fc1± Postny — Almagro,
Spain 2009)

9.♘e5 ♗e6 10.c5 (10.♗d2 dxc4
11.♘xc4 ♘bd7 12.b4 ♗xc4 13.♗xc4
e5= Shimanov — Solak, Stockholm
2012) 10...♘bd7 11.♘xd7

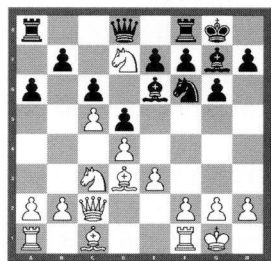

11...♗xd7!

a) 11...♘xd7 12.♗d2 (*12.b4 f6 13.e4 dxe4 14.♘xe4 ♗f7* Tomashevsky — Evseev, Sochi 2006 *15.♗b2±*) 12...f5

a1) 12...f6 13.f4 ♗f7 14.f5 ♕e8 I.Farago — Burmakin, Bad Woerishofen 2010 15.e4!± 15...e5 16.fxe6 ♗xe6 17.exd5 cxd5 18.♖ae1 ♕f7 (*18...f5 19.♘xd5 ♗xd4+ 20.♔h1 ♖c8 21.b4 ♘e5 22.♘f4+-*) 19.♖xe6 ♕xe6 20.♘xd5 f5 21.♘c7 ♗xd4+ 22.♔h1 ♕e5 23.♘xa8 ♖xa8 24.♕b3+ ♔h8 25.♕xb7 ♖d8 26.b4 ♗xc5 27.♕xa6+-;

a2) 12...♕c7 13.b4 ♖fe8 14.f4 (*14. a4±*) 14...f6 15.♗e1 (*15.a4±*) 15... ♗f7?! (*15...f5±*) 16.f5± Moiseenko — Burmakin, Sochi 2012;

13.b4 ♗f7 14.f4 (Also possible is *14.♘e2* and *14...e5 15.dxe5 ♘xe5 16.♗c3±* — The f5 pawn seriously restricts its white squared bishop, therefore White's chances are preferable, Macieja — Wojtaszek, Warsaw2009) 14...e5 15.a4 g5 16.fxg5 (*16. ♘e2±*) 16...♕xg5 17.♔h1± — Eventually White will play b4-b5, which

is always very unpleasant, Koneru — Stefanova, Ulan Bator 2010;

b) 11...♕xd7 12.♗d2

(12.♘a4 ♖ae8

(12...♕c7 13.f4 ♘g4

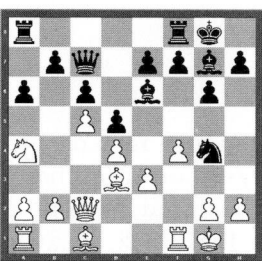

14.h3!N (*14.♘b6 ♖ae8 15.b4±* Giri — Kamsky, Beijing 2011) 14...♘h6 15.g4!± — The black knight remains out of play for the whole game.)

13.♘b6 Otherwise ♗e6-f5 and then e7-e5 13...♕c7

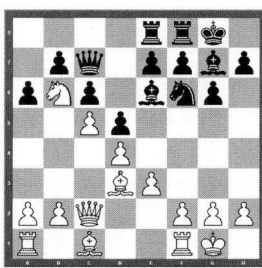

14.f4!N (*14.b4 ♘d7 15.♘xd7 ♗xd7 16.f4 f6=* Hracek — Kasparov, Prague (simultaneous) 2001; *14.f3 ♘d7 15.♘a4 f6 16.f4 ♔h8 17.♗d2 ♗f7 18.g4 e5 19.f5∞* Korchnoi —

Sakaev, Copenhagen 2005) 14...
♘d7 (*14...♘g4 15.h3 ♘h6 16.g4±*)
15.♘a4±)

12...♗f5 13.♗xf5 gxf5 (*13...♕xf5
14.♕xf5 gxf5 15.♘e2±* — The potential threat of advancing pawns of
the queenside is unpleasant) 14.♘e2
♔h8 15.♘f4 ♖g8 16.f3 ♗h6 17.♘d3±
Laznicka — Postny, Kolkata 2009;

12.♘a4

(The languid 12.♗d2 permits either e7-e5, or an exchange of the
white squared bishops advantageous for Black: 12...♘g4! 13.f4
♘h6 14.♕b3

(14.b4 ♗f5 15.a4 f6 16.♘d1?! (*16.
b5=*) 16...♗xd3 17.♕xd3 e5∓ Wang
Yue — Kamsky, Nice (blindfold)
2009)

14...♖b8 15.h3 ♔h8 16.♘a4 f6
17.♘b6 ♗f5 18.g4 ♗xd3 19.♕xd3
♘f7 20.♔g2 e5 21.dxe5 fxe5 22.♗c3
♕e7 23.b4 ♖be8 24.♖ae1 ♔g8∓ The
b6 knight is out of play so Black's
position is preferable, Le Quang
Liem — Khalifman, Moscow 2012)

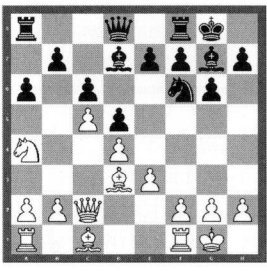

12...♖b8 It looks like this move is
the most exact. Before retreating
the knight from f6, Black tempts the
white knight to move to b6.

a) 12...♕c7 13.♘b6 ♖ae8 14.f4±;

b) 12...♘g4 13.♘b6 ♖b8 14.f3!

(14.♗d2 e5 (*14...♕c7 15.f4 ♘h6
16.♘xd7 ♕xd7 17.h3*) 15.f3 ♘h6
16.dxe5 ♗xe5 17.e4 dxe4 18.♗xe4
♗e6 19.♖ad1)

14...♘h6 15.g4! Restricting the black
knight very effectively. 15...♖e8 (*15...
e6 16.♗d2 ♕e7 17.h3 f5 18.♘xd7
♕xd7 19.g5 ♘f7 20.f4±; 15...f5 16.g5
♘f7 17.f4±; 15...e5 16.dxe5 ♗xe5
17.e4±*) 16.h3 f6 17.e4 ♘f7 18.f4 dxe4
19.♗xe4±;

c) 12...♘h5 13.f4!? (*13.f3 e5 14.g4 e4∓;
13.♘b6 ♖b8 — 12...♖b8 13.♘b6 ♘h5*)
13...♖b8 (*13...♗g4 14.h3 ♗f5 15.♗xf5
gxf5 16.♖f3 e6 17.g4±*) 14.♖f2!± (*14.
♗d2 ♗g4 15.h3 ♗f5 16.♗xf5 gxf5
17.♗e1 ♕d7=*) ;

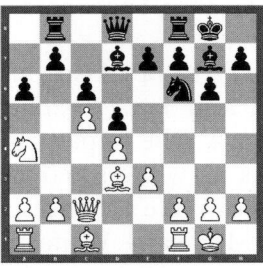

13.♘b6

(13.♗d2 ♘h5 (13...♘g4 14.h3 ♘h6 15.♘b6 ♗f5 16.e4 dxe4 17.♗xe4 ♕xd4 18.♖fe1↑) 14.♗c3 ♖e8 15.f4 ♗g4! 16.h3 ♗f5 17.♗xf5 gxf5 18.♗e1 ♕d7=)

13...♘h5 14.♘xd7

a) 14.f4 ♗g4! 15.h3 (15.♗d2 e6=) 15...♗f5 16.♗xf5 gxf5= — The white knight is stuck on b6. Black has an excellent game.;

b) 14.♗d2 e5 15.dxe5 ♗xe5 16.♗c3 ♗xc3 17.♕xc3 ♕e7=;

14...♕xd7 15.f4 f5 16.♗d2±/= — White has a plan of advancing the pawns in the queenside,therefore his position is preferable. However Black can resist after exchanging his a-pawn for b5 and placing the knight on e4.

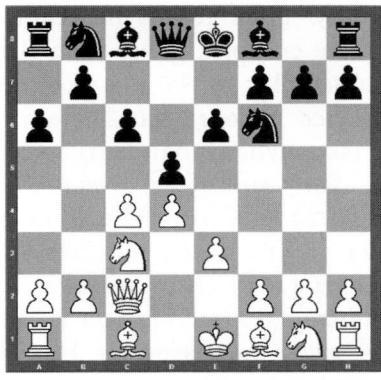

6.♘f3 c5
6...b5 7.c5 ♘bd7 8.♗d3±;

After 6...♘bd7 the best response for White is 7.b3 to recapture on c4 with a pawn making the move a7-a6 unnecessary. (7.♗d2 — 3.♘f3 ♘f6 4.e3 a6 5.♗d2 e6 6.♘c3 ♘bd7 7.♕c2) 7...♗d6 8.♗b2 0-0 (8...e5 9.dxe5! ♘xe5 10.0-0-0! ♕e7 11.cxd5 0-0 12.♘xe5 ♗xe5 13.dxc6± Aronian — Vallejo Pons, Khanty Mansyisk 2005) 9.♗d3

(The e2 square can later be profitably used by the c3 knight therefore the following is weaker : 9.♗e2 e5

(9...b5 10.0-0 ♗b7 (10...b4?! 11.♘a4 ♘e4 12.♗d3 f5 13.♘e5± Gelfand — Shirov, Monaco (rapid) 2003) 11.c5 ♗c7 12.♗d3 e5 13.dxe5 ♘xe5 14.♘xe5 ♗xe5 15.♘e2±)

10.cxd5 (10.dxe5 ♘xe5 11.0-0-0 ♕e7 12.c5 ♗c7 13.♘a4 Romanov — Jakovenko, Olginka 2011 13...♗g4∓ Comfortably completing development. Black should have a good game.) 10...cxd5 11.dxe5 ♘xe5 12.0-0 (12.♖d1 ♗e6 13.0-0 ♖c8 — The c3 knight is unstable giving Black active counter play.) 12...♗e6 13.♖ac1 ♖c8 14.♕d1 ♕e7 15.♘d4= — A complicated game with near equal chances lays ahead.)

9...e5 It's bette r that Black carries out this freeing move immediately, otherwise White will meet it with the counter-thrust e3-e4: (9...♖e8 10.0-0 e5 11.cxd5 cxd5 12.e4!± Al.Kharitonov — Kornev, Sochi 2006; 9...♕e7 10.0-0 e5 11.cxd5 cxd5

12.e4±) 10.cxd5 cxd5 11.dxe5 ♘xe5
12.♘xe5 ♗xe5 13.♘e2 ♕a5+ 14.♗c3
♗xc3+ 15.♕xc3 ♕xc3+ 16.♘xc3±

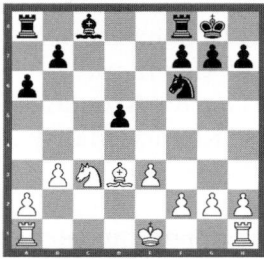

— A classical ending with an isolated pawn is unpleasant for Black,
though with good defence he should
be able to draw, Leko — Ni Hua,
Saratov 2011

7.cxd5
The following leads to simplifications and an equal game 7.dxc5 ♗xc5
8.a3 dxc4 9.♗xc4 b5 10.♗d3 ♘bd7
11.♘e4 (*11.b4 ♗e7 12.♗b2 ♗b7 13.♖d1
0-0 14.0-0 Sakaev — Izoria, Moscow
2003 14...♖c8=*) 11...♗e7 12.♘xf6+
♘xf6 (*12...♗xf6 13.♗e4 ♖a7=*) 13.e4
♗b7 14.0-0 ♘d7 15.♕e2 ♕b8 16.♗d2
0-0 17.♖ac1 ♗d6= Tomashevsky —
Ni Hua, Nizhnij Novgorod 2007

7...exd5 8.♗e2
8.g3 ♘c6 9.♗g2 ♘b4 10.♕d2 ♗f5
11.0-0 ♗d3 12.♖d1 ♗c2 13.♖f1 (*13.
♖e1 ♘e4 14.♘xe4 ♗xe4=*) 13...♗d3
14.♖d1 ♗c2= Blagojevic — Voiska,
Plovdiv 2010;
8.dxc5 allows the black bishop to
reach an active position in one move
after 8...♗xc5 9.♗e2 0-0 10.0-0

♘c6= White's pieces turn out to be
passive.

8...♗e6
8...cxd4 9.♘xd4

(9.exd4 ♘c6 10.0-0 ♗d6 (*10...
♗e7 11.♘e5 ♗d7 12.♗e3 0-0± —
White's game is a bit better?, Tomashevsky — Wang Yue, Nizhnij Novgorod 2007*) 11.♗g5 ♗e6=
Koneru — Stefanova, Plovdiv 2010)

9...♗d6

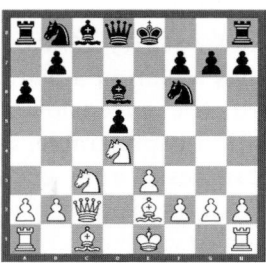

10.♘f5! (The following leads to
a more complex game with Black
counter play *10.0-0 0-0 11.b3 ♘c6
12.♘xc6 bxc6 13.♗b2± Hammer
— Iskusnyh, Dubai 2011*) 10...0-0
(*10...♗xf5 11.♕xf5 ♘c6 12.0-0 0-0
13.♖d1±*) 11.♘xd6 ♕xd6 12.0-0
♗g4 13.♖d1 ♗xe2 14.♘xe2 ♘c6
15.♗d2 (*15.b3 ♖ac8 16.♗b2 ♘d4
17.♕d2 ♘xe2+ 18.♕xe2±*) 15...♘g4
16.♘g3± Gustafsson — Handke,
Germany 2010;

8...♘c6 allows the unpleasant
9.♘e5!?

(9.0–0 ♗e6 — 8...♗e6 9.0–0
♘c6(9...cxd4 10.♘xd4±))

9...♕c7 (9...♗d7 10.0–0 cxd4 11.♘xc6
♗xc6 12.exd4± Tomashevsky —
Lintchevsky, Olginka (rapid) 2011)
10.♘xc6 bxc6 (10...♕xc6 11.0–0 ♗d6
12.dxc5 ♕xc5 13.♗d2 0–0 14.♖ac1±
Mamedyarov — Grischuk, Nalchik
2009) 11.e4!

(A completely unclear game arises after 11.0–0 ♗d6 12.h3 0–0
(12...cxd4 13.exd4 h6 14.♗e3 0–0
15.♖ac1∞ Bukavshin — Droz-
dowski, Albena 2011) 13.dxc5 ♗xc5
14.b3 ♗a7!?∞ — The threat ♗a7-b8
emerges provoking f2-f4.)

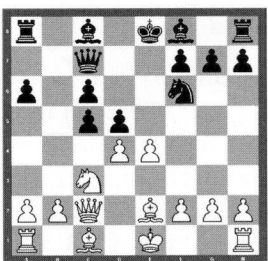

11...♗e6

a) 11...♗e7 12.0–0 0–0 13.dxc5±;

b) 11...cxd4 12.♘xd5 ♘xd5 13.exd5
♗b7 14.0–0 (14.♕e4+ ♗e7 15.♕xd4
0–0 16.0–0 ♗d6 17.♕h4 cxd5 18.♗d3
g6 19.♗e3±) 14...♗d6 15.♗f3 cxd5
16.♖e1+ ♔f8 17.♕xc7 ♗xc7 18.b3±
Zhou Weiqi — Ni Hua, Danzhou
2010;

12.♗e3

(12.0–0 cxd4 13.♘xd5 ♘xd5 14.exd5
♗xd5 15.♗c4 ♖d8 (15...♗xc4
16.♕xc4 ♗e7 17.♕xd4 0–0 18.♗f4±
Flear — Malakhatko, Calvi 2012)
16.♗g5 f6 17.♗d2 ♗e7=)

12...c4 (12...cxd4 13.♗xd4 ♘xe4
14.♘xe4 dxe4 15.0–0–0↑) 13.0–0
♗e7

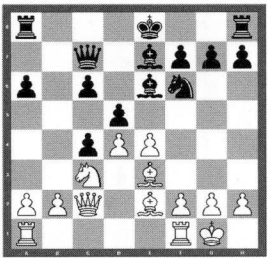

14.e5!N (14.b3 cxb3 15.axb3 dxe4
16.♘xe4 ♘xe4 17.♕xe4= Jovanic
— Svetushkin, Zadar 2011) 14...♘g4
(14...♘d7 15.f4 f5 16.♘a4±) 15.♗f4 g5
16.♗xg4 ♗xg4 17.♗e3± — White
has a good black squared blockade.
His chances are better.

9.0–0 ♘c6 10.♖d1
10.♘e5 ♖c8 11.♖d1 (11.♗f3 ♗d6
12.♘xc6 ♖xc6 13.dxc5 ♖xc5=; 11.♕a4
cxd4 12.exd4 ♕b6=) 11...cxd4 12.exd4
♗d6= Kornev — Ni Hua, Moscow
2012;

10.dxc5 ♗xc5 11.a3 (11.b3 ♖c8 12.♗b2
0–0 13.♖ac1 ♗a7 14.♖fd1 ♕e7 15.♕b1
♖fd8⩱ Gurevich — Morozevich,
Moscow 2001) 11...♗a7 (11...♖c8 12.b4
♗d6 13.♗b2 0–0=) 12.b4 ♖c8 13.♗b2
0–0 (13...♕e7 14.b5 axb5 15.♘xb5 ♘d4
16.♕d1 ♘xe2+ 17.♕xe2 ♗c5 18.♗d4

0-0 19.♕b2 ♗xd4 20.♘bxd4 ♘e4 21.♖fc1± Dreev — Wang Yue, Ergun 2006) 14.b5 axb5 15.♘xb5 ♘d4 (15... ♗b8=) 16.♕d1 ♘xb5 (16...♘xe2+ 17.♕xe2 ♗c5 18.♗d4 ♗e7 19.♕b2±) 17.♗xb5 ♘e4=

10...cxd4

10...♘b4 11.♕b1

(11.♕d2 ♘e4 12.♘xe4 dxe4

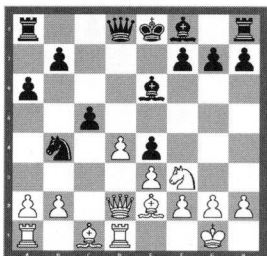

13.♘e5

(13.a3 exf3 14.♗xf3 ♘c6 15.d5 ♘e5 16.dxe6 ♘xf3+ 17.gxf3 fxe6 18.♕c2 ♕g5+ (18...♗d6 19.f4 0-0 20.♕e4 ♕e7 21.♗d2±) 19.♔f1 ♗e7 20.♕b3 ♔f7 21.♕xb7 ♖hd8 22.♗d2 ♖ab8 23.♕xa6 ♕f6= Matlakov — Lintchevski, St.Petersburg 2009)

13...cxd4 14.exd4

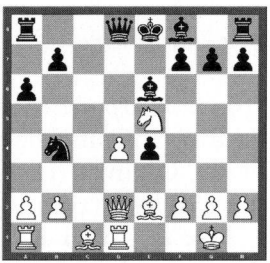

14...♗e7 The most accurate and reliable move though Black has other possibilities:

a) Risky is 14...♖c8?! 15.♕f4↑ — Black is behind in development.;

b) Sudden sharp tactics follow 14... f6!? 15.♗h5+ g6 16.♗xg6+ hxg6 17.♘xg6 ♖g8 18.♘xf8 ♗h3 19.g3 ♕e7 20.d5 ♕xf8 21.♕d4∞;

c) 14...♗d6 15.a3 ♘d5 16.♕c2 f5 17.f3 ♘f6 (17...e3!? 18.♕b3 f4 19.♗c4 ♗c7 20.♕xb7 0-0 Sulashvili — Guseinov, Baku 2008) 18.♗c4 (18.♗g5 0-0 19.♗c4 ♕e8=) 18...♖c8 19.♕b3 ♗xc4 20.♘xc4 ♗b8 21.fxe4 (21. ♗g5 ♕d5=) 21...fxe4 22.♘e3 ♕d7 23.♗d2 ♕f7=;

15.a3 ♘d5 16.♕c2 f6 17.♘c4 f5 18.f3 0-0 19.fxe4 fxe4 20.♕xe4 ♗f5 21.♕e5 ♗f6 22.♕d6 ♗c2 23.♖d2

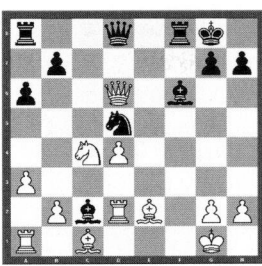

23...♕xd6!N (23...♗g6 Mamedyarov — I.Sokolov, Wijk aan Zee
2006 24.♕xd8 ♖axd8 25.♘e5 ♘e3
26.♘xg6 hxg6 27.d5 ♘f5 28.♖d1±)
24.♘xd6 ♗b3! 25.♖d3

(25.♗d1?! 25...♗xd1 26.♖xd1
♖ad8! 27.♘xb7 (27.♘e4 ♖de8
28.♘xf6+ ♖xf6∓) 27...♖de8∓ —
The black pieces have become
very active. White has to be concerned about maintaining equality.)

25...♗c2 26.♖d2=)

11...♕c8 12.♗d2

(12.e4 dxe4 13.♘xe4 ♗f5 14.♘fg5
♘xe4 15.♘xe4 cxd4 (15...♕e6!?
16.♗f3 0-0-0∞) 16.♖xd4 ♘c6
(16...♗e7 17.♗g5± Mamedyarov —
Grischuk, Baku 2008) 17.♖d1 ♗e7
18.♗d3 ♗g6=)

12...♗f5 13.♕c1 c4

(13...♘c2 14.♖b1 ♘b4 15.a3 (15.
dxc5!? 15...♗xb1 16.♕xb1 ♕xc5∞)
15...♘d3 16.♗xd3 ♗xd3 17.♖a1 c4
— 13...c4 14.a3 ♘d3 15.♗xd3 ♗xd3)

14.a3 ♘d3 15.♗xd3 ♗xd3 (15...cxd3
16.♘e5 ♗d6 17.♗e1 ♕c7 18.f4±)
16.♘e5 ♗f5

(16...♗g6

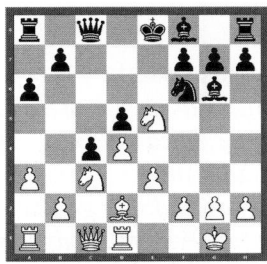

17.e4! dxe4 (17...♗xe4 18.♖e1 ♗e7
19.♗g5→) 18.♘a4! (18.♗f4 b5!= Jakovenko — Sakaev, St.Petersburg
2011) 18...♕e6 (18...♘d5 19.♘xc4
♕c6 20.♘cb6±) 19.♘xc4 ♗e7
(The fact that the bishop retreated
to g6 instead of f5 and doesn't participate in the queenside defence is
evident after 19...b5 20.♘cb6! ♖d8
21.d5 ♘xd5 22.♗a5!+-, with a decisive attack.) 20.♘c5 ♕c6 (20...♗xc5
21.dxc5 0-0 22.♘d6±) 21.♘a5 ♕d5
22.♘axb7 0-0 23.♕c3± Tomashevsky — Ni Hua, Saratov 2011)

17.e4 dxe4 18.♗g5 ♕e6

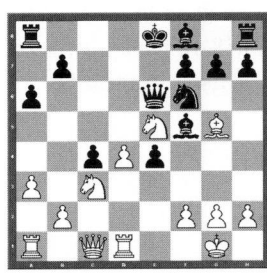

19.♖e1!N

(19.♘e2 ♖c8!

a) 19...b5 20.a4 h6 21.♗h4 ♖c8 22.axb5 axb5 23.♖a7 ♗e7 24.♕a1 0–0 25.♖a6↑;

b) 19...♘d5 20.♘f4 ♘xf4 21.♗xf4 ♖c8 (21...♕d5 22.♘xc4 ♖c8 23.♘b6 ♖xc1 24.♘xd5 ♖xa1 25.♖xa1 ♔d7 26.♘b6+±; 21...b5 22.d5 ♕b6 23.d6 ♖d8 24.g4 ♗e6 25.d7+ ♗xd7 26.♖xd7 ♖xd7 27.♘xd7 ♔xd7 28.♕d2+ ♔e6 29.♖d1 ♕c6 30.♕d8→) 22.d5 ♕f6 23.d6 ♗xd6 24.♖xd6 ♕xd6 25.♘xf7 ♕e6 26.♘d6+ (26.♘xh8 ♔f8=) 26...♔f8 Wojtaszek — I.Sokolov, Khanty Mansyisk 2010 27.♘xc8 ♕xc8 28.♗e5±/↑;

20.♘f4 ♕b6∞ — Black has sufficient counter play.)

19...♗e7 20.f3 h6 21.♗h4± — Winning back the pawn back and White gains the advantage due to his strong centre.

11.♘xd4 ♘xd4 12.♖xd4
12.exd4 yields nothing 12...♗e7 13.♕b3 (13.♗g5 0–0 14.♕b3 ♕d6! 15.♗f3 ♖fd8 16.g3 b5 17.♗f4 ♕d7=) 13...b5 14.♗g5 0–0 15.♗f3

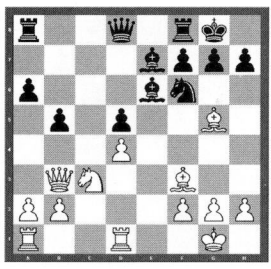

15...♖b8

a) 15...♖c8 16.a4 b4 17.♗xf6 ♗xf6 18.♕xb4 a5 (18...♖c4 19.♕b7± Sebenik — Jankovic, Zadar 2011) 19.♕a3 ♖c4 20.♘b5 ♕b6 21.♕d3 g6 22.b3 ♖b4 23.♖ac1 ♖d8;

b) 15...♕d6 16.♗xf6 ♗xf6 17.♗xd5 b4 18.♗xe6 bxc3 19.♗c4 cxb2 20.♕xb2± — White has an extra pawn though there is not much chance of realising it.;

16.♖ac1 ♖c8! Thanks to the opposition of rooks on the c-file, the d5 pawn is defended indirectly. (Passive is 16...♔h8 Volkov — Motylev, Novokuznetsk 2008. After a possible 17.g3 ♖e8 18.♘e2± White gets pressure on the black squares and the c-file.) 17.a4

(17.♘e2 ♖xc1 18.♖xc1 h6 19.♗e3 ♗g4 (o5Interesting is 19...g5!?, taking away the f4 square and creating a threat g5-g4.) 20.♗xg4 ♘xg4=)

17...h6 18.♗xf6 ♗xf6 19.axb5 axb5 20.♘xb5 (20.♕xb5 ♖b8 21.♕e2 ♖e8 22.♕c2 ♖b4∓ — Thanks to his great activity Blacks's position is even better.) 20...♖b8 21.♕d3 ♕d7 22.♘c7 ♖xb2=

12...♗c5

12...♖c8 13.♕a4+±;

12...♗d6 13.e4! ♗e5 14.♖d1 d4 15.f4 ♗b8 *(15...♘d7 16.fxe5 dxc3 17.♕xc3±)* 16.♗e3 ♗a7 17.♔h1 0-0 18.f5 ♗c8 19.♗xd4 ♗xd4 20.♕a4±

13.♖d1 ♕e7

13...♖c8 14.♕a4+±;

13...♕d6 14.♕a4+ ♗d7 15.♕b3 ♗c6 16.♗f3±

14.♗f3

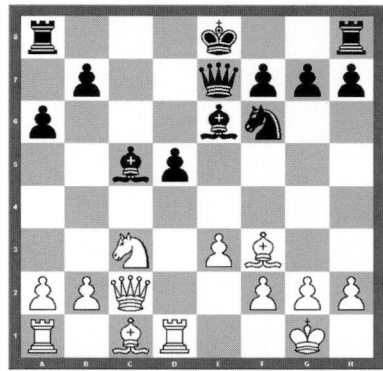

14...0-0!

14...♖d8 15.b3 0-0 16.♗b2 ♖c8 17.♕d3!

(17.♘xd5 ♗xd5 18.♗xd5 ♗xe3 19.♕e2 ♘xd5 20.♖xd5 ♗c5= *(20...♗g5 21.♖e5 ♕f6* Lenic — Rublevsky, Aix les Bains 2011 *22.♖d1↑)*)

17...♖fd8 18.♘e2 ♗a3 19.♗xa3 ♕xa3 20.♘f4±

15.♗xd5 ♘xd5 16.♘xd5 ♗xd5 17.♖xd5 ♖ac8 18.♗d2

18.♕d1 ♖fd8 19.g3 ♗b6=;

18.♕e2 ♕e4

18...♗xe3 19.♗c3 ♗b6±/=

White's osition is slightly more active but Black can maintain equality with accurate defence, for example:

20.♕f5

Or 20.♕b3 ♖fe8 21.h3 ♗c5 22.♖ad1 b5 23.♖d7 ♕e6 24.♕xe6 ♖xe6=

20...♕e6 21.♕f3 f6=

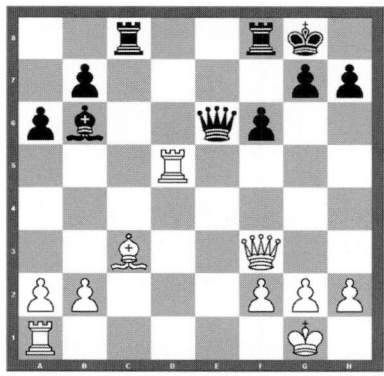

Gelfand — Anand, Moscow (match-06) 2012 Conclusion: The following can be said of the rare line 4.e3 ♗f5 5.cxd5 cxd5 6.♕b3 ♗c8 — It's sufficiently difficult for White to gain a substantial advantage. As for the main line 4.e3 a6 5.♕c2, it's quite a good choice for White as Black has to play with pinpoint accuracy for equality.

PART 8

3.♘f3 Variations, without early night development ♘f6

■ GAME 15

1.d4 d5 2.c4 c6 3.♘f3 dxc4

A rare move. However it deserves attention since it's better than its reputation and it's very difficult for White to gain an advantage.

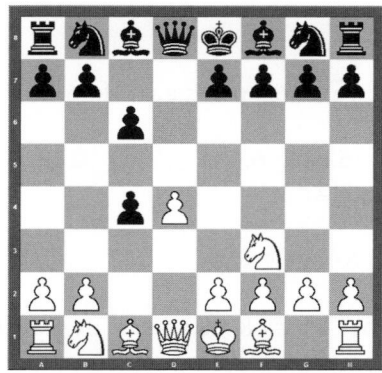

4.e3

4.a4 transposes e.g. 4...e6 (4...♘f6 5.♘c3 — 3...♘f6 4.♘c3 dxc4 5.a4) 5.e3 b5 — 4.e3 b5 5.a4 e6

4...♗e6

The experimental 4...b5 is dubious 5.a4 e6 6.axb5 (6.♘c3 ♗b4 — 3.♘c3 e6 4.♘f3 dxc4 5.e3 b5 6.a4 ♗b4; 6.b3 ♗b4+ 7.♗d2 ♗xd2+ 8.♘fxd2 cxb3 9.axb5 b2 10.♖a2 ♘e7 11.♖xb2 0-0= Neverov — Khenkin, Plovdiv 2012) 6...cxb5 7.b3 ♗b4+ 8.♗d2 ♗xd2+ 9.♘bxd2 a5 10.bxc4 b4 11.♘e5! (11.c5 ♘f6∞ Ledge — Khenkin, Frankfurt 2011) 11...♘f6

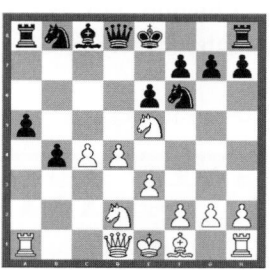

12.♕a4+!

(Less accurate is 12.♗e2 0-0 13.♗f3, in view of 13...♖a7!?

(13...♖a6 14.♕a4 (14.0-0 ♕c7 15.c5 ♘d5±/⇆ Leutwyler — Khenkin, Helsingor 2011) 14...♘fd7 — 12.♕a4 ♘fd7 13.♗e2 0-0 14.♗f3 ♖a6)

14.0-0 ♕c7 15.♕a4 ♗d7 16.♘xd7 ♘bxd7±/⇆ Kick — Khenkin, Bad Wiessee 2010)

12...♘fd7

(12...♗d7 13.♘xd7 ♘bxd7

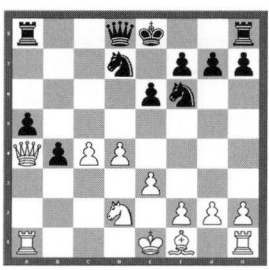

14.g3!N (*14. ♗e2 0-0 15. ♗f3 ♖a7 16.0-0 ♕c7±/⇆* Matthiesen — Pedersen, Copenhagen 1996) 14...0-0 15. ♗g2 It's hard fo r Black to support his pawns without the white squared bishop. For example: 15... ♖a7 16.♘b3 ♕c7 17.♕c6!±)

13. ♗e2 0-0 14. ♗f3

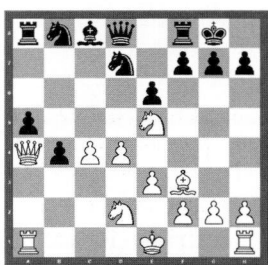

14...♖a6N (Very bad is *14...♖a7 15.♘d3* — the rook on a7 is not defended therefore the b4 pawn hangs *15...e5 16.d5 f5 17.♘xb4 ♘c5 18.♕a3±* Haba — Reefat Bin-Sattar, Yerevan 1996) 15.♘d3 e5 (*15...♘b6 16.♕c2±*) 16.d5 f5 17.e4 ♕b6 18.0-0 (*18. ♕c2 ♘c5 19.♘xc5 ♕xc5 20.0-0 ♘d7! 21.exf5 ♕b6∞*) 18...fxe4 19. ♗xe4 (*19.♘xe4? 19...♖xf3! 20.gxf3 ♕g6+ 21.♔h1 ♕h5 22.♔g2 ♘b6 23.♕d1 ♘xc4 24.♖g1 ♖h6 25.♔f1 ♖a6∓/→*) 19...♘d4 20.♕c2 ♘f6 21.♕b2!? (*21.♖ae1 ♘xe4 22.♖xe4 ♕c3 23.♕xc3 bxc3 24.♘b1 ♗f5 25.♖e3±/∞*) 21...♘xe4 22.♕xd4 exd4 23.♘xe4 ♘d7 24.f3 ♘b6 25.♖fc1±

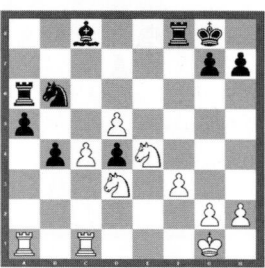

— White's central passed pawns are more dangerous than Black's wing pawns.

5.a4
On 5.♘c3 is a good option

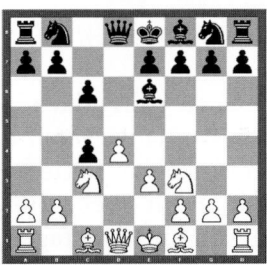

5...b5!?

(5...♘f6 6.a4 — 5.a4 ♘f6 6.♘c3

a) 6.e4?! 6...b5 7.♘g5 ♗g4 8.f3 ♗c8!±;

b) 6.♘g5!? ♗g4

b1) 6...♕c8 7.e4 (*7.a4 a5 8.e4 h6 9.♘xe6 ♕xe6 10.e5 ♘bd7 11. ♗e2 ♘d5 12.0-0 ♘7b6 13. ♗g4 ♕g6 14.e6±* Alekseev — Zhang Pengxiang, Nizhnij Novgorod 2007) 7...b5 8. ♗e2 ♗g4 9.e5 ♗xe2 10.♕xe2 h6 11.exf6 hxg5 12.fxg7 ♗xg7 13. ♗xg5 ♕e6 14.♕xe6 fxe6 15.0-0-0± Shimanov — Khairullin, Ulan Ude 2009;

b2) 6...♗d5 7.e4 h6 8.exd5 hxg5 9.dxc6 ♘xc6 10.d5 ♘e5 11. ♗xg5 a6 (*11...♕c7 12.♕d4 e6 13.0-0-0 (13.f4 ♘eg4∞) 13...♘xd5 (13... ♗c5? 14.♘b5+-) 14.♘xd5 exd5 15.♕xd5±*) 12.♕d4 ♕d6 (*12...♕c7*

13.0–0–0↑) 13.f4! (*13.♗xc4 ♘xc4 14.♕xc4± Gofshtein — Lalic, Neum 2000*) 13...♘d3+ 14.♗xd3 cxd3 15.♕xd3±;

7.f3 ♗d7

(*7...♗h5 8.♗xc4 e6 9.e4 ♗e7*

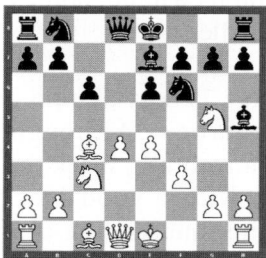

10.♗xe6!N (*10.♗e3± Pe.Nielsen — Rasmussen, Copenhagen 2004; 10.♘h3±*) 10...fxe6 11.♘xe6±/→)

8.♗xc4 e6 9.0–0 (*9.e4 b5 10.♗e2 h6 11.♘h3 c5 12.♗xb5 a6 13.♘c3 cxd4 14.♕xd4 ♘c6 Adhiban — Golod, New Delhi 2012*) 9...♗e7 (*9...c5 10.d5±*) 10.♘ge4 ♘xe4 11.♘xe4 0–0 12.♗d2±)

6.a4 (*6.♘g5 ♗f5 7.♘xf7 ♔xf7 8.♕f3 ♔g6 9.♕g3+ ♔f7 10.♕f3= Pe.Nielsen — Rausis, Germany 1998*) 6...b4

(*6...♕a5 7.♗d2 b4 8.♘a2 c3 9.bxc3 ♗xa2 10.c4! (10.♖xa2 bxc3 11.♗c1 e6 = San Segundo — Starostits, Bled 2002) 10...♗xc4 11.♗xc4±/⩲*)

7.♘e4

a) 7.♘a2 a5 8.♘g5 ♗c8 (*8...♗d5 9.e4 h6 10.exd5 hxg5 11.♗xc4 cxd5

12.♗b5+ ♘d7 13.♗xg5 ♘gf6 14.♘c1± Melkumyan — Av.Grigoryan, Yerevan 2012*) 9.♗xc4 e6 10.e4 ♗e7 11.♘f3 ♘f6= Filippov — Riazantsev, Krasnoyarsk 2003;

b) 7.♘e2 ♘f6 8.♘f4 ♗d5 9.♘e5 ♘bd7 10.♗xc4 ♘xe5 11.♗xd5 ♘xd5 12.dxe5± Kir. Georgiev — Varga, Austria 2008;

7...♘f6

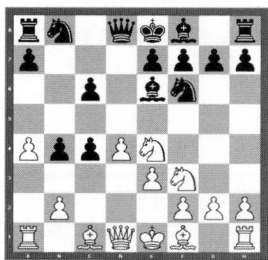

8.♘g3

a) 8.♘xf6+ exf6 9.♗d2 ♘d7 10.♖c1 c3 11.bxc3 b3∞;

b) 8.♘c5?! 8...♗d5 9.♕c2 (*9.♘e5 e6 10.f3 ♗xc5 11.dxc5 ♘fd7 12.♘xd7 ♘xd7 13.e4 ♗xe4 14.fxe4 ♕h4+∓ Izoria — Kupreichik, Istanbul 2003; 9.♗d2 e6 10.♗xb4 ♘bd7∓ Yakovich — Poluljahov, St.Petersburg 1998*) 9...e6 10.♗xc4 ♗xc5 11.dxc5 ♗e4∓ V.Georgiev — Kupreichik, Kish 2003;

c) 8.♘ed2 c3 9.bxc3 bxc3 10.♘c4 g6 11.♗a3 ♗g7 12.♗d3 0–0 13.0–0 ♘bd7 14.♖c1 ♖c8 15.♖xc3 c5 = Gyimesi — Varga, Pula 2000;

8...♗d5

(8...♛a5 9.♛c2

(9.e4!? Now a threat of ♘f3-g5 emerges 9...c3 (9...♘bd7 10.♘g5±) 10.bxc3 bxc3 11.♝d3 ♝g4 12.♛b3 ♘bd7 13.♛b7 ♜d8 14.♛xc6 ♝xf3 15.gxf3 e5 16.♝b5±)

9...♘bd7 (9...b3+ 10.♝d2 bxc2 11.♝xa5±; 9...c3 10.bxc3 bxc3 11.♝e2±) 10.♝xc4 b3+ 11.♛d2 ♛xd2+ 12.♘xd2 ♝xc4 13.♘xc4 c5 14.♝d2± — The b3 pawn can later be attacked.)

9.♝d2 e6 10.♜c1

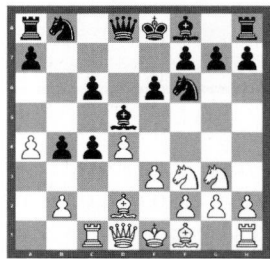

10...h5!

(10...c5 11.♝xc4 (11.dxc5 ♝xc5 12.♝xc4 ♘bd7= Landa — Braun, Germany 2009) 11...♝xc4 12.♜xc4 ♘bd7 13.0-0±)

11.h4 ♝d6

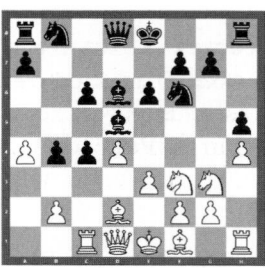

12.♝xc4!N

(12.♜h3 ♘bd7 13.♝xc4 ♝xc4 (13...c5 Konopka — Krenz, Germany 2003 14.♝xd5! ♘xd5 15.♘e4 ♛e7 16.♘xd6+ ♛xd6 17.♜g3↑) 14.♜xc4 c5 15.dxc5 ♝xc5 16.♝xb4 ♝xb4+ 17.♜xb4 ♛a5 18.♛d2 0-0 = — The rook on h3 will not come into play for a while.)

12...♝xg3 13.fxg3 a5 14.0-0 ♘bd7 15.♘g5 ♛b6∞ Although White has an advantage, Black too has his trumps with a good blockade on the white squares. The chances are equal.

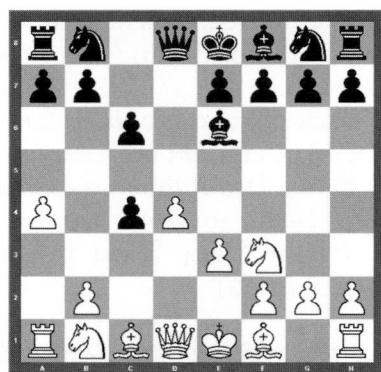

5...♘f6 6.♘c3
6.♘a3 does not pose any problems 6...♝d5 (6...c5=) 7.♘xc4 e6= — Black will soon push c6-c5.

6...g6
6...♝d5 7.♘d2±;

6...♝g4 7.♝xc4 e6 8.a5± Eljanov — Deutsch, Israel 2008;

6...h6 7.♘e5 ♘bd7 (7...c5 8.♕f3
♘bd7 9.♕xb7±) 8.♘xc4 ♗f5 9.f3!N
(9.♕b3 ♕c7 10.f3 e5 11.dxe5 ♘c5∞
Topalov — I.Sokolov, Sarajevo 1999)
9...e6 10.e4 ♗h7 11.♗e2±;

6...♘a6 7.a5

a) 7.♘e5 ♘b4 8.a5 — 7.a5 ♘b4
8.♘e5(8.♘xc4 ♗f5 9.♘a3 e5∓;
8.♗xc4 ♗xc4 9.♘xc4 c5=) ;

b) 7.♘g5 ♗g4 8.f3 ♗h5 9.♗xc4 ♘b4
Raykhman — Kovalenko, Alushta
2009 10.0-0±;

7...♗d5

(7...♘b4 8.♘e5 ♘d7 9.♘xc4 ♗xc4
(9...b5 10.axb6 axb6 11.♖xa8 ♕xa8
12.e4±) 10.♗xc4 e6 11.♕b3 (11.0-
0 ♗e7 12.e4 0-0 13.♗f4±) 11...b5
12.axb6 ♘xb6 13.0-0± Riazantsev
— Hamdouchi, France 2008)

8.♘d2 g6 9.e4 ♗e6 10.♘xc4± Karpov — Ljubojevic, Rotterdam 1989

7.e4
7.♘g5 ♗d5 8.e4 h6 9.exd5 hxg5
10.♗xc4 (10.dxc6 ♘xc6 11.d5 ♘a5
12.♗xg5 ♗h6 13.♗xh6 ♖xh6∓ Goganov — Bogdanovich, Donetsk 2010)
10...cxd5 11.♗b5+ ♘c6 12.♗xg5 ♗g7
13.0-0 0-0=;
7.♘e5 ♗g7 8.♗xc4

8...♘d5!N (8...♗xc4 9.♘xc4 0-0
10.0-0± Postny — I.Botvinnik, Israel
2008) 9.e4 ♘xc3 (9...♘c7!?) 10.bxc3
♗xc4 11.♘xc4 c5=

7... ♗g7
7...h6 8.♘e5± Zubov — Deutsch,
Petach Tikva 2011

8.♘g5
8.♗e2 0-0 9.0-0 ♘e8 (9...♘a6
10.♘g5 ♕d7 — 8.♘g5 ♕d7 9.♗e2
♘a6 10.0-0 0-0) 10.♗e3 ♘d6
11.♘g5± Fridman — Schuette, Nor-
dhorn 2009

8...♕d7
8...♕c8 9.e5 ♘g4 (9...♘d5 10.♗xc4±
San Segundo — Villavicencio, El Sauzal 2010) 10.♗e2 ♘h6 11.♘xe6 ♕xe6
12.0-0↑;
8...♗g4 9.f3 ♗c8 10.♗xc4 0-0
11.♕b3 e6 12.♗e3± Shimanov —
Rausis, Vilnius 2010

9.♗e2
9.♘xe6 ♕xe6 10.♕e2 ♘a6 11.♕xc4
♕xc4 12.♗xc4 ♘b4∓ Rakhmanov —
Kupreichik, Dubna 2007;
9.e5 ♘d5 10.♘xe6 ♕xe6 11.♗e2 (11.
♗xc4? 11...♘xc3 12.♕b3 ♘d5 13.♕xb7

0–0 14.♕xa8 ♕d7–+) 11...0–0 12.0–0 ♘a6∞

9...♘a6 10.0–0 0–0 11.e5
　11.a5!?

11...♘d5 12.♗xc4±

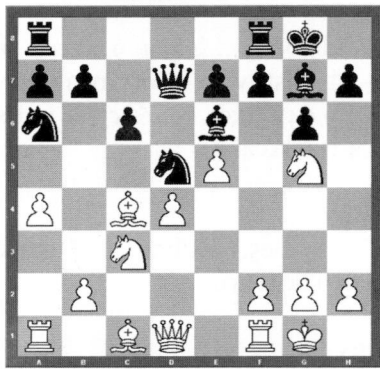

White's position is a little better. Conclusion: The line 3... dxc4 — is one of the lines which Black can prepare quickly, this is its advantage over other systems. At the same time it's not bad and frequently leads to a complex, full-blooded fight. Of course, with a good play White can count on a small opening advantage intrinsic to the player making the first move.

1.d4 d5 2.c4 c6 3.♘f3 e6

4.♕c2

4.g3 This gambit move is very demanding for White: 4...dxc4! The most principled (*4...f5 5.♗g2 ♘f6* leads to the Classical Stonewall, an opening whch is strategically risky for Black.; *4...♘f6 5.♗g2* Leads to a Catalan opening where Black has played an early c7-c6, depriving himself of the most promising defences in this opening.) 5.♗g2 b5 6.0–0 ♗b7 7.a4 ♘d7

a) After 7...a6 8.b3!? is interesting. Otherwise one of two transpositions can occur.

a1) 8.♘c3 ♘d7 — 7...♘d7 8.♘c3 a6(8...♘f6 9.♘e5 — 3.♘c3 e6 4.♘f3 dxc4 5.g3 b5 6.♗g2 ♗b7 7.♘e5 a6 8.0–0 ♘f6 9.a4) ;
a2) 8.♘e5 ♘f6 9.♘c3 — 3.♘c3 e6 4.♘f3 dxc4 5.g3 b5 6.♗g2 ♗b7 7.♘e5 a6 8.0–0 ♘f6 9.a4;

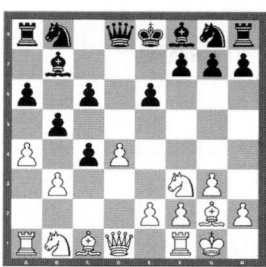

8...cxb3 9.♘bd2⯑ — White has good positional compensation and the b3 knight will be well-placed since it helps to blockade the c6 pawn.;

b) Quite good is 7...♘f6 8.♘e5 a6 9.axb5 (9.♘c3 — 3.♘c3 e6 4.♘f3 dxc4 5.g3 b5 6.♗g2 ♗b7 7.♘e5 a6 8.0-0 ♘f6 9.a4) 9...axb5 10.♖xa8 ♗xa8 11.♘c3 ♘d5 12.e4 ♘xc3 13.bxc3 ♘d7 14.♗f4 (*14.f4 ♗e7 15.♘xd7 ♕xd7 16.f5 exf5⯑* Too many exchanges have occurred so there are too few White pieces left to develop a kingside initiative.) 14...♘xe5 15.♗xe5 f6 16.♗f4 ♗e7 17.♕h5+ g6 18.♕h6 ♗f7 19.♖a1 ♗b7 — The compensation for a pawn is probably enough for equality but nothing else;

8.♘c3 a6 9.♘e5 ♕c8 This position has rarely occurred in practice. The most interesting seems to be

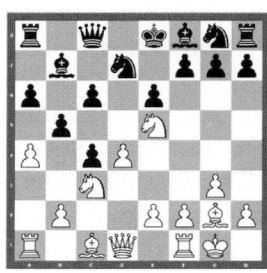

10.b3!?N

a) 10.♗f4 ♘gf6 11.e4 ♗b4 (*11... ♗e7!?*) 12.g4 0-0 13.g5 ♘xe5 14.♗xe5 ♘d7 15.♗g3 ♖d8 16.♕h5 g6 17.♕h4 ♗f8⯑ Khalifman — Timofeev, Sochi 2006;

b) 10.♘e4 is the sharpest 10...♘gf6 11.♘xf7 ♔xf7 12.♘g5+

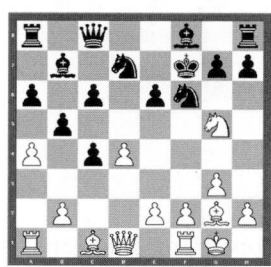

12...♔e7!

(12...♔g8 13.♗h3 g6 (*13...♗b4!?*) 14.e4 h6 15.♗xe6+ ♔g7 16.e5 ♘d5 17.♕f3 ♕e8 18.♗f7 ♘xe5 (*18...hxg5 19.♗xe8 ♖xe8 20.axb5 cxb5 21.♖xa6 ♗xa6 22.♕xd5+-* Grischuk — Timofeev, Sochi 2008) 19.dxe5 ♕xe5 20.♘e6+ ♔h7 21.♗e3±/↑)

13.♗h3 c5 14.♘xe6 cxd4 15.♘xd4 ♕c5⯑/∞ — It's hard for White to show that his initiative is worth a piece;

10...♘gf6

a) 10...b4 Risky is 11.♘e4 f5 (*11...c3? 12.♘c4!+-*) 12.♘d2 c3 13.♘dc4↑;

b) 10...cxb3 11.♘e4 (*11.♕xb3 ♘gf6 12.♗a3 b4 13.♗xb4 c5 14.♗xc5 ♘xc5 15.dxc5 ♗xg2 16.♔xg2 ♕xc5=*) 11...♘xe5 (*11...♘gf6 12.♘xf7 ♔xf7 13.♘g5+→*) 12.dxe5 c5 13.♕xb3⩲/∞;

11.axb5 cxb5 12.♗xb7 ♕xb7 13.bxc4 b4 14.♘xd7 ♘xd7 15.♘a4 ♗e7∞

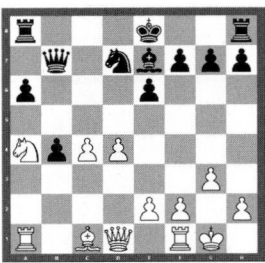

— The result ing positions structurally resemble the Noteboom Variation, but without possibilities for White to attack on the kingside;

4.♘bd2 Permits Bl ack to transpose to a good variation of either the Stonewall, or the Catalan opening — in both cases the knight has moved to d2 early and Black gains an equal game with accurate play. 4...f5

(*4...♘f6 5.g3 (5.e3 — 3...♘f6 4.e3 e6 5.♘bd2) 5...♗e7 6.♗g2 0-0 7.0-0 b6 8.♕c2 ♗b7 9.e4 ♘a6! From this square the knight can participate in the queenside battle, and d7 remains free for the retreat of the other knight. 10.e5*

(*10.a3 c5 11.exd5 (11.e5 ♘d7=) 11... exd5 12.dxc5 ♘xc5 13.b4 ♘ce4=*)

10...♘d7 11.a3 c5 12.cxd5 exd5 13.b3 ♘c7= Gelfand — Cifuentes Parada, Amsterdam 1988)

5.g3 ♘f6 6.♗g2 ♗d6 7.0-0

(After 7.♘e5 Black has an exchanging possibility 7...♘bd7 8.♘df3 ♘xe5! 9.♘xe5 (*9.dxe5 ♗b4+ 10.♗d2 ♗xd2+ 11.♕xd2 ♘e4 12.♕c2 ♕a5+ 13.♘d2 0-0=*) 9...♕c7=)

7...♘bd7 The most accurate because with this move the arrangement ♘f3-e5 and ♘d2-f3 is prevented although it's not too dangerous.

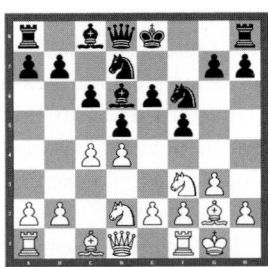

8.♘e1

(*8.♕c2 ♕e7 9.cxd5 (9.b3 0-0 10.♗b2 b6 11.♘e5 ♗b7 12.♖ac1 ♖ac8= Yevseev — Matlakov, Peterhof 2008) 9...cxd5 10.♘b1 ♘b6 11.♘c3 ♗d7 Kasimdzhanov — Galkin, Konya 2011*)

8...0-0 9.♘d3 ♕e7 The most soli d. Black continues development and has so far preventedqueenside expansion with the move b2-b4.

(9...♘e4 10.♕c2 ♕e7 11.f3 ♘xd2
12.♗xd2 c5 13.e4 dxc4 14.♕xc4
♘b6 15.♕c2 c4 (15...cxd4 16.e5
♕c7 17.♕b3 ♗e7 18.♖ac1±)
16.♘e5 ♗xe5 17.dxe5 ♕c5+ (17...
fxe4 18.♕xe4 ♗d7=) 18.♔h1 ♗d7
19.exf5 ♖xf5 20.f4 ♗c6= Bocharov
— S.Zhigalko, Moscow 2010)

10.♕c2 b6

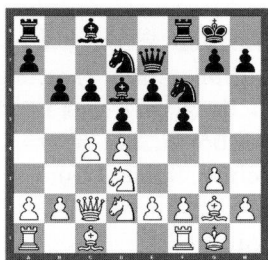

11.b4 (11.cxd5 cxd5 12.♘f3 ♗a6
13.♕a4 ♗c4= Matlakov — Riazantsev, St.Petersburg 2011) 11...♗b7
12.c5 ♗c7 13.♗b2 ♘e4 14.a4 bxc5
15.bxc5 a5= Lysyi — Huschenbeth,
Moscow 2011;

4.e3 ♘f6 — 3...♘f6 4.e3 e6

(4...f5 Leading to a typical Stonewall structure. However this structure with an early ♘g1–f3 is not
as good for Black as with ♘b1–
c3, since White has a plan of exchanging the dark squared bishops
via a3. 5.♗d3 ♘f6 6.0-0 ♗d6 7.b3
♕e7 8.♗b2 (8.a4 a5 9.♗a3 ♗xa3
10.♘xa3 0-0= It's very hard to
play b3-b4 but without it White's
queenside pawn structure has less
potential) 8...0-0

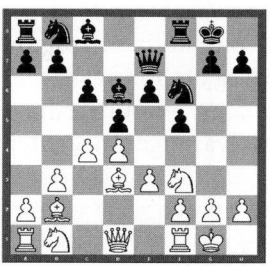

9.♕c1! (9.♘c3 ♘e4 10.♘e2 b6
11.♖c1 ♗b7 12.♘e5 ♘d7=) 9...
b6 10.♗a3 c5 (10...♗b7 11.♗xd6
♕xd6 12.♘c3 ♘bd7 13.cxd5 ♘xd5
14.♖d1± Ivanchuk — Nogueiras,
Habana 2007) 11.cxd5 exd5 12.♘c3±
Rodshtein — Schaefer, Rogaska
Slatina 2011)

4.♘c3, transposing to more dynam-
ic systems: Of course the most principled is 4...dxc4 — 3.♘c3 e6 4.♘f3
dxc4 (4...♘f6 — 3.♘f3 ♘f6 4.♘c3
e6 (Slav Defence, Part 2))

4...♘f6

4...dxc4 There is no sense in making the standard exchange before
developing the king's knight 5.♕xc4
b5 6.♕c2 ♗b7 7.e4± — White takes
the opportunity to quickly complete
kingside development. He will deter-
mine the position of the dark squared
bishop later.;

After 4...♗d6? with the idea of f7-
f5 and preventing ♗c1–f4. the most
promising is 5.♘c3

a) If 5.g3 f5 6.♗g2 ♘f6 Black's idea
works as he obtains a known standard position.;

b) 5.♗g5 ♘e7 (*5...f6 6.♗h4 ♘e7 7.♗g3±*) 6.e3 f6 7.♗h4 ♘f5 8.♗g3 ♘xg3 9.hxg3 f5 10.♘c3±;

5...f5 6.♗g5 — White has a comfortable advantage since after 6...♘f6 follows 7.♗xf6! and the queen recapture loses a pawn 7...♕xf6 8.cxd5 exd5 9.♘xd5±;

4...f5 5.♗f4 (*5.g3* {leads to a standard Stonewall line} *5...♘f6 6.e3 ♗e7 7.♘c3 0-0 8.♗d3 ♘e4 9.h3* (Many games have been played with *9.g4!?* which probably retains an advantage but gives Black counter chances due to the open lines.) *9...♘d7 10.0-0±* The bishop on f4 is perfectly placed with such a pawn structure while Black attempts to attack on the kingside with g7-g5 are speculative.

5.♗g5

5.e3 ♘bd7 (It's interesting but risky to make successive moves with the same piece: *5...♘e4!?* followed by f7-f5. For example *6.♘c3 f5 7.♘e5 ♘d7 8.♘d3 ♗d6 9.♘f4 ♘df6 10.f3 ♘xc3 11.bxc3 0-0∞*, with a good game for Black, Azmaiparashvili — Krasenkow, Groningen 1997) *6.♘c3* — *3.♘f3 ♘f6 4.♘c3 e6 5.e3 ♘bd7 6.♕c2* (Slav Defence, Part 2);

After 5.♘bd2 Black can confidently equalise with

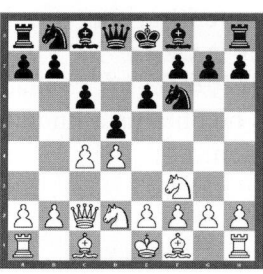

5...dxc4! 6.♘xc4 c5! 7.dxc5 ♗xc5 8.g3

(*8.a3 b5 9.♘ce5 ♕c7!* (*9... ♗e7 10.e3 0-0 11.♗d2!±*) *10.e4* (*10. ♗e3 ♗b4+ 11.♔d1 ♕xc2+ 12.♔xc2 ♗e7=; 10.e3 ♘bd7 11.♘d3 ♗d6 12.♕xc7 ♗xc7=*) *10...♘bd7 11.♗e3 ♕a5+ 12.♗d2 ♕b6 13.♗c3 0-0=*)

8...b5 9.♘ce5 ♕c7 10.♕b3 a6 (*10...0-0 11.♗g2 ♘bd7 12.♘d3 ♕b6 13.♘xc5 ♘xc5 14.♕c2 ♗b7 15.♗e3 ♕a5+ 16.♗d2 ♕b6 17.♗e3=*) *11.♗g2 ♗b7 12.0-0 ♗d5 13.♕c3 ♘e4 14.♕e1 0-0 15.♘d3 ♗b6 16.♗f4 ♕e7=* Carlsen — Ivanchuk, Sofia 2009;

5.g3 dxc4

(*5...♘bd7 6.♗g2 ♗d6* (*6... ♗e7 7.0-0 0-0 8.♖d1 b6 9.b3 ♗b7 10.♘c3±* leads to a favourable variation for White of the Catalan opening where e2-e4 can be played with ease.) *7.0-0 0-0 8.♘bd2 ♖e8 9.b3* (*9.e4 ♘xe4 10.♘xe4 dxe4 11.♕xe4 e5=*) *9...e5 10.cxd5 cxd5* (*10...e4? 11.dxc6+-*) *11.dxe5 ♘xe5 12.♗b2 ♘c6* (*12...♗g4 13.♗xe5 ♗xe5 14.♘xe5 ♖xe5 15.♘f3±*) *13.e3±*)

6.♕xc4 b5

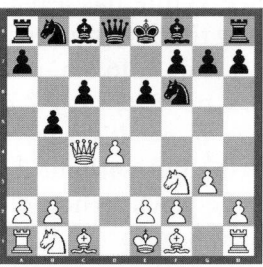

7.♕b3

a) 7.♕c2 is the least principled since it allows Black to play c6-c5 with ease : 7...♗b7 8.♗g2 ♘bd7 9.0-0 c5 10.♗g5

(10.a4 b4 11.♘bd2 ♖c8 12.♕d3 ♗e7 13.b3 cxd4 14.♘xd4 ♖c3 15.♕b1 (*15. ♕b5 ♗xg2 16.♔xg2 ♕a8+∓* Fridman — Grischuk, Mainz 2003) 15... ♗xg2 16.♔xg2 0-0 17.♗b2 ♕a8+ 18.♔g1 ♖cc8∓)

10...♖c8 11.dxc5 (*11.a4 cxd4 12.♕d1 bxa4 13.♕xd4 ♗c5 14.♕xa4 0-0=* Bareev — Kharlov, St.Petersburg 1998) 11...♗xc5 12.♕d3 a6 13.♘bd2 0-0 14.♘b3 ♗e7 (*14...♗b6 15.♖ac1 ♕e7=*) 15.♖fd1 h6 = Lerner — Lendwai, Oberwart 1996;

b) 7.♕d3 ♗b7 8.♗g2 ♘bd7 9.0-0 a6

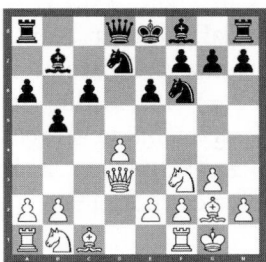

10.♘fd2!? An interesting move preventing c6-c5. (*10.a4 c5! 11.axb5 ♗e4=*) 10...♕b6

(10...♗e7 does not fully solve the problems. 11.♘c3 (*11.♘b3 0-0 12.♗g5 ♕b6 13.♘1d2 c5!=*) 11...0-0 12.♘b3 ♕b6 13.♗e3!N (*13.♘e4 ♘xe4 14.♗xe4=* Sakaev — Timo-

feev, Budva 2009) 13...♖fd8 (*13... ♘d5 14.♘e4±*) 14.♘e4 ♘xe4 15.♕xe4±)

11.a4 ♗e7!

(11...♖d8 12.♘b3 c5 13.♗xb7 ♕xb7 14.axb5 axb5

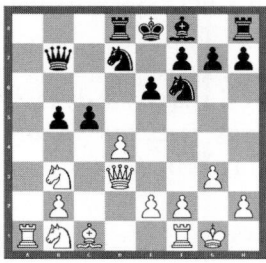

15.♘c3!N (*15.dxc5 ♘xc5 =* Burmakin — Khenkin, Bad Wiessee 2005) 15...c4 (*15...cxd4 16.♕xb5±*) 16.♘a5 ♕b6

(16...♕a6 17.♕f3 ♗b4 (*17... b4 18.♗f4!+-*) 18.♗f4 ♗xa5 19.♗c7+-)

17.♕f3 ♖c8 18.♗f4 b4 19.♘e4 ♘xe4 20.♕xe4 f5 21.♕e3 ♘f6 22.♖fc1 ♘d5 23.♖xc4 ♘xe3 24.♖xc8+ ♔f7 25.fxe3 ♕a6 26.♖c7+ ♔g6 27.♔f2±/↑)

12.axb5 (*12.♘b3 0-0 13.♗d2 c5 14.♗a5 ♕a7 15.♗xb7 ♕xb7 16.dxc5 ♘xc5 17.♘xc5 ♗xc5= Gyimesi — Pavasovic, Murska Sobota 2006*) 12...cxb5!N It's hard to exploit the backward pawn since the centre is not sufficiently closed and White hasn't strengthened it adequately. After apossible (*12...axb5 13.♖xa8+*

♗xa8 14.♘c3 0-0 15.♘b3± Landa — Galkin, Sochi 2009) 13.♗xb7 ♕xb7 14.♘b3 0-0 15.♗g5 ♖fd8 = the queen on d3 starts to look ineffectual. The game is about equal;

7...♗b7 8.♗g2 ♘bd7 9.0-0 a6 Black can never do without this move because it's necessary to play c6-c5. 10.♘e5

(10.a4 c5! 11.axb5 ♗d5 12.♕c2 ♗e4 (*12...axb5 13.♖xa8 ♕xa8 14.♘c3 ♗c6=*) 13.♕b3 ♗d5=)

10...♘xe5

a) 10...♕c8 11.♘xd7 (*11.a4!?±*) 11...♘xd7 12.♗e3 c5 13.♗xb7 ♕xb7 — 10...♕b6 11.♗e3 c5 12. ♘xd7 ♘xd7 13.♗xb7 ♕xb7;

b) 10...♕b6 11.♗e3 c5 12.♘xd7 ♘xd7 13.d5

(13.♗xb7 ♕xb7 14.♖c1 (*14.dxc5 ♘xc5* = Maletin — Grachev, Novokuznetsk 2008) 14...♖c8 15.dxc5 ♗xc5 16.♗xc5 ♘xc5 17.♕a3±)

13...exd5 14.♗xd5 ♗xd5 15.♕xd5 ♖d8 (*15...♖c8 16.a4 b4 17.♘d2±* Smirnov — Zontakh, Sochi 2012) 16.♖d1

(16.a4 ♗e7 17.axb5 axb5 18.♘c3 b4 (*18...0-0* Meier — Ponomariov, Dortmund 2011 *19.♕f5 ♖fe8 20.♘d5 ♕b7 21.♘xe7+ ♖xe7 22.♖fd1±*) 19.♘e4 0-0=)

16...♗e7 17.♕e4 (*17.♘c3 0-0 18.♕f5 ♘f6 19.b4 ♕e6 20.♕xe6 fxe6=*) 17...♕e6 18.♕xe6 fxe6 19.a4 b4 20.♘d2±;

11.dxe5

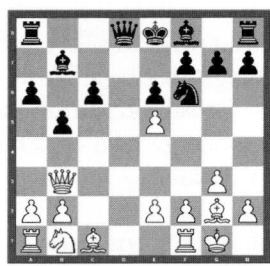

11...♘d5!

(11...♘d7 12.♘c3

(12.♖d1 ♕c7 13.♗f4 c5

(13...♗e7 14.♘c3 0-0 15.♘e4 ♘c5 16.♘xc5 ♗xc5 17.♗e4 ♗e7 18.♕d3! (*18.♕f3* Naiditsch — Riazantsev, Chisinau 2012 *18...♖ab8!=*) 18...♖fd8 (*18...♖ad8 19.♗xh7+ ♔h8 20.♕c2 g6 21.♗xg6 fxg6 22.♕xg6+-*) 19.♗xh7+ ♔h8 20.♕c2 c5 21.♗e4±)

14.♗xb7 ♕xb7 15.♘d2 c4 16.♕c2 ♗e7 17.♘e4 0-0= Despite the fact that White can move the knight to d6, he doesn't have any advantage as Black can undermine the knight's support with f7-f6.)

12...♕c7

a) 12...♕c8 13.♘e4 (*13.a4* Khalifman — Sargissian, Moscow 2010 *13...♘xe5 14.♗f4 ♘g6 15.♗e3 ♗e7 16.♖ac1 0-0 17.axb5 axb5 18.♘xb5 c5=*) 13...c5 14.♖d1±/↑;

b) 12...♘xe5 13.♗f4 (*13.♘e4 c5∞* Ehlvest — Vitiugov, Moscow 2009) *13...♘c4 14.♖fd1 ♕c8 15.♘e4* (*15. ♕c2 e5 16.♗c1 ♗e7 17.♘e4 0-0 18.b3 ♘b6 19.♘c5±*) *15...♗e7 16.♕c3 0-0 17.b3 ♘b6 18.♘d6 ♗xd6 19.♗xd6±/↑;*

13.♗f4 c5 14.♘e4 ♘xe5 15.♗xe5 (*15.a4 b4 16.♖fc1±* Agrest — Grandelius, Sweden 2012) *15... ♕xe5 16.♘f6+ gxf6 17.♗xb7 ♖a7 18.♗xa6±*)

12.♘c3 ♗e7

(12...♕b8 13.a4 b4 14.♘e4 (*14. e4 ♘xc3! 15.bxc3 a5=*) *14...♕xe5 15.♗e3 a5* (*15...♘xe3 16.♕xe3↑*) *16.♖fd1 ♕c7 17.♗d4 e5 18.♖ac1!* (*18.♗c5±* Fressinet — Gordon, Bremen 2012) *18...exd4 19.♕xd5 ♖d8 20.♕c4 ♗e7 21.♘c5±*)

13.♘e4 (*13.♖d1 ♕b8 14.♘xd5 cxd5=*) 13...♕c7 (*13...c5 14.♗g5 c4 15.♗xe7 ♕xe7 16.♕d1 0-0 17.♘d6 ♗c6 18.b3±* Meier — Blagojevic, Porto Carras 2011) *14.♗g5* (*14.♗f4 ♘xf4 15.gxf4 0-0 16.a4 ♖ad8 17.♖fc1 ♖d4 18.♕e3 ♖xa4 19.♖xa4 bxa4 20.♘c5 ♗xc5 21.♕xc5 ♖d8=* Ni Hua — Frolyanov, Moscow 2012; *14.♘d6+ ♗xd6 15.exd6 ♕xd6 16.e4 ♘b6 17.♖d1 ♕e7 18.♕c3 0-0 19.b3 ♘d7=*)

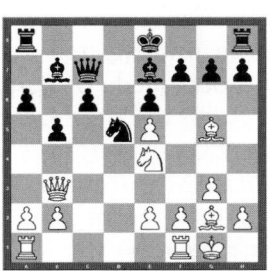

14...♗xg5 15.♘xg5 ♕xe5 16.♘e4 0-0 17.♘c5 ♕c7/= White has positional compensation but it's hardly enough for more than for equality, Bruzon — Leitao, Quito 2012

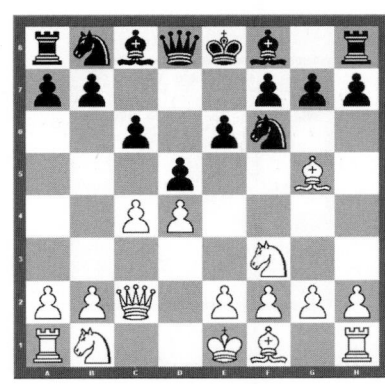

5...dxc4
5...♘bd7 6.e3

(Placing the knight on d2 is passive, 6.♘bd2 allows Black to equalise the game with simple development: 6...♗e7 7.e3 0-0 8.♗e2 h6 9.♗h4 c5 10.cxd5 ♘xd5 11.♗g3 b6 (The following leads to unclear game *11...♘b4 12.♕d1 cxd4 13.♘xd4 e5 14.♘4f3 ♘c6∞*, with the idea f7-f5.) 12.0-0 ♗b7 13.♖ac1 The most precise route to equality is 13...♘5f6!, so that if ♘d2-c4 then the unprotected square e4 can be occupied. (*13...a6 14.♘c4 ♘b4 15.♕b1 ♘f6 16.dxc5 ♗e4 17.♕a1 ♗xc5 18.a3 a5 19.♖fd1 ♘bd5 20.♘fd2±* M.Gurevich — Mala-khov, Saint Vincent 2002) 14.♖fd1 ♖c8 15.♕a4 a6!=)

6...♕a5+ (*6... ♗e7 7.♘c3±* Leads to a Queen's Gambit line favourable to White since instead of the already played c7-c6, it's more promising for Black to undermine White's centre with c7-c5.) 7.♘bd2 ♘e4

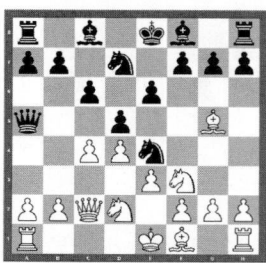

8. ♗h4

(8. ♗f4 is vulnerable to e6-e5,which could be played by Black: 8...♗b4 9.a3 (*9. ♗d3 ♘xd2 10.♘xd2 e5 11.dxe5 dxc4 12. ♗xc4 ♘xe5 =* Pelle-tier — Grischuk, Batumi 1999) 9...e5!

a) 9...♘xd2 10.♘xd2 dxc4 11. ♗xc4 e5 12.dxe5 ♘xe5 13.0-0 ♗xd2 14.b4! ♕c7 15.♗b3 0-0 (*15... ♗xe3 16.fxe3→*) 16.♕xd2±;

b) 9...g5 10. ♗g3 — 8. ♗h4 ♗b4 9.a3 g5 10. ♗g3;

10.dxe5

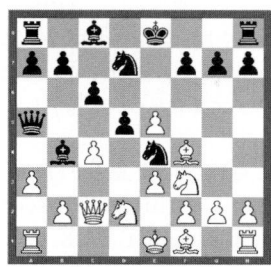

10...g5!N (*10...♘dc5 11.♖d1±* Volzhin — Rosich Valles, Terrasa 1999) 11.e6 (*11. ♗g3 ♘dc5 12.0-0-0 ♗xd2+ 13.♘xd2 ♗f5 14.♘xe4 ♗xe4 15.♕c3 ♕xc3+ 16.bxc3 dxc4 17.♖d6∞* — The endgame is double-edged.) 11...gxf4 12.exd7+ ♗xd7 13.0-0-0 ♗xa3 14.♘xe4 (*14.♘b3 ♕a4∓*) 14...dxe4 15.♕xe4+ ♗e7 16.♕e5 (*16. ♗d3 fxe3 17.♕xe3 ♕c5=*) 16...♕xe5 17.♘xe5 ♗e6 18.exf4 f6 19.♘f3 ♗c5 20.♘d4 ♗d7 21. ♗e2 0-0-0 22.f5 ♖he8 23.♘e6 ♗xe6 24.fxe6 ♔c7 25. ♗g4 ♗xf2 26.♔c2± — Thanks to the advanced passed pawn White stands better but Black should be able to resist.)

8... ♗b4

(8...h6!?N 9. ♗d3 (*9.cxd5 cxd5=*) 9...g5 10. ♗g3 ♘xg3 11.hxg3 g4 12.♘h4± — Although the knight on h4 has been out of play so far, White stands better due to a space advantage and the imminent e3-e4 possibility.)

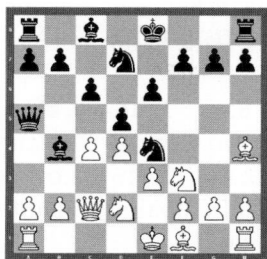

9.a3 g5 10. ♗g3 h5

(10...g4

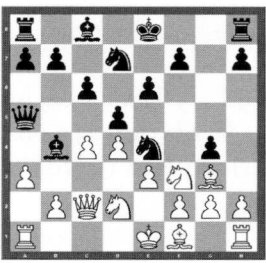

11.♕c1!N (If *11.♖d1 ♗e7∞* White cannot drive away the black queen with b2-b4, Stefanova — Areshenko, Giblartar 2007) 11...gxf3 (*11... ♗e7 12.b4 ♕d8 13.♘xe4 gxf3 14.♘d6+ ♗xd6 15.♗xd6 ♘b6 16.c5 fxg2 17.♗xg2 ♘c4 18.♗g3±*) 12.axb4 fxg2 13.♗xg2 ♕xb4 14.♗xe4 dxe4 15.0-0 f5 16.c5±/↑)

11.0-0-0 ♗xa3 12.bxa3 ♕xa3+ 13.♕b2 ♕xb2+ 14.♔xb2 h4 15.♘xe4 dxe4

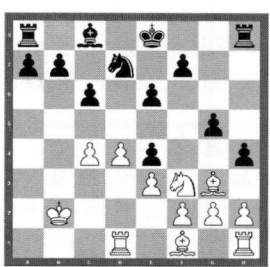

16.♘xg5!N (*16. ♗d6 exf3 17.gxf3±/⹌* Khalifman — Van Der Werf, Wijk aan Zee 1995) 16...hxg3 17.fxg3 ♘f6 18.♗e2 ♔e7 19.♖df1 ♗d7 20.♖f4 ♖ag8 21.h4±;

A good possibility is 5...h6 6. ♗xf6 (*6. ♗h4 dxc4 7.♕xc4 b5* — compared ith the line 5...dxc4 6.♕xc4 b5 the inclusion of the moves h7-h6 and ♗g5-h4 is favourable for Black.) 6...♕xf6 7.♘bd2 (*7.♘c3* — *3.♘f3 ♘f6 4.♘c3 e6 5.♗g5 h6 6.♗xf6 ♕xf6 7.♕c2* (Slav Defence 2)) 7... ♘d7 (*7...dxc4 8.♕xc4* — *5...dxc4 6.♕xc4 h6 7.♗xf6 ♕xf6 8.♘bd2 ♘d7*) 8.g3 ♗b4! 9.♗g2 0-0 10.0-0 ♗xd2 11.♕xd2 dxc4 12.♕c3 (*12. ♕b4 e5 13.♕xc4 ♖e8* = Huzman — Grachev, Moscow 2004) 12...b5 13.b3

(13.a4 ♗b7 14.♕a5 ♖fb8!± (*14... ♕d8 15.axb5 ♕xa5 16.♖xa5 cxb5*= I. Sokolov — Timofeev, Izmir 2004))

13...♖b8!N

(*13...♘b6 14.♘e5!N* (*14.bxc4 ♘xc4 15.♘e5 ♘xe5 16.dxe5 ♕e7 17.♕xc6 ♖b8 18.♕d6 ♕xd6 19.exd6 ♖d8 20.♖fd1 e5*= Fridman — Frolyanov,

Cappelle la Grande 2004) 14...♘d5 15.♕a5 ♕d8 16.♕xd8 ♖xd8 17.bxc4 bxc4 18.♖fc1 ♗a6 19.♘xc4±)

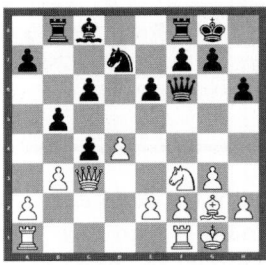

14.bxc4 bxc4 15.♕xc4 ♖b6 16.♕a4 ♗a6 17.♖fe1 ♕e7= — Black will play c6-c5 and equalise.

6.♕xc4 b5
6...h6 7.♗xf6 ♕xf6 8.♘bd2 ♘d7 9.g3 g6 10.♗g2 ♗g7 11.0-0 0-0 12.♘e4 ♕e7 13.♖fd1± White is ready to meet the pawn break e6-e5 with d4-d5. The fianchettoed bishop on g2 is quite well placed. White stands slightly better due to a space advantage.;

6... ♗e7 7.♘bd2

(7.e3 0-0 (7...b6 8.♕c2±) 8.♗d3 h6 9.♗xf6 (9.♗h4 b5!=) 9...♗xf6 10.♘c3 (10.0-0 ♕b6 11.♕c2 c5=) 10...b5!N (10...♘d7 11.♖d1± Kramnik — Lautier, Tilburg 1998)

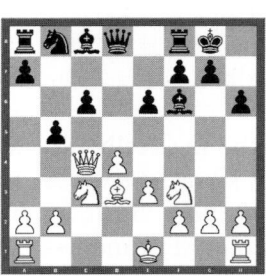

11.♕b3 ♗b7 12.0-0 ♘d7 13.♘e4 ♗e7 14.♖fd1 ♕b6=)

7...b6 8.e4 ♗a6 9.♕c2 ♗xf1 10.♖xf1 (10.♘xf1 0-0 11.♘e3±) 10... h6 11.♗xf6 ♗xf6 12.0-0-0 0-0 13.♔b1±/↑ Topalov — Lautier, Monaco 2000

7.♕c2 ♗b7 8.e3
8.♘bd2 ♘bd7 9.e4 — 8.e4 ♘bd7 9.♘bd2 (9.e3 — 8.e3 ♘bd7 9.♘bd2) ;

8.e4 ♘bd7

(8...a6 9.♘c3 ♘bd7 10.e5 h6 11.♗d2 ♘d5 12.♘xd5 cxd5 13.a4 b4 14.♗e2 (14.a5!?) 14...♖c8 15.♕d3±)

9.♗d3

(9.♘bd2

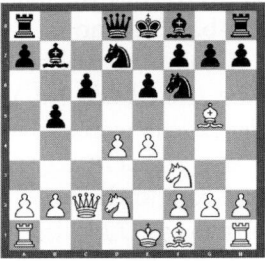

9...a6

a) 9...h6 10.♗xf6 ♕xf6 11.♗d3 (11. a4 a6 12.♗d3 ♗b4 13.0-0 0-0= Lerner — Malakhov, Bad Wiessee 2002) 11...e5 12.0-0 ♗d6= Tunik — Va.Popov, Toljatti 2001;

b) 9...♛b6 10.a4 a6 11.♗d3 ♜c8 12.0–0 c5∞ Zakhartsov — Va.Popov, Korolev 2000;

10.a4

(10.♗e2 c5 11.d5 h6 12.♗h4 ♛b6 *(12...♗d6 13.dxe6 fxe6 14.a4 c4∞; 12...exd5 13.e5 g5 14.♗g3 ♞e4 15.♞xe4 dxe4 16.♞d2 e3!∞)* 13.dxe6 ♛xe6 14.0–0 ♞h5=/∞)

10...h6 11.♗xf6 ♛xf6 12.e5 ♛d8 13.♗d3 ♗e7 14.0–0 0–0 15.♞e4 c5 16.axb5 axb5 17.dxc5 ♜xa1 18.♜xa1 ♗xe4 19.♗xe4 ♞xc5 = Karpov — Grischuk, Linares 2001)

9...a6! Black wants to play c6-c5, and to prevent this White is forced to play a2-a4. In the long term, the inclusion of these moves is favourable for Black since White aims for a blockading game and Black wants to open up lines.

a) 9...♛b6 10.♞c3±;

b) 9...h6 10.♗xf6 ♞xf6 *(10...♛xf6 11.0–0 e5 12.a4± Burmakin — Makarov, Toljatti 2003)* 11.0–0 ♗e7 12.♞bd2 ♛b6 13.♞b3 ♞d7 14.♜ac1± — Here the absence of the moves a7-a6 and a2-a4 could be to White's advantage Kharlov — Fressinet, Saint Vincent 2000;

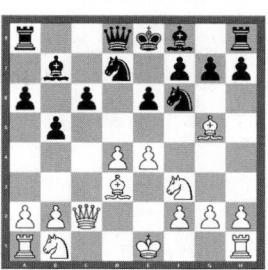

10.a4 h6 11.♗xf6

(11.♗h4

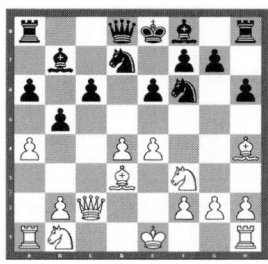

11...g5!N *(11...♜c8 12.♞bd2 ♛b6 13.0–0 c5∞ Ulibin — Galkin, Oberwart 1999; 11...♛b6 12.♞bd2 c5 13.axb5 axb5= Lastin — Grischuk, Elista 2000)* 12.♗g3 c5∓)

11...♞xf6 12.0–0 ♗e7 13.♞bd2 0–0=

8...♞bd7 9.♗d3

9.♗e2 a6 10.a4 ♗e7 11.0–0 0–0 12.♞bd2 ♜c8 13.♗xf6 gxf6!? *(13...♞xf6 14.♞b3 ♞d7=; 13...♗xf6 14.♞e4 ♗e7=)* 14.♛e4 ♚h8 15.♞b3 ♜g8∞ Wojtaszek — Adla, France 2009

9...a6

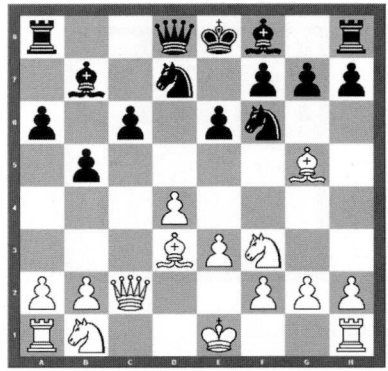

10.a4 ♖c8

10...♗b4+ 11.♘c3±;

10...c5 11.axb5

(11.♗xf6 gxf6 12.axb5 axb5 13.♖xa8 ♕xa8 14.dxc5 ♗xc5 15.♗xb5 ♗b4+ (15...♔e7 16.♗xd7 ♗b4+) 16.♔e2 0-0=/∞)

11...axb5 12.♖xa8 ♕xa8 13.♗xb5 ♗xf3 14.gxf3 ♕xf3 15.♖g1 ♕b7 16.♕a4 cxd4 17.♘d2 dxe3 18.♗xe3↑

11.0-0 ♗e7 N

11...h6 12.♗xf6 ♕xf6 13.♘c3± M. Gurevich — Bruno, Giblartar 2009; 11...c5 12.axb5 cxd4 13.♕e2 ♗xf3 14.gxf3 axb5 15.♗xb5±

12.♘bd2

12.♕e2 0-0 13.♘bd2 h6 14.♗h4 ♘d5 (14...g5!? 15.♗g3 ♘h5∞) 15.♗xe7 ♕xe7=

12...♘d5

The most reliable — Black makes use of the weakened b4 square and intends to play c6-c5 at an opportune moment.

12...c5!? The immediate breakthrough can lead to a double-edged play 13.axb5 cxd4 (13...axb5 14.dxc5 ♖xc5 15.♕b1±) 14.♕b1 dxe3 15.bxa6 exf2+∞

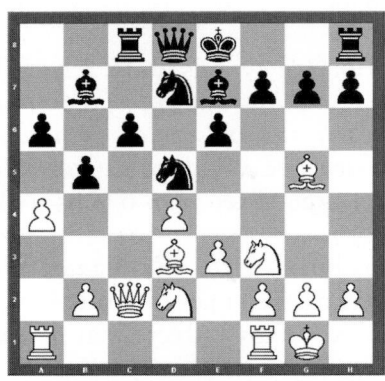

13.♗xe7

13.♘e4 ♘b4 14.♕e2 f6 15.♗f4 ♘xd3 16.♕xd3 c5=

13...♕xe7 14.♖fc1 ♘b4 15.♕b3 ♘xd3 16.♕xd3 0-0 17.♘e4

17.e4 ♕b4 (17...e5 18.axb5 cxb5 19.d5∞) 18.♕c3 ♕xc3 19.♖xc3 ♖fd8=

17...c5! 18.axb5 c4=

Black has no problems. Conclusion: The popularity of the Black development scheme analysed above has waned in recent years but nobody has refuted it yet. 4.♕c2 as well as 4.♘bd2 allow White to initiate a quiet positional battle but without serious pretensions to an advantage. 4.g3 is a gambit where White takes on large obligations and risks. The most dangerous is 4.♘c3 which tranposes after 4...dxc4 or 4...♘f6 to other systems.

PART 9

3.♘f3 ♘f6 What happens
if White declines
to follow the "main" road

■ GAME 17

1.d4 d5 2.c4 c6 3.♘f3 ♘f6 4.♕c2 g6
4...dxc4 5.♕xc4 — 4.♕b3 dxc4
5.♕xc4; 4...e6 — 3.♘f3 e6 4.♕c2
♘f6; 4...a6 5.♗f4±; 4...♗g4 5.♘e5
♗h5 6.cxd5

(6.♕b3 ♕b6 7.♘c3 dxc4 (7...e6
8.c5±) 8.♘xc4

(8.♕xc4 ♘bd7 9.♘xd7 (9.♘d3
♗g6=) 9...♘xd7=)

8...♕xb3 9.axb3 ♘a6! 10.♖a4 (10.f3
♘b4 11.♔f2 ♘c2∞) 10...♘c7 11.♘e5
a6 12.f3 ♘d7 13.♘xd7 ♔xd7 14.e4=)

6...cxd5 7.♗f4 e6 8.e3±

5.♗f4

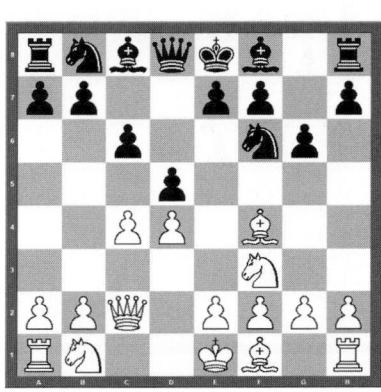

5...♗g7
5...♘a6 The idea of a piece sacrifice
is original but insufficient 6.e3 ♗f5
7.♕b3

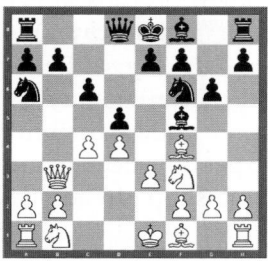

7...♘b4 (7...♕b6 8.♘c3±) 8.♕xb4 e5
9.♕xb7 ♖b8 10.♕xc6+ ♗d7 11.♕a6

(11.♕xf6 ♕xf6 12.♗xe5 ♕b6 13.b3
♕a5+ (13...♗b4+ 14.♘bd2 0–0
15.♗xb8 ♖xb8∞) 14.♘bd2 ♖xb3
15.♗xh8 ♗b4 16.♗e2 (16.axb3 ♕xa1+
17.♔e2 ♗g4 18.h3 ♗xf3+ 19.gxf3 ♕b2
20.f4 ♕xd2+ 21.♔f3 ♕d1+ 22.♔g3
♕xb3∓ — The passed a-pawn is very
dangerous.) 16...♗xd2+ 17.♘xd2 ♖b2
18.0–0 ♖xd2∓ D.Bischoff — Wang
Yu, Bad Woerishofen 2005)

11...exf4

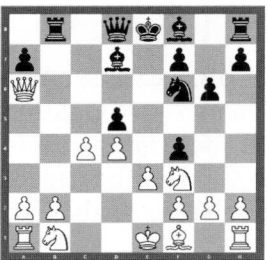

12.♘c3!N (12.c5 fxe3 13.fxe3 ♗h6 Meins — Schaller, Germany 2000) 12...fxe3 13.fxe3 ♖xb2 14.c5 ♗h6

(14...♖c2 15.♘d1 ♘e4 16.♖b1 ♗g7 (16...♗h6 17.g3+-) 17.♖g1+- — There is no defence to ♗f1–d3.)

15.♘d1 ♖b8 16.♘e5 0–0 17.♗e2± — There is insufficient compensation for a pawn.; 5...♗f5 6.♕b3 ♕b6 7.e3 (7.c5 ♕xb3 8.axb3 ♘a6! 9.♘c3 ♘h5 10.♗d2 ♗g7∞ Beliavsky — Van Wely, Groningen 1994) 7...♘a6 8.♘c3±; A good possibility is 5...dxc4, to get the queen to move to c4 with the bishop already developed on f4.

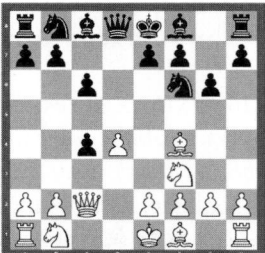

6.♕xc4 ♗g7 7.♘c3

a) 7.♘bd2 ♗e6 8.♕c2 (8.♕b4 ♕b6 9.♕xb6 axb6∓; 8.♕a4 ♕b6=) 8...♘h5 9.♗xb8 ♖xb8 10.e3 0–0 = Kamsky — Svidler, Khanty Mansyisk 2007;

b) 7.e3 0–0 8.♗e2 ♗e6 9.♕c2 (9.♕c1 ♘bd7 10.0–0 c5= Goldin — Jussupow, Tilburg 1992) 9...♗f5 10.♕b3 ♕b6 11.♘bd2 ♘bd7 12.♕a3 ♘d5 13.♘c4 ♕b4+ 14.♕xb4 ♘xb4 15.0–

0 c5 = Svidler — Ponomariov, Nice (rapid) 2010;

7...0–0 8.e4 b5 9.♕b3 ♕a5 (9...a5!? 10.♕c2 ♘a6=/∞ — Black has many chances to undermine White's centre and has decent counter play.) 10.♗d3 ♗e6 11.♕d1 ♗g4 12.0–0

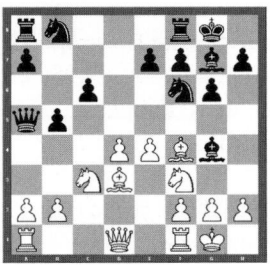

12...b4!N (12...♖d8 13.e5 ♘d5 14.♘xd5 cxd5 15.♖c1± Miles — Kasparov, Basel (match 02) 1986) 13.♕a4 (13.♘e2 is risky 13...♗xf3 14.gxf3 c5∓ and play on the dark squares begins.) 13...♕h5 14.♕xb4 ♗xf3 15.gxf3 ♕xf3 16.♗e3 ♕g4+ 17.♔h1 ♕f3+=

6.e3 0–0 7.♘c3

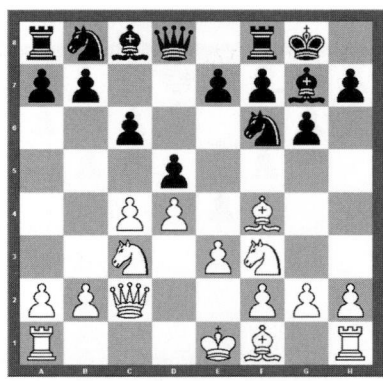

7...c5

7... ♗f5 8.♕b3 ♕b6 9.c5 (*9.h3±*) 9... ♕xb3 10.axb3 ♘bd7 11.h3 ♖fe8 12.b4± Dreev — Chekhov, Moscow 1991; 7... ♘a6 8.♗e2 c5 9.0–0± — When the centre is opened the knight on a6 stands badly.

8.dxc5 ♕a5

8... ♗f5!? 9.♗d3 (*9.♕b3 ♘bd7 10.♕a3 ♖c8 11.♖d1∞*) 9...♗xd3 10.♕xd3 ♘a6 11.cxd5 ♘xc5 12.♕d1 (*12.♕b5 ♘xd5 13.♕xc5 ♘xc3 14.bxc3 ♖c8 15.♕b5 ♗xc3+ 16.♔e2 ♗xa1 17.♖xa1 ♖c2+ 18.♔f1 ♕c8∞*) 12...♘ce4 13.♘xe4 ♘xe4 14.0–0 ♖c8=/⯑

9.♖d1

9.0–0–0?! 9...♘a6; 9.♘d2 dxc4 10.♗xc4 ♕xc5 11.0–0 ♘c6= Frolyanov — Danin, Taganrog 2011; 9.♖c1 ♘c6 (*9...♘a6!?*) 10.a3 (*10.♕a4 ♕xc5 11.♕b5 ♕xb5 12.cxb5∞*) 10...♗e6!? (*10...dxc4 11.♗xc4 ♕xc5=*) 11.♕a4

(11.♘d2 dxc4 12.♘xc4 ♕xc5 13.b4 ♘xb4 14.axb4 ♕xb4 15.♖b1 (*15.♕b2 a5 16.♕xb4 axb4 17.♘b5 ♖ac8⯑/↑*) 15...♕c5 16.♖b5 ♕c8 17.♕b3 a6! (*17...♘d7 Raetsky — I.Sokolov, Dubai 2012 18.♘d5∞*) 18.♖xb7 ♘h5⯑/↑)

11...dxc4 (*11...♕xc5 12.b4 ♕b6∞*) 12.♗xc4 ♘e4 13.♕xa5 ♘xa5 14.♗xe6 ♗xc3+ 15.bxc3 fxe6=/∞

9...dxc4

9...♘e4!? 10.cxd5 (*10.♗e5 ♘xc3 11.♕xc3 ♕xc3+ 12.♗xc3 ♗xc3+ 13.bxc3 dxc4=*) 10...♘xc3 11.bxc3∞; 9...

♗f5 10.♗d3 ♗xd3 11.♕xd3± Postny — Sasikiran, France 2009

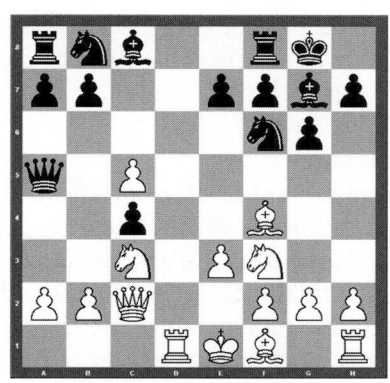

10.♗xc4 ♕xc5 11.♕b3

11.♘d5 ♘xd5 12.♖xd5 ♕b4+ 13.♖d2 ♘c6 14.a3 ♕b6 15.0–0 ♗g4 16.♘g5 ♖ad8=

11...♘c6 12.♕b5 ♕xb5 13.♗xb5 ♗d7=

Le Quang Liem — Tkachiev, Khanty Mansyisk 2009 ^013^010 Conclusion: After 4.♕c2, 4...g6 looks like a good choice. After 5.♗f4 Black already has two paths to ensure a decent game: 5... dxc4, and 5...g7 6. e3 0–0 7.♘c3 c5. The choice depends on the player's taste.

■ GAME 18

1.d4 d5 2.c4 c6 3.♘f3 ♘f6 4.♕b3

4.♕c2 dxc4 5.♕xc4 — 4.♕b3 dxc4 5.♕xc4

4...dxc4

4...g6 5.♘c3 (*5.cxd5 cxd5 6.♘c3 ♘c6 7.♗g5 ♘a5 8.♕d1 ♘e4=*) 5...♗g7 (*5...dxc4 6.♕xc4 ♗g7 7.e4± leads to a line of the Grunfeld Defence favourable to White*) 6.cxd5 cxd5 (*6...♘xd5 7.e4±*) 7.♗g5 e6 8.e3 0-0

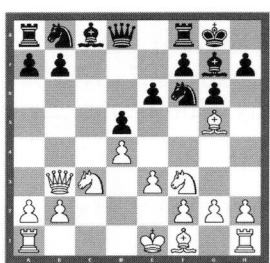

9.h3! Helping to prevent the dark squared bishop from being exchanged for the knight. 9...♘c6 10.♗e2 h6 11.♗f4 g5 12.♗h2 ♘e4 13.♖c1±; 4...♕b6 5.♘c3 ♗f5

(*5...♗g4 6.c5 (6.h3!?) 6...♕c7 7.♗f4 ♕c8 8.e4! (8.♘e5± Kasparov — Torre, Brussels 1987) 8...♘xe4 (8... dxe4 9.♘g5 e6 10.♘gxe4±) 9.♘xe4 dxe4 10.♘g5±*)

6.c5 (*6.♕xb6 axb6 7.cxd5 ♘xd5 8.e4 ♘xc3 9.exf5 ♘d5 10.♗d3±*) 6...♕c7 (*6...♕xb6 7.axb3±*) 7.♗f4 ♕c8 8.h3 h6 (*8...e6 9.♘h4±*) 9.g4!? (*9.e3±*)

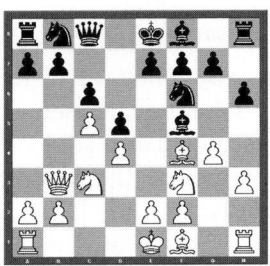

9...♗h7 10.g5±/↑; 4...e6 5.♘c3 — 3.♘f3 ♘f6 4.♘c3 e6 5.♕b3 (Slav Defence, Part 2)

a) The following is not dangerous for Black 5.g3 — Catalan positions with the queen on b3 do not constitute a threat. 5...♗e7 (*5...dxc4 6.♕xc4 — 3.♘f3 e6 4.♕c2 ♘f6 5.g3 dxc4 6.♕xc4*) 6.♗g2 0-0 7.0-0 b6 8.♗f4 ♗a6 9.♘bd2 ♘bd7= Durarbayli — S.Zhigalko, Nakhichivan 2012;

b) 5.♗g5 ♘bd7

b1) 5...dxc4 6.♕xc4 — 3.♘f3 e6 4.♕c2 ♘f6 5.♗g5 dxc4 6.♕xc4;

b2) 5...h6 6.♗xf6 (*6.♗h4 dxc4 7.♕xc4 — 3.♘f3 e6 4.♕c2 ♘f6 5.♗g5 dxc4 6.♕xc4 h6 7.♗h4*) 6...♕xf6 7.♘bd2 dxc4 8.♕xc4 (*8.♘xc4 c5 9.e3 cxd4 10.♘ce5 a6 11.exd4 ♗d6 12.♗d3 0-0 13.0-0 ♘c6 14.♘xc6 bxc6 15.♖ac1 ♖b8 = Khenkin — Roiz, Maalot-Tarshiha 2008) 8...♘d7 9.g3 g6 10.♗g2 ♗g7 11.0-0 0-0 12.♘e4 ♕e7 13.♖fd1±;*

6.♘c3

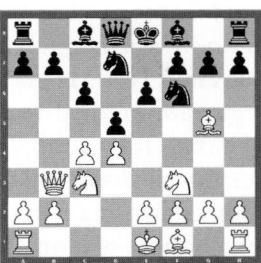

6...♗e7 A little passive but solid. No matter how Black plays, White stands just a little better.

(The following leads to more complicated play 6...♕a5 7.♗d2 (*7.cxd5 exd5 8.e3 ♘e4 9.♗d3 ♘xg5 10.♘xg5 ♗e7=* Krasenkow — Vallejo Pons, Lugo 2006) 7...♕b6

(*7...dxc4 8.♕xc4 ♕b4 9.e4 (9.♕xb4 ♗xb4 10.a3±) 9...♕xb2 10.♖b1 ♕a3 11.♗e2↑/± Landa — Yuzhakov, Khanty Mansyisk 2009)*

8.♕c2 (*8.e3 ♕xb3 9.axb3 b6! 10.♗d3 ♗b7=*) 8...dxc4 (*8...♘e4 9.c5 ♘dxc5 10.dxc5 ♗xc5 11.e3± Bareev — Morozevich, Monaco (rapid) 2004; 8...♗e7 9.e3 0-0 10.♗d3 dxc4 11.♗xc4 c5 12.0-0± Romanov — I.Sokolov, Budva 2009) 9.e4 (9.e3!? ♕a6 10.♗e2 b5 11.0-0∞) 9...e5 (9...c5 10.d5 exd5 11.exd5±) 10.♗e3 (10. dxe5 ♘g4 11.♗f4 ♕c5 12.e6 fxe6 13.h3 ♘ge5 Papaioannou — Graf, Plovdiv 2003 14.♘xe5 ♘xe5 15.0-0-0∞; 10.♗xc4!? exd4 11.♘a4 ♕c7 12.♘xd4 ♗d6 13.♘f5 b5 14.♘xg7+ ♔f8 15.♘f5 bxc4 16.0-0-0∞) 10...♘g4 11.♗xc4 ♘xe3 12.fxe3 ♗e7*

13.0-0 0-0 14.♔h1± Gustafsson — Haimovich, Herzelia 2000)

7.e3 0-0

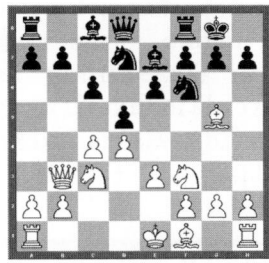

8.♗d3

b1) 8.♖d1 a6! (*8...b6 9.♗d3 ♗b7 10.0-0 dxc4 11.♗xc4 ♘d5 12.♗xe7 ♕xe7 13.e4 ♘xc3 14.bxc3± Landa — Svane, Copenhagen 2010) 9.a4*

(*9.♗d3 b5 10.cxd5 (10.c5 e5!±) 10...cxd5=*)

9...♕a5 10.♗d3 ♕b4=;

b2) 8.♗e2 h6

b21) 8...♘h5 9.♗xe7 ♕xe7 10.0-0 dxc4 11.♕xc4 e5 12.d5 ♘b6 13.♕h4± Khalifman — Hector, Germany 2000;

b22) 8...dxc4 9.♕xc4 ♘d5 10.♗xe7 ♕xe7 11.0-0 ♘5b6 12.♕d3 e5 13.♖fd1 ♖e8 14.♕e4 exd4 15.♕xe7 ♖xe7 16.♘xd4± Roiz- Malakhov, Sochi 2008;

b23) Interesting play arises after 8...a6!? 9.0-0 b5 10.c5 (*10.cxd5*

cxd5 11.♖fc1 ♗b7 12.h3 ♖c8=) 10...
a5 11.h3 e5 12.dxe5 ♘xc5 13.♕c2
♘fd7 14.♗f4±/∞;

9.♗h4 dxc4 (9...b6 10.0–0 ♗b7
11.♖fd1±) 10.♕xc4 ♘d5 11.♗xe7
♕xe7 12.0–0 ♘5b6 13.♕d3 e5
14.♖ad1 (14.♖fd1!?±) 14...♖e8
15.♕e4 exd4 16.♕xe7 ♖xe7 17.♖xd4
♘f6 18.♖d8+ ♖e8 19.♖xe8+ ♘xe8
20.♘d4±

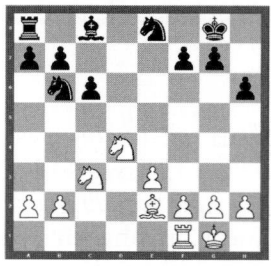

Accurate defence is required from
Black, T. Petrosian — Polugaevsky,
Yerevan 1975;

8...dxc4 9.♕xc4 (9.♗xc4 c5 10.0–0
a6 11.a4 cxd4 12.exd4 ♘b6 13.♗e2
♘bd5 14.♘e5± Landa — Moiseenko,
Serpukhov 2008) 9...c5

10.0–0

(10.dxc5!? ♘xc5 11.♗c2 ♕b6 (11...
♕a5 12.0–0 ♘cd7 13.♖fd1 ♘e5
14.♘xe5 ♕xe5 15.♘e4± Akopian —
San Segundo, Madrid 1997; 11...b5
12.♘xb5 ♕b6 13.0–0 ♗b7 14.♕e2±
— Black doesn't have full compensation for a pawn.) 12.0–0–0 h6∞/±
White's chances are on the kingside, Black's on the queenside. The
game is double-edged.)

10...cxd4 11.♕xd4 h6 12.♗h4 b6
13.♖fd1 ♗b7 Harikrishna — Dreev,
Melilla 2011. White could retain some pressure with the move
14.♖ac1±/=, though Black has good
chances to neutralise it.;

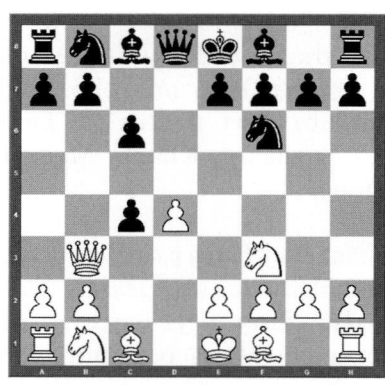

5.♕xc4 ♗f5

5...♗g4 6.♘c3 (6.♘bd2 An insufficiently ambitious move counting
on just a microscopically small advantage, 6...♘bd7 7.g3 e6 8.♗g2 ♗e7
9.0–0 0–0 10.♕b3 ♕b6 11.♘c4 ♕a6
12.♖e1 ♖fd8±/= — Black should
soon equalise with c6-c5) 6...♘bd7
7.e4 ♗xf3 (7...e6 8.♗e2±) 8.gxf3
e5 (8...e6 9.♗e3 ♗e7 10.0–0–0± —

White dominates the centre and has prospects of pressure on the g-file) 9.♗e3

(9.dxe5 ♘xe5 10.♕e2 ♗c5!

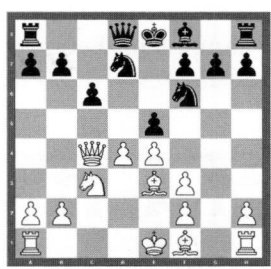

(10...♗b4 11.♗d2 ♕e7 12.f4 ♘g6 13.f5 ♗xc3 14.bxc3 ♘e5 (*14...♘h4 15.♗g5 ♕e5 16.♕e3 ♘g4 17.♕d3 ♘xf5 18.♗e2 ♘fh6 19.f4 ♕c5 20.0-0-0↑*) 15.f4!N (*15.♗g2 0-0-0 16.0-0∞ Bacrot — Potkin, Moscow 2010*) 15...♘xe4 16.f6 gxf6 17.fxe5 ♘xd2 18.♔xd2 0-0-0+ 19.♔c2±)

11.♗e3 (*11.♗d2 ♘h5 12.f4*

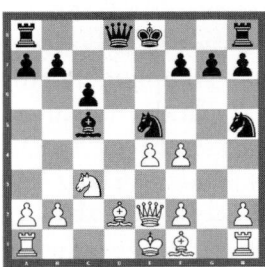

12...♕xd2+!! 13.♔xd2 ♘xf4 14.♕d1 0-0-0+ 15.♘d5 ♘xd5∓/↑ Caspi — Postny, Aix les Bains 2011; 11.♖g1 ♕b6 12.♖g5 ♘g6 13.♗d2 ♖d8∞ Krasenkow — Harikrishna, Nancy 2009) 11...♗xe3 12.fxe3 g5 13.f4 (13.♖g1 h6 14.f4 gxf4 15.exf4 ♘g6∓) 13...gxf4 14.exf4 ♘g6 15.♕f3∞ Kulaots — Buhmann, Khanty Mansyisk 2010)

9...exd4 (*9...♗d6 10.0-0-0 exd4 11.♕xd4!±*) 10.♗xd4 ♗d6 11.0-0-0 ♕c7

(11...♕e7

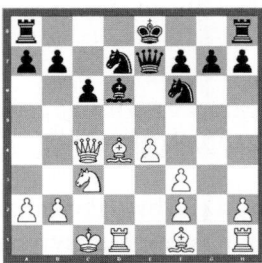

12.♕e2!?N

a) 12.♗e3 ♗c5 13.f4?! (*13.♕e2!?±; 13.♖g1±*) 13...b5 14.♕d3 b4 15.♘a4 ♗xe3+ 16.♕xe3 ♘b6! (*16...0-0 17.♖g1±/↑ Navara — Najer, Czech 2011*) 17.♘c5 (*17.♕c5 ♘fd7∓*) 17...♘g4 18.♕d4 0-0 19.f3 ♖ad8 20.♕g1 ♖xd1+ 21.♔xd1 ♘f6 22.♔c1 ♘fd7∓;

b) 12.♘e2 0-0 13.♗g2 ♖fd8 14.♔b1∞;

12...0-0 13.♕e3±/↑)

12.♘e2 (12.♖g1 0–0 13.♗h3 Almasi
— Le Quang Liem, Beijing 2011 13...
♗f4+ 14.♔b1 ♘e5 15.♕e2 ♖fd8∓)
12...0–0

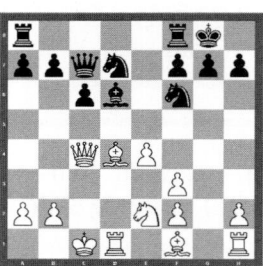

13.♕c2± — A double-edged game
with somewhat better chances for
White lies ahead, for example: 13...
♖ad8

a) 13...c5 14.♗e3 ♖fe8 15.♗g2± Landa — Szabo, Rijeka 2010;

b) 13...b5 14.♔b1± Ponomariov —
Gelfand, Khanty Mansyisk 2009;

c) 13...♘h5 14.♔b1 ♖ad8 15.♗e3±
Fridman — El Debs, Caleta 2011;

d) 13...♖fe8 14.h4 (14.♔b1±) 14...
♘h5 15.♗h3± Zvjagintsev — Boid-
man, Rogaska Slatina 2011;

14.♔b1 ♖fe8

(14...♘h5 15.♗e3 (15.♘g3!?) 15...
♘df6 16.♗g2 (16.h4!?) 16...♖fe8
17.h4± Macieja — Coleman, Fre-
mont 2012)

15.h4!? (15.♗h3 ♘h5∞ Khismatullin
— Potkin, Moscow 2010) 15...♘h5
16.♗h3±

6.g3 e6 7.♗g2 ♘bd7 8.0–0 ♗e7
After 8...♘b6 I like 9.♕b3 ♕d5

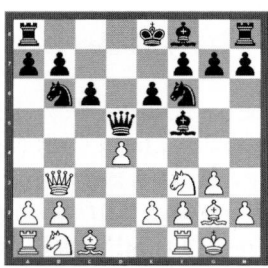

10.♘e5!? Aiming to find the Knight's
place in the centre and to avoid playing e2-e3.

(10.♘bd2 ♗e7 11.e3 (11.a4 ♕xb3
12.♘xb3 a5 13.♘e5 ♗c2 14.♘c5
♗xc5 15.dxc5 ♘bd7 16.♘xd7 ♘xd7
17.♗d2 ♔e7 18.♖fc1 ♗g6 = Fridman — Akopian, Porto Carras
2011) 11...♕xb3 (11...0–0 12.♘e5
♕xb3 13.♘xb3 a5 14.♘c5 ♗xc5
15.dxc5 ♘bd7 16.♘xd7 ♖xd7 17.e4
♗g6 18.♗e3±) 12.♘xb3 ♗e4 13.♘a5

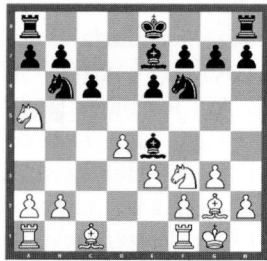

13...♖b8 (Interesting is 13...0–0–0!?
14.♗d2 ♘fd7 15.♖fc1 ♔b8) 14.♗d2
0–0 15.♖fc1 ♖fc8±/= — White's
advantage is minimal, Ponomariov
— Akopian, Astrakhan 2010)

10...♛xb3

a) 10...♝e4 11.♞c3 ♛xb3 (*11...♛xd4 12.♞xf7 ♚xf7 13.♜d1 ♛e5 14.♞xe4 ♞xe4 15.♛e3±*) 12.axb3 ♝xg2 13.♚xg2±;

b) 10...♛xd4 11.♞xc6 bxc6 12.♜d1 ♛b4 13.♝xc6+ ♞fd7 14.♛xb4 ♝xb4 15.♜xd7 ♞xd7 16.♝xa8 ♚e7 17.♝g2 ♜c8 18.♞c3!±;

11.axb3 ♝e4 (*11...♞bd5 12.♞a3 ♞b4 13.♝d2±*) 12.♞d2!?N

(12.♝xe4 ♞xe4 13.♞c3 ♞xc3 14.bxc3 c5 15.♝e3! (*15.♜d1 f6 16.dxc5 ♞d5 17.♞d3 ♞xc3 18.♜d2 ♞b5=* Sakaev — Akopian, Vrnjacka Banja 2010) 15...♞d5 16.c4 ♞xe3 17.fxe3 f6 18.♞d3 cxd4 19.exd4±)

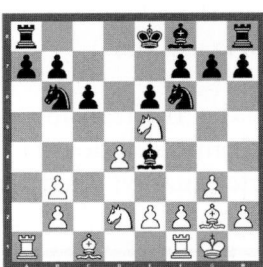

12...♝xg2 13.♚xg2± — White will play ♞d2-c4, after which he can move the knight to a5, or simply seize the centre with f2-f3 and e2-e4.

9.e3
The idea of not hurrying to develop the queen's knight has become fashionable recently.

9.♞c3 0-0 10.♜e1

(10.e3 b5 (*10...♞e4=*) 11.♛e2 (*11.♛xc6 b4 12.♞e2 ♝d3 13.♜e1 ♜c8 14.♛a4 ♛b6/↑*) 11...b4 12.♞a4 ♛a5 13.b3 ♛b5 14.♜e1 ♜ac8 = Vaganian — Cs.Horvath, Belgium 2011)

10...♞e4

(Also quite reliable is 10...♝g6

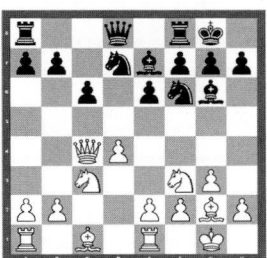

11.e4

a) 11.♛b3 ♛b6 12.e4 ♛xb3 13.axb3 ♝b4 14.♞h4 e5 = Bacrot — Hovhannisyan, Rijeka 2010;

b) 11.♝f4 ♞d5 12.♝d2 ♞b4 13.♞e4 ♞b6 14.♛b3 ♛d5∓ Fedoseev — Chadaev, Taganrog 2011;

c) 11.e3 ♞e4

(11...c5 12.♞h4!? (*12.♛b3 ♜b8=* Alekseev — Harikrishna, Motril 2008) 12...♞b6 13.♛f1 cxd4 14.♞xg6 hxg6 15.♜d1 ♞fd5 16.♜xd4 ♝f6 17.♜d3 ♝xc3 18.bxc3 ♛c7 19.e4±/↑)

12.♞d2 ♞d6 13.♛e2 e5=;

11...b5 12.♕xc6 b4 13.e5 bxc3 14.exf6 ♘xf6 15.bxc3 ♖c8 16.♕a6 (*16.♕a4 ♖xc3 17.♘e5 ♕b6 18.♘xg6 hxg6 19.♗e3 Landa — Acs, Hungary 2008 19...♖a3 20.♕c4 ♕b4=*) 16...♖xc3 17.♘e5 ♕b6 18.♕xb6 axb6 19.d5

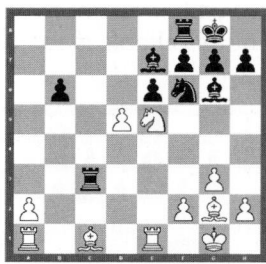

19...♗c5

(*19...♗f5 20.♘c6 (20.♗b2 ♖c2 21.♘c6 ♗d6 22.♗xf6 gxf6 23.♘d4 ♖d2 24.♖ad1 ♖xd1 25.♖xd1 ♗g4 26.f3 ♗h5 27.dxe6 ♗c5 28.♔f1 ♖d8 29.♔e2 ♖a8 30.♖d2 ♗b4 31.♖c2 ♗c5=) 20...♗d6 21.♗f4 ♗xf4 22.gxf4 g6*

a) *22...♗h3 23.♘e7+ ♔h8 24.♗xh3 ♖xh3 25.d6± Mamed-yarov — Gelfand, Plovdiv 2010(25. dxe6 fxe6 26.♖xe6 ♖f3±) ;*

b) *22...♖c4 23.d6↑;*

23.d6 ♘d7 24.a4 ♔g7± — White has the initiative but Black should not lose.)

20.dxe6 fxe6 21.♗d2 (*21.♘xg6 hxg6 22.♗e3 ♗xe3 23.♖xe3 ♖xe3*

24.fxe3 = Khairullin — Grachev, Irkutsk 2010) 21...♗xf2+ 22.♔xf2 ♘e4+ 23.♔g1 ♘xd2 24.♘xg6 hxg6 25.♖xe6 ♖f6 26.♖e2±/= — The game should end in a draw although White stands somewhat better.)

11.♕b3 (*11.♗f4 ♘xc3 12.bxc3 ♗e4 13.♕b3 c5= Brunello — Kobalia, Plovdiv 2012*)

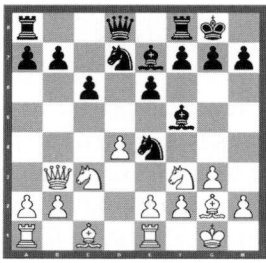

11...♕b6 12.♘h4 White's main idea is to gain the advantage of the two bishops. 12...♗xh4

(*12...♕xb3 The transformation to an endgame still doesn't promise absolute equality: 13.axb3 ♗b4*

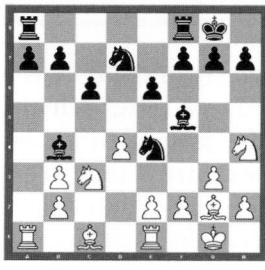

14.♖a4!

a) 14.g4 ♘xc3 15.gxf5 ♘a2! 16.♖d1
♘xc1 17.♖axc1 ♖ad8=;

b) 14.♘xf5 exf5

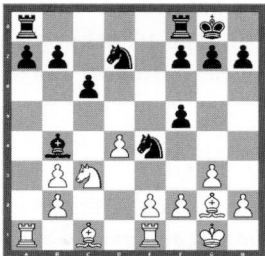

15.♗xe4

(15.♘xe4 ♗xe1

(15...fxe4 16.♖d1 f5 17.d5 ♘c5
(17...cxd5 18.♖xd5 ♘c5 19.♗e3
b6 20.♖ad1±) 18.dxc6 bxc6
19.♗e3 a5 20.♗xc5 (20.♖ac1
♘xb3 21.♖xc6 ♖fd8=) 20...♗xc5
21.♖ac1 ♗b4 22.♖xc6±)

16.♘d6 ♗b4 (16...♘f6 17.♘xb7
♘e4 18.♗e3±) 17.♘xb7 ♖fc8
18.♘a5 ♗xa5 19.♖xa5 g6 = —
White has sufficient compensation for the exchange but nothing more.)

15...fxe4 16.♗d2 ♖fe8 17.♘xe4
♖xe4 18.♗xb4 ♖xd4 19.♗c3 ♖d6
20.♖ed1 ♖xd1+ 21.♖xd1 ♘c5 22.b4
♘a4 23.♗d4 ♖d8 24.e3 (24.♖d3
f6=) 24...♘xb2 25.♖a1

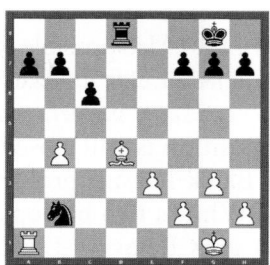

25...♘c4!N (25...♘d3 26.♖xa7
♘xb4 27.♖xb7 ♘d5 28.♔g2± —
The posit ion is drawish but Black
must defend accurately, Alekseev
— Leko, Dortmund 2007) 26.♖xa7
♖b8 27.♔f1 f6 28.♔e2 ♔f7=;

14...♗xc3 15.bxc3 ♘xc3 16.♘xf5
exf5 17.♖a5 g6

(17...♖fe8 18.♗b2 ♘b5 (18...♘e4
19.♖xf5± Krasenkow — Nezar,
Nancy 2009) 19.d5 ♖ac8 20.dxc6
bxc6 21.♗xc6 ♖xc6 22.♖xb5
♖b6 Miroshnichenko — De Jong,
Antwerpen 2007 (22...g6 23.♖b7
Stefanova — Houska, Dresden
2007 23...♖c2 24.♗d4 ♘e5 25.♔f1
♘c6 26.♗e3±) 23.♖xf5 ♖xb3
24.♗d4±)

18.♗b2 ♘e4

(18...b6 19.♖aa1 ♘d5 20.♖ec1 ♘b8
An unaesthetic move but it hangs
on to the pawn for a while and
Black hopes to regain space on
the queenside by advancing the
"a" pawn. 21.♗xd5 cxd5 22.♖c7
a5 (22...♖e8 23.e3±) 23.♖b7±)

19.g4!

(19.f3 ♘d6 (Also possible *19...♘ef6 20.e4 ♖fe8 21.♔f2 a6 22.exf5 ♖xe1 23.♔xe1 ♖e8+ 24.♔f2 ♘d5=* — The position is still closed, therefore Black has no problems despite White's two bishops.) 20.e4 ♖fe8 21.e5 Belov — Lintchevski, Krasnoyarsk 2007 *21...♘b6!±*)

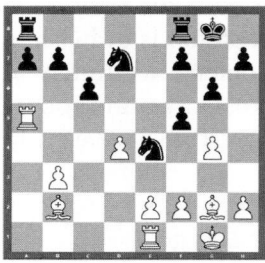

19...b6 (*19...♖fe8 20.gxf5 a6 21.f3 ♘d6 22.fxg6 hxg6 23.e4± Nyback — Kulaots, Jyvaskyla 2008*) 20.♖a6 ♘df6 21.gxf5 gxf5 22.♖ea1 ♖fe8 23.♖xa7 ♖xa7 24.♖xa7 ♘d5 25.♔f1± — The black knights have occupied good squares in the centre but the potential power of the bishop pair gives White some advantage.)

13.gxh4

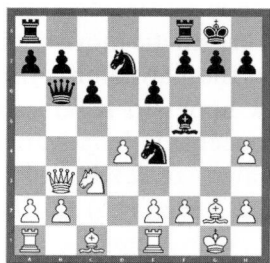

13...♘df6!

(*13...♘ef6 14.♕xb6 axb6 15.e4 (15.♗f4 permits 15...♘d5 =, after which the exchange on c3 spoiling White's pawn structureisunpleasant.) 15...♗g6 16.♗f4 b5 Yaksin — Volkov, Samara 2011 17.a3±*)

14.f3

(*14.♘xe4 ♗xe4 15.♕xb6 axb6 16.f3 ♗d5 (16...♗g6!? 17.e4 ♘h5, with f7-f5 to follow.) 17.a3 ♗c4 18.e4 (18.b3 ♗xb3 19.♖b1 ♗c4 20.♖xb6 ♖a7∓ Landa — Gasanov, Sochi 2010) 18...♘h5 (18...b5!?) 19.b3 ♗xb3 20.♖b1 ♗c4 21.♖xb6 ♖a7=*)

14...♘xc3 15.bxc3 ♕c7 (Double-edged is *15...e5!? 16.♕xb6 axb6 17.dxe5 ♘d7 18.e4 ♗e6 19.f4∞* Wojtaszek — Zherebukh, Warsaw (rapid) 2009) 16.e4 ♗g6

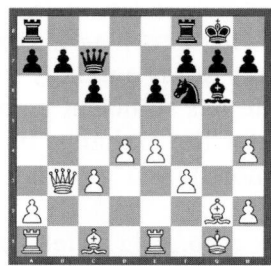

17.e5

a) 17.♖e2 ♘h5 18.♖f2 ♖fd8 19.♗e3 h6 20.a4 ♖d7∓ — Black prepares either f7-f5 or to attack h4 with ♕c7-d8, Khenkin — Karjakin, Dresden2008;

b) 17.a4 ♘h5 18.a5 ♖ab8 19. ♗a3 ♖fd8 20.♕b2 b6∓ Vitiugov — Motylev, Krasnoyarsk 2007;

c) 17.c4 ♘h5 It's more logical to leave the rook on f8 to support Black's main idea, the break f7-f5. *(17... ♖fd8 18. ♗e3 h6∞ Mamedyarov — Le Quang Liem, Dortmund 2010)* 18. ♗e3 f5∓;

17...♘d5 18. ♗a3 ♖fd8 19. ♗d6 ♕d7 *(19...♖xd6!? 20.exd6 ♕xd6 21.♕xb7 ♕d8)* 20.c4 ♘e7 21. ♗h3 ♘f5 22. ♗xf5 ♗xf5= Miroshnichenko — Gasanov, Moscow 2008

9...0–0 10. ♖d1
10.♕e2 ♕c7 11.♘c3 *(11. ♖d1 e5=)* 11...e5 12.♘xe5 *(12.h3 ♖fe8 = Ivanchuk — Karjakin, Beijing (rapid) 2011)* 12...♘xe5 13.dxe5 ♕xe5 14.e4 ♗e6 15.f4 ♕c5+ 16. ♗e3 ♕b4= Sargissian — Salgado Lopez, Villafranca 2010; 10.♘c3 — 9.♘c3 0–0 10.e3

10...♕c7!
Black plans not c6-c5 but e6-e5.

10... ♖c8 11.♕e2! *(11.♘c3 b5 12.♕e2 b4 13.♘a4 ♕a5 14.b3 ♕b5∓ Postny — Motylev, Plovdiv 2010)* 11...♘e4

a) 11...c5 12.♘c3 ♘e4 13.dxc5! *(13.♘e1 ♘xc3 14.bxc3 Kramnik — Smeets, Nice (rapid) 2010 14...♕c7=)* 13...♘xc3 14.bxc3 ♖xc5! *(14...♕e8 15.c6 ♖xc6 16.♘d4± Rakhmanov — Solak, Moscow 2012)* 15.♘h4 ♗xh4

16. ♗a3 ♗e7 17. ♗xc5 ♗xc5 18.g4 ♗xg4 19.♕xg4 ♕c7±;

b) 11...♕b6 12.♘c3 ♘e4 13.♘xe4 ♗xe4 14.♘e5 ♘xe5 15. ♗xe4±;

c) 11...♕c7 12.♘c3 ♘e4 13.♘e1 ♘xc3 14.bxc3±;

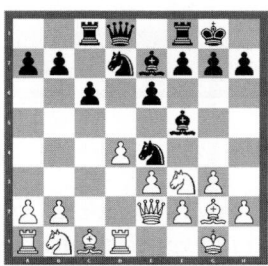

12.♘e1

(12.♘fd2 ♘xd2 13. ♗xd2 ♗g6 (13...e5 14.e4 ♗e6 15.d5 cxd5 16.exd5 ♗f5 17.♘c3±) 14.♘a3!?±)

12... ♗g6 *(12...c5 13.f3 ♘d6 14.dxc5 ♖xc5 15.e4 ♗g6 16. ♗e3 ♖c8 17.♘c3±)* 13.♘d3 ♕b6 14.♘f4 ♘ef6 15.♘c3 e5 16.♘xg6 hxg6 17.dxe5 ♘xe5 18.f4 *(18. b3±)* 18...♘ed7 19.♔h1 ♘c5 20.e4±; 10...e5 11.♘c3 ♕c7 — 10...♕c7 11.♘c3 e5; 10...♘e4 A typical blockading move for the given structure. 11.♕e2

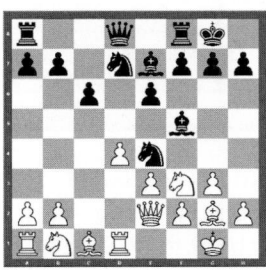

11...♕c7

(11...♕b6

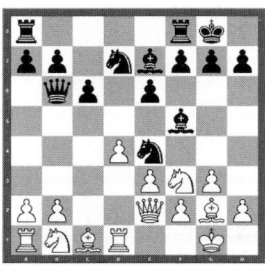

12.♘fd2!

(12.♘c3 ♖fd8 13.♘e1 (13.♘h4!? ♘xc3 14.bxc3 ♗xh4 15.gxh4±) 13... ♘df6 (13...♘xc3 14.bxc3 ♗g6 15.e4 c5 16.♗e3± Laznicka — Howell, Caleta 2012) 14.f3 ♘xc3 15.bxc3 e5 16.e4 ♗e6 17.♗e3±)

12...♘xd2 13.♘xd2 c5 (13...♗c2 14.♖e1 ♗g6 15.♘c4± Mista — Staniszewski, Poland 2011) 14.♘b3!N (14.dxc5 ♘xc5 15.e4 ♗g6 16.♘c4 ♕a6 17.♗f4 ♖fd8 18.b3= Matlakov — Andriasian, Magnitogorsk 2011)

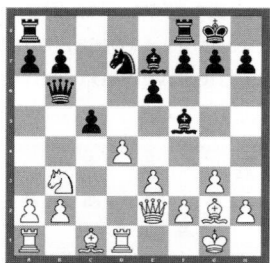

14...cxd4 (14...♖ac8 15.e4 ♗g6 16.♗e3±) 15.♘xd4 ♘c5 16.♘xf5 exf5 17.b3 ♗f6 18.♗b2±)

12.♘e1

(12.♘bd2 ♘xd2 13.♘xd2 ♗c2 14.♖e1 ♗g6! Black can break with c6-c5 as well as e6-e5. (14...c5 Atalik — Pavlidis, Kavala 2010 15.b3!±) 15.b3 a5 16.a3 e5 17.♗b2 ♖fe8=)

12...e5 (12...♗g6 13.f3 ♘ef6 14.e4±; 12...c5 13.f3 ♘d6 14.e4 ♗g6 15.dxc5±) 13.g4!?N

(13.♘d3

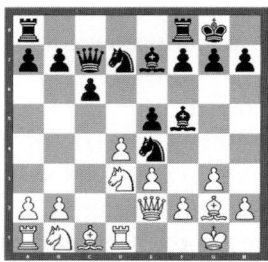

♘ef6!N (13...♖ad8 14.g4 ♗g6 15.f4± Alekseev — Inarkiev, Astrakhan 2010; 13...exd4 14.g4± Zatonskih — Sebag, Antalya 2010) 14.e4 ♗e6!=)

13...♗g6 14.dxe5

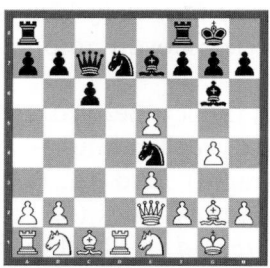

14...♘xf2!! A wonderful move! The knight sacrifices itself causing disharmony in the White camp. But with exceptionally accurate play it is somehow possible to make the pieces cooperate. (14...♘xe5 15.f4 ♖ad8 16.♖xd8 ♖xd8 17.f5 ♘xg4 18.♗xe4 ♗h5 19.♗f3 ♕a5 20.♘g2 ♕xf5 21.♘f4 ♗d6 22.♘xh5 ♘xh2 23.♘d2 ♕g5+ 24.♔h1 ♕h4 25.♔g2 ♘xf3 26.♕xf3 ♕h2+ 27.♔f1 ♗b4 28.♘xg7 ♗xd2 29.♘f5 ♗xc1 30.♕g4+ ♔f8 31.♖xc1 ♖d2 32.♕f3±; 14...♖ad8 15.f4 ♘dc5 16.♖d4±) 15.♕xf2 ♘xe5

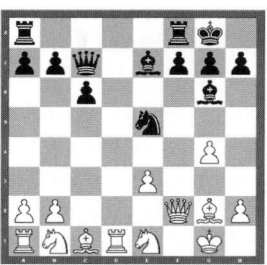

16.♗h3! the most accurate defensive move preventing Black from opening up the f-file with f7-f5. 16...♖ad8

a) 16...h5 17.gxh5 ♗xh5 18.♖d4 ♗c5 19.♘c3±;

b) 16...♗c5 17.♘c3 ♕e7 18.♘a4 ♗d6 19.♖d4 (19.e4!? ♗xe4 20.♗e3 f5 21.gxf5 ♘c4 22.♗f4 ♗xf5 23.♗xd6 ♘xd6 24.♗g2 ♗g4 25.♘f3 ♗xf3 26.♗xf3 ♖f5 27.♖f1 ♖af8 28.♕e2 ♖e5 29.♕c2±) 19...♖ad8 20.♘c3 ♗c5 — 16...♖ad8 17.♖d4 ♗c5 18.♘c3 ♕e7;

17.♖d4 (17.♘c3 ♖xd1 18.♘xd1 ♕d7 19.♕e2 f5 20.♘f2 ♗h4 21.g5 ♗xg5)

17...♗c5 18.♘c3 ♕e7 19.♖f4 ♖fe8 The position is very complicated and is of an unforcing nature. Black's positional compensation is very strong but White has managed to cover all the squares though his main problem is that the rook on a1 is still not in the game. Which side to prefer is a matter of taste as the chances are equal.

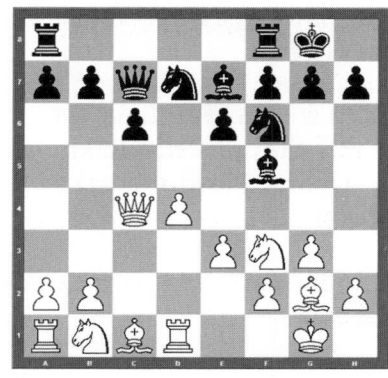

11.♘c3

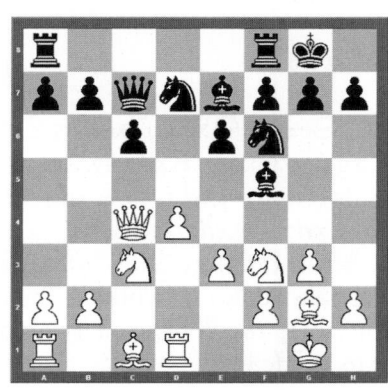

11...♘d5
11...e5 12.h3

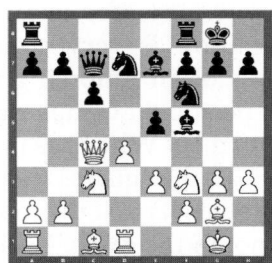

12...♖ad8

a) 12...♖fe8 13.dxe5 ♘xe5 14.♘xe5 ♕xe5 15.♕b3

(15.e4 ♗e6 16.♕e2 ♖ad8! *(16...♗b4 17.♗f4 ♕a5 18.♗d2± Rakhmanov — Dobre, Plovdiv 2012)* 17.♗e3 ♕a5=)

15...♕c7 16.e4 ♗e6 17.♕c2 ♖ad8 18.♗e3±;

b) 12...♗g6 13.dxe5 ♘xe5 14.♘xe5 ♕xe5 15.e4 ♕e6 16.♕xe6 fxe6 17.♗e3± Mamedyarov — Eljanov, Moscow 2010;

13.♕e2 h6

(13...♘e4 14.♘xe4 ♗xe4 15.♘xe5 ♗xg2 16.♘xd7 ♖xd7 17.♔xg2 c5 18.d5 *(18.b3 cxd4 19.♖xd4 ♗f6 20.♖xd7 ♕xd7 21.♗b2 ♗xb2 22.♕xb2 ♕d5+ 23.♔h2 ♖d8 24.♖c1 h5± Jakovenko — Volkov, Taganrog 2011)* 18...♕e5 19.e4 f5 20.d6! ♗f6 21.♕c4+±)

14.e4 ♗h7 15.♘xe5 *(15.dxe5 ♘xe5 16.♗f4 ♘fd7 17.♔h1 ♕a5 18.♘d4±)* 15...♘xe5 16.♗f4 ♘fd7 17.dxe5 ♘xe5

18.♗e3 b5 19.f4 ♘c4 20.♗f2± Rakhmanov — Magem Badals, Catalunya 2012;

11...♘e4 12.♘e1

(12.♘d2 ♘xc3

(12...♘b6 13.♕b3 ♘xd2 *(13...♘xc3 14.bxc3 e5 15.♗a3±)* 14.♗xd2 e5 15.d5±)

13.♕xc3 ♗g4! *(13...♖ac8 14.e4 ♗g4 15.f3 ♗h5 16.♘c4± Markus — Stamenkovic, Subotica 2008)* 14.f3 ♗h5 15.e4 f5 16.exf5 exf5 17.♘c4 ♘b6 18.♗f4 ♕d8=)

12...♘xc3 — 11...♘d5 12.♘e1 ♘xc3 *(12...♘b6 13.♕b3 ♘xc3 — 11.. ♘d5 12.♘e1 ♘b6 13.♕b3 ♘xc3; 12... ♘df6 13.f3 ♘xc3 14.♕xc3±)* ; 11... ♖ad8 12.h3 e5 — 11...e5 12.h3 ♖ad8

12.♘e1 ♘xc3!

12...♘7b6 13.♕b3 ♘xc3 14.♕xc3 ♘d5 15.♕b3 ♘f6 16.f3 e5 17.dxe5 ♕xe5 18.e4 ♗e6 19.♕xb7 ♕c5+ *(19...♗c4 20.♗f4 ♕c5+ 21.♔h1 ♘h5 22.♗e3 ♕xe3 23.♕xe7± Matlakov — Jakovenko, Taganrog 2011)* 20.♔h1 ♖ab8 21.♕a6±

13.bxc3

13.♕xc3 e5 14.e4 ♗g4! 15.f3 exd4 16.♖xd4 ♗e6 17.f4 *(17.♖d1 ♗f6 18.♕c2 ♘e5∓)* 17...♗f6! 18.e5 ♗e7 19.♗e3 f6∓

13...♘b6!N

13...e5 14.e4 ♗e6

(14...♗g4 15.♗f3 (15.♘f3∞ Bogo-
slavljevic — Solak, Valjevo 2011)
15...♘b6 16.♕e2 ♗e6 17.♘d3 ♘c4
18.♘b2 ♘xb2 19.♕xb2± — White
stands better due to his domination in the centre, Mamedyarov —
Karjakin, Beijing (rapid) 2011)

15.♕e2 ♘b6 16.♘f3 f6 17.♘h4

(17.h4 ♖ad8 (17...h6!?) 18.h5 h6
19.♘h4 ♖fe8 20.♗e3 ♗a3 21.d5
♗d7 22.c4 cxd5∞ Vitiugov — Negi,
Ningbo 2011)

17...g6 18.♗h6 ♖fe8 19.♘f3±

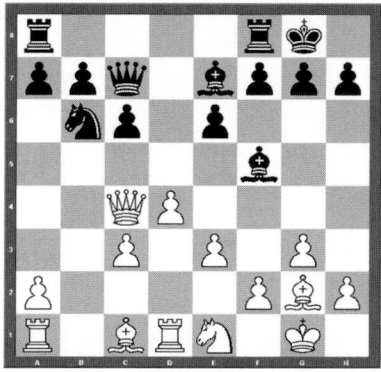

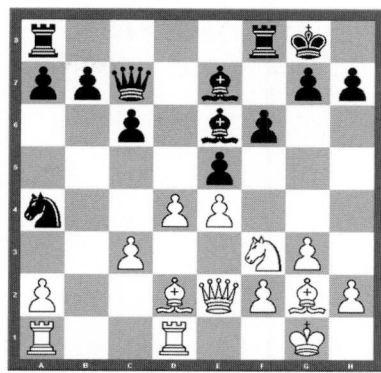

— In the forthcoming complicated
battle Black's chances are at least not
worse. Conclusion: The 4.♕b3 system does not require a large amount
of knowledge from White and there
are not so many forced lines. The
emerging positions as a rule have
a large margin of error but White
cannot count on posing serious
opening problems for Black. As for
Black, the most solid systems are 4...
e6 (though here one must be ready
for the double-edged move 5.♘c3) or
4...dxc4 5.♕xc4 ♗f5 — the choice is
a matter of taste.

14.♕e2 ♘a4!
It is useful to lure the white bishop
to d2, where it will be reduced to protecting the c3 pawn.

15.♗d2 e5 16.e4 ♗e6 17.♘f3 f6=/∞

■ GAME 19

1.d4 d5 2.c4 c6 3.♘f3 ♞f6 4.e3 g6 5.♘c3 ♝g7

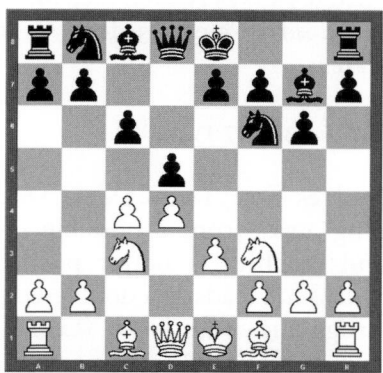

6. ♗e2

This unpretentious developing move is the most unpleasant for Black to face. One cannot expect much from 6.♕b3, with the idea of preventing the development of the c8 bishop. After 6...0–0 7.♗d2 e6 8.♗d3 b6 9.0–0 ♝b7= the game is about equal.;

6. ♗d3

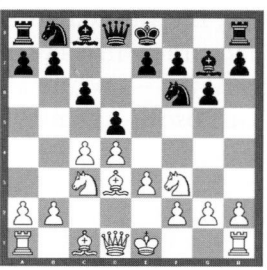

6...0–0 7.0–0 ♝g4 In other variations it's hard for Black to develop harmoniously.

a) 7...♘bd7 8.cxd5 cxd5 (8...♘xd5 9.e4±) 9.♕b3 ♞b6 10.a4 ♝f5 (10... a5 11.♗d2) 11.♗xf5 gxf5 12.♘e5± — White's pressure is very unpleasant.;

b) 7...♝e6 8.cxd5

(8.♕e2 ♘bd7 (8...dxc4 9.♗xc4 ♝xc4 10.♕xc4± Van Wely — S.Ernst, Netherlands 2011) 9.cxd5 cxd5 10.♘g5 ♝f5 11.♗xf5 gxf5 12.f3± Korchnoi — Nikolaevsky, Tbilisi 1966)

8...cxd5 9.♕b3 b6 10.♗d2 ♞e4 11.♖fc1 ♘xd2 12.♘xd2 ♘c6 13.♕a4 ♛d6

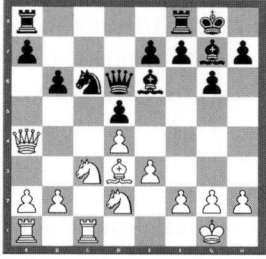

14.♘ce4!N (14. ♗b5 ♞b8±/= Wojtaszek — Volokitin, Karpacz 2008) 14...♛b4 15.♕xc6 dxe4 16.♘xe4 ♖fc8 17.♕b5 ♖xc1+ 18.♖xc1 ♛xb5 19.♗xb5 a6 20. ♗d3 ♝xa2 21.♖c6±;

c) 7...dxc4 8.♗xc4 — 6.♗e2 0-0
7.0-0 dxc4 8.♗xc4;

8.h3 ♗xf3 9.♕xf3

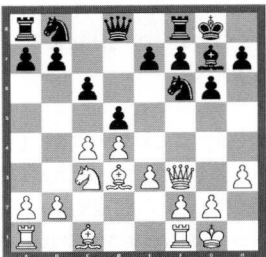

9...dxc4

(9...e6 leads to a very solid but passive position. White has many possible formations but his advantage is always minimal in a complicated manoeuvring battle. 10.♖d1 ♘bd7 11.b3 ♖e8 12.♗b2 ♕e7 13.♗f1!

(13.♕e2 allows a break in the centre: 13...♖ad8 (13...a6 14.♖ac1 ♖ad8 15.♕c2± Va.Popov — Mozharov, Sochi 2012) 14.♕c2 (It is better to play *14.f4!?*, even though it creates unwelcome weakness.) 14...e5! 15.dxe5 ♘xe5= Roiz — Ni Hua, Saratov 2011)

13...a6 14.♖ac1 h5 15.♖c2± Khismatullin — Matlakov, Magnitogorsk 2011)

10.♗xc4 ♘bd7 11.♖d1 e5

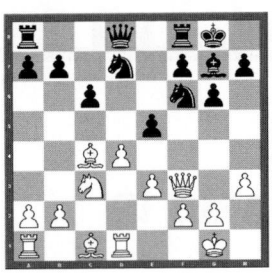

12.d5

a) 12.dxe5 ♘xe5 13.♕e2 ♕e7 14.♗b3 — 12.♗b3 ♕e7 13.dxe5 ♘xe5 14.♕e2;

b) 12.♗b3 ♕e7 13.♗d2

(13.dxe5 ♘xe5 14.♕e2 ♘ed7! Stepping away from a possible f2-f4 and reaching a better position. (*14...♖ad8* leads to a double-edged struggle *15.e4 ♖xd1+ 16.♗xd1 ♖d8 17.♗c2 ♕b4 18.f4 ♘c4 19.e5∞*) 15.e4 (*15.♗d2 ♘c5 16.♗c2 ♘fe4=* Markowski — Kempinski, Miedzybrodzie 2011) 15...♘c5 16.♗c2 ♖fe8 17.f3 ♖ad8 18.♗e3 ♘d5! 19.♘xd5 cxd5 20.♕f2 b6 21.♗xc5 ♕xc5=)

13...♖ad8 14.a3 ♖fe8 15.♖ac1 ♗h6! 16.♖c2 exd4 17.exd4 ♗xd2 18.♖cxd2 ♕d6!N= Black plans to play ♘d7-b6 and take hold of d5. The game is equal. (The immediate *18...♘b6* is an inaccuracy, in view of *19.♖e2 ♕d6 20.♖e5!±* — White seizes the e-file, Kurnosov — Danin, Moscow 2011);

12...e4

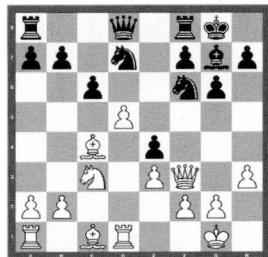

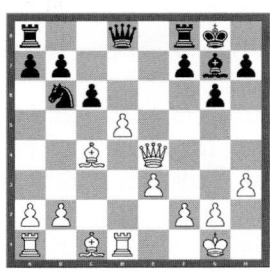

13.♘xe4

a) 13.♕e2 cxd5 14.♘xd5 ♘e5=;

b) 13.♕f4 cxd5 14.♘xd5

15.♗b3

(15.♖b1 allows Black to equalise in a forcing way: 15...♖e8 16.♕d3 ♘xc4 17.♕xc4 ♖e5 18.e4

(18.d6 ♖e6 19.♕b4 (*19.d7 ♕c7=*) 19...♕d7= — The d6 pawn will be lost soon.)

18...♕e8! 19.♗e3 (*19.f3 cxd5 20.♖xd5 ♖xd5 21.♕xd5 ♖d8 22.♕b3 ♕e6 23.♗e3 ♕xb3 24.axb3 ♖d3 25.♗xa7 ♖xb3=*) 19...♖xe4 20.♕b3 cxd5 21.♖xd5 b6 22.♖bd1 Kreisl — Pilaj, Austria 2011 22...♖c8=)

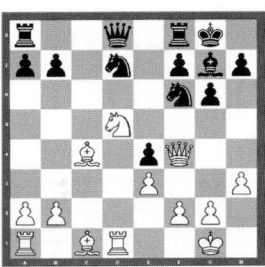

14...♘c5!N (*14...♘b6 15.♘c3 ♕e7 16.♗b3 ♖fd8 17.♗d2± D.Gurevich — Ziane, Dallas 1996*) 15.♖b1 ♖c8 16.b3 ♘d3 17.♘xf6+ ♗xf6 18.♕xe4 ♘xf2 19.♗xf7+ ♔g7 20.♖xd8 ♘xe4 21.♖xf8 (*21.♖xc8 ♖xc8 22.♗c4 b5 23.♗d3 ♘c3 24.♖b2 ♘xa2 25.♖xa2 ♖xc1+ 26.♔f2 ♖a1=*) 21...♔xf8 (*21...♖xf8 22.♗c4±*) 22.♗c4 ♘c3 23.♗a3+ ♔g7 24.♖c1 ♘xa2 25.♖d1 ♖d8 26.♖xd8 ♗xd8 27.♔f2 ♘c3 28.♔f3 b5 29.♗b2 ♗f6=;

13...♘xe4 14.♕xe4 ♘b6

15...cxd5

(If 15...♘xd5, it makes sense for White to be in no hurry to capture the pawn and to instead complete development retaining the two bishops: 16.♖b1 (*16.♕f3 ♕e7 17.♖b1 ♖ad8 18.♗d2 ♖d7=; 16.♗xd5 cxd5 17.♖xd5 — 15...cxd5 16.♗xd5 ♘xd5 17.♖xd5*) 16...♖e8 17.♕c2 Depending on what Black plays, White either solves the problem of the c1 bishop's development, or captures on d5. Therefore it's hard for Black to equalise, for example: 17...♕e7

(17...♕f6 18.e4 ♘b4 (*18...♘b6*
19.♗e3±) 19.♕c4 a5 20.a4±)

18.♗xd5 (*18.♗d2 ♖ad8 19.♗e1*
♖d6 20.♖d3 ♖ed8 21.♖bd1±) 18...
cxd5 19.♖xd5 ♖ac8 20.♕d3±)

16.♗xd5

(An interesting possibility is
16.♕b4!? White wants to prepare
development c1 bishop, or start
disturbing the knight by advancing the a-pawn. Only the following unobvious move allows Black
to equalise 16...♕c7! Black vacates
d8 for the rook and creates long-
term possibilities of a queen inva-
sion on the c-file. (*16...a5 17.♕b5 a4*
18.♗xd5 ♘xd5 19.♖xd5 ♕c7 Akes-
son — Ask, Taby 2007 The following would give a significant advantage *20.♗d2±*, and after *20...a3*
White has the intermediate move
21.♖c1!+-; 16...♖e8 17.a4±) 17.♗d2

(*17.♗xd5 ♘xd5 18.♖xd5 ♕c2*
19.♖d2 (19.♗d2 ♗xb2=) 19...♕c6
20.♖d6 ♕c7=)

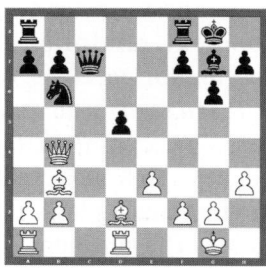

17...a5 18.♖ac1 ♕xc1 19.♕xf8+ ♖xf8
20.♖xc1 a4 21.♗d1 ♘c4=)

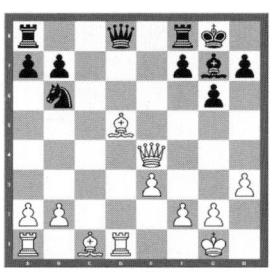

16...♘xd5 17.♖xd5 ♕b6 18.♕d3

(*18.♖b1 ♖ad8 19.♖d2 ♕a5 20.b4*
♕a4 21.♕c2 (21.♕c4 ♖c8=) 21...
♕xc2 22.♖xc2 ♖c8 23.♖xc8 ♖xc8
24.♗b2 ♖c2 25.♗xg7 ♔xg7 26.a4
b6= — Black easily obtains a draw
with his active rook.)

18...♖ad8!

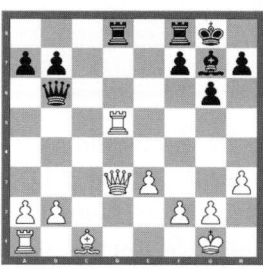

19.e4 ♗d4 20.♔h1 (*20.♗h6 ♕xb2*
21.♖d1 ♖xd5 22.exd5 ♕xf2+ 23.♔h1
♗g7 24.♗e3 ♕g3 25.♗xa7 ♕xd3
26.♖xd3 ♖d8= Shirov — Bareev,
Leon 1995; *20.♗e3 ♗xe3 21.fxe3*
♖xd5 22.exd5 ♖e8=; 20.♗g5 ♗xf2+
21.♔h1 ♖xd5 22.exd5 ♕d6 23.♖f1
♗g3 24.♗f6 ♖e8=) 20...♗xf2
21.♗h6 ♖xd5 22.exd5 ♖d8 23.♖d1
♕d6 24.♕c3 f6 25.♖f1 ♗h4 26.♕b3

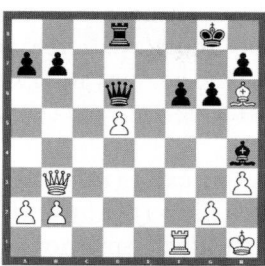

26...♖d7!N (26...♗g5 27.♗xg5 fxg5
28.♕xb7 ♕xd5 29.♕xa7 ♖a8 30.♕e3
♕xa2 31.♕xg5± Bareev — Kramnik, Novgorod 1994) 27.♕a4 ♗g5
28.♗xg5 fxg5 29.♕xa7 ♕xd5=;

6.h3 This continuation has been
popular in recent years. 6...0–0
7.♗d3 c5

a) 7...a6 8.0–0 b5 9.b3 ♘bd7 10.♕e2
♗b7 11.♖d1± e6 12. ♗a3 ♖e8 13. ♗d6
♘b6 14.c5 ♘c8 15.♗f4 (15.♘e5±)
15...♘d7 16.b4± Dreev — Mrkonjic,
Sibenik 2010;

b) 7...♗e6

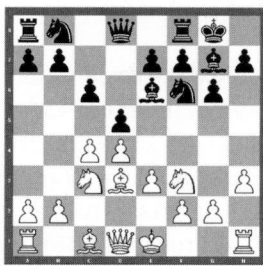

8.♘g5!?

  b1) 8.b3 c5=;

  b2) 8.cxd5 cxd5 9.♕b3 b6=;

b3) 8.♕b3 ♕b6 9.0–0 ♘a6=;

b4) Of the quiet continuations only
after 8.♕e2 can White hope to obtain a minimal advantage, for example 8...dxc4 (8...♘bd7 9.0–0±)
9. ♗xc4 ♗xc4 10.♕xc4 b5 11.♕b3
♘bd7 12.0–0± — It's not easy to
play c6-c5 favourably.;

8...♗f5 9.♗xf5 gxf5 10.♕b3 ♕b6
11.♕c2 e6 12.g4!? h6 (12...♘e4
13.h4↑) 13.♘f3 fxg4 14.hxg4 ♘xg4

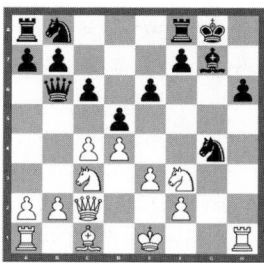

15.♖g1!N

(15.e4 dxc4 (15...♘a6!?) 16.e5 ♘d7
17.♗e3 f5 18.0–0–0 c5∞ Aronian —
Volokitin, Kallithea 2008)

15...f5 16.♘a4 ♕b4+ 17.♗d2 ♕e7
18.♘c5 ♘d7 19.♘xb7 (19.♗b4 b6
20.♘xd7 ♕xb4+ 21.♔e2 ♖fc8∓;
19.♘d3 c5 20.♘f4 ♖f7 21.cxd5 exd5
22.♘xd5 ♕d6∞) 19...e5 (19...♘df6
20.♘c5 ♘e4 21.♘d3±) 20.♘a5 ♖ac8
21.dxe5 ♘dxe5 22.♘xe5 ♕xe5 23.0–
0–0 ♘xf2 24. ♗c3 ♕xe3+ 25.♗d2
♕e5 26.♗xh6 ♘g4 27.♗xg7 ♔xg7
28.♕d2↑ — The black king is exposed and White's initiative is dangerous.;

c) Good for black is 7...♘bd7 8.0–0 dxc4 (8...♖e8 9.cxd5 cxd5 10.♕b3 e6 11.♗d2 a6 12.♖fc1± Pr.Nikolic — Thorfinsson, Kemer 2007; 8...♘b6 9.b3 ♗f5 10.♗xf5 gxf5 11.♘d2± The doubled black pawns do not beautify the position while White has a simple plan of developing play on the queenside — a2-a4, ♗c1-a3, etc.) 9.♗xc4 c5 It's not easy to set Black problems. The next move is a very interesting idea

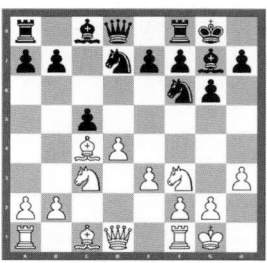

10.♗e2!?N to get piece play in the centre using the d-file instead of an isolated pawn position. Now d4-d5 threatens with subsequent e3-e4 — Black must prevent that.

c1) 10.♗b3 b6 11.d5 (11.♕e2 a5 12.♖d1 ♗a6 13.♗c4 ♗xc4 14.♕xc4 cxd4 15.exd4 ♕c8 16.♕b5 ♕b7=) 11...♗a6 12.♖e1 c4 13.♗c2 ♘c5 14.e4 ♘fd7 15.♗f4 ♘d3 16.♗xd3 cxd3 17.e5 ♖c8∞;

c2) 10.♕e2 a6 11.dxc5 (11.a4 cxd4 12.exd4 ♘b6 13.♗a2 ♘bd5 14.♗g5 ♗e6= Papin — Bryzgalin, Armavir 2011) 11...♘xc5 12.♖d1 ♗d7 13.b4 (13.e4 b5 14.e5 bxc4 15.exf6 ♗xf6

16.♗h6± Vitiugov — Wang Yue, Ningbo 2010) 13...♘fe4 14.♘xe4 ♘xe4 15.♗b2 ♘c3 16.♗xc3 ♗xc3 17.♖ac1 ♗xb4 18.e4±/↑;

c3) 10.♖e1 cxd4 (10...e6 11.e4 cxd4 12.♘xd4 ♘b6 13.♗b3 ♘fd7 14.♗e3 ♕e7 15.♘db5± Smirnov — Ponkratov, Magnitogorsk 2011) 11.exd4 ♘b6 12.♗b3 ♘bd5 13.♗g5 ♗e6 14.♘e5 (14.♖e5 h6 15.♗xf6 ♘xc3 16.bxc3 ♗xb3 17.axb3 ♗xf6=; 14.♖xe6!? 14...fxe6 15.♕e2 ♕d7 16.♖e1 ♘c7=/⯑) 14...♘c7 15.♖c1±;

10...cxd4 (10...e6 11.e4 cxd4 12.♕xd4 — 10...cxd4 11.♕xd4 e6 12.e4) 11.♕xd4 e6 (11...♕b6 12.♕h4!± — White can develop the black squared bishop on either side — both with e3-e4, or b2-b4.) 12.e4 (12.♕f4 b6 13.e4 ♗b7 14.♖d1) 12...♘d5 13.e5 ♘xc3 14.♕xc3 ♘b6 15.♗g5 ♘d5 16.♕d2 ♕b6 17.♗c4± — White has space and prospects of play on the black squares.;

8.0–0 cxd4

(8...♘c6 9.dxc5 dxc4 10.♗xc4 ♕a5 11.e4 ♕xc5 12.♕e2 ♘d7 13.♗e3 (13.♖d1±) 13...♕h5 14.♕c2 (14. ♖fd1 ♘de5 15.♘xe5 ♕xe2 16.♗xe2 ♗xe5± Sargissian — Bu Xiangzhi, Yerevan 2008) 14...♘de5 15.♘xe5 ♗xe5 (15...♘xe5 16.♗e2 ♕h4 17.♖ad1±) 16.f4 ♗d4 (16... ♗g7 17.♖ad1±) 17.♗xd4 ♘xd4 18.♕d3±)

9.exd4

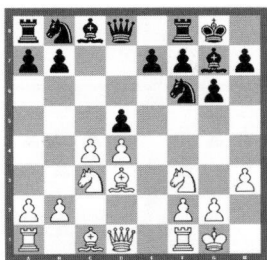

9...♘c6

a) 9...dxc4 10.♗xc4 a6 11.a4

a1) 11.♖e1 b5 12.♗b3 ♗b7 13.♗g5 ♘c6= Nepomniachtchi — Kamsky, Khanty Mansyisk 2011;

a2) 11.♘e5 b5 (*11...♘c6 12.♘xc6 bxc6 13.♗g5±*) 12.♗e2 ♗b7 13.♗f3± — It's hard for Black to keep control of the e5 square.;

11...♘c6 (*11...b6 12.♗f4 ♗b7 13.d5±*) 12.d5 (Also good is *12.♖e1± — The d-pawn is ready to move later restricting Black.*) 12...♘a5 13.♗a2±;

b) 9...b6 10.cxd5 ♘xd5 (*10...♗b7 11.♗g5 ♘xd5 12.♖e1±*) 11.♘xd5 ♕xd5 12.♖e1 ♗f5 13.♗xf5 ♕xf5 (*13...gxf5 14.♖xe7 ♘c6 15.♖e2±*) 14.♖xe7 ♘c6 15.♖c7 ♕d5 16.♗e3 ♕d6 17.♗f4 ♕d5 18.♗e5± — White succeeds in retaining the pawn, though it's not easy to realise.;

10.a3

a) 10.c5 b6∞ — Black's chances are not worse in the following sharp play.;

b) 10.♖e1 dxc4 (*10...♘b4 11.♗f1 dxc4 12.♗xc4± Wang Hao — Matlakov, Sochi 2010*) 11.♗xc4 ♘a5 12.♗d3 (*12.♗f1 b6=*) 12...b6 (*12...♘c6!?=*) 13.♗g5 ♗b7 14.♕e2 h6= Akopian — Yilmaz, Bursa 2010;

10...b6 Black prevents the space gaining c4-c5 and provides the b7 square for the bishop.

a) 10...♗f5 11.♗xf5 gxf5 12.c5 (*12.cxd5 ♘xd5 13.♕d3 e6 14.♗g5 ♕d6=*) 12...♘e4 13.♕d3 e6 14.b4 ♔h8 15.♗f4± Wojtaszek — Le Quang Liem, Wijk aan Zee 2011;

b) 10...dxc4 11.♗xc4 a6 12.d5 (*12. ♗a2 b5 13.♖e1 ♗b7 14.♗g5 ♖c8 15.♖c1 ♘a5 16.♘e5 ♘c4= Akopian — Gagunashvili, Khanty Mansyisk 2010*) 12...♘a5 13.♗a2 b5 14.♕e2 ♗b7 15.♖d1 ♖c8 16.♘e5 ♘d7 17.♗f4 ♘xe5 18.♗xe5 ♗xe5 19.♕xe5 ♕d6 Efimenko — Hammes, Rogaska Slatina 2011 20.♕xd6! exd6 21.♖d4±;

11.♖e1 (*11.♗g5 ♗e6!= — In this configuration White gains nothing from c4-c5, but otherwise Black gets piece control over the d5 square and a good game.*)

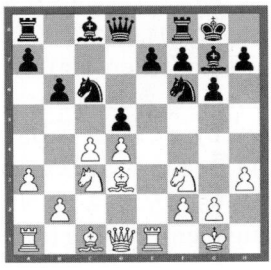

11...♗b7 (Not so good is 11...♗e6 in view of *12.c5! bxc5 13.dxc5 ♘d7 14.♗b5 ♖c8 15.♘a4±* — It's difficult for Black to advance the central pawns.) 12.♗g5 ♖c8 13.c5

(13.cxd5 ♘xd5 14.♗e4 ♘xc3 (*14... ♘f6=*) 15.bxc3 ♖e8=)

13...bxc5 14.dxc5 e5 15.♘xe5 ♘xe5 16.♖xe5 h6 (*16...♖xc5=*) 17.♗h4 ♕c7 18.♖e2 ♕xc5 19.♕b3 ♗a8= Ehlvest — Donaldson, Connecticut 2004.

6...0-0

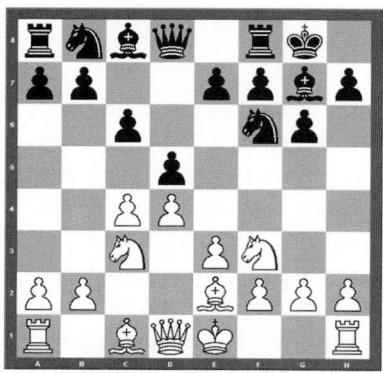

7.0-0 dxc4

Passive is 7...♘bd7 8.cxd5 (*8.b4?! 8... dxc4 9.♗xc4 ♘b6 10.♗e2 ♘fd5=; 8.b3 ♖e8 9.♗b2 ♘f8 10.h3 ♗f5 11.♖c1±* Wojtaszek — Bryzgalin, Warsaw (rapid) 2011) 8...cxd5 9.♕b3 (*9.a4!? ♘b8 10.b4 ♗g4 11.h3 ♗xf3 12.♗xf3 ♘c6 13.♗a3±* Kasimdzhanov — Dao Thien Hai, Mashhad 2011) 9...e6 10.♗d2 a6 11.♖fc1 b6 12.♖c2 ♗b7 13.♖ac1 ♖b8 14.♗e1 ♖e8 15.a4 ♖c8 16.♘a2 ♖xc2 17.♖xc2 ♕a8 18.a5 b5 19.♘b4± Pe.Nielsen — Le Quang Liem, Beijing (rapid) 2011;

7...♗g4

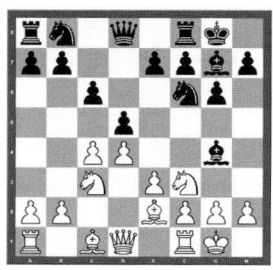

8.cxd5

(8.h3 ♗xf3 9.♗xf3 dxc4 (*9...e6 10.b3±*) 10.♕e2 ♘bd7 11.♖d1 (*11. ♕xc4 e5=*) 11...♘b6 12.e4 ♕c7∞ Giri — Timman, Leiden (rapid) match)

8...cxd5 (*8...♘xd5 9.h3 ♗xf3 10.♗xf3 e6 11.♕c2 ♘d7 12.♖d1±* Khalifman — Chadaev, Novokuznetsk 2008) 9.♕b3 9...b6

(*9...♗c8 10.♘e5 (*10.♗d2 ♘c6 11.♖ac1 e6 12.♖fd1±* Avrukh — Andonovski, Plovdiv 2010) 10...♘c6 11.f4 ♕b6 12.♕xb6! (*12.♗f3 ♕xb3 13.axb3 e6 14.♗d2 ♗d7 15.g4±* Caruana — Ortega, Perugia 2011) 12...axb6 13.b3± — The threat ♘c3-a4 is very unpleasant.)

10.♗d2!

(10.h3 ♗c8!

(10...♗xf3 11.♗xf3 e6 12.♗d2 ♘c6 13.♕a4 (*13.♖fc1 ♘a5 14.♕b4 ♘c4 15.♗e1 ♖e8 16.♗e2 ♗f8 17.♕b3 ♖c8* Nyback — P.Vorobjov,

Puhajarve 2011 *18.a4±*) 13...♘a5 14.b3± Kurnosov — Varga, Austria 2011)

11.♗d2 ♘c6 12.♘e5 ♗b7 13.♘xc6 ♗xc6 14.♖fc1 ♕d7 15.a4 ♖fc8±/= — Black can gradually extinguish White's initiative, Anand — Gashimov, Nanjing 2010)

10...♘c6 11.♖fc1 ♘a5 12.♕d1 ♖c8 13.b3± — Black's queenside white squares are weak and the g7 bishop is out of play. (*13.♘e5 ♗xe2 14.♕xe2 ♘d7 15.♘d3±* Tomashevsky — Sitnikov, Olginka 2011);

7...a6 Black does not decide on his plan waiting for White's response. White in his turn has several opportunities for a small advantage.

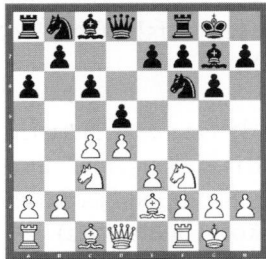

8.a4

a) Bad is 8.♗d2, in view of

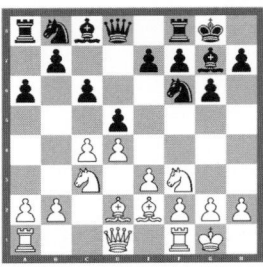

8...dxc4!

(8...b5 9.cxd5 (*9.b3 ♗g4 10.h3 ♗xf3 11.♗xf3 e6* Tregubov — Gashimov, Odessa (rapid) 2010 *12.♖c1±*) 9...cxd5 10.b4 ♘c6 (*10...♘e4 11.a4±* Potkin — Amonatov, Ulan Ude 2009) 11.a4 bxa4 12.♕xa4± — White's position is only slightly better.)

9.♗xc4 ♘bd7! Mainly to support the breaks e7-e5 or c6-c5. The d2 bishop blocking the d-file is badly placed.

a1) 9...b5 10.♗e2 ♘bd7 11.b4!± Bocharov — Vidit, St.Petersburg 2009;

a2) 9...♗g4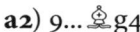

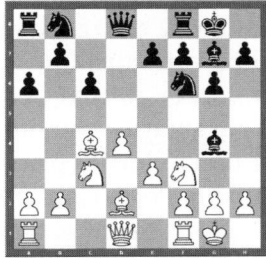

10.♗e2! The most important continuation, strengthening the centre.

(10.h3 ♗xf3 11.♕xf3 ♘bd7 12.♖fd1 e5 13.♗b3 ♕e7 14.dxe5!

(14.♖ac1 ♖fe8 15.♘a4 b5 (*15...exd4 16.exd4 ♕e4 17.♕xe4 ♘xe4 18.♗a5±*) 16.♘c3 ♖ac8= Tomashevsky — Bu Xiangzhi, Ningbo 2008)

14...♘xe5 15.♕e2± Av. Grigoryan — Ipatov, Moscow 2012)

10...♘bd7 11.♕b3! (*11.h3 ♗xf3 12.♗xf3 e5=; 11.e4 c5 12.d5 b5∞* Kazhgaleyev — Li Shilong, Manila 2008) 11...♕b6 12.♕xb6 ♘xb6 13.h3 ♗e6 (*13... ♗xf3 14.gxf3±*) 14.e4 ♘c4 15.♗c1± — White retains an advantage.;

10.b4 (*10.e4!? c5∞; 10.a4 c5=* Dzhumabaev — Fressinet, Khanty Mansyisk 2011) 10...♕c7 11.♗b3 (*11. ♖c1 e5=*) 11...e5 12.♖c1 ♕d6= Safyanovsky — Petrik, Bratislava 1993;

b) 8.b3 is also not energetic enough 8...♘e4 9.♗b2 ♘xc3 10.♗xc3 ♗g4 11.h3 (*11.♘e5 ♗xe2 12.♕xe2 ♘d7=* Bukavshin — Khairullin, Taganrog 2011) 11...♗xf3 12.♗xf3 e6±/= — White's advantage is minute and it's hard for him to form a plan, Postny — Buhmann, Porto Carras 2011;

c) 8.♕b3!? e6

(8...dxc4 9.♗xc4 b5 10.♗e2 ♘bd7 (*10...c5 11.dxc5 ♕c7 12.a4±* Karpov — Ljubojevic, Amsterdam 1988) 11.e4 ♘b6 12.♗f4± Carlsen — Malakhov, Khanty Mansyisk 2005)

9.♘e5!?N (*9.♖d1 ♘bd7 10.♕c2 ♕c7 11.h3 b6 12.e4 dxe4 13.♘xe4 c5=* Gelfand — Kamsky, Wijk aan Zee 2012)

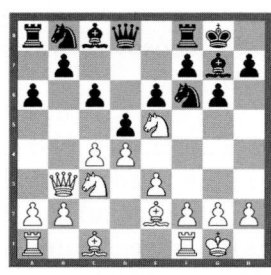

9...♘bd7 10.f4±;

8...a5 9.cxd5

(9.♕b3 e6 10.♖d1 (*10. ♗d2 ♘a6!?=*) 10...♘bd7 (*10...♘a6!?*) 11.♕c2 b6 12.cxd5 (*12.b3±*) 12...exd5= Wang Hao — Kamsky, Beijing 2011)

9...cxd5 10.♕b3 ♘c6 11.♗d2 e6

(11...♕d6 12.♖ac1

(12.♖fc1 ♗f5!? (*12...♖d8 13.h3 ♕b8*))

12...♗d7 (*12...♗f5!?*) 13.♘b5 ♕b8 14.♖fd1 ♖c8 15.♘e1 e6 16.♘d3 ♗f8 17.♗e1 b6 18.f3± Sargissian — Raznikov, Caleta 2012)

12.♖fc1 ♕e7 13.♕a3!?N (*13.♘e1* Wojtaszek — Bindrich, Czech 2012 *13...e5! 14.dxe5 ♘xe5=*) 13...♕xa3 14.bxa3!?±

8.♗xc4

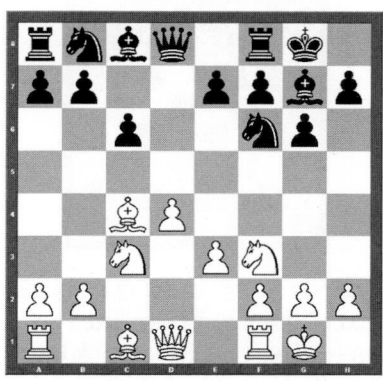

8...♗g4
8...♘bd7 9.e4 ♘b6 10.♗e2!

(10.♗b3 ♗g4 11.♗e3 e5 12.dxe5
♘fd7 (12...♕xd1 13.♖axd1 ♘fd7
14.e6 ♗xe6 15.♗xe6 fxe6 16.♘d4
♔f7 17.b3±) 13.e6 fxe6 14.♕d6 ♗xf3
15.gxf3 ♘e5∞ Giri — Almasi, Rieka
2010)

10...♗g4

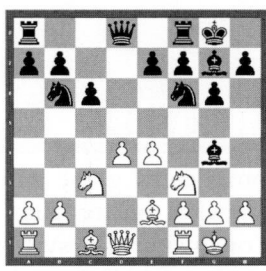

11.a4!

a) 11.♗e3 ♗xf3 12.♗xf3 (12.gxf3!?)
12...♘c4 13.e5 (13.♕b3 ♘xe3 14.fxe3
♗h6 15.♖ae1 ♕b6 16.♕xb6 axb6
17.e5 ♘d7=) 13...♘xe3 (13...♘d5
14.♗c1±) 14.fxe3 ♘d5 15.♗xd5 cxd5

16.♕b3 e6 17.♕xb7 ♖b8 18.♕xa7
♖xb2 19.♕a3 ♖b6;

b) 11.h3 ♗xf3 12.♗xf3 ♘e8

(12...♕c7 13.♕b3 ♘fd7 14.♗e3 (14.
e5 e6 15.♗e3±) 14...e5 15.d5± Khairullin — Romanov, St.Petersburg
2010)

13.e5 ♘c7±;

11...a5 12.♗g5 ♘e8 13.♕b3 ♗xf3
14.♗xf3 ♗xd4 15.♖ad1 ♘g7
16.♗g4!N (16.♘e2 c5 17.e5± Gelfand
— Nisipeanu, Fuegen 2006) 16...c5
17.♘b5±/↑

9.♗e2!
9.h3 ♗xf3 10.♕xf3 — 6.♗d3 0-0
7.0-0 ♗g4 8.h3 ♗xf3 9.♕xf3 dxc4
10.♗xc4

9...♘bd7
9...♘b6 10.♕c2 ♘bd7 11.♖d1 ♗xf3
12.♗xf3 e5 13.dxe5 ♘xe5 14.♗e2
♖fe8 15.h3± — Due to his two bishops White has a small but longlasting
advantage, Pe. Nielsen — Gashimov,
Khanty Mansyisk2011

10.e4 ♗xf3
10...♘e8 11.♗g5 ♘b6 12.♕d2 ♘c7
13.♖ad1 ♘e6 14.♗e3 ♗xf3 15.♗xf3
♘c4 16.♕e2 ♘xe3 17.fxe3± Tomashevsky — Romanov, Sochi 2010;
10...♕b6 11.♖b1 ♗xf3 12.♗xf3
e5 13.d5 cxd5 14.exd5 ♕d6 15.♗e3
a6 16.g3± Tomashevsky — Danin,
Olginka 2011

11.♗xf3 e5

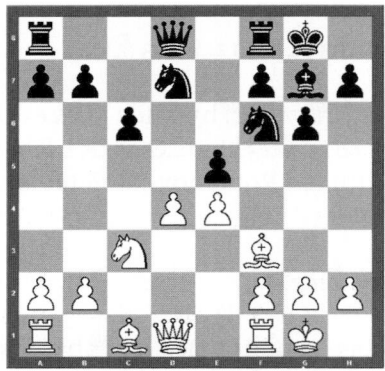

12.d5

12.♗e3 exd4 13.♗xd4 ♖e8= — The bishop on d4 could be attacked or exchanged.;

12.dxe5!? ♘xe5 13.♗e2 ♕e7 14.♕c2 ♖fe8 (After *14...b5* promising is *15.♘d1!*, escaping a potential pin after ♕e7-c5 with possibilities of f2-f4 followed by a strengthening ♘d1–f2 or a simple transfer of the knight to e3.) 15.♔h1!?

a) 15.f4 ♕c5+ (*15...♘eg4 16.♔h1 ♕c5* — *15...♕c5 16.♔h1 ♘eg4*) 16.♔h1 ♘eg4 17.♗d1 ♖ad8 18.e5 ♖xd1 19.♕xd1 ♘f2+ 20.♖xf2 ♕xf2∓ Delchev — Stojanovic, Plovdiv 2012;

b) 15.♖d1 ♖ad8 16.♗f4 c5 17.♖xd8 ♖xd8 18.♖d1 ♘c6 19.♖xd8+ ♕xd8 20.♗f1± — Despite Black's control of d4, White's chances are preferable due to his two bishops.;

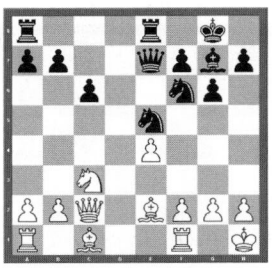

15...♘ed7 16.f3 ♘d5 17.exd5 ♗xc3 18.dxc6 ♕xe2 19.♕xe2 ♖xe2 20.cxb7 ♖b8 21.bxc3 ♖xb7 22.♗h6± — White has winning chances.

12...cxd5 13.exd5 ♖e8

13...♘b6 14.♕b3± Najer — Kovalevskaya, Tula 1999

14.♖e1 ♕b6 15.♖b1±

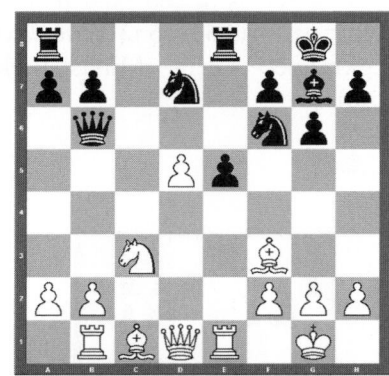

— A complicated game will follow with somewhat better chances for White. Conclusion: The system 4...g6 unlike the Grunfeld Defence in which Black makes the break c7-c5 as soon as possible, is passive, since Black has already made the move c7-c6. Nevertheless, with accurate play White can count on only a small advantage. In my opinion, the most promising for White is the line 6.♗e2.

■ **GAME 20**

1.d4 d5 2.c4 c6 3.♘f3 ♘f6 4.e3 e6

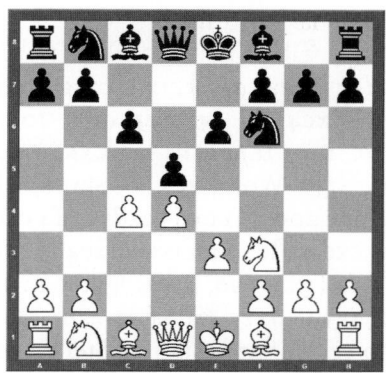

5.♘bd2

5.♕c2 — *3...e6 4.♕c2 ♘f6 5.e3;*

5.♘c3 — *3.♘f3 ♘f6 4.♘c3 e6 5.e3* (Slav Defence part 2);

5.♗d3 In most cases this move transposes to other lines.

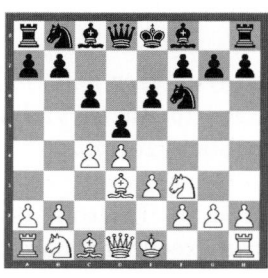

5...dxc4

(5...♘bd7 6.b3 — 5.b3 ♘bd7 6.♗d3

(6.0-0 ♗d6 7.♘bd2 — 5.♘bd2 ♘bd7 6.♗d3 ♗d6 7.0-0 (7.♘c3 — 3.♘f3 ♘f6 4.♘c3 e6 5.e3 ♘bd7 6.♗d3 ♗d6 7.0-0 (Slav Defence, Part 2))))

6.♗xc4 ♘bd7 *(6...c5 leads to the Queen's Gambit Accepted; 6...b5 7.♗d3 a6 8.a4±)* **7.0-0 ♗d6**

(7...b5 8.♗d3 a6 9.a4 ♗b7 10.e4 ♗e7 11.♘bd2 (11.♗g5 h6 12.♗h4 g5! 13.♗g3 ♘h5∞ Tregubov — J. Geller, Krasnodar 2001; 11.♘c3 b4 12.e5 bxc3 13.exf6 ♘xf6 14.bxc3 0-0=; 11.e5 ♘d5 12.♘c3±) 11...0-0 (11...♘c5 12.dxc5 ♕xd3 13.♖a3! ♕d8 14.♕c2±) 12.♕c2 (12.e5 ♘d5 13.♘e4 ♘b4±/⇄) 12...h6 13.♘b3 ♖c8 14.axb5 cxb5 15.♕e2±)

8.♘c3

a) 8.♖e1 0-0 9.e4 e5 10.♗g5 ♕c7 11.h3 exd4 12.♗xf6 gxf6 13.♕xd4 ♘e5 14.♘bd2 ♖d8∞ Black's chances are not worse Wang Yue — Akopian, Elista 2008;

b) 8.b3 e5 *(8...0-0 9.♗b2 ♕e7 10.♘e5 c5 11.♘d2 cxd4 12.exd4± Landa —*

Makarov, Krasnoyarsk 2007) 9.♗b2 ♛e7 10.♘bd2 0–0 11.♛c2 (*11.dxe5 ♘xe5 12.♘xe5 ♗xe5 13.♗xe5 ♛xe5 14.♘f3 ♛e7∓*) 11...e4 12.♘g5 ♗xh2+ 13.♔xh2 ♘g4+ 14.♔g1 ♛xg5 15.♛xe4 ♘b6=;

c) 8.♘bd2 0–0 9.♗b3 c5 10.♛e2 cxd4 11.exd4 ♘b6 (*11...b6=*) 12.♘e5 ♘bd5 = Miroshnichenko — Gasanov, Kharkov 2010;

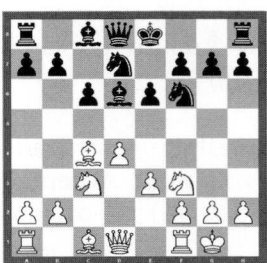

8...0–0 9.e4 (*9.♛c2 — 3.♘f3 ♘f6 4.♘c3 e6 5.e3 ♘bd7 6.♛c2 ♗d6 7.♗d3 0–0 8.0–0 dxc4 9.♗xc4* (Slav defence,Part 2)) *9...e5 — 3.♘f3 ♘f6 4.♘c3 e6 5.e3 ♘bd7 6.♗d3 ♗d6 7.0–0 0–0 8.e4 dxc4 9.♗xc4 e5* (Slav Defence,Part 2);

5.b3 c5! Despite having played c7-c6 and then c6-c5, the resulting simplification in this variation allows Black to equalise the game.

a) 5...♗b4+ 6.♘bd2 ♘e4 7.♛c2 (After the careless *7.♗b2?* follows *7...♛f6!*, and the threat ♗b4xd2+ appears. After *8.♛e2 dxc4 9.bxc4 0–0∓* White has problems completing development. Black's chances are better, Eljanov — Zherebukh,

Khanty Mansyisk 2011) 7...f5 8.♗b2 0–0 9.♗e2±;

b) 5...♘bd7 6.♗d3 ♗d6 7.♗b2 0–0 8.0–0 b6 9.♘c3 It's better to move the knight to a more active position, even if it loses the possibility of placing the other knight on e5.

b1) 9.♘e5 ♗b7 10.♘d2=/∞ — 9.♘bd2 ♗b7 10.♘e5;

b2) 9.♘bd2 ♗b7 10.♘e5 (*10.♛e2 ♛e7 11.e4 dxe4 12.♘xe4 ♘xe4 13.♛xe4 f5! 14.♛e3 c5=*) 10...c5 (*10...♛e7 11.f4 ♗a3 12.♗xa3 ♛xa3 13.♖f3↑* Wojtaszek — Stanojoski, Crete 2007) 11.cxd5 exd5 12.f4 cxd4 13.exd4 ♘e4 14.♘xe4 dxe4 15.♗c4 ♘f6 (*15...b5 16.♗xb5 ♘xe5 17.fxe5 ♗xe5 18.dxe5 ♛b6+ 19.♔h1 ♛xb5 20.♛g4±* Sargissian — Stellwagen, Wijk aan Zee 2007) 16.♛e2

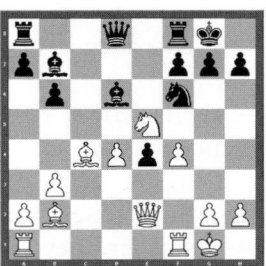

16...♖c8!

(16...a6 17.a4 ♛e7 18.f5 (*18.♖ac1±*) 18...♖ac8 19.♖ac1± Va.Popov — Papin, Sochi 2010)

17.♖ac1 ♖c7∞ The rook on c7 occupies an excellent square protecting f7 and putting pressure on the c-file. There are equal chances for both sides, for example: 18.♖c3 (It's very risky to weaken the long diagonal *18.g4?! 18...♘d5 19.♕xe4 ♘c3 20.♕e3 ♘xa2 21.♖a1 ♘b4 22.♖xa7 ♕b8 23.♖a4 ♕e8∓*) 18...♕c8 (*18... ♘d5!? 19.♖h3 f5 20.♕h5 h6∞*) 19.a4 a6 20.♖fc1 ♕f5 21.g3 Maletin — J.Geller, St.Petersburg 2011 Here Black could play 21...a5∞, removing the pawn from attack and maintaining the tension.;

9...♗b7 10.♕c2 (*10.♕e2 ♕e7 11.cxd5 exd5 12.♗a6 ♗xa6 13.♕xa6 ♖fc8=; 10.e4 dxe4 11.♘xe4 ♘xe4 12.♗xe4 ♘f6 13.♗c2 c5=* Konovalov — Grachev, Moscow 2006) 10...c5

b1) 10...♖c8 11.♖ad1 ♕e7 (*11...♕c7 12.e4 dxc4 13.♗xc4 e5 14.♘e2±* Avrukh — Piket, Biel 1999) 12.e4 dxe4 13.♘xe4 ♘xe4 14.♗xe4 ♘f6 15.♗d3 h6 16.♖fe1± Roiz — Robson, Caleta 2011;

b2) 10...♕e7 11.♖ad1

(11.♖fe1 ♖ac8 (*11...h6 12.e4±*) 12.e4 dxc4 13.♗xc4 e5 14.♘e2 b5 15.♗d3 c5 16.dxe5 ♘xe5 17.♘xe5 ♗xe5 18.♗xe5 ♕xe5 19.♗xb5 ♗xe4 20.♕c3± Dautov — Johannessen, Germany 2002)

11...♖fe8 (*11...e5 12.dxe5 ♘xe5 13.♘xe5 ♗xe5 14.cxd5 cxd5 15.♘b5±* Eljanov — Andreassen, Copenhagen 2010) 12.e4 dxe4 (*12...dxc4 13.♗xc4 e5 14.♘g5 ♖f8 15.f4 exd4*

16.♘e2→) 13.♘xe4 ♘xe4 14.♗xe4 ♘f6 15.♗d3 ♗a3 16.♗a1 h6 17.♖fe1 ♖ad8 18.h3± Kramnik — Van Wely, Monaco (blindfold) 2007;

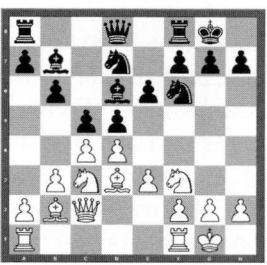

11.cxd5 exd5 12.♖fd1! (*12.♘b5 ♗e7 13.♖ad1 ♖e8 14.♘e5 a6 15.♘c3 cxd4 =* Grachev — Andriasian, Moscow 2009) 12...♕e7 (*12...♖c8 13.♕e2±; 12...♖e8 13.♗f5±*) 13.♗f5!N (*13. ♖ac1 g6 14.♗b5 ♖ac8=/∞* Dreev — Grachev, Sibenik 2009)

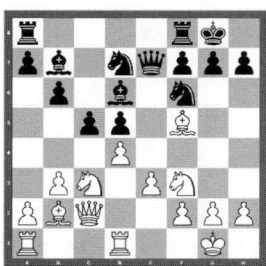

13...♖fe8 14.♖ac1± Sometimes the light squared bishop will retreat to h3 and after g2-g3 it can put pressure along the long diagonal. In the forthcoming complicated game White's chances are preferable.;

6.cxd5 (*6.♗d3 cxd4 7.exd4 ♗b4+ 8.♗d2 ♗xd2+ 9.♘bxd2 dxc4 10.bxc4 ♘c6 11.♘b3 0-0 12.0-0 b6=*

Leitao — Matsuura, Campinas 2011)
6...♘xd5!

(6...exd5 7.♗b5+ (7.♗b2 ♘c6
8.♘bd2 — 5.♘bd2 c5 6.cxd5 exd5
7.b3 ♘c6 8.♗b2) 7...♘c6 (7...
♗d7 8.♗xd7+ ♘bxd7 9.0-0 ♗e7
10.dxc5 ♗xc5 11.♗b2 0-0 12.♘c3±
Papaioannou — Dvirnyy, Porto Carras 2011) 8.0-0 cxd4 (8...
♗d7 9.♗a3 ♕a5 10.♗xc6 ♗xc6
11.♕c2± Volkov — Papin, Voronezh 2009) 9.♕xd4 (9.♘xd4 ♗d7=)
9...♗d7 10.♗xc6 bxc6 11.♗b2 (11.
♗a3 ♗xa3 12.♘xa3 ♕e7=) 11...♗e7
12.♘c3 0-0 13.♘a4± — Thanks
to his good control of the black
squares White's chances are better.)

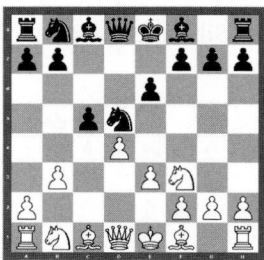

7.♗b2 (7.♗c4 ♘c6 8.0-0 cxd4
9.♘xd4 ♘xd4 10.♕xd4 ♗e7 11.♗b2
♗f6 12.♕d2 ♗xb2 13.♕xb2 ♕f6
14.♕xf6 ♘xf6 15.♗e2 ♗d7 16.♗f3
♖b8 17.♖c1 ♔e7 18.♘d2 ♖hc8=
Grachev — Dubov, Moscow 2011)
7...cxd4 8.♘xd4

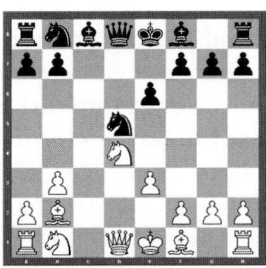

8...♗b4+! (8...e5 9.♘b5 ♗b4+
10.♘1c3 ♗e6 11.a3 ♗xc3+ 12.♘xc3
♘c6 13.b4±; 8...♗e7 9.♘d2 0-0
10.♖c1 ♗d7 11.♗c4 ♘b6 12.♗d3
♘c6±/= Meier — Le Quang Liem,
Lubbock 2011) 9.♘d2 0-0 10.a3 ♗c3
(10...♗e7=) 11.♗xc3 ♘xc3 12.♕c2
♘d5 13.♗d3 h6 14.0-0 ♗d7 = Volkov — Gopal, Dubai 2012

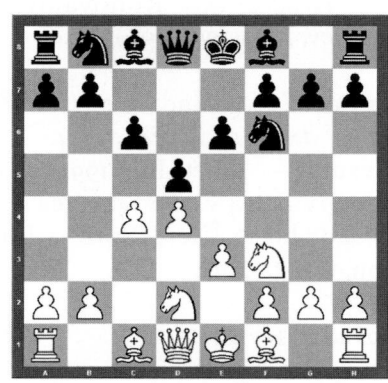

5...♘bd7
5...c5 6.cxd5

(6.b3 cxd4 7.exd4 b6 8.♗d3 ♗e7
(8...♗d6 9.0-0 0-0 10.♗b2 ♗b7
11.♕e2 ♘c6=) 9.0-0 ♗b7 10.♗b2
♘c6 11.♕e2 ♘b4 12.♗b1 0-0
13.a3 ♘c6 14.♗d3 ♖e8 15.♕e3 ♗f8
16.♖ac1 g6 = Zubarev — Grachev,
Moscow 2009)

6...exd5

(A very solid position without weaknesses arises after 6...♘xd5, but White still stands better due to his greater activity: 7.e4! It's useful to gain space with tempo.

(7.♗c4 ♘c6 8.dxc5 ♗xc5 9.0-0 0-0 10.♕e2 ♘f6 (*10...♗e7 11.♖d1 ♗d7 12.♘e4 ♘b6=*) 11.♖d1 ♕e7 = Sakaev — Papin, Taganrog 2011)

7...♘b6
(7...♘f6 8.e5 ♘d5

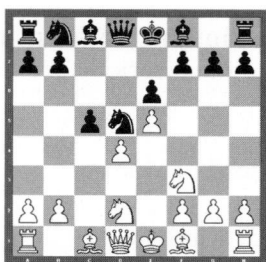

9.♘b3!N

(9.dxc5 ♗xc5 10.a3 (*10.♘e4 ♗e7 11.♗c4 0-0 12.0-0 ♘c6 13.♕e2 ♕c7 14.♘g3 ♖d8=*) 10...0-0 (*10... ♗e7!? 11.♕c2 ♗d7=*) 11.♕c2 ♗e7 12.♗d3 g6 (*12...h6 13.♕c4± Lysyi — Ter Sahakyan, Martuni 2009*) 13.0-0 ♘c6=)

9...cxd4 10.♘bxd4 ♗e7 11.♗c4 0-0 12.0-0 b6 13.♕e2 ♗b7 14.♗d2 ♘d7 15.♖ac1± — White's position is somewhat better due to his space advantage.)

8.♘b3 cxd4

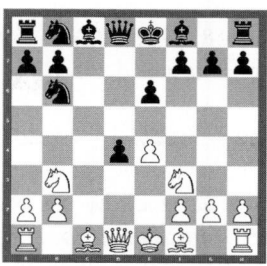

9.♘bxd4!

(9.♘fxd4 ♗b4+ 10.♗d2 ♗xd2+! (*10...♕e7 11.♗xb4 ♕xb4+ 12.♕d2 ♕xd2+ 13.♔xd2 ♔e7 M.Gurevich — Papin, Reykjavik 2011 14.♖c1! ♖d8 15.♔e3±*) 11.♕xd2 0-0 12.♗e2 e5 13.♘f3 ♘c6=)

9...♗d7 10.♗e2 ♗b4+ 11.♗d2 ♗xd2+ (*11...♗e7 12.0-0 0-0 13.a4± Onischuk — Steingrimsson, Dresden 2008*) 12.♕xd2 ♘c6 13.a4

(13.0-0 0-0 14.♖fd1 e5 15.♘xc6 (*15.♘b5 ♗g4 16.♕e3 ♕f6=*) 15... ♗xc6 16.♘xe5 ♕xd2 17.♖xd2 ♗xe4=)

13...a5 14.0-0 0-0 15.♖fd1 ♘xd4 16.♕xd4 ♗c6 17.♕e3 ♕c7 18.b3± — Black's minor pieces are badly placed. White retains pressure.)

7.b3

a) 7.dxc5 ♗xc5 8.a3 0-0 9.b4 ♗d6 10.♗b2 a5 11.bxa5 ♘c6 12.♗e2 ♘xa5 13.0-0 h6 14.♘d4 ♘c6 15.♘b5 ♗e5= Lysyi — Grachev, Serpukhov 2008;

b) 7.♗b5+ ♗d7

(7...♘c6 8.0-0 (8.♘e5 ♕c7=) 8...cxd4 9.♘xd4 ♗d7=)

8.♗xd7+ ♘bxd7=;

7...♘c6 8.♗b2 cxd4 9.♘xd4 ♗d6 10.♘xc6 (10.♗e2 0-0 11.0-0 ♖e8 12.♘2f3 a6 13.♖c1 ♗d7 14.h3 ♘e4 15.♘xc6 bxc6 16.♕d4 Onischuk — Andriasian, Moscow 2009 16...f6!=) 10...bxc6 11.♕c2 ♗d7 12.♗d3 0-0 13.0-0 h6 14.e4 ♖e8 15.♖fe1±

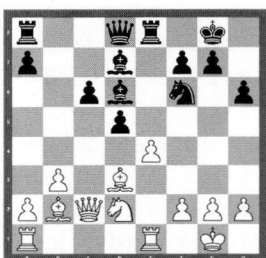

— White's advantage is minimal, Lysyi — Grigoryan, Martuni 2009

6.♗d3

6.b3 ♗d6 7.♗b2 0-0 8.♗d3 b6 (8...♕e7 9.♘e5±) 9.0-0 ♗b7 — 5.b3 ♘bd7 6.♗d3 ♗d6 7.♗b2 0-0 8.0-0 b6 9.♘bd2 ♗b7

6...♗d6 7.0-0

7.e4 e5 8.cxd5 cxd5 9.0-0 0-0 — 7.0-0 0-0 8.e4 e5 9.cxd5 cxd5

7...0-0 8.e4 e5

8...dxe4 9.♘xe4 ♘xe4 10.♗xe4 — 3.♘f3 ♘f6 4.♘c3 e6 5.e3 ♘bd7 6.♗d3 ♗d6 7.0-0 0-0 8.e4 dxe4 9.♘xe4 ♘xe4 10.♗xe4 (Slav Defence, Part 2)

9.cxd5 cxd5

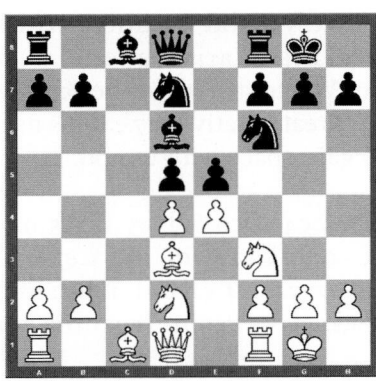

10.♖e1

This maintains the tension and poses the most serious problems for Black.

10.exd5 exd4 11.♘e4

(11.♘c4 ♘b6

a) 11...♘c5 12.♘xd6 ♕xd6 13.♗c4±;

b) 11...♗b8 12.♘xd4 (12.♗g5 h6 13.♗h4 ♘c5=) 12...♘c5 13.♗g5 ♘xd3 14.♕xd3 ♗xh2+ 15.♔xh2 ♘g4+ 16.♔g1 ♕xg5 17.♘f3 ♕f6=;

12.♘xd6 ♕xd6 13.♘xd4 ♘bxd5 Now White has the two bishops but Black equalises due to his greater activity, for example

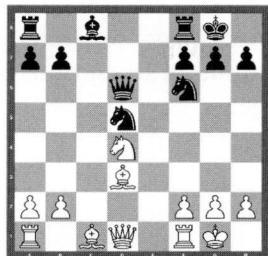

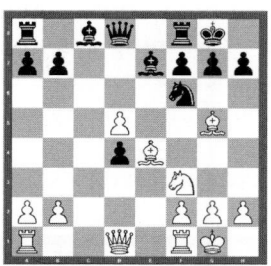

14.♘f5 ♗xf5! 15.♗xf5 ♕e5! Now White cannot move to d4. 16.♗d3 ♖fe8=)

11...♘xe4 12.♗xe4 ♘f6 13.♗g5

a) 13.♗c2 ♗g4 14.h3 ♗xf3 (*14... ♗h5=*) 15.♕xf3 ♖c8 16.♗b3 ♖e8 17.♗g5 h6 18.♗xf6 ♕xf6 19.♕xf6 gxf6=;

b) 13.♕xd4 ♘xe4 14.♕xe4 ♖e8 The d5 pawn isn't well supported by the white pieces and the compensation for it in the form of piece activity and two the bishops is sufficient: 15.♕d4 (*15.♕d3 ♕f6=*) 15...♗f5 16.♗e3 (*16. ♗g5 f6 17.♗h4 ♖e4=*) 16...♕d7 (*16... ♗e4=*) 17.♖fd1 ♗c2 18.♖e1 ♕f5= Kryakvin — Bukavshin, Moscow 2011;

13...♗e7 (There is another path : *13... h6 14.♗xf6 ♕xf6 15.♕xd4 ♕xd4 16.♘xd4 ♗d7 17.♖fd1 g6 18.g3 ♖ac8=* — The two bishops and a good blockade of the d5 pawn allow Black to hold the position, Sakaev — Kobalija, Sochi 2005)

14.♗c2 (*14.♗xf6 ♗xf6 15.♘xd4 ♕b6 16.♘b3 ♗d7 =* Volkov — Hamdouchi, Fuegen 2006) 14...♘xd5 15.♗xe7 ♘xe7±/= White has a minimal advantage due to his more active light squared bishop but it gradually evaporates. For example: (*15... ♕xe7 16.♖e1 ♕f6 17.♕xd4 ♕xd4 18.♘xd4±* Nanu — Pavasovic, Austria 2010) 16.♕xd4 (*16.♘xd4 ♕b6! 17.♖e1 ♘g6=*)

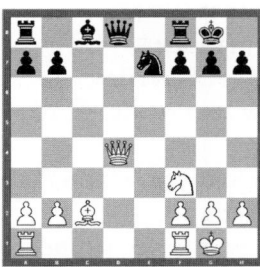

16...♕xd4 (*16...♗f5 17.♗b3 ♕xd4 18.♘xd4 ♗d7=*) 17.♘xd4 ♗d7 18.♗e4 ♖ac8 19.♖fe1 ♖fe8=

10...h6!

10...dxe4?! 11.♘xe4 ♘xe4 12.♖xe4±;
10...♖e8 This move does not equalise completely 11.exd5 exd4 12.♖xe8+ (White also stands better in the endgame after *12.♘e4 ♘xe4 13.♗xe4 ♘f6 14.♗g5 h6 15.♗xf6 ♕xf6 16.♕xd4*

♕xd4 17.♘xd4 ♔f8±, though the
chances of winning are small.) 12...
♕xe8 13.♘c4 ♗c5 14.a3± Levin —
Goikhman, St.Petersburg 2011

11.exd5 exd4 12.♘xd4

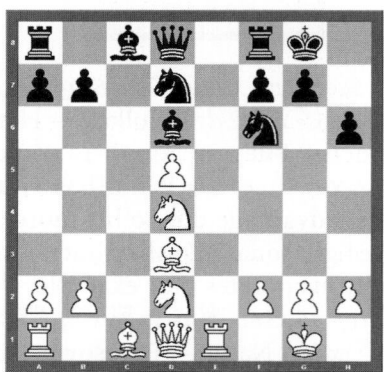

12...♘b6!N
  12...♘xd5 13.♘c4±;
  12...♘e5 13.♘e4±;
  12...♘c5 A.Gavrilov — Stukopin,
Moscow 2012 13. ♗c2 ♘xd5 14.♘c4±

**13.♘e4 ♘bxd5 14.♘xd6 ♕xd6 15.b3!
♗g4 16.♕d2**
White wants to support the d4
knight by placing the bishop on b2.
Black equalises only after very accurate play.

**16...♖fd8 17.♗b2 ♘b4 18.h3 ♘xd3
19.♕xd3 ♗d7 20.♕f3 ♕d5 21.♕g3
♘h5 22.♕h4 ♕g5 23.♕xg5 hxg5=**
Conclusion: Apart from 5.♘c3
which leads to complicated Meran
positions, White can choose one of
the quieter continuations analysed
above, leading to a positional struggle with a large safety margin. However if Black plays accurately, White
cannot count on any serious opening
advantage.

■ GAME 21

1.d4 d5 2.c4 c6 3.♘f3 ♘f6 4.e3 a6 5.♗d3

5.b3 is harmless

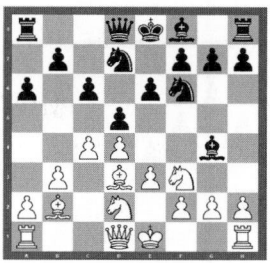

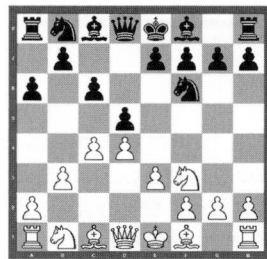

5...♗g4

(Also reliable is 5...♗f5 6.♗d3 ♗xd3 (6...♗g6 7.0-0 e6 8.♘c3 ♘bd7 9.♗b2 ♗d6 10.♕c2 ♗h5 Bareev — Carlsen, Moscow (blitz) 2009 11.♘d2±) 7.♕xd3 e6 8.0-0 ♘bd7 9.♘bd2 ♗e7 10.e4 dxe4 11.♘xe4 ♘xe4 12.♕xe4 0-0 = — The position without the moves b2-b3 and a7-a6 is more usual but their inclusion does not affect the evaluation of the position as close to equal.)

6.♘bd2 e6 7.♗b2 (7.♗d3 c5! — 5.♗d3 ♗g4 6.♘bd2 e6 7.b3 c5!) 7...♘bd7 8.♗d3

8...♗f5!

a) White stands slightly better after 8...♗d6 9.♕c2 ♕b8 to hinder ♘f3-e5. 10.0-0 0-0 11.h3 ♗h5 12.♘g5 ♗g6 13.♗xg6 hxg6± Dreev — Timman, Wijk aan Zee 2002;

b) 8...c5 9.0-0

(9.h3 ♗h5 10.0-0 ♗e7 11.cxd5 ♘xd5 12.♕b1 (12.♘e4 cxd4 13.♗xd4 0-0 = Pr.Nikolic — Karjakin, Amsterdam 2007) 12...cxd4 13.♗xd4 ♗f6=)

9...♗e7 10.♕c2± — 5.♗d3 ♗g4 6.♘bd2 e6 7.♕c2 ♘bd7 8.b3 c5 9.0-0 ♗e7 10.♗b2;

9.♕c2 ♗xd3 10.♕xd3 ♗e7 11.0-0 0-0 12.e4 dxe4 13.♘xe4 ♘xe4 14.♕xe4=;

Neither does the following pose any threat 5.♘bd2

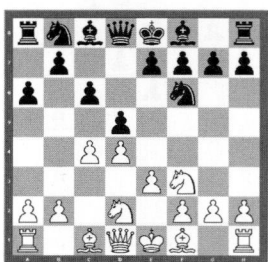

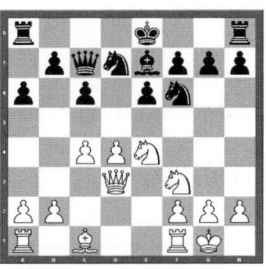

5...♗f5 6.♕b3

a) 6.♗e2 e6 7.0-0 ♘bd7 8.b3 ♗d6 9.♗b2 0-0 (9...♕b8=) 10.♘e5 ♘e4 11.♘xe4 ♗xe4=;

b) 6.♘h4 ♗e4! 7.♕b3 (7.f3 ♗g6 8.g3 e6 9.♘xg6 hxg6 10.♔f2 c5 11.dxc5 ♗xc5 12.♘b3 ♗b6∓ — Black has active pieces. His position is preferable, Bologan — Rublevsky, Poikovsky 2007; 7.♗e2 e6 8.0-0 ♘bd7=) 7...♖a7

(7...♕c7 8.f3 ♗g6 9.♗e2 (9.e4∞) 9...e6 10.e4 dxe4 (10...♗e7∞) 11.♘xg6 hxg6 12.♘xe4∞ (12.fxe4 Bareev — Kobalia, Sochi 2006 12...c5 13.e5 ♘fd7 14.d5 ♘xe5∓))

8.f3 ♗g6 = — The knight is badly placed on d2. Black has a good game.;

6...♕c7 7.♗d3 ♗xd3 8.♕xd3 e6 9.0-0 ♗e7 10.e4 dxe4 11.♘xe4 ♘bd7

12.♖e1

(12.♗g5 0-0 13.♗h4 ♖fe8 (13...♕d8 14.♘c3 b5 15.♖ac1 ♖c8 16.♖fd1 ♘h5 17.♗xe7 ♕xe7± — Black has nearly equalised but still stands somewhat worse, Ivanchuk — Svidler, Kemer 2007) 14.♗g3 ♕b6=)

12...0-0 13.♗g5 ♖fe8 14.♖ad1 ♘xe4 15.♕xe4 ♗xg5 16.♘xg5 ♘f6 17.♕e5 ♖e7= — The game is equal, Cheparinov — Svidler, Baku 2008;

5.♕c2

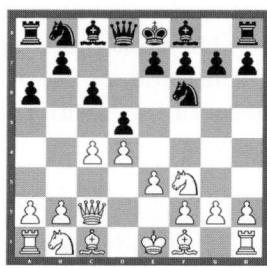

5...♗g4 (Bad is 5...e6, since White can arrange his pieces so that a7-a6 looks pointless: 6.♘bd2 ♘bd7 7.b3 ♗e7 8.♗b2 0-0 9.♗d3 h6 10.0-0 c5 11.♖ad1 b6 12.e4± Bologan — Movsesian, Sarajevo 2005; Quite possible is 5...g6 6.♗d3 ♗g7 7.0-0 0-0 8.♘c3

— 3.♘c3 ♘f6 4.e3 a6 5.♕c2 g6 6.♗d3 ♗g7 7.♘f3 0–0 8.0–0) 6.♘e5

(6.♘bd2 e6 7.b3 (7.♗d3 — 5.♗d3 ♗g4 6.♘bd2 e6 7.♕c2) 7...♗f5 8.♗d3 ♗xd3 9.♕xd3 ♘bd7 10.0–0 ♗e7 11.e4 dxe4 12.♘xe4 0–0=)

6...♗h5 7.♕b3

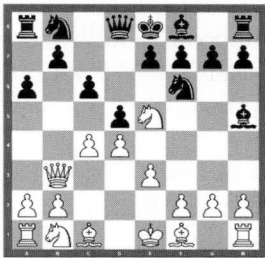

7...♕c7

(The other way of defending the pawn is awkward and not so convincing: 7...♖a7 8.cxd5

(The following leads to a very complicated game 8.♘c3 e6 9.f3 (*9.c5 ♘bd7 10.♘d3∞*) 9...♘fd7 (*9...♗d6 10.g4 ♗g6 11.h4±*) 10.♘d3 dxc4 (*10...♗d6 11.♘f4 ♗xf4 12.exf4±*) 11.♕xc4 b5 12.♕b3 c5 13.♘f4 ♗g6 (*13...♗d6!?∞*) 14.d5 (*14.a4∞*) 14...c4 15.♕d1 ♘c5∞)

8...cxd5 9.♗d2

(9.♘c3 e6 10.♗d3 ♘c6 (*10...♘fd7 11.♘xd7 ♘xd7 12.0–0±; 10...♘bd7 11.f4 ♗e7 12.0–0 0–0 13.♗d2±* El-janov — Wang Yue, Moscow 2005) *11.♘xc6 bxc6 12.♘a4±*)

9...e6 10.♗b4± Azmaiparashvili — Chen Fan, China 2005)

8.cxd5 cxd5 9.♘c3 e6 10.♗d2 ♘c6 11.♖c1 ♗d6 12.f4 0–0 13.♗d3

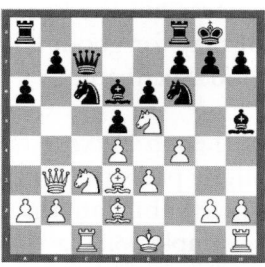

13...♘d7 The most reliable. Black sorts out the problematic kingside pieces.

a) Too straightforward is 13...♗xe5 14.fxe5 ♘d7 15.0–0 ♕b6 16.♕xb6 ♘xb6 17.♘e2 ♗g6 18.♘f4 ♗xd3 19.♘xd3 ♘d7 (*19...♘c4 20.♖c2 ♘xd2 21.♖xd2±*) 20.♖c2 f6 21.exf6 ♖xf6± — White stands a little better though Black should be able to draw without great difficulty, Toma-shevsky — Ni Hua, Ningbo 2008;

b) 13...♘a5!? leads to a double-edged game 14.♕c2 ♖ac8 15.h3 ♘c4

(After 15...♗g6 something similar can happen 16.♘xg6 hxg6 17.g4 b5 (*17...♘c4 — 15...♘c4 16.g4 ♗g6 17.♘xg6 hxg6*) 18.g5 ♘h5 19.♘e2 ♕d7 20.♕d1 ♘c4∞)

16.g4

(16.♗xc4 dxc4 17.e4 ♘e8 18.0–0
(*18.g4 f6 19.gxh5 fxe5 20.dxe5 ♗c5∓*)
18...f6 19.♘g4 b5∓)

16...♗g6 17.♘xg6 hxg6 18.g5 ♘h5
(*18...♘d7 19.h4 ♛b6 20.♖b1*) 19.♘e2
♛d7∞ — White has a cluster of
weak squares but the knight on h5
is out of play for good, Khairullin
— Gelfand, Sochi 2010;

14.♘xc6 (*14.0–0 ♘dxe5 15.dxe5 ♗e7*
Some slight pressure on the c-file
doesn't give White anything tangible, for example: *16.♖c2 ♗g6 17.♘e2
♗xd3 18.♛xd3 ♛d7 19.♖fc1 ♖fc8
20.♘d4 ♘xd4 21.exd4 f5 22.exf6
♗xf6 23.♗e3 ♗e7=* — The black
bishop moves to d6 where it protects
the c7 square.) 14...bxc6 15.♛c2 ♘f6
16.0–0 ♗g6= — Black has a backward pawn on c6, but White's weakening of the e4 square compensates
so the game is equal.;

5.♗d2 One of the ideas to counter
b7-b5. However committing the
dark squared bishop early has its
drawbacks, as it's often better to fianchetto the bishop on b2 or move
it to an active position after e3-e4.

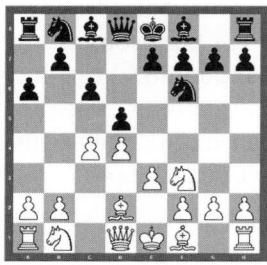

5...e6

a) The following is „non-Slav-like"
5...g6 6.♘c3 ♗g7 — Compared to
known examples, the inclusion of
a7-a6 and ♗c1-d2 gives the position a slightly different complexion.
The move ♗c1-d2 will always be of
use, and the position of pawn on a6
leads Black to consider playing b7-
b5 instead of the typical exchange of
the bishop on f3 followed by dxc4
and e7-e5. 7.♛b3!? is an interesting
development

a1) 7.♗e2 0–0 8.0–0 — 3.♘f3 ♘f6
4.e3 g6 5.♘c3 ♗g7 6.♗e2 0–0 7.0–
0 a6 8.♗d2;

a2) 7.♗d3 0–0 8.h3!? (*8.0–0 dxc4
9.♗xc4* — *3.♘f3 ♘f6 4.e3 g6
5.♘c3 ♗g7 6.♗e2 0–0 7.0–0 a6
8.♗d2 dxc4 9.♗xc4*) 8...♘bd7
(*8...dxc4 9.♗xc4 b5 10.♗e2 ♘bd7
11.b4±*) 9.cxd5 ♘xd5 10.♘xd5 cxd5
11.♛b3 ♘f6 12.0–0 ♘e4 13.♗b4±;

7...0–0 8.♖c1± Bocharov — Mona,
Abudhabi 2009;

b) The following experimental
move is playable although it doesn't
solve all problems 5...♘e4 — Black
gains the two bishops. 6.♘c3 ♘xd2
7.♛xd2 e6 (*7...♗f5 8.♗d3 ♗xd3
9.♛xd3 e6 10.0–0 ♗e7 11.e4 dxe4
12.♘xe4 0–0 13.♖ad1±* Cheparinov — Tkachiev, Khanty Mansyisk (blitz) 2007) 8.e4 (*8.♗d3 dxc4
9.♗xc4 c5 10.0–0 b5 11.♗d3 cxd4
12.♘xd4 ♗e7 13.♖fd1 ♖a7 14.♖ac1*

0-0 15.♕c2 g6 16.♘e4± Bocharov
— Gritsenko, Sochi 2012) 8...♗e7!N
(8...dxc4 9.♗xc4 b5 10.♗d3 c5 11.d5
c4 12.♗c2 ♗c5 13.0-0 0-0 14.♖ad1±
Ponomariov — Aronian, Moscow
(blitz) 2009)

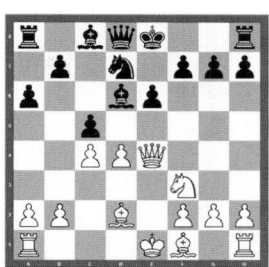

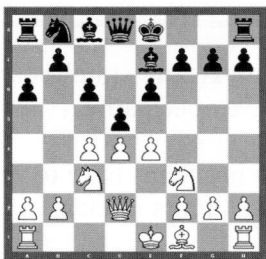

9.e5 0-0 — Thanks to to his two
bishops, Black has good chances of
counter play by opening up lines on
the queenside.;

6.♘c3 (6.♕c2 ♘bd7 7.♘c3 — 6.♘c3
♘bd7 7.♕c2) 6...♘bd7

(6...c5 7.cxd5 exd5 allows White to
train his sights on d5: 8.g3! ♘c6
(8...♘bd7 9.♗g2 b5 10.0-0 ♗b7
11.dxc5 ♗xc5 12.♘e2 0-0 13.♗c3±
Eljanov- Karjakin, Moscow (blitz)
2010) 9.♗g2 cxd4 10.♘xd4 ♘xd4
11.exd4 ♗e6 12.♕b3 ♕d7 13.0-0
♗e7 14.♘a4 ♕b5 Khismatullin —
Papin, Taganrog 2011 15.♘c5 ♕xb3
16.axb3 ♗xc5 17.dxc5 ♔d7 18.b4
♔c6 19.♗c3±)

7.♕c2 (7.c5 e5 =) 7...dxc4

(After 7...♗d6 8.e4 dxe4 9.♘xe4
♘xe4 10.♕xe4 c5

Most principled is 11.0-0-0!, ex-
ploiting the slight lead in development. (11.♗d3 ♘f6 12.♕h4 cxd4
13.0-0 Khismatullin — Ivakhi-
nova, St.Petersburg 2011. Black
should have completed her development: 13...b6! 14.♘xd4 ♗b7=,
with an equal game.; 11.♗c3 ♘f6
12.♕c2 cxd4 13.♘xd4 0-0 14.♗e2
Markus — Jurkovic, Rijeka 2005.
Black should have chosen 14...g6!?,
with the idea of e6-e5, or 14...♕c7,
followed by b7-b6.; 11.♖d1!?± deserves attention, with a slightly
better game.) 11...♗e7 (11...♘f6
12.♕h4 cxd4 Akatova — Girya,
Voronezh 2009 13.♕xd4±; 11...0-0
12.♗d3↑) 12.♗c3 0-0 13.♔b1±)

8.a4

(8.♗xc4 c5

(8...b5 9.♗e2 ♗b7 (9...c5 10.dxc5
♗xc5 11.♘e4±) 10.♘e4 ♘xe4
11.♕xe4 ♕b6

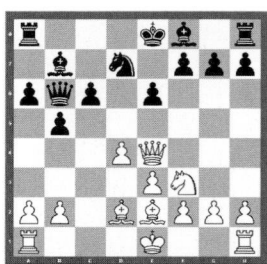

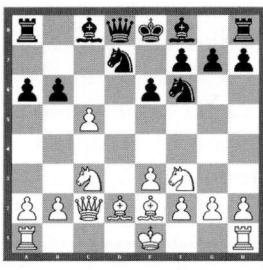

12.♘e5!N

(12.0-0 c5 13.♕f4 *(13.dxc5 ♘xc5 14.♕g4 ♘e4 = Dreev — Matla-kov, Aix les Bains 2011)* 13...♗e7 *(13...♕d6 14.a4!± Zhao Jun — Ni Hua, Xinghua 2012)* 14.dxc5 ♘xc5 15.♗b4 0-0=)

12...♘xe5 13.♕xe5 c5 14.0-0

(14.♖c1!? c4!∞ (14...cxd4 15.0-0↑))

14...♕d6 15.♕xd6 ♗xd6 16.dxc5 ♗xc5 17.♖fc1 ♗d6 18.♗a5 0-0 19.a4± — Black has to play accurately to achieve a draw.)

9.♗e2! *(9.dxc5 ♗xc5 10.♘e4 ♘xe4 11.♕xe4 ♘f6= L'Ami — Bacrot, Wijk aan Zee 2008; 9.a4 — 8.a4 c5 9.♗xc4)* 9...b6!

(9...b5 is vulnerable 10.dxc5 ♘xc5 (10...♗xc5 11.♘e4±) 11.b4 ♘cd7 12.a4 bxa4 13.♘xa4 ♗b7 14.0-0 ♖c8 15.♕b2± Black's queenside isn't solid enough and causes him some discomfort.)

10.dxc5

10...♘xc5!N The simplest way to a fully developed game.

(Some problems have to be solved after 10...♗xc5 11.♘e4 ♗e7

a) 11...♗b7 12.♘xc5 ♘xc5 13.0-0 ♖c8 *(13...♗e4 14.♕c4 ♗d3 15.♗xd3 ♕xd3 16.♕xd3 ♘xd3 17.♗c3±)* 14.♗b4± — White's position is somewhat better due to his two bishops.;

b) 11...♘xe4 12.♕xe4 ♖a7 13.♗c3±;

12.♕c6!N *(12.♘xf6+ ♘xf6 13.0-0 ♗b7 14.♖fd1 0-0 15.♗c3 ♕c7 16.♖ac1 ♗e4 17.♗d3 ♕b7 18.♗xe4 ♘xe4 19.♘e5 Bareev — Grischuk, Khanty Mansyisk 2007 19...♘f6 20.♗d4 ♖ac8 21.♕e2 ♖xc1 22.♖xc1 ♖c8=)*

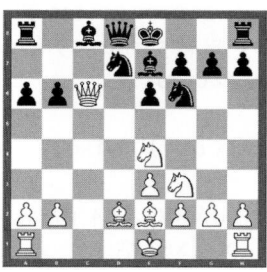

12...♖a7 13.♘d6+ ♗xd6 14.♕xd6
♘e4 15.♕d4 ♘xd2 16.♘xd2± —
White stands a little better.)

11.b4 ♘cd7 12.♕b3 ♗b7 13.0–0 ♗d6
= — The game is equal.)

8...c5 9.♗xc4

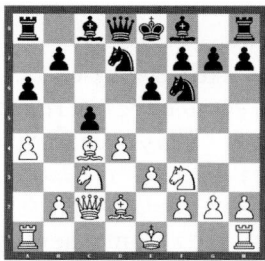

9...♕c7! It's better to not be in a hurry to remove the tension.

(9...cxd4 10.exd4

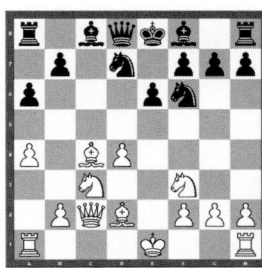

10...♗e7

(10...♘b6 11.♗d3 ♘bd5 12.♘xd5
♕xd5!

(12...♘xd5 13.0–0 (13.♗xh7±)
13...♘b4?! 14.♗xb4 ♗xb4
15.♗xh7± Carlsen — Nakamura, Monaco (rapid) 2011)

13.0–0 ♗e7 14.♘e5!? Only by ying
this pawn sacrifice can White
make it difficult for Black to develop his queenside. (14.♖fc1 0–0
15.♗g5 h6 16.♗xf6 ♗xf6 17.♗h7+
♔h8 18.♗e4 ♕d6=) 14...0–0
15.♘c4 ♕xd4 (15...♕d8 16.a5±;
15...♕c6 16.♖fc1±) 16.♖fd1± —
White has good compensation
due to the strong knight eyeing
b6.)

11.0–0 0–0 12.♖ac1

(12.♖fc1 ♘b8! (12...h6 13.♗a2
♘b6 14.a5 ♘bd5 15.♘xd5 exd5
16.♘e5± Jakovenko — Laznicka,
Poikovsky 2011) 13.♘e4 ♘c6
14.♘xf6+ ♗xf6=)

12...♘b6 13.♗b3

(13.♗d3 h6 14.♕b3 ♘bd5 15.♘xd5
♕xd5! (15...♘xd5 16.♗c4± Nakamura — Ni Hua, London 2009)
16.♗c4 ♕d6=)

13...♗d7 14.♘e5 ♖c8 15.♕d3± —
White's chances are preferable
in the forthcoming complicated
game.)

10.♗d3

a) 10.dxc5 ♗xc5 11.0–0 ♗e7 (11...
b6 12.♘e4 ♘xe4 13.♕xe4 ♗b7
14.♕g4±) 12.♗e2 b6 13.♖ac1 ♗b7
14.♕b1 ♕b8 15.♖fd1 0–0=;

b) 10.♗b3 ♗d6 11.0–0 0–0 12.♘e4 ♘xe4 13.♕xe4 cxd4

(13...♘f6 14.♕h4 ♗d7 (14...cxd4!=) 15.♖ac1± Hammer — V.Georgiev, Khanty Mamsyisk 2010)

14.♕xd4 ♘e5 15.♘g5 ♗e7 16.♗c3 ♗xg5 17.♕xe5 ♕xe5 18.♗xe5 ♗d7=;

10...b6 11.♘e4 ♗b7 12.0–0 Epishin — Cornette, Creon 2003 12...♘xe4 13.♗xe4 ♗e7 14.b4 ♗xe4 15.♕xe4 0–0 16.bxc5 bxc5 17.♖fc1 ♖ab8 = — Black has c5 fully covered. White cannot exploit the pin on the c-file.;

5.♘c3 — 3.♘f3 ♘f6 4.♘c3 a6 5.e3

5...♗g4 6.♘bd2
Not dangerous is 6.♕b3

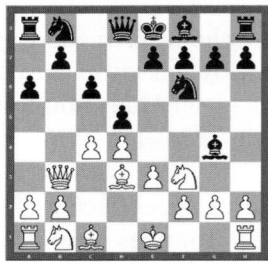

6...♕c7

(6...♗xf3!? is interesting but unnecessary 7.♕xb7 (7.gxf3 ♕c7=) 7...♗xg2 8.♖g1 dxc4 9.♖xg2 cxd3 10.♕xa8 ♕c7 (10...e5 11.dxe5 ♘d5 12.♕b7 ♘b4 13.♘a3+- Aleshin — S.Savchenko, Moscow 2005) 11.♘d2 (11.♘c3 ♘fd7 12.♘a4 ♕a5+ 13.♘c3 ♕c7= Hecht — Bjar-nason, Saint Vincent 2005) 11...e5 (11...g6 12.♘c4 ♗g7 13.♗d2 0–0 14.♖c1∞) 12.a3! (12.dxe5? 12...♘d5 13.♘c4 ♗b4+ 14.♗d2 0–0–+ So-rokin — Alavkin, St.Petersburg 2003; 12.♔f1 ♗b4 13.♖xg7 exd4/±) 12...exd4 13.♘c4∞ — The game is unclear.)

7.♘e5

(7.cxd5 cxd5 8.♘c3 e6 (8...♗xf3!? 9.gxf3 e6 10.e4 ♘c6 11.exd5 exd5 12.♘xd5 ♕a5+ 13.♘c3 0–0–0 14.♗e3 ♘xd4 15.♗xd4 ♖xd4 16.0–0–0 ♖d7=) 9.♘e5 ♘c6 10.f4 ♗d6 11.♗d2 Tomashevsky — Ni Hua, Sochi (rapid) 2009. After 11...♗h5=, with a later ♗h5-g6, Black could simplify the game.)

7...♗e6!

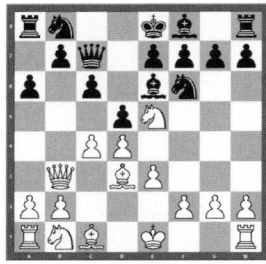

8.0–0 (8.♘c3 dxc4 9.♗xc4 ♗xc4 10.♕xc4 e6 11.0–0 — 8.0–0 dxc4 9.♗xc4 ♗xc4 10.♕xc4 e6 11.♘c3) 8...dxc4 (8...♘bd7 9.♘xd7 ♕xd7 10.♘d2±) 9.♗xc4 ♗xc4 10.♕xc4 (10.♘xc4 ♘bd7=) 10...e6 White has no time to strengthen his centre and Black wiil play the freeing c6-c5,for example,: 11.♘c3 ♗d6 It's worth provoking f2-f4 to restrict White's dark squared bishop. (White has a slightly better position after *11... ♘bd7 12.♘xd7 ♘xd7 13.e4±*, although the Black's position is very solid.) 12.f4 0–0 13.e4 c5 14.♗e3 cxd4 15.♕xc7 ♗xc7 16.♗xd4 ♖d8=, with an equal endgame.

6...e6 7.♕c2

7.0–0 ♘bd7 8.♕c2 (*8.b3 ♗f5! 9.♕c2 ♗xd3 10.♕xd3 ♗e7=*) 8...dxc4 9.♗xc4 — 7.♕c2 dxc4 8.♗xc4 ♘bd7 9.0–0(*9.♕xc4 — 7.♕c2 dxc4 8.♕xc4 ♘bd7 9.0–0*) ;

7.b3 c5! 8.0–0 ♘c6 9.♗b2 cxd4 10.exd4 ♗b4 (*10...♗d6 11.♖e1 0–0 12.c5 ♗c7 13.a3∞* Dreev — Bocharov, Krasnoyarsk 2003) 11.h3 ♗h5 12.♗e2 dxc4 13.bxc4 0–0 = Campos Moreno — Khalifman, Spain 2003

7...dxc4!

After 7...♘bd7 unpleasant for Black is 8.b3!, deterring the exchange on c4. 8...c5 (*8...♗d6 9.♗b2±*) 9.0–0 ♗e7 10.♗b2 ♖c8 11.♖ac1 0–0 12.cxd5 exd5 13.♕b1 ♗h5 14.♘e5 ♗g6 15.♘xg6 hxg6 16.♘f3±* Roiz — Karjakin, Drezden 2008

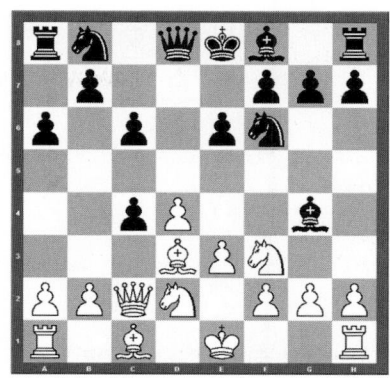

8.♕xc4

8.♗xc4 ♘bd7 9.0–0 ♗e7 10.e4 0–0 11.♗d3 h6!? (*11...♔h8=*) 12.h3 ♗h5 13.e5?! (Correct was *13.b3 c5 14.d5 exd5 15.e5⩱*, with unclear play.) 13...♘d5 14.g4 ♘b4 15.♗h7+ ♔h8 16.♕b1 f5 17.exf6 ♘xf6 18.gxh5 ♘xh7 19.♘e5 Carlsen — Karjakin, Wijk aan Zee 2009. Black could have developed the initiative with an exchange sacrifice *19...♘g5 20.♘g6+ ♔g8 21.♘xf8 ♗xf8∓*;

8.♘xc4 ♗xf3 9.gxf3 c5 10.dxc5 ♗xc5=

8...♘bd7 9.0–0 ♗e7 10.♘e5 ♗h5 11.♕c2 ♖c8

11...♘xe5!? 12.dxe5 ♘d7=

12.♘xd7 ♘xd7 13.b4 ♗g6 14.♖b1 ♗xd3 15.♕xd3 0–0=

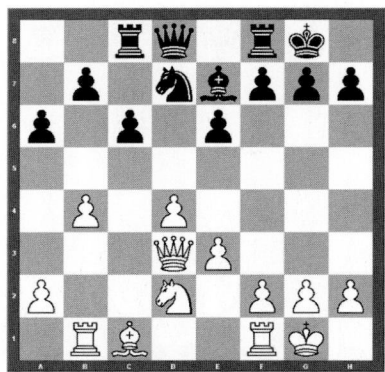

— The pawns on b4 and d4 restrict their own bishop, therefore Black has a completely satisfactory game, Grachev — Buhmann, Germany 2011 Conclusion: The unpopular and not very principled line studied in this chapter only leads to problems for Black if he plays inaccurately.

PART 12

■ GAME 22

1.d4 d5 2.c4 c6 3.♘f3 ♞f6 4.e3 ♗f5

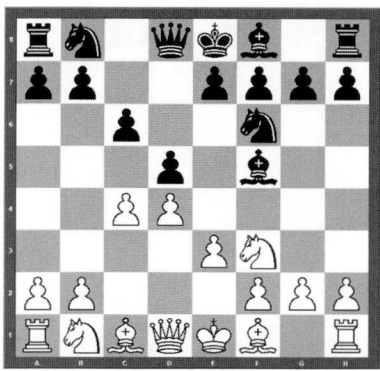

5.♘c3
5.♘bd2 e6 6. ♗e2 *(6.a3 ♞bd7 7.b4 a5 8.b5* Graf — D.Fernandez, Merida 2006 *8...c5=; 6.♘h4 ♗e4 7.f3 ♗g6 8.♕b3 ♕c7=* — The position of the knight on d2 is bad. Black has excellent play.) 6...h6 Now ♘f3-h4 loses is pointless as the black bishop has the h7 square. 7.0–0 ♞bd7 8.b3 ♗e7 9. ♗b2 0–0=;

5.♕b3 ♕b6 6.♘h4

a) 6.♘c3 e6 7.♕xb6 axb6 8.♘h4 ♗e4 *(8...♗c2!?)* 9.♗d2 h6 10.cxd5 exd5 11.f3 ♗h7 12.g4 b5∞ P. Nikolic — Beliavsky, Sarajevo 1982;

b) 6.cxd5 ♕xb3 7.axb3 ♞xd5 8.♘c3 ♞b4 9.♔d2 ♞d7 10.♘h4 ♗g6 11.♘xg6 hxg6= Salov — Bareev, Biel 1993;

6...♕xb3 7.axb3 ♗c2 8.b4 ♗xb1 9.♖xb1 dxc4 10.♗xc4 a6=;

5.cxd5 Since the c1 bishop is restricted by the e3 pawn, the exchange poses no threat even though Black has weakened his queenside by moving the white squared bishop. 5...cxd5 6.♕b3

(6.♘c3 e6 7.♘h4

a) 7. ♗b5+ ♞bd7 8.♘e5 a6∓;

b) 7.♘e5 ♗d6 8. ♗b5+ *(8.g4?! 8... ♗xe5 9.gxf5 ♗d6∓* — White lags in development.; *8.♕a4+ ♞bd7∓)* 8...♞fd7=;

7... ♗e4 8.f3 ♗g6 9.♕b3 ♕c7 10. ♗d2 ♞c6 11.♖c1 ♗e7 12.♘xg6 hxg6 13.f4 0–0 *(13...g5!?)* 14. ♗d3 a6 15.0–0 ♖fc8= V.Milov — Bareev, Ajaccio (rapid) 2006)

6...♕c7 *(6...♕b6 7.♕xb6 axb6 8.♘c3±)*

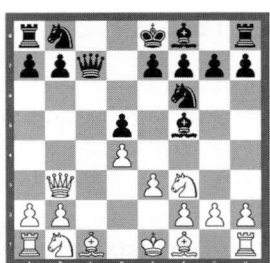

7.♗d2

(7.♘c3 e6 8.♗d2 (8.♘e5 ♘c6=; 8.♘h4 ♗e4=) 8...♘c6 9.♖c1 ♗e7 10.♘h4

a) 10.♗b5 0-0 11.♘h4 (11.0-0 a6 12.♗xc6 bxc6∓) 11...♗e4 12.♘xe4 ♘xe4 13.♘f3 ♗d6∓ Hebden — Shirov, France 1993;

b) 10.♘e5 0-0 11.♗b5

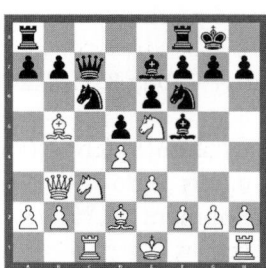

11...♘xe5! 12.♘xd5 ♕xc1+ 13.♗xc1 ♘xd5 14.e4

(14.dxe5? 14...♖ac8 15.♕d1 (15.0-0 ♗c2-+) 15...♗c2 16.♕h5 (16.♕d4 ♗d3-+) 16...g6 17.♕h6 ♗d3-+)

14...♗xe4 15.dxe5 ♗xg2 16.♖g1 ♗e4∓ P. Nikolic — Khalifman, Ter Apel 1994;

10...♗g4 (10...♗e4 11.f3 ♗g6=) 11.h3 ♗h5 12.g4 ♗g6 13.♘xg6 hxg6 14.♗e2 g5 15.♔f1 ♔f8 16.♔g2 g6 17.f3 ♔g7= Aleksandrov — Begunov, St.Petersburg 1994)

7...♘c6 (7...e6 8.♗b5+ ♘c6 — 7...♘c6 8.♗b5 e6) 8.♗b5 e6

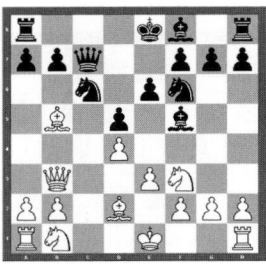

9.0-0

(9.♗b4 ♗xb4+ 10.♕xb4 ♕e7 11.♗xc6+ bxc6 12.♕xe7+ ♔xe7 13.♘c3 ♘d7 14.♘a4 ♖hc8 15.♖c1 ♖ab8 (15...♗e4=) 16.b3 f6 (16...♔d6=) 17.♔e2 ♔d6= — The backward c6 pawn is protected safely. Also Black is well centralised and after pushing e6-e5 or a preliminary space gain with g7-g5, the bishop becomes more active.)

9...♗d6 10.♗b4 0-0 11.♗xc6 bxc6 12.♘bd2 ♖ab8 (12...♘d7 13.♖fc1 ♖fc8 14.♕a3 ♗xb4 15.♕xb4 ♖ab8 16.♕a3±/= — The queen's position on a3 is good. It defends on b2 and prevents c6-c5, Ponomariov — Bacrot, Khanty Mansyisk 2009) 13.♗xd6 ♕xd6 14.♕c3 ♘d7 15.♖fc1 ♖fc8 16.♘b3 h6 (A more lively game

follows *16...f6!?=*, planning e6-e5.)
17.♘e5 (*17.♕a5 ♖c7=* Hebden —
Mellem, Oslo 2011) 17...♘xe5 18.dxe5
♕b4= — White cannot blockade on
the black squares since the b3 knight
is shielding the b2 pawn.;

5.♗d3 This exchange immediately
simplifies the game, and it's unlikely
that the position will become sharp.
Soon White plays e3-e4, after which
additional exchanges occur and the
pawn structure takes shape.

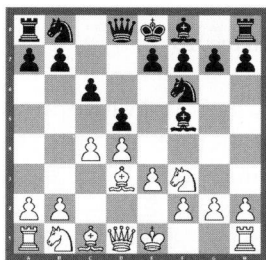

5...♗xd3

a) The next move is quite playable
but unnecessary 5...♗g6 After a possible 6.0–0 e6 7.b3 ♘bd7 8.♗b2 ♗d6
9.♘e5 (Another option is *9.♘c3 0–0
10.♗xg6 hxg6 11.♕c2,*with a later
e3-e4. I don't think the change in the
kingside pawn structure is beneficial
for Black, since the white knight potentially has the g5 square.) 9...♗xd3
(*9...dxc4 10.♘xc4 ♗e7 11.♘c3± Ili-
ncic — Korchnoi, Banja-Luka 2008*)
10.♘xd3 0–0 11.♘d2±/= White
stands just slightly better due to his
space advantage.;

b) The following allows doubled
pawns and needless strategic risk:
5...e6 6.0–0 ♗e7 7.♘c3 0–0 8. ♗xf5
exf5 9.cxd5 cxd5 (*9...♘xd5 10.♕b3±*)
10.♕b3± — Black can not comfortably to solve the problem of the b7
pawn.;

6.♕xd3 e6 7.0–0 ♘bd7

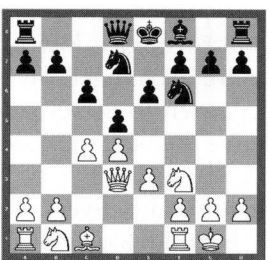

8.♘bd2

(8.♘c3 ♗e7

(There is hardly any point in preventing e3-e4, with 8...♗b4 For
White the most logical response
is 9.a3, forcing Black's immediate
decision. After

(*9.♗d2 a5 (9...0–0? 10.♘xd5+-)*
10.a3 ♗e7 11.e4 ♘c5 12.dxc5 dxe4
13.♕xd8+ ♖xd8 14.♘xe4 ♘xe4
15.♗xa5 ♖a8= Zysk — Pelletier,
Bad Wiessee 2006)

9...♗xc3 (If *9...♗e7 10.e4 dxe4*
11.♘xe4 — The move a2-a3 is
useful since the pawn is protected against a possible ♕d8-a5, and
White can play ♗c1–f4 followed
by ♖ad1.) 10.♕xc3 0–0 11.b3± By

retaining the bishop White has a minimal advantage.)

9.e4 (9.b3 0-0 10.♗b2 ♕a5=) 9...dxe4 10.♘xe4 — 8.♘bd2 ♗e7 9.e4 dxe4 10.♘xe4)

8...♗e7 (Less accurate is 8...♗d6, after 9.e4 dxe4 10.♘xe4 ♘xe4 11.♕xe4 The bishop turns out to be badly placed for several reasons. Control of g5 is lost, and if the knights are exchanged on e5, there is no d4 pawn to attack and Black must move the bishop.) 9.e4

(Internal manoeuvers are completely harmless: 9.b3 0-0 10.♗b2 a5 11.♗c3 ♕b6 (11...a4 12.b4±) 12.♖fd1 ♖fd8 (12...a4!? 13.b4 ♕a6∞) 13.♖ac1 ♕a6 14.a4 ♖ac8 15.♘e1 (15.♕c2 c5=) 15...♕b6

(15...♗a3!? 16.♖a1 (16.♖c2 c5=) 16...♗e7 17.cxd5 Otherwise Black will play c6-c5. 17...♕xd3 18.♘xd3 ♘xd5= — The pawn a5 is taboo. After 19.♗xa5? follows 19...b6 20.e4 bxa5 21.exd5 cxd5∓)

16.♕c2 ♕c7 17.♘d3 b6= — Black will play c6-c5 with equality, Karpov — Gelfand, Sanghi Nagar (match 08) 1995)

9...dxe4 10.♘xe4 ♘xe4 (10...0-0 usually transposes. White has only one additional idea 11.♘c3!? — Avoiding exchanges as he has more space. However after what follows there is also nothingveryserious

11...♕c7, with a later ♖a8-d8 and ♖f8-e8. Black has a solid position.) 11.♕xe4 0-0

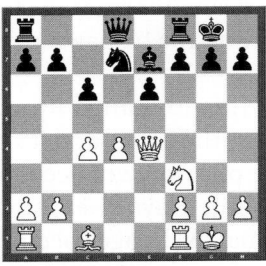

12.♗f4

a) 12.♖d1 ♘f6

(12...♕a5!? If White attacks the queen before playing the conventional ♗c1-f4 13.♗d2!?, then logical is (13.♗f4 — 12.♗f4 ♕a5 13.♖fd1) 13...♕h5!?)

13.♕e2 ♕a5 14.♘e5 ♖ad8 15.♗g5 ♖fe8 16.♖d3 ♘d7 17.♗xe7 ♖xe7 18.♖ad1 ♕c7 19.♘f3 ♘f8±/= White has more space but there are no weaknesses in Black's camp and he has no serious problems, Grachev — Vuckovic, Moscow 2011;

b) 12.b3 ♕c7 13.♗b2 ♗f6 14.♖ad1 ♖fd8= Gagunashvili — Balogh, Dubai 2010;

12...♕a5 (It's better not to hurry with 12...♘f6, so that ♘f3-e5 isn't allowed too soon. After 13.♕e2 pointed move 13...c5 leaves a small advantage to White: 14.♖fd1 cxd4 15.♘xd4 ♕b6 16.♖d3 ♖fd8 17.♖ad1

♖ac8 18.b3± Salov — Shirov, Dortmund 1992) 13.♖fd1 ♖ad8 (Also good is *13...♖fd8,* leaving c8 for the queen's rook which in the long term makes the idea b7-b5 possible. *14.♘e5 ♘xe5 15. ♗xe5 ♗d6=* Houska — Dreev, Aix les Bains 2011) 14.h3 ♖fe8 15.♕c2

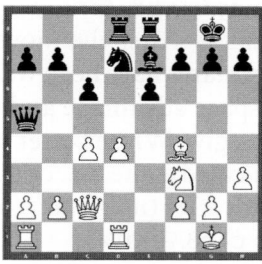

15...h6= — Black intends to place the bishop on f6. After that the knight may be activated by either ♘d7-f8-g6 and sometimes ♘e7-f5, or with the break c6-c5, or even b7-b5.(Risky is *15...♘f6 16.a3 ♕h5* Bu Xiangzhi — Carlsen, Bilbao 2007, in view of *17.♕b3! b5 18.♗e5±* — The queenside pawns are under immediate attack.)

5...e6

There is no point in playing 5...a6, transposing to the line 4.♘c3 a6 5.e3 ♗f5. The bishop has already moved to f5, and e7-e6 won't block it.

6.♘h4

This is White's main idea, to gain the two bishops, sometimes even at the cost of the weakening the kingside pawn structure.

6.♗d3 ♗xd3 7.♕xd3 ♘bd7 8.0–0 — 5.♗d3 ♗xd3 6.♕xd3 e6 7.0–0 ♘bd7 8.♘c3;

Passive is 6.♗e2 In reply it's best to defend against ♘f3-h4 with 6...h6 (6...♘e4 7.♕b3 ♕b6 8.♘h4±; If Black simply continues development 6... ♘bd7 7.♘h4, exchanging the bishop.) 7.0–0 ♘bd7 A possible continuation is 8.a3 ♗d6 9.b4 dxc4!? 10. ♗xc4 0–0=, and Black achieves the break e6-e5, or a7-a5.

6... ♗e4

Black provokes f2-f3, hoping that the weakening of White's black squares will be a problem later. However the move f2-f3 can be useful. There is the possibility of castling by hand, hiding the king on f2. Also Black always has to consider the break e3-e4.

6... ♗g4 With this move Black provokes the advance of the white wing pawns.

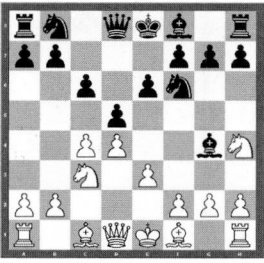

7.♕b3 ♕c7 (*7...♕b6 8.h3 ♗h5 9.g4 ♗g6 10.♘xg6 hxg6 11. ♗g2±* — compared to the line *4...♗g4 5.h3 ♗h5 6.♘c3 e6 7.♕b3 ♕b6 8.♘e5 ♗e7 9.g4 ♗g6 10.♘xg6 hxg6 11. ♗g2,* White has an extra tempo.) 8.h3

(Worth investigating is 8.f3!? ♗h5 (8...dxc4 9.♗xc4 ♗h5 10.e4±) 9.g4 ♗g6 Now interesting is

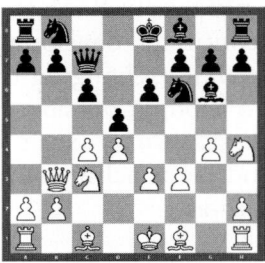

10.e4!?N (10.g5 dxc4 11.♗xc4 ♘d5 12.e4 ♘xc3 13.bxc3 ♘d7∞; 10.♗d2 ♘bd7 11.0-0-0 ♗e7 12.cxd5 ♘xd5 13.♘xg6 hxg6 14.♘xd5 exd5= Koneru — Postny, Budapest 2002) 10...dxc4 (10...dxe4 11.g5 ♘h5 12.♘xe4 ♘d7 13.♘xg6 hxg6 14.♗d2 c5 15.d5 exd5 16.cxd5 0-0-0 17.0-0-0±/∞) 11.♗xc4 ♘bd7

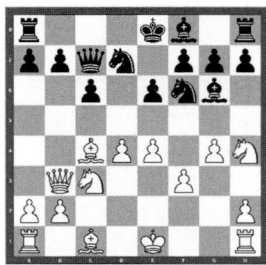

12.♗e3

a) 12.a4 Securing the bishop against b7-b5, and making possible a4-a5 depriving the knight of the b6 square. 12...♗e7 13.g5 ♘h5 14.♘e2 (14.♘g2 e5∓) 14...♗d6∞;

b) After 12.0-0 follows 12...♘b6 13.♗e2 ♕d8, attacking d4 and aiming at h4.;

12...♗e7 13.♘xg6 Other moves lead to an even more complicated game (13.♖c1 ♘xg4 14.♘xg6 ♘xe3 15.♘xh8 ♕f4∞; 13.g5 ♘h5 14.♘e2 ♗d6∞; 13.♗e2 ♘xg4 14.♘xg6 ♘xe3 15.♘xh8 ♕f4∞) 13...hxg6 14.♕c2± — After the move g4 the black squares have been weakened, but a space advantage and the two bishops give White better play in a complicated game. 14...c5 15.d5 exd5 16.♗xd5 ♘e5 (16...♘b6 17.0-0-0±) 17.0-0 c4 18.♔h1!∞)

8...♗h5 9.g4 ♗g6 10.♘xg6 hxg6 11.♗g2

(11.g5 dxc4

(11...♘fd7 12.♗d2!

(12.e4

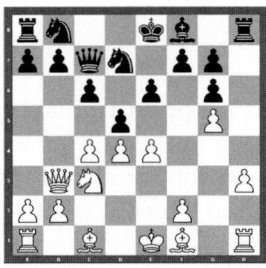

12...e5!N (12...dxe4 13.♘xe4↑ Vaganian — Gagunashvili, Calvia 2004) 13.cxd5

a) 13.♗e3 ♘c5! 14.dxc5 (*14.♕c2 exd4 15.♗xd4 ♘e6 16.0-0-0 ♘xd4 17.♖xd4 ♕f4+ 18.♔b1 ♗c5∓*) 14...d4∓;

b) 13.exd5 exd4 14.♘e2 ♘c5 15.♕f3 ♘bd7∓;

13...exd4 14.dxc6 bxc6 15.♘a4 ♘c5 16.♘xc5 ♗xc5∞)

12...♗e7 13.f4±)

12.♕xc4 ♘d5 13.♗g2 ♘d7± — 11.♗g2 ♘bd7 12.g5 dxc4 13.♕xc4 ♘d5)

11...♘bd7 12.g5 White forces Black to give up the centre or move the knight to the edge.

a) 12.cxd5

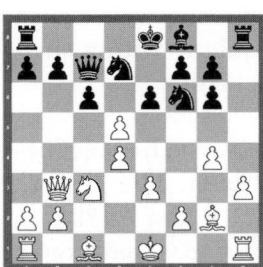

12...exd5 (*12...♘xd5 13.e4 ♘xc3 14.bxc3± M.Gurevich — De Vreugt, Haarlem 2006*) 13.♗d2 (*13.g5 ♘h5 14.♗d2 ♘b6=*) 13...♘b6 — 12.♗d2 ♘b6 13.cxd5 exd5;

b) 12.♗d2

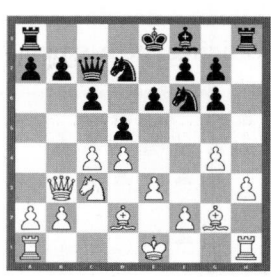

12...♘b6 13.cxd5 exd5 14.♖c1

(14.0-0-0 0-0-0 (*14...♗e7 15.♔b1 a5 16.♗c1 0-0 17.f3∞ Pashikian — Valeanu, Herceg Novi 2005*) 15.♔b1 ♔b8 16.♗c1 ♗d6

(16...♘h7 17.e4 (*17.f3 ♘g5 18.f4 ♘e6∞ Vidit — Grigoriants, Moscow 2012*) 17...dxe4 18.♘xe4 ♘f6 19.♘c5±)

17.g5 ♘h5 18.h4∞)

14...♕d7 15.g5 ♘h5 16.♗f1!? (*16.e4 dxe4 17.♘xe4 Volkov — Mainka, Bad Wiessee 2011 17...0-0-0!∓*) 16...♗d6 17.a4 0-0 18.a5 ♘c8 19.♗e2∞ The g5 pawn advance seriously weakens White's structure. The game is double-edged.;

12...dxc4

(12...♘h5 13.0-0 ♘b6 (*13...dxc4 14.♕xc4 ♘b6 15.♕e2 ♗e7 16.♘e4±*) 14.c5! (*14.cxd5 exd5 15.a4 a5 16.e4 dxe4 17.d5 ♗b4 18.dxc6 bxc6∞*) 14...♘d7 15.e4 0-0-0 16.exd5 exd5 17.♘e2 Preventing ♘h5-f4. 17...♗e7 18.♕d3↑

— White can develop an initiative by advancing the b-pawn.)

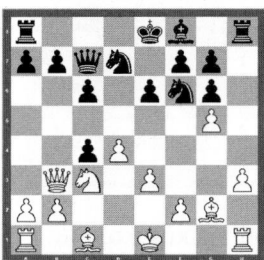

13.♛xc4 ♞d5 14.♝d2 0-0-0 (*14... ♞xc3 15.bxc3±; 14...♞7b6 15.♛b3 a5 16.a3 a4 17.♛a2 ♝e7 18.h4 ♖d8 19.♞e2± Dreev — M.Gurevich, Cap d'Agde (rapid) 2000) 15.0-0-0 (15. ♛b3 ♛b6 16.♛xb6 N7xb6 17.♞xd5 exd5 18.b3= Vorobiov — Gavrilov, Moscow 2011; 15.0-0!?∞) 15...♞7b6 16.♛b3 ♚b8 17.♚b1 f6 18.♞e2 f5 19.f3± Ionov — McShane, Stockholm 2010;*

6...♝g6 The most popular retreat.

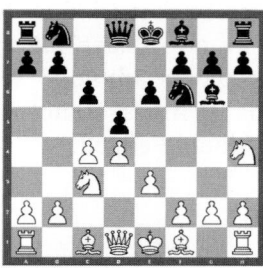

7.♞xg6 For a long time almost nobody played this, deterred by Black's potential play on the h-file.

a) 7.♝e2 ♞bd7 8.0-0 (*8.♞xg6 hxg6 9.♝d2 — 7.♞xg6 hxg6 8.♝d2 ♞bd7 9.♝e2*) 8...♝d6

(The following leads to quieter play 8...♞e4 9.g3 ♞d6 10.b3 (*10. cxd5 cxd5 11.f3 ♝e7 12.♞xg6 hxg6=* Neverov — Solak, Cappelle la Grande 2012) 10...♝e7 11.♞xg6 hxg6 12.♛c2 Navara — Gretarsson, Reykjavik 2012 12...♞f5±/= — The knight is now excellently placed on f5. Black's position is very solid.)

9.g3

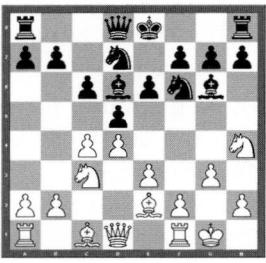

9...dxc4! Otherwise the game continues quietly with a small advantage for White:

a1) 9...♛e7 10.b3 (*10.♛b3 0-0-0!?*) 10...♞e4 11.♝b2 ♞xc3 12.♝xc3 ♝b4 13.♝xb4 ♛xb4 14.c5 0-0 15.a3 ♛a5 16.♞xg6 hxg6 17.b4 ♛c7 18.f4± Radjabov — Karjakin, Medias 2011;

a2) 9...0-0 10.♞xg6 hxg6 11.b3 (*11. ♛b3 ♖b8 12.♖d1 ♛e7 13.♛c2 a6 14.♝d2 dxc4 15.♝xc4 b5 16.♝f1 c5 17.dxc5 ♞xc5 18.♝e1 ♖fc8 19.♖ac1± Gelfand — Akopian, Jermuk 2009) 11...♛e7 12.♝f3 ♖ac8 (12...e5 13.cxd5±) 13.♝g2 ♖fd8*

14.♗d2± Gelfand — Kramnik, Moscow 2007;

10.♘xg6 (*10.♗xc4 ♗h5=*) 10...hxg6 11.♗xc4

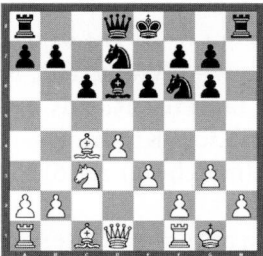

11...♕e7! The most promising way of preparing to castle long.

(11...♘b6 12.♗e2 ♕d7 13.♗f3 e5 14.♗g2 0-0-0 (*14...exd4 15.exd4 0-0 16.♗g5 ♗e7=*) 15.a4 a6∞ To-mashevsky — Rublevsky, Olginka (rapid) 2011)

12.♗e2 0-0-0!∓ — The position is double-edged but in practice it's easier to play Black, Lysyi — Rublevsky, Apatity (rapid) 2011;

b) 7.♕b3 ♕c7 (*7...♕b6 8.♘xg6 hxg6 — 7.♘xg6 hxg6 8.♕b3 ♕b6*) 8.♘xg6 hxg6 — 7.♘xg6 hxg6 8.♕b3 ♕c7;

c) 7.♗d2 ♘bd7 8.♘xg6 hxg6 — 7.♘xg6 hxg6 8.♗d2 ♘bd7;

7...hxg6 8.♗d3 This new trend is a direct and active move posing serious problems for Black.

a) 8.♗d2 8...♘bd7 9.g3

a1) 9.c5 e5 10.b4 a6 (*10...♖h4!?∞*) 11.a4 ♗e7 12.g3 exd4 13.exd4 ♘f8 14.♗g2 ♘e6 15.♗e3 ♘g8 16.0-0 ♗f6= Salgado Lopez — Alsina, Barcelona 2011;

a2) 9.♗e2 dxc4 10.♗xc4 ♗d6 11.♕c2 ♕e7 12.♗e2 e5 13.dxe5 ♗xe5 14.0-0-0 0-0-0= Zhao Jun — Bu Xiangzhi, China 2011;

a3) 9.♖c1 ♗d6

(9...♗e7 10.♗d3 (*10.♕b3 ♖b8 11.cxd5 exd5=*) 10...dxc4 11.♗xc4 ♖c8 12.0-0 c5 13.dxc5 ♖xc5 (*13...♘xc5!?*) 14.♗e2 ♕b8 15.g3 0-0= — It's hard for White to unravel and transfer his black squared bishop to a more active position, Zakhartsov — Bareev, Krasnoyarsk 2007)

10.g3 ♕e7 11.c5 ♗c7 12.f4 ♗a5 (*12...g5 13.♗g2 gxf4 14.exf4±* Campos Moreno — M.Gurevich, Andorra 2005) 13.♘b1 ♗xd2+ 14.♘xd2 ♘e4 15.♘xe4 dxe4 16.h4 f5= Bareev — Dreev, Moscow 2004;

a4) 9.♕c2 ♗d6 10.♗e2 dxc4 11.♗xc4 ♕e7 12.h3 ♘b6 13.♗e2 e5 14.dxe5 ♗xe5 15.0-0-0 0-0-0= Roiz — T.Petrosyan, Tashkent 2011;

a5) 9.♕b3 ♕c7 10.cxd5 exd5 11.♖c1 ♘b6 12.h3 ♗e7 13.♗d3 ♖d8= Mozharov — Dreev, Moscow 2007;

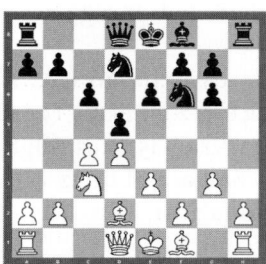

9...♗b4!

a1) After 9...♗d6, promising is
10.♕b3 ♖b8 11.♗g2± since Black
doesn't have ♘d7-b6, Caruana —
N.Nguyen, Biel 2010;

a2) 9...♗e7

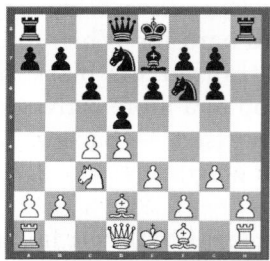

10.b3! 0–0

(10...e5 11.cxd5 cxd5 12.♗g2 e4
13.0–0 (*13.f3±*) 13...0–0 14.h4 ♘b6
15.♕e2 a6 16.a4± Wang Yue —
Dreev, Ergun 2006)

11.♗g2 dxc4 (*11...a6 12.0–0 b5
13.♕e2±* Wang Yue — Megaran-
to, Zaozhuang 2012) 12.bxc4 e5
13.♕b3 (*13.0–0±*) 13...♖b8 (*13...exd4
14.exd4 ♖e8 15.0–0 ♘c5 16.dxc5
♕xd2 17.♖ad1 ♕g5 18.♕xb7 ♗xc5*

19.♘a4) 14.♖d1± Kramnik — Gelfand, Monaco (blindfold) 2005;

10.♕b3 (*10.♕c2 0–0=*) 10...♗xc3
11.♗xc3 ♘e4 12.♗g2 ♘xc3 13.♕xc3
(*13.bxc3 ♕c7=*) 13...dxc4! is simplest

(13...f5 14.0–0 (*14.0–0–0 ♘b6*
Tregubov — Wang Yue, Kallithea
2008) 14...♕e7 15.cxd5 exd5 16.b4
♘f6 17.♖fc1± Kramnik — Topalov,
Elista (match–12) 2006)

14.♕xc4 a5±/= — White's advantage
is minute, Yakovich — Dubov, Voronezh 2010;

b) 8.g3

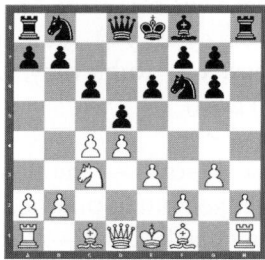

8...♘bd7 9.a3

b1) 9.♗d2 — 8.♗d2 ♘bd7 9.g3;

b2) 9.♕e2 ♗b4 10.♗d2 ♗xc3
11.♗xc3 ♘e4= Mustafaev — Kuzubov, Tashkent 2009;

b3) 9.♗g2 dxc4 10.♕e2 ♘b6
11.0–0 ♗e7 12.♖d1 ♕c7 13.e4 e5
14.♗e3 (*14.dxe5 ♕xe5∞* Shirov
— Khairullin, Riga (rapid) 2012)
14...♘fd7 15.f4 exd4 16.♗xd4 ♗c5

17.e5 ♗xd4+ 18.♖xd4 ♘c5 19.♘e4 ♘xe4 20.♗xe4 ♖d8 21.♖xd8+ ♕xd8 22.♖d1 ♕e7= — White's compensation is only sufficient for equality, Nyback — Stupak, Rogaska Slatina 2011;

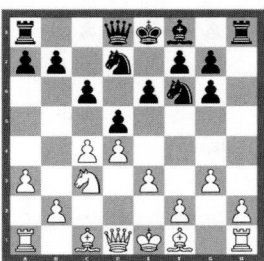

9... ♗d6 The most active and correct square. c4-c5 is not dangerous, because there will then be counter play in the centre or on the kingside.

b1) 9...dxc4 10.♗xc4 ♘b6 11.♗b3±;

b2) 9...♗e7

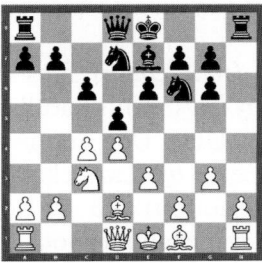

10.b3!

(10.f4 dxc4 (10...0-0 11.c5 b6 12.b4 a5 13.♗d2 ♕c7 14.♗d3±) 11.♗xc4 ♘b6 (11...c5 12.d5 exd5 13.♘xd5 ♘b6 14.♘xb6 ♕xb6 15.♕f3 0-0 16.0-0±; 11...♕c7!? 12.0-0 0-0-0∞; 11...0-0 12.e4 b5 13.♗e2± Topalov — Kramnik, Elista 2006) 12.♗a2 ♘bd5= Khismatullin — Dreev, Ramenskoe 2006)

10...e5 11.♗g2 (11.dxe5 ♘xe5 12.cxd5 ♘xd5 13.♘xd5 cxd5 14.♗g2 ♕a5+= Harikrishna — Shirov, Sestao 2010)

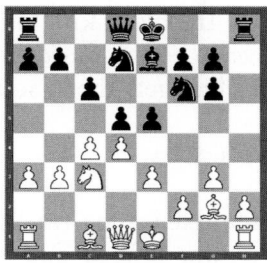

11...♕a5

b21) 11...e4 12.0-0 (12.f3 exf3 13.♗xf3 ♘f8 14.0-0 ♘e6=) 12...0-0 13.f3 exf3 14.♗xf3 ♘b6 (14...dxc4 15.bxc4 c5 16.♗xb7 ♖b8 Khismatullin — Yevseev, Voronezh 2010 17.♗f3 ♘b6 18.♗e2) 15.♕d3±;

b22) 11...dxc4!? 12.bxc4 ♘b6 13.♕d3 (13.♖b1 exd4 14.exd4 ♕d7=) 13...0-0 (13...♕d7 14.0-0 0-0-0 15.d5±) 14.0-0 exd4

(14...♕d7 15.♖b1 ♖ad8 16.♖d1 (16.♕e2 ♕e6±) 16...♖fe8±)

15.exd4 c5 16.d5 ♘e8 17.♘e4 (17. ♗f4 ♘d6 18.♗xd6 ♗xd6±/=) 17...f5 18.♘d2 ♘d6∞ Tomashevsky — Roiz, Bursa 2010;

12.♕c2 exd4 13.exd4 dxc4 14.bxc4 ♕a6 (*14...♗f5 15.♕xf5 gxf5 16.0-0 0-0-0 17.♖e1±*) 15.c5 ♕c4∞;

10.b3

(10.c5 ♗c7 11.♗g2 e5 12.b4 0-0 (*12... e4 13.b5* N.Nguyen — Wang Yue, Zaozhuang 2012 *13...♘f8±*) 13.0-0 ♖e8= — The black knight is ready to move to e6 via f8. If b4-b5 the black bishop gets the a5 square.)

10...♘e4 11.♗b2

(11.♘xe4 dxe4 12.b4 (*12. ♗g2 f5=*) 12...f5 (*12...a6 13.♕g4 ♘f6 14.♕e2±* Dreev — Maletin, Delhi 2010) 13.c5 ♗c7 14.b5 ♘f6 15.♖b1 ♗a5+ 16.♗d2 e5= Lysyi — Matlakov, Ulan Ude 2009)

11...f5 12.♗g2 g5 13.♘xe4 dxe4 14.♕c2 g4 15.h3 gxh3 16.♗xh3 ♖xh3 17.♗xh3 ♕e7= Ni Hua — Rublevsky, Ningbo (rapid) 2010;

c) 8.♕b3

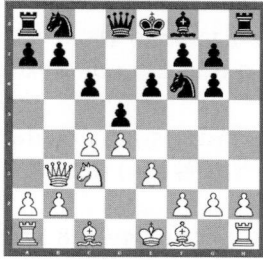

8...♕c7

(The b6 square is bad for the queen as Black gets the worse game consistently : 8...♕b6 9.♗d2 (*9.g3 ♘bd7 10.♗d2 — 9.♗d2 ♘bd7 10.g3*) 9...♘bd7

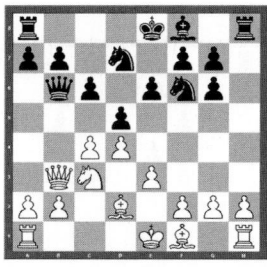

10.♕c2

c1) 10.g3 ♗e7 11.♗g2 ♕a6 12.cxd5 cxd5 13.♕b5± — White has a small endgame advantage due to his two bishops.;

c2) 10.♗e2 ♗e7 11.♕c2 0-0 12.0-0 dxc4 (*12...♖fe8 13.c5 ♕c7 14.f4±* Grachev — Chadaev, Sochi 2009) 13.♗xc4 c5 14.♘a4 ♕c7 15.♗e2±;

10...g5 (*10...♗b4 11.♗d3 e5 12.a3 ♗xc3 13.bxc3±* Khismatullin — Romanov, Ulan Ude 2009; *10...♕c7 11.g3 ♗e7 12.b3±* Laznicka — Agrest, Plovdiv 2010) 11.0-0-0± Koneru — Stefanova, Istanbul 2009)

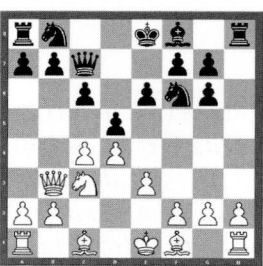

9.g3

c1) 9.♗d2 ♘bd7 10.cxd5 (*10.h3 — 9.h3 ♘bd7 10.♗d2*) 10...exd5 11.0-0-0 a5 12.f3 a4 13.♕c2 a3 14.b3 ♗b4∞ Cheparinov — Grischuk, Sochi 2008;

c2) 9.h3 ♘bd7 10.♗d2 ♘b6 (*10...0-0-0!?; 10...♗e7 11.♖c1 ♘b6 12.cxd5 exd5 13.♗d3 Khismatullin — Dreev, Tomsk 2006 13...g5=*) 11.cxd5 exd5 12.♗d3 ♗e7 13.0-0-0 a5 (*13...0-0-0!?*) 14.♔b1 a4 15.♕c2 ♘c4∞= Harikrishna — Gelfand, Bermuda 2005;

9...♘bd7 10.♗g2 (*10.♗d2 ♗e7 11.♗g2 ♘b6 12.cxd5 exd5= — The d2 bishop will be attacked by ♘b6-c4 and is badly placed, Mchedlishvili — Motylev, Germany 2012*) 10...♗e7 11.0-0 0-0 12.♖d1

(12.cxd5 cxd5= (*12...exd5 13.♕c2±* — In a complicated battle White's chances are just a little better, Eljanov — Malakhov, Olginka 2011))

12...♘b6 13.c5 ♘bd7= Tregubov — Sakaev, France 2005;

d) 8.♗e2 ♘bd7 9.♗d2 — 8.♗d2 ♘bd7 9.♗e2;

8...♘bd7

(The problems aren't solved by 8...c5 9.♕b3 (*9.cxd5 exd5 10.dxc5 ♗xc5 11.0-0 ♘c6 12.♗d2 0-0*

13.♖c1 ♕e7=*) 9...♕d7 10.cxd5 exd5 11.dxc5 ♗xc5

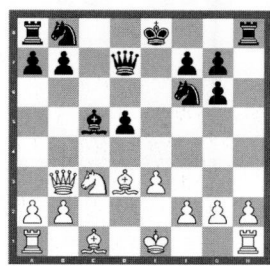

12.♕b5! In the endgame the activity of the black pieces not important. 12...♕xb5 13.♘xb5 ♔d7 14.0-0 ♘c6 15.♖d1 ♗e7 16.♗d2± — It's difficult for Black to defend, Kramnik — Gelfand, Saint Vincent 2005)

9.0-0

(9.♗d2 ♗d6 10.h3 dxc4 (*10...a6 11.c5 ♗c7 12.f4 ♘h5 13.♕f3 f5 14.g4± Khairullin — Jumabayev, Moscow 2012*))

9...♗d6 10.h3 ♕e7

a) 10...g5 11.cxd5 exd5 12.e4 dxe4 13.♖e1±;

b) 10...dxc4 11.♗xc4 ♘b6 (*11...♕e7 12.e4 e5 13.d5 ♘b6 14.dxc6 bxc6 15.♗b3± Huzman — Deutsch, Israel 2012*) 12.♗b3 e5

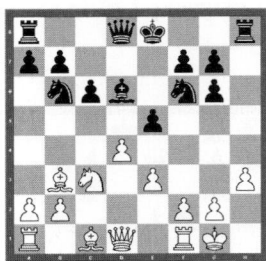

13.d5

b1) The following leads to immense complications 13.♕c2 ♕e7 14.♗d2 0–0–0 15.d5 (*15.♘b5 ♗b8∞*) 15...e4 16.dxc6 ♕e5 17.f4 exf3 18.♖xf3∞ Carlsen — Gelfand, Moscow 2011;

b2) 13.dxe5 ♗xe5 14.♕c2 ♕e7 15.♖d1±;

b3) 13.a4!?±;

13...♘fxd5 14.♘xd5 ♘xd5 15.♗xd5 cxd5 16.♕xd5 ♕e7 17.e4 (*17.♖d1±*) 17...0–0 18.♗e3± — with a bad bishop it's hard for Black to defend.;

c) 10...0–0 11.c5!?

(11.♕c2 ♕e7 (*11...dxc4 12.♗xc4 ♕e7 13.♖d1 — 11...♕e7 12.♖d1 dxc4 13.♗xc4*) 12.♖d1 (*12.c5 ♗c7 13.b4 e5 14.b5 ♖fe8∞*) 12...dxc4 (*12... ♖ac8 13.c5 ♗b8 14.f4± Gelfand — Anand, Moscow (match–03,rapid) 2012*) 13.♗xc4 ♖ac8 (*13...♖fd8 14.♗d2±*) 14.♗d2 c5 (*14...♘b6 15.♗f1 e5 16.dxe5 ♗xe5 17.♖ac1 ♖cd8 18.♗e1 ♖xd1 19.♖xd1 ♖d8 20.♖xd8+ ♕xd8 21.g3±*) — White has a small but stable advantage,

Carlsen — Gelfand, Wijk aan Zee 2012) 15.dxc5 ♘xc5 16.♖ac1 a6 17.♗e1 b5 18.♗f1 ♘a4 19.♕b1 ♘xc3 20.♗xc3 ♘d5 21.♗e1 ♗b4±/= — After exchange of one of the bishops, Black is close to equality, Melkumyan — Akopian, Albena 2012)

11...♗c7 12.b4 (If *12.f4* then *12...♗a5,* and the weakness of e4 is apparent.) 12...e5 13.b5 ♖e8 (*13...♗a5 14.♗d2 exd4 15.exd4 ♗xc3 16.♗xc3 ♘e4 17.♗e1! ♕c7 18.bxc6 bxc6 19.♕a4±*) 14.♕a4 ♖e6 15.bxc6 bxc6 16.♗d2± The e6 rook prevents Black's usual plan of ♘d7-f8-e6 to attack the d4 pawn;

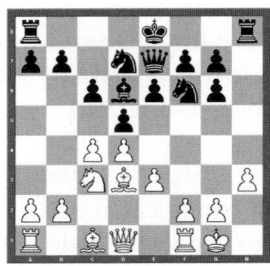

11.c5

a) 11.♗d2 dxc4

(11...0–0 12.c5 ♗c7 13.f4 (*13.b4 e5 14.b5±*) 13...♗a5 14.♕b1!± A typical move in such a structure. White threatens b2-b4, and takes control of e4.)

12.♗xc4 e5 (*12...0–0 13.♕b3 ♘b6 14.♗d3±*) 13.♕c2 ♗c7 14.d5 e4 15.dxc6 bxc6 16.♘e2 g5 17.♘g3 g4

18.♗e2 Gustafsson — Zhu Chen, Caleta 2012 18...♗xg3 19.fxg3 gxh3 20.gxh3 ♕e6 21.h4∞;

b) 11.♕c2 dxc4 (*11...g5!?*) 12.♗xc4 g5 13.e4 e5 14.d5 g4;

11...♗c7 12.f4 (One must not underestimate Black's play: *12.b4? 12...e5 13.♗b2 e4 14.♗e2 g5∓* Black hasn't castled yet and this is his advantage — White is under attack!) 12...♘h5 (Very slow is *12...♘g8 13.b4 a6* Sargissian — Brunello, Caleta 2012, and now the simple *14.a4±*) 13.♘e2 f5 14.♗d2∞ — White's developing play on the b-file looks more dangerous than Black's on the kingside, Movsesian — Motylev, Sochi 2012.

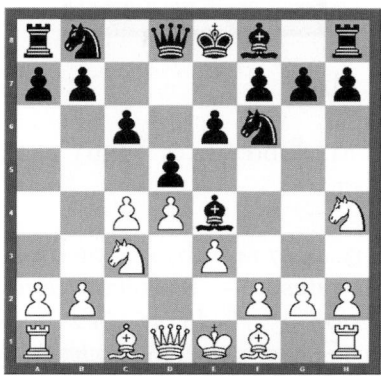

7.f3
7.♕b3 ♕b6=

7...♗g6 8.♕b3
White develops with tempo putting pressure on b7 and d5.

8...♕c7

The most principled.

8...♕b6 provokes a transition to an endgame favourable for White.

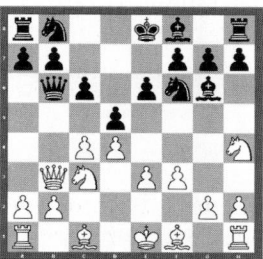

9.♘xg6 hxg6 10.♗d2

a) The immediate king evacuation is a good and straightforward idea: 10.♔f2 ♘bd7 11.g3 (*11.♗d2 — 10.♗d2 ♘bd7 11.♔f2*) 11...g5 (*11...♕c7 12.♗d2 — 10.♗d2 ♘bd7 11.♔f2 ♕c7 12.g3*) 12.♔g2 g4 Sakaev — Danin, Taganrog 2011 13.fxg4 ♘xg4 14.♗d3±;

b) 10.g3 ♘bd7 11.♗d2 — 10.♗d2 ♘bd7 11.g3(*11.♔f2 — 10.♔f2 ♘bd7 11.g3*) ;

10...♘bd7

(Too hasty is 10...♗d6 11.f4 The most so lid continuation as the weakening of the e4 square is not too significant. White also starts to threaten on the queenside.

a) No advantage is given by 11.h3 ♘bd7 12.0-0-0 ♕xb3 13.axb3 a6 (or start with *13...♘h5=*) 14.♔c2 ♘h5! 15.♗d3 ♘g3 16.♖he1 — 10...

♘bd7 11.0–0–0 ♕xb3 12.axb3 ♗d6
13.h3 ♘h5 14.♗d3 ♘g3 15.♖he1 a6
16.♔c2;

b) An interesting positional pawn
sacrifice follows 11.c5!?

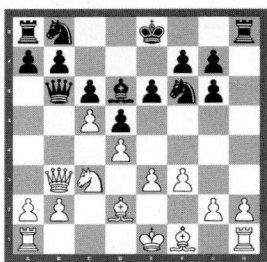

11...♕xb3 12.axb3 ♖xh2

(12...♗xh2 13.♗d3 (13.♘e2 ♘bd7
14.♔f2 g5 15.g3 g4 16.♗g2 ♔e7=
— The bishop is stuck on h2 but
White has trouble capturing it
and the black rooks are ready
to support it.) 13...♗g3+ 14.♔e2
♖xh1 15.♖xh1 ♘h5 16.♖h3 e5
17.dxe5 ♗xe5 18.g4 ♘f6 19.♖h8+
♔e7 20.b4↑ White's initiative is
dangerous.)

13.♖xh2 ♗xh2

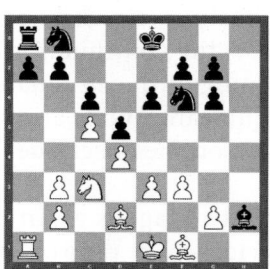

14.♔f2!N Before launching an attack on the queenside, it's useful to
drive the black bishop there so that
it can be attacked. (Less accurate
is *14.b4* Hillarp Persson — Hector,
Denmark 2012 *14...♗g3!+ 15.♔d1
♔e7 16.b5 cxb5∓*) 14...♗c7 15.b4 b5
16.cxb6 ♗xb6 17.♘a4 ♘bd7 18.b5
cxb5 19.♘xb6 ♘xb6 20.♗xb5+
♔d8 21.b3↑ — Black has a bor-
ing defence, and the extra pawn is
small consolation.;

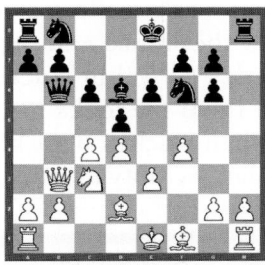

11...dxc4

a) 11...♘bd7 12.c5 ♕xb3 13.axb3
♗e7

(13...♗c7 14.b4 b5 15.cxb6 (*15.♗d3
Istratescu — Baekelant, Avoine
2004 15...♔d8 16.♔e2 ♔c8±;
15.♘xb5 cxb5 16.♗xb5±*) 15...
♗xb6 16.♗d3±)

14.b4 b5 15.♘xb5! cxb5 16.♗xb5
♘e4 17.♗c6 ♖c8 18.b5 ♖c7 (18...
♘exc5 19.♖xa7+- Dautov — Hector, Goteborg 2005) 19.♗a5 ♖c8
20.♗b4 ♖c7 21.♔e2±;

b) 11...♕xb3 12.axb3 ♗b4 13.♗d3
♘bd7 14.♔e2±;

12.♗xc4 ♘bd7 13.0-0±)

11.g3 The most flexible move. White can hide the king on f2 or castle long.

a) The next frequently played move neglects the pawn structure and gives the black pieces squaresfor-regrouping 11.0-0-0 11...♕xb3 12.axb3 ♗d6 13.h3 ♘h5! 14.♗d3 ♘g3 15.♖he1 a6

(The plan with short castling is less reliable 15...0-0, primarily in view of

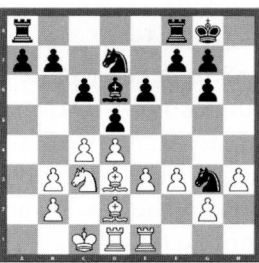

16.♗c2±!N, with the idea of quickly playing e3-e4 in a very favourable configuration.

a1) 16.c5 ♗e7 17.b4 e5 (17...a6 18.e4 ♗h4 19.♗e3± Tregubov — Kritz, Kallithea 2009) 18.♘e2 (18.b5!?) 18...♘xe2+ 19.♖xe2 ♗f6 20.♗c3 a6= Dautov — Gagunashvili, Mainz (rapid) 2005;

a2) 16.♔b1 a6 17.♖c1 (17.e4 dxe4 18.♘xe4 ♘xe4 19.♗xe4 ♘f6= Cheparinov — Malakhov, Vil-

larrobledo (rapid) 2007) 17...♖ac8 18.♖ed1 ♖fe8 19.♗e1±/= Gelfand — Eljanov, Jermuk 2009;)

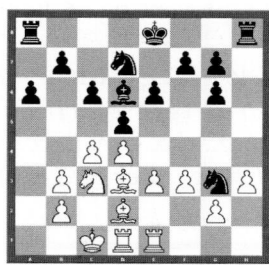

16.♔c2 0-0-0 17.e4

(17.♖a1 ♘f5! (17...♘f6 Granda Zuniga — Hillarp Persson, Porto Mannu 2008 18.e4±) 18.♘e2 ♗c7 19.e4 dxe4 20.fxe4 ♘xd4+ 21.♘xd4 ♘e5 22.♘xe6 ♘xd3 23.♖e3 fxe6 24.♖xd3 ♖df8=)

17...dxe4 18.fxe4 c5 19.d5 ♖de8= — In a complex endgame both sides have their trumps, Carlsen — Vallejo Pons, Bilbao 2011;

b) 11.♔f2

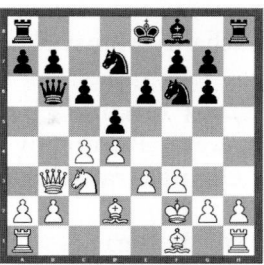

11...♕c7

(After 11...♗e7, the next move is interesting 12.♕xb6!? (*12.g3 — 11.g3 ♗e7 12.♔f2*) 12...axb6 13.♗e2, with the idea after 13...dxc4 to reply 14.a4!±, preventing b6-b5.)

12.g3 ♗d6 — 11.g3 ♗d6 12.♔f2 ♕c7 (*12...0-0-0 13.c5 e5 14.♕a4 ♔b8 15.b4↑; 12...dxc4 13.♗xc4 0-0-0 14.♖ad1±; 12...♗e7 13.♔g2±*) ;

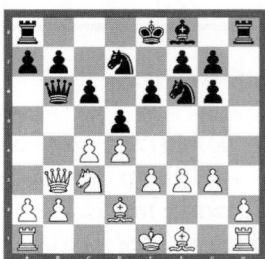

11...♗d6

a) 11...♗e7 12.♔f2 (*12.0-0-0 ♕xb3 13.axb3 0-0-0 14.♔c2±* Av.Grigoryan — Yilmaz, Moscow 2012) 12...♖d8 (*12...c5 13.cxd5 exd5 14.♕xb6±* Hillarp Persson — Hector, Vaxjo 2008) 13.♔g2 (*13.♕xb6 axb6 14.a4±*) 13...0-0 14.♕xb6 axb6 15.cxd5 exd5 16.a4± Grachev — Romanov, Khanty Mansyisk 2011;

b) 11...♕xb3 12.axb3 ♗b4 13.♗g2 0-0 14.♔e2± P.Smirnov — Romanov, Olginka (rapid) 2011;

12.♔f2 ♕c7 13.♔g2

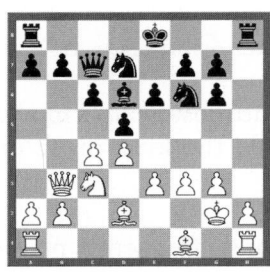

13...dxc4

(13...a6 14.cxd5! (*14.♖c1±* Eljanov — Solak, Banja Vrucica 2009) 14...cxd5 (*14...exd5 15.e4 dxe4 16.fxe4 c5 17.♗c4 0-0-0 18.♖ac1→*) 15.♗d3 ♖c8 16.♖ac1 ♕b8 17.e4± Fridman — Ravichandran, Mesa 2010)

14.♗xc4 ♘b6 (*14...0-0 15.♖hd1±*) 15.♗e2 e5 16.dxe5 ♗xe5 17.♖ad1 0-0-0 18.f4 ♗xc3 (*18...♗d6 19.e4 ♗c5* Kurnosov — Danin, Taganrog 2011 *20.♗c1±*) 19.♗xc3 ♘bd5 20.♗d4± — In an open position the advantage of the two bishops is an important factor.

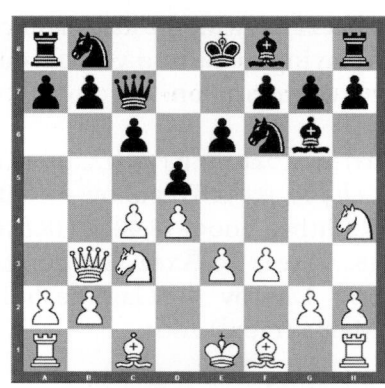

9.♗d2 ♗e7

The most flexible. In comparison with the development of the knight to d7, Black can capture on c4, push c6-c5, and then place the knight on the active square c6.

9...♗d6 10.♖c1 a6 (10...♗xh2 11.♖xh2 dxc4 12.♗xc4 ♕xh2 13.♕xb7 ♕xh4+ 14.♔f1 0-0 15.♕xa8±) 11.♘xg6 hxg6 12.f4±;

9...♘bd7

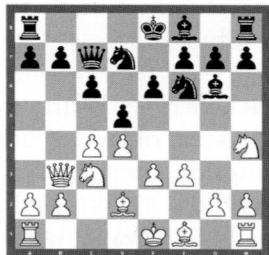

10.♖c1

a) 10.0-0-0 dxc4! Otherwise White will capture on d5 himself and play e3-e4. (10...♗e7 — 9...♗e7 10.0-0-0 ♘bd7; 10...a5 11.cxd5∞) 11.♕xc4 ♗e7 12.♘xg6 hxg6 13.g3 0-0-0 (The next move leads to sharper play, though also with near equal chances 13...0-0 14.e4∞ Mchedlishvili — Sulypa, Alushta 2000) 14.♔b1 ♘b6 15.♕b3 ♔b8= — White has no advantage, since his pawn structure is not solid enough.;

b) 10.cxd5 ♘xd5

(10...exd5 11.e4! dxe4 12.♘xg6 hxg6 13.fxe4 ♘b6 (13...♖xh2 14.♖xh2 ♕g3+ 15.♔d1 ♕xh2 16.e5± Legky — Verat, Saint-Quentin 2003) 14.e5 ♘fd5

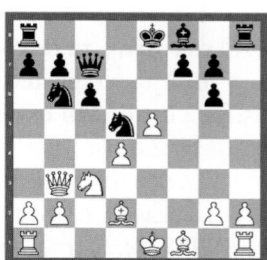

15.a4!N Now Black either gives up the centre by capturing on c3, or allows a weakeness in his camp with a7-a5. (15.♘xd5 ♘xd5 16.♗c4 0-0-0= Krush — Zhu Chen, Shanghai 2002) 15...a5 16.♘xd5 ♘xd5 17.♗c4 0-0-0 18.0-0 f5 19.♗xd5 ♖xd5 20.♕xd5! cxd5 21.♖ac1 b6 22.♖xc7+ ♔xc7 23.♖c1+ ♔d7 24.e6+ ♔xe6 25.♖c6+ ♔d7 26.♖xb6±)

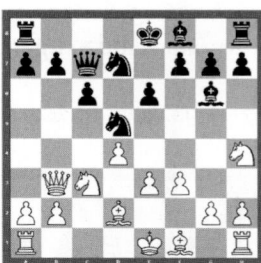

11.e4

b1) 11.0-0-0 ♘xc3 12.♕xc3 a5= — Black wants to enable a useful exchange of the black squared bishops.;

b2) 11.♘xg6 hxg6 12.g3 0-0-0∞/=;

b3) 11.g3 ♗e7 — 9...♗e7 10.g3 ♘bd7 11.cxd5 ♘xd5;

b4) 11.♘xd5 exd5 12.0-0-0 ♗e7 (*12...0-0-0∞*) 13.♘xg6 hxg6 14.e4 dxe4 15.fxe4 c5 16.♔b1 cxd4 17.♖c1 ♕b6 18.♗b5 ♖d8∞;

11...♘xc3 (*11...♘5b6 12.0-0-0 0-0-0 13.♔b1 ♔b8 14.♖c1 ♔a8 15.g3± Ftacnik — Banusz, Hungary 2010*) 12.♘xg6

(*12.bxc3 ♗h5!? 13.g4 (13. ♗e2 ♗e7 14.g3 ♗xh4 15.gxh4 0-0=) 13...♗e7 14.♘g2 ♗g6∞ Dziuba — Zawadski, Lublin 2009*)

12...hxg6 13.bxc3 ♗e7 14.g3 — 9...♗e7 10.g3 ♘bd7 11.cxd5 ♘xd5 12.♘xg6 hxg6 13.e4 ♘xc3 14.bxc3;

c) 10.g3 ♗e7 (*10...♘b6 11.cxd5 exd5 12.♘xg6 hxg6 13.♗d3±*) 11.♖c1 — 9...♗e7 10.♖c1 ♘bd7 11.g3;

10...♗e7 — 9...♗e7 10.♖c1 ♘bd7

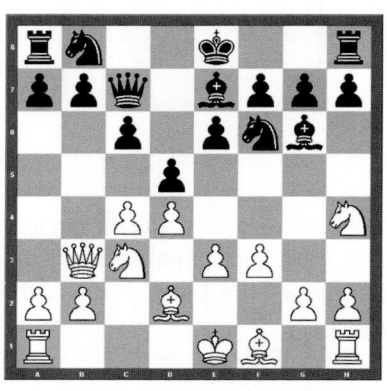

10.♖c1

10.cxd5

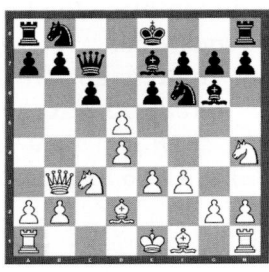

10...cxd5 11.♘xg6 hxg6 12.0-0-0 ♘c6 13.♔b1 a6

(If Black cast les White immediately has an object of attack on the kingside after 13...0-0 14.♖c1 ♖fc8 15.♕d1∞ the kingside pawns are ready to advance and central action after 15...e5 16.g4 (*16. ♗e1 exd4 17.exd4 Tregubov — Grachev, Olginka (rapid) 2011 17...a6=; 16.h4!?*) 16...exd4 17.exd4± leads to a somewhat better game for White.)

14.♖c1 ♖c8 15.♗d3 Socko — Kindermann, Porto Carras 2011 (*15.g4 ♘d7 16.f4 ♘a5= Praveen — Siddarth, Mumbai 2011*) 15...0-0!? Black plans a quick manoeuvre with knight to c4 which will give sufficient counter play. If White exchanges on c4, he will lose a tempo since he just played ♗d3.(*15...♘d7 16.♘e2 ♕b6 17.♕a4±*) ;

The next line is commital and risky 10.0-0-0

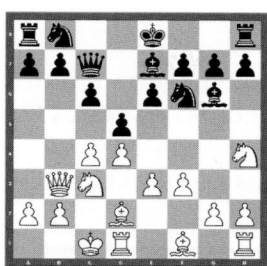

10...dxc4! The central exchange is very timely.

a) The following allows the queen-side to be blocked and is therefore dubious 10...a6

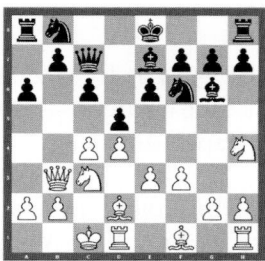

11.c5 ♘bd7 12.♘a4 One needn't hurry with the exchange on g6 — White can make it at any time. 12...♖b8

(12...e5 13.♗e1

a1) 13.♘xg6 hxg6 14.♔b1 0-0 *(14...e4 15.♗e1± Potkin — Bu Xi-angzhi, Ningbo 2010; 14...♖b8 15.♗e1 b5 16.cxb6 ♘xb6 17.♗a5 ♘fd7 18.dxe5 0-0 19.e4±)* ;

a2) 13.♗c3!? ♖b8 14.dxe5 ♘xe5 15.♗d4 ♘ed7 16.♕c3± Karpov — Caruana, Cap d'Agde 2008;

13...♖b8 — 12...♖b8 13.♗e1 e5)

13.♗e1 e5

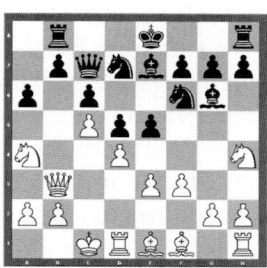

14.dxe5!N

a1) 14.g4 b6 15.cxb6 ♘xb6 16.♘xb6 ♘d7 17.♘xg6 hxg6 18.♗a5 *(18. dxe5 ♖xb6 19.♗a5 ♖xb3 20.♗xc7 ♖xe3∓ Lysyi — Esen, Plovdiv 2012)* 18...♘xb6 19.dxe5 0-0 20.f4∞ — Black's initiative on the b-file compensates for the sacrificed pawn.;

a2) 14.♘xg6 hxg6 15.♔b1 0-0 *(15... b5 16.cxb6 ♘xb6 17.♗a5 ♘fd7 18.dxe5 0-0 19.e4±)* ;

14...♘xe5 15.♕c3 ♘fd7 16.♘xg6 hxg6 17.♗g3 ♗f6 18.e4 dxe4

(18...0-0 19.f4 ♘g4 20.e5 ♗e7 21.♗e2 ♘h6

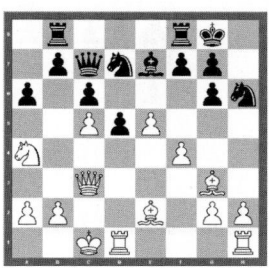

22.♖hf1! The idea of the move is unobvious and deep — it allows ♗g3-f2. (*22.h4 b6 23.cxb6 ♘xb6∞; After the immediate 22.♗f2 follows 22...f6!∓, and Black takes the initiative.) 22...b6 Black has no other plan anyway. 23.cxb6 ♘xb6 24.♘xb6 ♕xb6 25.♗f2 ♕b7 26.g4± — Without the knight's support, Black's initiative on the queenside comes to a dead end.)*

19.♖e1 exf3 20.gxf3 ♔f8 21.♘b6 ♕d8

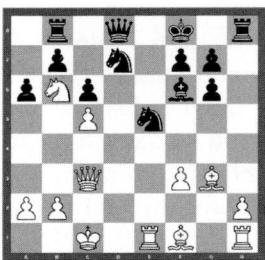

22.♖e4!! The point of the move is that when the bishop moves to e2 it won't block the e-file. 22...♖h5 23.♗e2 ♘xb6 24.cxb6 ♘d7 25.♕e3 ♖a8 26.♗c7 ♕c8 27.f4±/↑;

b) 10...♘bd7

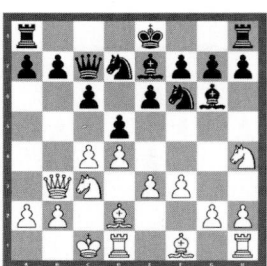

11.cxd5

(11.♘xg6 hxg6 12.♔b1 dxc4 (*12... ♖d8 13.cxd5±*) 13.♗xc4 ♘b6=)

11...♘xd5 12.♘xg6 hxg6

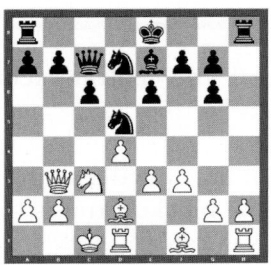

13.♘xd5

b1) 13.h3 a5 14.a3 b5 15.♘xd5 exd5 16.♔b1 ♘b6∓ Bareev — Ivanchuk, Dubai (rapid) 2002;

b2) 13.♔b1 ♘xc3+ 14.♗xc3 ♘b6 (*14...a5 15.e4∞* Van Wely — I. Sokolov, Amsterdam 2002) 15.h3 ♘d5 16.♗d2 ♕b6= Grachev — Miton, Sochi 2008;

b3) 13.e4 ♘xc3 14.♗xc3 0-0-0 15.g3 ♔b8 16.♔b1 ♘b6 17.♗e2± Kramnik — Vallejo Pons, Monaco (rapid) 2007(*17.f4!?±; 17.a4!?*) ;

13...exd5 (*13...cxd5+ 14.♔b1 ♘b8 15.e4 ♘c6 16.exd5 exd5 17.h4!?↑*) 14.e4 0-0 (*14...♘b6 15.g3 0-0-0 16.♗f4 ♗d6 17.e5 ♗e7 18.h4±* Najer — Wang Yue, Moscow 2006) 15.♔b1 dxe4 16.fxe4 c5 17.e5! cxd4 18.e6 ♘c5 19.exf7+ ♖xf7 20.♕c2↑ Nyback — Ladva, Harjumaa 2010;

11.♗xc4

(11.♕xc4 a6

(11...♘bd7 12.♕b3 (*12.g4 ♘d5 13.♘xg6 hxg6 14.f4 g5∓* Schlosser — Balogh, Austria 2010) 12...c5 13.♘xg6 hxg6 14.♔b1∞)

12.g4 b5 13.♕e2 c5 14.♘xg6 hxg6 15.dxc5 ♕xc5 16.♔b1 ♘c6∞ Gustafson — Ragger, Rijeka 2010)

11...b5 12.♗e2 a6 13.♘xg6 hxg6 14.♘e4 (*14.f4 ♘bd7 15.♗f3 ♖c8 16.♔b1 c5 17.♘e4 ♘xe4 18.♗xe4 ♘f6 19.♗f3 c4 20.♕c2 ♘d5∓* Burmakin — Malakhov, Sochi 2012; *14.♔b1 c5 15.dxc5 ♘bd7∞*) 14...♘xe4 15.fxe4 c5 16.♔b1 c4 (*16...♖xh2? 17.♗a5 ♕g3 18.♗xb5+ axb5 19.♕xb5+ ♘d7 20.dxc5+-* Potkin — Goganov, Rijeka 2010) 17.♕c2

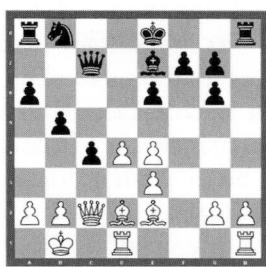

17...♘c6

(17...♘d7 18.e5 (*18.h4!?*) 18...♖c8 Shomoev — Kargin, St.Petersburg 2010 19.h4 (*19.♕e4!?*) 19...b4 20.h5∞)

18.e5 Black can choose between 18...♖c8, and 18...♘b4, with a double-edged struggle in both cases.;

The exchange on g6 makes no sense, since this can be done later with practically any chosen development scheme. The immediate exchange will at best transpose to some other line and one must always consider Black's pressure on the h-file. 10.♘xg6 hxg6 11.0-0-0 dxc4 12.♗xc4 a6 13.♗e2 b5 14.♕c2 c5 15.dxc5 ♕xc5= — It's hard for White to activate his bishops, Bareev — Grachev, Moscow 2010;

10.g3

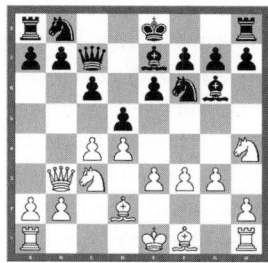

10...♘bd7

a) 10...♗h5 11.♗e2 (*11.0-0-0!?*) 11...g5 12.♘g2 h6 13.♖c1 ♕b6 Karpov — Bacrot, Cannes 2000 14.g4 ♗g6 15.h4±;

b) 10...a6 11.♖c1 dxc4 12.♗xc4 0-0 13.0-0 ♘bd7 14.♘xg6 hxg6 15.♘e2 (*15.♘e4±; The next move is premature 15.e4, since it exposes the black squares. After 15...e5 16.dxe5*

♕*xe5* Black has counter play.) 15...
e5 16.♕c2±;

11.cxd5 (*11.♖c1 — 10.♖c1 ♘bd7
11.g3*) 11...♘xd5 (*11...exd5 12.♘xg6
hxg6 13.e4±*) 12.♘xg6 hxg6

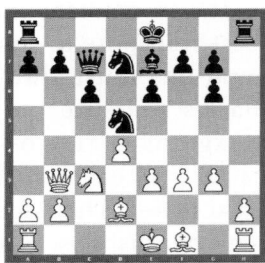

13.♔f2

a) 13.0-0-0 a5! (*13...b5 14.e4 ♘xc3
15.♕xc3 ♖c8 16.♔b1±* Dautov —
Abel, Germany 2012) 14.e4 ♘xc3
15.♗xc3 a4 16.♕c2 a3 17.b3 0-0
18.♔b1 ♖fd8= — The restricted
white squared bishop and the weakened black squares in White's camp
give Black good counter play, Sulashvili — Darmarakis, Rethymno
2010;

b) 13.e4 ♘xc3 14.bxc3 ♖xh2! 15.♖xh2
(*15.♗f4 ♕xf4 16.gxf4 ♗h4+ 17.♔d1
♖xh1∓*) 15...♕xg3+ 16.♖f2 ♗h4
17.0-0-0 ♕xf2 18.♕xb7 ♖d8
19.♕xc6 ♕xf3 20.♗b5 ♗e7 (*20...
♔f8 21.♕c7±*) 21.♖f1 (*21.e5 ♕xc6
22.♗xc6 ♔f8 23.♖h1 ♔g8=* Werle
— S.Ernst, Leeuwarden 2009) 21...
♕g2= — Black wants to move the
king to f8, or exchange the bishops
on g5, solving the problem of the
pinned knight. White has sufficient

compensation for a pawn, due to his
domination of the centre, but nothing else.;

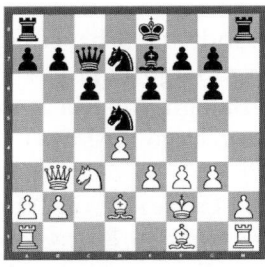

13...♘5f6!?

a) 13...0-0 14.e4 ♘5b6!?∞ (*14...♘xc3
15.bxc3 b5 16.♗e2±* McShane — Yilmaz, Khanty Mansyisk 2010) ;

b) 13...♖d8 14.♔g2 ♘5f6 — *13...♘5f6
14.♔g2 ♖d8;*

c) 13...0-0-0 14.♔g2 f5 15.♖e1 ♔b8
16.e4±;

14.♔g2 ♖d8! (*14...0-0 15.♗e2 e5
16.dxe5 ♘c5 17.♕c2 ♕xe5 18.♖ad1±*)
15.♖d1 e5 16.dxe5 (*16.♗c4 0-0=*)
16...♘c5 17.♕c2 ♕xe5∞ The game
is unclear since after 18.♗e2 Black
needn't be in a hurry to castle and
can use the rook on the h-file to develop counter play 18...♗d6 (Also
of interest is *18...g5!?*, controlling
the black squares and threatening
g5-g4.) 19.♗e1 (*19.f4 ♕f5 20.♕xf5
gxf5=*) 19...♕f5 (*19...g5 20.♗f2±; 19...
♕xe3 20.♘b5 cxb5 21.♗xb5+ ♔f8
22.♗f2 ♕e5 23.♗xc5 ♔g8 24.♗a4
♖c8 25.♖xd6 ♖xc5 26.♕d2 ♘e4
27.♖d8+ ♔h7 28.♖xh8+ ♔xh8*

29.♕e2±) 20.e4 ♕h3+ 21.♔g1 ♘e6 22.♗f2 0-0 23.♖xd6 ♖xd6 24.e5 ♘d4 25.♗xd4 ♖xd4 26.exf6 gxf6 27.♘e4 ♕e6 28.♕c3 ♕e5 29.♔f2 ♖fd8= — Black has sufficient counter play due to his control of the central black squares.

10...♘bd7 11.g3

11.cxd5 ♘xd5 12.♘xg6 hxg6 13.g3 ♘xc3! *(13...a5 14.♔f2 ♘xc3 15.bxc3±* Mchedlishvili — Mamedyarov, Baku 2011) 14.♗xc3 *(14.bxc3 ♖xh2)* 14...0-0-0!∓ — The black King will hide on b8 and there are many weaknesses in White's camp.

11...♘b6

11...♖c8 12.♔f2 0-0 13.♘xg6 hxg6 14.cxd5 ♘xd5 15.♗e2 ♘xc3 16.bxc3± Miroshnichenko — Sandipan, Dubai 2012;

11...dxc4 12.♗xc4 ♖d8

a) 12...0-0 13.♗e2 ♖ad8 14.♘xg6 hxg6 15.f4± Wang Yue — Durarbeyli, Nakhichivan 2011;

b) 12...a6 13.a4 *(13.♗e2 e5 14.♘xg6 hxg6 15.dxe5 ♘c5 16.♕c2 ♕xe5 17.0-0 0-0-0∞)* 13...0-0 *(13...♗h5 14.0-0±)* 14.0-0 e5 15.♘e2± Meier — Hautot, Antwerpen 2010*(15.a5!?±)* ;

13.♘xg6 hxg6 14.0-0 *(14.f4* Lysyi — Kobalia, Khanty Mansyisk 2011 *14...a6 15.♗e2 c5=)* 14...a6 15.a4 0-0 16.♘e2±

12.cxd5 exd5

12...♘fxd5 13.♘xg6 hxg6 14.♔f2 *(14.♘e2±)* 14...♗f6 15.♘e2 *(15.♘e4 ♗e7 16.♘c5±)* 15...♖d8 16.e4 ♘e7 17.♗e3 e5 18.♖d1± Sakaev — Lastin, Moscow 2008

13.♘xg6 hxg6

13...fxg6 14.e4 dxe4 15.fxe4 ♕d7 16.♖d1± White indirectly defends d4, since the capture is bad, after 16...♕xd4 follows 17.♗h6!±

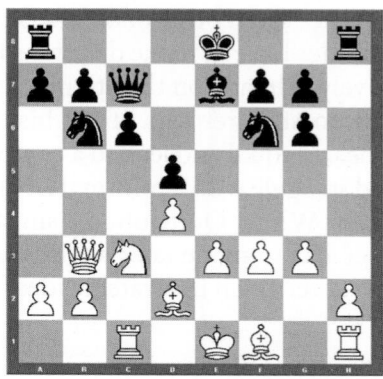

14.♗d3!

In this case there is no sense in hiding the king on f2. White plans to

castle and move the knight to e2. After that he may bolster the centre with
his pieces and play e3-e4.

14...♕d7
14...♖d8 15.0-0±;
14...g5 15.0-0±

15.0-0
15.♘e2 g5 16.e4 dxe4 17.fxe4∞ Galli-
amova — Shadrina, Sochi 2007

15...0-0 16.♘e2±
— sooner or later, White will play
e3-e4, gaining the upper hand. The
variation 4...♗f5 is solid and can be
recommended for both colours and
players keen on a complicated, positional struggle. The main line is
definitely 5.♘c3 e6 6.♗h4, in which
White gains the advantage of two
bishops. In compensation Black has
the more harmonious development
and an excellent pawn structure. At
times there are neither concrete variations nor strict positional criteria —
both sides have to make decisions in-
tuitively. Already on the 6th move all
three possible retreats of the bishop
are nearly equal and lead to a complicated struggle with a minimal advantage for White. Quite often a similar
choice has to made later as the variation is very rich in strategic ideas.

■ GAME 23

1.d4 d5 2.c4 c6 3.♘f3 ♘f6 4.e3 ♗g4 5.h3

5.cxd5 ♗xf3 (White's ideas emerge in the line 5...cxd5 6.♕b3 ♕c7 7.♘c3 ♗xf3 Otherwise ♘f3-e5 is possible. *8.gxf3 e6 9.e4↑*, with an initiative.) 6.♕xf3 cxd5= — Compared to the line 5.h3 ♗h5 6.cxd5 ♗xf3 7.♕xf3 cxd5 White has not played the useful h2-h3, Karimov — Grachev, Tashkent 2012.;

5.♘c3 e6 6.♕b3

(6.h3 ♗h5 — 5.h3 ♗h5 6.♘c3 e6 (6... ♗xf3 7.♕xf3 — 5.h3 ♗xf3 6.♕xf3 e6 7.♘c3))

6...♕b6

(After 6...♕c7, the opposition of the queen and rook on the c-file comes into consideration: 7.♗d2! *(7.♘e5 ♗f5 8.♗d2 ♘bd7=)* 7...♘bd7 8.♖c1 ♖c8 9.♘h4 *(9.h3 ♗xf3 10.gxf3 ♗e7 11.cxd5 ♘xd5 12.f4 0-0 13.♗g2±* Miroshnichenko — Sandipan, Zuerich 2009) 9...dxc4 10.♗xc4 ♘b6 11.♗d3 ♗e7 12.h3 ♗h5 13.g4 ♗g6 14.♘xg6 hxg6 15.g5 ♘fd7 16.♘e4 ♘d5 17.h4± Volkov — I.Sokolov, Nakhichivan 2011)

7.♘h4 *(7.♘e5 ♗f5=)* 7...♗e7 (7... ♘bd7 8.h3 ♗h5 9.g4 ♗g6 10.♘xg6 hxg6 — 5.h3 ♗h5 6.♘c3 e6 7.♕b3 ♕b6 8.♘e5 ♘bd7 9.g4 ♗g6 10.♘xg6 hxg6; 7...♗h5 8.h3 — 5.h3 ♗h5 6.♘c3 e6 7.♕b3 ♕b6 8.♘h4) 8.h3 ♗h5 9.g4 ♗g6 10.♘xg6 hxg6 — 5.h3 ♗h5 6.♘c3 e6 7.♕b3 ♕b6 8.♘e5 ♗e7 9.g4 ♗g6 10.♘xg6 hxg6;

5.♕b3 ♕b6

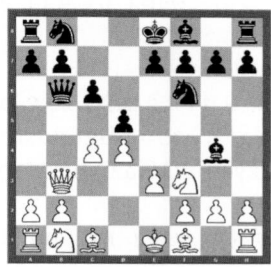

6.♘c3

a) 6.cxd5 ♘xd5

(6...♕xb3 7.axb3 ♗xf3 8.gxf3 cxd5 9.b4 e6 10.♗d2 ♘bd7 (Probably more accurate is 10...♗d6=, keeping the option of ♘b8-c6.) 11.♗c3 ♗d6 12.♘d2 0-0 13.♗e2± Burmakin — Tikkanen, Lille 2011)

7.♘c3 ♕xb3 8.axb3 ♘b4 9.♖a4 e6=;

b) 6.♘e5 ♗f5 7.cxd5 ♕xb3 8.axb3 ♘xd5

9.♘c3

b1) 9.♘a3 f6 (9...♘d7 10.♘xd7 ♗xd7 11.♘c4 a6=) 10.♘ec4 b5 11.♘a5 e5 12.dxe5 ♗b4+ 13.♗d2 Vaganian — Jussupow, Germany 2007 13...fxe5 14.♖c1 0–0∓/↑;

b2) 9.♘d2 ♘b4 10.♖a4 e6 11.e4 ♗g6=;

b3) 9.♗d3 ♗xd3 10.♘xd3 e6 11.♗d2 ♘a6= Batsiashvili — A.Muzychuk, Gaziantep 2012;

9...♘d7 (9...♘b4 10.♖a4 e6 11.e4 ♗g6∞) 10.e4 ♘xc3 11.exf5 ♘d5 12.♗d2 g6=;

6...e6 — 5.♘c3 e6 6.♕b3 ♕b6

5...♗xf3
5...♗h5 6.♘c3

a) 6.cxd5 isn't dangerous 6...♗xf3

(6...cxd5 also leads to equality 7.♕b3 (7.♗b5+ ♘bd7=; 7.♕a4+ ♘bd7 8.♘e5 a6 9.♘c3 e6=; 7.♘c3 e6 8.g4 ♗g6 9.♘e5 ♘fd7 10.♘xg6 hxg6 11.♕b3 ♘b6= Khismatullin

— Ponkratov, Sochi 2008) 7...♕c7 8.♘c3 e6

(8... ♗xf3 is risky 9.gxf3 e6, in view of 10.e4! ♘c6 11.♗f4 ♕d7 12.0–0–0 ♖c8 13.♔b1 ♘a5 14.♕b5 ♘c4 15.exd5 (15.♖c1 ♘h5= I.Popov — Inarkiev, Moscow 2010) 15...♘a3+ 16.bxa3 ♖xc3 17.dxe6 fxe6 18.♕b2 ♕c8 19.♗d2 ♘d5 20.♗b5+ ♔f7 21.♖c1 ♖xc1+ 22.♖xc1 ♕d8 23.f4 g6 24.♗c4±)

9.♘e5 ♘c6 10.♗d2 ♗e7 11.♖c1 0–0=)

7.♕xf3 cxd5 8.♘c3 ♘c6 9.♗d3 (9.♗d2 e6 10.♖c1 ♗d6 11.♗d3 0–0 12.0–0 ♖c8 13.♕e2 a6 14.f4 ♗b4 15.♕f3 ♘a5= Lintchevski — Potkin, Taganrog 2011) 9...e6 10.0–0 (10.g4 g6 11.♗d2 ♖c8 12.♕g2 J.Geller — Ovod, Sochi 2010 12...a6= — Potentially White could have problems later as he has weakened his pawns.) 10...♗e7 11.♗d2 0–0 12.♕e2 ♖c8 13.♖ac1

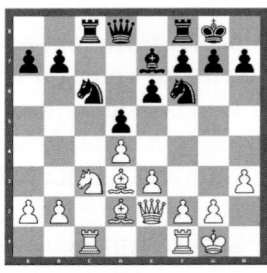

13...g6 With the black squared bishop it's a good idea to place the pawns on white squares. Additionally this is a prophylaxis against f2-f4-f5.

(Also interesting is *13...a6!?*, with the idea of b7-b5 and ♘f6-e8-d6, developing a queenside initiative Tukmakov — Arkhangelsky,Biel2003) 14.♖fd1 ♕d7 15.♗e1 ♖fd8 16.f4 a6= Lenic — Bareev, Rijeka 2010;

b) 6.♕b3 transposes 6...♕b6 (*6... ♕c7 7.♘c3 e6 — 6.♘c3 e6 7.♕b3 ♕c7*) 7.♘c3 (*7.♘e5 e6 8.♘c3 — 6.♘c3 e6 7.♕b3 ♕b6 8.♘e5*) 7...e6 — 6.♘c3 e6 7.♕b3 ♕b6;

6...e6

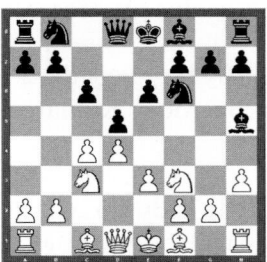

7.♕b3 Only after this move, which has recently become popular, does White have good chances to fight for a small opening advantage.

(7.g4 ♗g6 8.♘e5

(8.♘h4 ♗e4

a) 8...♘bd7 9.♗d2 — 8.♘e5 ♘bd7 9.♘xg6 hxg6 (*9.♘xg6 hxg6; 9.♕b3 ♕c7=*) 9...♗b4 10.♘xg6 hxg6 11.♕b3± Svetushkin — Kazhgaleyev, France 2009;

b) 8...♘fd7 9.♘xg6 — 8.♘e5 ♘fd7 8.♘xg6;

c) 8...♗b4 9.♕b3 c5 10.♘xg6 hxg6 11.♗g2± Rodshtein — Gelfand, Natanya (rapid) 2009;

9.f3

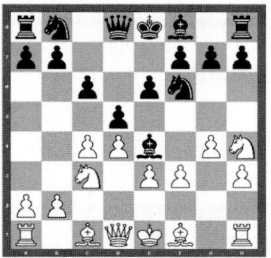

9...♘fd7

(*9...♘h5* N 10.♘g2 ♘g3 11.fxe4! (*11.♖g1 ♗g6 12.♗d3 ♗xd3 13.♕xd3 dxc4 14.♕xc4 h5∞*) 11...♘xh1 12.cxd5⇄/↑ — In addition to a pawn White has a strong central position for the exchange.)

10.♘g2

(10.fxe4 ♕xh4+ 11.♔d2 dxc4 12.♗xc4 b5 13.♗d3 e5 (*13...b4 14.♘e2 c5∞*) 14.♕f3 ♗d6∞ Lysyi — Najer, Zvenigorod 2008)

10...♗g6 11.♕b3

(11.h4 h6 (*11...h5 12.♘f4 hxg4 13.♘xg6 fxg6 14.♗d3±*) 12.♘f4 ♗h7 13.♕b3 ♕c7∞)

11...♕c7 (*11...♘a6 12.a3±*) 12.♘f4

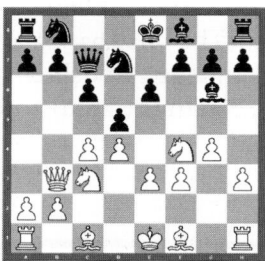

12...dxc4 N

(12...e5

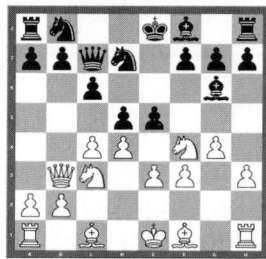

13.♘xg6!N (13.♘cxd5 cxd5 14.♘xd5 ♕c8 15.♗g2 ♘c6 16.f4∞ Khismatullin — Ponkratov, Khanty Mansyisk 2009) 13... hxg6 14.cxd5 exd4 15.exd4 ♗e7 16.♗e3 ♘b6 17.0-0-0 ♘xd5 18.♘xd5 cxd5+ 19.♔b1 ♕d7 20.♗d3 ♘c6 21.h4±/↑)

13.♗xc4 ♗d6 (13...♘b6 14.h4 ♗c2 15.♕xc2 ♘xc4 16.♘e4±) 14.h4 (14. ♘xg6 hxg6 15.♗d2 ♘b6 16.♗e2=) 14...♗xf4 15.exf4 h5 16.♗xe6 0-0 17.♗c4∞)

8...♘bd7 (8...♘fd7 9.♘xg6 hxg6 10.e4 dxe4 11.♘xe4 ♘f6 12.♘c3± Lysyi — Ponkratov, Zvenigorod 2008)

9.♘xg6 (9.h4 dxc4 10.♘xg6 hxg6 11.♗xc4 ♗b4∓ — White's centre is shaky and the kingside pawns are at risk, Rozum — Grachev, Sochi 2012) 9...hxg6 10.a3

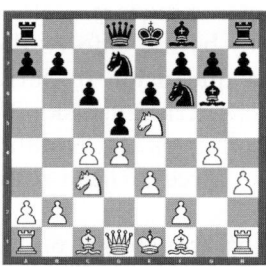

a) 10.♗g2 dxc4 11.♕e2 ♘b6∓;

b) 10.♕b3 ♕c7 11.g5 dxc4 12.♗xc4 ♘d5= Bacrot — Komarov, France 2009;

c) 10.cxd5 exd5 (10...♘xd5 11.e4±) 11.g5 ♘e4!?N (11...♘g8 — 10.g5 ♘g8 11.cxd5 exd5) 12.♘xe4 dxe4 13.h4 ♗b4+ 14.♗d2 ♗xd2+ 15.♕xd2 ♘b6 (15...♕e7=) 16.♕c2 ♕e7 17.♗g2 0-0-0=;

d) 10.♗d2

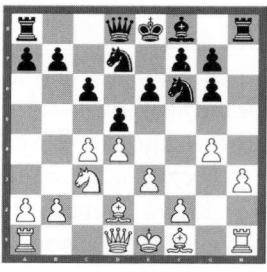

10...♗b4 11.♕b3

d1) 11.cxd5 exd5 12.♗g2

(12.♗d3 ♕e7 13.f3 c5 (13...0-0-0!?) 14.♕e2 0-0 15.0-0 ♖ac8=/∞ Rustemov — Smeets, Germany 2008)

12...♕e7 13.a3

(13.♕c2 ♘b6 14.0-0-0 ♘c4= Exchanging off the black squared bishop or driving it to the extremely miserable square e1.(14...0-0-0 15.♔b1 ♘c4 16.♗c1 ♗xc3 17.♕xc3 ♘e4 18.♕c2 f5 19.f3 ♘ed6± Campos Moreno — M.Gurevich, Lanzarote 2003))

13...♗xc3 14.♗xc3 ♘e4 15.♕c2 ♘xc3 16.♕xc3= Bareev — Nepomniachtchi, Moscow 2010;

d2) 11.♕f3 ♗xc3 12.♗xc3 ♘e4=;

d3) 11.♖c1 ♕e7 12.a3 ♗xc3 13.♗xc3 ♘e4 14.♗g2 (14.♗b4 ♕h4∓) 14...♘xc3 15.♖xc3 ♘b6= Bareev — Najer, Philadelphia 2009;

11...a5 The most reliable

(11...♗xc3 leads to a sharp play 12.♗xc3 ♘xg4

d1) 12...♕c7 13.♗g2 ♘e4 14.cxd5 exd5

(14...cxd5 15.♗xe4 (15.♖c1 ♘df6±) 15...dxe4 16.d5 0-0=)

15.♗xe4 dxe4 16.♕c2 f5 17.♕b3 ♘f6 (17...0-0-0 18.♕e6 ♔b8 19.♕xg6±) 18.gxf5 gxf5 19.♕e6+ ♕e7 20.♕xf5 ♖h5 21.♕g6+ ♕f7±/= The h3 pawn will soon be lost, so material will be equal. Black has many pawn islands but his knight is stronger than the bishop, therefore the position should be equal.;

d2) 12...♘e4 13.♕xb7±;

13.♗g2 (13.♗e2 ♘xf2!? 14.♔xf2 ♕h4+ 15.♔g2 ♕g5+ 16.♔f1 0-0-0∞; 13.♕xb7 ♖b8 14.♕xc6 ♕f6∓) 13...♘h6 14.♕xb7 ♘f5 15.c5 (15.♕xc6 ♖c8 16.♕a6 ♖xc4 17.♕xa7 0-0) 15...♖c8 (15...♕c8 16.♕xc8+ ♖xc8∞) 16.0-0-0 (16.♕xa7 ♕g5∞) 16...0-0∞ Levin — Evseev, St.Petersburg 2012)

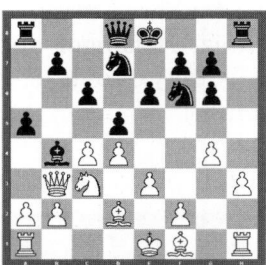

12.♗g2

d1) 12.g5 dxc4 (12...♘e4 13.♘xe4 dxe4 14.♗xb4 axb4 15.h4 ♕a5 16.♗g2 f5 17.gxf6 ♘xf6 18.c5± Vallejo Pons — Najer, Baku 2011) 13.♗xc4 ♘d5 14.e4 a4 15.♕c2 ♘5b6 16.♗e2 a3∞;

d2) 12.f3 dxc4 13.♗xc4 ♘d5= Fridman — Balogh, Germany 2011;

12...♘b6 13.cxd5 exd5 14.g5 ♘fd7 15.h4 ♘c4=;

e) 10.g5

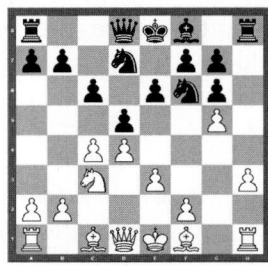

10...♘g8

(10...♘e4 11.♘xe4 dxe4 12.♕g4 ♕a5+

(A less reliable but interesting move 12...♗b4+ 13.♔d1 ♕a5 14.h4 *(14.♕xe4 ♕xg5∞ Nguyen — Roiz, Helsingor 2008)* 14... ♕f5 15.♕g3 0-0-0 16.♔c2 ♗e1 17.♖h2∞)*

13.♔e2

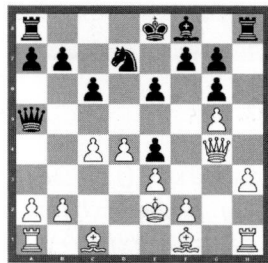

13...♗e7

e1) 13...♕b4 14.♔d1±;

e2) 13...♘b6 14.c5 ♘d5 15.♕xe4±;

e3) 13...0-0-0!? 14.♗g2 ♘b6

*(14...e5 15.♖d1 (15.♗xe4 ♔b8)
15...exd4 16.exd4 ♖e8*

(16...f5 17.gxf6 gxf6 18.♔f1 ♕h5 (18...f5 19.♕xg6 ♗e7 20.d5±) 19.♕xh5 ♖xh5 20.♗xe4 ♖xh3 21.b3±)

17.♗e3±/∞)

15.b3 ♗b4 16.♗b2 ♘d5 17.♕xe4 ♘c3+ 18.♗xc3 ♗xc3 19.♖ac1 ♕xa2+ 20.♖c2 ♕a5 21.♖hc1 ♗b4 22.d5 ♕c5±;

14.♗g2 ♕xg5 *(14...♗xg5 15.♗d2 ♕d8 16.♕xe4±)* 15.♕xg5 ♗xg5 16.♗xe4 0-0-0±/= — e h3 pawn is an island so Black has good counter play, Lysyi — Potkin, Taganrog 2011)

11.♕b3

e1) 11.e4 dxe4 12.♘xe4 ♗b4+ 13.♗d2 ♖h4 14.♗g2 ♕a5 15.a3 *(15.♘d6+ ♔f8∓)* 15...♗xd2+ 16.♕xd2 ♕xd2+ 17.♔xd2 ♘e7 18.♔c3 0-0-0=;

e2) 11.cxd5 exd5 *(11...cxd5!?N 12.♕b3 ♕b6 13.♕xb6 ♘xb6=)* 12.h4 ♘e7 13.♕g4 *(13.h5 gxh5 14.♖xh5 ♖xh5 15.♕xh5 g6 16.♕g4 ♘f5=)* 13...♘b6= Kosic — Jovanic, Zadar 2004;

11...♕c7!N

(11...♕b6

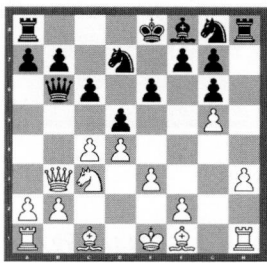

12.c5!N

e1) 12.♕xb6 axb6 13.cxd5 exd5=;

e2) 12.♕c2 ♗b4 (12...♘e7!?) 13.a3
♗xc3+ 14.bxc3 ♘e7= Luukkonen
— Tikkanen, Stockholm 2011;

12...♕c7 (12...♕xb3 13.axb3 a6
14.b4 0-0-0 15.f3±) 13.e4 b6
14.cxb6 axb6 15.♗g2±)

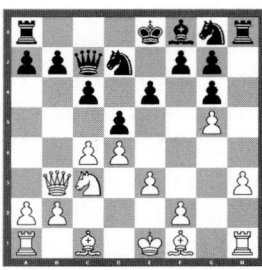

12.♗d2 ♘e7 13.♖c1 ♕b6!=;

10...g5 Black fixes the wing pawn
structure to his advantage and
makes the constricting move g4-
g5 impossible.

a) 10...♗d6 11.g5 ♘h5 12.♕g4±;

b) 10...♕c7 11.g5 ♘g8 12.cxd5 exd5
13.♗d2 ♘e7 14.♗d3± Bareev —
Nepomniachtchi, St.Petersburg
2009;

c) 10...dxc4 11.♗xc4 ♗d6 12.♕f3
(12.g5 ♘d5 13.♘e4 ♗e7∞ Goldin
— D.Gurevich, San Diego 2006)
12...♕e7 13.♗d2 0-0-0 14.0-0-0±;

d) 10...♗e7 11.♕f3 (11.♗d2 g5
12.♕f3 — 10...g5 11.♗d2 ♗e7
12.♕f3) 11...g5 12.♗d2 — 10...g5
11.♗d2 ♗e7 12.♕f3;

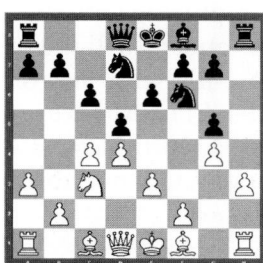

11.♗d2 ♗e7

(It's possible to move the bishop
to a more active square and consider a plan with long castling:
11...♗d6 12.♕f3 (12.c5 ♗c7 13.b4
a6 14.a4 e5= — Black is ready to
transfer the knight via f8 to e6
increasing the pressure on the d4
pawn) 12...♕e7 13.0-0-0 0-0-0
14.♔b1 ♔b8 15.♖c1 ♗c7 16.♖c2
dxc4!? (16...g6 17.♗g2± Ivanchuk
— Potkin, Havana 2012; An interesting plan is 16...♘f8!?, aiming

for g6.) 17.♗xc4 ♘b6=, planning
a future e6-e5 break.)

12.♕f3

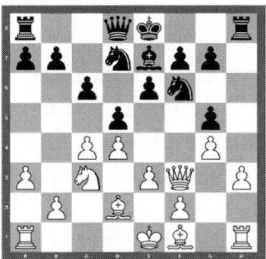

12...g6

a) 12...♕c7 13.cxd5! Now it's not
worth capturing with the c6 pawn
as the queen will be attacked
on the c-file with loss of tempo.
(*13.0-0-0 b5 14.cxb5 cxb5 15.♔b1 b4
16.axb4 ♗xb4 17.♖c1=/∞* Alekseev
— Inarkiev, Olginka 2011) 13...exd5
14.♗d3±/∞;

b) A good option for Black is 12...
♔f8, with possibilit ies of g7-g6
and ♔f8-g7 or simply ♔f8-g8. The
main reply is following idouble-
edged move: 13.0-0-0!?±/∞ (*13.
♖d1 ♔g8 14.♗d3 ♘b6 15.c5 ♘bd7
16.♕g3 e5 17.dxe5 ♘xc5 18.♗f5
♘fd7 19.b4 ♘e6∞* Tomashevsky —
Eljanov, Saratov 2011) ;

13.♗d3 It's worth waiting for some
move with the black king before castling long. (*13.0-0-0 dxc4
14.♗xc4 b5 15.♗d3 a5 16.♘e4 ♘d5
17.♔b1 a4∞* Bareev — Bruzon,
Khanty Mansyisk 2005) 13...♔f8

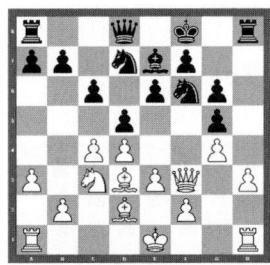

14.0-0-0

a) 14.0-0 ♘c5 (*14...♔g7 15.♖fd1±*)
15.dxc5 dxc4 16.♗xc4 ♕xd2
17.♖fd1 ♕c2 18.♖ab1 ♔g7 19.♖dc1
♕d2 20.♖d1 ♕c2=;

b) 14.cxd5 cxd5 15.0-0 ♔g7=;

14...♔g7 15.♔b1±/∞ — The position is extremely double-edged.
White's chances look slightly preferable.)

7...♕b6

(*7...♕c7 8.♘h4 (8.g4 ♗g6 9.♘e5
♘bd7 10.♘xg6 hxg6 11.♗g2 ♗e7
12.♗d2 ♘b6 13.cxd5 exd5=* Ev-
dokimov — Dubov, Moscow
2012; *8.♗d2 ♘bd7 9.♖c1 ♗xf3
10.gxf3 dxc4 11.♗xc4 ♗e7 12.f4 0-0
13.0-0 ♖ad8 14.♖fd1 ♕b8 15.♗f1
g6 16.♗g2±* Ftacnik — Vitiugov,
Czech 2011) *8...♘bd7 9.♗d2 ♘b6
10.cxd5 exd5 11.♖c1 ♗g6 12.♘xg6
hxg6 13.♗d3 ♗e7 14.0-0±* Bartel
— Caruana, Moscow 2012)

8.♘e5

(After 8.♘h4, a good option is

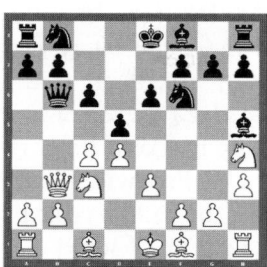

8...g5 (8...♘bd7 9.g4 ♗g6 10.♘xg6 hxg6 — 8.♘e5 ♘bd7 9.g4 ♗g6 10.♘xg6 hxg6; 8...♗e7 9.g4 ♗g6 10.♘xg6 — 8.♘e5 ♗e7 9.g4 ♗g6 10.♘xg6) 9.♘f3

(9.g4 gxh4 10.gxh5 ♘a6

(10...♘bd7 11.♕c2 (11.♗e2 ♕c7 12.♗d2 0-0-0 13.0-0-0 ♖g8=) 11...♗b4 (11...♘xh5=) 12.♗d2 ♗xc3 13.♗xc3 ♘e4 14.♖g1± Dziuba — Nepomniachtchi, Moscow 2009)

11.♗d2 (11.c5 ♕xb3 12.axb3 ♘c7 13.♗e2 ♖g8=) 11...♖g8 12.0-0-0 ♕xb3 13.axb3 ♘e4 14.♘xe4 dxe4= Postny — Sandipan, Germany 2010)

9...h6 10.♘e5

a) 10.♗d3 ♖g8 11.c5

a1) 11.♗d2 ♘bd7 12.♕a4

(12.♕c2 dxc4 (12...♗g6 13.e4 dxe4 14.♘xe4 ♘xe4 15.♗xe4 ♗xe4 16.♕xe4 Le Quang Liem — Paragua, Vietnam 2012 16...0-0-0=) 13.♗xc4 0-0-0 14.0-0-0

♔b8 (14...c5=) 15.e4 ♗g6 16.h4 g4 17.♗f4+ ♔a8 18.♘e5 ♘xe5 19.♗xe5 ♘d5= Nyback — Ragger, Porto Carras 2011)

12...♕b4 13.♕xb4 ♗xb4= Lenic — Hovhannisyan, Martuni 2010;

a2) 11.♕c2 dxc4 12.♗xc4 ♘bd7=;

11...♕c7 12.♕c2 ♘bd7 13.b4 ♗g6 (13...a5 14.b5 e5 15.b6 ♕b8 16.g4 ♗g6 17.♗xg6 ♖xg6 18.♗b2 e4 19.♘d2± S.Zhigalko — Diermair, Plovdiv 2012) 14.♗xg6 ♖xg6 15.♗b2

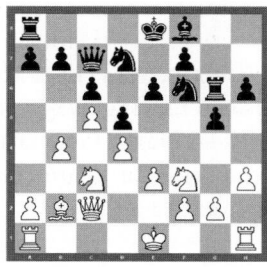

15...h5 (15...♗e7 16.a4 h5 17.♘d2± Ftacnik — Ruck, Germany 2009) 16.♘e2 g4 17.♘e5 ♘xe5 18.dxe5 ♘d7 19.hxg4 ♖xg4 20.♘f4 ♘xe5 21.♖xh5= Eljanov — Sandipan, Plovdiv 2010;

b) 10.g4 ♗g6 11.h4 ♕xb3 12.axb3 gxh4 (12...♘xg4 13.hxg5 ♘a6∞; 12...♖g8 13.hxg5 hxg5 14.c5 ♘xg4 15.b4∞ Morozevich — Smeets, Wijk aan Zee 2009) 13.♖xh4 ♘bd7=;

10...♘fd7 11.♘d3 ♗g6 (11...♘a6 12.h4 ♗g7 13.♕a4 dxc4 14.♕xc4 ♗g6 15.♗d2± Giri — Zontakh, Sochi 2012) 12.h4 (12.♗d2 ♘a6 13.♖c1 ♕xb3 14.axb3 ♘b4 15.♘xb4 ♗xb4= Wang Yue — Aronian, Dresden 2008) 12...g4 13.♗d2 ♘a6 14.♗e2 ♘f5 15.0–0 Mchedlishvili — Smeets, Sestao 2010 15...♕xb3 16.axb3 ♘b4 17.♘xb4 ♗xb4=)

8...♗e7

a) 8...♘fd7 9.♘d3 ♗g6

a1) 9...f6 10.c5 ♕xb3 11.axb3 e5 12.b4± Sakaev — Ovod, St.Petersburg 2010;

a2) 9...♘a6 10.♕a4 (10.♕xb6 axb6 11.♘f4 ♗g6 12.♘xg6 hxg6 13.♗d2± Parligras — Najer, Germany 2010) 10...dxc4 11.♘f4 ♗g6 12.♘xg6 hxg6 13.♗xc4±;

a3) 9...♕xb3 10.axb3 ♗g6 11.♗d2 ♘a6 12.c5 ♘c7 13.b4 a6 14.♘f4 ♗c2 15.♗d3 ♗xd3 16.♘xd3 g6= Caruana — Balogh, Plovdiv 2012;

10.♕d1

a1) 10.♕a4

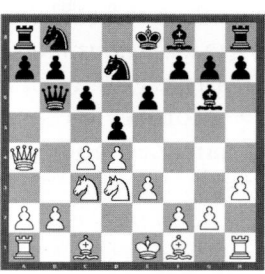

10...♕d8!N (10...♕a6 11.♕xa6 ♘xa6 12.♘f4 ♘b4 13.♘xg6 hxg6 14.♖b1±; 10...♕c7 11.♘f4 ♘b6 12.♕a5 dxc4 13.♗xc4±; 10...dxc4 11.♘f4 e5 12.♘xg6 hxg6 13.♗xc4± Navara — Froewis, Plovdiv 2012) 11.♘f4 ♘b6 12.♕b3 dxc4 13.♗xc4 ♘xc4 14.♕xc4 ♘d7=;

a2) 10.♗e2 ♗e7 11.0–0 0–0 12.♕d1 ♕c7 13.b3± Reshetnikov — A.Kharitonov, Moscow 2011;

10...h6 (10...dxc4 11.♘f4 ♕a6 12.h4 e5 13.h5 ♗f5 14.g4 exf4 15.gxf5±/↑) 11.♘f4 ♗h7 12.♘h5 ♕d8

(12...♗g6 13.♗e2 (13.a3±) 13...♗xh5 14.♗xh5 ♘f6 (14...dxc4 15.♗e2 ♕a6 16.0–0±) 15.♗e2± Efimenko — Shaw, Khanty Mansyisk 2010)

13.♗e2± Lupulescu — Najer, Germany 2011;

b) 8...♘bd7 9.g4

(9.♘d3 ♗g6 10.♕xb6 axb6 11.♘f4 ♗d6 (11...♗c2=) 12.♘xg6 hxg6 13.♗d2 0–0= Azmaiparashvili — Movsesian, Moscow 2001)

9...♗g6 10.♘xg6 hxg6 11.♗g2 g5 (11...♕c7 12.♗d2 ♘b6 13.cxd5 exd5 14.0–0–0 0–0–0 15.♔b1 ♔b8 16.♗c1±/∞ Vidit — Grigoriants, Moscow 2012) 12.0–0 ♗e7 — 8...♗e7 9.g4 ♗g6 10.♘xg6 hxg6 11.♗g2 g5 12.0–0 ♘bd7;

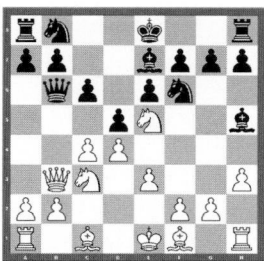

9.g4 ♗g6 10.♘xg6 hxg6 11.♗g2 g5 12.0–0

(12.♗d2 ♘bd7 13.0–0–0 (13.♕a4 ♕c7 14.cxd5 exd5 15.♕c2 ♘b6 16.b3 a5 17.♖c1 ♕d7±/∞ Tomashevsky — Sjugirov, Moscow 2009) 13...a5 (13...0–0–0!?) 14.♕xb6 ♘xb6 15.c5 ♘bd7)

12...♘bd7 13.♖d1

(The next move doesn't really make sense 13.♖e1 — Black can counter the threat of opening the e-file in various ways. 13...♔f8 (13...0–0–0!?; 13...dxc4 14.♕xc4 ♘d5= — Black intends to castle short and play ♖ac8. Then c6-c5 could be played at an opportune moment.) 14.cxd5 ♕xb3 15.axb3 ♘xd5 16.♘xd5 exd5 17.e4 dxe4 18.♖xe4 ♘b6 19.♗d2 a6= Dreev — Inarkiev, Sochi 2012)

13...♕b4 14.♕xb4 ♗xb4 15.cxd5 ♘xd5 16.♘xd5 exd5 17.e4± Lysyi — Inarkiev, Moscow 2012

6.♕xf3

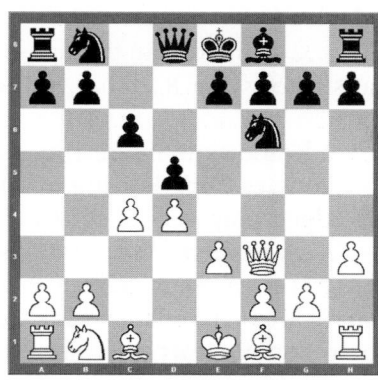

6...e6 7.♘c3

7.♗d3 ♗b4+

(7...♘bd7 8.0–0 ♗d6 9.♘c3 — 7.♘c3 ♘bd7 8.♗d3 ♗d6 9.0–0(9. ♘d2 0–0 10.e4 dxe4 11.♘xe4 — 7.♘c3 ♘bd7 8.♗d3 ♗d6 9.0–0 0–0 10.e4 dxe4 11.♘xe4))

8.♘d2 (8.♘c3 ♘bd7 — 7.♘c3 ♘bd7 8.♗d3 ♗b4; 8.♗d2 ♗xd2+ 9.♘xd2 0–0 10.0–0 ♘bd7 11.♖fd1 ♕e7 12.♖ac1 ♖fe8 13.♗b1 g6 14.a3 a5= Zhou Weiqi — Ni Hua, Beijing 2012) 8...0–0 9.0–0 ♘bd7 10.a3

(10.♕d1 ♗d6 11.c5 (11.♘f3 ♘e4=) 11...♗c7= Lysyi — Vasquez, Moscow 2009)

10...♗a5 (10...♗xd2 11.♗xd2 dxc4 12.♗xc4 e5 13.♗c3± Ni Hua — Paragua, Vietnam 2012) 11.b4 ♗c7 12.♗b2 e5=

7...♘bd7

7...♗e7 8.♗d2 (8.♗d3 0–0 9.0–0±) 8...0–0 9.g4 ♘bd7 10.g5 ♘e8 11.h4 f5±/∞ Vallejo Pons — Acs, Germany 2012

8. ♗d3

After 8. ♗d2, Black can transpose to a satisfactory line: 8... ♗b4

(8... ♗d6 allows an interesting plan with long castling leading to double-edged play: 9.0-0-0!? (9.♕e2 0-0 10.g3 dxc4 11.♕xc4 e5 12.dxe5 ♗xe5 13.♗g2 ♘b6 14.♕e2 ♘bd5 15.0-0 ♕e7= Landa — Makarov, Sochi 2009; 9.cxd5 exd5 10.g4 0-0 11.g5 ♘e8 12.h4∞ Potkin — Caruana, Sochi 2010; 9.g4) 9...0-0 (9...♕e7 10.♔b1 0-0 11.g4 dxc4 12. ♗xc4 ♘d5±/∞ Meier — Berkes, Paks 2009) 10.♔b1 a5 (10...dxc4 11.♗xc4 c5 12. ♗b3±/∞ Kazhgaleyev — Stellwagen, France 2009) 11.g4 dxc4 (11... ♗b4 12.g5 ♗xc3 13.gxf6 ♗xd2 14.fxg7 ♔xg7 15.♖xd2 ♕f6 16. ♕d1± Tregubov — Laznicka, Germany 2007) 12. ♗xc4 ♘d5∞)

9.♗d3 0-0 — 8.♗d3 ♗b4 9.♗d2 0-0

8... ♗b4

8...dxc4 9.♗xc4 ♗d6 10.0-0 0-0 11.e4 e5 12.d5 ♘b6 13.♗d3 cxd5 14.exd5 h6 15.♗e3± Ivanchuk — Gelfand, Moscow 2009;

8...g6 9.0-0 ♗g7 10.cxd5 cxd5 11. ♗d2 0-0 12.♖fc1 a6 13.♕d1± — White has serious pressure in the queenside, Jakovenko — Postny, Spain 2008;

8... ♗d6

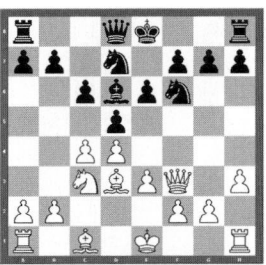

9.cxd5

a) 9.g4 It's interesting but risky to start a flank attack with an undefined centre: 9...dxc4 10. ♗xc4 0-0 11. ♗d2 ♘d5=/∞ Riazantsev — Grachev, Novokuznetsk 2008;

b) 9.0-0 The straightforward approach yields nothing tangible: 9...0-0 10.e4

(10. ♗d2 ♖e8 (10...♕e7 11.cxd5 cxd5 12.♖ac1 ♖ac8 13.e4 dxe4 14.♘xe4 ♘xe4 15. ♗xe4 Malakhov — So, Khanty Mansyisk (rapid) 2009 15... ♘f6! 16.♗g5 h6 17. ♗xf6 ♕xf6=) 11.♕d1 (11.cxd5 exd5=) 11...dxc4 12. ♗xc4 ♕e7 13.♕c2 e5= Cheparinov — Aronian, Sochi 2008)

10...dxe4 11.♘xe4 ♘xe4 12. ♗xe4 (12.♕xe4 ♘f6 13.♕f3 e5 14.♗g5 h6 15. ♗xf6 ♕xf6 16.♕xf6 gxf6= Bu Xiangzhi — Ni Hua, Biel 2011) 12...♘f6

(12...♕h4 13.♗e3 (13.♖d1 ♘f6 14. ♗c2 ♖fd8 15. ♗e3 ♗c7 16.b4± Bu Xiangzhi — Aronian, Sofia 2008) 13...♘f6 14. ♗c2 ♖ad8 15.♖ad1±)

13. ♗c2

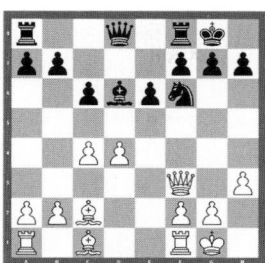

13...h6

(13...♕a5 14.♖d1 ♖fd8 15.♗d2 (15. g4!?) 15...♗b4 16.♗e3 ♗f8 17.a3 ♖d7 18.b4 ♕d8 19.♖ab1 ♖c8 20.a4! (20. ♖b3 b5!= Bu Xiangzhi — Aronian, Yerevan 2008) 20...h6 21.♗d3± After ♗d3-f1 White plans the advance b4-b5 to create weaknesses on Black's queenside.)

14.♗d2

(14.♖d1 ♖e8 15.♗d2 ♕e7 16.a3 (16. ♗c3 ♗b4=) 16...e5 17.♖e1 e4 18.♕b3 ♖ad8=)

14...e5 (14...♗c5 15.♕g3!±; 14...♕e7 15.a3!±) 15.dxe5 ♗xe5 16.♖ad1 ♕c7 17.b4 ♖fe8 18.♖fe1 ♖ad8±/= — Black must be equal due to his piece centralisation.;

9...exd5

(9...cxd5 10.0-0 ♗e7

a) 10...♕b6 11.a3 ♖c8 12.♗d2 0-0 (12...♕xb2 13.♕e2±) 13.b4 ♗b8 14.g3± Melkumyan — Caruana, Moscow 2008;

b) 10...0-0 11.e4± — If the knights are exchanged on e4, the pawns at b7 and h7 will be simultaneously attacked, Aronian — Fressinet, Paris 2009;

11.e4 dxe4

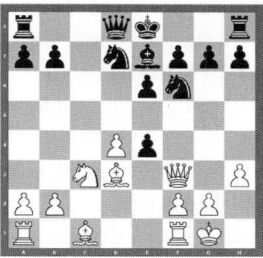

12.♗xe4! ♘xe4 13.♕xe4 b6

a) 13...♕b6 14.d5 0-0 (14...♘c5 15.♕e2 0-0 16.♗e3±) 15.dxe6 (15. ♗e3 ♕xb2 16.dxe6 ♘f6 17.♕e5±/↑) 15...fxe6 16.♗e3±;

b) 13...0-0 14.♕xb7 ♗f6 15.♖d1± Grachev — Predojevic, Rijeka 2008;

14.d5±)

10.g4! Expansion on the kingside is almost the main path in this variation. Chasing away the f6 knight is possible because e4 is well controlled.

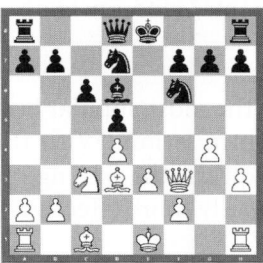

10...g6

a) 10...0–0 11.g5 (*11.♗d2 ♗b4*) 11...
♘e8 12.h4 ♕e7 (*12...♗b4 13.♕f5 g6
14.♕h3↑*) 13.♗d2 f5 14.0–0–0±/∞
Malakhov — Beliavsky, Sibenik
2010;

b) 10...♘b6 11.♗d2 ♕e7 12.0–0–
0 0–0–0 13.g5 ♘e8 14.e4 dxe4
15.♘xe4± Khismatullin — Romanov, Zvenigorod 2008;

11.♗d2 ♘f8 (*11...♕e7 12.0–0–0 ♗b4
13.♔b1± Malakhov — Kuzubov,
Helsingor 2009*) 12.0–0–0

(12.g5 ♘h5 (*12...♘6d7 13.e4±/↑*)
13.e4 ♘e6 14.exd5 cxd5 15.h4∞)

12...♘e6 13.♔b1 ♕e7 14.♕g2 0–0–0
15.f3 ♘d7 16.f4 ♘b6 17.♖hf1±/∞

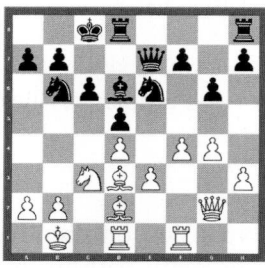

White plans the constricting advance of the f-pawn, Riazantsev —
Grigoriants, Moscow 2009

9.0–0

9.♗d2 The most popular but not the
best continuation. With the white
bishop on d2, the freeing break e6-
e5 is usually more effective.

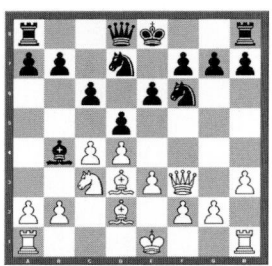

9...0–0 (*9...dxc4 10.♗xc4 e5 11.0–0
0–0 12.♖ad1 ♖e8 13.♗b3± Sargissyan — Navara, Germany 2008*) 10.a3

(After 10.0–0 the following equalises immediately 10...♘c5! 11.dxc5
dxc4 12.♘e4 (*12.♗xh7+ ♘xh7
13.♖fd1 ♗xc5 14.♕e4 ♘f6 15.♕xc4
♕e7=*) 12...♗xd2 13.♗xc4 ♘xe4
14.♕xe4 ♗a5=)

10...♗a5

a) 10...♗xc3 11.♗xc3 c5 12.dxc5 (*12.cxd5
♘xd5 13.0–0 ♖c8±/= Bareev — Gustafsson, Mainz (rapid) 2010; 12.b3±*) 12...
♘xc5 13.♖d1 ♘a4 (*13...♘fe4 14.♗b4±*)
14.♗d4!N (*14.♗xf6 ♕xf6 15.♕xf6 gxf6
16.cxd5 ♘xb2= Landa — Gustafsson,
Reggio Emilia 2008*)

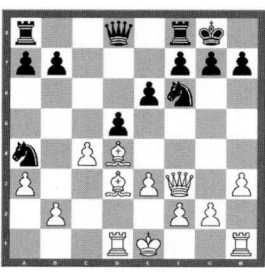

14...dxc4 15.♗xc4 ♖c8 16.b3 ♕a5+
17.b4 ♕c7 18.♗b3 e5 19.♗a1±;

b) 10...dxc4 11.♗xc4 ♗d6

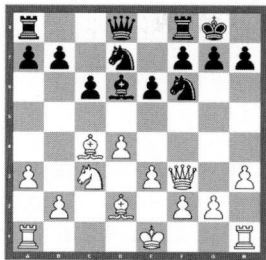

12.♘e4!N

b1) 12.♗a2 ♕b6 13.♖b1 c5 14.dxc5 ♘xc5∓ Tregubov — Smeets, Germany 2008;

b2) 12.♕e2 e5

(12...♕e7 13.0-0 (13.f4 c5=) 13...e5 14.dxe5 ♗xe5 15.♖fd1 ♘c5= Tregubov — Huzman, Kallithea 2008)

13.d5 e4 14.dxc6 bxc6=;

12...♘xe4 13.♕xe4±;

11.0-0

a) 11.b4 dxc4 12.♗xc4 ♗c7 13.♗b3 ♖e8 14.0-0 e5= Kazhgaleyev — I.Sokolov, Baku 2008;

b) 11.cxd5

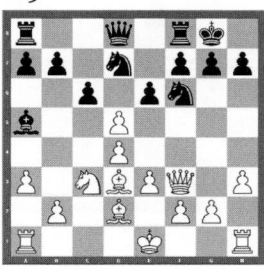

11...exd5!

(11...cxd5 12.0-0 — 9.0-0 0-0 10.a3 ♗a5 11.cxd5 cxd5 12.♗d2

(12.b4 ♗c7 (12...♗b6 13.0-0 ♖e8 14.♗c2 ♖c8 15.♗b3 ♗c7 16.♖fc1 ♗b8= Sargissyan — Roiz, Crete 2007) 13.0-0 ♘b6 14.♖ac1 ♖c8= Rustemov — Postny, Germany 2007))

12.b4 ♗c7 13.b5 ♖e8 14.bxc6 bxc6 15.0-0 ♘f8 16.♕d1

b1) 16.g3 ♘e6 17.♕g2 ♘g5 18.f3 ♖b8∓/∞ — White's kingside pawn structure is too vulnerable, Lysyi — Vitiugov, Serpukhov2008;

b2) 16.♖fc1 ♘e6 17.h4 ♖b8 18.♗f5 ♕d6 (18...g6=) 19.g3 c5= Van Wely — Potkin, Sochi 2008;

16...♘e6 17.♕c2 (17.♕a4 c5 18.♘b5 ♗b6 19.dxc5 ♘xc5 20.♕c2 ♘fe4 21.♗b4 ♘xd3 22.♕xd3 ♕d7= Gelfand — Kramnik, Nice (blindfold) 2008) 17...c5 18.dxc5 ♘xc5 19.♘b5 ♗b6= Lysyi — Movsesian, Moscow 2011;

11...♖e8 (11...♘c5 12.dxc5 dxc4 13.♗xh7+ ♔xh7 14.♖fd1± Meier — I.Popov, Budva 2009) 12.♕d1

a) 12.♖fd1 e5=;

b) 12.b4 ♗c7 13.♖ac1 dxc4 14.♗xc4 e5 15.♗b3 exd4 (15...♕e7=) 16.exd4 ♘b6 17.♗g5 h6 18.♗xf6 ♕xf6

19.♕xf6 gxf6±/= Aronian — Cheparinov, Sofia 2008;

12...♗c7 (12...e5 13.cxd5 cxd5 14.♖c1 e4 15.♗e2 ♘f8 16.♕a4 ♗b6 17.♕b3± Efimenko — Movsesian, Germany 2011) 13.♕c2

a) 13.b4 e5 14.cxd5 cxd5 15.♘b5 e4 16.♘xc7 ♕xc7 17.♖c1 ♕d6 18.♗e2 ♖ec8 19.♕a4± (19.♕b3 ♘b6 20.a4 ♕e6= Potkin — Andriasian, Belgorod 2010) ;

b) 13.♖c1 a6 (13...dxc4 14.♗xc4 ♘b6 15.♗e2 e5 16.dxe5 ♗xe5 17.♕c2±/=; 13...♕e7!?) 14.♕b3 ♖b8 15.♖fd1 ♘b6 16.♗e1 dxc4 17.♗xc4 ♘xc4 18.♕xc4 ♕d6 19.g3±/= Roiz — Harikrishna, Bursa 2010;

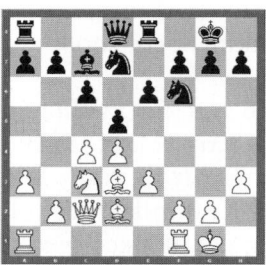

13...♕e7 14.♖fd1 dxc4 15.♗xc4 ♘b6 16.♗f1 e5 17.♗e1 (17.dxe5 ♕xe5 18.g3 h5 19.h4 19...g5! If White is allowed to regroup his pieces or exchange the queens, his position will become better because of the two bishops. 20.hxg5 ♕xg5 21.e4 ♕g4 22.♗e2 ♕h3 23.♗f1 ♕g4= Navara — Le Quang Liem, Wijk aan Zee 2011) 17...h5 (17...♖ad8 18.dxe5 ♕xe5 19.g3 h5 20.♗g2 h4 21.♖xd8 ♖xd8 22.g4±

Alekseev — Ragger, Khanty Mansyisk (rapid) 2011) 18.♘e4 ♘xe4 19.♕xe4 ♖ad8 20.♗c3 ♘d5=;

9.a3 ♗a5

(9...♗xc3+ 10.bxc3 ♕a5 (10...0-0 11.0-0 — 9.0-0 0-0 10.a3 ♗xc3 11.bxc3) 11.♗d2 ♘b6 12.c5 ♘c4 13.♗xc4 dxc4 14.0-0 0-0 15.♖fb1 ♖ab8 16.e4± Vitiugov — Ragger, Germany 2012)

10.0-0 0-0 — 9.0-0 0-0 10.a3 ♗a5

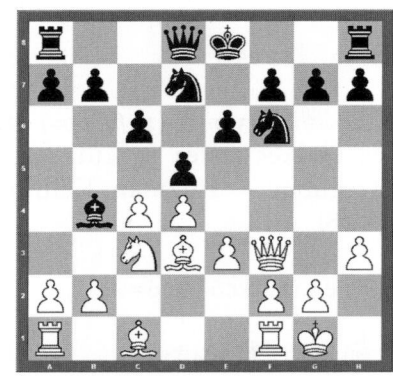

9...0-0

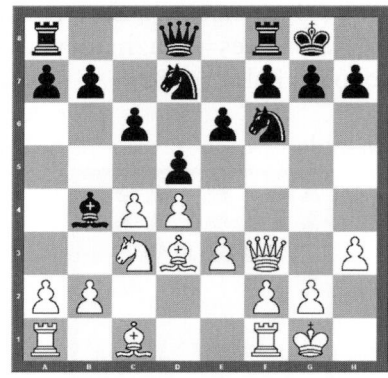

10.a3

10.♕d1 dxc4 (*10...♕e7 11.♕b3 dxc4 12.♗xc4 ♘b6 13.♗e2 ♖fd8 14.♖d1 ♖d7*= Rodshtein — Ruck, Crete 2007) 11.♗xc4 e5 12.♕b3 (*12.a3 ♗d6*=) 12...♕b6 13.♖d1 ♖ad8! (*13...exd4 14.exd4 ♗a5 15.♗f4 ♕xb3 16.axb3 ♗b4 17.d5 ♗xc3 18.bxc3 cxd5 19.♗xd5 ♘xd5 20.♖xd5 ♘f6 21.♗b5 b6* Roiz — Pikula, Zlatibor 2008 *22.c4±*) 14.♗d2 ♗a5!=;

10.♖d1 ♘b6! (*10...♖e8 11.♕e2 a6 12.♗d2 ♗a5 13.♗e1 ♗c7 14.♖ac1 ♕e7 15.♕c2 ♖ad8 16.♕b3 dxc4 17.♗xc4 ♘b6 18.♗f1 e5 19.dxe5 ♕xe5 20.g3±* Ivanchuk — Karjakin, Nice (rapid) 2010) 11.c5 (*11.cxd5 cxd5 12.♗d2 ♖c8*=) 11...♘bd7 12.a3 ♗a5 13.b4 ♗c7= Anand — Gelfand, Nice (rapid) 2008

10...♗a5

10...♗xc3 11.bxc3 e5 (*11...♘b6 12.c5 ♘bd7 13.c4 ♖e8 14.♕d1 e5 15.cxd5 ♘xd5 16.♕c2±* Sakaev — Kreisl, Budva 2009; *11...♕a5 12.♗d2 e5 13.cxd5 cxd5 14.♕e2±* Malakhov — Harikrishna, Montcada 2009) 12.♕d1 e4 13.♗e2 ♘b6 14.c5 ♘c4 (*14...♘bd7 15.c4±* Ponkratov — Semcesen, Stockholm 2009) 15.♕a4±

11.b4

11.cxd5 cxd5 (*11...exd5 12.b4 ♗c7 13.b5 ♖e8 14.a4 ♘f8 15.♗a3!±* Black cannot play ♕d8-d6, weakening White's kingside, Wang Yue — Aronian, Nice (rapid) 2009) 12.♗d2 ♖c8

a) 12...♖e8

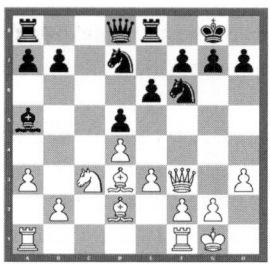

13.♖ac1 ♖c8 — 12...♖c8 13.♖ac1 ♖e8

(13...e5 14.♕d1±

a1) 14.♗b1 exd4 15.exd4 ♗xc3 16.♕xc3 (*16.♗xc3 ♘e4*= Lysyi — Shimanov, Ulan Ude 2009) 16...♘e4 17.♕d3±;

a2) 14.♗c2 exd4 15.exd4 ♗xc3 16.♕xc3 Bacrot — Karjakin, Khanty Mansyisk 2007 16...♘e4 17.♕d3 g6 18.♗f4±;);

b) 12...e5

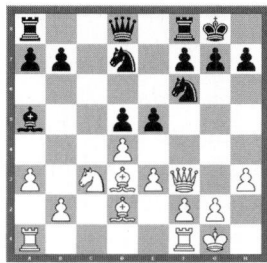

13.♗c2!N

b1) 13.♕d1 ♗b6 14.♕a4 exd4 15.exd4 ♘b8 16.♗g5±;

b2) 13.♕f5 ♖e8 14.♖ac1

b21) 14.♖fd1 g6 15.♕g5 exd4 16.exd4 ♘f8 (*16...♗xc3 17.♗xc3*

♘b6 18.♗a5± Lysyi — Bindrich, Moscow 2008) 17.♕h4 ♘e6=;

b22) 14.♗b5 g6 15.♕g5 a6 (*15... ♖e6* Bacrot — Harikrishna, Wijk aan Zee 2008 *16.♖ad1±*) 16.♗xd7 (*16.♗a4 b5 17.♗b3 exd4 18.exd4 ♘b6=*) 16...♘xd7 17.♕xd8 ♖axd8 18.b4 ♗b6 19.♘xd5 exd4=;

14...g6 15.♕g5 ♗b6= Pelletier — De La Riva Aguado, Dresden 2008;

13...♖c8 14.♖ac1±;
c) 12...♘b8

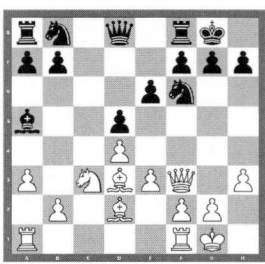

13.♕e2 ♘c6 14.b4 ♗c7 15.f4 a5 (*15... ♖c8 16.♖fc1 ♗d6 17.♖c2 a6 18.♘a4 ♘e4 19.♘c5±*) 16.b5 ♘e7 17.♖fc1 ♗d6 18.♘a4 b6 19.♗e1± V.Popov — Smeets, Aix les Bains 2011;

13.♖ac1

(*13.♖fd1 ♖e8 (13...♘b8!?) 14.e4 dxe4 15.♗xe4 ♘xe4 (15...♗xc3 16.♗xc3 ♘xe4 17.♕xe4 ♕b6 18.d5±* Bareev — Grigoriants, Serpukhov 2007) *16.♘xe4 ♗xd2 17.♘d6 ♗g5 18.♕xf7+ ♔h8=*)

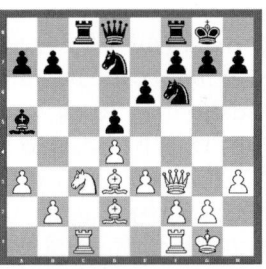

13...♖e8 14.b4 (*14.♕d1 ♗c7 15.♕b3 ♘b6 16.♖c2 ♗b8 17.♖fc1±/=*) 14...♗b6

(14...♗c7 15.e4 (*15.♘b5 ♗b8 16.♖xc8 ♕xc8 17.♖c1 ♕d8 18.♘c3±*) 15...dxe4 16.♘xe4 ♘d5 17.♘c5 b6 18.♘e4±)

15.a4 (*15.♘a4 ♗c7 16.♘c5 ♘xc5 17.bxc5 e5 18.♗f5 ♖b8 19.♗c2±/=*) 15... e5 16.♗b1 exd4 17.exd4 ♘f8 18.♗a2 ♗xd4 19.♘xd5 ♘e6 20.♘xf6+ ♗xf6

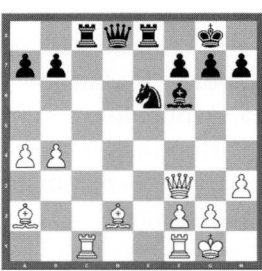

21.♗e3!± (*21.♗xe6 fxe6 22.♖xc8 ♕xc8 23.♗e3 a6±/=* Bacrot — Shaw, Liverpool 2008)

11... ♗c7 12. ♗b2
12.cxd5 cxd5 13.e4 dxe4

(13...e5 14.♗g5 (*14.♘xd5 ♘xd5 15.exd5 exd4 16.d6 ♗xd6 17.♕e4*

♘f6 18.♕xb7±) 14...h6 15.♗h4
g5 16.♗g3 exd4 17.♘xd5 ♗xg3
18.♕xg3± Timofeev — Balogh,
Moscow 2008)

14.♘xe4

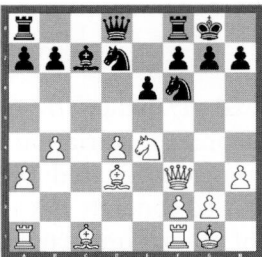

14...h6 (14...♖c8 15.♖e1 ♘xe4
16.♗xe4 b5 17.♗c6±) 15.♘c5 Weakening the white squares in the
Black's camp.

(15.♗d2 ♘xe4! (15...♘d5 16.♖ac1±)
16.♗xe4 ♘e5! 17.dxe5 ♕xd2
18.♗xb7 ♖ad8= — The e5 pawn
will be lost so the game is equal.)

15...b6 (White has a small advantage after 15...♘xc5 16.dxc5 ♗e5
17.♖a2 ♕c7 18.♖c2± — the advanced
queenside pawns pose a potential
threat.) 16.♘xd7 ♘xd7

(16...♕xd7 17.♗xh6 ♕xd4 18.♖ac1
♕d5 19.♗xg7 (19.♕xd5 ♘xd5
20.♗d2 ♗f4 21.♗xf4 ♘xf4 22.♗a6
♖fd8=) 19...♕xf3 20.gxf3 ♔xg7
21.♖xc7 ♘d5 22.♖c4 ♖h8 23.♔h2
f5 24.♖fc1 ♖ad8±/= White has an
extra pawn so he can play for a win.
But his bishop is restricted and his
king is out of play on the h-file.
Black should be able to draw.)

17.♗e4

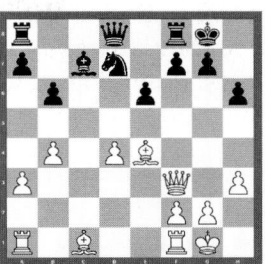

17...♖c8!N (17...♖b8 doesn't neces-
sitate ♗e4-b7 and therefore gives
White other possibilities, Schlosser
— Levin, Austria 2008) 18.♗b7 ♖b8
19.♗c6 ♘f6 20.♗b2 ♘d5=

12...♖e8

12...♘b6 13.c5 ♘bd7 14.b5 e5
15.♕d1±;

12...♕e7 13.♖ac1 dxc4 14.♗xc4
e5 15.♘e4 exd4 16.♘xf6+ ♘xf6
17.♗xd4± Harikrishna — Neelotpal,
Goa 2002

13.♖fd1

13.cxd5 cxd5 (13...exd5 14.b5 ♘f8 15.a4
♘e6 16.♗a3 ♗d6 17.bxc6 bxc6= — The
extra time White spent on transferring
the bishop to a3 is evident. Black has
no problems.) 14.♖ac1 ♘b6 15.♕d1
♖c8 (15...a6=; 15...♘c4!?∞) 16.♘a4 (16.
♘b5 ♗b8=) 16...♕d6 17.g3 ♘c4 (Less
accurate is 17...♘xa4 18.♕xa4 ♗b6
Wang Yue — Rodshtein, Pamplona
2007 19.♖c2± The bishop's position on
b6 is bad, and White has succeeded in
controlling the c-file. Therefore his position is better.) 18.♕e2 ♘xb2 (18...♕c6
19.♘c5 b6 20.♘b3 b5=) 19.♕xb2 ♕e7=;

13.♖ac1 ♘b6! 14.c5 ♘bd7 15.♕d1 e5 16.b5 exd4 17.exd4 ♘f8= Black has a good game and after the straightforward 18.♕a4 strong is 18...h5! 19.bxc6 ♕g5!↑, developing an initiative.

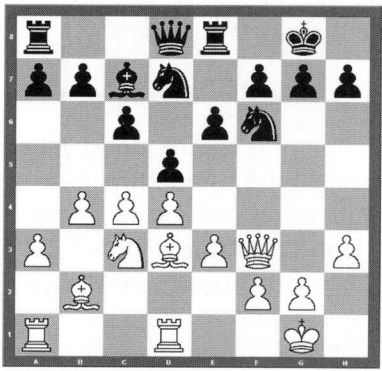

13...♘b6!N

A typical manoeuver which has not been played in this variation yet.

13...♕e7 14.♕e2 e5 (14...♖ad8 15.♖ac1 a6 16.♕c2±) 15.dxe5 (15.♕c2? 15...exd4 16.exd4 dxc4 17.♗xc4 ♘b6∓ Dao Thien Hai — Wang Rui, Kuala Lumpur 2007) 15...♕xe5 16.g3 dxc4 17.♗xc4±

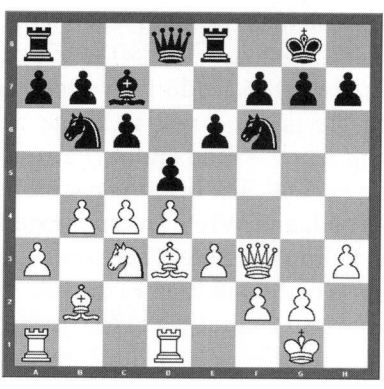

14.c5

14.♕e2 dxc4 15.♗xc4 ♕d6 16.g3 ♘xc4 17.♕xc4 ♘d5=

14...♘bd7 15.b5 e5

The d1 rook occupies the square which the queen could use to reach a4.

16.♗c2 exd4 17.exd4 ♘f8=/∞

Conclusion: The variation 4...♗g4 leads to a complicated positional struggle. Also concrete lines are usually not of crucial importance. There are several nearly equal possibilities and plans in many positions. Regarding the popular variation 5. h3 ♗xf3 6.♕xf3 e6 7.♘c3 ♘bd7 8.♗d3 ♗b4, here not developing the bishop on d2 is the key, only this development scheme looks interesting. Another important line 5.h3 ♗h5 6.♘c3 e6 provides White with options depending on the player's style. One possibility is 7.g4 ♗g6 8.♘e5 ♘bd7 9.♘xg6 hxg6, and here the line 10.a3 g5 11.♗d2 is of principal interest. Later the queen moves to f3, after which a plan with long castling leads to an interesting double-edged struggle. Another line — 7.♕b3 ♕b6 8.♘e5, leads to a quieter game with slightly better chances for White.

■ GAME 24

1.d4 d5 2.c4 c6 3.♘f3 ♘f6 4.♘c3 ♛b6

This rare move is regularly defended at the top level by Gata Kamsky. Black prevents the development of White's black squared bishop and wants to place his bishop on g4. After the exchange of bishop for knight, Black plans to play e7-e6 building a very strong fortress. The next move deserves particular attention

The following is bad 4...♗g4, since Black cannot continue with comfortable development. 5.♘e5 ♗h5

a) 5...♗f5 6.cxd5 cxd5 7.e4! ♘xe4 (7...dxe4 8.♛b3+-) 8.♘xe4 dxe4 9.♗c4 e6 10.♗b5+±/→;

b) 5...e6 6.cxd5±;

c) 5...♗e6 6.cxd5 cxd5 7.♗f4±;

6.f3! Problems have appeared for the white squared bishop. (Also leading to a better game is *6.cxd5 ♘xd5 7.♛b3 ♘b6 8.g4 ♗g6 9.♗f4±*)

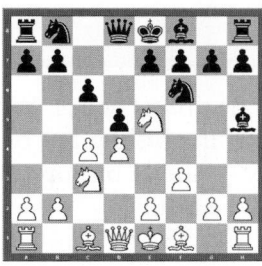

6...e6 (6...♘bd7 7.g4 ♗g6 8.h4±; 6...♘fd7 7.cxd5 cxd5 8.♛b3±) 7.g4 ♗g6 8.h4 h6 9.♘xg6 fxg6 10.♛d3 ♔f7 11.g5±;

Also not very good is 4...♗f5, as the white queenside squares are unprotected. 5.cxd5 (*5.e3 — 4.e3 ♗f5 5.♘c3*) 5...cxd5 6.♛b3 ♛b6 (6...♗c8 7.♗f4±; 6...b6 7.♘e5±) 7.♘xd5 (*7.♛xb6 axb6 8.♗f4 ♘c6 9.e3±*) 7...♘xd5 8.♛xd5 e6 9.♛b3 ♘c6 (9...♗b4+ 10.♗d2 ♘c6 11.e3± Gelfand — Adly, Dresden 2008) 10.♗d2 (*10.e3 ♘b4 11.♛a4+ ♔e7 12.♘e5 ♘c2+ 13.♔d1 ♛c7∞*) 10...♛xb3 (*10...♘b4 11.♖c1 ♘c2+ 12.♔d1±; 10...♗b4 — 9...♗b4 10.♗d2 ♘c6*) 11.axb3 ♗c2 12.♗c3 (*12.♖c1 ♗xb3 13.e4±*) 12...♖c8 (*12...b5 13.e3+-; 12...♗xb3 13.e4 a6 14.♗d3±*) 13.♘d2!N (*13.♘e5 a6 14.♘xc6 ♖xc6 15.b4 ♖b6 16.♔d2 ♗e4=* Atalik — Kekov, Voronezh 1998)

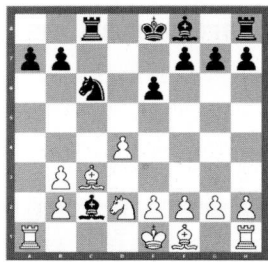

13...b5 14.e4 b4 15.♗c4± White has sacrificed the bishop but only temporarily — the c2 bishop is trapped and will be lost.;

4...g6 5.cxd5

a) After 5.♗f4 one must consider

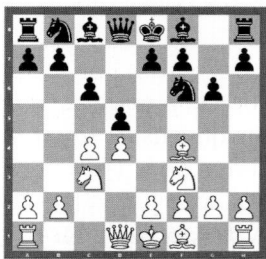

5...dxc4!? (*5...♗g7 6.e3 0-0 7.h3±*) 6.e3 (*6.a4 ♘d5 7.♗d2 ♘b4 8.e4 ♗e6∞*) 6...♗e6

(*6...b5 A dubious move 7.a4 ♕b6 (7...b4 8.♘b1 ♘d5 9.♗e5 f6 10.♗g3 c3 11.bxc3 bxc3 12.♗e2±; 7...♘d5 8.axb5 ♘xc3 9.bxc3 cxb5 10.♘e5↑) 8.♗e2 It's important for White to castle quickly, so that after b2-b3 the knight on c3 will not be pinned by ♗b4. (8.♘e5 ♘h5∞; 8.axb5 cxb5 9.b3 e6∞) 8...♘d5 9.♘xd5 (9.♗e5 f6 10.♗g3↑) 9...cxd5 10.b3 ♕a5+ 11.♔f1 b4 12.bxc4↑*)

7.♘g5 ♗d5

(A double-edged fight follows 7...♕d7!? 8.♗e2 (*8.♘xe6 ♕xe6 9.♕a4 b5 10.♕a5 ♘d5 11.♗e5 f6 12.♗g3 ♕d7 13.e4 ♘xc3 14.bxc3∞*) 8...♗d5 (*8...♗g7 9.♘xe6 ♕xe6 10.♕a4 b5 11.♕a5±*) 9.0-0 ♗g7∞)

8.e4 h6 9.exd5 hxg5 10.dxc6 ♘xc6 11.♗xg5 ♕xd4 12.♕xd4 ♘xd4 13.0-0-0 ♖d8 14.♗xc4 ♗h6=;

b) 5.e3 — 3.♘f3 ♘f6 4.e3 g6 5.♘c3;

c) The following is a good choice providing a small but stable advantage 5.♕b3± — 4.♕b3 g6 5.♘c3;

d) After 5.♗g5 also possible is

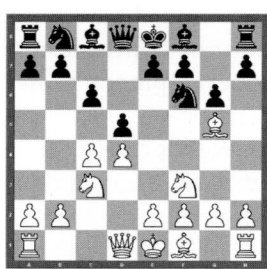

5...dxc4!?

(*5...♗g7 After this White's position is just a little better 6.e3 0-0 7.♗d3 ♗g4 (7...♗e6 8.♕e2 ♘bd7 9.0-0 h6 10.♗h4 ♗g4 11.cxd5 cxd5 12.h3 ♗xf3 13.♕xf3 e6 14.♖fc1± Kasparov — Smyslov, Vilnius (match 01) 1984) 8.h3 ♗xf3 9.♕xf3 dxc4*)

(9...e6 10.0-0 ♘bd7 11.cxd5 cxd5 (11...exd5 12.b4±) 12.♖fc1 ♖c8 13.♕d1±)

10.♗xc4 ♕a5 11.♗h4 ♘bd7 12.0-0 e5±)

6.a4 ♗g7 7.e4 ♗e6 — While White wins back the c4 pawn, Black can create counter play.;

5...cxd5

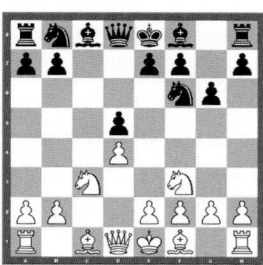

6.♗f4 ♗g7 7.e3 (7.♗xb8?! 7...♖xb8 8.♕a4+ ♗d7 9.♕xa7 0-0) 7...0-0 8.♗d3 ♘c6 (8...♗g4 9.h3 ♗xf3 10.♕xf3±) 9.h3 9...♗e6 (9...♗f5 10.♗xf5 gxf5 11.g4!→; 9...♕b6 10.a3±) 10.0-0 ♖c8 11.♖c1 ♘a5 12.♕e2± — The black bishops are ineffectual as they are restricted by pawns therefore White has a small but stable advantage, Taimanov — Lilienthal, Baku 1951.

5.h3!?
Depriving the black bishop of the g4 square.
5.g3 dxc4 6.♗g2 g6 7.♘e5 ♗g7 (7...♕a6!?) 8.♘xc4 ♕a6 9.♘e5 0-0 10.0-0 ♘bd7 11.♘d3± Sakaev — Kamsky, Khanty Mansyisk 2005;

The following is a quiet and solid way to achieve a slight advantage.
5.e3

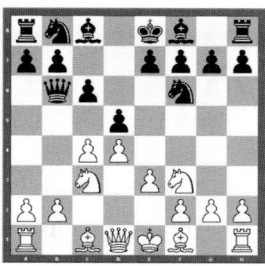

5... ♗g4

(5...♗f5 6.♘e5! (6.♘h4 ♗g4 7.f3 ♗e6=; 6.♗d3 ♗xd3 7.♕xd3 e6 8.0-0±) 6...♘bd7

(If 6...e6, White can start to chase the bishop: 7.g4 ♗g6 8.h4 dxc4 9.♗xc4

(9.♘xc4 ♕c7 10.h5 ♗e4 11.♖h4 g5 (11...h6 12.g5 hxg5 13.♖xe4±) 12.hxg6 ♗xg6 13.g5 ♘d5 14.e4 ♘xc3 15.bxc3 ♘d7 16.♗f4 ♕d8 17.♗g2±)

9...♗e4 10.f3 ♗d5 11.♗e2 c5 12.g5 cxd4 13.♕xd4 ♕xd4 14.exd4 ♘fd7 15.♘xd5 exd5 16.♗e3±)

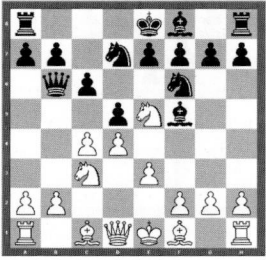

7.cxd5! (*7.♘xd7 ♗xd7 8.♗d3 e6 9.0–0 I.Sokolov — Nakamura, Stepana-kert 2005 9...dxc4 10.♗xc4 c5=*)

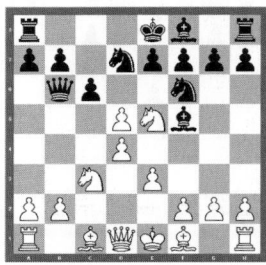

7...♘xd5 (*7...cxd5 8.♗b5±*) 8.♕f3! *♗e6 (8...♘xe5 9.♕xf5±) 9.♘c4 ♕d8 10.e4 ♘xc3 11.♕xc3± —* White's dominance in the centre is very real.)

6.h3 ♗xf3 7.♕xf3 e6 8.♗d3 ♘bd7 9.0–0 ♗e7 10.b3 0–0 11.♕e2 a5 12.♖d1± Gelfand — Kamsky, Jer-muk 2009;

A small advantage can also be achieved after 5.♕b3± — 4.♕b3 ♕b6 5.♘c3;

5.♕c2

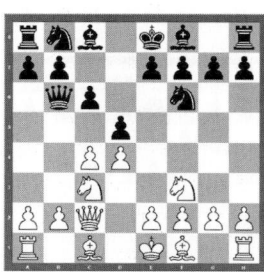

5...♘a6

a) 5...dxc4 6.e4 ♗g4 7.♗xc4 ♗xf3 8.gxf3 g6 (*8...♕xd4? 9.♕b3+-*) 9.♗e3± Navara — Jirovsky, Czech 2011;

b) 5...♗g4 6.c5 ♕c7 7.g3 (*7.♘e5 ♘bd7 8.♘xg4 ♘xg4 9.e3 e5 10.♗e2 ♘gf6 11.b4 g6 12.b5 ♗g7 13.0–0 0–0 14.♖b1± Shipov — Vysochin, Yalta 1996) 7...♗xf3 8.exf3 g6 (8...e5 9.♕e2 ♗e7 10.dxe5 ♘fd7 11.f4↑) 9.b4 (9.♗f4 ♕c8 10.0–0–0±) 9...♗g7 10.f4±* Van Wely — Zaura, Munich 1992;

6.a3 g6 7.e3 ♗f5 8.♕a4

(*8.♗d3 ♗xd3 9.♕xd3 ♗g7 10.0–0 0–0 11.b4 (11.c5 ♕d8 12.b4 ♘c7=) 11...dxc4 12.♕xc4 ♘c7 13.♗d2±*)

8...dxc4 9.♗xc4 ♗g7 10.♘e5 0–0 11.♘xc6 bxc6 12.♕xa6 ♕c7 13.0–0 ♖ab8± — Black has some compen-sation for a pawn though it's not completely sufficient, Mamedyarov — Kamsky, Baku (rapid) 2010.

5...♗f5
5...dxc4 6.e4 ♕a6 7.♗e2↑;

5...♗e6 6.e3 (Also promising is *6.cxd5!? cxd5 7.e3 ♘c6 8.♗d2±* — Although the bishop has not moved to f4, White has good chances of developing an initiative along the c-file.) 6...dxc4 7.♗e2 (*7.♘g5 ♗d5 8.e4 h6 9.exd5 hxg5 10.♗xc4∞*) 7...g6 8.0-0 ♗h6 (*8...♗g7 9.e4↑*) 9.♘d2 0-0 10.♘xc4±

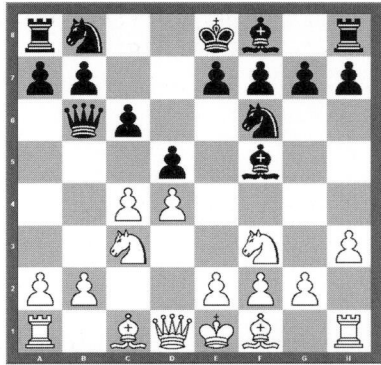

6.g4! ♗e4

6...♗e6 7.c5 (*7.♘a4!? ♕c7 8.♘c5 ♗c8 9.cxd5 cxd5 10.♗d2±; 7.♕c2!?*) 7...♕c7 8.♗g2± Structurally Black stands quite well but he is considerably behind in development. White is better prepared if the game opens up.

7.g5 ♘fd7 8.e3

8.c5 ♕c7 9.♘xe4 dxe4

8...♗xf3

8...e5 9.♘xe4 dxe4 10.c5 ♕d8 11.♘d2± Zhao Xue — Munguntuul, Ho Chi Minh 2012.

9.♕xf3 e6

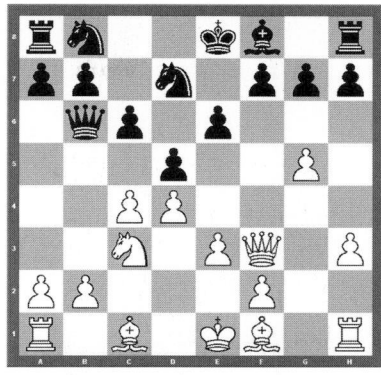

10.♗d2!

10.c5 ♕d8 11.h4 (*11.e4 e5*) 11...b6 12.cxb6 ♘xb6 (*12...axb6 13.e4↑*) 13.♗d2±;

10.h4 dxc4 11.♗xc4 c5 12.♕e4 cxd4 13.exd4±/↑

10...♗e7 11.h4 0-0 12.0-0-0±/↑

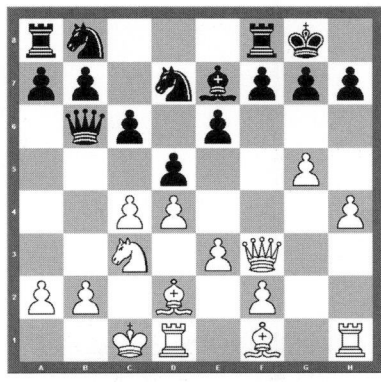

— White is better prepared for sharp play on both flanks. Conclusion: If he rejects the main lines on move four, Black cannot count on a fully satisfactory game. At best he gains a solid but passive position.

PART 15   Chebanenko variation

■ GAME 25

1.d4 d5 2.c4 c6 3.♘f3 ♘f6 4.♘c3 a6
5.e3 e6

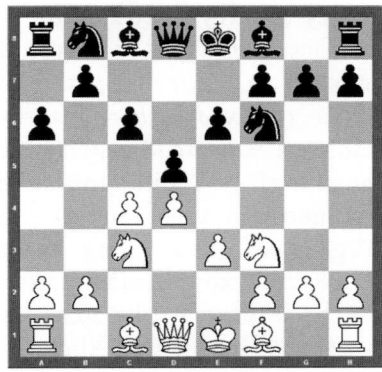

6.b3

6.♕c2 — 3.♘c3 ♘f6 4.e3 a6 5.♕c2
e6 6.♘f3;

Straightforward development does
not pose any danger for Black after
6.♗d3 dxc4 7.♗xc4 b5, with c6-c5
to follow Black has an easy game,
since the white knight has already
moved to c3 and if a2-a4 Black can
always reply b5-b4.;

6.c5

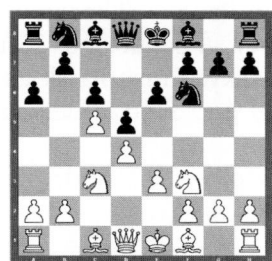

6...♘bd7

(6...b6 7.cxb6 ♘bd7

(White stands slightly better after 7...♕xb6 — The queen can
be attacked with tempo by ♘c3-
a4 and the c6 pawn will remain
backward. 8.♗d3 (The id ea of
delaying the development of the
f1 bishop deserves attention, so
that after an early a6-a5 and ♗c8-
a6, ♗f1xa6 can be played without loss of tempo,. For example:
8.♕c2 ♗d6 9.♗d2 a5 10.♖c1 0–0
11.♘e5!?±) 8...a5 9.♘a4 (9.0–0
♗a6 10.♘a4 ♕c7 11.♗xa6 ♘xa6
12.b3 ♗d6 13.♗b2±) 9...♕c7
10.♗d2 ♗a6 11.♕e2 ♗d6 12.♖c1
0–0 13.0–0 ♗xd3 14.♕xd3 ♘bd7
15.♖c2 ♖fc8 16.♖fc1 ♕b7 17.♗e1±
Kraemer — Rublevsky, Germany
2011)

8.♗d3

a) 8.♘a4 ♘xb6 9.♗d2 ♘xa4 (*9...♘bd7 10.♗d3±*) 10.♕xa4 ♗d7 11.♘e5 c5 12.♘xd7 ♕xd7 13.♕xd7+ ♔xd7 14.dxc5 ♗xc5 15.♖c1 (*15. b4 ♗d6 16.f3 ♔e7 17.♗d3 ♘d7=* Vallejo Pons — Tkachiev, France 2007) 15...♖hc8 16.♗d3 Kornev — Rublevsky, Krasnojarsk 2007 16...♗b4 17.♔e2 ♖xd2 18.♔xd2 a5=;

b) 8.♕c2 — *6...♘bd7 7.♕c2 b6 8.cxb6;*

8...c5 9.0-0 (The following is premature prior to castling *9.b3 cxd4 10.exd4 ♗b4 11.♗d2 0-0 12.0-0 a5 13.♘a4 ♘xb6 14.♘c5 ♘bd7 15.♕c2 ♘xc5 16.dxc5 ♕c7 17.a3 ♗xd2 18.♘xd2 e5∞/=* — The central black pawn pair is no less dangerous than the white passed wing pawns, Khismatullin — Galkin, Taganrog 2011) 9...♘xb6

a) 9...c4 10.♗e2! ♖b8 (*10...♘xb6 11.b3±*) 11.e4 ♘xe4 12.♘xe4 dxe4 13.♘d2± Riazantsev — Vitiugov, Moscow 2009;

b) 9...♕xb6 10.b3 cxd4 11.exd4 ♗d6

(11...♗e7 is passive 12.♗f4! 0-0 13.♘a4 ♕a7 14.♖c1 ♗b7

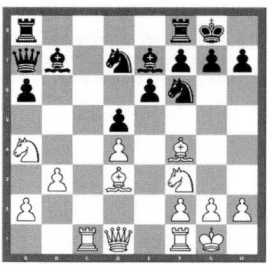

15.b4! ♗xb4 (*15...♖fc8 16.♘c5 ♕b6 17.a4±* Gelfand — Feller, Ohrid 2009) 16.♕b3 ♘h5 17.♕xb4 ♘xf4 18.♗xh7+ ♔xh7 19.♖c7 ♘e2+ 20.♔h1 ♘f6 21.♕b2 ♘e4 (White has an obvious advantage after *21...♖ab8 22.♕xe2 ♖bc8 23.♖e7 ♖ce8 24.♖xe8 ♖xe8 25.♘c5±*) 22.♘c5 (*22.♖xb7? 22...♕xb7 23.♕xb7 ♖ab8 24.♕xa6 ♘xf2+ 25.♖xf2 ♖b1+-+; 22.h3 a5! 23.♖xb7 ♕a6 24.♖e1 ♘f4 25.♘c5 ♘xc5 26.dxc5 ♘d3 27.♕b1 ♔g8 28.♘g5 ♘xf2+ 29.♔g1 ♕d3 30.♖e3 ♕xb1+ 31.♖xb1 ♘e4 32.♘xe4 dxe4 33.♖xe4 ♖fb8=; 22.♕xe2 ♖ac8 23.♖d7 ♖cd8 24.♘c5 ♖xd7 25.♘xd7↑* — White's initiative is dangerous.) 22...♘2c3 23.♘g5+ ♔g8 24.♘gxe4 ♘xe4 25.♘d7 ♖fc8 26.♖xb7 ♘xf2+ 27.♕xf2 ♕xb7 28.♕xf7+ ♔h8 29.h3 ♖ab8 30.♕xe6 ♖c6 31.♕g4 ♖bc8

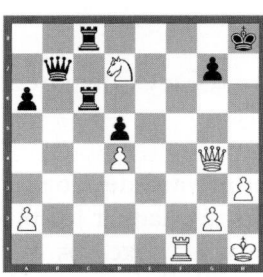

32.♔h2! — White has a strong attack, and the knight on e5 is worth a rook.)

12.♘a4 ♕a7 13.♗b2 (*13.♗e3 0-0 14.♘e5 ♗b7 15.♘xd7 ♘xd7 16.♘c5±*) 13...♗b7 14.♖c1 0-0

15.♘c5± Fressinet — Kempinski, Germany 2009;

c) 9...♗b7 10.♘a4 (*10.b3 ♘xb6 — 9...♘b6 10.b3 ♗b7*) 10...c4

(The following is bad 10...♗d6?! in view of 11.b3! cxd4 (*11...0–0 12.♗a3±*) 12.exd4 ♘xb6 13.♘c5±)

11.♗c2 (*11.♗e2 ♗c6 12.♗d2±*) 11...♘xb6 12.♗d2 ♘bd7 13.b3 cxb3 (*13...♗e7 14.bxc4 dxc4 15.♖b1±*) 14.axb3 a5 15.♘e5 ♗d6 16.f4± — White is much more active, Caruana — Rublevsky, Dagomys 2010;

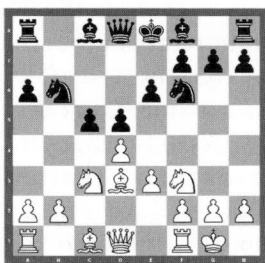

10.b3

(An interesting move is 10.e4!?N, whereon the correct response is the reinforcement of the centre

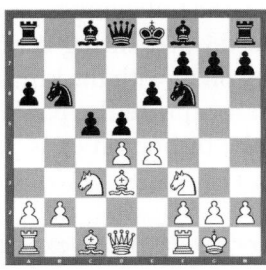

10...♗b7!

(Black cannot solve the problems by simplifying the position: 10...cxd4 11.♘xd4 dxe4 12.♘xe4 ♗b7 13.♘xf6+ ♕xf6 14.♗e3 ♗d6 15.♖e1 ♕e5 (If *15...0–0 strong is 16.♕g4!↑, and it's hard to simultaneously defend against ♗e3-g5 and ♘xe6.*) 16.f4 ♕d5 17.♕g4 0–0 18.♕h3 g6 19.♗f2,with the unpleasant threat ♗d3-e4.)

11.♗g5 (If *11.e5 ♘fd7=* A complicated, near equal game arises. In the long term Black plans to exchange the white squared bishops by means of a6-a5 and ♗b7-a6.) 11...cxd4 12.♘xd4 ♗d6 13.♘f3 (*13. ♕b3 ♗e5 14.♘f3 ♗xc3 15.e5 ♗a5 16.♗h4! d4 17.exf6 gxf6 18.♕a3∞; 13.♖e1 ♗e5 14.♗c2 dxe4 15.♗xe4 ♗xe4 16.♖xe4 ♕c7=*) 13...h6 14.♗xf6 ♕xf6 15.exd5 ♗xd5 16.♘xd5 ♘xd5 17.♕a4+ ♔e7=)

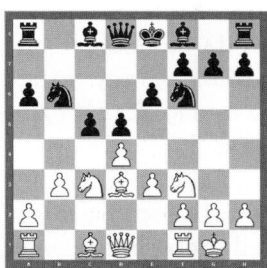

10...♗b7 11.♗a3

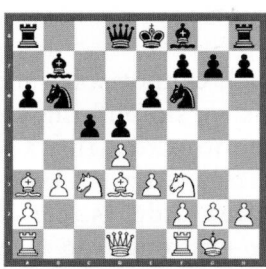

11...♘fd7

a) 11...cxd4 12.♗xf8 dxc3

(Probably bad for Black is 12...♔xf8 13.exd4 — The mobility of the b6 knight and b7 bishop is greatly restricted. 13...g6 14.♕e2 ♔g7 15.♖ac1 ♕e7 16.♖c2 ♖hc8 17.♖fc1 ♕b4 18.h3 a5 19.♘b5 (Also strong is *19.♕e3,* with the idea of ♘f3-e5. The following reply leads nowhere *19...a4 20.♘xa4! ♘xa4 21.bxa4±*) 19...♖xc2 20.♖xc2 ♖c8 21.a3 ♕e7 22.♖xc8 ♘xc8 23.♕d2! *(23.♕e1 ♕d8 24.♕e5 ♗a6=* Markus — Kempinski, Agios Kirykos 2009) 23...♕d8 24.♘e5±)

13.♗b4 d4 14.♘xd4 ♘bd5 15.♗c5 ♘d7 16.b4 ♘xc5 17.bxc5 ♕d7 18.♗c2 0-0 19.♗a4 ♕c7 20.c6 ♗c8 21.♗b3±;

b) An active move also cannot solve all problems: 11...♘e4 12.♖c1 ♖c8 13.♘b1! ♘d7 14.♘e5± — The knight on e4 has become vulnerable;

12.♖c1 ♗e7 (*12...♖c8 13.♘b1! ♗e7 14.♕e2* — *12...♗e7 13.♘b1 ♖c8*)

13.♘b1!N (After *13.♖c2 0-0 14.♕b1±* White's advantage is too small, Berkes — Rublevsky, Kragujevac 2009)

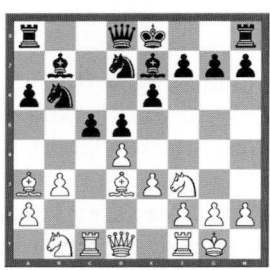

13...♖c8 14.♕e2! Suddenly the problem of defending the queenside pawns emerges for Black. 14...a5 (*14...0-0 15.♗xa6 ♗xa6 16.♕xa6 c4 17.♗xe7 ♕xe7 18.♕a5±* — White retains an extra pawn.) 15.dxc5 (*15.♗b5 0-0 16.♕d2 cxd4 17.exd4 ♗xa3 18.♘xa3 ♕e7 19.♘c2 ♖a8 20.♘e5±*) 15...♗xc5 16.♖c3 (*16. ♕d2 0-0 17.♗b5 ♗xa3 18.♘xa3±*) 16...♗xa3 17.♖xc8 ♕xc8 18.♘xa3 0-0 19.♘b5 ♕c5 20.♕d2 ♕b4 21.♕xb4 axb4 22.♖c1± — The b4 pawn is potentially weak. Black faces a struggle for a draw.)

7.b4

a) Harmless is 7.♗e2 after which, for example, the following is good 7...b6 8.cxb6 ♗d6, preventing White from invading on e5 with the knight. Now Black can capture the pawn b6 later and the bishop on e2 is passively placed.;

b) After 7.♗d3 Black executes the break

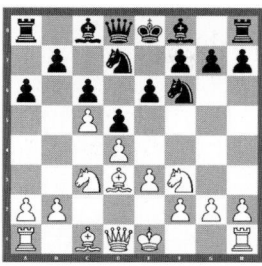

7...e5! (7...b6 8.cxb6 — 6...b6 7.cxb6 ♘bd7 8.♗d3) 8.dxe5 ♘g4 9.♘a4 ♘gxe5 10.♘xe5 ♘xe5 11.0-0 ♗g4! It's worth provoking f2-f3 to make it difficult for White to play on the black squares. (The superficially aggressive 11...♕h4? is unproductive (Zhu Chen — Stefanova, Ulan Bator 2010), due to the simple reply 12.♗c2 ♗e7 13.♕d4 ♕f6 14.f4 ♘d7 15.♗d2± — Black is severely constricted; In case of 11...♘xd3 12.♕xd3 ♗e6 13.e4 has to be considered; However quite reliable is 11...♗e7=) 12.f3 ♘xd3 13.♕xd3 ♗e6 14.♗d2 (14.e4 doesn't help 14...dxe4 15.♕xe4 ♕d5 — f3 has turned out to be weakening.) 14...♗e7 15.♗c3 0-0= Li Shilong — Wang Hao, Beijing 2009;

c) 7.♕c2 hardly presents a serious danger. In reply Black has two possible plans — the break b7-b6 or to fianchetto the bishop on g7 and prepare e6-e5. 7...g6 I like this best

c1) 7...b6 8.cxb6 ♘xb6 (8...c5 9.♘a4±) 9.♗d2 c5 10.♖c1 cxd4 (10...c4 11.b3 cxb3 12.♕xb3±) 11.exd4 ♗d6 12.♗g5 0-0 13.♗d3 h6 14.♗h4± — Black's white squared bishop is confined to quarters

while White has outposts on e5 and c5. Black must play very accurately to achieve equality, Gelfand — Anand, Moscow (match 07) 2012;

c2) 7...e5 This break does not solve all problems and looks premature 8.dxe5 ♘g4 9.♘a4 ♘gxe5 10.♘xe5 ♘xe5

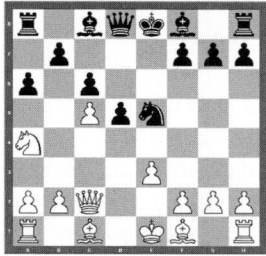

11.e4!?N

(11.♗d2 ♗e7 12.♗c3 (12.♘b6 ♖b8 13.♗a5∞ Koneru — Zhu Chen, Caleta 2012) 12...♗f6 13.0-0-0 ♕e7 14.e4 dxe4 15.♘b6 ♖b8 16.♘xc8 ♖xc8 17.♕xe4 0-0 18.f4 ♘g6 19.♕xe7 ♗xe7 20.♖d7 ♗xc5 21.♖xb7 ♘xf4 22.♗xa6 ♘xg2 23.♖f1±)

11...dxe4 12.♘b6 ♕e7 (12...♘d3+ 13.♗xd3 exd3 14.♕c3 ♖b8 15.0-0 ♕f6 16.♕xf6 gxf6 17.♗f4 ♗xc5 18.♘a4 ♗a7 19.♗xb8 ♗xb8 20.♖ad1 ♗f5 21.♘c5±) 13.♗e3 ♖b8 14.♕xe4 g6 15.♘xc8 ♖xc8 16.0-0-0±;

8.b4 (After the break 8.e4 follows the counter-break 8...e5!=, solving all problems, Krasenkow — Avrukh,

Plovdiv 2003) 8...♗g7 9.♗b2 0-0
10.♗e2 ♖e8 11.♘a4 ♘e4= — Black
will play e6-e5 and equalise;

7...b6!

(7...g6 8.♗b2

(8.♗d3 ♗g7 9.0-0 0-0 10.e4 e5!
11.♗e3 (*11.dxe5 ♘xe5! 12.♘xe5
♘xe4 13.♘xe4 dxe4∓* Cvitan
— Kobalia, Biel 2006) 11...dxe4
12.♗xe4 a5=)

8...♗g7 9.♗e2

(9.♗d3 0-0 (*9...e5 10.♘xe5 ♘xe5
11.dxe5 ♘g4 12.f4 ♘xe3 13.♕e2±*)
10.h3 (*10.0-0 e5=*) 10...♗e7 (*10...
♖e8 11.♘a4±*) 11.♘e2 ♘e8 12.0-0
e5 13.♘xe5 ♘xe5 14.dxe5 ♗xe5=
I.Sokolov — Wang Hao, Sarajevo
2009)

9...0-0 10.0-0 ♕c7

(10...♖e8 11.♘a4 ♕c7 — 10...♕c7
11.♘a4 ♖e8(*11...♘e4 12.♘e5±*))

11.♘a4 ♘e4 (*11...♖e8 12.♘e5 ♘xe5
13.dxe5 ♘d7 14.f4 ♖b8* Fridman —
Delorme, Rijeka 2010 *15.♖c1 f6
16.exf6 ♗xf6 17.♕d2±*) 12.♗d3!

a) 12.♘d2 ♘xd2 13.♕xd2 e5 14.dxe5
♗xe5 15.♗xe5 ♕xe5 16.♕d4 ♖e8=
Psakhis — Gofstein, Ashdod 2004;

b) 12.♘e1

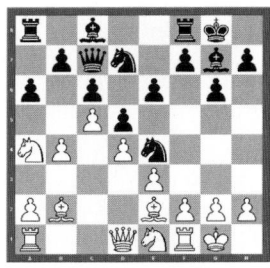

12...b5!N (*12...e5 13.dxe5 ♘xe5 14.f3±*
Bologan — Grischuk, Poikovsky
2004) 13.cxb6 ♘xb6 14.♘xb6
♕xb6 15.♘d3 a5=;

12...a5 (*12...b5 13.cxb6 ♘xb6
14.♖c1±; 12...e5 13.♗xe4 dxe4
14.♘xe5 ♘xe5 15.dxe5±*) 13.b5 b6
(*13...e5 14.b6 ♕d8 15.♗xe4 dxe4
16.♘d2±*) 14.cxb6 ♘xb6 15.♖c1
♘xa4 16.♕xa4 cxb5 17.♖xc7 (*17.
♗xb5±*) 17...bxa4 18.♗a3 ♖d8
19.♘e5±)

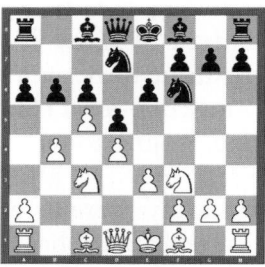

8.♗b2 a5 9.a3 ♗e7 10.♗d3 0-0
11.♕c2

(11.0-0 ♗a6 12.♕e2 (*12.b5 ♗b7=*)
12...♗xd3 13.♕xd3 ♕c7 14.h3 ♖fb8
15.♖fb1 ♖b7 16.♕c2 h6 17.♘d2
♖ab8 18.♗c1 axb4 19.axb4 e5= —
Black plans to exchange pawns on
c5 and d4, followed by ♘d7-f8-e6,

Matlakov — Jakovenko, Dagomys 2010)

11...♕c7 12.0–0 ♗a6 13.♗xa6 ♖xa6 14.♖fc1 ♕b7 15.♖ab1 axb4 16.axb4 ♖fa8 17.h3 ♗d8= -Black has solved all problems, Onischuk — Motylev, Poikovsky 2010

6... ♗b4

It's worth making the white bishop move to d2 so that it cannot go to the more promising square b2.

The following doesn't look very logical 6...c5 — The advance c6-c5 with loss of tempo is only worthwhile when the white knight is on d2 instead of c3. Regarding b2-b3. It is desirable move for White in the resulting isolated black queen's pawn formation. After the possible moves 7.cxd5 exd5 8.♗b2 ♘c6 9.♗e2 cxd4 10.♘xd4 ♗d6 11.0–0 0–0 12.♖c1 ♕c7 13.h3 ♖d8 14.♗f3 ♕e7 15.♘xc6 bxc6 16.♘a4 ♗b7 17.♕d4± White has a stable advantage, San Segundo — Jakovenko, Drezden 2008

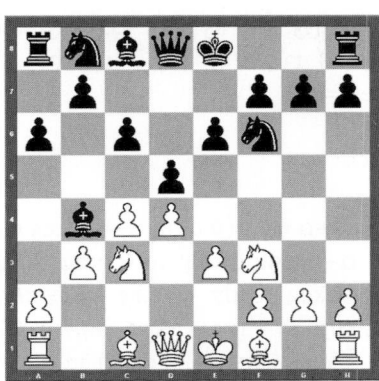

7. ♗d2

7.♗b2? leads to an endgame with a pawn deficit 7...♕a5 8.♕c2 ♘e4 9.♖c1 ♕xa2∓

7...♘bd7

7...0–0 8.♗d3 ♘bd7 — 7...♘bd7 8.♗d3 0–0;

In recent years the following has gained in popularity 7...♗d6 8.♗d3

a) 8.♕c2

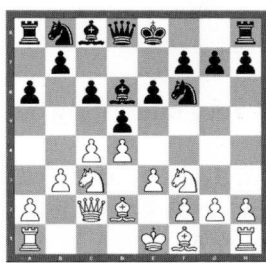

8...♘bd7

a1) 8...c5 9.dxc5 ♗xc5 10.cxd5 exd5 11.♘xd5! ♕xd5 12.b4±;

a2) 8...0–0

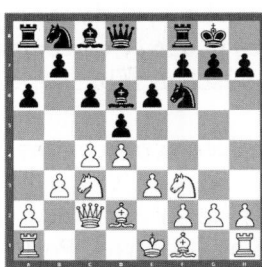

9.c5!N

a21) 9.♗d3 ♘bd7 10.0-0 -7... ♘bd7 8.♗d3 0-0 9.0-0 ♗d6 10.♕c2;

a22) 9.e4 dxe4 10.♘xe4 ♘xe4 11.♕xe4 c5= Sriram — Agrest, Cutro 2007;

a23) 9.g3 c5 (*9...♘bd7 10.♗g2 e5 11.0-0±*) 10.♗g2 ♘c6 11.0-0± Sasikiran — Roiz, Pamplona 2008;

9...♗c7 10.e4 dxe4 11.♘xe4 ♘xe4 12.♕xe4 ♘d7 13.♗d3 ♘f6 14.♕e2±;

9.g4!?N Very interesting but risky.

a1) 9.♗d3 e5 10.cxd5 cxd5 11.e4 dxe4 12.♘xe4 ♘xe4 13.♗xe4 exd4 14.0-0 ♘f6=;

a2) 9.g3 e5 10.cxd5 (*10.♗g2 e4=/∞*) 10...cxd5 11.dxe5 ♘xe5 12.♘xe5 ♗xe5 13.♗g2 0-0=;

a3) 9.e4 e5 10.exd5 cxd5 11.♘xd5 ♘xd5 12.cxd5 ♕e7 13.♗c4 exd4+

a31) 13...b5 14.♗d3 (*14.0-0 bxc4 15.bxc4 0-0 16.c5 ♘xc5=*) 14...♗b7 15.0-0 ♖c8 16.♕b1±;

a32) 13...e4 14.0-0 0-0 15.♖fe1±;

14.♔f1 0-0 15.♖e1 (*15.♗g5 I.Sokolov — Bartel, Porto Carras 2011 15...f6!±*) 15...♕d8 16.♘xd4 (*16.♕e4 h6=*) 16...♘f6 17.h4 ♖e8=

while White develops the h1 rook, the d5 pawn will be lost.;

9...♘xg4

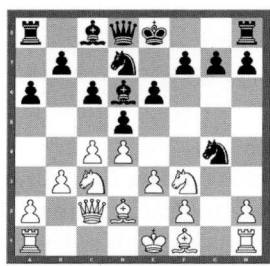

10.♖g1 ♘xh2 11.♘xh2 ♗xh2 12.♖xg7∞ — White plans to castle long and open up the centre.;

b) Leading to a complicated game is 8.g3 ♘bd7 (*8...c5 9.♗g2 0-0 10.0-0 ♘c6 11.♕e2±*) 9.♗g2 ♘e4 10.0-0 f5 11.♘e1 0-0 12.♘d3 b6

(12...♘xd2 13.♕xd2 dxc4 14.bxc4 e5 15.c5 (*15.f4 e4 16.♘f2∞ Wojtaszek — Bartel, Warsaw 2011*) 15...♗c7 16.♖fd1±)

13.♖c1 (*13.♗e1 a5 14.f3 ♘xc3 15.♗xc3 ♗a6=*) 13...♕e7 14.♗e1 ♗b7 15.f3 ♘ef6=/∞;

8...c5

(8...0-0 9.e4 (*9.0-0 c5 — 8...c5 9.0-0 0-0*) 9...dxe4 10.♘xe4 ♘xe4 11.♗xe4 ♘d7 (*11...c5 12.♗xh7+! ♔xh7 13.♘g5+ ♔g6 14.h4 ♔f6 15.♘e4+ ♔e7 16.♕g4→*) 12.0-0 — 7...♘bd7 8.♗d3 0-0 9.0-0 ♗d6 10.e4 dxe4 11.♘xe4 ♘xe4 12.♗xe4)

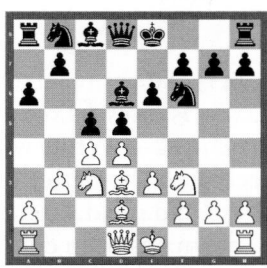

9.0-0 0-0 Perhaps the most promising path for White is to continue development and maintain tension in the centre:

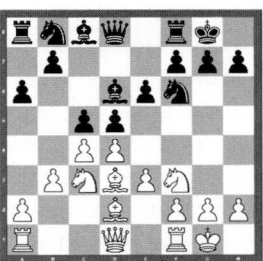

10.♕c2

(10.cxd5 exd5 11.e4

(11.dxc5 ♗xc5 12.♘e2 (12.♕c2 ♘c6=) 12...♘c6 13.♘ed4 (13.♕c2 ♕e7 14.♘ed4 ♘b4 15.♗xb4 ♗xb4 16.♘f5 ♗xf5 17.♗xf5 g6 18.♗h3 ♘e4= Bacrot — Bartel, Germany 2011) 13...♘b4

(13...♗xd4 14.♘xd4 ♘xd4 15.exd4 ♗g4 16.f3 ♗h5 17.♖e1 ♗g6 18.♗f1!± — By retaining the two bishops White gains a small but long-lasting advantage.(18.♗xg6 hxg6 19.♗g5 ♕d6

20.♕d2 ♖fe8= Markos — Najer, Germany 2009))

14.♗b1

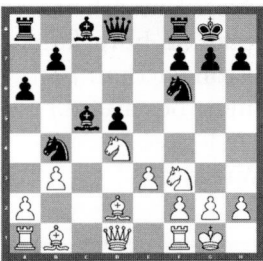

14...♖e8! (14...♗d6 15.a3 ♘c6 16.♗c3±; 14...♘e4 15.a3 ♘c6 Donchenko — Malakhatko, Nuernberg 2011 16.♘xc6! bxc6 17.♗b4 ♗xb4 18.axb4 ♕e7 19.♕d4±) 15.a3 ♘c6 16.♗c3 ♘e4 17.♘xc6 (17.♗xe4 dxe4 18.♘xc6 ♕xd1 19.♖fxd1 exf3=) 17...bxc6 18.♗xe4 dxe4 19.♕xd8 ♖xd8 20.♘e5 ♗e6±/= — Black should achieve a draw with an accurate defence.)

11...cxd4 (11...dxe4 12.♘xe4 ♘xe4 13.♗xe4 cxd4 14.♗g5 f6 15.♕xd4 fxg5 16.♖ad1 ♗xh2+ 17.♔xh2 ♕xd4 18.♖xd4 h6 19.♘e5 ♘c6 20.♘xc6 bxc6 21.♗xc6 ♖a7 22.♖c1± — Despite the limited remaining material, White retains winning chances.) 12.♘xd5 ♘xd5 13.exd5 ♗g4 14.h3 ♗h5 15.g4 ♗g6 16.♗xg6 hxg6 17.♘xd4 (17.♖c1 ♘d7 18.♖c4 ♘e5 19.♖xd4 ♗c5 20.♖e4 ♘xf3+ 21.♕xf3 ♕xd5= Akobian — Shulman, Saint Louis 2012) 17...♗e5 18.♗e3 ♕xd5 19.♘f3

♕e6 20.♘xe5 (*20.♗d4 ♗xd4 21.♕xd4 ♘c6 22.♕f4 ♖ad8=* Matlakov — Inarkiev, Plovdiv 2012) 20...♕xe5 21.♕d4 ♕xd4 22.♗xd4 ♘c6 23.♗b6± — Although the endgame is drawish, it's not equal. With play on both flanks a bishop is stronger than a knight, and Black must be careful.)

10...♘c6 11.a3 h6

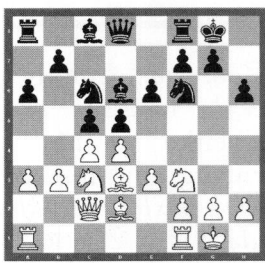

12.h3!N This subtle move not yet committing White's forces is the most unpleasant.

a) 12.♖fd1 cxd4! (*12...♖e8 13.dxc5 ♗xc5 14.h3 dxc4 15.♗xc4 ♕e7 16.b4 ♗a7 17.♘e4±* S.Zhigalko — Vysochin, St.Petersburg 2010) 13.exd4 e5!

(*13...♖e8 14.c5 (14.♖e1!?±) 14...♗c7 15.♘e2 e5 16.dxe5 ♘xe5 17.♘xe5 ♗xe5 18.♗c3±*)

14.dxe5 ♘xe5 15.♘xe5 ♗xe5=;

b) 12.dxc5 ♗xc5 13.♘a4 (*13.♖fd1 ♕e7=; 13.b4 ♗d6=*) 13...♗e7 14.♖fd1 dxc4 15.bxc4 ♕c7 16.♗c3 ♖d8=;

12...♕e7

(*12...cxd4 13.exd4 e5 14.♘xd5 ♘xd4 (14...♘xd5 15.dxe5 ♘xe5 16.♘xe5 ♗xe5 17.♖ae1±* — White wins back the piece with the better development.) 15.♘xd4 exd4 16.♗e4± — The d4 pawn has been cut off from its army and risks being lost.)

13.♘a4!

a) 13.♗c1±;

b) 13.cxd5 exd5 14.dxc5 ♗xc5 15.b4 ♗d6 16.♘a4 (*16.e4 dxe4 17.♘xe4 ♘e5 18.♘xe5 ♗xe5 19.♖ae1 ♖d8 20.♖e2 ♗d4 21.♗c3 ♗xc3 22.♘xc3 ♗e6 23.♗c4 ♖ac8 24.♗xe6 fxe6±/=* — Thanks to the weakness on e6, White's position is somewhat better however he has almost no chances to win.) 16...♗e6 17.♗c3± — A complicated game where White's position is preferable.;

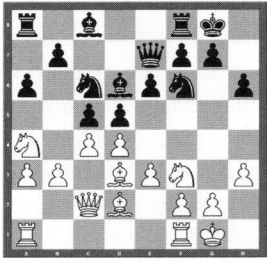

13...cxd4 14.exd4 e5

(*14...♗xa3 15.♘b6 ♖a7 (15...♖b8 16.c5 ♘xd4 17.♘xd4 ♗xc5 18.♘xc8 ♖bxc8 19.♕b2±) 16.♖fe1 (16.c5 ♗b4 17.♗f4⩲) 16...♖d8 17.cxd5 ♘xd5*

18.♘xd5 ♖xd5 19.♗h7+ ♔h8
20.♗e4±/↑)

15.♖fe1 ♕c7 (*15...e4 16.cxd5 ♗f5*
17.dxc6 exd3 18.♖xe7 dxc2 19.♖xb7±)
16.dxe5 ♘xe5 17.♘xe5 ♗xe5 18.♖ac1
dxc4 19.♕xc4 ♗h2+ 20.♔h1 ♕xc4
21.♗xc4 ♗d6 22.♘b6 ♖b8 23.♘xc8
♖fxc8 24.b4± — White has winning
chances.

8.♗d3 0–0 9.0–0 ♗d6

9...♕e7

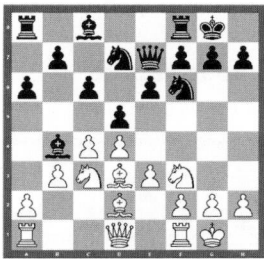

10.♕c2

a) An original move leading to
a complicated game is 10.♕e1

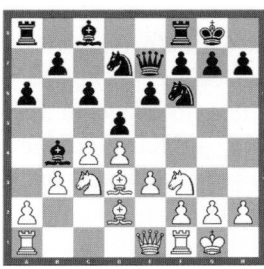

10...a5!? A non-standard but quite
decent possibility.

a1) 10...♖e8 11.♗c2

a11) 11.e4 dxc4 12.bxc4 e5 13.♘d5
♘xd5 14.exd5 ♗xd2 15.♕xd2 cxd5
16.cxd5 e4 17.♗xe4 ♘f6 18.♗c2
(*18.♗d3 ♕d6=*) 18...♕d6=;

a12) 11.♘xd5 ♘xd5 12.cxd5 ♗xd2
13.♕xd2 exd5 14.b4 ♘f6=;

11...dxc4 12.bxc4 e5 — 10...dxc4
11.bxc4 e5 12.♗c2 ♖e8;

a2) 10...dxc4 11.bxc4 e5 12.♗c2 ♖e8
13.♕b1

(13.c5

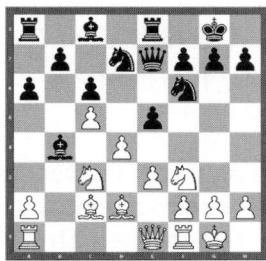

13...a5!N∞

(*13...exd4 14.exd4 b6 15.cxb6*
(*15.♕xe7 ♖xe7 16.cxb6 ♘xb6*
17.♖ab1 a5= Sargissian — Ga-
gunashvili, Warsaw 2005) *15...*
♘xb6 16.♘e4 ♘fd5 17.♗xb4
♘xb4 18.♗b3 ♗f5 19.♘c5 ♘4d5
20.♕a5±))

13... ♗d6 14.♘g5 (*14.h3 h6 15.♘h4*
♘f8 16.♘f5 ♗xf5 17.♗xf5 Mala-
khatko — Drozdovskij, Warsaw
2006 17...b5!±) 14...h6 15.♘ge4 b5

16.d5 Dreev — Khenkin, Saint Vincent 2005

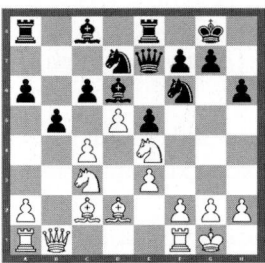

16...♞b6! 17.♞xf6+ ♛xf6 18.♞e4 ♛e7 19.♞xd6 ♛xd6 20.cxb5 cxd5=;

11. ♗c2

a1) 11.e4 dxc4 12.bxc4 e5 13.d5∞;

a2) 11.a3 ♗xa3!? 12.e4 (*12.c5 ♗b4 13.e4 dxe4 14.♞xe4 ♞d5∓*) 12...dxc4 13.bxc4 e5∞;

a3) 11.♞e5 ♞xe5 12.dxe5 ♞d7 13.f4 ♞c5 14.♗c2 b6 15.a3 ♗xc3 16.♗xc3 ♗a6= Grachev — Dreev, Sochi 2006;

11...e5! 12.a3 ♗d6 13.♞h4 g6∞ Stefanova — I.Sokolov, Khanty Mansyisk 2005;

b) 10.♞e5, has a good reputation but after

10...♞xe5 11.dxe5 ♞d7 12.f4 g6! White's advantage is very small.

b1) 12...dxc4 13.bxc4! ♗xc3 14. ♗xc3 ♞c5 15.♗c2± Najer — Se.Ivanov, Moscow 2004;

b2) The locking move 12...f5 does not solve the problems in view of 13.♞e2! (This move is more promising than, *13.cxd5 cxd5 14.♞e2±*, although here too White stands better.) 13...♗xd2 14.♛xd2 dxc4 15.bxc4! 15...♞c5 16. ♗c2± — Black's white squared bishop is bad.;

b3) 12...f6 13.♛c2 h6

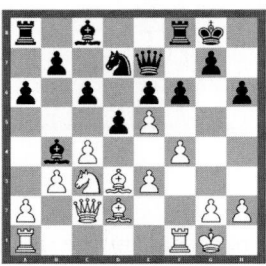

14.a3!

(14.exf6 ♞xf6 15.♔h1 ♗d7 16.e4 d4 (*16...♞g4!?*) 17.e5 ♗xc3 (*17...dxc3 18.exf6 ♛xf6 19.♗e1∞* Moiseenko — Kir.Georgiev, Zlatibor 2006) 18.♗xc3 dxc3 19.exf6 ♛xf6=)

14... ♗c5

(A losing move is 14...♗xa3? 15.♖xa3! ♛xa3 16.b4! — The queen cannot get back: 16...dxc4

(16...♘b6 17.♖b1 dxc4 18.♗h7+ ♔h8 19.♗c1 ♕xc3 20.♕xc3 ♔xh7 21.exf6 ♖xf6 22.e4+-; 16...♕xb4 17.♘xd5 ♕c5 18.♗b4 ♕a7 19.♘e7+ ♔h8 20.♘g6+ ♔g8 21.♘xf8 ♕xe3+ 22.♔h1 ♘xf8 23.exf6 gxf6 24.♖f3+-) 17.♗xc4 ♘b6 18.♗b3 ♕xb4 19.♘d5 ♕b5 20.♘c7 ♕e2 21.♖f2 ♕g4 22.♕c5+-)

15.b4 ♗a7

(15...♗b6

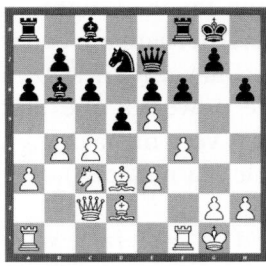

16.♘a4!?N

(16.c5 ♗c7 17.exf6 ♘xf6 18.e4 dxe4 (18...e5 19.exd5 cxd5 20.fxe5 ♗xe5 21.♖ae1± Roiz — Drozdovskij, Port Erin 2007) 19.♘xe4 ♘d5 20.♖ae1±)

16...♗c7 17.cxd5 exd5 18.e4 fxe5 19.exd5 exf4 *(19...♘b6 20.dxc6 ♘xa4 21.♕xa4 exf4 22.♖ae1±)* 20.dxc6 ♘e5 21.♖ae1 f3 22.♗c3 ♕g5 23.♗xe5 ♗xe5 24.♔h1 bxc6 25.♘b6 ♖b8 26.♘xc8 ♖bxc8 27.gxf3± — The weakness of the white squares in the Black camp is obvious.)*

16.exf6 ♘xf6 17.c5

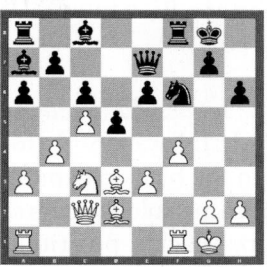

17...b6

b31) After 17...e5 the next move follows with great effect 18.e4! Taking advantage of his better development, White opens up lines in his favour: 18...♗e6 19.fxe5 ♘g4 20.exd5 cxd5 21.♘e2 b6 22.♘f4 ♖xf4 23.♖xf4 bxc5 24.bxc5 ♕xc5+ *(24...♗xc5+ 25.♔h1 ♘f2+ 26.♖xf2 ♗xf2 27.♗b4 ♕h4 28.♕c6+-)* 25.♕xc5 ♗xc5+ 26.♔f1 ♘xe5 27.♗e2± — White has winning chances.;

b32) 17...a5 18.♘a4±;

18.cxb6 ♗xb6 19.♘a4 ♗a7 20.♖ae1 e5 21.fxe5 ♕xe5 22.♘c5± Aronian — Navara, Sochi 2008;

b4) 12...b5 13.cxd5 *(13.♘e2±)* 13...cxd5 14.♘e2 ♗c5 15.b4 ♗a7 16.a4±;

13.cxd5!?N Only thus can White aspire to something tangible.

b1) Black has preventively protected his kingside, therefore the c2 square turns out to be bad for the queen: 13.♕c2 b5! 14.cxd5 cxd5 15.♘e2 ♗c5 16.♘d4 ♗b7 17.♗c3 b4 18.♗b2 a5= Riazantsev — Eljanov, Sochi 2012;

b2) 13.♘e2 ♗xd2 (*13...a5 14.♘d4±*) 14.♕xd2 f6! 15.exf6 ♘xf6 — Even though the black pawns are placed on the same colour squares as their bishop, Black's position is quite defendable since it's difficult for White to prevent the freeing move e6-e5. 16.♘g3 ♗d7 (*16...e5 17.f5±*) 17.e4 ♘g4 18.cxd5 ♕c5+ 19.♔h1 cxd5=;

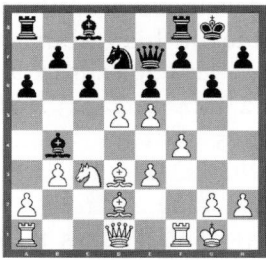

13...exd5 (*13...cxd5 14.♖c1±* — Besides ♘c3-e2 White has the idea ♘c3-a4, putting pressure on the queenside.) 14.♕c2 ♖d8 15.♘a4±/∞ — The position is complicated but White's chances look preferable.;

10...h6 Black waits for e3-e4, in order to capture on c4 in response and play e6-e5.

a) The following doesn't solve the problems 10...dxc4 11.bxc4 e5 — The move a7-a6 is not only pointless but it's even harmful.

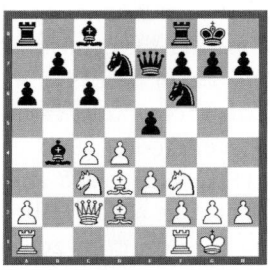

12.♘e2

(Also good is 12.♘e4 ♗xd2 13.♘fxd2! ♘xe4 (Otherwise the move c4-c5 will follow, providing a station for the knight on the d6 square. Alternatively, bad is *13...c5?! 14.dxe5! ♕xe5 15.f4! ♕e7 16.♖ae1↑* — The power of the pieces and pawns is very menacing.) 14.♘xe4 f5 15.♘c3 e4 16.♗e2±)

12...a5 (*12...e4 13.♗xb4 ♕xb4 14.♗xe4 ♘xe4 15.♕xe4 ♕xc4 16.♘f4 ♘f6 17.♕b1±*) 13.♘g3 ♖e8 Cmilite — Stefanova, ACP Cup 2012 14.a3! ♗xd2 15.♘xd2±;

b) 10...e5 11.dxe5 ♘xe5 12.♘xe5 ♕xe5 13.cxd5 cxd5 14.♘e2 ♗d6 15.♘g3 ♕g5 (*15...♕e7 16.♗c3 h6 17.♕b2 ♖e8 18.♗xf6 ♕xf6 19.♕xf6 gxf6 20.♖ac1±* Ivanchuk — Riazantsev, Moscow 2005) 16.f4! (*16. ♗c3 ♘g4!=* Dreev — Riazantsev, Sochi 2005) 16...♕h4 (*16...♕h6 17.♖ad1 ♖e8 18.♘f5 ♗xf5 19.♗xf5±*) 17.♖f3 ♖e8 (*17...g6 18.♗e1±* Pinter — M.Gurevich, France 2004) 18.♗c3±;

c) 10...♖e8 is bad in view of 11.♘e5 — Black will not be able to make a freeing break.;

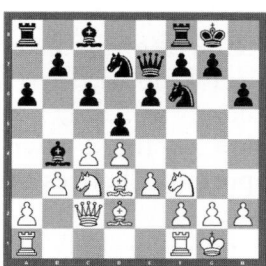

11.♖fe1 (11.♘e5 ♘xe5 12.dxe5 ♘d7 13.f4 b6=) 11...♖e8 12.e4

a) 12.♖ad1 e5 13.♘xe5 (13.dxe5 dxc4!=) 13...♘xe5 14.dxe5 dxc4! (14...♘g4 15.h3 ♘xe5 16.cxd5 ♗xh3 17.gxh3 ♘f3+ 18.♔g2 ♘xd2 19.♖xd2 ♕g5+ 20.♔h1 ♕e5 21.♖c1 ♖ac8 22.♗h7+ ♔h8 23.♗f5 ♗xc3 24.f4 ♕f6 25.♖g2 cxd5 26.♗xc8 ♖xc8 27.♕d3+-) 15.exf6 cxd3 16.♕xd3 ♕xf6 17.♘d5 (17.♘e4 ♕g6 18.♗xb4 ♖xe4=) 17...cxd5 18.♗xb4 ♗e6= — White's position is better but Black can hold the fort easily.;

b) 12.h3 e5 13.e4 dxc4 14.bxc4 — 12.e4 dxc4 13.bxc4 e5 14.h3;

12...dxc4

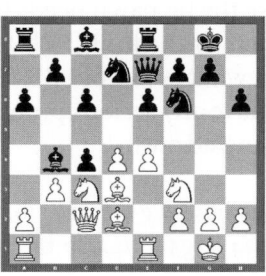

13.bxc4!N (13.♗xc4 b5 14.♗f1 e5= Lautier — Sakaev, Khanty Mansyisk (rapid) 2005) 13...e5 14.h3! In the impending fierce battle it's very important to take the square g4 away from the black knight. 14...♖d8!? An interesting attempt to put pressure on d4. (14...exd4 15.e5 ♘g4 16.♘a4 ♗xd2 17.♕xd2 b5 18.♘b2 ♘gxe5 19.♘xe5 ♘xe5 20.f4±; 14...b5 15.♖ab1 ♗d6 16.♘e2↑; 14...♗d6 15.c5 ♗c7 16.♘e2 exd4 17.♖ac1±) 15.♖ab1!

a) 15.d5 ♘c5 16.♗f1 ♗d7 17.♖ab1 ♗a5=;

b) 15.a3 ♗d6 16.♘a4 (16.♘d1 ♖e8 17.♘e3 exd4 18.♘f5 ♕f8 19.N5xd4 ♘e5 20.♖ad1 ♘xd3 21.♕xd3 ♗xa3 22.e5 ♘d7∞) 16...b5 17.c5 ♗c7 18.♘b6 ♘xb6 19.cxb6 ♗xb6 20.♘xe5 ♗b7∞;

c) 15.♘e2 ♗xd2 16.♕xd2 ♘h7 17.♖ad1 ♘g5 18.♘xg5 hxg5 19.d5 ♘c5 20.♗c2±;

15...a5 (15...♗d6 16.♘e2 exd4 17.♘exd4 ♘e5 18.♘xe5 ♗xe5 19.♘f3±) 16.♘a4! (16.d5 ♘c5 17.♗f1 ♗d7 18.♕b2 ♘a6=) 16...exd4 17.e5 ♘e8 18.e6 fxe6 19.♘xd4 ♘c5 20.♘xc5 ♖xd4 21.♘a4±/↑ — White has a strong initiative for a minimal material loss.

10.♖e1
10.♖c1

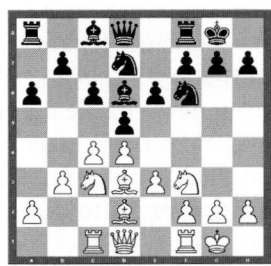

10...♖e8

a) 10...e5 11.cxd5 cxd5 12.dxe5!

(12.e4 This leads to mass exchanges and simplifications 12...dxe4 13.♘xe4 ♘xe4 14.♗xe4

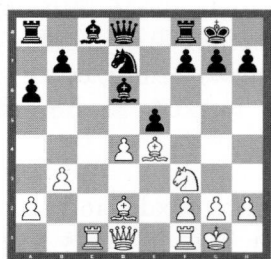

14...♘f6

(Not so convincing but also sufficient is 14...exd4 15.♖c4

(15.♗g5 f6! (15...♘f6 — 14...♘f6 15.♗g5 exd4) 16.♗h4 ♘c5 17.♗d5+ ♔h8 18.♕xd4 ♘e6=)

15...♘f6

(Also possible is 15...♘c5 but in the following play Black must be very accurate: 16.♗g5 ♕e8!N (16...f6 Riazantsev —

Antoniewski, Warsaw (rapid) 2011 17.♗xh7+! ♔xh7 18.♖xd4 fxg5 19.♖xd6 ♕e7 20.♖e1 ♘e6 21.♖e5±/→) 17.♗d5 ♘e6 18.♗c1

(18.♗h4 ♗e7 19.♗xe7 ♕xe7 20.♖e1 ♕d6 21.♖e5 (21.♗xe6 ♗xe6=) 21...♗d7 22.♗xb7 ♖ad8= — The d-pawn is well supported. Chances are about equal.)

18...♕b5 19.♗xe6 ♗xe6 20.♘xd4 ♕d7 21.♘xe6 ♕xe6 22.♖e1 ♕f6 23.♕d5 b5! 24.♖c6 (24.♗g5 ♖ae8 25.♖xe8 ♖xe8 26.g3 ♕a1+ 27.♔c1 ♖e1+ 28.♖xe1 ♕xe1+ 29.♔g2 ♗f8=) 24...♖ad8! 25.♕e4 ♖c8 26.g3 ♖xc6 27.♕xc6 ♗e5 28.♕c5 ♗d6 (28...♗d4? 29.♕xf8+ ♔xf8 30.♗a3++-) 29.♕d5 h6=)

16.♗b1 (16.♗g5 — 14...♘f6 15.♗g5 exd4 16.♖c4) 16...♗g4 17.♗g5 h6 18.♗h4 ♗xf3 19.♕xf3 ♖e8!N (19...g5 20.♗g3 ♗xg3 21.fxg3 ♔g7 22.♕xb7± Riazantsev — Matlakov, St.Petersburg 2011) 20.♗xf6 ♕xf6 21.♕xf6 gxf6 22.♖xd4 ♖ad8 23.♖fd1 ♗c7 24.♔f1 ♖xd4 25.♖xd4 ♖d8 26.♖g4+ ♔f8 27.♔e2±/= — Because the h6 pawn needs to be defended by the king, White stands somewhat better but Black should not have any serious problems obtaining a draw.)

15.dxe5 (15.♗g5 exd4 16.♖c4 h6 17.♖xd4 hxg5 18.♖xd6 ♕e7= Goga-

nov — Rublevsky, Taganrog 2011)
15...♘xe4 16.exd6 ♕xd6 17.♗e3
♗f5 18.♕xd6 ♘xd6 19.♘d4 ♖fe8
20.♘xf5 ♘xf5 21.♗c5 h5= Gelfand — Anand, Moscow (match
02) 2012)

12...♘xe5 13.♘xe5 ♗xe5 14.♘e2
♘e4 (*14...♗d7 15.♗c3 ♕b8 16.h3
♖c8 17.♕d2± Goloshchapov — Antoniewski, Germany 2011; 14...♗g4
15.f3 ♗h5 16.♗c3 ♕d6 17.h3 ♗g6
18.♗xg6 hxg6* Wojtaszek — Perez,
Spain 2008. Here it makes sense to
induce simplifications: *19.♗xe5!
♕xe5 20.♕d4±* — Black faces an
unpleasant, patient defence.) 15.♗e1!
(*15.♗xe4 dxe4 16.♗c3 ♗g4=* Najer
— Jakovenko, Olginka (rapid) 2011)
15...♖e8 16.f3 ♘f6 (*16...♕d6 17.h3 ♘g3
18.♘xg3 ♗xg3 19.♕c2 h6 20.f4 ♗xe1
21.♖fxe1±*) 17.♕d2!N (*17.♗c3? Hern-
andez Holden — Gomez Ledo, Bala-
guer 2011 17...♗xc3 18.♖xc3 d4!±*)

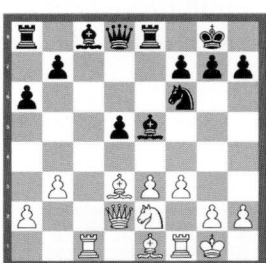

17... ♗d7 18. ♗f2

(If 18.♗g3 ♗xg3 19.♘xg3 (*19.hxg3!?*
deserves attention *19...♕e7 20.♔f2,*
however the king feels uncomfort-
ably close to the centre.) *19...♕b6
20.♖fe1 ♖e5=* The white pieces are
tied to the defence of the e3 pawn.)

18...♕e7 19.♘d4± — White has
a small advantage.;

b) 10...h6 11.h3 ♖e8 — 10...♖e8 11.h3
h6.;

11.h3

(11.e4 This leads to double-edged
play with near equal chances 11...
dxc4 12.♗xc4 (*12.bxc4 e5 13.d5
♘c5 14.♗g5 h6 15.♗h4 g5 16.♗g3*
Grachev — Victor Ivanov, Moscow 2006 *16...cxd5 17.cxd5 b5∓* —
The g3 bishop is out of play.) 12...
e5! (A passive move is *12...♗a3?
13.♖c2 ♗e7 14.e5 ♘d5 15.♘e4±*
Shomoev — Danin, Taganrog 2011;
12...b5 13.e5± Wojtaszek — Cram-
ling, Stockholm 2009) 13.♘g5 ♖f8
14.♗e3 exd4 15.♗xd4 ♕c7 16.g3
♘e5 17.f4 ♘xc4 18.bxc4∞)

11...e5

(11...h6 12.e4 (*12.♖e1* — 10.♖e1 h6
11.♖c1 ♖e8 12.h3) 12...dxc4 13.bxc4
e5 14.c5 ♗c7 15.♗e3± Jakovenko —
Vitiugov, Poikovsky 2010)

12.dxe5 ♘xe5 13.♘xe5

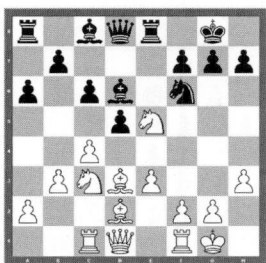

13...♖xe5! From here the rook can be deployed tor a kingside attack.

(13...♗xe5 14.cxd5 ♘xd5 (14... cxd5 15.♘e2 ♘e4 16.♗xe4 dxe4 17.♗c3 ♗d6! The exchange of black squared bishops is disadvantageous. 18.♕d4 ♗f8 Sargissian — Rublevsky, Khanty Mansyisk 2010 19.♖fd1±) 15.♘xd5 ♕xd5 16.♕c2 g6 17.♖cd1± — White puts pressure on the d-file and plans to gain space by advancing the e and f-pawns.)

14.cxd5

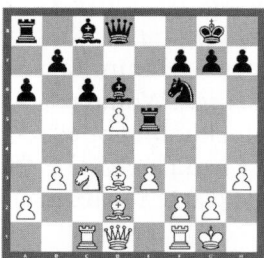

14...♗xh3!N (14...♗a3 15.♖b1 ♘xd5 16.e4± Wojtaszek — Bellon Lopez, Stockholm 2009) 15.gxh3 ♖g5+ 16.♔h1 ♕c8 17.♕f3 ♖h5 18.♔g2 ♖g5+ 19.♔h1 ♖h5= with a draw by repetition.;

10.e4

10...dxc4

(10...dxe4 11.♘xe4 ♘xe4 12.♗xe4 e5 13.♕c2 (13.dxe5 ♘xe5 14.♗c3 ♘xf3+ 15.♕xf3 ♕g5± Onischuk — A.Ramirez, Saint Louis 2012) 13... exd4 (13...h6 14.♗c3 exd4 15.♗h7+ ♔h8 16.♗xd4 ♘f6 17.♗f5±) 14.♗xh7+ ♔h8 15.♗d3±/↑)

11.bxc4 e5 12.c5 (12.d5 ♘c5∓) 12... ♗c7 13.♘a4 exd4 14.h3 ♖e8 15.♖e1 h6 This vacates h7 for the knight, from where it can go to g5 to fight for the key kingside squares. 16.♖b1 Black has several near equal options. Most of all I like the waiting move 16...♖b8, evading a potential ♘a4-b6 and protecting b7, thereby freeing the white squared bishop.

a) Also leads to a completely unclear game is 16...♘h7 17.♗c4 (17. ♘xd4 ♘g5; 17.♖b4 ♘g5∓) 17...♕f6 18.♖b3 ♘hf8 (18...♖b8!?; 18...♘g5!?) 19.♗c1∞ Kasparov — Gelfand, Linares 1991;

b) 16...♘f8

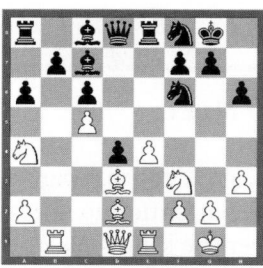

17.♕c2

(17.♖b4 ♘6d7

(A move to equalise is 17...♘e6 — in the long term Black wants to free the queenside. After 18.♖c4 it's most best for Black to prepare the advance of the b-pawn. 18...♖b8! For example, the following is possible (Not so strong is *18...♘d7 19.e5 b5 20.cxb6 ♘xb6 21.♘xb6 ♗xb6 22.♖xc6 ♗b7 23.♖d6 ♕c7 24.♘h4* Rodshtein — Delorme, Biel 2011, though here too if he had continued *24...♗a5!*, with the idea of exchanging on d2 and penetration to c3 with the queen, Black would have had good chances to equalise.) 19.e5 ♘d5 20.♕c2 b6 21.cxb6 ♘xb6 22.♘xb6 ♗xb6 23.♖xc6 ♗b7 24.♖d6 ♕c7=, with a near equal game.)

18.♕c2 ♕f6 19.♘xd4 ♗a5 20.♘f5 ♗xb4 21.♗xb4 ♘e5 22.♘d6 22...♗xh3!N (*22...♖d8 23.♘b6 ♖b8 24.♖e3⩲* Van Wely — Bacrot, Germany 2006) 23.♖e3 ♗e6 24.♗c3 ♘fg6∓ — White's compensation looks insufficient.)

17...♘6d7 18.♖bd1 (*18.♖b3 ♕f6 19.♗c4 ♘g6∓* Braun — M.Gurevich, Dresden 2008) 18...♕f6

(18...♘e5 is less sharp but also a good option 19.♘xe5 ♖xe5 20.♗f4 (*20.f4 is risky 20...♖e8* — White has weakened his king.) 20...♖e8 (*20...♕f6!?*) 21.♗xc7 ♕xc7 22.♘b6 ♖b8= — White has suffi-cient compensation for a pawn but nothing more. If the knight moves to d6 via c4, then Black will un-dermine its support with the move b7-b6.)

19.♘xd4 ♘e5 20.♗e2! (*20. ♗f1 ♗xh3∓/↑* Riazantsev — Sakaev,Moscow 2008) 20...♘fg6∞;

17.♖b4

(17.♕c1 ♘e5! (*17...♘f8 18.♖b4∞* Moiseenko — M.Gurevich, Trom-soe 2007) 18.♘xe5 ♖xe5∓/↑ — Black not only has an extra pawn but also prospects for a kingside attack.)

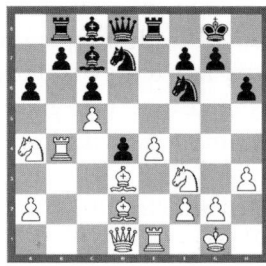

17...♕e7 18.e5!? (Besides quieter continuations the next move is of interest *18.♖c4,* After *18...g5!?* Black weakens the king but now the idea g5-g4 arises, and if the knights are exchanged on e5, White will not have the move f2-f4. The follow-ing is possible *19.♖xd4 ♘e5 20.♗c3 ♘fd7=*,with an excellent game on the black squares.) 18...♘d5 19.e6 fxe6 20.♖xd4⩲ White has good compensation since the black king is badly protected. But Black has his trumps — there are no concrete threats and there is the extra material. The chances are equal.;

10.♕c2 This continuation is the most natural and popular but allows central exchanges in a way which is favourable for Black.

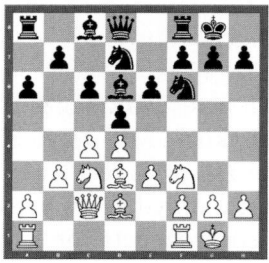

10...e5

a) 10...b6 11.♖ad1 ♕c7 12.h3 ♗b7 13.e4 dxc4 14.bxc4 e5 15.dxe5 ♘xe5 16.♘xe5 ♗xe5 17.f4± Lysyi — Kobalia, Khanty Mansyisk (rapid) 2011;

b) 10...♖e8 11.♖fe1 h6 — 10.♖e1 h6 11.♕c2 ♖e8;

c) 10...h6 11.♖ad1

c1) 11.h3 e5 12.cxd5 cxd5 13.e4 dxe4 14.♘xe4 ♘xe4 15.♗xe4 exd4 16.♘xd4 ♘f6 17.♗f3 ♗e5 18.♗c3 ♕b6 19.♖ad1 ♗d7= — Black can maintain equality with accurate play, Tomashevsky — Jakovenko, Moscow 2010;

c2) 11.e4 dxc4 12.bxc4 e5 13.c5 ♗c7 Leads to a ion of the sharp line 10.e4 dxc4 11.bxc4 e5 12.c5 ♗c7

— The move h7-h6 is very useful when White has already determined his queen's position.;

c3) 11.♖fe1 — 10.♖e1 h6 11.♕c2;

c4) After 11.♘e2, with the idea of transferring the knight to g3, a good choice for Black is

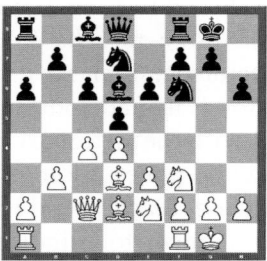

11...♕e7

c41) 11...♖e8 12.♖ad1

(12.♘g3 c5!? (12...e5 13.cxd5 cxd5 14.dxe5 ♘xe5 15.♘xe5 ♗xe5 16.♗c3±) 13.♗c3!? (13.cxd5 exd5 14.♗c3 b6 15.♖fd1± Navara — Dreev, Greece 2006) 13...b6 14.♘e5 ♗b7 15.f4± In the forthcomi ng complicated game White's chances are a little better, Eljanov — Rublevsky, Foros2007)

12...e5 13.dxe5 ♘xe5 14.♘xe5 ♗xe5 15.cxd5 cxd5 16.h3 ♗d7 17.♗c3 ♖c8 18.♕b2 ♗xc3 19.♘xc3± Jakovenko — Rublevsky, Poikovsky 2011;

c42) 11...c5 12.cxd5 exd5 13.♘g3± Navara — Kempinski, Czech 2009;

c43) Interest is 11...e5!? 12.cxd5 ♘xd5! (*12...cxd5 13.dxe5 ♘xe5 14.♘xe5 ♗xe5 15.♗c3±*) 13.e4 (*13. ♖ad1 exd4 14.♘exd4 ♖e8=*) 13... ♘b4 14.♗xb4 ♗xb4 15.♘xe5 ♘xe5 16.dxe5 ♕e7 17.f4 ♖d8/= — The weakness of the black squares in White's camp is very evident and the compensation for a pawn looks sufficient.;

12.♘g3 (*12.c5 ♗c7 13.♘g3 e5 14.♘f5 ♕d8 15.dxe5 ♘xe5 16.♘xe5 ♗xe5=*) 12...b6! 13.♖ad1 (*13.e4 dxe4 14.♘xe4 ♘xe4 15.♗xe4 ♗b7=* Ftacnik — Erenburg, Germany 2006) 13... ♗b7 14.♖fe1 ♖fd8=, with a level game, Volkov — Rodshtein, Dresden 2007;

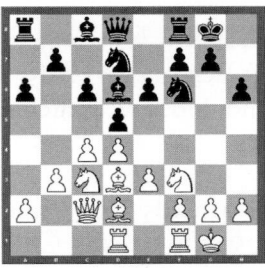

11...e5 12.cxd5 cxd5 13.dxe5

(13.e4 dxe4

(13...exd4 also leads to equality 14.♘xd5 (*14.♘xd4 dxe4 15.♘xe4 ♘xe4 16.♗xe4 ♘f6* — 13...dxe4 14.♘xe4 ♘xe4 15.♗xe4 exd4 16.♘xd4 ♘f6=*) 14...♘xd5 15.exd5

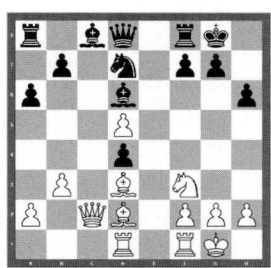

15...♕f6!N (*15...♘f6 16.h3 ♘xd5 17.♘xd4±* Banikas — Motylev, Khanty Mansyisk 2010) 16.h3 ♘c5 17.♗b4 ♘xd3 18.♗xd6 ♕xd6 19.♕xd3 ♕xd5=)

14.♘xe4 ♘xe4 15.♗xe4 exd4 16.♘xd4 ♘f6 17.♗f3 (*17.♘f5 ♘xe4 18.♕xe4 ♖e8 19.♕f3 ♗xf5 20.♕xf5 ♕c7=* Sanikidze — M.Gurevich, Izmir 2008) 17...♗g4 (*17...♗xh2+ 18.♔xh2 ♕xd4 19.♔g1 ♗g4 20.♗xh6 ♕b6 21.♗e3 ♕e6=*) 18.♗xg4 ♘xg4 19.g3 (*19.♘f3 ♕c7=*) 19...♕c8!=)

13...♘xe5 14.♘xe5 ♗xe5 15.♘e2

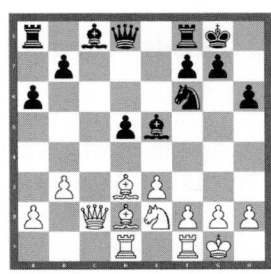

15...♗g4

c1) If 15...♗d7 White can manage to exchange the black squared bishops in time 16.♗c3 ♖c8 17.♕d2

(Bad is *17.♕b2? 17...♖xc3 18.♘xc3 ♕c7 19.♖c1 ♗xh2+ 20.♔h1 ♕e5 21.♗e2 ♘g4 22.♗xg4 ♗xg4 23.f3 ♗g3 24.fxg4 ♕e7 25.♖f2 d4!±*) 17... ♗xc3 (An exchange sacrifice does not succeed in this version. *17... ♖xc3 18.♘xc3 ♕c7 19.♖c1 ♗xh2+ 20.♔h1±*) 18.♘xc3± — White has a small but stable advantage.;

c2) The same holds true for 15... ♗e6 16.♗c3 ♖c8 17.♕d2 ♗xc3 18.♘xc3±;

16.f3 ♖c8 17.♕b1 ♗d7 18.♖c1 ♖e8 19.♖xc8 ♕xc8 20.♖c1 ♕b8 21.g3 h5=/∞1 White's kingside is weakened so Black has sufficient counter play.;

11.cxd5 cxd5 12.e4

(12.dxe5 ♘xe5 13.♘xe5 ♗xe5 14.♖ad1 (*14.f4 ♗d6=*) 14...♗g4 15.f3 ♗h5 16.♘e2 ♖c8 17.♕b1 ♗g6= Arlandi — Godena, Reggio Emilia 1995)

12...exd4 13.♘xd5 ♘xd5 14.exd5 ♘f6 15.h3

a) 15.♕c4 ♗g4 16.♕xd4 ♗xf3 17.gxf3 ♘xd5= Avrukh — Wang Hao, Sochi 2008;

b) 15.♖ae1 ♗g4 16.♘xd4 (*16.♘e5 ♖c8 17.♕b2 ♖c5=*) 16...♖c8 17.♕b1 ♖c5= Kaidanov — Hess, Saint Louis 2012;

c) 15.♖fe1 ♗g4 16.♘xd4 ♖c8 17.♕b2 ♖c5= Aleksandrov — Kharlov, Moscow 2009;

15...♗d7 16.♖ad1

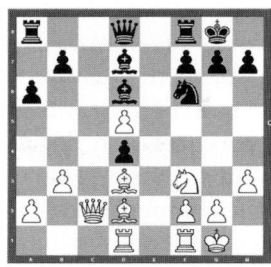

16...♖e8!

(16...♖c8 17.♕b2! (*17.♕b1 ♖c5=* Levin — Martynov, St.Petersburg 2012) 17...♕b6 18.♕xd4 ♕xd4 19.♘xd4 ♗c5 20.♘f3 ♘xd5 21.♗e4 ♗c6 22.♘e5 ♖ce8 23.♗xd5 ♖xe5 24.♗xc6 bxc6 25.♖fe1±)

17.♘xd4 ♖c8 18.♕b1 h6 19.♘f5 ♗xf5 20.♗xf5 ♖c5 21.♖fe1 ♖xd5= Gelfand — Anand, Moscow (match–04) 2012

10...h6

10...e5?! 11.cxd5 cxd5 12.e4 exd4 13.♘xd5 ♘xd5 14.exd5 ♘f6 (*14...h6 15.♘xd4 ♘f6 16.♘f5 ♗xf5 17.♗xf5±*) 15.♖c1! (*15.♘xd4 ♗g4! 16.♘f3 ♖c8!∞*) 15...♗g4 16.h3 ♗h5 17.♗g5 h6 18.♗xf6 ♕xf6 19.g4 ♗g6 20.♖c4± Sasikiran — Moradiabadi, Guanzhou 2010;

10...dxc4 11.bxc4 b6 12.♖b1 ♕c7 13.a4± Giri — Wang Hao, Wijk aan Zee 2011;

10...b6!? 11.h3 ♗b7 12.e4 dxc4 13.bxc4 e5 14.♗e3 ♖e8 15.♖b1 (No advantage is given by *15.d5* — Black takes hold of the c-file as well as the c5 square for his minor pieces.) 15...b5 16.♕c2± — In the forthcoming complicated game White's chances are preferable.;

10...♖e8 11.♕c2 h6 — 10.♖e1 h6 11.♕c2 ♖e8

White faces the threat of the rook's deployment on the kingside. Black has active counter play.)

12.cxd5 cxd5 13.e4 dxe4 14.♘xe4 ♘xe4 15.♖xe4 (*15.♗xe4 exd4 16.♘xd4 ♘f6 17.♗f3 ♗xh2+ 18.♔xh2 ♕xd4 19.♖c4 ♕d6+ 20.♗f4 ♕xd1 21.♖xd1 ♗g4=* Chadaev — Rublevsky, Taganrog 2011) 15...♘f6 16.♖h4 e4! 17.♗xe4 ♘xe4 18.♖xe4 ♗f5/= — Black has good compensation for a pawn thanks to his good blockade and bishop pair.;

11.e4 dxc4 12.bxc4 e5 13.c5 ♗c7 14.♕c2 (*14.♘a4 exd4 15.h3 ♖e8* — 10.e4 dxc4 11.bxc4 e5 12.c5 ♗c7 13.♘a4 exd4 14.h3 ♖e8 15.♖e1 h6) 14...exd4 15.♘e2 ♖e8 (*15...♘g4 16.♘exd4 ♘de5 17.h3 ♘xd3 18.♕xd3 ♘e5 19.♘xe5 ♗xe5 20.♗e3 ♕f6 21.♖ad1 ♖d8 22.♕c4±* Bacrot — Rublevsky, Poikovsky 2011) 16.h3 (*16.♘exd4 ♘e5=*) 16...b6!N (*16...♘h7 17.♘exd4 ♘e5 18.♖ad1±* Laznicka — Matlakov, Czech 2012)

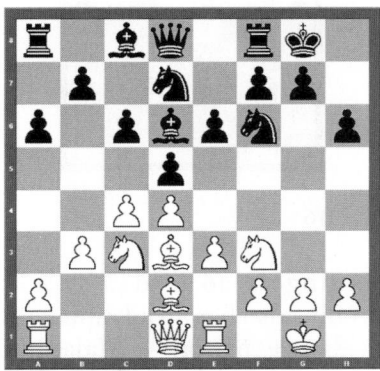

11.♕c2

11.♖c1 e5

(Black can start a more complicated battle if he wants 11...♖e8 12.h3

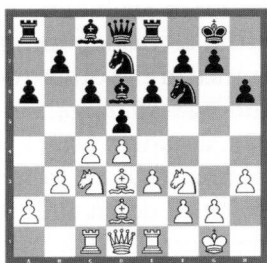

12...e5!N (*12...dxc4 13.bxc4 e5 14.♕c2 ♕e7 15.♘h4 ♘f8 16.♘f5 ♗xf5 17.♗xf5±* Nepomniachtchi — Inarkiev, Sochi 2012) 13.dxe5 ♘xe5 14.♘xe5 ♖xe5 15.cxd5 cxd5=/∞ —

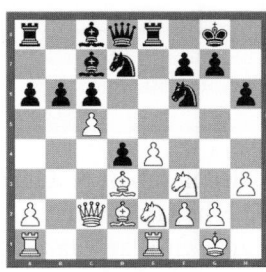

17.cxb6 ♗xb6∓ — The black pieces have gained some room to manoeuver, while White still has to play a pawn down since the following is bad 18.♕xc6? 18...♗b7! 19.♕xb7 ♘c5∓

11...b6!?N
11...♖e8 12.♖ad1

(12.h3 e5 (12...♕e7 13.c5! ♗c7 14.e4 dxe4 15.♘xe4 ♘xe4 16.♗xe4 ♘f6 17.♗d3±; 12...dxc4 13.bxc4 e5 14.♖ab1 ♖b8 15.a4 exd4 16.exd4 ♖xe1+ 17.♖xe1 ♘f8 18.♘e4 ♘xe4 19.♗xe4± — White has an advantage mainly on account of the backward b-pawn, which can be fixed with the move a4-a5, Lou Yiping — Moradiabadi, Iran 2011) 13.cxd5 cxd5 14.e4 dxe4 15.♘xe4 ♘xe4 16.♗xe4 exd4 17.♗h7+! White drives the black king to h8, and in some lines the weakening of f7 will become evident. 17...♔h8 18.♖xe8+ ♕xe8 19.♖e1 ♕d8

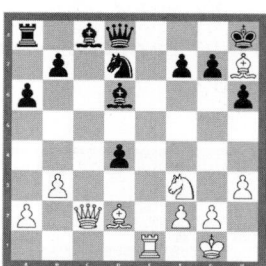

20.♘xd4!N (20.♗f5 Gelfand — Dreev, Khanty Mansyisk (blitz) 2005 20...♘f6 21.♘xd4 ♗d7!=) 20...♘f8 (20...♘f6 21.♗d3 ♗d7 22.♘f5±) 21.♗c3 ♘f6 22.♗d3 ♘d5 23.♗d2 ♘b4 24.♗xb4 ♗xb4 25.♖e3↑ — The threat of the queen entering via c4 is very unpleasant.)

12...e5 (12...♕e7 13.c5 ♗c7 14.e4 dxe4 15.♘xe4 ♘xe4 16.♗xe4 ♘f6 17.♗d3±) 13.cxd5 cxd5 14.e4 dxe4 15.♘xe4 ♘xe4 16.♖xe4!

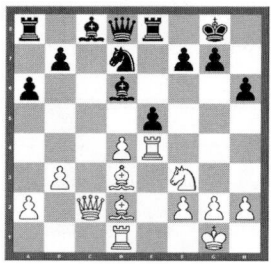

16...♘f6

(Losing is 16...exd4? 17.♗a5!N (White also has an advantage after 17.♖xd4±, Miron — Malakhatko, Eforie Nord 2011) 17...b6 18.♕c6 ♖b8 19.♕xd6 bxa5 20.♘xd4 ♗b7 21.♖xe8+ ♕xe8 22.♘f5 ♕e6 23.♕c7+-)

17.dxe5! ♘xe4 18.♗xe4 ♗xe5 19.♘xe5 ♖xe5 20.♗c3 ♕xd1+ 21.♕xd1 ♖xe4 22.♕d8+ ♔h7 23.h4! ♖e6 The black rook aims for c6 to protect the c8 bishop and prepare the entrance of the other rook with a6-a5 and ♖a8-a6. 24.g4!± — White conducts a pawn attack on the kingside,and it's hard to fend it off as Black is tied down with the bishop's pin.;

11...dxc4 12.bxc4 c5 13.a4 (13.h3±) 13...b6 14.♘e4 ♘xe4 15.♗xe4 ♖b8 16.a5±

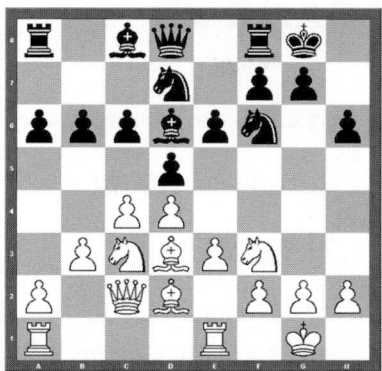

12.e4!?

It leads to an interesting game.

A quieter option is 12.♖ad1 ♕c7 13.h3 ♗b7 14.e4 dxc4 (*14...dxe4 15.♘xe4 ♘xe4 16.♗xe4±*) 15.bxc4 e5 16.c5 bxc5 17.dxe5 ♘xe5 18.♘xe5 ♗xe5 19.♘a4±

12...dxc4 13.bxc4 e5 14.♘a4!

White puts pressure on c5, preventing Black from using this important square for his pieces.

14...♖b8

14...♗c7 15.d5±

15.♗f1!

A useful prophylaxis, as forcing lines are unproductive: 15.♘xb6 ♕xb6 16.c5 ♘xc5 17.dxc5 ♕xc5 18.♕xc5 ♗xc5 19.♘xe5 ♘g4 20.♘xg4 ♗xg4 21.♗xa6 ♗d4 22.♖ac1 ♖b2 23.♗e3 ♗xe3 24.♖xe3 ♖xa2=;

15.♖ac1 b5 16.c5 ♗c7 17.♘b6 ♘xb6 18.♘xe5 (*18.cxb6 ♗xb6 19.♘xe5 ♕xd4 20.♗f4 ♘h5 21.♗g3 ♗b7 22.♘f3 ♕d8 23.♗xb8 ♕xb8*) 18...♘g4 19.cxb6 ♗xe5 20.dxe5 ♘xe5 21.♗e2

♕xb6 22.♗b4 ♖e8 23.♗c5 ♕d8 24.f4 ♘c4=

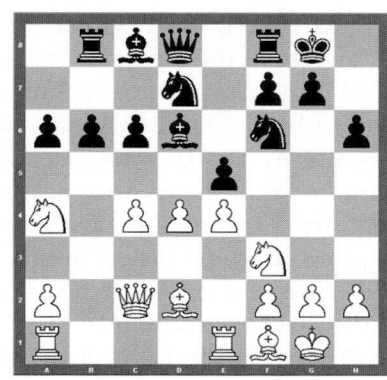

15...b5

15...♗c7 16.♖ad1±

16.♘b2 c5 17.d5±

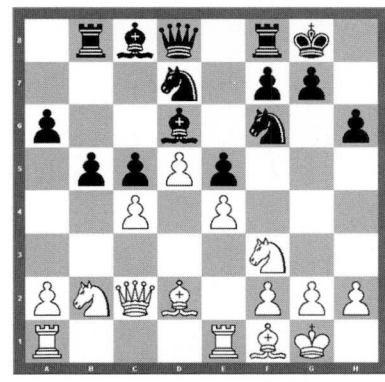

— In the forthcoming manoeuvering game, White's chances are somewhat better. Conclusion: The line 4...a6 5.e3 e6, usually leads to a full-blooded battle. The variation 6.♕c2 is analysed in a separate chapter and requires accurate play from Black to achieve equality. The line 6. c5 looks quite satisfactory for Black, if he knows up to 6...♘bd7! 7.b4 b6! Regarding the system 6.b3 ♗b4 7.♗d2 0–0 8.♗d3 ♘bd7 9.0–0 with 9...♕e7, then instead of the reputable 10.♘e5, 10.♕c2 is more promising, intending after 10.. .h6 11.♖fe1 ♖e8 12.e4! dxc4 13.bxc4!N e5 14.h3! With 9...♗d6, many similar branches and transpositions arise. I think the most promising out the whole variety seems to be 10.♖e1, and if 10...h6, then 11.♕c2, making Black think about e3-e4, and correctly preparing to meet the potential break e6-e5 with the counter break e3-e4!

■ GAME 26

1.d4 d5 2.c4 c6 3.♘f3 ♘f6 4.♘c3 a6 5.e3 b5
5...♗g4?! is bad 6.♕b3 b5

a) 6...♕c7 7.♘e5±;

b) 6...♖a7 7.♘e5 ♗e6 8.cxd5 cxd5 (8...♘xd5 9.e4±) 9.♗d2 g6 10.♖c1± Bruzon — Cuartas, Montcada 2010;

7.cxd5 ♗xf3 (After 7...cxd5 8.♘e5 is strong,and after the retreat of the bishop, a2-a4.) 8.gxf3 cxd5 9.a4 b4 10.♕xb4 ♘c6 11.♕b3± — Black has no compensation for the pawn.;

Ineffective is 5...g6 — as it tranposes to the line 3.♘f3 ♘f6 4.e3 g6 5.♘c3, where instead of the developing move 5...♗g7 Black has made the move a7-a6.;

5...♗f5

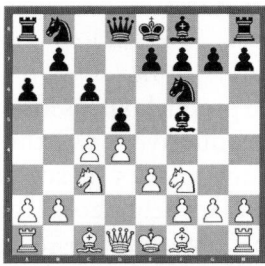

6.♕b3

a) A little tame is 6.♗d3 ♗xd3 7.♕xd3 e6 8.0–0 ♗e7 9.e4 dxe4 10.♘xe4 0–0 11.♗f4 ♘xe4 12.♕xe4

♘d7± — Black has nearly equalised.;

b) 6.♗e2 e6 7.♘h4 ♗e4 8.0-0 ♘bd7 9.g3 (*9.cxd5 cxd5 10.f3 ♗g6 11.♘xg6 hxg6 12.e4 dxe4 13.fxe4 e5= leads to an comfortable game for Black.*) 9...♗d6 10.f3 ♗g6= — The move a7-a6 has turned out to be useful. Black has an easy game.;

6...b5 7.c5

(7.cxd5 leads to a double-edged game with equal chances *7... cxd5 8.a4 b4 9.♕xb4 ♘c6 10.♕c5 ♘a5 11.♗xa6 ♖xa6 12.♕b5+ ♖c6 13.♘e5 ♗d7 14.♘xd7 ♘xd7 15.♗d2 ♖c8 16.♘xd5 ♘c4 17.♖c1 ♘d6 18.♖xc8 ♕xc8 19.♕a5 (19. ♕a6 ♕xa6 20.♘c7+ ♔d8 21.♘xa6 e5∞) 19...♘c4 20.♕a7 (20.♘c7+ ♔d8 21.♘e6+ ♔e8= In the game continuation White only has enough compensation for equality: 22.♕c7 ♕xc7 23.♘xc7+ ♔d8 24.♘b5 ♘xb2 25.a5 e6 26.♔e2 ♘c4 27.♖b1=) 20...e6 21.♘c7+ ♔d8 22.♘b5 ♗d6 23.♘xd6 ♘xd6 24.0-0 ♔e7= Tregubov — Vallejo Pons, France 2004)*

7...a5

(*7...♘bd7 It's quite risky to allow a queenside clamp: 8.a4 e5 9.♘a2 With the knig ht on b4 Black will be tied to the defence of the c6 pawn. Also there is always the threat of sacrificing the knight on c6 creating a pair of passed pawns.*

(9.♕a3 ♖b8

(9...♖c8 10.b4 g6 11.axb5 axb5 12.♘xb5 (*12.dxe5 ♘g4 13.♗b2 ♗g7 14.e6±*) 12...cxb5 13. ♗xb5 e4 14.♘e5± Vallejo Pons — Svidler, Monaco (blindfold) 2006)

10.♘a2±)

9... ♗e7 (*9...♕c8 10.♘b4 e4 11.axb5 axb5 12.♖xa8 ♕xa8 13.♘d2±*) 10.♘b4 ♕c8 11.axb5 axb5 12.♖xa8 ♕xa8 13.♕a3 ♕xa3 14.bxa3 e4 15.♘xc6 exf3 16.gxf3± Bacrot — Bologan, Porto Carras 2011)

8.♘e5 a4 9.♕d1 g6

(9...♘e4

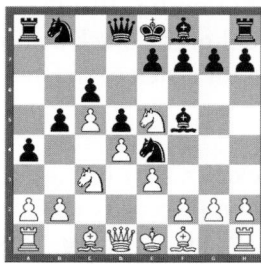

10.g4 (*10.♕f3 g6 11.g4 ♗e6 12.♘xe4 dxe4 13.♕xe4∞ Lintchevsky — I.Popov, Dagomys 2009*) 10...♗e6

(10...♗c8 11.♗g2 ♘xc3 12.bxc3 f6 (*12...e6 13.e4 ♗e7 14.0-0 0-0 15.f4± Svidler — Prie, France 2009*) 13.♘d3 g6 14.h4 (*14.e4 dxe4 15.♗xe4 ♗g7 16.0-0 0-0 17.♗f4±*) 14...♗g7 15.h5 f5 (*15...♕d7 16.h6*

♗f8 17.g5±) 16.♕e2± Khismatul-lin — I.Popov, Voronezh 2009)

11.♗g2 ♘xc3 12.bxc3 ♕c8 13.h3 ♘d7 14.♘d3±)

10.g4

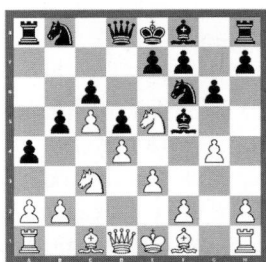

10...♗e6 11.♗g2 (*11.f3 ♗g7 12.♘d3±*) 11...♗g7 12.f4 ♕c8 13.h3 h5 14.g5 ♘fd7 (*14...♘e4 15.♘xe4 dxe4 16.♕c2± Al.David — Bologan, Ca-leta 2012*) 15.♘f3± — By placing the knight on h4, White deters the placement of the black bishop on f5. It's hard for Black to defend.

6.b3
6.cxd5 cxd5 7.♗d3 (*7.♘e5 e6 8.♗d3 ♗b7 9.0-0 — 7.♗d3 e6 8.0-0 ♗b7 9.♘e5*) 7...e6 (*7...♗g4 leaves the queenside weakened: 8.♘e2 ♗xf3 9.gxf3 ♘c6 10.a4 b4 11.a5± Jussupow — Reuss, Osterburg 2006*) 8.0-0

(*8.♗d2 ♗b7 (8...♗d6 9.e4!±) 9.0-0 — 8.0-0 ♗b7 9.♗d2*)

8...♗b7 (*8...♘bd7* It's better not to play ♘b8-d7 before White knight plays ♘f3-e5. Now White can change his plan and try to exchange

the bishops via b4: 9.♗d2 ♗b7 10.a3 ♘e4 11.♗e1 ♗d6 12.♘a2 0-0 13.♗b4 a5 14.♗xd6 ♘xd6 15.♕e2 ♕b6= — White's game is somewhat bet-ter due to the potential use of the weakened c5 square, Damljanovic — Sakaev, Zlatibor 2007) 9.♗d2

(*9.♘e5*

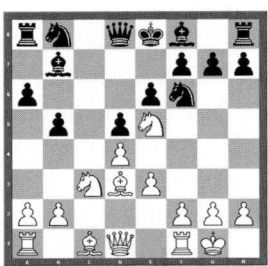

9...♗d6

(When the knight stands on e5, Black can move his knight to d7: 9...♘bd7 10.f4 ♗e7 (*10...♗d6 11.♗d2 0-0 12.♕e2 ♘e4 13.a4 ♘xd2 14.♕xd2 b4 15.♘a2 ♘f6 16.♕e1 a5 17.♘c1 ♘e4=* Jussupow — V.Milov, Switzerland 2007) 11.♗d2

(*11.♕f3 0-0*

(A near equal game arises when Black loses a tempo but regains the e4 square: 11...b4 12.♘d1 (*12. ♘e2 ♘e4 13.♘g3 ♘df6=*) 12... ♘e4 13.♘f2 ♘df6=)

12.a3 ♘e8!? The most reli-able path to d6. Only with the knight which can potentially be attacked on the f-file, if White pushes f4-f5. (12...b4 13.axb4 ♗xb4 14.♗d2 a5 Jussupow — Lautier, Germany 2003 15.♗e1±; 12...♘b6 13.♗d2 ♘c8 14.f5 exf5 15.♕xf5 ♘d6 16.♕h3∞ Vaganian — Sakaev, Toljatti 2003) 13.e4 (13. f5 ♘xe5 14.dxe5 exf5∓) 13...♘ef6! 14.♘xd7 ♕xd7 15.e5 ♘e4=)

11...0-0 12.♕e2

(12.♖c1 ♖c8 13.a3 ♘b6 (13...♘e4=) 14.♕f3 ♗a8 (14...♘c4∓) 15.♗e1 ♘c4 16.♖c2 ♘e4 17.♘xc4 bxc4 18.♗e2 f5∓ Jussupow — Grischuk, Mainz (rapid) 2005)

12...♘e4 13.a4 b4 (13...♘xd2 14.♕xd2 b4=) 14.♘xe4 dxe4 15.♗c4 ♘b6= Bocharov — B.Savchenko, Serpukhov 2008)

10.f4 0-0 11.♗d2 (11.♖f3 ♘e4 12.♖h3 ♘d7∓; 11.♕f3 b4 12.♘a4 ♘e4∓) 11...♘e4 — 9.♗d2 ♗d6 10.♘e5 0-0 11.f4 ♘e4)

9...♗d6! Black doesn't commit the queen's knight.

a) 9...♗e7 is too passive 10.♘e2 0-0 11.a4 b4 12.a5 ♘e4 13.♗e1±;

b) 9...♘bd7 10.♘e2 ♘e4 11.a4 b4 12.a5 ♗d6 13.♗e1! (13.♗xb4 ♗xb4 14.♕b3 ♕e7 15.♖a4 ♘dc5 16.dxc5 ♗xc5 17.♗xe4 dxe4 18.♘g5 ♗d5 19.♕c3 ♕xg5 20.♕xc5 ♕e7 21.♕d4 0-0 22.♘c3 ♖fd8 23.♘xd5 ♖xd5 24.♕xe4 ♖b8= — White cannot save

the backward pawn.; 13.♕a4 ♘xd2 14.♘xd2 0-0 15.f4 ♕e7 16.♘f3 ♖fc8 17.♘e5 ♘f6∓ M.Gurevich — Bareev, Germany 1992) 13...0-0 14.♘d2

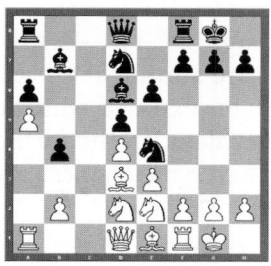

14...♖c8!?N

b1) 14...♕e7 15.f3 ♘ef6 16.♘b3 e5 17.♗h4 ♕e6 18.♖e1±;

b2) 14...♕b8 15.♔h1 ♗c6 16.♘b3 ♗b5 17.f3 ♘ef6 18.♗g3 ♗xg3 19.♘xg3 ♖c8 (19...♗c4 20.♘c1 ♕b5 21.b3 ♗xd3 22.♘xd3 ♖fc8 23.♘e2 ♘b8 24.♖a4 ♘c6 25.♕d2±) 20.e4± Belyavsky — Laznicka, Austria 2007;

15.♘b3 (15.f3 ♕g5 16.♘f4 ♘xd2 17.♕xd2 e5) 15...♕g5!? Preventing White from driving away the knight with f2-f3. (15...e5 16.f3 ♘ef6± — Black has more weak squares in his camp and a bad bishop on b7.)

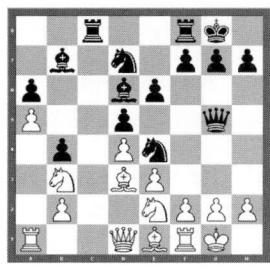

16.♘f4 e5 17.dxe5 ♕xe5 18.g3

(18.♘d4 g5 19.♘f3 ♕e7 20.♘h5 (20. ♗xe4 dxe4 21.♘xg5 ♘f6 — Black has a space advantage and active pieces. Also the threat ♗b7-c6-b5 is strong.) 20...f5∞ — All Black's pieces are aiming at an attack but his king is exposed which can become evident. In the forthcoming sharp battle the chances are about equal.)

18...g6 19.♘d4 ♖fe8 20.♕e2 ♘b8∞ — Black has sufficient counter play since the White's black squared bishop is confined.;

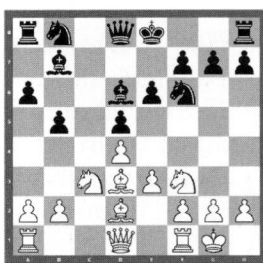

10.♘e5 0–0 11.f4

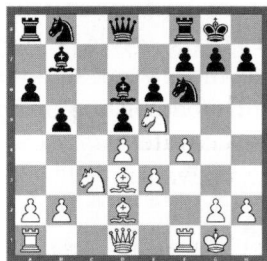

11...♘e4! The most exact move obtaining an easy game.

(Not so convincing is 11...♘bd7 12.♕f3 (12.♖c1 ♖c8=) 12...♘b6 (12... b4 13.♘a4 ♘e4 14.♕e2±) 13.a3± In the forthcoming complicated battle White's chances are somewhat better. He plans the redeployment ♗d2-e1–h4, or the break f4-f5.)

12.♕c2

(12.♗e1 f6 (12...♘d7 13.a4 b4 14.♘xe4 dxe4 15.♘c4 ♗e7 16.♗e2 ♘b6=) 13.♘f3 ♘d7∓)

12...♘xd2 13.♕xd2 ♘d7 (13...f6 14.♕c2! f5 15.a4 b4 16.♘e2 ♘d7= Moiseenko — Bareev, Ekaterinburg 2002) 14.♖ac1 ♖c8= — It's impossible to use the weakness of the c5 square, Black even stands nominally better.;

6.c5 First introduced to practice at the top level by Vadim Zvyaginzev. White gains space and later plans either to put pressure on the queenside, where Black often faces the problem of protecting c6, or to play e3-e4. 6...♘bd7

a) Dubious is 6...♗f5?!

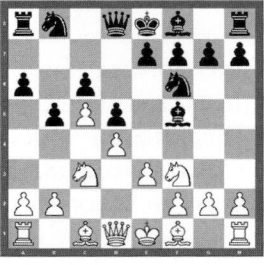

7.♘e5 h5 8.♕b3 ♘g4 9.e4! (9.♗d3 e6 10.♗xf5 exf5 11.♘d3 a5 12.f3 ♘f6 13.0-0±) 9...♗e6 10.exd5 cxd5 11.♘f3 ♘c6 12.♗d3 g6 13.0-0 ♗g7 14.♘e2 0-0 15.a4 bxa4 (15...b4 16.♘f4 ♕c8 17.h3 ♘f6 18.♗e3±) 16.♖xa4 a5 17.h3 ♘f6 (17...♘h6 18.♗d2±) 18.♗f4± — It's not easy to maintain the blockade on c6. White has an advantage.;

b) 6...♗g4 Strangely enough, exchanging off the white squared bishop is strategically risky

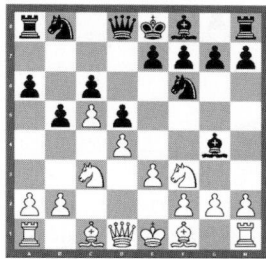

7.♕b3

(7.h3 ♗xf3 8.gxf3

(8.♕xf3 g6!

b1) The natural move 8...♘bd7 is bad, in view of 9.g4! g6 (Black is severely constricted after *9...e5 10.g5 ♘g8 11.h4± Sakaev — Bryzgalin, Kazan 2005*) 10.g5 ♘h5 11.e4±;

b2) The immediate 8...e5 is quite possible, and after 9.g4 g6! — 8...g6 9.g4 e5;

9.g4 It's difficult to expect anything without gaining space. 9...e5 10.♕g3 ♘bd7 11.♗g2 ♕e7 12.0-0 ♗g7= — Black has enough counter play due to the pressure on d4, Sakaev — Gruenenwald, Fuegen 2006)

8...♘bd7 9.f4 a5! The most exact, guaranteeing a blocked queenside. Otherwise b2-b4 comes into consideration, after which Black must either open up the game with the move a6-a5, or give up the a-file. 10.♗d3 e6 11.♗d2 g6= — In the long term, Black can play ♘f6-h5 and f7-f5, building an unassailable fortress.)

7...♘bd7 8.a4 e5 (8...♗xf3 9.gxf3 e5 10.♕a3 — 8...e5 9.♕a3 ♗xf3 10.gxf3) 9.♕a3

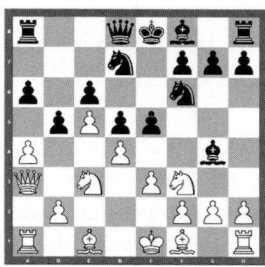

9...♖b8 This move requires exceptionally accurate play from White to gain an advantage.

b1) In practice Black most frequently parts with the bishop: 9...♗xf3 10.gxf3 ♖c8 (*10...♖b8 11.♘a2! ♖c8 12.♗d2±*) 11.axb5 axb5

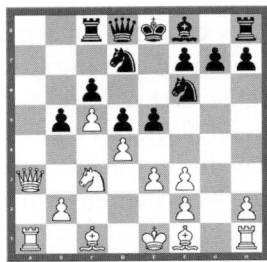

12.♗d2! The impending threat of capturing on b5 is very strong.

b11) Black's chanc es are in the middlegame, where the doubled pawns on the f-file can be exploited, therefore after 12.♕a5 follows 12...♖c7;

b12) 12.♗h3 ♗e7 13.♕a5

(13.dxe5 b4!

(13...♘xc5 14.♘xb5 ♘fd7 15.♘d6+ (15.♘d4 ♘xe5 Nisipeanu — Sanduleac, Predeal 2006) 15...♗xd6 16.exd6 ♕h4 17.♗g2 0-0 18.0-0±)

14.♕xb4 ♘xe5 15.♔f1 (15.♔e2 0-0! 16.♗xc8 ♕xc8 17.♖d1 ♖e8 — Black's play on the white squares is very dangerous.) 15...♘fd7 16.f4 ♗xc5 17.♕b7 ♖c7 18.♕a8 ♖c8 19.♕b7=)

13...♖c7 14.0-0 0-0 15.♘a2 ♘h5 16.♘b4 ♗f6 (16...f5 17.f4 e4 18.♗d2± — White's position is better due to the a-file and the strong knight on b4.) 17.♖d1 g6 18.f4 exf4 19.exf4 ♖e8 20.♖a3!± — White's chances are better.;

12...exd4

(12...g6 13.♘xb5 cxb5 14.♗xb5 exd4 15.exd4 ♖b8 (15...♗xc5 16.dxc5 0-0 17.b4+-) 16.♗a4! ♗e7 17.♗h6 ♕a5+ 18.♔f1 ♕b4 19.♕d3+- — White has a decisive attack.)

13.exd4 ♗e7

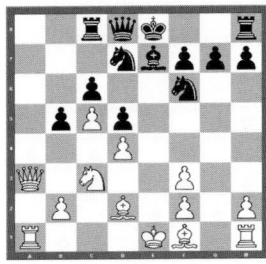

14.♘xb5! 0-0 (14...cxb5 15.♗a5 ♖c7 16.♗xb5 0-0 17.0-0± — The connected queenside pawns are a menacing force.) 15.♘c3 ♖e8 16.♘e2 ♘b6 17.b3 ♖a8 18.♕b2 ♘bd7 19.b4± — Black has insufficient compensation for a pawn.;

b2) A very interesting pawn sacrifice is 9...b4!? 10.♕xb4 ♖b8 11.♕a3 a5 12.♗e2

b21) 12.h3 ♗xf3 13.gxf3 ♘h5;

b22) 12.♗d2 ♗e7 13.♗e2 0-0 (It's disadvantageous to completely block the centre, 13...e4 14.♘g1± gives White the better game.) 14.h3 ♗f5 — Black has good compensation.;

12...♘e4! (12...♗e7 benefits White 13.♘xe5 ♗xc5 14.♘xf7!±) 13.♘d2

(13.♘xe5 ♘xe5 14.♘xe4 ♗xe2 15.♔xe2 dxe4 16.dxe5 ♕g5 17.♗d2 ♕xg2 18.♖hg1 ♕xh2 19.♗xa5 ♗e7

(19...♕h5+ 20.♔e1 ♕h2 21.♖f1!? (21.♔e2=) 21...♕xe5 22.♗c3 ♕g5 23.b4 ♗e7±/∞)

20.♕c3 ♗h4 21.♖gf1= — The chances are equal. Black will probably take a perpetual check soon.)

13...♘dxc5!? (13...♗xe2 14.♘xe2±)

14.dxc5 ♘xc5 15.♕a2 ♗xe2 16.♔xe2 e4 17.b3 ♘d3 18.♕c2± — Black has powerful positional compensation but it's very difficult to prove that it's worth a whole piece.;

10.♘a2!

(10.axb5 axb5 11.♕a5 (11.b4 transposes after 11...e4 12.♘d2 ♗e7 13.♕a6 ♕c7=) 11...♕c8 Going into an endgame is not benefi-

cial for Black. 12.♕a6 ♕c7 13.b4 e4 14.♘d2 ♗e7= — Black plans to castle and play ♖fc8, ♕c7-d8 and ♖c8-a8.)

10...♘e4 11.axb5 axb5 (11...exd4 12.bxc6 ♘dxc5 13.b4±) 12.♘b4 ♕f6 13.♗e2 ♗e7 14.h3! ♗xf3 (14...♗h5 The move is bad for Black 15.g4! ♗g6 16.♕a7±) 15.gxf3 ♘g5 (15...♘exc5 16.dxc5 ♘xc5 17.♘d3±) 16.f4!

(16.♕a6 exd4 17.exd4 (17.f4 ♘xc5 18.♕xc6+ ♘d7 19.♕xf6 ♗xb4+ 20.♔f1=) 17...0-0 (17...♘xf3+? 18.♗xf3 ♕xf3 19.0-0-0+- — The white rook enters via a3.) 18.♗xg5

(18.♘xc6 ♘xf3+ 19.♗xf3 (19.♔f1 ♘xd4 20.♘xb8 ♕f5 21.♘xd7 ♕e4 22.♔g1 ♕xe2 23.♗e3 ♘f3+ 24.♔g2 ♘h4+ 25.♔h2 ♘f3+=) 19...♘xc5 20.dxc5 ♗xc5 — Despite a temporary two piece deficit Black is safe.)

18...♕xg5 19.♘xc6 ♖be8 20.♕xb5 ♕f4 — The white king is very weak. Black has compensation sufficient for equality.)

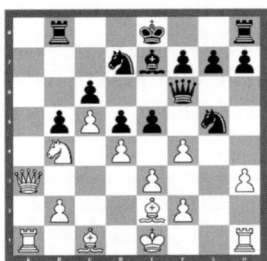

16...♘e4 *(16...exf4 17.♕a6! fxe3 18.♗xe3 0-0 19.♘xc6 ♖be8 20.♘xe7+ ♕xe7 21.♕d6 ♕xd6 22.cxd6±)* 17.♗g4 ♘dxc5 18.dxc5 ♗xc5 19.♕b3 exf4 *(19...♘xf2 20.♔xf2 ♕xf4+ 21.♔e2 ♕xb4 22.♕xb4 ♗xb4 23.♖a7 0-0 24.♖f1±* — The white squares in the Black's camp are vulnerable.; *19...0-0 20.♘d3 exf4 21.♘xc5 ♘xc5 22.♕c2±)* 20.♘a6 0-0 *(20... fxe3 21.♗xe3 ♗xe3 22.♕xe3 ♖d8 23.f3 h5 24.fxe4 hxg4 25.exd5+ ♔f8 26.0-0-0±; 20...h5 21.♗e2 0-0 22.♘xc5 ♘xc5 23.♕c2 ♘e4 24.exf4±)* 21.♘xc5 ♘xc5 22.♕c2 fxe3 23.♗xe3± — The position is complicated but the piece is still stronger than the pawns.;

c) 6...g6 7.♘e5

c1) 7.♗d3 ♗g4! 8.h3 ♗xf3 9.♕xf3 ♗g7= Svidler — Malakhov, Khanty Mansyisk 2009;

c2) 7.b4 also gives nothing 7...a5 8.bxa5 ♕xa5 9.♗d2 b4 10.♘b1 ♘e4 11.a3 *(11.♗e2? 11...♗g7 12.a3 ♘a6!±* — Black threatens to exchange on d2 and then to capture on c5.) 11...♘xd2 12.♘fxd2 e5 *(12...♕c7=)*

13.♘b3 ♕a4 14.♗d3 bxa3 15.♖xa3 ♕b4+ 16.♕d2 ♕xd2+ 17.♔xd2 ♖xa3 18.♘xa3 exd4 19.exd4 ♔d8= Panarin — Rublevsky, Moscow 2010;

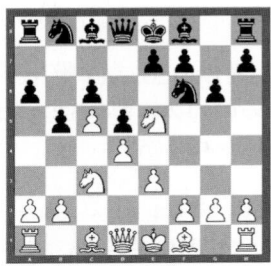

7...♗g7 8.f4

(8.♗d3 0-0 9.0-0 (9.f4 — 8.f4 0-0 9.♗d3) 9...♘fd7

(9...♗f5?! 10.♗xf5 gxf5 11.b4 (Also good is 11.♗d2±, with a later f2-f3 and the transfer of the bishop via e1 to g3 or h4.) 11...a5 12.bxa5 ♕xa5 13.♗d2 ♕c7 14.a4 bxa4 Gashimov — Laznicka, San Sebastian 2012 15.♖xa4! The a-file is worth fighting for. 15...♘bd7 16.♘xd7 ♘xd7 (16...♕xd7 17.f3±) 17.♕a1 ♖xa4 18.♕xa4± White has the unpleasant manoeuvre ♘c3-a2-b4 at hand, which gives him a slightly better game.)

10.f4 ♘xe5 11.fxe5 f6 12.exf6 exf6 13.♕b3 *(13.♗d2 f5 14.♕f3 ♘d7 15.♗e1 ♘f6 16.♗g3 ♖e8=)* 13...f5 14.a4 ♗b7= Dreev — Dautov, Mainz (rapid) 2005)

8...0-0 (A plan without castling can hardly be considered a good one: 8...a5 9.♗e2 ♕c7 10.0-0 h5 11.h3 ♗f5 12.♗d2 ♘bd7 13.♗f3 h4 14.♕e1 ♘e4 15.♘xe4 dxe4 16.♗e2 f6 17.♗xa5 ♖xa5 18.♘xc6± Caruana — Giri, Wijk aan Zee 2012; 8...♘fd7 9.♘d3±) 9.♗d3

(More popular is 9.♗e2 . In my opinion, it makes sense to associate this move with the following transfer of the bishop to f3, keeping control of the e4 square and preparing an additional gain of space with the move g2-g4. If Black plays b5-b4 aiming to fight for the e4 square, it creates a target on the queenside. 9...♕c7

c1) 9...♘fd7 10.♘d3 a5 11.h4 (11.a3 f5±) 11...h5 12.g4 hxg4 13.♗xg4 ♘f6 14.♗f3 ♗f5 15.♘e5! (15.h5 Gelfand — Levin, Austria 2009 15...♘xh5 16.♗xh5 gxh5 17.♕xh5 ♗g6 18.♕e2 ♘d7) 15...♕c8 16.h5 gxh5 17.♕e2!↑;

c2) 9...♗e6 10.♗f3 ♕c7 11.♘d3 a5 12.a3 ♕c8 13.h3 ♗f5 14.♘f2± P.Smirnov — Chadaev, Irkutsk 2010;

c3) 9...a5 10.0-0 ♗e6 11.♗f3 (11.♗d2 ♘e4 12.♗e1 f6 13.♘d3 f5= Melkumyan — Volkov, St.Petersburg 2009) 11...♕c7 12.♘d3±;

10.0-0 a5

c1) 10...♘bd7 11.♗d2 ♘xe5 (11...a5 12.a3 ♘xe5 13.fxe5 ♘e8 14.♗e1 ♗h6= Moiseenko — Amonatov,

Belgorod 2010) 12.fxe5 ♘e8 13.b4 f6 Moiseenko — Amonatov, Belgorod (rapid) 2010 14.♕b3±;

c2) 10...♗e6 11.♗f3 (11.g4 ♘e4 12.♗f3 f5= Gelfand — Bareev, Khanty Mansyisk 2005; 11.♗d2 ♘e4= Eljanov — Malakhov, Moscow 2006) 11...♘bd7 12.♘d3 ♗f5 13.♘f2 h5 14.h3 b4 15.♘a4 ♘e4 16.♗xe4 dxe4 17.♗d2 ♖ab8∞ Wang Yue — Malakhov, Ningbo (rapid) 2010;

11.♗f3!? (11.a3 ♘e4 12.♘xe4 dxe4 13.a4 b4 14.♕c2 f5 15.♕b3+ e6= Vitiugov — Malakhov, Moscow 2010) 11...♗e6 12.♗d2 ♘bd7 13.♘d3± — White stands better since after

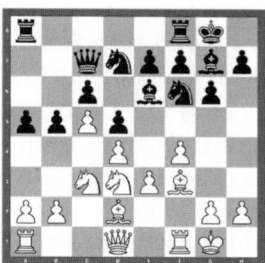

13...♗f5 he can play 14.♘f2! h5 15.h3, preparing expansion with g2-g4.)

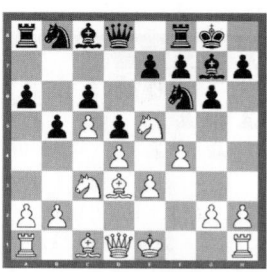

9...♕c7 (9...♗f5 10.♗xf5 gxf5 11.0−0± Sargissyan — Zhou Jinchao, Moscow 2009; 9...a5 10.♗d2 ♗e6 11.♕c2 ♕c8 12.h3 ♘a6 13.a3 ♘d7 14.♘f3± Anand — Buhmann, Germany 2012) 10.0−0 ♗e6 11.♗d2 (11.g4 ♘bd7! 12.f5 ♘xe5 13.dxe5 ♘d7 14.fxe6 fxe6∓ Eljanov — Malakhov, Khanty Mansyisk (rapid) 2009) 11...a5

(11...♘bd7 12.b4 a5 (12...♘xe5 13.dxe5 ♘g4 14.♘e2 f6 15.h3 ♘h6 16.♘d4 ♕c8 17.exf6 ♗xf6 18. ♗c3±) 13.bxa5 ♖xa5 14.a4 bxa4 15.♖xa4± — Problems remain with defence of the c6 pawn, Malakhov — So, Khanty Mansyisk 2009)

12.♕c2! (12.♗e1 ♘bd7 13. ♗h4 ♘xe5 14.fxe5 ♘g4 15.♕e2 ♘h6=; 12.a3 ♘bd7 13.b4 axb4 14.axb4 ♗f5 15.♗xf5 gxf5 16.♕c2 ♘e4 17.♘xe4 dxe4 18.♘xd7 ♕xd7 19.♖a2 ♖xa2 20.♕xa2 e6=) 12...♘bd7 13.♘f3± — White controls the e4 square and retains a space advantage.;

7.a3! Stabilising the c3 knight before playing e3-e4. Also White wants to make the cementing move b2-b4 and the a3 pawn is prophylaxis against the break a6-a5.

a) 7.♗d2

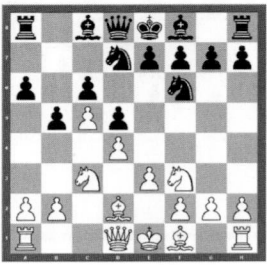

7...a5 8.a3

(8. ♗d3 e5!

(8...g6 9.0−0 ♗g7 10.e4 (10.a3 0−0 11.b4 e5!± Dubov — I. Popov, Moscow 2012) 10...dxe4 11.♘xe4±)

9.dxe5 ♘g4 10.e6 fxe6 11.♘d4 ♘xc5∓)

8...♕c7 9.b4 e5= Bareev — Jakovenko, Moscow 2005;

b) 7.♗d3

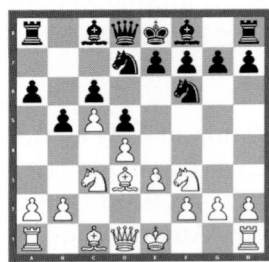

7...e5 8.♘xe5 ♘xe5 9.dxe5 ♘d7

(The following leads to an unclear, irrational position 9...♘g4 10.f4 ♗xc5 11.♕f3 ♕b6 12.♘d1 (12.♔e2 ♘h6 13.h3 ♘f5∓ Bacrot — Karjakin, Baku 2008) 12...♗b4+!

(12...♘h6 13.0−0 0−0 14.♘f2 ♘f5 (14...f6 15.exf6 ♖xf6 16. ♗d2± Kazhgaleyev — Gundavaa, Subic Bay 2009) 15.♕h3 ♘h6 16.g4 f6 17.exf6 ♖xf6 18. ♗d2±)

13.♔e2 (13.♘c3 ♗c5=; 13.♔f1 0−0 14.h3 ♘h6 15.g4 c5∞) 13...0−0 14.h3 ♘h6 15.g4∞)

10.e6 (*10.f4 ♘xc5 11.0-0 ♘xd3 12.♕xd3 ♗e7∞* — The game is double-edged but it's more pleasant to play with the two bishops.) 10... ♘xc5 11.exf7+ ♔xf7 12. ♗c2 (*12.b3? 12...♘xd3+ 13.♕xd3 ♕g5∓* Anand — Aronian, Moscow 2009) 12...g6 13.0-0 ♗g7= — in the forthcoming double-edged battle White's chances are no worse, Aronian — Movsesian, Nanjing 2008;

c) 7.b3

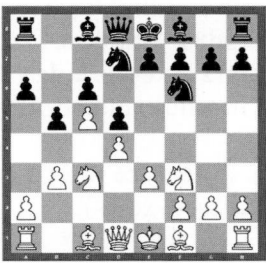

7...g6 8. ♗b2 ♗g7 9.b4 a5 10.a3 0-0 11. ♗e2 ♕c7! Black's main strategical aim is to push e7-e5 and after exchanging in the centre to move the white squared bishop to the kingside. If Black moves the bishop to b7, his position will always be worse, regardless of whether he pushes e7-e5 or not. (*11...♘e4 12.0-0 axb4 13.axb4 ♖xa1 14.♕xa1±* Gashimov — Movsesian, Porto Carras 2011) 12.0-0 ♖e8= — Black will inevitably play e7-e5 equalising.;

d) 7.b4

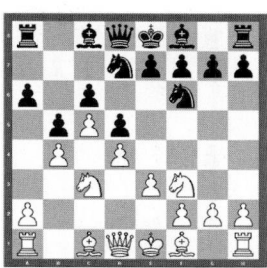

7...a5 (The following is bad *7...g6 8.a4 ♗b7 9. ♗b2 ♗g7 10.♕c2 0-0 11. ♗e2±* — The bishop on b7 will remain passive for the whole game, Ponomariov — Gashimov, Warsaw (blitz)2010) 8.bxa5

(8.♕b3 axb4 9.♕xb4 e5 10.a4 exd4 11.exd4 ♘e4 12. ♗e3 Miroshnichenko — Sakaev, Kragujevac 2009 12...♕a5! 13.♕xa5 ♖xa5 14. ♗d2 (If White sacrifices a piece *14.♘xd5 cxd5 15. ♗xb5 ♔d8* he takes the bigger risk.) 14...♘xd2 15.♘xd2 bxa4 16.♘b3 ♖a8 17.♖xa4 ♖xa4 18.♘xa4 ♔d8= — By transferring the king to c7, Black safely solves the problem of defending the c6 pawn.)

8...♕xa5 9. ♗d2 b4 10.♘b1 (*10. ♘e2 ♘e4 11.♘c1 e5 12.a4 ♘xd2 13.♘xd2 ♗e7 14.♘db3 ♕c7 15.♘d3 0-0 16. ♗e2 ♗a6=* — Black has no problems, Wang Yue — Karjakin, Nice (rapid) 2009) 10...♘e4 11.a3 (*11. ♗e2 e5 12.0-0 ♗e7 13.a3 ♖b8* — 11.a3 ♖b8 12. ♗e2 e5 13.0-0 ♗e7) 11... ♖b8! (*11...♘xd2 12.♘fxd2 e5 13.♘b3 ♕a4 14. ♗d3 bxa3 15.♖xa3 ♕b4+ 16.♕d2±*)

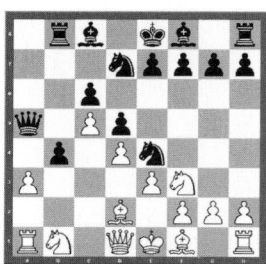

12.♖a2 (*12.♗e2 e5 13.0–0 ♗e7 14.♖a2 ♘xd2 15.♘fxd2 0–0=*) 12...♘xd2 13.♕xd2 ♖a8 14.♗e2 e5 15.0–0 ♗e7 16.♖b2 bxa3 17.♕xa5 ♖xa5 18.♖a2 ♗a6 19.♗xa6 ♖xa6 20.♖xa3= Aronian — I.Sokolov, Goteborg 2005;

7...a5!

(7...g6 8.b4 a5 Otherwise the move a3-a4 is unpleasant. 9.♗b2 ♗g7 10.♗d3! (*10.♗e2 0–0 11.0–0 ♕c7 12.♕c2 ♖e8 13.h3 e5=*) 10...0–0 11.h3± — It's difficult to play e7-e5. White stands better.)

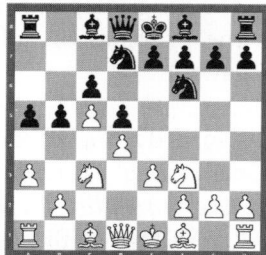

8.♕c2

(8.♗d3

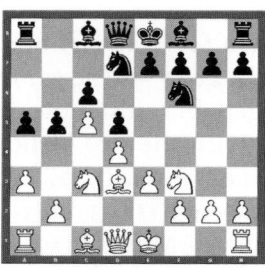

8...e5 9.dxe5 ♘g4 10.e6

(10.♗xb5 cxb5 11.♕xd5 ♖a6

(11...♖b8? 12.h3 b4 (*12...♘h6 13.c6 ♘c5 14.♕xd8+ ♔xd8 15.♘d4±*) 13.axb4 axb4 14.♘e4 ♘xc5 15.♕xd8+ ♔xd8 16.♘xc5 ♘xf2 17.♔xf2 ♗xc5 18.♗d2± Aronian — Grischuk, Bilbao 2009)

12.h3 ♘h6 13.c6 ♘c5 14.e4 ♗e6 15.♕xd8+ ♔xd8∓)

10...fxe6 11.♘d4 ♘xc5 (*11...♘ge5 12.♗xb5±*) 12.♗e2

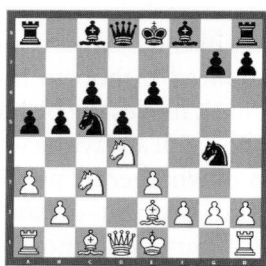

12...♘xf2!

a) 12...♘f6 13.♘xc6 ♕b6 14.♘e5 ♗a6 15.b4 ♘cd7 16.♘xd7 ♘xd7 17.bxa5 ♕xa5 18.♗d2±;

b) 12...♘e5 13.f4 ♘c4 14.b3 ♘d6 15.♘xc6 ♕b6 16.♘d4 ♗d7 (16...♗e7 17.♘cxb5±) 17.♗b2!N (Less convincing is *17.0-0* Lputian — Jakovenko, Fuegen 2006, whereon *17...g6* was possible preventing f4-f5. Though after *18.♗b2 ♗g7 19.f5! gxf5 20.♗h5+ ♔d8 21.b4→* White still has a strong attack.)

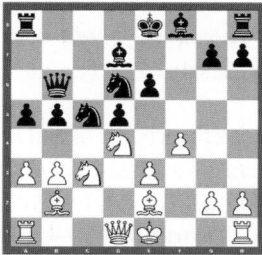

17...♗e7 18.f5±;

13.♔xf2 ♗d6 14.♘xc6 0-0+

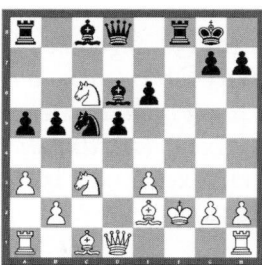

15.♗f3!

(*15.♔g1 ♕h4 16.♗f3 (16.g3 ♕f6 17.♕e1 ♘b3 18.♖b1* Krasenkow — Gozzoli, Ustron 2007 *18...b4! 19.axb4 axb4 20.♘b5 ♗c5-+)* 16...♘e4 17.♕e2 ♗a6 18.♗xe4 dxe4 19.g3 ♕h6 (19...♗xg3 20.hxg3 ♕xg3+ 21.♕g2 ♕e1+ 22.♔h2 ♕h4+=) 20.♘xe4 ♖ac8 21.♘xa5 b4 22.♕xa6 ♖xc1+ 23.♖xc1 ♕xe3+ 24.♔g2 ♕xe4+ 25.♔h3 ♕f5+ 26.♔g2=)*

15...♕d7! (*15...♕c7 16.♘d4 ♗xh2 17.♕c2±; 15...♕h4+ 16.g3 ♕f6 17.♔g2 ♗b7 18.♘d4 e5 19.♖f1 exd4 20.exd4 ♘e4 21.♗xe4 ♕xf1+ 22.♕xf1 ♖xf1 23.♗xh7+ ♔xh7 24.♔xf1±) 16.♘d4 ♗a6 (16...e5 17.♘dxb5+-) 17.♔g1 (17.a4 bxa4 18.♔g1 ♔h8 19.♘xa4 e5!≥) 17...b4 18.♘ce2 (18.♘xd5 exd5 19.♗xd5+ ♔h8 20.♗xa8 ♖xa8 21.axb4 axb4 22.♗d2 ♖f8 23.♗xb4 ♕e8 24.♗d2 ♗b7) 18...♔h8!≥* — Black has sufficient compensation for a piece but he must play energetically and accurately.)

8...♕c7

(8...g6 9.e4

(9.♗d3 ♗g7 10.0-0 0-0 11.e4 (*11.♖e1 e5!*) 11...dxe4 12.♘xe4 ♘xe4 13.♗xe4 ♕c7=)

9...dxe4 10.♘xe4 ♗g7 11.a4 b4 12.♗c4 0-0 13.0-0± Eljanov — Movsesian, Sochi 2012)

9.e4 dxe4 10.♘xe4 ♘xe4 11.♕xe4 ♘f6

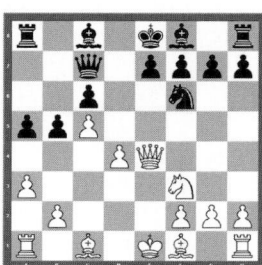

12.♕e5 ♛xe5+ 13.♘xe5 ♝b7 14.a4 b4 15.♝f4 ♘d5

(15...♘d7 16.♘c4 ♝a6 17.♘b6 (17.0-0-0±) 17...♖a7 18.♝xa6 ♖xa6 19.♘c4 ♖a7 20.0-0-0± Gelfand — Karjakin, Nalchik 2009)

16.♝g3 g6 17.h4 (17.0-0-0 ♝g7 18.♘c4±) 17...♝g7 18.h5 g5 19.♝c4± E.Gasanov — O.Ivanov, Alushta 2009

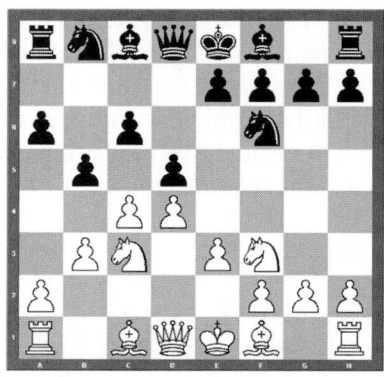

6...♝g4
    6...♝f5

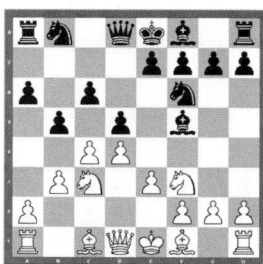

7.♘e5

(Somewhat unenergetic is 7.♝d3, after which White can expect only a minimal advantage: 7...e6 (7... ♝xd3 8.♕xd3 e6 9.0-0 ♝e7 10.e4 b4 11.e5 bxc3 12.exf6 ♝xf6 13. ♝a3± Pe.Nielsen — Postny, Khanty Mansyisk 2011) 8.0-0 ♘bd7

(8...♝d6 9.♕c2

a) 9.cxd5 cxd5 10.♘xd5!? ♘xd5 11.e4 ♝xe4 12.♝xe4 0-0 13.♕d3 g6 14.♝xd5 exd5 15.a4±;

b) 9.♝xf5 exf5 10.♕d3 (10.♕c2 g6 11.♝d2 0-0 12.♖fc1 ♘bd7 13.cxd5 cxd5 14.a4 b4 15.♘e2 ♖c8 16.♕d3 ♕b6= Radjabov — Ivanchuk, Wijk aan Zee 2003) 10...g6 11.a4 dxc4 12.bxc4 b4 13.♘e2 (13.e4 bxc3 14.e5 ♝b4 15.exf6 0-0=) 13...♘bd7 14.♝b2 0-0= Kasimdzhanov — Sakaev, Germany 2003;

9...♝xd3 (9...♝g6 10.e4 b4 11.e5±) 10.♕xd3 ♘bd7 (10...0-0 11.e4 ♝b4 12.e5 ♝xc3 13.♕xc3 ♘e4 14.♕e3±) 11.e4 dxe4 (11...dxc4!? 12.bxc4 e5±) 12.♘xe4 ♘xe4 13.♕xe4 ♖c8 14.♝g5±)

9.♝xf5 (9.♝b2 ♝d6 10.♝xf5 exf5 — 9.♝xf5 exf5 10.♝b2 ♝d6) 9... exf5 10.♝b2 (10.♘e5 ♝d6! 11.f4 ♖c8=) 10...♝d6 11.♕c2 g6 12.cxd5 cxd5 13.♘xd5 ♘xd5 14.♕c6 ♝xh2+ 15.♔xh2 ♘b4 16.♕d6 ♕e7 17.♕xe7+ ♔xe7±)

7...h6

(7...e6? is bad. 8.g4 ♗g6 9.h4 ♗b4

(9...♘e4 10.♘xe4 ♗xe4 11.f3 f6 12.fxe4 fxe5 13.cxd5 cxd5 14. ♗g2 ♗b4+ *(14...dxe4 15.0-0±)* 15.♗d2 ♗xd2+ 16.♕xd2 ♘c6 *(16...dxe4 17.0-0±)* 17.exd5 exd5 18.dxe5 ♘xe5 19.0-0±)

10.♗d2 ♗xc3

(10...♕a5 11.♖c1 ♘e4 12.♘xe4 ♗xe4 13.f3 f6 *(13...dxc4 14.♗xb4 ♕xb4+ 15.♔f2 ♗d5 16.bxc4 bxc4 17. ♗xc4±)* 14.fxe4 fxe5 15.cxd5 exd4 16.exd4 exd5 17. ♗xb4 ♕xb4+ 18.♕d2 ♕xd2+ 19.♔xd2 dxe4 20.♗g2±)

11.♗xc3 ♘e4 12. ♗b4 a5 *(12... f6 13.h5±)* 13. ♗a3 b4 14.♗b2 f6 15.♘xg6 hxg6 16.cxd5 cxd5 17.f3 ♘d6 18.♖c1±)

8.g4 (White also retains a space advantage after *8. ♗d3 ♗xd3 9.♕xd3 e6 10.0-0 ♗d6 11.f4 0-0 12. ♗b2±* Savina — Aldokhin, Moscow 2009) 8...♗h7 9.♗g2 e6 10.0-0

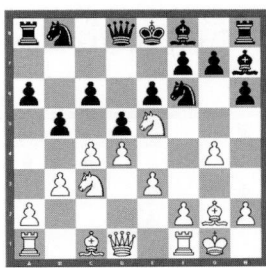

10...♗d6

(10... ♗e7 11.f4

(11. ♗b2 ♖a7 *(11...0-0±)* 12.c5 ♕c8 13.f4 ♘bd7 14.g5 ♘g8 15.g6 fxg6 Sakaev — Saltaev, Germany 2007 16. ♗h3±)

11...♘fd7 *(11...0-0 12.g5!? hxg5 13.fxg5 ♘fd7 14.g6 fxg6 15.♖xf8+ ♗xf8 16. ♕g4 ♘xe5 17.dxe5±)* 12.cxd5 ♘xe5 13.d6 ♕xd6 Kramnik — Bareev, Monaco (blindfold) 2003 14.fxe5 ♕c7 15. ♗b2±)

11.♗b2 *(11.f4 0-0 12. ♗b2 ♘fd7 13.cxd5 cxd5 14. ♖c1±)* 11...0-0 12.♖c1 ♖a7 13.c5 ♗c7 14.♘e2 a5 15.f3 ♘fd7 16.f4 f6 17.♘d3 ♘a6 18.a3 b4 19.a4 ♖e8 20.♕d2± Grischuk — Morozevich, Sochi 2004

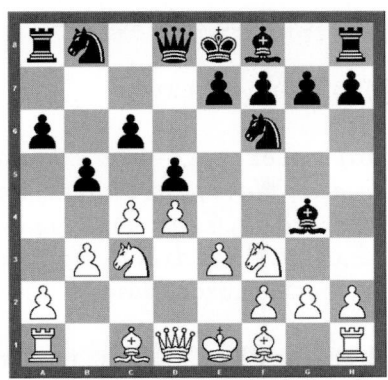

7. ♗e2
7. ♗d2 ♘bd7

(7...e6 8.h3 ♗xf3 *(8... ♗h5 9.g4 ♗g6 10.♘e5 ♘fd7 11.♘xg6 hxg6 12. ♗g2 f5 Sadler — Volkov, Oslo 2011 13.♘e2!±)* 9.♕xf3 ♗b4

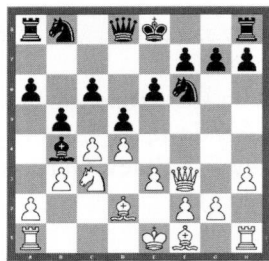

10.♗d3! This entails a pawn sacrifice but no other move gives any chance for an advantage.

a) 10.♖c1 0–0 11.♗d3

(11.♗e2 ♕a5 12.0–0 (12.♖c2 bxc4 13.bxc4 ♗xc3 14.♗xc3 ♕a4=) 12...♗xc3 13.♗xc3 ♕xa2=)

11...dxc4 12.bxc4 e5 13.0–0 exd4 14.exd4 bxc4 15.♗e2 ♕xd4 16.♖fd1 ♘bd7 17.♗f4 ♕a7 18.♘e4 ♘xe4 19.♕xe4 ♖ae8 20.♕xc4 a5=;

b) 10.♕d1 0–0 11.a3

b1) 11.♗e2 c5 12.0–0 (12.cxb5 cxd4 13.exd4 ♕a5 14.♖c1 ♖c8) 12...bxc4 (12...cxd4 13.♘xd5 ♘xd5 14.cxd5 ♗xd2 15.♕xd2 dxe3 16.♕xe3 exd5 17.♕c5±) 13.bxc4 ♕a5=;

b2) 11.c5?! 11...♗xc3 12.♗xc3 ♘e4∓;

b3) 11.♗d3?! 11...dxc4 12.bxc4 c5∓;

10...♗xc3 12.♗xc3 ♘e4 13.♖c1 dxc4 14.bxc4 c5=;

10...♕a5 11.♖c1 ♗xc3 12.♗xc3 (12.♖xc3 ♕xa2 13.♕d1 0–0 14.0–0 ♕a3

15.♕b1 ♕e7 16.♖c2∞) 12...♕xa2 13.♕d1 bxc4 14.bxc4 dxc4

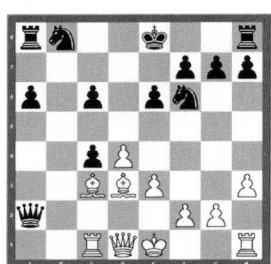

15.♗e2! (15.♖a1 ♕b3 16.♕xb3 cxb3 17.♔e2 ♘d5 18.♗d2 ♘d7 19.♖hb1 c5 20.♖xb3 cxd4 21.exd4 ♔e7 22.♖xa6 ♖xa6 23.♗xa6 ♖a8=) 15...♕b3 (15...♘bd7 16.0–0 ♘b6 17.♗b4 ♘fd5 18.♗c5±; 15...a5 16.0–0 0–0 17.♖a1 ♕b3 18.♕c1±) 16.♗a5 ♕xd1+ 17.♗xd1± — Since Black will not be able to keep the extra material, White will obtain a positional advantage.)

8.h3 ♗xf3 (8...♗h5 9.g4 ♗g6 10.♘h4 e6 11.♘xg6 hxg6 12.♗g2 bxc4 13.bxc4 ♘b6 14.c5 ♘c4 15.♕a4 ♕c7 16.♗c1± Lysyi — Dominguez, Khanty Mansyisk 2011) 9.♕xf3 b4 10.♘a4

(10.♘e2 e5 11.♘g3 g6 12.cxd5 cxd5 13.dxe5 ♘xe5 14.♕f4 ♗d6 15.♕h6

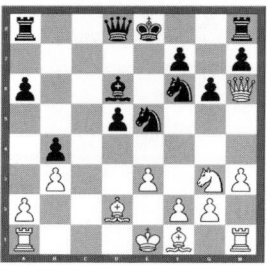

15...♘ed7!N Black has created the threat 16...♘g8 17.♕g7 ♗e5 (*15... ♖g8 16.♖c1±* Morozevich — Ivanchuk, Reggio Emilia 2012) 16.♕h4 0–0 17.♗e2 (*17.♗xb4 ♘e4–+*) 17... ♖c8 18.0–0 ♖c2 19.♗xb4 ♗xg3 20.♕xg3 ♖xe2 21.♗xf8 ♕xf8∓)

10...e5

(10...♘e4

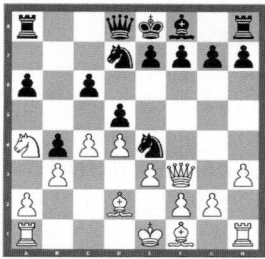

11.♕d1

a) 11.♗xb4?! 11...e5 12.c5 ♖b8 13.♗c3 ♘xc3 14.♘xc3 g6∓;

b) 11.♖d1 e6

(11...e5 12.cxd5 cxd5 13.♗d3 ♘ef6 (*13...♘xd2 14.♕xd5+-*) 14.♕e2±)

12.♗d3 f5∞;

c) 11.♗d3 ♘xd2 12.♔xd2 e6 13.cxd5 cxd5 14.♖hc1 ♗d6 15.♖c6 ♘b8 16.♖c2 0–0 17.♖ac1 ♖a7 18.♔e1±;

d) 11.♗c1!? e6 12.♗d3 f5 13.♕h5+! (*13.g4* Bauer — Fontaine, Chartres 2005 *13...♕f6∞*) 13...g6 14.♕e2±;

11...e5 12.♗d3 — 10...e5 11.♕d1 ♘e4 12.♗d3)

11.♕d1

a) 11.c5?! 11...a5 12.0–0–0 ♗e7∓;

b) 11.cxd5 cxd5 12.dxe5

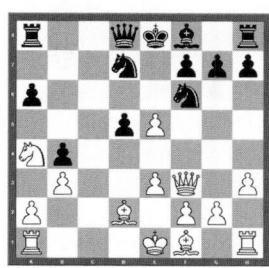

12...♘e4!N

(12...♘xe5 13.♕f4 ♗d6 14.♕d4 0–0 (*14...♘c6 15.♕b6 ♕xb6 16.♘xb6 ♖b8 17.♘a4 a5 18.♖c1 ♔d7 19.♗d3±*) 15.♖c1 ♖e8 (*15...♕e7 16.♗e2±* Ponomariov — Ni Hua, Saratov 2011) 16.♗e2 ♘g6 (*16... ♘e4 17.0–0±*) 17.0–0 ♘f4 18.exf4 (*18.♗f3 ♗e5 19.♕b6 ♘d3=*) 18... ♖xe2 19.♖fe1 ♖xe1+ 20.♖xe1 ♖b8 21.♖d1±)

13.♕f4 g6 14.♗c1 (Risky is *14.♖d1 ♗g7 15.♗xb4 ♗xe5 16.♕f3 ♖b8 17.♗d2 ♗c7 18.♗d3 ♘xd2 19.♔xd2 ♘e5 20.♕e2∞* — White is vulnerable to attack.) 14...♗g7 15.♗b2 0–0 16.♗d3 ♘c3 17.♘xc3 ♘xe5 18.♖d1 bxc3 19.♗xc3 ♘xd3+ 20.♖xd3 ♗xc3+ 21.♖xc3 ♕a5 22.♕c7 ♕xa2 23.0–0 ♖ab8=;

11...exd4

a) 11...♘e4 12.♗d3 ♘xd2 13.♕xd2 exd4

(13...♕g5 14.0-0 exd4 15.cxd5 cxd5

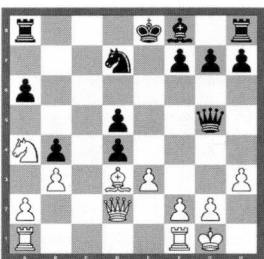

16.♕c2!N (*16.f4 ♕f6 17.e4 dxe4 18.♗xe4 ♖d8∞* Schlosser — Dzhakaev, Pardubice 2011) 16...dxe3 17.♖ae1 ♗e7 18.♗f5 ♖d8 19.♗xd7+ ♖xd7 20.♘b6 ♕g6 21.♕xg6 hxg6 22.♘xd7 ♔xd7 23.♖xe3±)

14.0-0! (*14.cxd5 cxd5 15.0-0 ♗d6 16.♗f5 ♘f6 17.♕xd4 0-0 18.♖ac1 g6 19.♗d3 a5 20.♖c6±* Kramnik — Karjakin, Nice (rapid) 2009)

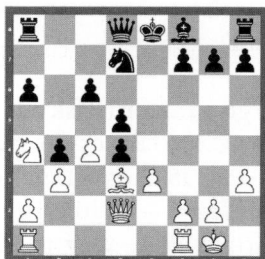

14...♗e7 15.cxd5 cxd5 16.exd4

(16.♗f5

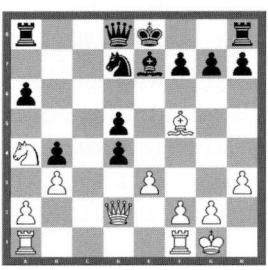

16...♘b6!N (*16...♖b8 17.♕xd4 ♘f6 18.♖ac1 0-0 19.♖c6±* Alekseev — Svidler, Nalchik 2009) 17.♖ad1 ♘xa4 18.bxa4 dxe3 19.♕xe3 0-0 20.♗e4±)

16...0-0 17.♖fe1±;

b) 11...♗d6 12.♗d3 0-0 13.0-0 a5 14.cxd5 cxd5 15.dxe5 ♗xe5 16.♖c1 ♕e7 17.♖c2 ♖ad8±/= The queenside structure is in Black's favour as the c3 square can be used by a knight eventually. In addition White's dark squared bishop is out of play. Therefore despite an isolated pawn, Black is nearly equal, Roiz — Wang Yue, Ningbo 2011;

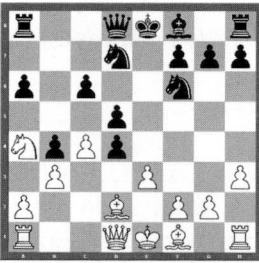

12.exd4 ♘e4 13.♗d3 (*13.g3 ♗d6 14.♗g2 ♘df6 15.0-0 a5 16.cxd5 cxd5 17.♘c5 0-0=* Aronian — Svidler, Nalchik 2009) 13...♗d6!?

a) 13...♕f6 14.♗e3 ♗d6 15.♕c2 0-0 16.♗xe4 dxe4 17.♕xe4 ♖fe8 18.♕g4±;

b) 13...♗e7 14.0-0 0-0 15.♗xe4 dxe4 16.♕e1 ♘f6 17.♗xb4 ♗xb4 18.♕xb4 ♘h5 (18...♕xd4 19.♖ad1 ♕e5 20.♕c5±) 19.♕d2 ♕h4 20.♘c5 ♘f4 21.♔h2±;

c) 13...♘xd2 14.♕xd2 dxc4 15.♗xc4 ♗e7 16.0-0 0-0 17.♖fe1±;

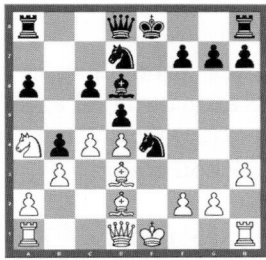

14.c5 (14.0-0 0-0 15.♗xe4 dxe4 16.♕e1 ♕e7 17.c5 ♗c7 18.♗xb4 a5 19.♗d2 ♖fe8 20.♖d1 h6) 14...♗c7 15.♗xb4 0-0 16.0-0

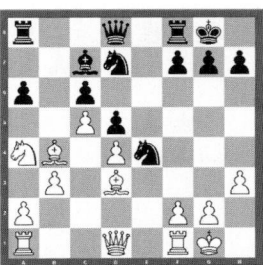

16...a5!N (After 16...f5 the next move is unpleasant 17.♘b6±, and Black's attacking potential decreases, Legky — Vidoniak, Lvov 2009) 17.♗d2

f5 — Black has sufficient compensation for a pawn.;

7.h3 ♗xf3

(7... ♗h5?! 8.g4 ♗g6 9.♘e5 e6 10.h4 ♗b4 (10...♘bd7 N 11.♘xd7! ♔xd7 12.h5 ♗b4 13.♗d2 ♕a5 14.♖c1 ♘e4 15.hxg6 ♘xc3 16.♕c2 ♘e4 17.♗xb4 ♕xb4+ 18.♔e2±) 11.♗d2 ♗xc3 (11...dxc4 12.h5 ♗d3 13.♗xd3 cxd3 14.♘xd3±) 12.♗xc3 ♘e4 13.♗b4 a5 (13...f6 14.♘xg6 hxg6 15.cxd5±) 14.♗a3 b4 15.♗b2 f6 16.♘xg6 hxg6 17.cxd5 cxd5 18.f3 ♘d6 19.♖c1 f5 20.g5±)

8.♕xf3

(The creative move gives nothing 8.gxf3

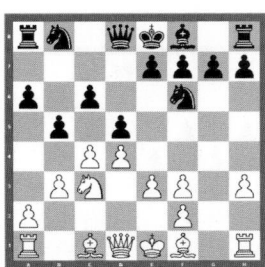

8...♘bd7 9.f4 (9.♗b2 e6 10.♗d3 ♗e7=) 9...e6 10.c5 (10.♗d2 ♗e7 11.c5 ♘e4 12.♘xe4 dxe4 13.♗g2 f5 14.f3 exf3 15.♗xf3 ♖c8 16.♕e2 ♗h4+ 17.♔d1 ♘f6 18.♖g1 0-0= Van Wely — So, Amsterdam 2010) 10...g6

(The following is not so reliable 10...♘e4 11.♘xe4 (11.♗d2 ♘xc3 12.♗xc3 a5 13.♗d3 f5= Ivanchuk

— Gelfand, Dresden 2008) 11...
dxe4 12.♗g2 f5 13.f3 exf3 14.♗xf3
♖c8 15.♕e2 ♘f6 16.♗d2 ♕d7
17.♖g1 ♔f7 18.0-0-0 g6± Gustafsson — Ni Hua, Reggio Emilia
2008)

11.♗d3 ♗g7 (There is another
way of building a fortress *11...♗e7
12.♕c2 0-0 13.♗b2 a5 14.♘e2 ♘h5
15.♘g1 f5 16.♘f3 ♗h4= Gurevich
— Postny, Kusadasi 2006) 12.♗b2
♘g8 13.♕c2 ♘e7 14.a4 b4 15.♘e2
a5 16.♘g1 ♘f5 17.0-0-0 ♘h4= El-
sness — Volkov, Oslo 2011)*

8...e5! (*8...e6 9.♗d3 ♗b4 10.♗d2 —
7.♗d2 e6 8.h3 ♗xf3 9.♕xf3 ♗b4
10.♗d3; 8...bxc4 9.bxc4 e5 10.♖b1
♕a5 11.♕f5 ♘bd7 12.♗d2 ♗b4
13.♖xb4 ♕xb4 14.♘xd5± Ortiz —
Gomez Camilo, Panama 2011)*

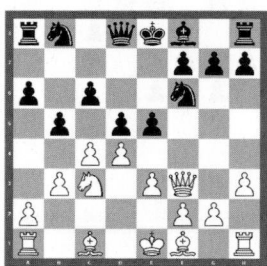

9.dxe5 (*9.c5 ♘bd7 10.♗e2 g6∓*) 9...
♗b4 10.♗d2 ♗xc3 11.♗xc3 ♘e4
12.♗b4 bxc4

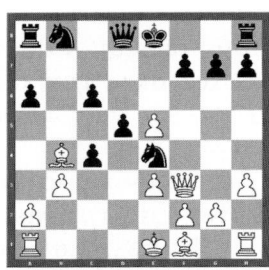

13.♕g4

a) 13.bxc4? 13...♕b6 14.a3 a5 15.e6 (*15.
cxd5 cxd5 16.♗d6 ♕b2 17.♖d1 ♕c3+
18.♔e2 ♘d7!↑*) 15...fxe6 16.♕h5+
♔d8 17.♗d2 ♘d7∓;

b) 13.♗xc4 ♕b6 14.a3 a5 15.♗d6
♘xd6 16.exd6 0-0 17.♗e2 ♕c5 18.0-
0 ♕xd6 19.e4 ♘d7= Wang Yue — Ni
Hua, Jin Zhou 2009;

c) 13.e6 fxe6 14.bxc4 ♘d7 15.cxd5
cxd5 16.♗d3 ♖b8 17.♗xe4 ♖xb4
18.♕h5+ ♔f8 19.♗d3 g6= So —
Malakhov, Khanty Mansyisk 2009;

13...c5 14.f3

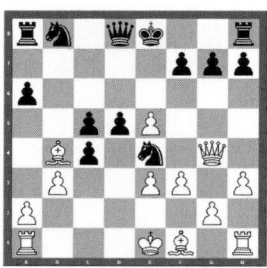

14...♘c6!

(Another route to equality is less
convincing: 14...cxb4 15.fxe4 0-0

16.exd5 cxb3 (16...♕xd5 17.♗xc4
♕xe5 18.0-0± Jakovenko —
Laznicka, Plovdiv 2010) 17.♕d4
(17.axb3 ♕xd5 18.♗c4 ♕xe5∓) 17...
♘d7 18.axb3 ♕g5

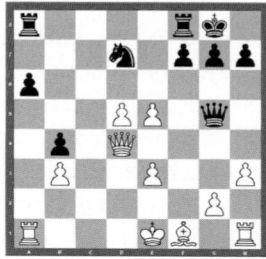

19.♔f2!?

(19.♕f4 ♕g6 (19...♕xe5 20.♕xe5
♘xe5 21.♗xa6± Kramnik — Ni
Hua, London 2009) 20.♖d1 (20.
♕g4 ♕h6 21.♕f4 ♕g6= Grisc-
chuk — Aronian, Bursa 2010)
20...♖ae8! (20...♕c2 21.♗c4 ♕c3+
22.♔e2 ♘xe5 23.d6± Le Quang
— Bacrot, Moscow 2010) 21.♗d3
♕b6 22.0-0 ♖xe5 23.d6 g6= Ni
Hua — Malakhov, China 2010)

19...♘xe5!N (19...a5 20.♗e2 ♕f5+
21.♕f4 ♕xe5 22.♕xe5 ♘xe5
23.♖hc1± Shulman — Malakhov,
Khanty Mansyisk 2010)

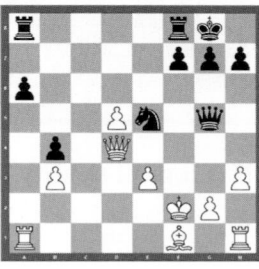

20.♕f4

(20.♖xa6 ♖xa6 21.♗xa6 ♕f6+
22.♕f4 (22.♔g3 ♕g6+ 23.♔h2
♕d6 24.♕f4 g5 25.♕g3 f6∓) 22...
♕xa6 23.♕xe5 ♕a2+=)

20...♕e7 21.♖xa6 ♖ad8 (21...♖ac8
22.♗e2 ♖c2 23.♖d1 ♕b7 24.♖a5
♕b6 25.♕e4 ♖xe2+ 26.♔xe2
♕xa5 27.♕xe5 ♕a2+ 28.♔f3 ♕xb3
29.♖d4±) 22.♕d4 ♕g5 23.d6 (23.
♗c4 ♕f5+ 24.♔g3 ♘xc4 25.bxc4
♖de8=) 23...♖fe8 24.♗e2 ♕f5+
25.♔g3 ♕c2 26.♗c4 ♘xc4 27.bxc4
♖e4

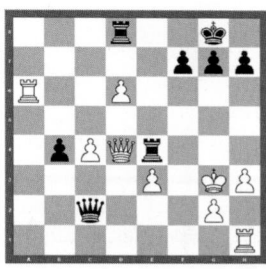

28.♖c1 ♖xd4 29.♖xc2 R4xd6
30.♖xd6 ♖xd6 31.♖b2 ♖b6
32.♔f4 ♔f8 33.♔e5 ♔e7 34.♔d4
♔d7 35.♔c5 ♔c7 36.♖xb4 ♖c6+
37.♔d4 ♖d6+ 38.♔e4 ♖e6+ 39.♔f3
♖f6+ 40.♔e2 ♖g6 41.♔f2 ♖f6+
42.♔g1±/= — Black must play accurately to achieve a draw.)

15.fxe4 (15.♕xg7 ♕h4+ 16.♔d1 cxb4
17.fxe4 0-0-0∓) 15...♘xb4 16.♕xg7
♖f8 17.exd5 (17.♕h6 ♖g8 18.♔f2
♖g6∓; 17.♔f2 ♕h4+∓) 17...♕h4+

(17...♘c2+ 18.♔f2 ♘xa1 (*18...*
♛xd5 19.♗e2 ♘xa1 20.♖xa1± Le
Quang — Nguyen, Vietnam 2010)
19.♗xc4 ♘c2

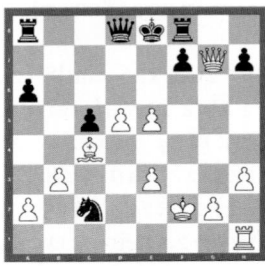

20.♛g4!N (*20.♛h6 ♖g8∞ Shi-*
manov — Linchevsky, Dagomys
2010) *20...♛a5 21.♖d1±*)

18.♔e2 ♘xd5

(*18...♛e4*

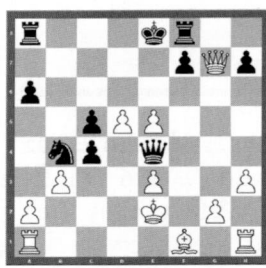

19.♛f6!N (*19.♔f2 ♘c2 20.♛h6 ♛g6*
21.♛f4 ♘xa1 22.♗xc4↑ Vitiugov
— Rodshtein, Bursa 2010) 19...♖d8
(*19...♖g8 20.e6 ♖a7 21.exf7+ ♖xf7*
22.♛e6+ ♛xe6 23.dxe6±) *20.bxc4*
♛xc4+ 21.♔f2 ♛xd5 22.♗e2±)

19.♛g4

a) 19.♔f3 f5 20.♗xc4 ♛e4+ 21.♔g3
♖a7 22.♛g5 ♛xe5+ (*22...♘xe3*
23.♔h2 ♛xe5+ 24.♛g3=) 23.♔f2
♛b2+ 24.♗e2 ♖g7∓/↑;

b) 19.♖c1 c3 20.♛g4 ♛h6 21.♛f3

(*21.♛e4 0-0-0 (21...♖d8 22.♔f2±)*
22.g4 f5 23.gxf5 ♖g8 24.♔f2 ♘xe3
25.♛a8+ (25.♖g1 ♘xf1 26.♛a8+
♔c7 27.♛a7+ ♔c8=) 25...♔d7
26.♗b5+ axb5 27.♖hd1+ ♘xd1+
28.♖xd1+ ♔c7 29.♛a7+ ♔c8
30.♛a8+=)

21...♖d8 — 19.♛g4 ♛h6 20.♛f3
♖d8 21.♖c1 c3(*21...0-0-0!?*) ;

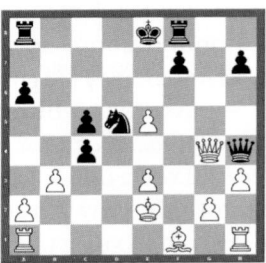

19...♛h6 20.♛f3 ♖d8

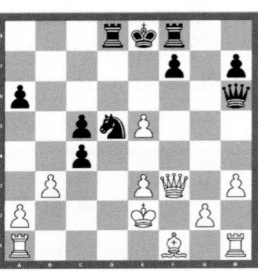

21.♔f2 N A logical novelty.

(21.♖c1 has also been played 21...
c3 22.g3 ♖g8 (22...f5 23.♗g2 f4
24.♖hf1 ♘xe3 25.♕c6+ ♕xc6
26.♗xc6+ ♔e7 27.♖xf4 ♘f5
28.♔e1 ♖d3 29.♗e4 ♖xg3 30.♔f2
♘d4 31.♖xf8 ♔xf8 32.♔xg3 ♘e2+
33.♔f2 ♘xc1=) 23.♔f2 ♖g5 (23...
♕g5=) 24.♗c4 (24.e4 ♖xe5 25.exd5
♖dxd5= — With such major pieces
Black has a guaranteed perpetual
check.) 24...♖xe5= Le Quang —
Kasimdzhanov, Guanzhou 2010)

21...f5! 22.♗xc4

(22.♖d1 f4 23.e4 ♕h4+ 24.♔g1
♘e3 25.♖xd8+ ♔xd8 26.♗xc4
♕g3 27.h4 (27.♗xa6? 27...♕xf3
28.gxf3 ♖g8+ 29.♔f2 ♖g2+ 30.♔e1
♖xa2 31.♗f1 ♔e7∓; 27.♕f2 ♘xc4
28.bxc4 ♔d7=) 27...♕e1+ 28.♔h2
(28.♗f1 ♖g8=) 28...♕xh4+ 29.♔g1
♕e1+ 30.♔h2=)

22...f4

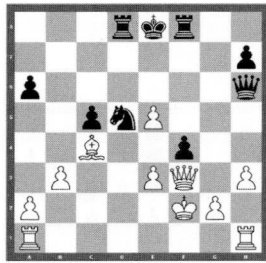

23.e4

(23.♔g1 fxe3 (23...♘xe3 24.e6±)
24.♕g4 ♘c3 (24...♘e7!?) 25.♖e1
♔e7 26.♔h2 (26.e6 ♖d2 27.♕g3
♖ff2 28.♕c7+ ♔e8 29.♕c8+ ♔e7=)

26...e2 27.e6 (27.♗xe2 ♖d4 28.♕g3
♘e4 29.♕g4 ♘f2 30.♕g3 ♘e4=)
27...♖d2 28.♗a6 ♘f4 29.♕g8
♘e4 30.♕b8 ♕g5 31.♕c7+ ♔f6
32.♕f7+ ♔e5 33.♕c7+ ♔f6=)

23...♘e3 24.♗d5

(24.♖he1 ♘xc4 (24...♖d7!?)
25.bxc4 ♖g8=)

24...♖g8! 25.♗xg8 ♖d2+ 26.♔e1 (26.
♔g1 ♖xg2+ 27.♕xg2 ♘xg2 28.♔xg2
♕g6+ 29.♔f1 ♕xe4 30.♖g1 ♕f3+
31.♔e1 ♕e3+=) 26...♖xg2 27.♖f1
♘c2+ 28.♔d1 ♘e3+ 29.♔e1=

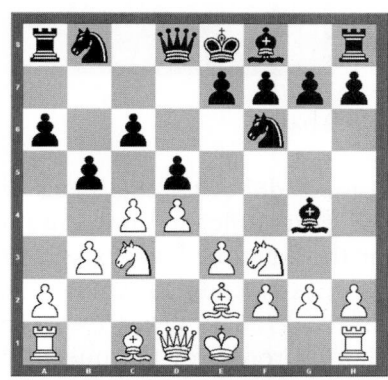

7...e6
7...♘bd7 8.0-0 e6 — 7...e6 8.0-0
♘bd7

8.0-0
8.h3 ♗h5 (8...♗f5 9.0-0 ♘bd7 —
8.0-0 ♘bd7 9.h3 ♗f5) 9.0-0 ♘bd7
— 8.0-0 ♘bd7 9.h3 ♗h5

8...♘bd7 9.h3

9.♗b2 is not of independent significance 9...♗d6 10.h3 ♗h5 — 9.h3 ♗h5 10.♗b2 ♗d6(10...♗f5 — 9.h3 ♗f5 10.♗b2 ♗d6)

9...♗h5
9...♗f5 10.♗b2

(After 10.♗d3 Black achieves equalisation with accurate play:

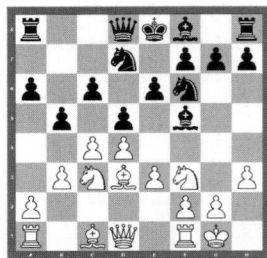

10...♗b4!

a) 10...♗d6? After this Black will not gain sufficient compensation for the pawn 11.♗xf5 exf5 12.♕c2 g6 13.cxd5 cxd5 14.♘xd5 ♘xd5 15.♕c6 ♕b8 16.♕xd5 0-0 17.b4! Making room for the queen. 17...♘b6 18.♕b3 ♘c4 19.♗d2±;

b) 10...♗xd3 11.♕xd3 ♗e7 12.e4 White has no other active move. 12...b4 13.e5 (13.exd5 bxc3 14.dxe6 fxe6 15.♕xc3∞) 13...bxc3 14.exf6 ♘xf6 15.♕xc3 0-0 16.♘e5 (16.♗f4 c5=) 16...♖c8 17.c5 ♘e4± — A complicated game lies ahead with slightly better chances for White.;

c) Possible is 10...♗g6 then 11.♕c2 It's best for Black to exchange

c1) 11.♗b2 ♗e7 12.♗xg6 hxg6 13.♘e5 ♖c8=;

c2) 11.♗xg6 hxg6 12.♕d3 ♗e7 13.e4 (13.cxd5 cxd5 14.a4 b4 15.♘e2 0-0 16.♗d2 ♕b6 17.♖fc1 ♖fc8 18.♖c2 ♘e4 19.♖ac1 ♕b7 20.♗e1 Aronian — Karjakin, Moscow 2004. The following might solve the problems 20...♘d6, preparing exchanges on the c-line. After 21.♘e5 ♘xe5 22.dxe5 ♖xc2 23.♖xc2 ♘e4=, with ♖a8-c8 to follow, the game is equal.) 13...bxc4 (13...b4 14.exd5 exd5 15.♘a4±) 14.bxc4 dxe4 15.♘xe4 c5=;

11...♗xd3 — 10...♗xd3 11.♕xd3(11...♗e7 12.♗xg6 hxg6 13.e4 b4 14.exd5 cxd5 15.♘e2± Riazantsev — Van Wely, France 2009; 11...♗b4 12.♗d2± Riazantsev — I.Sokolov, Poikovsky 2010; 11...♗h5 12.♘d2 ♖c8 13.c5± Riazantsev — Sakaev, Moscow 2005) ;

11.♗b2

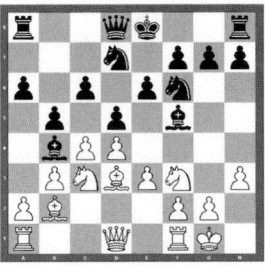

11...♗xd3!

(After the following Black's pawn structure starts to crumble. 11...0-0 12.♗xf5! (12.♘e5 ♘xe5 13.dxe5 ♗xd3 14.♕xd3 bxc4 15.bxc4 ♘d7=) 12...exf5 13.cxd5 cxd5 14.♕d3 g6 15.a4 bxa4 16.♘xa4 (16.♖xa4 ♕b6 17.♖fa1 a5 18.♘e5 ♖fd8= Harika — Volkov, Moscow 2007) 16...♕e7 (16...♕b8 17.♘e5 ♖c8 18.♘xd7 ♘xd7 19.♘c5!↑) 17.♖fc1±)

12.♕xd3 0-0 13.♖fc1 ♕e7 (13...♗e7 14.♖c2 ♕b8 15.cxd5 cxd5 16.♖ac1 ♕b7 17.♘e2 ♖fc8 18.♘e5 ♘xe5 19.dxe5 ♘d7 20.♕d1± Yevseev — Lovkov, Peterhof 2007) 14.♖c2 (14. cxd5 cxd5 15.a4 bxa4=) 14...♖fc8 15.♖ac1 dxc4 16.bxc4 ♘b6 17.♘d2 ♖d8=)

10...♗d6

(10...♕b8 11.♘h4 ♗e4 (11...♗g6 12.♘xg6 hxg6 13.♖b1± Wojtaszek — Lintchevsky, Warsaw (rapid) 2010) 12.♘xe4 (12.cxd5 cxd5 13.♖c1±) 12...dxe4 13.g3± (13.f4 bxc4 14.♗xc4 ♗e7= Acs — Laznicka, Paks 2010))

11.♘h4 (After 11.♗d3 White cannot expect anything, in view of the simple 11...0-0=) 11...♗e4 (11...♗g6 12.♘xg6 hxg6 13.♗f3 0-0 14.♕e2± — White is ready to play e3-e4, Wang Hao — Ni Hua, Xinghua 2010) 12.f3

(12.♘xe4 dxe4

(Also possible is 12...♘xe4 13.♘f3 0-0 14.♗d3 Vitiugov — Wirig, Aix les Bains 2011 (14.♕c2 f5 15.a4 bxc4 16.bxc4 a5!=; 14.a4 bxc4 15.bxc4 a5!=) 14...f5!= — The white pawns are positioned badly. White cannot drive out the black knight with the move f2-f3 because g3 would become weak.)

13.d5!? (13.g3 0-0) 13...cxd5 14.cxd5

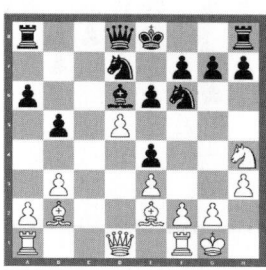

14...♗e5!N

a) 14...♕b8 15.a4 bxa4 16.♖xa4 g5 17.dxe6 fxe6 18.♖xe4 ♘xe4 19.♗xh8 ♔e7 20.♗b2 gxh4 21.♗f3±;

b) 14...♘xd5 15.♘f5 ♘7f6 (15...♗f8 16.♘g3±) 16.♘xg7+ ♔e7 Ni Hua — Malakhov, Ningbo 2010 17.♘h5±;

15.♗xe5 ♘xe5 16.dxe6 fxe6 17.a4 bxa4 (17...g5 18.f4!±; 17...♕xd1 18.♖fxd1 bxa4 19.f4 exf3 20.♘xf3 ♘xf3+ 21.♗xf3 ♖a7 22.bxa4±) 18.♖xa4 ♕xd1 19.♖xd1 ♔e7 20.f4 exf3 21.♘xf3 ♘xf3+ 22.♗xf3 ♖a7=)

12...♗g6 13.♘xg6 hxg6

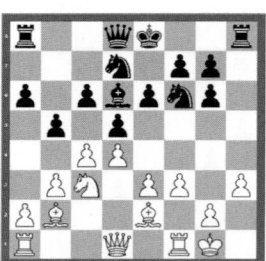

14.♗d3

a) 14.c5 ♗c7 15.♗d3 e5 16.f4 e4 (*16...
b4 17.♘a4 e4 18.♗e2 ♘h5 19.♕e1± Lysyi — Kritz, Biel 2010*) 17.♗e2 ♘h5=;

b) 14.cxd5 cxd5 15.♗d3 0–0 16.a4 bxa4 17.♖xa4 ♕b6= Haba — Khalifman, Germany 2002;

14...0–0 15.c5 ♗c7 16.f4 b4 17.♘e2 ♘e4 18.a3 bxa3 (*18...a5 19.♗xe4 dxe4 20.axb4 axb4 21.♕c2 ♘f6 22.♖xa8 ♕xa8 23.♖a1 ♕b7 24.♔f2 ♖a8 25.♖xa8+ ♕xa8 26.g4±*) 19.♖xa3 a5

20.♘c3!?N (*20.♕c2 f5∞ Riazantsev — S.Savchenko, Chisinau 2012*) 20... ♘g3 (*20...f5 21.♘xe4 fxe4 22.♗e2 ♕e7 23.♗g4±*) 21.♖f3 ♘f5 22.♘e2 g5 23.♕c2± — A complicated positional game across the whole board lies ahead. On the queenside White wants to play ♗b2-c3, tying Black to the defence of the a5-pawn, and on the kingside White plans to play g2-g4, ejecting the black knight and gaining space.

10.♗b2

10.♘e5 ♗xe2 11.♘xe2 dxc4 12.♘xd7 (*12.♕c2 ♘xe5 13.dxe5 ♕d3 14.♕xd3 cxd3 15.♘f4 Krasenkow — Erenburg, Reykjavik 2004 15...♘e4 16.♘xd3 0-0-0∓*) 12...♘xd7! (*12...♕xd7 13.bxc4 ♗e7 14.♕c2 0-0 15.c5± — White's chances are better due to his central domination.*) 13.bxc4 ♘b6 14.c5 ♘c4 15.a4 ♗e7= — Black can try e6-e5 after completing development.

10...♗d6

10...♕b8 11.♘e5 ♗xe2 12.♕xe2 ♘xe5 13.dxe5 ♘d7 14.cxd5 cxd5 15.♖ad1

a) 15.f4 ♗c5=;

b) The following riskier move also deserves attention 15.♖fd1!?

15...♘xe5

b1) 15...♗e7 16.♕g4 g6 17.e4! (Too academic is *17.♘e2±* — White's advantage is minimal, Radjabov — Braga, Bled 2002) 17...d4 18.♘e2± — White is better prepared for an opening up of lines.;

b2) 15...b4 16.♘a4 ♕b7 17.♖ac1 ♗e7 18.♕c2 0-0 19.♕c7 ♖a7 20.♕xb7 ♖xb7 21.♗d4±;

16.♘xd5! (*16.e4 d4 17.♖xd4 ♗e7=*) 16...exd5 17.♖xd5 ♘c6 18.♕f3↑ — White's initiative is very dangerous and fully compensates for the sacrificed piece. However the game is of an unforcing nature and Black retains practical chances for successful defence.;

15...♗e7

16.f4 (*16.e4 d4 17.♖xd4 ♘xe5=;* *16.♕g4 g6 17.e4 ♘xe5 18.♕f4 d4* *19.♘e2 ♘c6 20.♕c1 ♕b7 21.♘xd4* *♘xd4 22.♖xd4 0-0=*) 16...0-0

(16...b4 17.♘a4 0-0 (*17...♕b5 18.♕c2* *0-0 19.♖c1±* — White stands better thanks to his control of the c-file.) 18.e4 ♕b5 19.♕d2 ♘b6

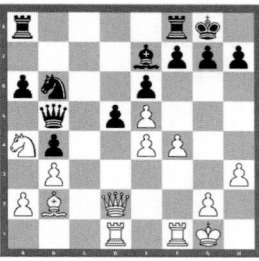

20.♘xb6!N (*20.♗d4 ♘xa4 21.bxa4* *♕b7 22.f5 ♖fd8 23.f6 ♗f8=* Dobrov — Amonatov, St.Petersburg 2004) 20...♕xb6+ 21.♗d4 ♕b5 22.f5 ♖fd8 23.f6 ♗f8 (*23...♗c5 24.♕f2* *♗xd4 25.♖xd4±*) 24.fxg7 ♗xg7 25.♖f4 dxe4 26.♖xe4±)

17.♕g4 ♕a7 18.♔h1 ♖ac8 (*18...b4* *19.♘e2 ♕xe3 20.♘d4↑*) 19.e4!N

(19.f5 is weaker 19...♘xe5 20.♕g3 exf5! (Less accurate is *20...f6 21.fxe6* *♕b6 22.♘xd5 ♕xe6 23.♗xe5 fxe5±* — Black can resist but White's position is more solid Tomashevsky — Malakhov, Moscow 2010) 21.♘xd5 ♘g6 22.♖xf5 ♖c2= — Black has enough counter play to equalise.)

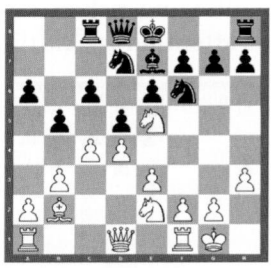

19...b4 20.♘a4 dxe4 21.f5 exf5 22.♕xf5 ♘c5 23.♘xc5 ♕xc5 24.♖c1 g6 25.♕d7 ♖cd8 26.♕b7 ♖b8 27.♕xe4 ♕b6 28.♖c6 ♕b5 29.♖fc1± — Black faces an unpleasant defence.;

10...♗e7 11.♘e5 ♗xe2 12.♘xe2

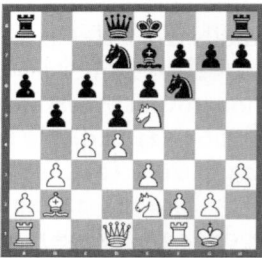

12...♘xe5

a) 12...♕b6 13.cxd5 (Also good is *13.c5 ♕b7 14.♘d3±*) 13...cxd5 (13...♘xe5 14.dxe5 ♘xd5 15.♘g3 0–0 16.♕g4±) 14.♖c1 ♕b7 15.♕c2 0–0 16.♕c7 ♖fb8 17.♕xb7 ♖xb7 18.♖c6± — Black faces an unpleasant defence, Gelfand — Bareev, Monaco (blindfold) 2003;

b) 12...♖c8

13.c5!

(13.♖c1 The most promising move although after what follows White stands also better 13...bxc4 (13...dxc4 14.bxc4 ♘xe5 15.dxe5 ♘d7 16.♘g3 0–0 17.♘e4±) 14.bxc4 0–0 15.♘xd7 (15.♕a4 ♘xe5 16.dxe5 ♘e4=) 15...♕xd7 16.c5 ♖b8 17.♕c2±)

13...a5 14.♘d3! (14.a3 Additional strengthening of the queenside pawn structure 14...0–0 15.b4 This move is not mandatory, Korotylev — Reshetnikov, Moscow 2011. In this case the time lost would have been better spent playing in the centre.) 14...0–0 15.f3± — White has a space advantage and the possibility to increase it later by playing e3-e4.;

13.dxe5 ♘d7 14.cxd5 cxd5 15.♘f4 (After 15.♖c1 ♖c8 16.♘d4 Black must play 16...♘c5!±, protecting the c6 aquare with the possibility of moving to e4 — White has only a minimal advantage.) 15...0–0 16.♕g4 ♔h8

a) 16...♖c8 17.♖ac1 ♔h8 — 16...♔h8 17.♖ac1 ♖c8;

b) 16...♖e8

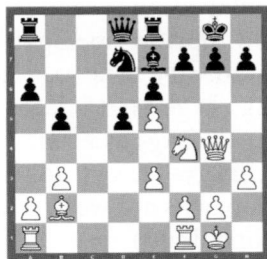

17.e4!N (*17.♖fd1 ♘c5 18.♘h5 g6 19.♘f6+ ♗xf6 20.exf6↑* Gallego — Almagro, Madrid 2010) 17...dxe4 18.♖fd1±;

c) 16...♗g5 17.♘d3 (*17.♖ac1±*) 17...♗e7 18.♖ac1 ♕a5?! (*18...♖c8 19.♘f4±*) 19.♘f4 ♕xa2 20.♗d4± Avrukh — Pasman, Israel 2003;

17.♖ac1 ♖c8 18.♘xe6!? (*18.♘h5±*) 18...fxe6 19.♖xc8 ♕xc8 20.♕xe6 By capturing on d5, White gains a third pawn for the piece and retains the initiative. 20...♗c5 21.♕xd5 ♘b6 22.♕e4 ♕a8 23.♕xa8 ♖xa8 24.♖c1 ♖c8 Marin — D. Horvat, Romania 2011 The strongest appears to be 25.g4!±, later bringing the king to the centre via g2 and f3 to e4and-maintaining winning chances.

11.♘e5 ♗xe2 12.♘xe2 bxc4
After 12...♖c8 most promising is 13.c5 ♗b8 14.b4, restraining Black as much as possible. Then after 14...a5 White has a tactical trick:

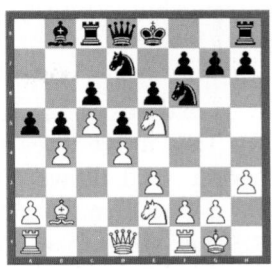

15.a4!?

(A quieter move is also possible 15.♘xd7 ♘xd7 (*15...♕xd7 16.a4 ♕c7 17.f3±*) 16.a4 bxa4 17.♕xa4 ♕c7 18.f3 (Less aesthetic is *18.f4 axb4 19.♕xb4±* — The b8 bishop is severely restricted and the c6 pawn is weak. However one still doesn't like to weaken e4.) 18...axb4 19.♕xb4 0–0 20.♗c3 e5 21.♕a5± — The endgame is unpleasant for Black due to the chronic weakness of c6.)

15...♘xe5 16.dxe5 ♘d7

17.♘f4! The point of the plan! The capture on e5 now is bad for Black, otherwise the knight moves to the cementing square d3. (*17.axb5 axb4∞*) 17...axb4 (*17...♘xe5 18.axb5±*) 18.♘d3! bxa4 19.♕xa4 0–0 20.♕xb4 f6 21.exf6 ♘xf6 22.f3 — The position is complicated but White has the advantage.;

12...♕c7 13.cxd5 cxd5 14.♖c1 ♕b8 (*14...♕b7 This move does not put pressure on e5 and allows White after 15.♕c2 0–0 16.♕c6 ♕xc6 17.♖xc6 ♝b4 18.♖fc1± to gain a comfortable advantage in the endgame, Neverov — Rogozenko, Bucharest 1993) 15.♘xd7 ♘xd7* (More serious problems emerge for Black after *15...♔xd7?! 16.f3* — The provocative king position and weakening of the c5 square is evident, for example: *16...♕b7 17.♘f4 ♖hc8 18.♘d3 ♔e8 19.♘c5± Riazantsev — Ponkratov, Cheliabinsk 2007)* 16.e4 dxe4

(*16...0–0 17.e5 ♝e7 18.♖c6* (A sharper move is also possible *18.♘f4!? ♕b7 19.♕g4↑* — A deployment of the rook via c3 to g3, the advance of the h-pawn and a threat to sacrifice the knight on e6 are among the ideas for White.) *18...♖c8 19.♕c2 ♕b7 20.♖c1 ♖xc6 21.♕xc6 ♕xc6 22.♖xc6 ♔f8 23.f4±* — White's pressure in the endgame is very unpleasant.)

17.d5 0–0 18.dxe6 ♘c5

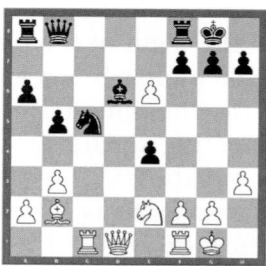

19.♘f4

(The next move, which has not been played in practice yet, is a good option *19.♘g3!?N 19... ♘xe6 20.♘f5 ♝f4 21.♕g4 ♕d8 22.♘xg7 ♕g5 23.♘f5 ♖fd8 (23...h5 24.♕xg5+ ♝xg5 25.♖ce1±)* 24.♖c2 h5 25.♕xg5+ ♝xg5 26.♘g3± — Black's pawns are weak. He has to fight for a draw.)

19...♖a7 (*19...fxe6 20.♕g4 e5 21.♘e6± Sasikiran — Sakaev, Copenhagen 2003; 19...♝xf4 20.♖xc5 fxe6 21.♕g4± Pert — Sarakauskas, Liverpool 2006)* 20.♝d4 (*20.♕d5 ♝xf4 21.♖xc5 e3= Bu Xiangzhi — Ni Hua, China 2004; 20.♘h5 ♘xe6 21.♘f6+ gxf6 22.♕g4+ ♘g5 23.♝xf6 h6 24.♖c6 ♝h2+ 25.♔h1 ♝e5 26.h4 ♝xf6 27.♖xf6 ♕c8= Morovic Fernandez — Leitao, Santos 2004)* 20...♝xf4 21.♝xc5 ♝xc1 22.♝xf8 (A similar position arises after *22.♝xa7 ♕xa7 23.exf7+ ♕xf7 24.♕xc1± Kharlov — Leitao, Tripoli 2004)* 22...♕xf8 23.♕xc1 ♖e7 24.exf7+ ♖xf7 (*24...♕xf7 25.♕c8+ ♕e8 26.♕xa6 e3 27.fxe3 ♖xe3 28.♕d6± Kanep — Kulaots, Tallinn 2005)* 25.♕d2±

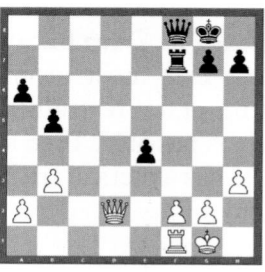

— Black can obtain a draw with very accurate defence.

13.bxc4 0–0 14.♖c1

A similar position also arises after 14.♕c2 ♕c7 15.♘xd7 (After *15.♘d3* the following equalises: *15...c5* White cannot profit from the opposition of major pieces on the c-file: *16.dxc5 ♘xc5 17.♖ac1 ♖fc8 18.cxd5 ♘xd5=*) *15...♕xd7 16.♖ab1* — White can always play c4-c5.;

14.♖b1 ♕c7 15.♘xd7 ♘xd7 — 14.♖c1 ♕b8 15.♘xd7 ♘xd7 16.♖b1 ♕c7

14...♕b8 15.♘xd7 ♘xd7 16.♖b1 ♕c7

16...dxc4 17.d5 cxd5 18.♗xg7 ♕c7 (*18...♕xb1 19.♕xb1 ♔xg7 20.e4±*) 19.♗xf8 ♗xf8 20.e4±

17.c5 ♗e7 18.♗c3 ♖fb8 19.♕a4 ♖xb1 20.♖xb1 ♖b8 21.♖xb8+ ♘xb8 22.♗a5 ♕b7

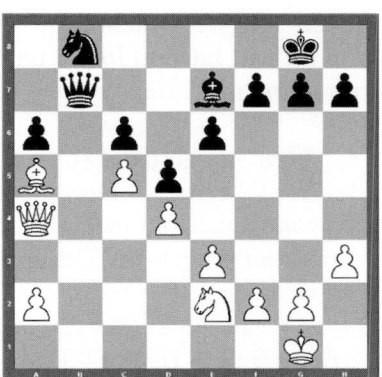

23.♕b3!?N±
— Poses some problems for Black. It's not profitable to abandon the b-

file, and if Black exchanges on b3 White has the plan of moving the king to a5, as well as the transfer of the knight to b4. Conclusion: The line analysed with e2-e3 against the a7-a6 system can be regarded as classical as such a formation looks the most solid. In many variations Black is close to equalising but still does not fully achieve it, so the variation appears to be a good choice for White.

23.♗b6 The penetration with the bishop hardly makes sense 23...♘d7 24.♕a5 ♔f8 25.♘c1 ♘xb6 26.♕xb6 ♕a8±/= — White's advantage is negligible, Tomashevsky — Romanov, Moscow 2011.

■ GAME 27

1.d4 d5 2.c4 c6 3.♘f3 ♘f6 4.♘c3 a6 5.c5

A very ambitious and strategically demanding attempt to constrain Black. Usually the battle revolves around whether Black can play the freeing break e7-e5 advantageously. If he succeeds, he has no problems and in some cases gains an advantage. If he fails, then he remains constrained without counter play.

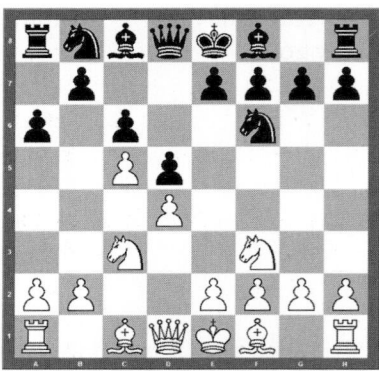

5...♘bd7

5...♗g4 The straightforward attempt to quickly exchange the bishop and play e7-e5 turns out badly

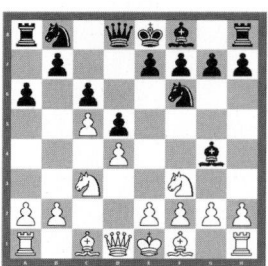

6.h3!? This unobvious move immediately determining the pawn structure is very unpleasant. However Black has problems with other replies too.

(6.♘e5

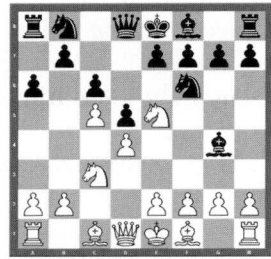

6...♗e6 Other bishop retreats are bad:

a) 6...♗f5 7.f3

(7.♕b3 It is also possible to tie Black to the defence of b7 pawn first, however the move e2-e4 will then not be so effective, since the queen will be attacked by ♗e6 and he will have to lose a tempo retreating it. 7...♖a7

(7...♕c8 8.f3 g6 9.g4! (9.e4 ♗e6 10.♕c2± Lerner — Dreev, Moscow 1985) 9...♗e6 10.♘a4 ♘fd7 (10...♘bd7 11.g5+-) 11.♘d3±)

8.f3 g6 9.e4 ♗e6 10.♗e3 ♗g7 (10...dxe4 11.♗c4±) 11.♕c2± Lysyi — I.Popov, St.Petersburg 2007)

7...g6

a1) 7...♘bd7 8.g4 ♗e6 (*8...♗g6 9.h4+-*) 9.♘d3± Pe.Nielsen — Agrest, Malme 2004;

a2) 7...b6 8.e4 ♗e6 9.♘a4± Mamedyarov — Agrest, Antalya 2004;

8.e4 ♗e6 9.♗e3± Sakaev — Epishin, St.Petersburg 2004;

b) 6...♗h5 7.♕b3 ♖a7 8.e4! dxe4

b1) 8...♘xe4 9.♘xe4 dxe4 10.♕h3 ♗g6 11.♗c4+-;

b2) 8...e6 9.exd5 exd5

(*9...cxd5 10.♕a4+ ♘fd7 (10...♘bd7 11.c6+-) 11.g4 ♗g6 12.♗f4 ♗e7 (12...♕c8 13.♘b5+-) 13.♘b5+-*)

10.♗d3 ♘bd7 11.0-0 (*11.f4↑; 11.♗f4 ♘xe5 12.♗xe5 ♗e7 13.0-0 0-0 14.♖fe1± Topalov — I.Sokolov, Wijk aan Zee 2004*) 11...♗e7 (*11...♘xe5 12.♖e1 ♘fd7 13.♗f4±*) 12.♖e1 0-0 13.♗f4±;

9.♗e2 e6 10.♗xh5 ♘xh5

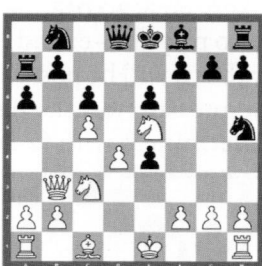

11.♗g5!! A most beautiful distraction motif. 11...♕xg5 12.♕b6 ♗e7 13.♕xa7 0-0 14.g3+-;

7.♗f4

(*7.♕b3 ♖a7 8.♗f4 g6 9.h3 (9.e3 ♘h5= Akopian — I.Sokolov, Kemer 2007) 9...♗g7 10.e3 0-0 11.♗e2 ♘bd7 12.♖d1±*)

7...♘bd7

(*7...♘h5 8.♗d2 (8.e3 g6 9.h4 ♘xf4 10.exf4∞ Potkin — Agrest, El Sauzal (rapid) 2008) 8...♘f6 9.♕b3 ♖a7 10.f3 ♘bd7 11.♘d3 ♗f5 12.e3 e5 13.0-0-0 ♗e7 14.g4 ♗e6 15.♕c2±*)

8.e3 (*8.♘d3!?*) 8...♘xe5 9.♗xe5 ♘d7 10.♗g3 g6 11.♗d3 ♗g7 12.0-0 0-0 13.b4 f5 14.♕c2 ♗f7 15.♗h4 h6 16.f4± Eljanov — Kanep, Goteborg 2005)

6...♗xf3 (If *6...♗h5* Black's minor pieces will be attacked with tempi, for example: *7.♕b3 ♖a7 8.g4 ♗g6 9.g5 ♘e4 10.♘e5 ♘xc3 11.♘xg6 hxg6 12.♕xc3 ♘d7 13.♗g2 e5 14.dxe5 ♕e7 15.♗e3 ♕xe5 16.♕xe5+ ♘xe5 17.f4 ♘d7 18.♖c1±* — The two bishops provide an advantage for White.)

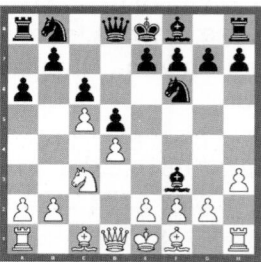

7.exf3 ♘bd7 (*7...e5 8.dxe5 ♘fd7 9.f4 ♘xc5 10.♗e3± Grigorov — Tzekov, Sunny Beach 2005*) 8.f4 b6 9.b4± —

Black is short of space and it's hard for him to defend.;

General opinion seems to underestimate 5... ♗f5 6. ♗f4 (It doesn't make much sense for White to move the queen to b3 as It just hampers his own pawns. 6.♕b3 ♕c8 7.♗f4 ♘bd7 8.h3 e6 9.e3 ♗e7 10. ♗e2 0–0 11.0–0 ♖e8= — Black is ready with the equalising manoeuver ♗e7-d8-c7.) 6...♘bd7 7.h3 This quiet move appears to be the strongest for White

(Of course one doesn't want to spend a tempo on prophylaxis instead of development but it's necessary. Much more frequently the following move is played 7.e3, which al lows Black to start chasing the black squared bishop and obtain a completely satisfactory game: 7...♘h5! (7...e6 8.♘d2 ♗e7 9. ♗e2± — White intends to press Black on the kingside with g2-g4 and then h2-h4.) 8.♗e5

a) 8.♗d3 ♘xf4 (8... ♗xd3 9.♕xd3 ♘xf4 10.exf4 g6 11.0–0 ♗g7±) 9.exf4 ♗g4! 10.h3 ♗xf3 11.♕xf3 g6 12.0–0 ♗g7 13.♘e2 Datu — Nguyen Huynh, Olongapo 2010 13...0–0=;

b) 8.♗g5 h6 9.♗h4 g5 10.♘d2 ♘df6 11. ♗e2 gxh4 12. ♗xh5 ♖g8 13. ♗f3 ♕c7∓;

c) 8.h3 ♘xf4 9.exf4 e6 10. ♗d3 ♗xd3 11.♕xd3 g6 12.0–0 ♗g7 13.b4 0–0 14.♖fe1 b6 15.cxb6 ♕xb6

16.♖ab1 ♕c7 17.g3 ♖fb8= Radjabov — Wang Yue, Linares 2009;

8...f6!

(8...♘hf6 9. ♗g3 ♘e4

(9...♘h5 10. ♗h4 h6 11.♘d2 ♘hf6 12. ♗g3! (12. ♗e2 e5=) 12... e6 13. ♗e2± — The bishop on g3 and knight on d2 are very well placed effectively stopping ♘f6-e4 and ♘f6-h5.)

10.♘xe4 dxe4!? (10... ♗xe4 11.♘d2 ♗g6 12.b4 f6 13. ♗e2 e5 Grischuk — Collins, Khanty Mansyisk 2010 14.♘f3 appears to be promising, making Black to decide on his plan in the centre.) 11.♘d2 e5 12. ♗e2 (12.♕b3 exd4 13.exd4 b5 14.cxb6 ♘xb6 15.f3 exf3 16.♕xf3 ♕d7=; 12.♘c4 exd4 13.exd4 b5 14.♘d6+ ♗xd6 15. ♗xd6 ♘b6!= — The knight will move to c8 driving the bishop from d6.) 12... exd4 13.exd4 ♗e7 14.♘c4 0–0 15.♕b3 ♖a7 16.0–0 ♗e6 17.♕e3 ♗d5 18.♘d6 ♗xd6 (18...f5 19.f3!±) 19. ♗xd6 ♖e8 20.b3± — White wants to play ♖a1–e1 and ♗e2-c4. After that it will be possible to increase pressure on the e4 pawn, or undermine it with f2-f3.)

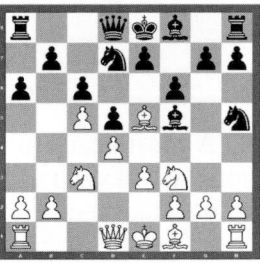

9. ♗g3 (9.♘h4 ♗e6!=) 9...e5 10.♘h4

(After 10. ♗h4 Black can seize the initiative with the bold 10...g5!N (10... ♗e7 11. ♗e2 g6 12.h3± Vitiugov — Matlakov, Sochi 2010) 11.♘xe5 (11. ♗g3 ♘xg3 12.hxg3 ♗g7∓) 11...♘xe5 12.dxe5 gxh4 13. ♕xh5+ ♗g6 14. ♕xh4 fxe5 15. ♕xd8+ ♖xd8 16.♘a4 d4/±)

10... ♗g6 11. ♗e2

a) 11. ♕b3 ♕c7=;

b) 11.♘xg6 hxg6 12. ♕c2 ♖h6! (12... e4 13.♘xe4! dxe4 14. ♕xe4+ ♕e7 15. ♕xg6+ ♕f7 16. ♕xf7+ ♔xf7 17. ♗c4+ ♔g6 18. ♗c7!±) 13. ♖g1 ♘xg3 14.hxg3 f5 15.0-0-0 ♕f6=;

c) 11.f4 ♘xg3 12.hxg3 ♗f7= Halkias — Svetushkin, Kallithea 2009;

11...♘xg3 12.hxg3 ♗f7 13.♘f5 g6 (Also good is 13...h5!?) 14.♘h6 ♗e6∞ — A complicated battle lies ahead in which the Black's chances don't look any worse.)

7...e6

(7...g6 8.e3 ♗g7 9. ♗e2 ♗e4 (9... ♘e4 10.0-0-0 0-0 11. ♕b3 ♕c8 — 5... g6 6. ♗f4 ♗g7 7.h3 0-0 8.e3 ♗f5 9. ♕b3 ♕c8 10. ♗e2 ♘bd7 11.0-0 ♘e4) 10. ♕b3

a) 10.♘h4 e5 11. ♗g3 (11.dxe5 ♘h5 12.♘f3 Alekseev — Kamsky, Mos-

cow 2007 12...♘xf4 13.exf4 ♘xc5∓) 11...exd4 12.exd4 0-0 13.f3 ♗f5 14.♘xf5 gxf5∞ Mamedyarov — Kamsky, Moscow 2007;

b) 10.0-0 ♗xf3 11. ♗xf3 0-0±;

10...♖a7 (10... ♕c8 11.♘h4±; 10... ♗xf3 11. ♗xf3 ♕c8 12.0-0 0-0 13.♘a4 ♖e8 14. ♖fd1±) 11.0-0 ♗xf3 12. ♗xf3 0-0 5...g6 6. ♗f4 ♗g7 7.h3 0-0 8.e3 ♗f5 9. ♕b3 ♖a7 10. ♗e2 ♗e4 11.0-0 ♗xf3 12. ♗xf3 ♘bd7)

8.e3 ♗e7 9.♘d2! The most move. White prevents ♘f6-e4 simplifyng the game and has possibilities of play on both flanks.

a) 9. ♗d3 This aspires to nothing

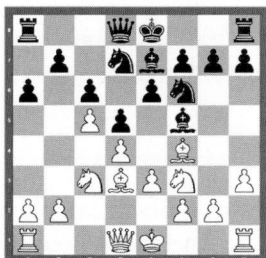

9... ♗xd3

(After 9... ♕c8 Black also doesn't have any problems 10.0-0 0-0 11.b4 ♖e8!

(11...b6 12. ♗xf5 (12.g4?! Black has chances of a later e6-e5 and the weakening of the king may become evident. 12... ♗xd3 13. ♕xd3 a5 14.a3 ♖e8= 15. ♖ab1? 15...axb4

16.axb4 bxc5 17.bxc5 ♗xc5∓ Jobava
— Bu Xiangzhi, Turin 2006) 12...
exf5 13.♕c2±)

12.a4 (*12.♗xf5 exf5 13.♕c2 ♘e4=*)
12...♗xd3 13.♕xd3 a5 14.b5 ♗xc5
15.dxc5 e5= Cebalo — Kritz, Biel
2007)

10.♕xd3 b6 11.cxb6 (*11.b4 a5 12.b5
♖c8 13.cxb6 ♕xb6 14.0–0=* Stohl
— Dautov, Germany 2002) 11...
♕xb6 12.b3 (After *12.0–0* Black can
capture a pawn *12...♕xb2 13.♖ab1
♕a3=*) 12...♗a3!? The most reliable
way to equalise — the white rook is
deprived of the c1 square.

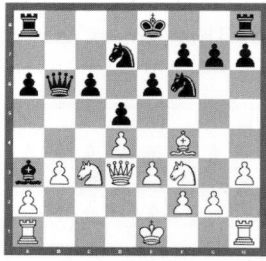

13.0–0 0–0 — Black can play ♖a8-c8
and c6-c5. The game is equal.;

b) 9.♗e2

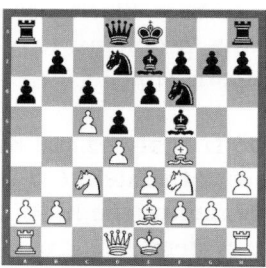

9...♘e4 10.0–0 0–0 11.♕b3 (*11.♘xe4
♗xe4 12.♕b3 ♕c8=*, intending
♗d8-c7) 11...♕c8 12.♖fd1 ♖e8

(*12... ♗d8 13.♘xe4 (13.♖ac1 ♗c7
14.♘xe4 ♗xe4 15.♘d2 ♗g6=) 13...
♗xe4 14.♗d6 ♖e8 15.♖ac1 ♗c7
16.♘e5±*)

13.♘a4! h6 14.♘e5 ♘ef6 15.♖ac1
♗d8 16.♘b6 ♗xb6 17.cxb6 ♘xe5
18.♗xe5± — In the forthcoming
long, manoeuvering battle White's
chances are preferable due to the
two bishop, Kir.Georgiev — Hodg-
son, Groningen 1994;

9... ♗g6 Prophylaxis against g2-g4

a) 9...h6 10.♗e2 g5?! 11.♗g3 h5
12.♕b3 h4 13.♗h2 b6 14.cxb6 ♘xb6
15.♖c1± Postny — Moutousis, Peris-
teri 2010;

b) 9...♕c8 10.♗e2 (*10.♘b3 ♗d8
11.♗d3 ♗xd3 12.♕xd3 ♗c7 13.0–0–0
♗xf4 14.exf4 ♕c7 15.g3 0–0 16.♖he1
a5=* Ivanchuk — Kritz, Greece 2010)
10...♗g6 (*10...♗d8 11.g4! ♗g6 12.g5
♘g8 13.h4±; 10...h6 11.g4 ♗g6 12.h4±*)
11.g4!± — 9...♗g6 10.♗e2 ♕c8 11.g4;

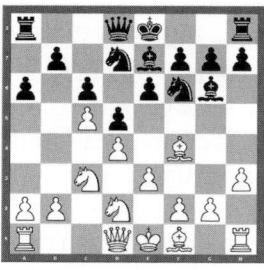

10.♗e2

(10.b4 ♕c8 11.♗e2 (Too indiscrim-
inate is *11.g4*, as White has already
made the sharp move b2-b4 on the
queenside *11...♗d8 12.a4 h5 13.♖g1
hxg4 14.hxg4 ♗c7 15.♗xc7 ♕xc7=*
Klimov — Vysochin, Sochi 2009)
11...♗d8 12.0-0 ♗c7 13.♗xc7 ♕xc7
14.f4= — White has prevented e6-
e5 but weakened the white squares
which may be exploited in the play
to follow.)

10...♕c8 (*10...0-0 11.g4!?*) 11.g4!± —
Only by pressing Black on the kingside can White pose any problems
for him. Both sides face a wide-
ranging, complicated battle with
somewhat better chances for White.;

5...g6 6.h3 (After *6.♗f4* one must
consider *6...♘h5!?*) 6...♗g7 7.♗f4
0-0 8.e3 ♗f5 (*8...♘bd7 — 5...♘bd7
6.♗f4 g6 7.h3 ♗g7 8.e3 0-0; 8...♘fd7
9.♗e2 e5 10.♗g5 f6 11.♗h4±* — The
knight on d7 hinders the development of the other pieces.) 9.♕b3
leads to a stodgy positional struggle

a) 9.♗e2 ♘e4 (*9...♗e4 10.0-0 ♗xf3
11.♗xf3 ♘bd7 12.♗g3 ♖e8 13.♕b3±*)
10.0-0 ♘d7 11.♕b3 ♕c8 — 9.♕b3
♕c8 10.♗e2 ♘bd7 11.0-0 ♘e4(*11...
♖a7 — 9.♕b3 ♖a7 10.♗e2 ♘e4
11.0-0 ♘d7*) ;

b) 9.♘h4 ♗c8 10.♗e2 ♘e4 11.♘f3
♘d7 — 5...♘bd7 6.♗f4 g6 7.h3 ♗g7
8.e3 0-0 9.♗e2 ♘e4;

c) Double-edged play arises after
9.♘d2 ♘e4!

(*9...♘bd7 10.g4 (10. ♗e2 e5 11.dxe5
♘e8 12.e4 dxe4 13.♘dxe4 ♕e7=)*
10...♗e6 11.♗e2 (*11.b4* Carlsen —
Kamsky, Nice (blindfold) 2009
11...♘e4! 12.♘dxe4 dxe4∞) 11...b6
12.cxb6 ♕xb6 13.♘a4± — The c-
pawn remains backward. White's
chances are better.)

10.♘dxe4

(10.g4 ♘xd2 11.♕xd2 ♗c8 12.0-
0-0 ♘d7 13.e4 dxe4 14.♘xe4 ♘f6
15.♘xf6+ ♗xf6 16.♗c4 b5 17.♗b3
a5 18.a3 b4 19.a4 (*19.axb4 axb4
20.♕xb4 ♗a6*) 19...♗e6 20.♗xe6
fxe6=)

10... ♗xe4

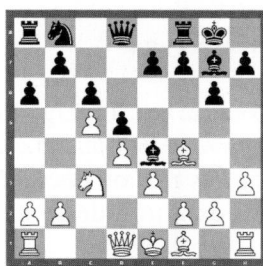

11.h4!?

(11.♘xe4 dxe4 12.♗c4 ♕a5+!

(*12...♘d7 13.0-0 e5 14.♗g3± (14.
dxe5 ♗xe5 15.♗h6 ♗g7 16.♗xg7
♔xg7 17.♕d4+ ♘f6 18.♕c3 ♕e7
19.b4±/=))*

13.♕d2 ♛xd2+ 14.♔xd2 ♘d7=)

11...♘d7 12.f3 ♝f5 13.g4 e5 14.♝xe5 ♝xe5 15.dxe5 ♝e6 16.♕d4±/∞;

9...♖a7 (9...♛c8 10.♝e2 ♘bd7 11.0–0 ♘e4 12.♖fd1 ♖e8 13.♘xe4 ♝xe4 14.♘g5 ♝f5 15.g4 Potkin — Kamsky, Mainz (rapid) 2009 15...e5! 16.♝xe5 ♘xe5 17.dxe5 ♝d7 18.f4±/∞)

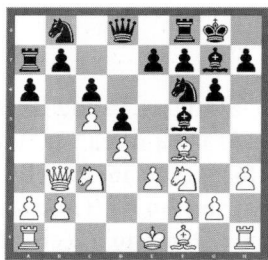

10.♝e2 ♘e4 (10...♝e4 11.0–0 ♝xf3 12.♝xf3 ♘bd7 13.♖ad1 ♛c8 14.♖fe1 e6 15.e4 dxe4 16.♝xe4± Eljanov — Kamsky, Sochi 2008) 11.0–0 ♘d7 12.♖ad1 ♖e8 13.g4

(13.♘xe4 ♝xe4 14.♘g5 (14.♘d2 ♝f5 15.g4 ♝e6 16.♖fe1±) 14...e5 (14... ♝f5 15.g4 e5 16.dxe5 ♝e6 17.e4±/∞) 15.♘xe4 exf4 16.♘d6±)

13...♝e6 14.♕c2± White's chances are a little better. He has weakened his king position but Black will not be able to play the freeing e7-e5.

6.♝f4

6.h3 gives Black time to immediately break out advantageously 6...b6 (Bad is 6...e5?! 7.dxe5 ♘e4 8.♘xe4 dxe4 9.♘g5±; Better is 6...♛c7 7.♝g5

— 6.♝f4 ♘h5 7.♝d2 ♘hf6 8.h3 ♛c7 9.♝g5) 7.cxb6 (7.b4 a5 8.b5 ♝b7=) 7...e6=;

6.♝g5 h6 7.♝h4 g5 8.♝g3 ♘h5 9.♝e5 (9.e3 ♘xg3 10.hxg3 ♝g7=; 9.e4 dxe4 10.♘xe4 ♝g7 11.♝c4 ♘xg3 12.hxg3 g4 13.♘h4 ♘f6=) 9...♘xe5 10.♘xe5 ♝g7=

6...♘h5

6...g6 allows White to place his pieces on suitable squares 7.h3 (7.e3 invites 7...♘h5, which is obviously undesirable.) 7...♝g7 8.e3 0–0 9.♝d3

(The following occurs more frequently in practice 9.♝e2 and is weaker as control of the e4 square is quite important. 9...♘e4

a) 9...♘e8 10.0–0 ♘c7 11.♖c1 (11. b4 ♖e8 12.♕d2 e5 13.♘xe5 ♘xe5 14.dxe5 ♝xe5 15.♝xe5 ♖xe5 16.e4 a5 17.a3 axb4 18.axb4 ♖xa1 19.♖xa1 ♛f6= Gelfand — Shirov, Linares 1994) 11...♖e8 12.♝g5 ♘e6 13.♝h4 f5 14.♝g3± Roiz — Najer, Sochi 2006;

b) 9...b6 10.cxb6 ♛xb6 11.0–0! ♛xb2 12.♘a4 ♛a3 13.♖c1 (13. ♛c2!?±) 13...♝b7 14.♖c3 ♛b4 Najer — Shimanov, Moscow 2007 A small advantage can be gained from 15.♝d3!?± protecting the square e4 and threatening ♕d1-c2, ♖f1-b1.;

10.0–0 (10.♕c2 e5 11.♘xe5 ♘xe5 12.♘xe4 ♝f5=) 10...e5 11.♘xe5 ♘xc3 12.bxc3 ♘xe5 13.♝xe5 ♝xe5 14.dxe5

♕e7 15.♖d4 ♖e8±/= — Black is close to equalisation, Rodshtein — Burmakin, Dresden 2007)

9...♘e8

(9...b6 10.cxb6 ♕xb6

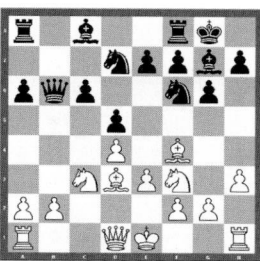

11.0-0! If White makes a passive move protecting the b2 pawn then Black will play c6-c5 and the advantage will be lost. 11...c5 (11...♕xb2 12.♖c1±) 12.♘a4 ♕a5

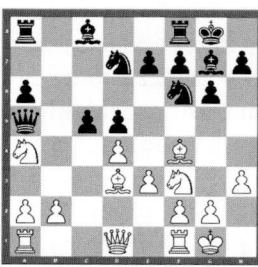

13.b3!N White prevents c5-c4 and starts fighting for the c5 square. (White only has a minimal advantage after *13.dxc5 ♘xc5 14.♘xc5 ♕xc5 15.♖c1 ♕b6 16.♗e5± Matlakov — Lovkov, St.Petersburg 2007)* 13...♗b7 14.♖c1 ♖fc8 15.a3 cxd4 16.♖xc8+ ♖xc8 17.b4 ♕d8 18.exd4

♘e4 19.♕b3 ♘f8 20.♗e3! ♘e6 21.♘c5±)

10.0-0 ♘c7

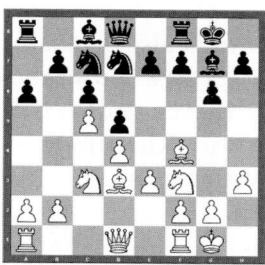

11.♕d2! The most promising way to prepare e3-e4. (*11.♖e1 ♖e8 12.e4 ♘e6 13.♗e3 ♘dxc5 14.dxc5 d4=; 11.e4 ♘e6! 12.♗e3 ♘dxc5 Babula — Beikert, Germany 2009 13.dxc5 d4=*) 11...♖e8 12.e4 e5 13.♘xe5 ♘xe5 14.♗xe5 ♗xe5 15.dxe5 ♖xe5 16.♗c2 ♕e7 17.exd5 cxd5 (*17...♘xd5 18.♖ae1±*) 18.b4 a5 19.a3±

7.♗d2

White has tried many other continuations: 7.♕d2?! After this the game is somewhat better for Black 7...♘xf4 8.♕xf4 ♘f6 After the exchange of the bishop it's impossible to keep control of the black squares: (*8...f6 9.e4 e5 10.dxe5 ♗xc5 11.exd5 cxd5 12.♘xd5 ♘xe5 13.0-0-0±*) 9.♘e5 g6 (*9...♗e6=*) 10.g4 ♗e6 11.h4 ♕b8 (*11...♗g7!? 12.h5 ♘e4∓*) 12.♗h3 ♗g7 13.♕e3 ♘e4 14.f4= Khalifman — Malakhov, Sochi 2007;

After 7.g3?! almost any reasonable option gives Black an easy game: 7...g6 (*7...b6 8.b4 a5 9.a3 ♘xf4 10.gxf4 e6*

11.e3 ♗e7 12.♗d3 0-0 13.0-0 ♕c7=)
8.♕d2 ♘xf4 9.gxf4 ♘f6= — There's
no question of a White advantage.;

7.♗e3 g6

(7...♘hf6 is also a reliable option
8.h3 (*8.♗f4=*) 8...b6 9.cxb6 e6 10.g3
♕xb6 11.♖b1 ♗d6 12.♗g2 0-0
13.0-0 a5= Khalifman — Najer,
St.Petersburg 2004)

8.g4

(8.g3 ♗g7 9.♗g2 0-0 10.0-0 ♖e8
(*10...e5=*) 11.♘a4 Postny — Sarakauskas, Olomouc 2004 11...e5=)

8...♘hf6 (*8...♘g7!?*) 9.h3 ♗g7 10.♗g2
0-0 11.0-0 h5 12.g5 ♘h7 13.♕d2
(*13.h4 f6 14.♕d2 e5 15.gxf6 ♕xf6
16.♖ad1 ♕e7 17.b4 exd4 18.♗xd4
♗xd4 19.♕xd4 ♘df6=* Sakaev —
Malakhov, Sochi 2004) 13...e5!

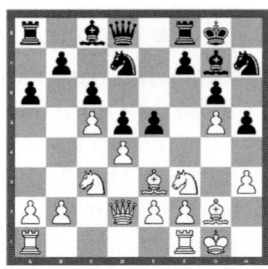

14.♘xe5 ♘xe5 15.dxe5 ♗xe5 16.f4
♗g7 17.♗d4 ♗xd4+ 18.♕xd4 ♗f5=
Lputian — Bacrot, Moscow 2004;

7.♗g5 Sometimes White tries to
provoke h7-h6 before a retreat to d2:
7...h6 8.♗d2 ♘hf6 9.♕c2 ♕c7!

(9...g6 10.♗f4 ♘h5 (*10...g5 11.♗g3
♘h5 12.e3±*) 11.♗e5 ♘xe5 12.♘xe5±
h7-h6 has turned out to be weakening as Black cannot drive out the
white knight with f7-f6, Eljanov —
Prie, France 2008)

10.e4

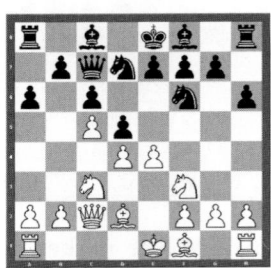

10...e5!

(10...dxe4 11.♘xe4 ♘xe4 12.♕xe4
♘f6 13.♕c2 ♗e6 14.0-0-0 (*14.♘e5
♘d7 15.♗f4 ♘xe5 16.♗xe5 ♕a5+
17.♕c3 ♕xc3+ 18.bxc3 ♗f5 19.0-0-
0 0-0-0 20.♗e2 f6 21.♗g3 e5±/=*
Ponomariov — Malakhov, Khanty
Mansyisk 2009) 14...g6

a) 14...♘d7 15.h4 ♗d5 (*15...b6
16.♗c4 ♗xc4 17.♕xc4 e6 18.♖he1
♗e7 19.g4↑* Vaganian — Movsesian, Kemer 2007) 16.♗c4 ♗xc4
17.♕xc4 e6 18.♔b1± Eljanov —
Malakhov, Sochi 2007;

b) 14...♗d5 15.♘e5 e6 16.♗f4 ♕a5
17.♗c4 ♗e7 (*17...♗xc4 18.♘xc4
♕xa2 19.♔d2 ♘d5 20.♖a1 ♕xa1
21.♖xa1 ♘xf4 22.g3 ♘d5 23.♕b3*

0-0-0 24.♘e5 ♘c7 25.♖a4±)
18.♔b1±;

15.♗d3 ♗g7 16.♖de1 ♗d5 17.♘e5
♘d7 18.f4∞ Eljanov — Laznicka,
Dresden 2007)

11.exd5 cxd5 12.b4 (12.♘a4 ♗e7!±)
12...♗e7! (12...e4 13.♘xd5! ♘xd5
14.♕xe4+ ♘e7 15.♗c4 ♘f6 16.♕e2
♗e6 17.♗xe6 fxe6 18.0-0↑) 13.g3
(13.♗e2 e4 14.♘h4 ♘b8∓ — h7-h6
is now useful as g7-g5 is a threat.)
13...0-0 (13...b6 14.♗g2 bxc5 15.bxc5
exd4 16.♘xd4 ♘xc5 17.0-0 ♕d7=)
14.♗g2 a5! 15.♘xe5 ♘xe5 16.♗f4
axb4 17.♗xe5 ♕c6 18.♘e2 ♗e6 (18...
♘g4∓) 19.0-0 ♘d7∓ Navara — Bacrot, Baku 2008;

7.e3 b6

(One may also begin with 7...g6
and later Black will play ♗f8-g7,
exchange on f4 and follow up with
b7-b6. Usually play transposes to
the line 7...b6 8.b4 ♘xf4 9.exf4 ♕c7
10.g3 g6. However with the 7..g6
move order Black allows extra double-edged possibilities such as 8.h4!?
♘xf4 (8...♗g7 9.♗h2±) 9.exf4 b6

a) 9...♗g7 10.h5 b6 11.cxb6 ♕xb6
(11...♘xb6 12.h6!±) 12.♕d2 ♖b8
13.b3± Gelfand — Bacrot, Cap
d'Agde 2003;

b) 9...♕c7 10.g3 ♗g7 11.h5∞
Krasenkow — Delchev, Calvia
2004;

10.cxb6 ♕xb6 11.♕d2 ♖b8 12.b3
e6∞)

8.b4 (8.cxb6 ♘xf4 9.exf4 e6 10.♗d3
♗d6 11.g3 c5= Krylov — Kobalia,
Moscow 2010) 8...♘xf4 9.exf4 ♕c7
10.g3

(10.♕d2 g6 11.♖c1 ♗h6 12.g3 bxc5
13.bxc5 0-0 14.h4 14...f6!N (14...e5
15.dxe5 ♘xe5 16.♘xe5 ♖e8 17.♗e2
♖xe5 18.h5 gxh5 19.♔f1∞ Avrukh —
Malakhov, Helsingor 2009) 15.h5
g5 16.♘xg5 fxg5 17.fxg5 ♗g7 18.h6
♗h8∓/∞)

10...g6 11.♗e2 ♗g7 12.♖c1 0-0 13.0-
0 ♖b8! (13...a5 14.b5!± I.Sokolov —
Bacrot, Wijk aan Zee 2006) 14.♖e1
bxc5 15.bxc5 ♖e8=

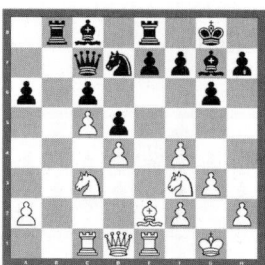

— A convenient square is vacated
for the knight, after which the problem of the white squared bishop is
solved.

7...♘hf6

7...g6 8.e4 dxe4 9.♘xe4 ♘df6
10.♘xf6+ exf6 (10...♘xf6 11.♗c4
♗g7 12.♕b3 0-0 13.0-0 ♘d5 14.♖fe1±
Sakaev — Lastin, Moscow 2005)
11.♗c4 ♕e7+

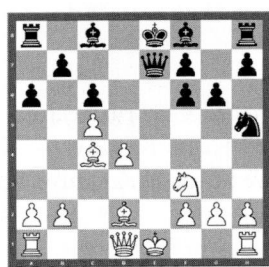

12. ♗e2!N As usual exchanges are not profitable for the side with more space. (12. ♗e3 ♗h6 13. ♕b3 ♗xe3 14.fxe3 0-0 15.0-0 ♗g4 16.♘d2 ♖ad8 17.♖ae1 ♘g7± — White's position is preferable but his centre is shaky. Black has counter play, Bagaturov — Volkov,Jermuk2010) 12...♗e6 (12... ♗g7 13.0-0 0-0 14.h3 ♕c7 15. ♗c4 ♘f4 16. ♗xf4 ♕xf4 17.♖e1 ♕c7 18. ♕b3±) 13.0-0 ♕d7 14.♖e1 ♗e7 (14...♘g7 15. ♗c3 ♗e7 16.♘d2 0-0 17.♘c4 ♖ad8 18. ♕c2 ♘f5 19. ♖ad1±) 15. ♗h6 0-0-0 16. ♗e3 ♖hg8

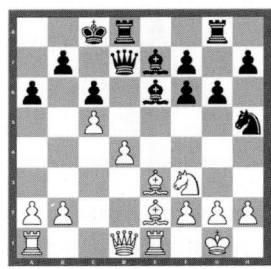

17. ♗f1! An important prophylaxis. (17.b4 g5 18. ♕c1 g4 19.♘d2 f5 20.♘c4 ♕c7 21.g3 f4 22.gxf4∞) 17...g5 (17...f5 18. ♗d2! With the intention of ♗d2-a5 driving the rook from d8. 18... ♗f6 19. ♗a5 ♖de8 20.a4± — It's very hard to deal with the threat b2-b4-b5.) 18.♘xg5 fxg5 19. ♕xh5±;

7... ♕c7 8.e4 dxe4 9.♘xe4 ♘hf6 (9...♘df6 10.♘eg5! h6 11.♘xf7 ♔xf7 12.♘e5+ ♔g8 13. ♗e2+-) 10.♘g3 g6 11. ♗c4 ♗g7 12.0-0 0-0 13.♖e1±;

7...e5 8.♘xe5 ♘xe5 9.dxe5 ♕e7 10.♘a4 (10.e4 ♕xe5 11. ♗e2 ♘f6= Bologan — Morozevich, Tomsk 2006; 10. ♗e3 ♕xe5 11. ♗d4 ♕g5 12.e3 ♗e7= Wojtaszek — Morozevich, Pamplona 2006) 10...♕xe5 11.e3 ♘f6 12. ♗c3 ♕e4 13.♘b6 ♖b8 14.♘xc8 ♖xc8 (14... ♗xc5 15. ♕d4!!+-) 15. ♕d4 (15. ♗d4 ♗e7 16.f3 ♕e6 17. ♕c2 0-0 18. ♗d3 g6 19.0-0±) 15... ♗e7 (15...♕xd4 16. ♗xd4±) 16.f3 ♕xd4 17.exd4 ♘h5 18.g3 g6 19.♔e2± — The white king moves to d3 and after having coordinated his forces, White can prepare to advance the queenside pawns.

8. ♕c2
After 8.h3 a good move, preparing ♗d2-f4, is

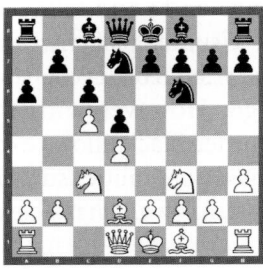

8...e5!

(If 8...♕c7 preparing the break, then it's White who can become active first: 9.e4!

(9. ♗g5 h6! (9...e5 10.e3!± Kazhga-leyev — Kozlov, Pavlodar 2006)

10.♗h4 ♘h5 11.g4 g5 12.gxh5 gxh4 13.♖g1 b6 14.b4 a5 15.a3 e5 16.e3 axb4 17.axb4 ♖xa1 18.♕xa1 bxc5 19.bxc5 ♗e7∓ — Black has the two bishops, at the same time the d4 pawn is potentially weak, Postny — Borovikov, Rethymno 2010)

9...♘xe4 (9...dxe4 10.♘g5 b6 11.♘cxe4 e6 12.cxb6 ♕xb6 13.♗d3±) 10.♘xe4 dxe4 11.♘g5 ♘f6 (11...h6 12.♘xe4 g6 13.♗c4 ♗g7 14.0-0 0-0 15.♖e1± Borovikov — I.Schneider, Boeblingen 2009) 12.♗c4 e6 13.♕c2±)

9.♘xe5

a) 9.b4 a5 (9...♕e7= Dreev — Volkov, Samara 1998) 10.a3 e4 11.♘g1 ♗e7 12.e3 b6!±;

b) 9.dxe5 ♘e4 10.e6 (10.♘xe4 dxe4 11.♘g5 ♘xc5 12.b4 ♗e7∓) 10...fxe6 (10...♘dxc5 11.exf7+ ♔xf7=) 11.♘xe4 dxe4 12.♘g5 ♘xc5 13.♕c2 ♕d5∓;

9...♘xe5 10.dxe5 ♘d7 11.e4 ♗xc5= Shengelia — Laznicka, Dresden 2007;

8.♖c1

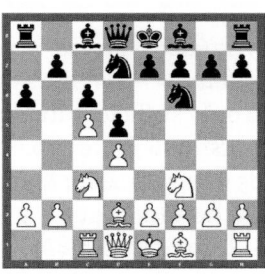

8...g6

a) 8...♕c7 9.g3 e5 (9...g6 10.♗f4 ♕d8 11.♗g2 ♘h5 12.♗g5 ♗g7 13.0-0 0-0 14.e4± Vitiugov — Va.Popov, St.Petersburg 2006) 10.♘xe5 ♘xe5 11.dxe5 ♘d7

a1) 11...♕xe5 12.♗f4 ♕f5 13.♘a4± Knott — Hagesaether, Hastings 2006;

a2) 11...♘g4 12.♘a4 ♘xe5 13.♘b6 ♖b8 14.♘xc8 ♕xc8 (14...♖xc8 15.♗h3±) 15.♗c3 ♕e6 16.♗g2±;

12.♘a4 ♕xe5 13.♗g2 ♗e7 14.♗c3 ♕g5 15.0-0±;

b) 8...e5 9.♘xe5 ♘xe5 10.dxe5 ♘g4 11.♘a4 ♘xe5 12.♗c3 f6 13.♘b6 ♖b8 14.♘xc8 ♕xc8 (14...♖xc8 15.g3± Topalov — Bacrot, Sofia 2006) 15.e3!N (15.♗xe5 fxe5 16.e4± Cmilyte — Stefanova, Fuegen 2006) 15...♕e6 16.♗e2 ♗e7 17.0-0 0-0 18.♕d4±;

9.h3

(9.g3 ♗g7 10.♗g2 0-0 (10...♘e4 11.♗f4 ♘xc3 12.bxc3!±) 11.0-0 ♖e8 12.♗f4 ♘h5 13.♗g5 h6 14.♗d2 ♘hf6 15.♘e5 ♘e4 (15...♘xe5 16.dxe5 ♘d7=) 16.♘xe4 (16.♘xd7 ♕xd7 17.♘xe4 dxe4 18.♗c3 ♕d5=) 16...♘xe5 17.dxe5 dxe4 18.♗c3 Illescas Cordoba — Huerga Leache, Villava 2009 18...♗f5=)

9...♕c7

a) 9...♘e4 10.♗f4 ♘xc3 11.bxc3±;

b) After 9...♗g7 White places the bishop on a ideal position 10.♗f4 0–0 11.e3 Compared to the line 5...♘bd7 6.♗f4 g6 7.h3 ♗g7 8.e3 0–0, White has played 9.♖c1 instead of developing the white squared bishop. Nevertheless it's still hard for Black to equalise. 11...♖e8!?

b1) 11...♘e4 12.♘xe4 dxe4 13.♘g5! (13.♘d2 e5 14.dxe5 ♕a5∞ Gagarin — Iljushin, Moscow 2008) 13...♘f6 14.♗e5 ♗h6 15.♗xf6 exf6 16.♘xe4 f5 17.♘d6 f4 18.e4± Lysyi — Iljushin, Budva 2009;

b2) 11...♘e8 12.♗e2 ♘c7 13.0–0 ♖e8 14.♗g5±;

12.♗e2 ♘e4 13.0–0 e5 14.♘xe4 exf4 15.♘d6 fxe3 16.♘xe8 ♕xe8 — Black has good compensation for the exchange.;

10.g3 ♗g7 11.♗f4 ♕d8 The bishop cannot stay long on the h2-b8 diagonal because of the pawn on g3. 12.♗g2 0–0 13.0–0 ♘h5 14.♗d2 (14. ♗g5 f6 15.♗d2 f5 — 14.♗d2 f5) 14...f5 (14...e5 15.dxe5 ♘xe5 16.e4 dxe4 17.♘xe4↑) 15.♕b3

a) 15.♘a4 e5 16.dxe5 (16.♗g5 ♕e8=) 16...♘xe5 17.♘xe5 ♗xe5 18.e3 ♗e6 19.♗c3 ♕f6 20.♗xe5 ♕xe5 21.♘c3 ♖ae8= — Black wants to retreat the bishop to f7, after which the idea of g6-g5 and f5-f4 emerges, Mozharov — Malakhov, Sochi 2012;

b) 15.♘g5 White can prevent the pawn advance e7-e5 for a time, but after ♘d7-f6 the black knight can go to e4, after which the break e7-e5 becomes possible again.;

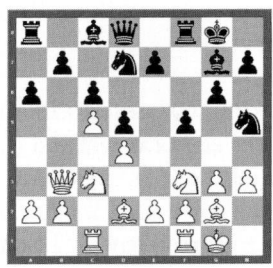

15...♔h8 (15...e5? is bad. 16.♘g5!± — A fork on e6 and a capture on d5 are threatened.; 15...♖b8 16.e4! fxe4 17.♘xe4↑) 16.♘g5 (16.♘a4 e5=) 16...♗xd4!?N (16...♘df6 17.♘a4 h6 18.♘b6 ♖b8 19.♘f3 ♘e4 Vallejo Pons — Malakhov, Pamplona 2008 20.♗a5± — Both sides face a long manoeuvering struggle in which White's chances are better.)

17.♘xd5 (17.♘e6 ♘xc5 18.♘xc5 ♗xc5 19.♘xd5 ♗d4/= — White's compensation is only sufficient for equality.) 17...cxd5 18.♘e6 ♘xc5 19.♘xc5 b6 20.♗xd5 ♘xg3 21.♖fe1 ♖a7 22.♘d3 ♘e4 23.♗h6 ♕d6 24.e3 ♗g7 25.♖c6 ♕d8 26.♗xg7+ ♔xg7∞/= — In the forthcoming complicated game the chances are about equal.

8...g6

8...♛c7

9.e4

(9.♗g5 e5

(9...h6 10.♗xf6 (10.♗h4 ♘h5 11.e4 g5 12.♗g3 ♘xg3 13.hxg3 g4 14.♘h4 b6 15.exd5 bxc5 16.0-0-0 cxd4 17.♖xd4 cxd5 18.♘xd5 ♛xc2+ 19.♔xc2 ♖a7=) 10...♘xf6 11.e3 g6 (11...♘d7 12.e4±) 12.♗d3 ♗g7 13.0-0 0-0 14.♘e5 ♘g4 15.♘xg4 ♗xg4 16.f3 ♗d7 17.f4±)

10.e3

(10.♗xf6 ♘xf6 (10...gxf6 11.e3∞ Aronian — Arizmendi Martinez, San Sebastian 2006) 11.♘xe5 ♗xc5 12.e3 ♗d6=)

10...♘h5 11.0-0-0 h6 12.♗h4 g5 13.♗g3 ♘xg3 14.hxg3 g4! (14...♗g7 15.e4↑) 15.♘xe5

a) 15.♘h4 ♘f6∞;

b) 15.♘e1 e4! (15...♗g7 16.♘d3) 16.♗e2 ♘f6=;

15...♘xe5 16.e4 ♗e6 17.dxe5 0-0-0 18.exd5 cxd5=)

9...e5 10.exd5 cxd5

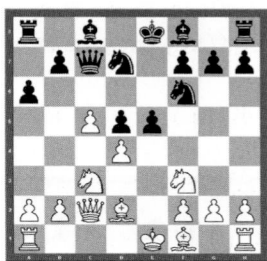

11.b4

a) 11.♘xd5 ♘xd5 12.♗c4 exd4 13.♗xd5 ♘f6 14.♗b3 ♗xc5=;

b) 11.♗g5 exd4 12.♕e2+ ♘e5 (12...♗e7 13.♕xe7+ ♔xe7 14.♘xd5+±; 12...♔d8 13.♘xd4 h6 14.♗e3 ♗xc5 15.♕d2 ♖e8 16.♗e2 ♔e7 17.0-0 ♔f8 18.♖ac1=) 13.♗xf6 gxf6 14.♘xd5 ♕xc5 15.♘xf6+ ♔e7 16.♘xe5 ♔xf6 17.f4=;

c) 11.0-0-0 exd4 (11...♗e7 12.g4!?∞ Najer — Savchenko, Moscow 2006) 12.♖e1+ ♗e7 13.♘xd4 ♘xc5 14.g4 ♘e6∓;

d) 11.♘a4 e4

d1) 11...b5 12.c6±;

d2) 11...exd4 12.♖c1 ♗e7 (12...g6 13.♗e2 ♗g7 14.♘xd4 ♘e4 15.♗e3

♕a5+ 16.♔f1 0–0 17.f3 ♘ef6 18.♔f2 ♖e8 19.♖hd1 ♕c7 20.g3±) 13.♗e2 ♘e4 14.♘xd4 0–0 (14...♗xc5 15.♘xc5 ♕xc5 16.♕xc5 ♘dxc5 17.♗b4 ♘e6 18.♘xe6 ♗xe6 19.f3 ♘f6 20.♖c7±) 15.0–0 ♗xc5 (15... ♕e5 16.♘f3 ♕e6 17.♗d3±) 16.♘xc5 ♘dxc5 17.♗b4 b6 18.f3 a5 (18...♕e5 19.♖fd1±) 19.♗a3 ♕e5 20.♖fd1 ♘d6 21.♗xc5 bxc5 22.♕xc5±;

12.♘h4

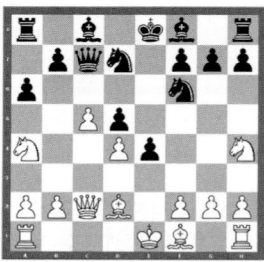

12...b5! (12...g6 13.♗e2±) 13.♘c3 ♘b8! 14.♗e2 ♘c6 15.♗e3 ♗e7∞ — In the complicated game which follows Black's chances are no worse.;

11...♗e7

a) After 11...e4 the piece sacrifice appears to be promising: 12.♘xd5! (12. ♘h4 ♘b8 13.♕a4+ ♕d7 14.b5 ♗e7 15.g3±) 12...♘xd5 13.♕xe4+ ♘e7 14.♗c4 ♘f6 15.♕e2 ♗e6 16.♗xe6 fxe6 17.0–0↑ — White's initiative is very strong.;

b) 11...exd4 12.♘xd4 b6 13.c6 ♘e5 14.♕a4±;

12.♕c1 Now Black has to decide on the pawn structure in the centre.

(Alternatively White can quietly continue development 12.♗e2 e4

(12...0–0 13.0–0 (13.g3 a5 14.♘b5 ♕b8 15.0–0 ♘e4 16.a3±) 13...e4 14.♘e1 ♘b8 15.♕c1 ♗e6 16.♘c2 ♘c6 17.♖b1 ♗d8 18.a4± Alekseev — Bacrot, Biel 2008)

13.♘g5 b6

(13...♘f8 14.f3 h6 15.♘xf7 ♔xf7 16.fxe4 dxe4 (16...♘e6 17.♘xd5±) 17.0–0 ♔g8 18.♗f4 ♕d8 19.d5±)

14.♘h3 (14.f3 bxc5 15.bxc5 ♘xc5! 16.dxc5 ♕xc5 17.fxe4 d4 18.♕b3 dxc3 19.♕xf7+ ♔d8 20.♗f4 c2 21.♖c1 ♖f8 22.♕b3 ♕b4+ 23.♗d2 ♕xb3 24.axb3 h6 25.e5 ♘d5 26.♘f3 ♘f4 27.♗xf4 ♖xf4 28.♖xc2 ♗e6=) 14...♗b7 15.0–0 0–0 16.♖ab1± — White has good prospects for queenside play.)

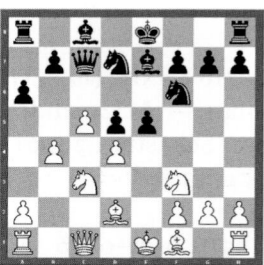

12...e4 (12...0–0 13.♘xe5 ♘xe5 14.♗f4±; 12...exd4 13.♗f4 ♕d8 14.♘xd4 0–0 15.♗d3 ♘h5 16.♗e3 ♘e5 17.♗e2±) 13.♗f4 ♕d8 14.♘e5

♘h5 15.♘xd7 ♕xd7 16.♗e3± —
White's p lay on the queenside is
more serious than the Black's play
in the centre.;

8...e5

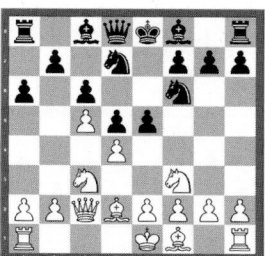

9.dxe5 ♘g4 10.♘a4 ♘gxe5

a) 10...♕e7

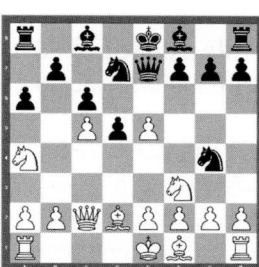

11.♗c3!N (11.♗g5 f6 12.exf6 gxf6∞
Lugovoi — Najer, Moscow 2005)
11...♘xc5 (11...♘gxe5 12.♘xe5 ♘xe5
13.0-0-0±) 12.♘xc5 ♕xc5 13.e3± —
The black knight will be driven to h6
and remain out of play.;

b) 10...♗e7 11.♕c3 0-0 12.♕d4 ♘h6
13.e4± f6 Avrukh — Erenburg, Caleta 2005 14.e6 ♘e5 15.♘b6+-;

11.0-0-0 ♘xf3

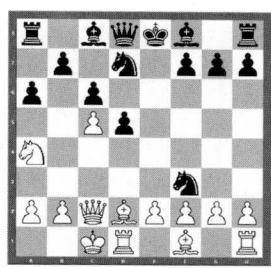

12.exf3!N

(12.gxf3 ♗e7 13.♖g1 0-0 14.e4 (14.
♗c3 g6 15.♗d4 Laznicka — Huerga, Pamplona 2009 15...♗f6=) 14...
♕c7 15.exd5 cxd5 16.♗e3↑)

12...♗e7 13.♗d3 h6 14.♖he1 0-0
15.♔b1±

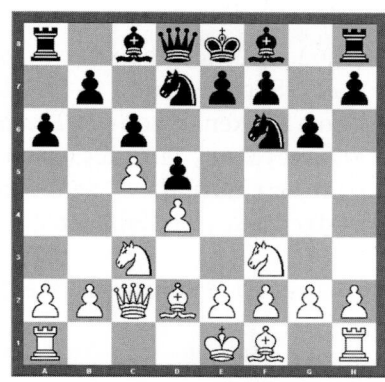

9.g3
9.h3 ♕c7

(Also possible is 9...♗g7 10.♗f4
0-0 11.e3, which leads to the line
5.. ♘bd7 6.♗f4 g6 7.h3 ♗g7 8.e3
0-0 when White plays ♕d1-c2.

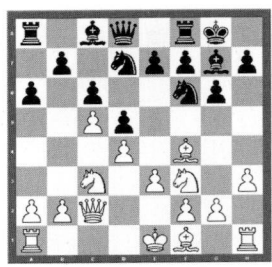

11...♘e4! The most precise way to equalise

(11...b6 12.cxb6 ♕xb6 13.♗d3 c5 14.0-0 cxd4 (*14...c4 15.♗e2 ♗b7 16.♖ab1 ♖fc8 17.b3 cxb3 18.♖xb3 ♕a7 19.♕b2±* Najer — Chuprikov, Sochi 2005) 15.exd4 ♗b7 16.♘a4 ♕a7 17.b4 ♖fc8 18.♕b3 ♘e4 19.♖ac1

(19.♘c5 ♘exc5 20.bxc5 e5 (*20...♗c6?* San Segundo — Malakhov, Sanxenxo 2004 *21.♖ac1±*) 21.♘xe5 ♗xe5 22.♗xe5 (*22.dxe5 ♘xc5 23.♕a3 d4∞*) 22...♘xe5 23.dxe5 ♖xc5 24.♖ab1 ♗c8!=)

19...♖xc1 20.♗xc1 ♖c8 21.♗e3±)

12.♘xe4

a) 12.♗e2 e5 13.♘xe5 ♘xe5=;

b) 12.♖d1 e5 (*12...♘xc3 13.♕xc3 b6=* Dzagnidze — Stefanova, Fuegen 2006) 13.♘xe5 ♘xe5 14.♗xe5 ♗xe5 15.dxe5 ♕a5=;

12...dxe4 13.♘d2 (*13.♕xe4 ♕a5+ 14.♘d2 e5*) 13...e5 14.dxe5 ♘xe5 (*14...♕a5 15.e6 ♘xc5∞* Lagowski

— Stefanova, Gibraltar 2006) 15.♘xe4 ♗f5 16.♗e2 ♘d7 17.0-0 ♕e7 18.♗d3 ♗xe4 19.♗xe4 ♘xc5 20.♗f3 ♖fd8=)

10.e4 ♘xe4 (*10...dxe4 11.♘g5!? ♗g7 12.♗c4 0-0*) 11.♘xe4 dxe4 12.♕xe4 (*12.♘g5 ♗g7∓*) 12...♘f6 13.♕e5 ♕xe5+ 14.dxe5

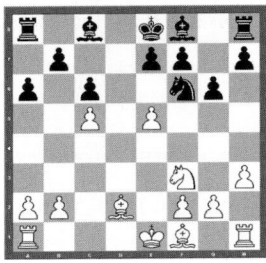

14...♘d7

a) 14...♘d5 15.♗c4 ♗e6 16.♘d4± Topalov — Najer, Ajaccio 2004;

b) 14...♘e4 15.♗e3 ♗e6 16.♘d4 (*16.♗d3 ♗d5 17.0-0 0-0-0=* Huzman — Volkov, Moscow 2006) 16...♘xc5 17.♖c1 ♘d7 18.♘xe6 fxe6∞ Khenkin — Volkov, Fuegen 2006;

15.e6 (*15.♗e3 ♗g7 16.e6 fxe6 17.0-0-0 ♘f6∓* Lugovoi — Malakhov, Moscow 2005) 15...fxe6 16.♗c3 ♖g8 17.♗d4 ♗g7 18.♗xg7 ♖xg7 19.♖c1 ♖f7 20.♗d3 ♖f4=

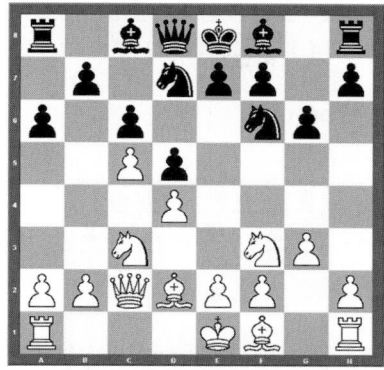

9...e5

9... ♗g7 10. ♗g2 0–0 11.0–0 ♖e8 (*11... b6 12.b4 ♗b7 13.♖ab1 ♖e8 14.♖fd1± ♕c8 15.♘a4 b5 16.♘c3 e5 17.dxe5 ♘xe5 18.♘xe5 ♖xe5 19.e4 dxe4 20.♘xe4 ♘xe4 21.♗xe4±* — It's difficult for the b7 bishop to enter the game. White has a serious advantage, Sakaev — Malakhov, Krasnoyarsk 2007) 12.♖ad1 b6

(12...♘f8 So far neither side threatens to carry out a break in the centre, therefore in my opinion, the best option is simply to strengthen the position a little with an indefinite move

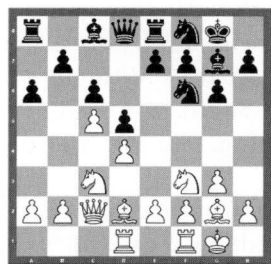

13.♖fe1!N

a) 13.h3!? ♗f5 14.♕b3 ♕c8 15.g4 (*15. ♘a4 ♘6d7=; 15.♔h2 ♘e4=*) 15... ♗e4 16.♘xe4 ♘xe4 17.♗f4 ♘d7= Korotylev — Bryzgalin, Voronezh 2008;

b) 13.♕b3 ♘e6 14. ♗e3 ♕c7 15.♘a4 ♘e4 16.♘b6 ♖b8 17.♘h4± Najer — Volkov, Moscow 2010;

13... ♗f5

(*13...♗g4 14.♘e5 ♗f5 15.♕b3 ♖b8 (15...♘6d7 16.♕xb7 ♘xe5 17.dxe5 ♕d7 18.♕xd7 ♘xd7 19.f4 ♘xc5 20.♖c1±) 16.e4 ♗e6 17.exd5 ♘xd5 18.♘xd5 ♗xd5 19.♗xd5 ♕xd5 20.♕xd5 cxd5 21.b4±*)

14.♕b3 ♖a7 15. ♗f4 ♘e6 16. ♗e5 ♗g4 17.h3 ♗xf3 18. ♗xf3±)

13.b4!

(*13.cxb6 ♘xb6 14.♘e5 ♗f5 15.♕b3 ♖c8 16.♘a4 ♘bd7!? (16...♘xa4 17.♕xa4 ♕b6 18.♕b4!± Sargissian — Malakhov, 2007 18...♕xb4 19.♗xb4 ♘d7 20.♘xd7 ♗xd7 21.♖d2 ♖b8 22. ♗c3±) 17.♖c1 ♘xe5 18.dxe5 ♘e4 19. ♗f4 g5 20. ♗xe4 ♗xe4 21. ♗xg5 ♗xe5 22.♖fd1±*)

13...bxc5

a) 13...e5 14.e4±;

b) 13...a5 14.b5 cxb5 (*14...bxc5 15.bxc6 ♘b8 16.c7 ♕xc7 17. ♗f4±*) 15.♘xb5

(15.c6 ♘b8 16.♘e5 (*16.♘xb5 ♘xc6!*)
16...b4 17.♘b5⯑)

15...bxc5 16.dxc5 ♗a6 17.a4±;

14.bxc5 e5 15.e4 ♘xe4 16.♘xe4 dxe4
17.♕xe4 exd4 18.♕xc6 ♖b8 19.♗g5
♕a5 20.♖fe1 ♖xe1+ 21.♖xe1 ♘f8
22.♗d2±

10.dxe5 ♘g4 11.e6

11.♗f4 ♗xc5 12.e3 ♕e7∓;

11.♗g2 ♗xc5

(*11...♘gxe5 12.♘xe5 (12.♘a4 ♗g7
13.0-0 0-0=) 12...♘xe5 13.0-0 ♗g7
(13...♗e6 14.e4 d4 15.♘a4±) 14.e4!N
(14.♖ad1 0-0 15.♗e3 ♗f5 16.♕c1
♖e8∓ Pashikian — Laznicka, Yerevan 2007)*)

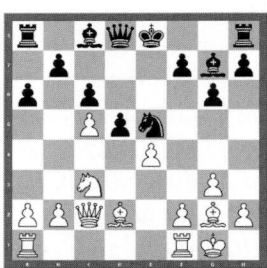

14...d4 15.♘a4 0-0 16.♘b6 ♖b8
17.♘xc8 ♖xc8 18.♖ad1± — White
has two strong bishops, and the d4
pawn lacks support.)

12.0-0 0-0 13.♖ad1

(*13.h3 ♘gxe5 14.♘xe5 ♘xe5
15.♘xd5 ♗d4! (15...♗xf2+ 16.♖xf2*)

cxd5 17.♗f4⯑/±; 15...♗d6 16.♘f4±)
16.♘f4 ♕b6! 17.♗c3 ♕c5=)

13...♕b6 14.e3

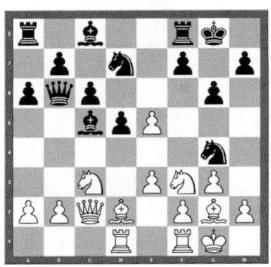

14...♕a7!N

(*14...♕c7 15.e4 ♘dxe5 (15...d4
16.♗f4 ♘dxe5 17.♘xd4 ♖d8
18.♘b3±) 16.♘xe5 ♕xe5 17.exd5
♗f5*)

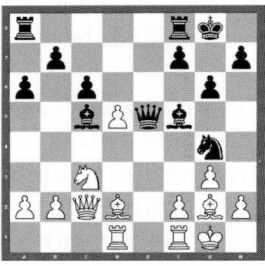

18.♕c1!N ± Black cannot play by
analogy with this game (*18.♕b3
♗d3 19.♗f4 ♕f5 20.♖xd3 ♕xd3
21.dxc6 bxc6∓ Vitiugov — Malakhov, Sochi 2010*) 18...♗d3?, in
view of 19.♗f4 ♕f5 20.h3!+-)

15.♘a4 ♗e7 16.e4 b5 17.exd5 bxa4
18.d6 ♗d8 19.♗c3 ♗b6 20.h3 ♘xf2
(*20...♘h6 21.g4±*) 21.♖xf2 ♗xf2+
22.♕xf2 ♕xf2+ 23.♔xf2⯑/± —

White has full compensation for the exchange.;

11.♘a4

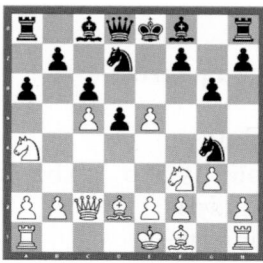

11...♘gxe5 (11...♘dxe5!?N The idea of immediately freeing the white squared bishop appears to be good 12.♗c3 ♕e7 13.♗g2 ♘xf3+ 14.♗xf3 ♘e5 15.0-0-0 ♗h6+ 16.♔b1 0-0=) 12.♗c3 ♗g7 13.0-0-0 0-0 14.♘xe5 ♗xe5!

(14...♘xe5 15.e4 ♗e6 16.♘b6 ♖b8

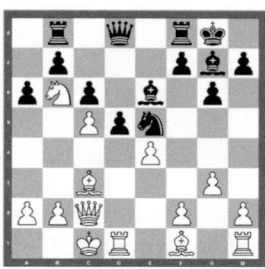

17.♗g2!N (17.f4 ♘d7 18.♗xg7 ♔xg7 19.exd5 cxd5= Miton — Bacrot, Lugo 2007) 17...♕e7 (17... ♘d7 18.♗xg7 ♔xg7 19.exd5 cxd5 20.♗xd5+-) 18.♗xe5 ♗xe5 19.exd5 ♗f5 (19...cxd5 20.♖he1±) 20.d6±)

15.♗xe5 ♘xe5 16.♘b6 ♖b8=

11...♘xc5

11...fxe6 12.♗h3 ♘gf6 (12...♘ge5 13.♘xe5 ♘xe5 14.♘a4±) 13.♘g5 ♕e7 14.♘a4 ♘xc5 15.♘b6 ♖b8 16.♘xc8 ♖xc8 17.♗b4 ♘d3+ 18.exd3 ♕xb4+ 19.♔f1 ♗h6 20.♘xe6 ♔f7 21.♔g2±

12.exf7+ ♔xf7

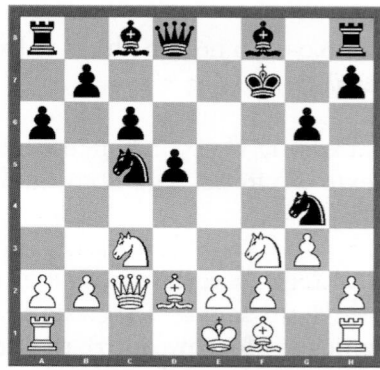

13.♗g2!N
It's better for White not to force events. The following gains nothing 13.e4 ♗g7!

(13...♗e7 14.h3 ♘f6 15.♘e5+ ♔g8 16.♗g2 d4 (16...♗d6 17.♘g4↑) 17.♘a4 d3 18.♕d1 ♘fxe4 19.♘xc5 ♘xc5 20.0-0↑)

14.♘xd5

a) 14.h3 ♘f6 15.♘g5+ ♔g8 16.♘xd5

a1) 16.♗e3 ♕a5

(16...♘cxe4? Aronian — Bacrot, Mainz (rapid) 2007 17.♘gxe4! dxe4 (17...♘xe4 18.♘xe4 ♗f5

19.f3!+-) 18.♗c4+ ♘d5 19.♘xd5 cxd5 20.0-0-0 ♗e6 21.♖xd5 ♗xd5 22.♖d1 h6 23.♖xd5 ♕c8 24.♖d8+ ♔h7 25.♖xc8 ♖hxc8 26.♕xe4 *(26.♗c5 ♖xc5 27.♗g8+ ♖xg8 28.♕xc5±)* 26...b5 27.♔b1 bxc4 28.h4±)

17.♗d2 ♕b6 18.♗e3=;

a2) 16.0-0-0 h6 17.b4 hxg5 18.bxc5 ♗g4!±;

16...cxd5 17.♕xc5 h6 18.e5 hxg5 19.exf6 ♗xf6 20.♗g2 ♗e6 21.♖d1 ♖c8=;

b) 14.♗g2 ♗xc3! *(14...♖e8 15.0-0 ♔g8 16.♗g5±* Sargissian — Laznicka, Moscow 2007)* 15.♗xc3 dxe4 16.♗xh8 ♘d3+ 17.♔f1 exf3 18.♗xf3 ♘gxf2 19.♕b3+ ♔e7 20.♗g7 ♗h3+ 21.♗g2 *(21.♔g1 ♕d7 22.♗h6 ♖h8!!∓)* 21...♕d7∓ Ivanchuk — Bacrot, Crete 2007;

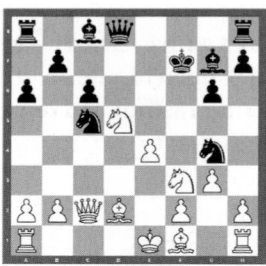

14...♘xe4 15.♘f4 ♘xd2 16.0-0-0 ♗f5 17.♗c4+ ♔f8 18.♗d3 ♗xd3 19.♕xd2 ♗h6 20.♖he1 ♕d6 21.♕xd3 ♕xd3 22.♖xd3 ♖g8= Leko — Karjakin, Nalchik 2009;

13.b4 ♗f5 14.♕c1 ♘e6 15.♗g2 ♗g7 *(15...♗xb4 16.h3 ♘f6 17.g4 ♗xc3 18.♕xc3 ♗e4 19.♘e5+ ♔g8 20.f3 d4 21.♕b3 ♗d5 22.♕xb7±/∞; 15...♘f6!?)* 16.0-0 ♖e8 17.h3 ♘f6=

13... ♗f5

13...♗g7? 14.♘xd5+-

14.♕d1 ♗d6

14...♕b6? 15.0-0 ♕xb2 16.♘g5+ ♔g8 17.♘xd5!+-;
  14...d4 15.♘a4±;
  14...♗g7 15.♘g5+! ♔g8 16.0-0 h6 17.♘f3 ♔h7 18.♘h4±

15.0-0 ♖e8 16.b4 ♘e6 17.♘h4±

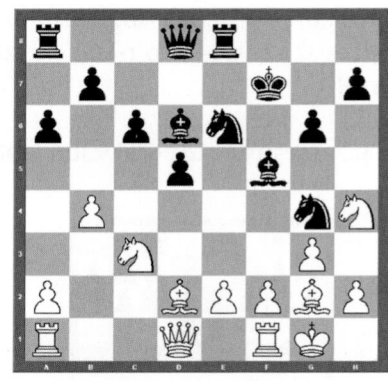

— Black has active pieces but his king is badly protected. Conclusion: The system 5.c5 leads to an interesting, and very complicated strategic struggle. The evaluation of many key positions is complicated and still controversial.

■ GAME 28

1.d4 d5 2.c4 c6 3.♘f3 ♘f6 4.♘c3 a6
5.a4

5.♕c2

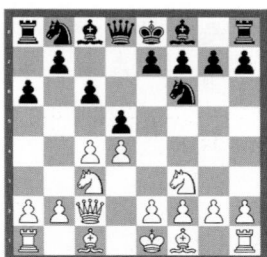

5...dxc4 6.a4

(An less promising move is 6.e4
b5 7.♗e2 e6 8.0-0 ♘bd7 9.b3 cxb3
10.axb3 ♗b7 11.e5 ♘d5 12.♗g5 (12.
♘xd5 cxd5 13.♗g5 ♖c8∓; 12.♘e4 c5
13.dxc5 ♖c8 14.♗g5 ♕c7∓) 12...♘b4
(12...♕b6 13.♘xd5 cxd5 14.♖fc1
♗b4∓) 13.♕e4 ♗e7 14.♕g4 ♗xg5
15.♘xg5 0-0 16.♘ge4 c5 17.♘xc5
♘xc5 18.dxc5 ♘c6 19.♕f4 ♕d4∓)

6...e6 7.♗g5 (If 7.e4 Black has
a strong initiative 7...b5 8.axb5 cxb5
9.♘xb5 axb5 10.♖xa8 ♗b7 11.♖a1
♘xe4 12.♗e2 ♗b4+ 13.♔f1 0-0∓/↑)
7...♕a5 8.e4 b5∓ — It's hard for
White prove that there's enough
compensation for a pawn, Korobov
— Kobalia, Amman 2006;

5.♕b3, usually transposes to lines
which will be considered in the second book:

5...dxc4

a) 5...e6 6.♗g5 dxc4 7.♕xc4 b5
8.♕b3 — 4...e6 5.♕b3 dxc4 6.♕xc4
b5 7.♕b3 a6 8.♗g5(8.♕d3 — 4...e6
5.♕b3 dxc4 6.♕xc4 b5 7.♕d3 a6
8.♗g5) ;

b) If Black doesn't want the complicated game which arises after dxc4
or some other variations, he can
choose a passive but solid move 5...
b5 6.cxd5 (6.c5 a5 7.♘e5 g6=) 6...cxd5
7.♗g5

b1) 7.♗f4 e6 8.♖c1 ♗b7 9.e3 ♘c6
10.♗e2 ♗e7±/=;

b2) 7.a4 bxa4 8.♘xa4 ♘c6 9.♗f4
e6 10.♖c1 ♗d7 (10...♗b4+ 11.♔d1
♗d6 12.♗xd6 ♕xd6 13.♕b6
♗d7∞) 11.♘c3 (11.♘c5?! 11...♘e4∓)
11...♗e7=;

7...e6 8.e3 ♘c6 9.♗d3 ♗e7 10.0-
0 0-0 11.♗xf6 gxf6 (Bad is 11...
♗xf6? 12.♕c2, with an attack on h7
and threatening to capture on d5.)
12.♖ac1 Kryakvin — Bryzgalin,
Belorechensk 2010 12...♗d7±/= —
Black is very close to equalising.;

6.♕xc4 b5 7.♕d3 e6 — 4...e6 5.♕b3 dxc4 6.♕xc4 b5 7.♕d3 a6;

5.♗g5

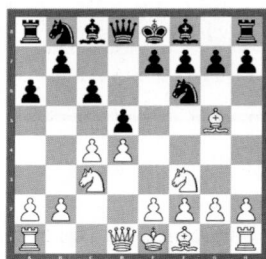

5...♘e4

a) 5...e6 is bad 6.e3 — It now looks like a7-a6 has been made prematurely.;

b) But the rare 5...dxc4 is quite reliable 6.a4 (If *6.e4 b5∓* It's difficult for White to prove that his initiative is worth a pawn.) 6...♗f5 (*6...♗e6 7.e4 ♘bd7 8.a5!±*) 7.e3

(*7.♘e5 ♘e4*

(*7...h6 8.♗f4 (8.♗h4 ♘bd7 9.♘xc4 b5 10.♘e3 ♗e6=) 8...e6=)*

8.♘xe4 ♗xe4 9.♘xc4 ♕d5 10.♕b3 ♘d7 11.♗f4 b5 12.axb5 cxb5 13.f3 bxc4 14.fxe4 ♕xe4 15.♕f3 ♕xf3=)

7...♘e4 8.♗xc4 ♘xg5 9.♘xg5 e6 10.♘f3 ♘d7= S.Ivanov — Khalifman, Krasnoyarsk 2003;

6.♗f4

a) 6.cxd5 ♘xg5 7.♘xg5 cxd5=;

b) 6.♗h4 ♘xc3 7.bxc3 dxc4 8.e4 b5 9.♗e2 g6 10.0-0 ♗g7∓;

c) 6.h4 An original but inadequate move

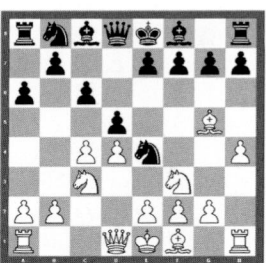

6...♘xc3

c1) The next move hasn't been very successful 6...h6, for after 7.♗f4 ♘xc3 8.bxc3 dxc4 9.♘e5 b5 10.g3 Black cannot drive away the knight with the move f7-f6.;

c2) 6...♕a5 7.♕c2!? (*7.cxd5 cxd5 8.♕b3 e6 9.e3 Bocharov — Burmakin, Tula 2001 9...♗b4! 10.♖c1 ♗d7 11.a3 ♗xc3+ 12.bxc3 ♗b5∓; 7.♗d2 ♘xd2 8.♘xd2 e6=*) 7...b5 (*7...♗f5 8.♕b3±*) 8.cxd5 cxd5 9.♘d2 ♘xc3 10.bxc3±;

7.bxc3 dxc4 8.g3 (*8.e4 b5 9.♘e5 ♘d7 10.♘xc6 ♕c7 11.d5 ♗b7∓ Mamedyarov — Fontaine, Istanbul 2003*) 8...b5 9.♗g2 ♗b7 10.0-0

(*10.♘d2 ♘d7 (10...h6 11.♗f4 ♘d7 12.♘e4⩲) 11.♘e4 f6 12.♗f4 (12.♗e3 e6 13.0-0 ♗e7∓) 12...e5 13.dxe5 ♘xe5∓*)

10...♘d7 11.e4 h6 12.♗f4 e6∓ — White do esn't have full compensation for a pawn, Dreev — Malakhov, Khanty Mansyisk 2005;

6...♘xc3 (After 6...♕a5 strong is 7.♕c2!±, and now entirely bad is 7...♗f5 8.♕b3±) 7.bxc3 dxc4

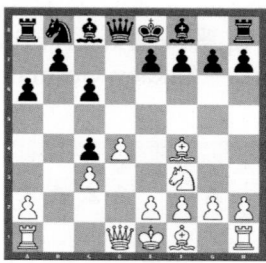

8.g3

(8.e4 b5 9.♘e5 ♕a5 (Not too bad is 9...♗e6 10.♗e2 f6 11.♘f3 ♘d7 12.0−0 ♗f7∓ — White's compensation looks insufficient.) 10.♗d2 (10.♖c1 g6 11.♕f3 f6∓ Argandona — Prie, Montpellier 2005) 10...♘d7 11.♘xc6 ♕c7 12.d5 (12.♘b4 e6∓) 12...e6

(12...♘c5 13.a4! (13.♕f3 e5∓ Nakamura — Volkov, Santo-Domingo 2002) 13...♘xa4 14.♕f3⩲)

13.g3 (13.a4 ♗b7∓; 13.♘d4 ♘c5∓) 13...♗b7 14.♗g2 ♗xc6 15.dxc6 ♘e5 16.0−0 ♗d6∓)

8...b5 9.♗g2 ♗b7 10.♘e5

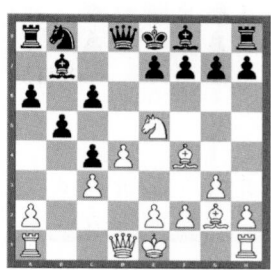

10...♕c8!

(Complications unnecessary for Black arise after 10...f6 11.♘xc4 g5 (11...bxc4 12.♖b1 ♕c8 13.♕a4 g5∞) 12.♗e3! bxc4 13.♖b1⩲ Anand — Shirov, Monaco (blindfold) 1997)

11.♖b1 ♘d7 12.0−0

(Too reckless is 12.♘xc4? 12...bxc4 13.0−0 (13.♕a4 e6 14.0−0 ♖a7∓) 13...e6 14.♕a4 ♖a7 15.♗e3 c5−+ Shirov — Movsesian, Sarajevo 2002)

12...♘xe5 13.♗xe5 f6 14.♗f4 g6!± There are no weaknesses in Black's camp and he can complete development. White doesn't have full compensation for the pawn. (Not so convincing is 14...e6 15.e4 ♗a3 16.♕h5+ g6 17.♕h6 ♕d7 18.♗c1 ♗f8 19.♕f4 ♗e7 20.♕h6 ♗f8= Khalifman — P. Nikolic, Germany 1999) ;

5.cxd5

5...cxd5 6.♗g5 (6.♗f4 ♘c6 — 3.cxd5 cxd5 4.♗f4 ♘f6 5.♘c3 ♘c6 6.♘f3 a6) 6...♘e4

a) Passive is 6...e6 7.e3± — the bishop is left on c8.;

b) If there is another move, its better not to allow doubled pawns. After 6...♘c6 7.e3

b1) 7.♗xf6 exf6!? (*7...gxf6 8.e3 ♗g4=*) 8.e3 ♗e7 9.♗d3 0-0 10.0-0 ♗e6=;

b2) 7.♘e5 ♕b6!

(*7...♘xe5 8.dxe5 d4 9.♕a4+ ♕d7 (9...b5 10.♘xb5 ♗d7 11.♕xd4±) 10.♖d1 ♕xa4 11.♘xa4 ♘d7 12.e6 fxe6 13.♖xd4±*)

8.♘xc6 bxc6 9.♕d2 ♖b8 10.b3 ♘e4

(*10...e5 11.dxe5 ♘e4 (11...♘g4 12.e3 ♘xe5 13.♗e2±) 12.♘xe4 ♗b4 13.♘c3 d4 14.♖c1∞ Graf — Dautov, Germany 2004*)

11.♘xe4 dxe4= — The threat e7-e5 is very unpleasant. It's now White who must be concerned about maintaining the balance.;

7...♗g4 8.♗xf6 gxf6 9.♗e2 e6±/= White has a microscopic advantage.;

7.♗h4

(*7.♗f4 ♘c6 8.e3 ♗f5 (8...♗g4 9.♕b3 ♘xc3 10.bxc3 ♘a5 11.♕c2 e6=) 9.♕b3 ♘xc3 10.bxc3 ♘a5 11.♕b2 e6 12.♗e2 ♗d6 13.♗xd6 ♕xd6 14.♕b4 ♕xb4 15.cxb4 ♘c6= Ftacnik — Sakaev, Germany 2004*)

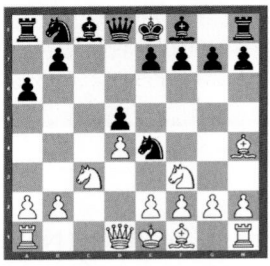

7...♕a5 8.♕b3 (*8.e3 ♘xc3 9.♕d2 ♗f5 10.bxc3 e6= Guliev — Volkov, Moscow 2004; 8.♖c1 e6 9.e3 ♘xc3 10.bxc3 ♗a3 11.♖c2 0-0 12.♗e2 ♗d7 13.♘d2 b5∓*) 8...e6 9.e3 ♗b4 10.♗d3 (*10.♖c1 ♗d7 11.a3 ♗xc3+ 12.bxc3 ♗b5= Beliavsky — Khalifman, Moscow (rapid) 2002*) 10...♘xc3 11.a3 ♘c6 12.0-0 ♘e4

(*12...♕a4 13.♕xa4 ♘xa4 14.axb4 ♘xb2 15.♗e2 ♘c4 16.♗xc4 dxc4 17.b5 ♘a7 (17...♘e7!?) 18.bxa6 b5∞ Ljubojevic — Bacrot, Bled 2002*)

13.axb4 ♕xb4 14.♕c2 0-0 15.♗xe4 dxe4 16.♕xe4 ♗d7= ;

5.h3

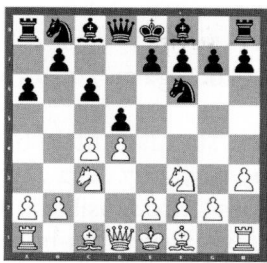

5...e6

a) 5...b5 6.c5±;

b) 5...dxc4 6.a4 e6 (*6...c5 7.d5 e6 8.e4 exd5 9.exd5±; 6...♘d5 7.a5 ♗f5 8.e3 ♗d3 9.♗xd3 cxd3 10.♕xd3± Eingorn — Volkov, St.Petersburg 1996*) 7.e3 c5 8.♗xc4±;

c) 5...♗f5 6.♕b3±;

6.e3

(After 6.cxd5 Black can transform the structure to that of the Exchange Variation 6...cxd5 — The e6 pawn blocks the c8 bishop but White has made the unnecessary move h2-h3. (*6...exd5 7.♗f4±*) 7.♗f4 ♘c6 8.e3 ♗d6 9.♗d3 0-0 10.0-0 b5 11.♖c1 ♗b7= Timman — Laznicka, Carlsbad 2007)

6...♘bd7 (*6...c5 7.cxd5 exd5 8.♗d3! — h3 prevents Black's pin. 8...♘c6 9.0-0 ♗e6 10.♘e5± Ivanisevic — Campos Moreno, Khanty Mansyisk 2010*) 7.♕c2 7...dxc4

(Leading to a more complicated game is 7...♗d6 8.b3

(If White begins an attack on the kingside with 8.g4,then after 8...dxc4 the move h2-h3 frequently becomes redundant 9.e4

(*9.♗xc4 b5 10.♗e2 ♗b7 11.e4 (11.g5 ♘d5 12.♘e4 ♗e7 13.a3 ♕b6∓) 11...c5 12.e5 cxd4 13.exf6 dxc3 14.fxg7 ♖g8∓*)

9...c5 10.e5 cxd4 11.exf6 dxc3 12.fxg7 ♖g8 13.♕xc3 ♕f6 14.♕xf6 ♘xf6 15.♗xc4 b5 (*15... ♖xg7 16.♗h6 ♖g6 17.♗e3 ♗d7 18.♗d3 ♗c6 19.♔e2 ♖g8 20.g5 ♘h5 21.♗xh7 ♖h8 22.♗d3 ♘f4+ 23.♗xf4 ♗xf4 24.h4 e5 25.♗f5 ♗b5+ 26.♔e1 ♗c6 27.♔e2 ♗b5+=*) 16.♗d3 ♗b7 17.♔e2 h5= Ivanisevic — S.Atalik, Valjevo 2007)

8...e5 (One needn't hurry with the break: *8...0-0 9.♗b2 ♕e7 10.♗e2 b6 11.0-0 ♗b7= N.Nguyen — So, Vietnam 2009*) 9.♗b2 e4 (*9...0-0=*) 10.♘d2 ♘f8 (*10...0-0∞*) 11.0-0-0 ♘e6 12.♗e2 0-0 13.g4∞ Ivanisevic — Morozevich, Neum 2008)

8.a4 (*8.♗xc4 b5 9.♗d3 c5 10.a4 b4 11.♘e4 ♗b7 12.♘xf6+ ♘xf6 13.dxc5 ♖c8=*)

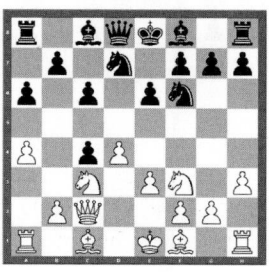

8...c5 9.♗xc4 ♕c7 (*9...b6 10.d5 exd5 11.♘xd5± Ivanisevic — Svetushkin, Subotica 2008; 9...cxd4 10.exd4 ♘b6 11.♗b3 ♗e7 12.0–0 0–0 13.♖d1 ♗d7 14.♘e5 ♖c8 15.♕d3 ♗c6 16.♗g5 ♘fd5 17.♗d2* Tkachiev — Bacrot, Porto Vecchio (match) 2008 *17... ♗g5!=*) 10.♕e2 ♗d6 11.0–0 0–0 12.dxc5

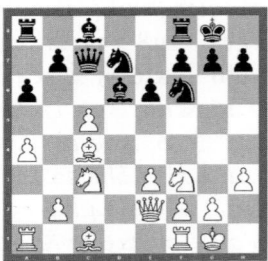

12...♗xc5!N (*12...♕xc5 13.b3 ♘e5 14.♗a3 ♕c7 15.♗xd6 ♕xd6 16.♖fd1 ♕c7 17.♘xe5 ♕xe5 18.♖d4 ♗d7 19.♖ad1 ♗c6 20.e4± Kir.Georgiev — Tkachiev, Crete 2007) 13.b3

(*13.e4 b6 (13...♘e5 14.♗f4±) 14.e5 ♘h5=*)

13...b6 14.♗b2 ♗b7=;

5.g3

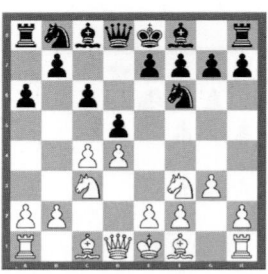

5...dxc4

a) 5...♗f5 6.♗g2 e6 7.0–0±;

b) White stands a little better after 5...b5 6.c5 g6 7.♗g2 ♗g7 8.0–0 0–0 9.♘e5 (Also sensible is 9.a3±, as prophylaxis against b5-b4.) 9...♗e6 10.h3 ♕c8 11.♔h2± Sakaev — Najer, Istanbul 2003;

6.♘e5 (6.♗g2 b5 7.♘e5 ♗b7 8.0–0 e6 — 3.♘c3 e6 4.♘f3 dxc4 5.g3 b5 6.♗g2 ♗b7 7.♘e5 a6 8.0–0 ♘f6; 6.a4 e6 — 4...a6 5.a4 e6 6.g3 dxc4) 6...b5 7.♗g2 ♗b7 8.0–0 e6 — 3.♘c3 e6 4.♘f3 dxc4 5.g3 b5 6.♗g2 ♗b7 7.♘e5 a6 8.0–0 ♘f6;

One cannot expect an advantage after making two moves with the same piece: 5.♘e5 e6 The simplest way to equalise.

(5...♘bd7 6.♗f4

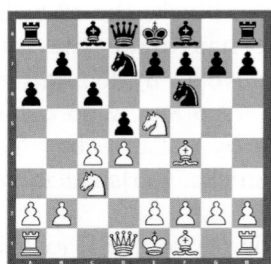

6...dxc4

a) 6...♕a5 7.e3 ♘xe5 8.♗xe5 ♘e4 9.♕a4 ♕b6 Gleizerov — Wirig, Biel 2011 10.♕c2±;

b) 6...e6 7.e3 ♘xe5 8.♗xe5 ♗e7 9.♗d3 0-0 10.0-0± Potkin — Le Quang Liem, Moscow 2008;

c) 6...♘h5!? 7.♗e3

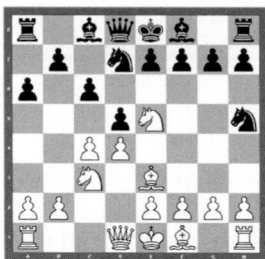

♘hf6! 8.g3 (8.♗g5 ♘xe5 9.dxe5 d4 10.exf6 exf6 11.♗d2 dxc3 12.♗xc3= Gleizerov — Mohannad, New Delhi 2009) 8...e6 9.♗h3 Otherwise the exchange on e5 followed by ♘f6-g4 is unpleasant. 9...♗e7 10.0-0 0-0 11.♕c2 ♘xe5 12.dxe5 ♘d7 13.f4 b5 14.cxd5 cxd5=;

7.♘xc4

(7.e3 ♘xe5 8.dxe5 ♕xd1+ 9.♖xd1 ♘d5 10.♗xc4 (A showy but dubious move is 10.♖xd5?! 10...cxd5 11.♘xd5 ♖a7 12.♘b6 ♗e6∓ — It's hard to keep the a7 rook trapped, Timofeev — Jakovenko, Moscow 2009) 10...♘xc3 11.bxc3 e6=)

7...b5

(7...♘d5 8.♗d2 e6 9.♖c1 (9.a4±) 9...b5 10.♘xd5 cxd5 11.♘a5 (11. ♗a5 ♕f6=) 11...♘b6 12.♘c6±)

8.♘e5 ♗b7 9.e3 e6

(9...♘xe5 10.♗xe5 (10.dxe5 ♕xd1+ 11.♖xd1 ♘d5=) 10...♘d7 (10... c5 11.dxc5 ♘d7 12.♗g3 ♘xc5 13.♕xd8+ ♖xd8 14.♘xb5! axb5 15.♗xb5+ ♘d7 16.0-0 e5 17.♖fd1± Gleizerov — Voinov, Saratov 2006) 11.♗g3 e6 (11...c5 12.dxc5 — 10...c5 11.dxc5 ♘d7 12.♗g3) 12.♗e2 c5 13.0-0 cxd4 14.♕xd4± Riazantsev — Bouchet, France 2007)

10.♕f3

(10.♗e2 c5 (10...♗e7 11.0-0 0-0 12.♗f3 ♘d5 13.♘xd5 cxd5 14.♘d3±) 11.♗f3 (11.0-0 ♘xe5 12.♗xe5 cxd4 13.exd4 ♗e7= Gleizerov — Panarin, Voronezh 2006) 11...♗xf3 12.♕xf3 cxd4 13.exd4 ♗b4 14.♗g5 (14.0-0 ♗xc3 15.bxc3 ♘d5= Babula — Keitlinghaus, Lazne Bohdanec 1996) 14...♗xc3+ 15.bxc3 ♕c8 16.♘xd7 ♘xd7 17.0-0 ♘b6= Riazantsev — Erenburg, Moscow 2005)

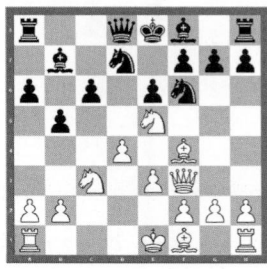

10...♖a7! This awkward looking move is the best means of playing c6-c5.

a) 10...♘xe5 11.♗xe5 ♘d7 12.♗f4±;

b) 10...♘d5 11.♘xd5 ♘xe5 12.♗xe5 ♕xd5 13.♕xd5 cxd5 14.♗d3±;

c) 10...♕b6 11.♘xd7 ♘xd7 12.♗d3 c5

(12...♘f6 13.0-0 (*13.♗e5 ♘d7 14.0-0 ♘xe5 15.dxe5 ♗e7=/∞* B.Savchenko — Deviatkin, Voronezh 2007) 13...c5 14.♘e4±)

13.♗e4 ♗xe4 14.♘xe4 ♖c8 15.0-0± Vitiugov — I.Popov, Krasnoyarsk 2007;

d) 10...♗b4 11.♗d3 ♕c8 12.0-0 c5 13.♘e4 c4 14.♘xd7 (*14.♗c2 Timoshenko — Kamsky, Romania 2011 14...♘xe5 15.♗xe5 ♘xe4 16.♗xe4 ♗xe4 17.♕xe4 0-0=*) 14...♕xd7 (*14...♘xd7 15.♗d6!+-*) 15.♘xf6+ gxf6 16.♗e4 ♗xe4 17.♕xe4±;

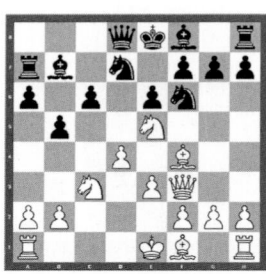

11.♗d3 (*11.♕h3 c5 12.dxc5 ♘xc5 13.♗e2 Gyimesi — Movsesian, Germany 2008 13...b4!±*) 11...c5 12.♕h3 Here exchanging in the centre looks the most reliable method for Black

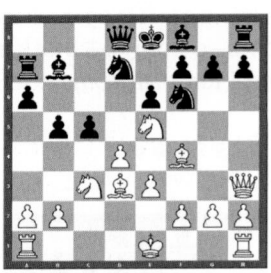

12...♘xe5

(Alternatively — 12...♗e7 13.0-0

(13.♖d1 cxd4 14.exd4 ♘b6 (*14...♘d5=*) 15.0-0 b4 16.♘e2 0-0∞ I.Sokolov — Movsesian, Sarajevo 2008)

13...g5!? — looks risky but interesting (*13...♘xe5 14.♗xe5 c4 15.♗c2 h6 16.f4!, with f4-f5 to follow. White has the initiative.*) 14.♗g3 h5 15.f3 h4 16.♖ad1±/∞))

13.♗xe5 ♘d7 14.♗g3 cxd4 15.exd4 g6!

(15...♘c5 16.♗e2 ♕xd4 (*16...b4 17.♘b5 axb5 18.dxc5±*) 17.♖d1 ♕b4 18.♗e5± — White's initiative is very strong.)

16.0-0 ♗e7!= — The game is nearly equal. (After *16...♗g7* a pawn sacrifice can be considered *17.♗d6!? ♗xd4 18.♕g3↑*))

6.g3

a) 6.cxd5 exd5 7.e4 ♗e6 8.exd5 ♘xd5 9.♗d3 ♘d7= I.Sokolov — Sasikiran, Croatia 2008;

b) 6.♗f4 dxc4 7.♘xc4 b5 8.♘e5 ♗b7 (*8...c5 9.dxc5 ♕xd1+ 10.♖xd1 ♗xc5* Papin — Volkov, Moscow 2010 *11.g4! ♗b7 12.♖g1±* — White stands somewhat better.) 9.e3 c5 (*9...♘bd7 — 5... ♘bd7 6.♗f4 dxc4 7.♘xc4 b5 8.♘e5 ♗b7 9.e3 e6*) 10.dxc5 ♕xd1+ 11.♖xd1 ♗xc5=;

6...♘bd7 7.♗g2

(7.♘xd7 ♗xd7 8.♕d3

(8.c5 b6 9.b4 (*9.cxb6 ♕xb6 10.♗g2 c5 11.dxc5 ♗xc5 12.0-0 0-0 13.♘a4 ♗xa4 14.♕xa4 ♖fc8∓* E.Vladimirov — Safin, Sangli 2000) 9...bxc5 (*9...e5 10.dxe5 ♘g4 11.e4∞*) 10.bxc5 e5 11.e3 ♗e7=)

8...dxc4 (8...c5 9.♗g2 dxc4 10.♕xc4 b5 11.♕d3 ♖c8 — 8...dxc4 9.♕xc4 b5 10.♕d3 c5 11.♗g2 ♖c8)

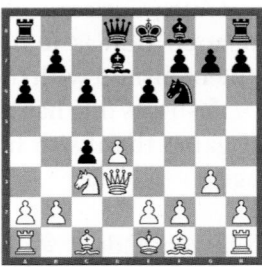

9.♕xc4 b5 10.♕d3 c5 11.♗g2 ♖c8 12.dxc5 ♗xc5 13.♗e3 ♗xe3 14.♕xe3 ♗c6= Riazantsev — Rogozenko, Drezden 2007)

7...♘xe5 8.dxe5 ♘d7 9.cxd5 exd5 (*9... cxd5 10.e4 d4 11.♕xd4 ♗c5 12.♕d1 ♘xe5 13.♕xd8+ ♔xd8 14.f4 ♘c6 15.e5±* Yevseev — Matlakov, Peterhof 2008) 10.e4

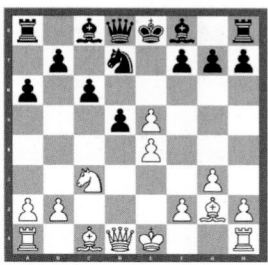

10...d4! 11.♕xd4 ♗c5 12.♕d3 ♘xe5 13.♕xd8+ ♔xd8 14.f4 ♘d3+ 15.♔e2 ♘xc1+ 16.♖axc1 ♗a7!= — Leaving the square e7 for the king, and if White plays e4-e5, Black can undermine the white centre with f7-f6, Harika — Stefanova, Ohrid 2009 (*16...♗g4+ 17.♗f3 ♗xf3+ 18.♔xf3 ♔e7 19.e5±* Riazantsev — Dunis, Bastia 2005)

5...e6

5...♗f5 6.♕b3 ♖a7 7.a5! (*7.g3±*) 7... e6 8.♕b6 ♕xb6 9.axb6 ♖a8 10.c5± — The threat of moving the white knight from f3 to a5 is very strong, Gelfand — Morozevich, Astana 2001; 5...g6 6.♗f4 (*6.e3 ♗g7 7.♗e2 0-0 8.0-0 a5 9.♕b3 e6 10.♗d2 ♘a6 11.♖fd1±* — White has some advantage but Black's position is very solid, Melkumyan — Thorfinnsson, Aix les Bains 2011) 6...♗g7 7.e3 0-0 8.♕b3 (*8.a5 c5 9.dxc5 ♘e4∞*) 8...♕a5 9.♕a3± — White is ready to increase his space advantage with b2-b4.

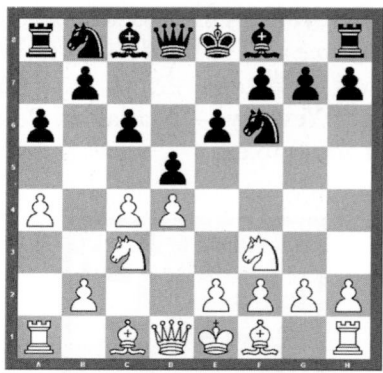

6.♗g5

6.a5 c5 7.cxd5 ♘xd5 8.♘e5 ♘c6 9.♘xc6 bxc6= Azmaiparashvili — Epishin, Burgas 1994;

After 6.e3 the following is good 6...c5 — in some cases a2-a4 might turn out to be even harmful. (Not so convincing is 6...♘bd7 7.♗d3 ♗d6 8.0-0 0-0 — The inclusion of a7-a6 and a2-a4 can be to the advantage of either side. White has weak black squares, Black has no possibility of a capture on c4 followed by b7-b5.) 7.♗d3 ♘c6 8.0-0 ♗e7

a) 8...cxd4 9.exd4 ♘b4 10.c5 (*10.b3±*) 10...b6 11.cxb6 ♕xb6 12.♗f4 ♘xd3 13.♕xd3± — White has prospects of play on the black squares, and it's hard for Black to solve the problem of the c8 bishop, Shmelev — Erenburg, Berkeley 2011;

b) 8...dxc4 is possible 9.♗xc4 ♗e7, leads to a variation of the Queen's Gambit Accepted favourable to Black, where the white knight has moved to c3 early. 10.♕e2 0-0

11.♖d1 ♕c7= Euler — Grischuk, Mainz (rapid) 2007;

9.cxd5 exd5 10.dxc5

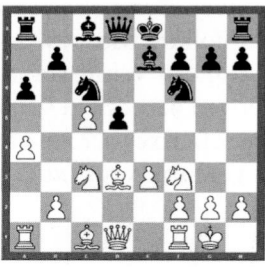

10...0-0! (*10...♗xc5 11.e4±*) 11.b3 (*11.e4 d4=*) 11...♗xc5 12.♘e2 ♗g4 13.♗b2 ♕e7 14.♖c1 ♗xf3 (*14...♗d6 15.♘g3 ♘e4 16.♗e2 ♖fd8 17.♘d4±* Kramnik — Movsesian, Moscow (blitz) 2010) 15.gxf3 ♗a3= — The remaining white bishop is not too strong. Black is doing fine.;

6.♗f4 yields nothing. In reply it's best to immediately attack the centre 6...c5

a) 6...a5 is passive 7.e3 ♘a6 8.♗e2 ♗e7 9.0-0 ♘b4 Carlsen — Kamsky, Moscow 2008 Best is 10.h3±, providing the f4 bishop with a defence against ♘f6-h5. White has the more pleasant game thanks to his space advantage.;

b) 6...dxc4 7.e3 ♘d5 8.♗xc4 ♘xf4 9.exf4 ♗e7 10.0-0 ♘d7 11.a5± Carlsen — Movsesian, Moscow (blitz) 2008;

c) A good option is 6...♗b4 7.e3 c5

(7...♕a5 8.♖c1 c5 9.dxc5 (*9.♗e2±*)
9...♘bd7

(*9...♘e4 10.cxd5 (10.♗d3 ♘xc3*
11.bxc3 ♗xc3+ 12.♔e2 dxc4
13.♗xc4± Maslak — Potkin,
Novokuznetsk 2008) 10...♘xc3
11.bxc3 ♗xc3+ 12.♔e2 exd5
13.♕xd5 ♗e6 14.♕d3 ♗f6 15.♘d4
♗xd4 16.♕xd4 0-0 17.f3 ♘c6
18.♕c3 ♕xa4 19.♔f2±)

10.♗e2 ♗xc3+ 11.♖xc3 ♘e4
12.♕d4 0-0 13.♗d6 ♘xc3 14.bxc3
♖e8 15.cxd5 exd5 16.0-0±/↑)

8.♗d3 cxd4 9.exd4 dxc4 10.♗xc4
♘d5 11.♗d2 ♘c6 12.0-0 0-0=
Kramnik — Gashimov, Nice (rapid) 2010;

d) 6...♗e7 7.e3 ♘h5 8.♗d3

(8.♗e5 ♘d7 9.♗d3 (*9.h3 ♘xe5*
10.dxe5 g6 11.♗e2 0-0 12.0-0 f6=)
9...0-0 10.0-0 ♘xe5 11.♘xe5
♘f6=)

8...♘xf4 9.exf4 a5 10.0-0 ♘a6
11.♖c1 ♘b4 12.b3 0-0 13.♗b1 ♗f6
14.♖e1 b6= Nakamura — Carlsen,
Wijk aan Zee 2012;

7.e3 ♘c6 8.♗e2 dxc4 9.♗xc4 cxd4
10.exd4 ♗e7 11.0-0 0-0= A typical
isolated queen's pawn position has
arisen with a formation favourable
for Black, Carlsen — Movsesian,
Kallithea 2008;

6.g3

6...dxc4

a) 6...♗b4 7.♗g2 ♘bd7 8.0-0 0-0

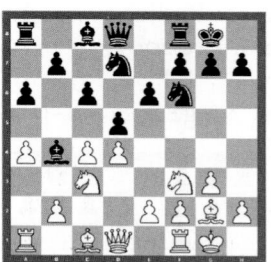

9.♕c2

a1) 9.♕b3 a5 10.♗f4 b6 11.cxd5
exd5!= (*11...cxd5 12.♘b5± Fridman*
— Kindermann, Germany 2009) ;

a2) 9.♗f4!? dxc4 (*9...b6 10.♘e5*
♗b7 11.♕b3± I.Sokolov — Lender-
man, Reykjavik 2010) 10.♕c2 ♘d5
(*10...c5 11.♘a2± Ivanchuk — Shi-*
rov, Tilburg 1993) 11.♗d2 a5 12.e4
♘5b6∞/=;

a3) 9.♘d2 ♖e8 (*9...a5 10.e4 dxe4*
11.♘dxe4 ♘xe4 12.♘xe4 e5 13.d5
cxd5 14.♕xd5± Ruck — Burmakin,
Bad Woerishofen 2004) 10.♕c2 (*10.*
e4 e5 11.dxe5 d4∞) 10...a5 11.♖d1
♕e7=;

9...a5 10.♗f4

(10.♖d1 b6!=(10...dxc4 11.♘a2±; 10...♖e8 11.♗f4±; 10...♕e7 11.e4 dxc4 12.e5 ♘d5 13.♗g5 f6 14.exf6 gxf6 15.♗h6↑ Yevseev — Ponomarev, Voronezh 2010))

10...b6 11.cxd5 cxd5 (11...♘xd5 12.♗d2±) 12.♘b5 ♗a6 13.♖fc1 ♕e7 14.♕d1 ♖ac8 15.♘a7 ♖xc1 16.♖xc1 ♖a8 17.♘c6 ♕f8 18.♗f1 ♗d6 19.♘fe5 ♗xe5 20.♘xe5 ♘xe5 21.♗xe5± Radjabov — Karjakin, Wijk aan Zee 2009;

b) 6...a5 7.♗g2 ♗e7 8.0–0 0–0

9.♗f4! This developing move strengthens White's position in the centre most effectively.

b1) 9.♘e5 The knight can exchanged off: 9...♘fd7! 10.♘xd7 (10.f4 ♘xe5 11.fxe5 dxc4 12.♘e4∞) 10...♘xd7 11.b3 f5!= — The Whi te queenside is compromised, therefore Black gains a smooth game after placing the knight on f6 and moving the bishop to b7 or a6 after b7-b6.;

b2) 9.♘d2 ♘a6 10.e4 ♘b4 11.e5 ♘d7 12.cxd5

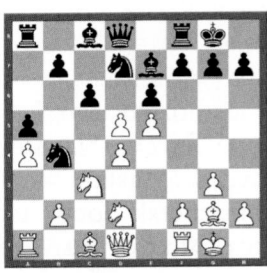

12...exd5!N (12...cxd5 13.♘db1 ♘b8 14.♘a3 ♘8c6 15.♘ab5± Ruck — Morozevich, Mainz 2006) 13.f4 c5∞;

b3) 9.b3 This helps to retain a small advantage but is still not energetic enough 9...♘a6 10.♗f4 ♘b4 11.♘e5±;

9...♘a6 (After 9...dxc4 follows 10.e4, and Black cannot save the c4 pawn, since if 10...b6 11.♘e5 ♗a6 strong is 12.d5!±/↑) 10.♘e5 ♘b4 11.e4 ♘xe4 12.♘xe4 dxe4 13.♗xe4 f6 14.♘g6!± Cheparinov — Malakhov, Villafranca de los Barros 2010;

c) The following has become fashion 6...c5 7.cxd5 cxd4 8.♘xd4 (8.♕xd4 ♘xd5 9.♘xd5 ♘c6= Nester — Karalkin, Russia 2006) 8...♘xd5, and here White can only pose some problems for Black with the retreat

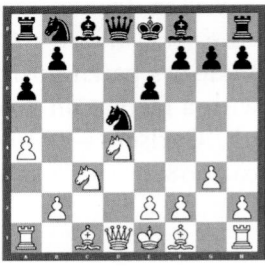

9.♘c2!

c1) 9.♘b3 ♗b4 10.♕c2

(10.♗d2 ♘xc3 11.bxc3 ♕d5! (11...
♗e7 12.♗g2 ♕c7 13.0-0 ♗d7
14.♕c2 0-0 15.c4 ♗c6 16.e4=
Cheparinov — Shimanov, Plovdiv 2012) 12.♖g1 (12.f3 ♗e7 13.e4
♕c6∓) 12...♗e7∓ White hasn't
castled and can therefore forget
about an advantage.)

10...0-0 11.♗g2 ♘xc3 12.bxc3 ♕c7!
13.♗d2 ♗e7 14.0-0 ♗d7=, followed
by ♗d7-c6;

c2) 9.♗g2 ♘xc3 10.bxc3 e5 11.♘b3
♕xd1+ 12.♔xd1 ♘c6 13.♗e3 (13.
♗a3 ♗e6 14.♘c5 0-0-0+ 15.♔c2
♗d5∓ Miton — Wirig, France 2011)
13...♗f5!N

(13...♗e6 14.♔c2 0-0-0 (14...♖c8
15.♖hd1±) 15.♗b6

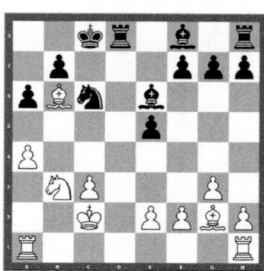

15...♖d6!?N (15...♖d7 16.♖hd1±
Grischuk — Movsesian, Ningbo
2011) 16.♘c5 ♘b4+ 17.cxb4 ♖xb6
18.♘xe6 fxe6 19.b5 axb5 20.♖hb1
b4 21.♔b3 ♗e7±/= — Black can
obtain a draw without problems.)

14.♗b6 ♗e7 15.♔c1 h5 (15...♖c8
16.♔b2 ♗d8 17.a5 h5=) 16.h4 Otherwise Black gains an opportunity to
play h5-h4, and the pressure on the
h-file becomes unpleasant. 16...♖c8
17.♔b2 ♗d8= — The cramping bishop is ejected from b6 and Black has
no more problems. Sometimes the
rook can to enter the game via h6.;

9...♘c6 (9...♘xc3 10.♕xd8+ ♔xd8
11.bxc3 ♗d7 12.♗g2 ♗c6 13.0-0±)
10.♘xd5 (10.♗g2 ♘xc3 11.♕xd8+
♘xd8 12.bxc3 ♗d7 13.0-0 ♖c8
14.♗d2 ♗e7= Ftacnik — Kindermann, Austria 2006) 10...exd5
11.♗g2 ♗e6 12.0-0 ♗e7

(12...♗c5 is vulnerable to 13.b4!
♘xb4 14.♘xb4 ♗xb4 15.♖b1 (15.
♗b2 f6 16.♕b3±) 15...a5 16.♗d2
♗xd2 17.♕xd2 ♕d7 18.♖b5 0-0
19.♖d1± — Black's defence is unpleasant.)

13.b4 (13.♗e3 0-0 14.♘d4±/= —
e has a minimal advantage but
Black should equalise thanks to the
weakeness caused by a2-a4.) 13...0-
0!N

(13...♗f6 14.♖b1 0-0 15.b5 axb5
16.axb5 ♘a5 17.♘d4 ♕d7 N The
most natural option

(17...♗g4 has also been played
18.h3 ♗d7 19.g4 (19.♕d3 ♖e8
20.♖d1±) 19...♕b6 20.♗e3 ♘c4,
and now strong is

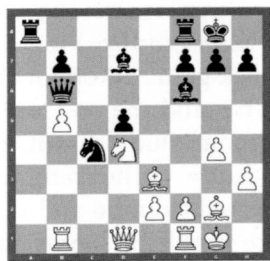

21.♘c2!N (21.♘f5 ♕a5 22.♕xd5 ♗xf5 23.♕xf5 ♘xe3 24.fxe3 Wirig — A.Ramirez, Cappelle la Grande 2012 24...♖ae8!=) 21... ♘xe3 22.♘xe3 d4 23.♘d5 ♕d6 24.♕d3!± — White intends to increase pressure on d4 with ♖fd1 and ♖b4, after which the capture on f6 will be threatened.)

18.♘xe6 fxe6 19.e4 d4 20.e5 ♗xe5 21.♖e1 ♗f6 22. ♗h3 ♖fe8 (22...♖ae8 23.♕a4 b6 24.♕a2!+-) 23.♕e2 ♔h8 24.♗d2 d3 25.♕e4 ♕d4 26.♕xd4 ♗xd4 27.♗xe6 ♖f8 28.♗e3± The knight on a5 is out of play and the d-pawn is in danger. The endgame is worse for Black)

14.♗b2 ♖c8 15.♕d2± The advanced queenside pawns are a nuisance. Therefore White has a slightly better position regardless of the isolated pawn on d5.;

d) 6...b6 7.♗g2 ♗b7 8.0-0 ♗e7 9.a5! (9.♘e5 ♘bd7 10.♘xd7 ♘xd7 11.e4 dxc4 12.♕g4∞ Kramnik — Bareev, Belgrade 1993) 9...b5 10.c5± — Later White will play e2-e4, and the b7 bishop will still be bad.;

7.♗g2

a) The simplest way to give Black an excellent game is to play 7.e4 After g2-g3 has been played this move is not in the spirit of the position. 7... b5!± — It's hard for White to prove that his compensation is sufficient;

b) 7.♘e5 c5 8.dxc5 (8.♗e3 cxd4 9.♕xd4 ♕xd4 10.♗xd4 ♘c6 11.♘xc6 bxc6= Pe.Nielsen — Johannessen, Copenhagen 2003) 8... ♕xd1+ 9.♘xd1 ♗d7! (9...♗xc5 10.♗g2 — 7.♗g2 c5 8.dxc5 ♕xd1 9.♘xd1 ♗xc5 10.♘e5) 10.♗g2 — 7.♗g2 c5 8.dxc5 ♕xd1 9.♘xd1 ♗d7 10.♘e5(10.♗e3 ♘c6 11.♘xc4 ♘b4 12.♖c1 ♘fd5=) ;

7...c5 8.dxc5

(8.0-0

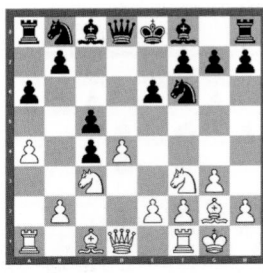

8...♘c6! Development is a priority.

(8...cxd4 9.♘xd4 ♕c7 10.♘c2 (10. a5∞) 10...♘bd7 11.♕d4 (11.♘a3∞; 11.♗f4 e5 12.♗g5 h6 13.♗xf6 ♘xf6 14.♘e3 ♗c5 15.♘ed5 ♘xd5 16.♘xd5 ♕d6=) 11... ♗c5 12.♕h4

♗e7 13.♘a3 ♘e5 Kramnik — Gelfand, Linares 1997 14.♕d4∞)

9.♘e5 ♘a5 The most reliable way to equalise. (The game is more complicated after 9...♗d7∞) 10.dxc5 (*10.d5 ♗d6∓*) 10...♕xd1 11.♖xd1 ♗xc5

(11...♘d7 12.♘xd7! (*12.♗f4 Joba-va — Svetushkin, Istanbul 2004 12...♘xc5∓*) 12...♗xd7 13.♗e3 ♖c8 14.♖d2 ♘b3 15.♖xd7 ♘xa1 16.♖xb7 ♘c2 17.♗f4 ♗xc5 18.♘e4 0-0 19.♘xc5 ♖xc5 20.♗d6±)

12.♗f4 0-0 13.♖ac1 (*13.♘e4 ♘xe4 14.♗xe4 Del Rio Ange-lis — Espinosa, Las Palmas 2012 14...f6! 15.♘d7 ♗xd7 16.♖xd7 ♖ad8 17.♖xd8 ♖xd8 18.♗c7 ♖d4 19.♗xh7+ ♔xh7 20.♗xa5 ♖d5∓*) 13...♖a7 14.♘e4 ♘xe4 15.♗xe4 b5 16.♘c6 16...♘b3 17.♘xa7 ♘xc1 18.♖xc1 ♗xa7 19.axb5 axb5 20.♗c6 ♗d4 21.♗xb5 ♗xb2 22.♖xc4 ♗b7=)

8...♕xd1+

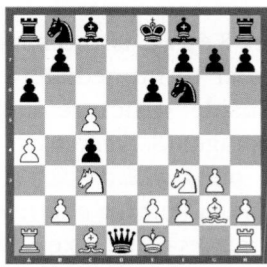

9.♘xd1 ♗d7!

a) The least successful way of neutralising the Catalan-style pressure of White is 9...♘c6 10.♘e3 ♗xc5 (*10...♘a5 11.♘d2±*) 11.♘xc4 ♔e7 12.0-0± Aronian — Movsesian, Wijk aan Zee 2009;

b) 9...♗xc5 is quite reliable even though it doesn't have a very good reputation,

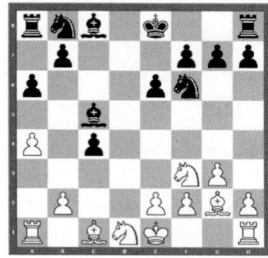

10.♘e5 ♘d5 11.♘e3

b1) 11.0-0 ♘c6=;

b2) 11.♘xc4 ♘c6 12.0-0 ♘d4=;

b3) 11.♗d2 0-0! (*11...♔e7 12.♘xc4 ♘c6 13.♘c3±* Pelletier — Aronian, Novi Sad 2009) 12.♘xc4 ♘c6 13.♘c3 ♖d8 14.0-0 ♘b6 15.♘xb6 ♗xb6=;

11...♘xe3 12.♗xe3 ♗xe3 13.fxe3 c3 (*13...♘d7 14.♘xc4 ♔e7 15.0-0 ♖b8 16.♖ac1 ♖d8* Zhou Jinchao — Malakhov, Ningbo 2011 If *17.b4* or *17.a5* had been played here White would have maintained unpleasant pressure.) 14.b4 (The following deserves attention although it's not very dangerous: *14.b3!?*, to keep the queenside pawns protected. Then possible is *14...f6 15.♘d3 ♗d7* Now if White aspires to something, he must capture the pawn *16.♗xb7,* but after *16...♖a7 17.♗f3 ♔e7 18.♔d1 a5 19.♔c2 ♖c8=* Black has sufficient counter play.) *14...♘d7 15.♘d3*

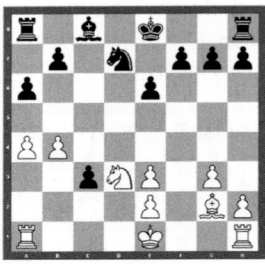

15...♘f6!N (15...♖b8 16.0–0± Anand — Wang Yue, Linares 2009) 16.♖c1 ♗d7 17.♖xc3 ♘d5 18.♗xd5 exd5 19.a5 ♗c6= — Black has a bad bishop but White has doubled pawns. The game should end in a draw.;

10.♘e5

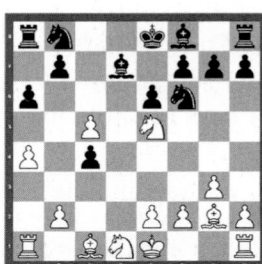

10...♘c6 (10...♗c6 11.♘xc6 ♘xc6 12.♗d2 ♘d5 13.♖c1 ♗xc5 14.♖xc4± Sasakiran — Aronian, Bursa 2010) 11.♘xc4 (11.♘xc6 ♗xc6 12.♗xc6+ bxc6 13.a5 ♗xc5 14.♖a4 ♗e7 15.♖xc4 c5= D.Rombaldoni — D'Amore,

Arvier 2012) *11...♗xc5 12.♗e3 (12.0–0 ♔e7 13.♗e3 ♗xe3 14.♘dxe3 ♖hd8=* Tregubov — Movsesian, Odessa (rapid) 2009) *12...♗xe3 13.♘dxe3 ♔e7 14.f4 ♖hd8 (14...♖ab8* looks about equal *15.♔f2 ♘b4 16.♘e5 ♖hc8±/=* Moiseenko — Postny, France 2011) *15.♔f2 ♖ab8 (15...♗e8±/=* Maletin — Malakhov, Olginka 2011) *16.♖hd1 (16.♖hc1 ♘d4=* Ernst — Movsesian, Plovdiv 2012) *16...♗e8±/=* — White's advantage is minute so Black should obtain a draw.

6...♘bd7
6...h6

7.♗h4

(7.♗xf6 gives little 7...♕xf6 8.a5

(After 8.e3 a5! is the most exact in order to immediately fix the queenside structure to Black's advantage. *(8...♘d7 9.a5! —* *8.a5 ♘d7 9.e3)* *9.♗d3 ♗b4 10.0–0 ♘d7 11.e4 (11.♕e2 0–0 12.e4 dxc4 13.♗xc4 e5∓)* *11...dxe4 12.♘xe4 ♕f4 13.c5 (13.♗c2 0–0 14.♕d3 ♖d8=)* *13...0–0 14.♖c1 ♖b8=* Huzman — Karjakin, Kallithea 2008)

8...dxc4!

(8...♘d7 9.e3 (9.g3 dxc4=) 9...g5
10.♗d3 ♗g7 11.0–0 0–0 12.cxd5
exd5 13.h3± Gagunashvili — Kobalia, Rijeka 2010)

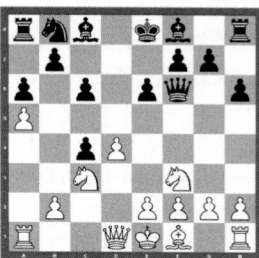

9.e3 (9.e4 ♗b4 10.e5 ♕e7 11.♗xc4
c5= — The a5 pawn can soon be attacked.; 9.♕a4 ♘d7 10.e3 e5=) 9...
♗b4 10.♗xc4 c5 11.0–0 0–0 12.♘e4
♕e7 13.♘xc5 ♗xc5 14.dxc5 ♕xc5
15.♕d4 ♕xd4 16.♘xd4 ♗d7±/=
— White stands better but Black
should obtain a draw.)

7...dxc4 8.e4! Other continuations
do not give an advantage.

a) 8.a5

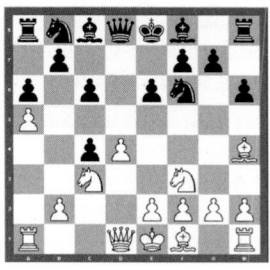

8...b5!N

a1) 8...c5 9.♗xf6 ♕xf6 10.d5± Shulman — Shabalov, Chicago 2006;

a2) 8...♗b4 9.e3!? (9.♕a4 ♕e7 10.e3
♗d7= — Black will play c6-c5 and
solve all problems, Shulman —
Yermolinsky, Chicago 2008) 9...
♗xa5 10.♗xc4⩲⩱ — The a5 bishop
is cut off from the black squares,
whose weakness can soon be exploited by White with e3-e4-e5.;

9.axb6 ♕xb6 10.♖a2 ♘bd7 11.e3 c5
12.♗xc4 cxd4 13.♘xd4 ♗d6 14.0–0
0–0= — The game is equal.;

b) 8.e3 b5 9.axb5 cxb5 10.♗xf6 gxf6
11.♘xb5 axb5 12.♖xa8 ♗b4+ 13.♔e2
(13.♘d2 ♗b7 14.♖a1∞) 13...♗b7
14.♖a1 f5↑ Van Wely — Topalov,
Wijk aan Zee 2006;

8...g5

9.♗g3 b5 10.axb5 cxb5 11.♘xb5 axb5
12.♖xa8 ♗b4+ 13.♔e2 ♘c6 14.♘e5
♘a5 15.♖b8

a) 15.f3!?N

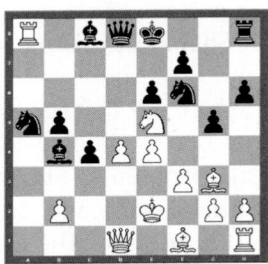

15...0–0 16.h4

a1) 16.♗f2 ♘d7 17.♘xd7 (*17.h4 ♘xe5 18.dxe5 ♕c7 19.♗e1 ♖d8 20.♗xb4 ♖xd1 21.♔xd1 ♘c6∓* — The black king is better protected than his counterpart therefore his chances are preferable.; *17.♖xa5 ♕xa5 18.♘c6 ♕a2 19.♘xb4 ♕xb2+ 20.♘c2 b4∓)* 17...♕xd7 18.h4 g4 19.♗e3 ♘b3 20.♔f2 ♕c6 21.♖a2 ♖d8 — The capture on d4 cannot be prevented.;

a2) 16.♖xa5 ♕xa5 17.♘c6 ♕a2 18.♘xb4 ♕xb2+ 19.♘c2 ♗b7;

a3) 16.♔f2 ♕b6 (*16...♗c5? 17.♖xa5+-*) 17.h4 ♘b3 18.♔g1 g4 19.♘xg4 ♘xg4 20.fxg4 ♘d2!

a31) 20...♕c6 21.♖b8 ♘xd4 22.g5 (*22.♖h3∞*) 22...♕xe4 23.gxh6 e5 24.♕h5 f6 25.♗f2 ♔h7 26.♖xc8 ♖xc8 27.♕f7+ ♔xh6 28.♖h3 ♖f8 29.♕d7 ♕f5 30.♕b7 ♘e6 31.♕xb5± Winning a pawn and retaining the initiative.;

a32) 20...♘xd4 21.♔h2±;

21.g5 (*21.♗f2 ♘xe4 22.♗e3 e5 23.♖h3 ♗d2 24.♗e2 ♗xe3+ 25.♖xe3 ♗b7 26.♖xf8+ ♔xf8 27.♗f3 exd4 28.♖xe4 ♗xe4 29.♗xe4 d3+ 30.♔f1 ♕d4 31.♗f3 ♕xb2 32.♗d5 ♕a1+ 33.♔f2 ♕d4+ 34.♔f1 f6 35.♕f5=*) 21...♕xd4+ 22.♗f2 ♕xe4 (*22...♗xb2 23.gxh6∞*) 23.gxh6 ♘xf1 24.♔xf1 ♗b7 25.h7+ ♔xh7 26.♕h5+ ♔g7 27.♕g5+ ♔h7 28.♕h5+=;

16...g4! — 15.h4 g4 16.f3 0–0

a1) 16...♕b6 17.hxg5 ♘b3 18.♗f2 hxg5 19.♗e3+-;

a2) 16...♘h5 17.♗e1 ♗xe1 18.♔xe1 ♘b3 19.hxg5 ♕xg5 20.♔f2 ♘g3 (*20...♕g3+ 21.♔g1 ♕g5 22.♕e1 ♘xd4 23.♖xh5 ♕xh5 24.f4+-*) 21.♖h3 ♘xf1 22.♔xf1 ♕e3 23.♕e2 ♕xd4 24.♘c6 ♕c5 25.♕f2+-; ;

b) 15.h4!?N

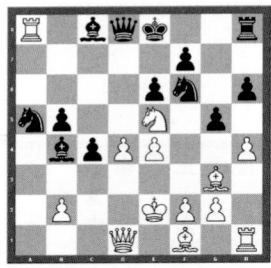

15...♘xe4!

(15...g4 16.♗f4!

(16.f3 0–0 17.♗f2 (*17.♖xa5 ♕xa5 18.♘c6 ♕a2 19.♘xb4 ♕xb2+*

20.♘c2 ♗b7 21.♔f2 ♖a8; 17.♖b8
♗d6 18.♖xc8 ♕xc8 19.♘xg4
♘xg4 20.♗xd6 ♖d8=; 17.♔f2
♗c5 18.♖xa5?! 18...♗xd4+
19.♔e2 ♘h5 20.♗h2 g3 21.♘c6
♘f4+ 22.♔d2 ♗c3+ 23.♔c2
♕xd1+ 24.♔xd1 ♗xa5 25.♘xa5
gxh2 26.♖xh2 f5∓) 17...♕c7!
(17...♘h5 18.g3±) 18.h5 (18.♗e3
♘b3 19.♔f2 ♖d8; 18.♕c1 ♔h7∞
19.♕f4? 19...♘h5 20.♕xg4 c3-+)
18...♘b3 19.♖h4 ♔h7 20.♕b1 g3

(20...gxf3+ 21.♘xf3 (21.gxf3 ♖d8)
21...e5 22.♘xe5∞)

21.♗e3 ♖d8 22.♘xf7 ♘xd4+
23.♗xd4 ♖xd4 24.e5+ ♖d3
25.exf6 ♕c5 26.♕xd3+ cxd3+
27.♔xd3 ♕c1 28.♖xc8 ♕d2+
29.♔e4 ♕d5+ 30.♔e3 ♕d2+=)

16...0-0 (16...♘xe4 17.g3 0-0
18.♗g2 — 16...0-0 17.g3 ♘xe4
18.♗g2) 17.g3! ♘xe4 (17...♘b3
18.♗g2 ♕xd4 19.♕xd4 ♘xd4+
20.♔f1 h5 21.♘xc4 bxc4 22.♗e5+-
; 17...♕b6 18.♗g2 ♕b7 19.♖xa5
♗xa5 20.♗xh6+-) 18.♗g2 ♕d5
19.♔f1 f5 20.♖xc8 ♖xc8 21.♘xg4
♖f8 22.♘e3 ♕b7 23.d5 exd5
24.♘xf5+-)

16.hxg5 0-0 17.gxh6 ♔h7! The position is exceptionally rich in possibilities and chances are nearly
equal. From a practical standpoint
though, I think White's play is
a little easier. The following looks
the mostattractive

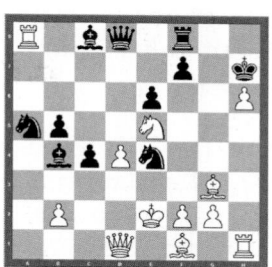

18.♖h4 but from here the game is
eventually drawn:

b1) 18.♗h4 ♕d5 19.♖xa5 ♗xa5
20.f3 f6 21.♘g4∞;

b2) 18.♖xc8 ♕xc8 (18...♘xg3+
19.fxg3 ♕xc8 20.♔f2±/∞) 19.♗f4
♕b7 (19...♕a8 20.g4 f6 21.♘f3 ♖g8
22.♗h3±/∞) 20.g4 f6 21.♘f3 ♖g8
22.♗h3∞;

18...♕d5 19.♖a7 ♘b3 20.♘f3 e5
21.♗xe5 ♗f5 22.♖f4 ♗g6!

(The alternative looks more risky
but leads to the same result: 22...
♖e8 23.g4 ♗d2 24.♕xd2 ♘exd2
25.♖xf7+ ♕xf7 26.♘g5+ ♔g8
27.♘xf7 ♗d3+ 28.♔e1 ♘xf1
29.g5 (29.♘d6 ♖e7 30.♘e4 ♗xe4
31.♖xe4 ♘fd2 32.♖e3 ♔h7 33.♔e2
c3 34.bxc3 ♘c4 35.♗f6 ♘c1+
36.♔f3 ♘d2+ 37.♔f4 ♘e2+ 38.♔f5
♖xe3 39.fxe3 ♘xc3=; 29.♘g5
♘xd4 30.h7+ ♗xh7 31.♘xh7
♖xe5+ 32.♔xf1 ♘e6 33.♖e4 ♖xe4
34.♘f6+ ♔g7 35.♘xe4 b4±/= —
Black should achieve a draw with
accurate play.) 29...♘fd2

(29...♖a8 30.f3 ♘e3 (*30...♖a1+*
31.♔f2 c3 32.h7+ ♔xh7 33.♘d6+-)
31.♖f6→)

30.♖f6 (*30.♘d6 ♘f3+ 31.♖xf3*
♘xd4 32.♖e3 ♖xe5 33.♖xe5 ♘f3+
34.♔d1 ♘xe5=) 30...♖a8 31.f3 (*31.*
h7+ ♔xh7 32.♖h6+ ♔g8 33.♖h8+
♔xf7 34.♖xa8 b4=) 31...c3
32.bxc3 ♖a2 33.h7+ ♔xh7 34.g6+
♔xg6 35.♘g5+ ♔h6 36.♘e6 ♖c2
37.d5 ♘c4 38.♗f4+ ♔h7 39.d6
♘b6 40.♘f8+ ♔g7 41.d7 ♘xd7
42.♘xd7 ♘c5=)

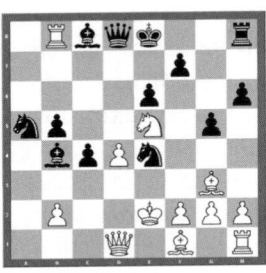

16.♖xb5! (*16.f3 ♘d6!*± Ivanchuk —
Topalov, Monaco (2006)) 16...♗d2
17.♕c2 ♘xg3+

(*17...f5N*

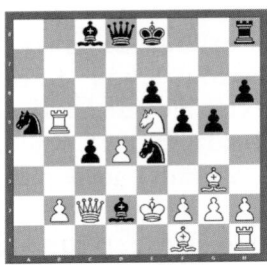

18.♘f3! Only this immediate
knight move gives White an advantage.

a) 18.♘xc4 ♗a6 19.♕a4 ♕d7
20.♘a3 ♕c6 21.f3 0–0 22.fxe4
♕c1 23.♕d1 ♕xb2 24.♕xd2 ♕xa3
25.♔e1 ♕a1+ 26.♕d1 ♕c3+ 27.♕d2
♕a1+=;

23.♘h4 (*23.g4 c3 24.♔e3 cxb2*
25.♗d3 ♘bd2 26.♖xe4 ♘xe4
27.♕c2 ♗c3∞ — The position unclear but White takes the greater
risk.) 23...♖e8 24.♘xg6 ♔xg6
25.♖g4+ (*25.h7 ♖xe5 26.dxe5*
♘d4+ 27.♔e3 ♗d2+ 28.♕xd2
♘xd2 29.♔xd2 ♘b3+ 30.♔e3
♕xe5+ 31.♖e4 ♕c5+ 32.♔e2 ♕d5∓;
25.♖axf7 ♖xe5 26.dxe5 ♗d2 27.♕b1
♘d4+ 28.♔d1 ♗xf4 29.♖d7 ♕xd7
30.♕xe4+ ♘f5+ 31.♔e2 ♔g5 32.g3
♗xg3 33.♔e1 ♗f4 34.♕g2+ ♔xh6
35.♕h3+ ♔g5 36.♕g2+ ♘g3 37.fxg3
♗xe5 38.♕d2+ ♕xd2+ 39.♔xd2
♗xb2 40.♗g2 ♗e5 41.♗c6 b4
42.♗d5 c3+ 43.♔c2=) 25...♔xh6
26.♖a6+ f6 27.f3 ♘d6 28.♔f2 ♖xe5
29.♗d3 ♖e1 30.♖g6+ ♔h7 31.♖a7+
♘f7 32.♗e4 ♕xe4 33.fxe4 ♖xd1
34.♖xf6=;

15...♘xe4

b) 18.f3 ♗a6 19.fxe4 ♗xb5 20.♔xd2
♕xd4+ 21.♔e1 f4 22.♘xc4
♘xc4 (*22...fxg3 23.♘d6+ ♕xd6*
24.♗xb5+±) 23.♗f2 ♕d6 24.♕c3
0–0 25.♗xc4 ♖c8= — White has
lost the right to castle therefore
Black maintains the balance.;

18...0–0 19.♘xd2 ♘c6 20.♗e5 ♘xd2 21.♔xd2 ♘xe5 22.♔c1 ♘d3+ 23.♗xd3 cxd3 24.♕c3 ♗d7 25.♖a5± — The position is still sharp but White has an obvious advantage.)

18.hxg3

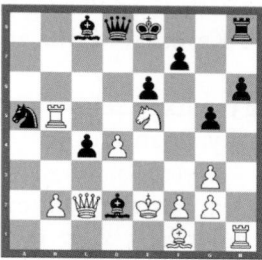

18...♗a6 19.♕xd2 ♗xb5 20.♕b4 ♕b6 21.♔e3 ♘b3 (21...♘c6 22.♘xc6 ♕xc6 23.b3 f5 24.f3+– Berkes — Wang Hao, Taiyuan 2006) 22.♕c3 0–0 23.♗xc4 ♗xc4 24.♘xc4 ♕b7 25.♖xh6 ♖d8 26.f3 ♘xd4 27.♔f2±;

Black has a solid but very passive position after 6...a5

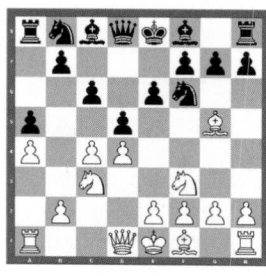

7.e3

a) 7.e4 dxe4 8.♘xe4 ♗b4+ 9.♘c3 h6 10.♗xf6 ♕xf6= Shulman — Kamsky, Saint Louis 2011;

b) 7.g3 h6 (7...♘bd7 8.♗g2 h6 9.♗f4∞ Miton — Prie, France 2007) 8.♗xf6 ♕xf6 9.♗g2 ♗b4 10.0–0 ♘d7=;

7...♗e7 (Black can also begin with 7...♘a6, which usually leads to a transposition.) 8.♗e2

a) 8.♖c1 0–0 9.♗d3 ♘a6 10.0–0 ♘b4 11.♗b1 ♘d7 (11...b6 12.♕e2 ♗a6 13.b3 ♘d7 14.♗f4 f5= Gelfand — Malakhov, Sochi 2005) 12.♗xe7 ♕xe7 13.♘a2 ♘xa2 14.♗xa2 b6= Sasikiran — Kazhgaleyev, Dubai 2011;

b) 8.♗d3 ♘a6 9.0–0

(9.e4 dxe4 10.♘xe4 ♘xe4 11.♗xe7 ♕xe7 12.♗xe4 f5 (12...♕b4+ 13.♕d2 ♕xc4 14.♘e5 ♕b4 15.♘xc6 ♕xd2+ 16.♔xd2± Grischuk — Bacrot, Odessa 2007) 13.♗d3 c5=)

9...♘b4 10.♖e1 0–0 11.e4 dxe4 12.♗xe4 (12.♘xe4 c5! 13.♗xf6 gxf6∞) 12...♘xe4 13.♘xe4 f6 14.♗d2 ♗d7= Kamsky — Bacrot, Baku 2008;

8...0–0

(8...b6 9.0–0 ♗b7 10.cxd5 exd5 11.♘e5!? (11.♗d3 ♘a6 12.♖c1 ♘b4 13.♗b1 0–0 14.♘e5 Beliavsky — Stefanova, Gibraltar 2008) 11...0–0 12.f4 ♘a6 13.♖f3↑ — by deploying the rook on the kingside White develops a dangerous initiative.)

9.0-0 ♞a6 10.♕b3 ♞b4

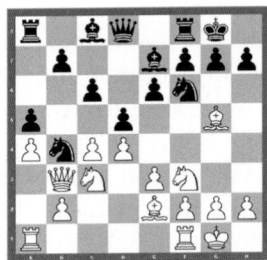

11.♞a2

a) 11.♖fd1 b6 (*11...♞h5 12.♗xe7 ♕xe7 13.♞a2 ♞xa2 14.♕xa2 ♞f6 15.♕a3 ♕xa3 16.bxa3!?± Zhou Jin-chao — Malakhov, Sochi (rap-id) 2009*) 12.♖ac1 ♗b7 13.♞e5 h6 14.♗h4 ♞d7= Kir.Georgiev — Mir-zoev, Pamplona 2009;

b) 11.♖ac1 h6 12.♗h4 b6 13.♞a2 c5=;

c) 11.♞e5 ♞d7 12.♗xe7 ♕xe7 13.♞d3 dxc4 14.♕xc4 e5= Kramnik — Bacrot, Paris (rapid) 2002;

11...♞a6 The following preventive move gives a small advantage

(*11...♞xa2 12.♕xa2 ♞d7 (12... dxc4 13.♕xc4 ♞d5 14.♗xe7 ♕xe7 15.♞e5± Shulman — Izoria, Las Vegas 2008) 13.♗xe7 (13.♗f4 ♞b8 14.♖ac1 ♞a6± Wang Yue — Mala-khov, Sochi 2009) 13...♕xe7 14.♕b3 b6 15.cxd5 exd5 16.♖fc1± Beliavsky — Wang Hao, Amsterdam 2006*)

12.h3!± prevent ing the black squared bishop being exchanged for the black knight.

a) 12.♖ac1 h6! (*12...♞e4 13.♗xe7 ♕xe7 14.♖fd1± Sargissian — Volk-ov, Rijeka 2010*) 13.♗h4 g5! 14.♗g3 ♞e4 15.♞c3

(*15.♖fd1 ♞xg3 (15...h5!?) 16.hxg3 ♗f6 17.♞c3 ♗g7 18.e4 g4!± Aro-nian — Kamsky, Mainz 2010*)

15...♞xg3 16.hxg3 ♗f6∞/= Ivanchuk — Kamsky, Bazna 2009;

b) 12.♞e5 ♞e4 13.♗xe7 ♕xe7 14.♕c2 f6 15.♞f3 ♗d7 16.♗d3 El-janov — V.Milov, Kallithea 2008 16...♗e8!=; ;

6...♗e7 7.e3 0-0 8.♗e2 (*8.♗d3 a5 9.0-0 ♞a6=*) 8...a5 9.0-0 ♞a6 — 6...a5 7.e3 ♗e7 8.♗e2 0-0 9.0-0 ♞a6(*9...♞bd7 10.♖c1 b6 Postny — Panarin, Internet 2005 11.cxd5 exd5 12.h3±*)

7.e3
7.a5

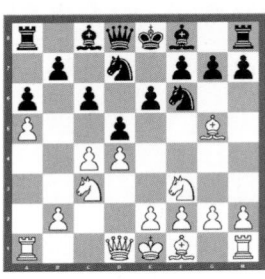

7...h6!

a) 7...♗b4 8.♕a4 ♗e7 9.e3 0–0
10.♗e2 b5 11.axb6 ♘xb6 12.♕c2
(*12.♕a2±*) 12...♘xc4 13.♗xc4 dxc4
14.0–0 c5 15.dxc5 ♗xc5 16.♖fd1 ♕c7
Bu Xiangzhi — Movsesian, Nanjing
2008 17.♗xf6 gxf6 18.♖a4±;

b) 7...dxc4 8.e4

(8.e3 b5 (*8...h6 9.♗xf6 ♘xf6
10.♗xc4 ♗b4 11.♕a4 ♕e7 12.0–0
0–0 13.♘e5 ♗d6 14.♘d3 c5=* Dautov — Morozevich, Bled 2002)
9.axb6 ♕xb6 10.♕c2 ♖b8= Miton
— Lastin, Moscow 2004)

8...h6 9.♗xf6 (*9.♗h4 ♗b4 10.♕a4
♗xc3+ 11.bxc3 g5∓* Gagunashvili — Carlsen, Wijk aan Zee 2004)
9...♘xf6 10.♕a4 ♗d7 11.♕xc4 (*11.
♘e5 c5∓* Gelfand — Kasparov,
Moscow (rapid) 2002) 11...♕e7
(*11...♖c8 12.♗e2 ♗e7 13.0–0 0–0
14.b4±*) 12.♗e2 ♕b4 13.♖a4 ♕xc4
14.♖xc4± Gagunashvili — Haslin-
ger, Hastings 2006;

8.♗xf6

(8.♗h4 dxc4 9.e3 b5 10.axb6 ♕xb6
(*10...♘xb6 11.♘e5 c5 12.♗e2 cxd4
13.♗h5 ♖a7 14.♘c6 ♕c7 15.♘xa7
dxc3∞* Akobian — Kacheishvili,
Las Vegas 2008) 11.♖a2 c5=)

8...♘xf6 9.c5 g6= — It's better to develop the bishop to g7 to facilitate
the move e6-e5.(*9...g5* has the same
idea however it gives White a target on the kingside and is therefore

risky *10.e3 ♗g7 11.h4±* Shulman —
Epishin, Minneapolis 2005) ;

7.cxd5!?

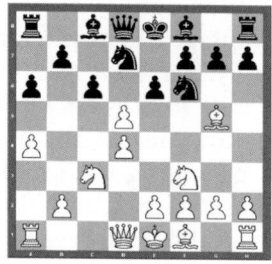

7...cxd5

(7...exd5 8.e3 a5

(*8...♗e7 9.♗d3 0–0 10.♕c2 ♖e8
11.0–0 ♘f8 12.♖ae1 ♗e6 13.♘e5
♘6d7 14.♗xe7 ♕xe7 15.♘xd7
(15.f4 f6 16.♘f3±) 15...♕xd7 16.f4
f6 17.a5±* Kramnik — Gelfand,
Novgorod 1997)

9.♗d3 ♗e7 10.♕c2 0–0 11.0–0 ♖e8
12.♖ae1 ♘f8 13.♘e5 (*13.h3 ♘e4=*)
13...♘g4 14.♗xe7 ♖xe7 15.♘f3!N
Exchanges are not good for White
as he has more space. (*15.f4 f6
16.♘xg4 ♗xg4 17.h3 ♗h5 18.g4 ♗f7*
White tries to seize more space but
thanks to the exchange of a pair
of knights, the black pieces have
enough freedom, for example:
*19.♕f2 ♕d6 20.♖e2 ♖ae8 21.h4
♔h8=*, Ponomariov — Movsesian,
Carlsbad 2007) 15...♘f6 16.h3±
White plans to retreat the f3 knight
to e5 or d2 in order to advance the
f pawn to f5. After that White can

prepare a kingside attack by advancing the g-pawn.)

8.e3 h6 9.♗h4 ♗d6 10.♗d3 b6 11.0-0 ♗b7 The only plan allowing White to fight even for a minimal advantage lies in 12.♘d2!N *(12. ♖c1 0-0 13.♖e1 ♕b8 14.♗g3 ♗xg3 15.hxg3 ♕d6 16.♕b3 ♖fc8= Pelletier — Karjakin, Merida 2005)* 12...0-0 13.f4!±, providing the knight with the strong square e5, and sometimes with possibilities of developing the initiative with f4-f5.;

7.♕b3

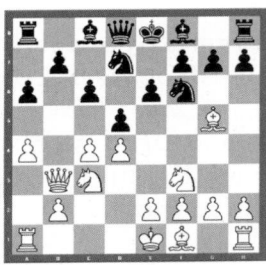

7...h6 8.♗xf6

(If 8.♗h4, Black takes advantage of the bishop's absence from the queenside: 8...dxc4 9.♕xc4 ♕b6 10.e4 *(10.♖b1 ♗b4∓)* 10...♕xb2 11.♖b1 ♕a3∓ -It's hard for White to prove that he has sufficient compensation.)

8...♘xf6 9.a5 c5 10.e3 cxd4 11.exd4 dxc4 12.♗xc4 ♗d6 13.0-0 0-0= Hillarp Persson — Khalifman, Dresden 2007;

7.♕c2

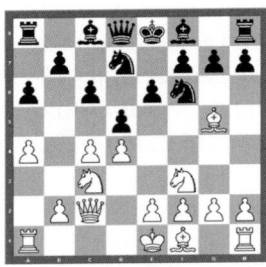

7...♗e7

a) After 7...♕a5,besides the conventional move 8.cxd5 leading to a small advantage, the following is interesting 8.♗d2!? ♗b4 9.e3 0-0 10.cxd5 exd5 *(10...cxd5 11.♗d3±)* 11.♗e2±;

b) 7...h6 8.♗h4 ♕a5 9.e3 ♘e4 10.♗d3 f5 11.0-0 ♗d6 12.c5 ♗b8 13.♗xe4 fxe4 14.♘d2 0-0 15.f3 exf3 16.♘xf3± Van Wely — Karjakin, Merida 2005;

c) 7...♗b4 8.cxd5 cxd5 *(8...exd5 9.e3 a5 10.♗d3 ♗e7 11.0-0 0-0 12.h3 ♖e8 13.♖ae1 ♘f8 14.♘e5 ♘6d7 15.♗xe7 ♖xe7 16.f4 f6 17.♘f3± — White intends to play f4-f5, after which he will either prepare to open up the centre with e3-e4, or advance the g-pawn and organise a kingside attack, Tkachiev — Chuprikov, Sochi 2005)* 9.e3 h6 10.♗h4 0-0 11.♗d3 b6 12.0-0 ♗b7 Gustafsson — Volkov, Internet 2004 13.♘e5 ♗e7 14.f4±;

8.e3 0-0 9.a5 *(9.♗e2 dxc4 10.♗xc4 ♘d5 11.♗xe7 ♕xe7 12.0-0 ♘b4 13.♕b3 a5!±/= — Later on Black* will play b7-b6 and c6-c5, or e6-e5, equalising almost completely.) 9... h6 10.♗h4 c5 11.cxd5 (*11.dxc5 ♘xc5 12.cxd5 ♘xd5 13.♘xd5 exd5 14.♗xe7 ♕xe7 15.♗e2 ♗g4 16.0-0 ♖ac8=* Van Wely — Ivanchuk, Monaco (rapid) 2006) 11...♘xd5 12.♗xe7 ♘xe7= Van Wely — Najer, Minneapolis 2005

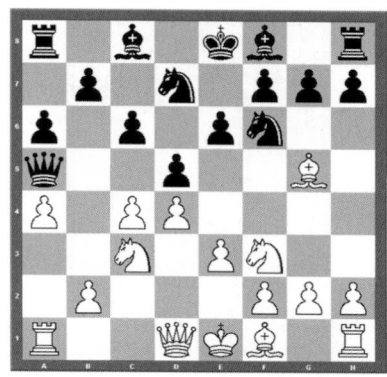

7...♕a5

After the the knight has moved to d7, the idea of developing the bishop is even less promising 7...♗e7, since after the simple move 8.♗d3± Black doesn't have the standard option of transferring the knight to b4 after a6-a5.;

7...♗b4 8.cxd5 exd5 (*8...cxd5 9.♗d3 h6 10.♗h4 b6 11.0-0 ♗b7 12.♘e5±*) 9.♗d3± — The bishop's position on b4 turns out to be bad.

8.♘d2
8.cxd5 ♘xd5!

a) 8...cxd5

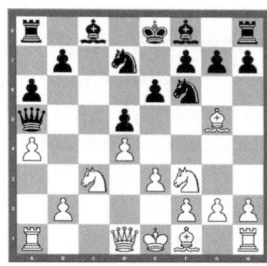

9.♗d3 (*9.♘d2 ♗b4 10.♖c1 ♘e4 11.♘dxe4 dxe4 12.♗f4 ♘f6=*) 9...♘e4 10.0-0 ♘xg5 11.♘xg5 ♘f6 12.f4!? (*12.♘f3 ♗b4 13.♕c2 ♗d7 14.♘e5 ♖c8 15.♖fc1 ♖c7 16.♕b3 0-0 17.♘xd7 ♘xd7 18.♘a2 ♗d6 19.♖xc7 ♕xc7 20.g3=* Jakovenko — Dominguez, Khanty Mansyisk 2010) 12...♗b4 13.♖c1 0-0 (*13...♗d7 14.f5↑*) 14.♕e1 ♗d7 15.♕h4 h6 16.♘f3 ♖fc8 17.g4→ Vaganian — Shirov, Istanbul 2000;

b) 8...exd5

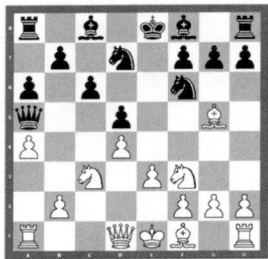

9.♘d2

(9.♗d3 ♘e4 10.0-0 ♘xg5 11.♘xg5 ♗e7 (11...♘f6 12.f4 ♗e7 13.♕c2 h6 14.♘f3 ♗e6 15.♘e5 ♖d8 16.h3 h5!? — Black prepares a shelter for the king on f8 instead of castling in order to escape an attack. 17.♘f3 ♔f8±/∞ — Both sides face a complicated manoeuvering struggle with a small advantage for White, Gelfand — Kamsky, Elista 2007) 12.♕h5 (12.f4 ♘f6 — 11...♘f6 12.f4 ♗e7) 12...g6 13.♕h6 ♗f8 14.♕h4 ♗e7 15.♕f4 (15.♕g3 0-0 16.♕h4 — 15.♕f4 0-0 16.♕h4) 15...0-0 16.♕h4 ♗xg5 (16...h5 17.f4↑ Moiseenko — Roussel-Roozmon, Monreal 2009) 17.♕xg5 ♕b4= Harikrishna — Movsesian, Sarajevo 2009)

9...♗d6 (9...♗e7 10.♗d3 0-0 11.0-0 ♖e8 12.♕c2 ♕d8 13.a5!± Jakovenko — Laznicka, Pamplona 2006) 10.♗d3 0-0 11.0-0 (11.♕c2 ♖e8 12.♗h4 h6= Gelfand — Aronian, Linares 2010) 11...♕c7 12.♘f3 h6 13.♗h4 a5 Eljanov — Movsesian, Sarajevo 2009 14.♖c1± — In view of the threat ♘c3-b5, the black queen

has to move to a lesspromising position.;

9.♕c2

(9.e4 ♘xc3 10.bxc3 ♘f6 11.♗d3 (11. e5 ♘e4∓ Sandipan — Luther, Port Erin 2003) 11...♕xc3+ 12.♔e2 ♕a5 13.♕c2 ♗e7= — White has sufficient positional compensation for the pawn but nothing more, Yermolinsky — Izoria,Mesa2009)

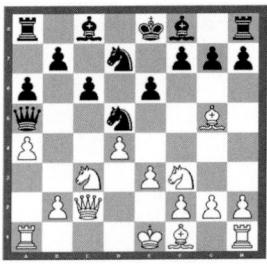

9...♗b4 10.♖c1

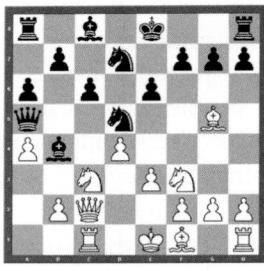

10...c5!N (10...♘7b6 11.e4 ♘f6 12. ♗d2 c5 13.dxc5 ♕xc5 14.♗d3± Lautier — Piket, Monaco (rapid) 1997) 11.♗d3 h6 12.♗h4 cxd4 13.exd4 ♘f4 14.0-0 ♘xd3 15.♕xd3 0-0=

8...♗b4

8...c5 9.dxc5 ♘e4 10.♘dxe4 dxe4 11.♗e2 ♘xc5 12.0-0 ♗d7 13.f4!?

(13.♗h4 ♕b4 (13...♗c6 14.♘b5!± Naiditsch — Kuzubov, Plovdiv 2012) 14.♕c2±)

13...♗c6 14.f5±/→;

8...dxc4

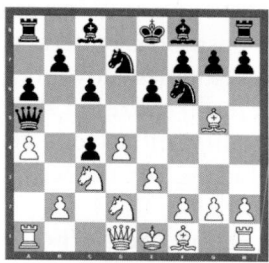

9.♗h4! Only if he is ready to sacrifice a pawn can White aspire to an advantage.

(A quiet move leads to an equal game: 9.♗xf6 ♘xf6 10.♘xc4 ♕c7 11.♗e2 (11.♗d3 c5 12.0-0 cxd4 13.exd4 ♗e7=; 11.a5 ♗d7= — Black plays c6-c5, solving all his problems, Van der Velden — Kuipers, Arnhem 2007; 11.g3 c5 12.♗g2 cxd4 13.♕xd4 ♗d7=) 11...c5 12.0-0 ♗d7 13.♖c1 ♖d8=)

9...♗b4

a) 9...♕b4 10.♕c2 b5 11.♗e2 ♗b7 12.0-0±/↑ — Apart from the standard option of seizing the centre with e3-e4, White has a strong positional idea in the break b2-b3. After that

the black queen will face the unpleasant prospect of an opposing rook on b1.;

b) 9...♘d5 10.♗xc4 ♗b4 (10...♘xc3 11.bxc3 ♕xc3 12.0-0↑) 11.♘a2 — 9...♗b4 10.♗xc4 ♘d5 11.♘a2;

10.♗xc4 ♘d5

a) 10...c5 11.0-0 cxd4 12.exd4 (Also good is 12.♘b3!?±, giving the possibility of capturing on d4 with a piece.) 12...♗xc3 (After 12...0-0 13.♗e2, is strong with a later ♘d2-c4.) 13.bxc3 ♕xc3 14.d5±/↑ Dao Thien Hai — Keitlinghaus, Budapest 1997;

b) 10...♗xc3 11.bxc3 ♕xc3 12.0-0 0-0 13.♗e2 e5 14.♘c4 exd4 15.♖c1 ♕b4 16.♖b1 ♕e7 (16...♕c5 17.exd4±) 17.♕xd4↑;

11.♘a2 e5 (11...♗xd2+ 12.♕xd2 ♕xa4 13.b3 ♕a3 14.0-0↑) 12.♘xb4 ♕xb4 13.♕b3 ♘7b6 14.e4 ♕xb3 15.♗xb3 ♘f4 16.♗g3 ♘xg2+ 17.♔e2 ♘f4+ 18.♗xf4 exf4 19.♖hg1 g6 (19...0-0 20.a5 ♘d7 21.♔f3±) 20.a5 ♘d7 21.♘c4 ♘f6 22.♘b6 ♖b8 23.♔f3±

9.♖c1

9.♕c2 c5 (Black also achieves equality after 9...dxc4 10.♗xf6 ♘xf6 11.♘xc4 ♕c7 12.♗e2 c5 13.0-0 cxd4 14.exd4 0-0 15.♕b3 ♗d6= Naumkin — Friedrich, Montecatini 1998) 10.♘b3 (10.♗xf6 ♘xf6 11.♘b3 ♕c7 12.dxc5 dxc4 13.♗xc4 0-0= Ftacnik

— Postny, Germany 2006) 10...♕c7 11.dxc5 (*11.♘xc5 ♘xc5 12.♗xf6 gxf6 13.dxc5 dxc4 14.♗xc4 ♗d7=; 11.0-0-0?! Beliavsky — Handke, Germany 2005 11...cxd4∓*) 11...0-0 12.♗xf6 ♘xf6 13.cxd5 ♘xd5 14.♗d3 h6 15.0-0 ♘xc3 16.bxc3 ♗xc5 17.♘xc5 ♕xc5= Vaganian — Movsesian, Germany 2005

9...c5

10.♗h4!N

A possib ilit y to fight for the initiative which has not been tested in practice yet. White protects his bishop from being exchanged.

10.♗e2 cxd4 11.exd4 dxc4 12.♗xf6 ♘xf6 13.♘xc4 ♕d8 14.0-0 0-0 15.♗f3 ♖b8 16.♕b3 ♕e7 17.♘e5 ♖d8 18.♖fd1 ♗d7 19.d5 (*19.♘e4 ♘xe4 20.♗xe4 ♗e8∓ Moiseenko — Laznicka, San Sebastian 2012*) 19... ♗d6 20.♘xd7 ♖xd7 21.dxe6 ♕xe6=;

10.dxc5 ♘e4 11.♘dxe4 dxe4 12.♗e2 ♘xc5 13.0-0 f6∓ Moiseenko — Laznicka, San Sebastian 2012

10...0-0

10...♕b6 11.dxc5!

(11.cxd5 cxd4 (*11...♘xd5 12.♘c4 ♕c6=*) 12.♘c4 (*12.dxe6 ♕xe6 13.♗c4 ♕c6 14.exd4 ♕xg2 15.♗e2+ ♔f8 16.♕f3 ♕xf3 17.♘xf3 ♘b6 18.♗b3 ♗e6=*) 12...dxc3 13.bxc3 ♗xc3+ 14.♖xc3 ♕b4=)

11...♗xc5 12.cxd5 (*12.♕c2 0-0 13.♗d3 d4 14.exd4 ♗xd4 15.0-0±* — White's position is preferable thanks to his development advantage, and if *15...♘c5 16.♘f3 ♗xc3 17.♕xc3 ♘xa4 18.♕d2±* his initiative is very dangerous.) 12...♘xd5 13.♘ce4±

11.♗e2 cxd4 12.exd4 ♕b6

12...dxc4 13.♘xc4 ♕d8 14.0-0 ♗e7 15.♗f3 ♘b6 16.♘e3±

13.c5 ♕c6 14.♘a2!

Otherwise Black breaks the white pawn chain with b7-b6,.

14...♗xd2+ 15.♕xd2 ♕xa4 16.♘c3 ♕c6 17.0-0↑

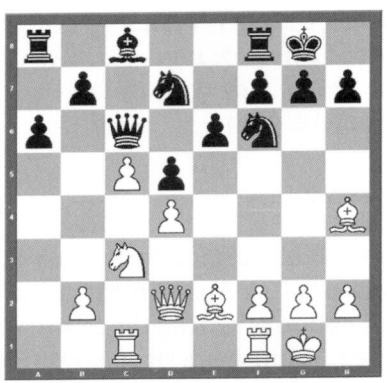

— White's longlasting initiative fully compensates for the pawn deficit. Conclusion: The line 5.a4 is at the moment probably the best way in the 4...a6 system to set Black opening problems. In the main line 5...e6 6.♗g5 there are several paths: 6... a5 leads to a very solid position but with a small stable advantage for White. 6...h6 7.♗h4! dxc4 8.e4! is a sharp line which develops to White's advantage. After 6. ..♘bd7, if White wants to play with a large safety margin, he can choose 7. cxd5, but in my opinion the continuation: 7.e3 ♕a5 8.♘d2 is the most principled. The lines analysed later after 8...dxc4 9.♗h4! and 8...♗b4 9.♖c1 c5 10.♗h4!N are promising and unified by the idea that White tries to retain his black squared bishop, frequently at the cost of a pawn.

Notes